COLONIALISM IN AFRICA
1870–1960

VOLUME 5
A BIBLIOGRAPHICAL GUIDE
TO COLONIALISM
IN SUB-SAHARAN AFRICA

by
PETER DUIGNAN
Senior Fellow, Hoover Institution, Stanford University

AND

L. H. GANN
Senior Fellow, Hoover Institution, Stanford University

CAMBRIDGE
AT THE UNIVERSITY PRESS
1973

Published by the Syndics of the Cambridge University Press
Bentley House, 200 Euston Road, London NW1 2DB
American Branch: 32 East 57th Street, New York, N.Y.10022

Library of Congress Catalogue Card Number: 75–77289

ISBN: 0 521 07859 8

Printed in Great Britain by
The Eastern Press Limited
London and Reading

CONTENTS

v

Contents

Contents

PART III
AREA GUIDE
(BY COLONIAL POWER, REGION AND COLONY) *p.* 165

vii

Contents

Contents

PREFACE

The present guide aims to provide a bibliographic overview of the 'New Imperialism' in sub-Saharan Africa. We have stressed historical material, but also have cited works from many other disciplines such as anthropology, law, economics and geography. We have done so knowing full well that the old academic spheres of influence, derived from the traditional university faculty structure, do not meet current Africanist needs. In addition we have tried to show by our choice of titles the incredible range of material produced during the colonial period – not just on history and politics or on ethnography and linguistics, but on subjects as diverse as biology and botany, medicine and natural science, geology and geography.

In undertaking this work, we have necessarily been selective. More than sixty years ago Sidney Mendelssohn, a diamond dealer from the Kimberley 'Diggings' turned book collector and savant, produced the greatest bibliography on southern Africa. Mendelssohn took account only of printed works. Though he wrote before the great 'knowledge explosion' of the twentieth century had got fully under way, he needed two massive tomes to complete his labours. Were he to venture on a similar task today, he would have to compile a multi-volume bibliographical encyclopaedia.

With the tide of books showing no sign of abating, the production of African reference books and bibliographies has at last begun to meet the demands of scholars. Our one-volume survey of the sources for the study of colonialism will probably be the last of its kind to cover colonialism in sub-Saharan Africa. The future will surely lie with more specialized bibliographies concerned with particular colonial powers, regions or topics. The present volume is thus bound by its very nature to have distinct limitations. It can make no claims to being exhaustive. The criteria of selection and annotation have necessarily been subjective. This work cannot possibly satisfy the requirements of any particular scholar concerned with a specific power, region or subject. We do hope, however, to provide a comprehensive introduction that will help students to find their way through the maze of colonial literature as a whole, and to furnish scholars and reference librarians with sources for comparative studies.

The bulk of our work was done during the 1960s. We originally intended to include only works published up to 1969. Delays, however, proved inevitable. As more and more scholarly works made their appearance in bookshops, we decided to include the more important contributions printed through 1971, and a few that came out in early 1972.

When we started in 1964 there were few guides to even individual colonial powers. But by 1972 some excellent surveys of Belgian colonialism (by Bustin), of British and German colonialism (by Pogge von Strandmann) and of French colonialism (by Gardinier) had appeared. We felt there still was a need for a one-volume survey that covered all the colonial powers and included material on archives and library resources, on serials and government documents, on library catalogues and thesis lists – sources not well represented in even the most recent bibliographies. We therefore offer this guide to serve some unmet needs.

In selecting our material we have tried to satisfy the requirements of the inter-disciplinary approach, and we have gone beyond the traditional requirements of a historian. We have tried also to bring to the notice of American and British students a good deal of material in French, Portuguese, German, Italian and Afrikaans. We have been impressed by the extent of the continental literature that has been little used by scholars in the United States and in the Commonwealth. Having surveyed the wealth of these sources, we have come to the conclusion that Africanists should spend at least as much time learning European languages as the more recondite African tongues.

In view of the complexity of the subject, we have furnished explanatory notes concerning such details as documentation, administrative history and archives. Again our treatment may be somewhat uneven. The average student knows more about the workings of British than, say, of German or of Portuguese rule. Hence we have provided extensive information on the German and the Portuguese background. We have supplied also a good deal of bibliographical information obtained from such sources as journals, printed book lists and bibliographical sections of published works. While we could not possibly include even a fraction of the works found in library stacks, we hope that our readers will at least find their way to such sources indirectly, through the bibliographical information provided in works which we cite. We admit to our individual predilections; hence we have not hesitated to bestow praise or criticism on individual authors, as the occasion seemed to warrant.

This volume is organized in three parts. Part I, 'Guide to Reference Materials', surveys libraries and archives in Western Europe, the United States and Africa, centres of research and various kinds of general bibliographies (library catalogues, thesis lists, etc.). Part II is a 'Subject Guide' to the literature regarding history, anthropology, geography, religion, missions, etc. Part III, an 'Area Guide', is arranged by colonial power, region and country. First we deal with British Africa in general, then by region and colony, as West Africa, the Gambia, etc. Then follow French Africa, the Belgian Congo, German Africa, Italian Africa, Portuguese Africa, Spanish Africa and finally a section of miscellaneous items on north-eastern Africa. Each colonial section usually has four parts: atlases, serials, bibliographies, reference works. As many works could be categorized by either subject or area, it would be wise for the reader to check through both Parts II and III.

The task of selection has not been an easy one. In compiling this work, we have found ourselves going far beyond our original aim, which was simply to provide a bibliographical annex to the four volumes of the 'Colonialism in Africa' series. Yet unavoidable gaps remain. There was not enough room to include even all the relevant material within our stated terms of reference, and vast areas remain to be covered. We hope, however, that for all its omissions, the present work will serve as a reference tool useful both to students and to librarians who must consult bibliographies and reference works and to those who compile them.

There remains the pleasant task of thanking our friends and assistants. We are indebted to Mrs. Mildred Teruya Stevenson and Ms. Carol Bain for typing the manuscript. Mrs. Edna Halperin has assisted us with the copy editing. Ms. Liselotte Hofmann prepared the index. Miss Karen Fung checked a great number of titles for accuracy. Numerous scholars read parts of the manuscript; we thank them all for their help: John E. Flint, David Gardinier, Richard Hammond, Martin Klein, René Lemarchand, Claudio Segre, Jake Spidle and Douglas Wheeler. Finally we should once again like to acknowledge the financial generosity of the Relm Foundation of Ann Arbor which enabled us to complete this work.

Peter Duignan
L. H. Gann

June 1972

INTRODUCTION

COLONIAL RESEARCH
ON AFRICA

AN OVERVIEW

Every generation writes its own history. Most scholars would agree that the historiography on colonialism, like that on every aspect of human affairs, has been influenced to a large degree by the period during which it was written. Only two generations ago, for instance, European writers were extolling Western imperialism as a source of light for 'Darkest Africa'. More recently, however, decolonization and its aftermath have produced strikingly different assessments. Westerners are being accused not only of economic exploitation of the African continent but also of 'cultural imperialism'. The erstwhile colonial rulers have been variously charged with ethnocentric bias, with having taken little or no interest in the history and culture of their subjects and with having perpetuated all manner of myths about the African continent. Although many Europeans did indeed produce works of a biased or racist nature, exploration and commerce, evangelization and conquest between them nevertheless occasioned a vast intellectual effort of a scholarly nature. The modern study of African ethnology and archaeology, of veterinary science and tropical medicine, of geography and agronomy, of history and politics and a host of related sciences, was the product – directly or indirectly – of the Western imperial impact on the continent. The eighty-year span between the scramble for Africa and the process of decolonization produced an outpouring of documents and of research on a scale paralleled by no other empire-builders in history.

No comprehensive history as yet exists of the Western intellectual endeavours in Africa during the colonial era,[1] although there are monographs on particular subjects, such as medical histories of individual colonial territories. But the subject of all Western research in Africa is so extensive that it would require a major study of its own. The present introductory essay can make no claim to filling the gap. We shall give merely a brief outline of some of the most important official or semi-official institutions created by the imperial powers that were concerned with sub-Saharan Africa. We have touched only lightly upon the intellectual history of South Africa on the grounds that South Africa came to form an imperial sub-system of its own, no longer politically dependent on Europe.

European efforts in the intellectual sphere were as unco-ordinated as the political initiatives. A variety of organizations whose collective impact was as uneven as that of economic development were initiated by Europeans. The total effect of these efforts was nevertheless impressive. The 'New Imperialism' struck Africa at a time when Westerners held an undisputed pre-eminence in the world of science and technology. European, and to some extent American, research during the colonial era represented a major transfer of skills and knowledge. It accomplished a great deal at a relatively small price; little or no relationship existed between the cost of intellectual investment and the value of its output.

The motives for research covered a wide spectrum. Many investigations, such as geological surveys or experiments regarding specific crops, had purely utilitarian value. Rumour and legend fascinated European gold-seekers by

---

[1] The best survey of colonial research remains Lord Hailey, *An African survey revised 1956: A study of problems arising in Africa south of the Sahara* (London, Oxford University Press, 1957), 1,676 p.

3

depicting Central Africa as the source of King Solomon's wealth. European archives perhaps contained the key that might unlock doors to the treasure chamber of the ' Far North '. Cecil John Rhodes therefore commissioned George McCall Theal, a South African historian, to compile the *Records of Southeastern Africa* (Cape Town, Government Printer, 1898–1903, 9 v.), a major documentary collection. Missionary enterprise occasioned research on a large scale. Evangelization clearly required not only a knowledge of African languages; but the more enlightened clergymen also became convinced that they could not preach the Gospel without understanding African beliefs and folkways. Many gifted missionaries thus became amateur ethnographers, translators and grammarians and even printers, in order to disseminate the Gospel to greater effect. The concern with disease led to intense medical research for human survival and to the study of plant and animal health to increase productivity. District officers in remote stations would accumulate ethnographic or historical data for reasons of administrative convenience, antiquarian inquisitiveness or general intellectual curiosity; and with the passage of time, their researches gradually became more systematized. The years following the Great War especially saw the emergence of an influential group of scholar-administrators. Men such as Lord Lugard, Lord Hailey or Maurice Delafosse looked to scholarship not only to provide intellectual illumination, but to humanize imperial rule and to make colonial governance more efficient.

In addition, a good deal of material was put out for avowedly propagandistic purposes to glorify colonial expansion or to defend the imperial record of a specific colonial power against critics at home and enemies abroad. For instance, the petitioners who in 1875 called upon the king of Portugal to incorporate the Sociedade de Geografia had no compunction about explaining to their sovereign the need for a body that would not only serve science, but would also do justice ' in the light of Modern Criticism ' to the ' grandiose but now sadly forgotten, slandered and mutilated labors ' which the Portuguese nation had performed for civilization. Later, the chauvinist and self-glorifying element was particularly marked in fascist Italy, where the state, as opposed to private corporations, took a particularly militant stand in spreading nationalism as a kind of secular religion. Italian as well as Portuguese scholars also turned out scores of highly legalistic studies concerned with subjects such as colonial legislation, administrative organization, and constitutional law. These subjects naturally appealed to civil servants who, unlike their British opposite numbers, had received all their academic training in jurisprudence. In addition, specialists wrote a good deal on subjects such as finance or linguistics. But even fascist Italy was not a fully totalitarian state. Italian fascism produced hard-line chauvinists, but no Lysenko – not because Italian scholars were braver than their Russian counterparts, but because there was no official fascist party line in fields like plant-breeding or geology or linguistics.

In the Western democracies, research during the colonial era was not constrained by officially imposed ideology or by governmental directives, anti-colonial propaganda notwithstanding. This is not to say that British or French inquirers were free from bias, or that they were not influenced by the prevailing climate of opinion or hindered by officials at times. But despite the pressure of prejudice, there was also a spirit of independent, disinterested scholarship whose intellectual origins reached back to the age of Thucydides. The impact of this scholarship was sufficiently strong and sufficiently independent of current orthodoxies to defy prevalent errors and misconceptions.

To give a specific example, many white Rhodesians remain convinced to this day that the mysterious Zimbabwe ruins must be of enormous antiquity, and

4

that they must be of Asian rather than African inspiration. Impelled by a mixture of racism and romanticism, or because of faulty interpretation of half-forgotten Scriptural passages or adventure stories about King Solomon's mines, whites used to insist that the ancient Hebrews, the Phoenicians or some even more exotic people must have designed the great Zimbabwe complex. Their views did not prevail. No British governor, no cabinet minister, or for that matter no banker or mining magnate could ever impose a specific line, say, on historical inquiry. Intellectual pioneers such as Gertrude Caton-Thompson could elaborate their findings concerning the Bantu origins of Zimbabwe without fear or favour from governments. Official bodies such as the Historical Monuments Commission of Rhodesia played an important part in elucidating the history of Rhodesia's Bantu-speaking peoples. Government publications, such as the *Guidebook to Zimbabwe* (Bulawayo, Historical Monuments Commission, 1971) or the *Handbook to the Federation of Rhodesia and Nyasaland* (London, Cassell, 1960), publicized their researches without fear, despite some bigoted comments in the Rhodesian press. Western archaeology in turn filtered back into African consciousness as part of a neo-traditional revival that exalted the Zimbabwe heritage for political as well as historical reasons.

The record of Western scholarly endeavour during the latter part of the eighteenth century, viewed from today's vantage-point, stands out as an intellectual watershed. The combined labours of naturalists, cartographers, antiquarians, travellers, medical men and others vastly lengthened the known span of history. At the same time, Western scholars became increasingly interested in the so-called 'exotic' parts of the world, including Africa. In 1788 the British set up the 'Association for Promoting the Discovery of the Interior Parts of Africa', commonly called the African Association. Its object was to send travellers to the interior, to collaborate with mission bodies and to further commerce and Christianity. The bulk of this and subsequent exploratory work owed its existence to the private enterprise of missionaries and of explorers (including large numbers of medical doctors), who drew on the generosity of private contributors and sometimes also on government subsidies. Travellers such as Heinrich Barth (who had a background of classical philology), Gustav Nachtigal, Emil Holub and David Livingstone (all trained physicians), produced an immense amount of literature. Many of these pioneers were not only men of resourcefulness and energy, but also acute observers. Their findings remain of value to students of African history.

The researches of explorers provided the raw material required by academic geographers whose scholarship in turn helped to give a wider unity to the work of individual explorers. From the beginning of the last century, scholars like Alexander von Humboldt and Karl Ritter turned the study of geography into a scientific subject with a great theoretical undergirding. The creation of new geographical societies provided organizational support for their endeavours. These bodies included the Société de Géographie de Paris, formed 1821, the Gesellschaft für Erdkunde zu Berlin (1828) and others. In Great Britain the African Association merged into the Royal Geographical Society founded in 1830. This organization played a major part in the exploration of Africa by serving as a centre of debate and study and also by subsidizing travellers like Sir Richard Burton, David Livingstone and Joseph Thomson. Later on the Society also promoted the creation of departments of geography at the universities of Oxford and Cambridge. Other famous bodies included the German Centralverein für Handelsgeographie, created in 1863, which emphasized the economic value of the geographical sciences. In Italy the Società Geogràfica

Introduction : colonial research on Africa

Italiana was founded in 1867, just a year after the new kingdom had acquired Venetia, a major step on the way to unification. In Portuguese colonial history an important part was played by the Sociedade de Geografia, initiated in 1875. These and allied organizations acted as vehicles for promoting exploration, scientific research and colonial propaganda.

At the same time, the rising interest in 'native races', a concern stimulated alike by humanitarianism and by missionary zeal, as well as by commercial and scientific endeavour, led to the formation of a number of specialized bodies. These included the Ethnological Society of London, founded in 1843, and later the Aborigines Protection Society, partly a humanitarian lobby, partly an ethnographic study group, that manfully proclaimed its belief in the unity of the human race by taking for its motto *ab uno sanguine*. Other similar organizations were the Société d'Anthropologie de Paris (dating from 1859) and the Anthropologische Gesellschaft of Vienna (founded in 1870).

During the era of the 'New Imperialism' this group was augmented. New societies included the Colonial Society (formed in 1868, renamed Royal Colonial Institute in 1910; Royal Empire Society in 1928 and Royal Commonwealth Society in 1958), the Royal African Society founded in 1901, and the Union Royale Coloniale Belge (later the Union Royale Belge pour le Congo et les Pays d'Outremer) first established in 1912 and the Institut Royal Colonial Belge. The German Colonial Society (Deutsche Kolonialgesellschaft) was founded in 1887 as a result of merging two other groups. These bodies published periodicals of their own and often also learned monographs, held meetings, listened to lectures on the colonies and lobbied for colonial interests.

The world-wide proliferation of knowledge and the improvements both in the means of physical communication of publicity as well as the growth of a public endowed with some education and a good deal of curiosity concerning exotic lands, strange people and outlandish animals, gave a new stimulus to the growth of public museums. To some extent these bodies took the place of privately owned 'curiosity cabinets' of earlier and more aristocratic ages. Museums such as the Musée de l'Homme at Paris (thus named in 1938, formerly known as the Institut d'Ethnologie of the Université de Paris), and the Musée Royal de l'Afrique Centrale at Tervuren in Belgium (started in 1897), became important centres of learning in their own right.

Above all, the nineteenth and early twentieth centuries became the golden age of international congresses and exhibitions. The Great Exhibition of 1851 served both as a British national pageant and as a symbol of hope for a 'machine-minded' future. World Expositions, such as those held at Paris in 1889 and 1900, shed reflected glory on the Third Republic. Most of these exhibitions had a colonial dimension, and to their number may be added several colonial expositions as well. For instance, the Exposition Coloniale Nationale, held at Marseille in 1906, issued a fifteen-volume set of reports illustrating the social and economic progress made in the colonies. The series culminated in a three-volume survey entitled *Les colonies françaises au début du 20e siècle*. (The entire set was published by Baratier, Marseille, 1906–1907.) Another important exposition was held at Paris in 1931, the Exposition Coloniale Internationale, which sponsored a whole series of studies, including major geographic surveys and an important multi-volume history of the colonial army.[2] Later on, in the 1930s, the Portuguese organized the Exposição Colonial Portuguesa at Oporto (1934), which published a major report on Angola.

[2] France. Armée. Etat-major, *Les armées françaises d'outre-mer* (Paris, Impr. Nationale, 1931–32), 21 v.

An overview

Equally important were colonial congresses, which produced an extensive literature. These congresses served a variety of purposes: imperially minded enthusiasts assembled to promote the colonial idea and to debate, argue and hammer out colonial policies; scholars lectured with regard to their findings; organizers used the congresses as a means of creating new and more lasting institutions. For instance, the Congresso Coloniale Italiano, held at Asmara in 1905, led to the creation of the Istituto Coloniale Italiano. The same congress also produced an important series, the *Atti del Congresso Coloniale Italiano in Asmara . . . 1905* (Rome, 1906, 2 v.). During the same period, the influential German colonial society sponsored three major congresses, whose proceedings were published as *Verhandlungen des deutschen Kolonialkongresses* (Berlin, 1903, 1906, 1911, 3 v.). French *congrès coloniaux* were held almost every year; the 1889–1890 *Congrès*, for example, was important for devising the policy of assimilation.

The pioneering days of empire provided opportunities for intelligent amateurs in the field of scholarship as well as in governance. The academic dilettante tradition, in the best sense of the word, was represented by such men as Sir Harry Johnston, Her Majesty's first Commissioner and Consul General in Nyasaland in the 1890s. Johnston was a remarkable man. A former art student, under-sized and squeaky-voiced, he was as unlike the muscular, rugger-playing empire-builder of British fiction as might be imagined. But Johnston was good at everything, at improvising an army or a government, at photography and draftsmanship, at botany, linguistics or a host of other pursuits. He wrote a shelfful of books that would have made the reputation of an academic. His works ranged from an autobiographical novel (*The Gay Dombeys*) that H. G. Wells considered worthy of a laudatory preface, to studies of colonial history, ethnography and Bantu linguistics such as *A comparative study of the Bantu and semi-Bantu languages* (Oxford, Clarendon Press, 1919–22, 2 v.).

Missionaries, too, played an important part in African research. In fact the first European intellectuals to write on Africa were expatriate clergymen. Missionary motives, of course, varied widely. Christian preachers wrote in order to spread the Gospel; they were interested also in raising funds for the purpose of sustaining their various activities. The early missionaries thus displayed a tendency both to exaggerate the effectiveness of their evangelical labours and to paint the assumed horrors of 'heathen darkness' in the grimmest colours. Yet the old-time missionary's sociological naïveté can be overestimated. He stayed with 'his' people over long periods of time; he shared in the vicissitudes of African life. The depredations of civil or interethnic strife within precolonial communities represented far more than a mere historical reconstruction worked out in the safety provided by the *Pax Britannica* or the *Pax Belgica*; they were an ever-present reality to the pioneer of the Gospel. Clerical training moreover placed a tremendous emphasis on the manners, laws and customs of at least one ancient, cattle-keeping people – the Hebrews. Missionaries knew *Leviticus* inside out, and some of them applied their knowledge in a surprisingly modern scientific manner.

The missionaries of colonial days thus made a major contribution to the study of African linguistics, ethnography and anthropology. The yellowed pages in old volumes of *Congo* or *Anthropos* are full of valuable articles compiled by learned clergymen; major missionary journals such as *Neue Allgemeine Missionszeitschrift* (1874–1939), the *International Review of Missions* (1912–), or *Portugal em Africa; Revista de Cultura Missionária* (1894–) merit careful perusal by any student of African history or ethnography. Missionary scholars such as E. W. Smith, Diedrich Westermann and Henri Alexandre Junod compiled anthropological classics (see, for example, Junod, *The life of a South African tribe*, London, Macmillan, 1912–13, 2 v.). If among their numbers might be found such men as Robert Moffat, who regarded most African customs and habits as evil, there were many more of the stamp of John MacKenzie, who studied and made major contributions in the area of tribal religion and tribal rites. Missionaries moreover played a major role in linguistic work in Africa. The various mission societies produced scores upon scores of intellectual pioneers, unknown for the most part, who rendered the Bible, the Shorter Catechism and other works into indigenous African tongues. These men were usually the first to reduce various types of Bantu speech to writing and to compile dictionaries and grammars. By this means they helped to lay the foundations of new literary languages. Missionary scholars such as S. W. Koelle (1823–1902), author of the *Polyglotta Africana*, an early pioneer work derived from information supplied by freed slaves in Sierra Leone, also made a major contribution to general linguistics.

In addition, the missionaries furnished much valuable information on the social condition of the peoples they tried to serve. For instance, the *Deputation reports* compiled by investigators sent to British Central Africa by the London Missionary Society remain useful sources of information. So are more ambitious inquiries such as that of J. Merle Davis, *Modern industry and the African : An enquiry into the effect of the copper mines of Central Africa upon native society and the work of the Christian missions* ... (London, Macmillan and Co., 1933).

Research produced by the private enterprise of missionaries, scholars and explorers was gradually supplemented and sometimes superseded by research controlled directly by colonial governments. The process of conquest, in fact, stimulated research. When Napoleon launched his great expedition to Egypt in 1798, he took with him a distinguished group of scholars who laid the foundations of modern Egyptology. Though the French occupation of Egypt lasted but a few years, permanent colonial occupation led to more sustained efforts.

The nature of colonial conquest varied a great deal from area to area. In some cases the European powers met with speedy submission; others entailed a process of lengthy campaigns accompanied by rapine, cruelty and bloodshed. In the first phases of empire-building, physical courage and endurance stood at a premium among the white administrators; so did their ability to raise revenue for fledgling governments. In time, however, the imperialists tried to develop their patrimony. Unlike previous conquerors in Africa, the Europeans brought in new means of production, far more advanced than those known to their subjects. The whites were able to draw on large scientific, technological and academic resources, which were applied to a wide variety of problems created by the drive for a new economy.

The *mise en valeur* of the colonies engendered extensive administrative changes. Businessmen-politicians such as Bernhard Dernburg, the German colonial secretary, and administrators like Sir William Milton in Southern Rhodesia, introduced a great variety of governmental reforms. Numerous investigations were launched into existing deficiencies in colonies (for example. in the French Congo, the Belgian Congo and German East Africa). The first decade of the present century may be styled as an era of ' capitalist self-criticism ' in the African colonies. Between 1907 and 1912 Germany, Belgium, Portugal and Italy all improved their machinery of governance and set up separate colonial ministries. Such men as Dernburg called openly for a more constructive colonial policy that would eschew simple coercion and rule instead by drawing on the skills of missionaries, medical men, railway engineers, mechanics, and above all on the tools provided by the theoretical and applied sciences in all fields.

The new emphasis on the *mise en valeur* of the colonies and self-criticism, and on greater efficiency and humanity in governance often went along with subsidized research. Well-organized expeditions left for remote parts of the colonies. These included ventures such as the two Central African missions commanded by Adolf Friedrich, Duke of Mecklenburg, respectively between 1907–08 and 1910–11. Above all, the colonizers intended to solve problems of health of men and of animals and plants and to throw light on a wide variety of technical problems relating to African traditional societies, administration, agriculture, veterinary science, railway building and many other practical matters. Studies with a predominantly utilitarian slant tended to dominate most colonial research until at least the outbreak of World War II.

In addition to carrying on investigations undertaken for such purposes as safeguarding health and increasing productivity, some European authorities began to take an interest in such subjects as the study of African history, archaeology and indigenous institutions. Here again, the Europeans' motives for financing this kind of work differed immensely. Romanticism and mere curiosity might mingle with the desire for fame and profits. Rhodes, for instance, helped in founding the National Museum at Bulawayo, which opened in 1901. His original grant was made on condition that there be a geologist on the staff to assist prospectors and miners. From 1911, however, the emphasis changed: the museum took a wider interest in natural history, and later on, in the prehistory of Central Africa.

Administrative problems afforded another avenue for research. After initial periods of pacification, often carried out by professional soldiers or adventurers, the various colonial powers gradually began to revise their methods. Administration became more sophisticated. Governors such as Albrecht von Rechenberg in German East Africa or Ernest Roume in French West Africa tried to make colonial rule more efficient, more humane, and at the same time more acceptable to their subjects than old-style governance by force. In doing so, government officers drew increasingly on the ethnographic work of missionary pioneers, such as Jakob Spieth's classic study *Die Ewestämme : Material zur Kunde des Ewevolkes in Deutsch-Togo* (Berlin, 1906). In addition they began to carry out investigations of their own. In 1912 Maurice Delafosse, a French official, published a major three-volume study (*Haute-Sénégal-Niger*) based on an extensive on-the-spot inquiry carried out with a view to the preparation of a civil code for the use of courts dealing with African cases. Paul Marty, on the other hand, carried out numerous studies on Islam in the various colonies of French West Africa. During the same period the Germans, to give another example, made studies of indigenous law that was edited in two volumes after the war by Erich Schultz-Ewerth and Leonhard Adam, in *Das Eingeborenenrecht* ... (Stuttgart, 1929–30). Robert Delavignette, Hubert Deschamps and Lord Hailey were scholar-administrators of a more recent vintage.[3] Hailey's encyclopaedic *African survey*, first published in 1938 and revised in 1956, remains unsurpassed as a reference work.

The growth of governmental activities gave rise to numerous investigations intended to aid policy makers. These inquiries, sometimes launched to find

[3] See Robert Delavignette, *Freedom and authority in French West Africa* (London, 1950), 152 p.; and by the same author, *Les paysans noirs* (Paris, 1946), 263 p.; also Hubert J. Deschamps, *Les Antaisaka* (Tananarive, 1936), 220 p.; and his *Traditions orales et archives au Gabon : Contribution à l'ethno-histoire* (Paris, 1962), 172 p.

remedies for specific abuses, were frequently published. They continue to provide students with a vast body of historical evidence that illustrates the failings as well as the achievements of colonialism. In their objectivity and scope many of these documents commonly paralleled the government investigations of the Victorian era that had provided social critics such as Marx and Engels, and later the Hammonds, with a large body of data. The inspiration for these studies derived from many sources and covered a variety of subjects. Investigators wished, for example, to come to grips with pressing practical problems. Their deliberations sometimes owed a great deal to the ' overspill ' of the social conscience from domestic to colonial responsibilities. (For instance, Sir Roger Casement, whose consular investigations into the atrocities of the Congo Free State in 1903 played a major part in arousing the British conscience against Belgian methods, brought to his task a bitter hostility to ' landlordism ' that was engendered by his Irish nationalism.) Again, the great rebellion of the Shona and the Ndebele in Rhodesia during the 1890s produced the command paper *British South Africa Company's territories : Report by Sir Richard Martin on the native administration of the British South Africa Company* ... (Great Britain, Parliamentary Paper, C. 8547, 1897), a dispassionate inquiry which remains a basic document for the period. West African questions occasioned investigations such as the *Report of the Northern Nigeria Lands Committee* ... (Great Britain, Parliamentary Paper, Cd. 5102, 1910), a document considerably influenced by the moral and political concepts advocated by the Congo Reform Association. Reports of a similar kind continued to be printed by government presses as long as the colonial era lasted. In the Belgian Congo, for instance, a Labour Commission was set up in 1930 to study the question of labour recruitment. This body collaborated with the ' Commission for the Colonial Charter in 1925 ', and amassed a wealth of factual material. Indeed, they remain today the basic source of information concerning the theories and practice of colonial governments, although they are not always accurate or unbiased.

The 1930s witnessed a spate of additional inquiries into the problems of particular colonies. For example, the *Report* ... *into the financial and economic position of Northern Rhodesia* ... (London, H.M. Stationery Office, 1938) still remains the best economic history of Zambia under colonial auspices. Similarly, there were investigations into African chieftaincy, land law and marriage customs, or into riots. Thus the 1940 Copper Belt disturbances in Zambia, or the African rail strike in Rhodesia six years later, may be studied because colonial governments themselves published documents such as the *Report of the commission to investigate* ... *the strike amongst African employees of the Rhodesian railways* ... (Salisbury, Government Printer, 1946).

Government inspiration led to research into a great variety of other topics. During the 1930s, for example, C. G. Trapnell and J. N. Clothier began their brilliant work on the soils, vegetation and ecological problems of what is now Zambia. During the same period meteorological observations became more systematic; the technique of census-taking improved; and colonial demography became less of a hit-or-miss affair than it had been in the early days of imperial governance.

From the beginning of the colonial period, all the European governments concerned began issuing laws, reports, ordinances and directives. Gradually the whole paraphernalia of modern government institutions was transferred to Africa along with their publications. These included gazettes, sessional papers, reports, committees of inquiry, and annual reports of departments and research institutes. At least in British Africa there were proceedings of executive councils, of legislative councils and assemblies. Similarly all colonial governments launched medical and health research and investigations into plant and animal diseases with a view to rendering life in the colonies safer, healthier and more productive. Before 1946 these services had reached limited numbers; still a constant effort was sustained to increase the range of operation of government services and to spread the benefits to more and more people. Lack of resources had limited the impact of modern science and technology on African peoples, but with the end of World War II this situation was changed.[4]

At the same time, public or semi-public bodies stepped in to provide or supplement a whole range of services originally furnished by missionary societies (education, medicine, agricultural training). To give just one example, missionary pioneers had rendered a major service to Africa by reducing a large number of languages to writing and by laying thereby the foundations of many vernacular forms of literature. This work was later extended in the secular sphere by bodies such as the East African Literature Bureau, set up in 1948.

From the 1930s onward governments drew increasingly on the assistance of professional anthropologists and sociologists, as well as archaeologists and others to supplement the information previously amassed by missionaries, civil servants and geographers. In 1936, for example, the Portuguese founded the Junta das Missões Geográficas e de Investigações do Ultramar, concerned with a great variety of topics connected with arts and sciences. In the French empire, during the same period, institutionalized research received a great impetus through the creation of the Institut Français de l'Afrique Noire (IFAN), first set up in Dakar in 1938. In the British colonies, to give another example, the Rhodes-Livingstone Institute was organized in 1937 in what is now Zambia. The Institute was designed to promote research in all disciplines but especially anthropological and sociological research in Central Africa.

These new intellectual endeavours rested on an increasing degree of specialization in academic labour. Anthropologists, museum curators and archaeologists became professional men for whom scholarship was a career rather than a form of intellectual relaxation or an administrative tool. Much of their effort was characterized by a spirit of critical inquiry that frequently merged into social criticism. Anthropological research was often accompanied, consciously or unconsciously, by a sense of self-identification with the African peoples who formed the subject of the scholar's professional studies. Most anthropologists tended to be critical of settlers and governments alike, whereas governments on the whole took but little notice of anthropological findings. As a result the rift between expatriate intellectuals and specific local 'establishments' tended to widen. At the same time, anthropological inquiries, by recording African indigenous institutions and customs as they existed at a given time, made a major contribution to African history. In addition, the new scholarship affected the intellectual climate of opinion overseas. Academic pioneers such as Max Gluckman and a score of others helped to persuade their countrymen that Africans, far from being primitive savages subject to the irrational desires of a 'pre-logical' personality, had developed their own cultures, that African economies made good sense within their accustomed context, or that African judges, with their notion of the 'reasonable man', would judge a case as competently and as justly as any jurist steeped in the tradition of Roman law.[5]

[4] See Commission for Technical Cooperation in Africa, *Directory of scientific institutes, organizations and services in Africa* (Paris, CCTA, 1954); and E. B. Worthington, *Science in the development of Africa: A review of the contributions of physical and biological knowledge south of the Sahara* (London, CCTA, 1958), 462 p.

[5] See, for instance, Max Gluckman, *The judicial process among the Barotse of Northern Rhodesia* (Manchester University Press, 1955), 386 p.

Introduction : colonial research on Africa

The new field of study was painfully developed over several generations by learned missionaries, by government officials with an academic bent and by professional scholars. African academic pioneers also began to make their contribution to the study of their own continent. In the nineteenth century the foundations of African scholarship had been laid by European-educated men such as Surgeon-Major James Africanus Horton, a British Army officer of Ibo origins and author of numerous studies, such as *West African countries and their peoples: British and native* ... (London, W. J. Johnson, 1868). During the 1920s, Samuel Johnson, a Yoruba, compiled another classic, *The history of the Yorubas from the earliest times to the beginning of the British protectorate* (London, G. Routledge and Sons, 1921); and Joseph Boakye Danquah, an Ashanti, published *Akan laws and customs and the Akim Abuakwa constitution* (London, G. Routledge and Sons, 1928).

Slowly these studies hardened into recognized disciplines whose syllabi found acceptance in academic institutions. This was a long process extending over many decades. In 1887 the Germans, who were among the pioneers of 'scientific' colonial education, set up the Seminar für orientalische Sprachen at the University of Berlin, deliberately designed as an institution of applied science for the colonies. Impressed by the German example which they had studied, the British later founded the School of Oriental Studies in London in 1916 (in 1938 the name was changed to School of Oriental and African Studies). The new body was created to provide instruction in the languages of Asia and Africa and to offer courses in the history and cultures of different areas. The school at first remained small and underfinanced and played an unimportant role until after the end of World War II. Paradoxically the institution then grew and exerted its greatest influence when the empire was being dissolved. But its scholars made important contributions in many fields. Its *Bulletin* was highly regarded. Most of its publications, however, were started after 1950, when periodicals such as the *Journal of African History*, the *Journal of African Law* and the *Journal of African Languages* began to publish. After World War II, the universities of Oxford and London each established its own Institute of Commonwealth Studies (in 1945 and 1949, respectively).

British academic pioneers also played an important part in developing university education in Africa. To do justice to an academic history of South Africa, for example, would require a full chapter. Suffice it to say that in 1873 Cape Town University came into being as an examining body modelled on the University of London, and came to serve a number of constituent colleges that gradually acquired independent university status of their own. The requirements of the South African mining industry, to give another example, led to the formation in 1903 of a technical school at Johannesburg that became known as the South African School of Mines and Technology. This school, in turn, was the nucleus of a great institution of higher learning, Witwatersrand University. The University of Cape Town pioneered in many fields of African research. In 1918, for instance, Cape Town founded its own School of African Life and Languages. South African universities attracted a number of expatriate scholars from overseas, men such as W. M. Macmillan, one of the founders of modern South African historiography. The South African Institute of Race Relations, established in 1933, published a journal and numerous monographs on all aspects of race relations. In later years South Africa was to make its influence felt on the academic world by a 'brain drain' in reverse. In addition, South African academics made a not inconsiderable contribution in other parts of Africa. And a small but influential South African diaspora played an important part, too, in developing anthropology, colonial economics, and other Africa-related disciplines in Great Britain.

On the European continent, German learned bodies played a major part in the development of what the Germans called *Völkerkunde* and in a host of other new studies such as *Missionskunde*. Indeed the German Kolonialinstitut at Hamburg (founded under the inspiration of Bernhard Dernburg's 'scientific' colonialism and with financial aid from Alfred Beit, Rhodes's Hamburg-born collaborator) became the nucleus around which the University of Hamburg was founded in 1919. The French greatly extended the scope of their own academic work and, among other things, turned their *Ecole Coloniale* (founded in 1887 to train colonial officials) into a prestigious body, academically almost on a par with the other *grandes écoles* at Paris and served by men with the intellectual standing of Georges Hardy and Henri Labouret. During the 1940s, and to an even greater extent during the 1950s, the number of academic institutions concerned with African studies expanded still further. The pioneer in British Africa had been Fourah Bay College in Sierra Leone, which had an affiliation with Durham University. Finally, toward the end of the colonial era, European universities such as London and Louvain took the initiative in creating new universities in Africa; and many Africans, among them the historians Ajayi, Anene, Ayandele, Boahen, Cox-George, Dike and others, took their advanced degree work in England or in France during the 1950s.

ARCHIVES

Historians and social scientists concerned with the imperial era in Africa can draw on a vast storehouse of information recorded in secondary sources of the kind we have been describing. Archives in Europe and Africa moreover contain reports prepared by administrative, commercial, ecclesiastical or other bodies. In the course of administrative or executive transactions these records formed a part, and they were subsequently preserved for future reference. Admittedly, the use of official sources presents many pitfalls. The records in departmental files were not prepared initially for the purpose of making a theoretical analysis. Official memoranda naturally reflected all the biases and preconceptions of their authors. Unlike published reminiscences or other kinds of secondary material, archives have a quality peculiarly their own. They are at the same time both instruments for and products of administrative action. They are less self-conscious than books or published reports. The correspondence of an official or the confidential proceedings of a board may conceivably have been drafted to deceive another office, but they are hardly ever composed with an eye to deceiving posterity.[6]

RECORDS AND REPOSITORIES

The nature of official archives has passed through certain well-defined stages which in turn corresponded to changes in the administrative systems of the various colonies. The earliest white administrators in remote outposts lived in close contact with the indigenous people. They might run their district for

[6] See L. H. Gann, 'Archives and the study of society', in *Rhodes-Livingstone Journal*, v. 20, 1956: 48–67.

months on end without seeing another white. Most of their time was spent touring the district, where they maintained order by moral or if necessary by physical force. They tramped around with African carriers, hunted, adjudicated disputes or on occasion tried to settle a succession quarrel over a disputed chieftainship. Unfortunately men of this type did not usually commit very much to writing; and such records as they did make fell victim to rats, white ants, climatic factors or to neglect occasioned by primitive office facilities.

As time went on, the administration became more complex. District commissioners were required to enforce the law and to collect taxes, and they sometimes supervised the census taking. Gradually technical services came into existence. As the volume of correspondence increased, the white officials had to spend more and more time inside the office, and documents were preserved more efficiently. At the same time, however, the direct and informal contacts between the official and the indigenous people might diminish, with the result that the reliability of the official's observations was likely to suffer.

By the twentieth century in Europe, the flood of official documents had become a torrent. This was true not only in the state administration but in industry as well, and both were forced to upgrade their administrative techniques. The invention of the typewriter ushered in the mechanization of the office. This was followed in due course by the introduction of accounting machines, devices for the rapid duplication of documents and, finally, by the installation of electronic equipment. More clerks had to be employed. The development of mass production made staff work of tremendous importance. Work schedules, staff manuals and lengthy instructions had to be printed, and new forms had to be devised in large quantities. Much the same development occurred in government services, though in this area colonial administrations lagged behind the more developed metropolitan departments. The state extended its activities into the social and economic spheres in a way that would have horrified most Victorian civil servants. Information was required on an ever-broadening range of subjects. The most trivial transactions could now be recorded and ultimately filed away, in the process cluttering up office space and often enough, by its sheer bulk, concealing vital information. By the mid-1950s, for example, the governments of the Federation of Rhodesia and Nyasaland among them produced something like 270 tons of paper a year. Only about one-tenth of this material could be permanently preserved, and record-keepers had to become skilled in determining which papers should be kept and which should be weeded out and put through the shredding machine.

The problem of the research worker also became much more complex. The inflation in the number of records made them more difficult to consult for his purposes. The neatly arranged ' inletter ' and ' outletter ' series formally kept in an old-fashioned governor's office, with copper-plate writing on linen paper, gave way to mass-produced files, an untidy jumble of carbon copies, enclosures and scribbled memoranda, all hastily filed under one subject heading. The change in the volume and character of records was often accompanied by a sharp fall in value as a research tool. An investigator could no longer plough through all the papers relating to a specific era because there was simply too much material. At the same time he had to reckon with the possibility that some important decisions – possibly made over the telephone or in a personal meeting after a hurried plane journey – might not be recorded at all.

The mass of documents produced by colonial governments, as well as by private organizations, nevertheless remains the best source of historical evidence available. The historian's work, then, was determined to a considerable extent by the existence of archives that made some attempt to preserve and classify historical records and on the willingness of governments to make this material available to scholars once the records had ceased to be of current use. The growth of archives in sub-Saharan Africa closely followed the evolution of modern administrative organization, and paralleled each country's general economic development. The lead in this activity was taken by the Cape Colony, where an archival institution was first set up in 1876. The Transvaal followed in 1887, and the Orange Free State made a beginning after the South African War, in 1903. The next advance was made in French West Africa, where steps for the proper preservation of records were taken just before World War I. During the inter-war years, Southern Rhodesia opened its government archives in 1935. The end of World War II was followed by dramatic expansion. In 1946 the archives of the Gold Coast (now Ghana) came into being. During the same year the Southern Rhodesian Government Archives was empowered to extend its work into Northern Rhodesia (now Zambia) and Nyasaland (now Malawi). In 1947 archives were established in what was then the Belgian Congo (now Zaïre) and two years later in Uganda. The 1950s brought further growth, with the government archives being reorganized in various territories. Sierra Leone, for instance, created facilities of its own between 1950 and 1951; Nigeria followed suit in 1954, Kenya and Zanzibar in 1956. In 1957 Basutoland (now Lesotho) appointed a government archivist; a year later Mauritius and Madagascar set up services of their own. By the end of the colonial period, the framework had been laid for most of the existing archives in Africa.

ARCHIVAL FINDING AIDS AND PUBLICATIONS

All archivists, whether British, Bemba, French or other, by the very nature of their calling, must establish a certain number of similar basic operational procedures. When an archives institution is set up, the uncontrolled destruction of files must cease and holdings in district offices must be safeguarded. Material is then assembled in central repositories. Files are then carefully combed through and weeded, put in order according to the original arrangement used by originating offices, and finally boxed and shelved. The next step is to create finding aids for in-house use. In a few of the more advanced institutions, such as the National Archives of Rhodesia, arrangements are also made for the management and control of current records. Archives may ultimately be able to provide published lists, guides, calendars (that is to say, précis of important documents), or documentary collections published *in extenso*.[7]

In most African countries trained manpower and money for archives have remained scarce. Hence the supply of finding aids lags far behind the scholarly demand. Furthermore the records of Africa's past are scattered throughout the world in private, organizational and government depositories. For many African countries, researchers in need of information on specific territories still have to seek out general descriptive articles in learned journals such as *Archives* (London) or the *Gazette des Archives* (Paris). Nevertheless, a start has been made, especially in West Africa and in Southern Africa, to produce and publish finding aids.

[7] See Peter Duignan, ' Bibliographical control of African manuscripts and archives collections ', in J. D. Pearson and Ruth Jones, eds., *The bibliography of Africa: Proceedings and papers of the International Conference on African Bibliography, Nairobi, 4–8 December 1967* (London, Frank Cass, 1970), p. 194–209, for a survey of archival finding aids and projects in Europe and Africa.

Introduction : colonial research on Africa

Since 1961, for instance, the Nigerian Archives has been publishing a valuable series of Special Lists of Records, providing information concerning the activities of particular agencies such as the police, the army and the medical service. Lesotho, to give another example, has issued a *Catalogue of the Basutoland Government Archives* (Rome, 1962), and Senegal has published *Répertoire des archives* by J. F. Maurel. The best and most complete African guide in existence is *A guide to the public records of Southern Rhodesia under the regime of the British South Africa Company 1890–1923* (Salisbury, Central African Archives, 1956). This consists of descriptions of all official records produced during a specific period of history, together with detailed administrative histories of each unit of government. The *Guide to the historical manuscripts in the National Archives of Rhodesia*, edited by T. W. Baxter and E. E. Burke (Salisbury, National Archives of Rhodesia, 1970), provides a survey of documents of prime provenance in the Archives; it also provides calendars (that is to say, précis) of the more important items. Calendars of this kind, however, remain rare. Though they are more useful as a finding aid than a catalogue or a guide, they are extremely expensive to produce.

Documentary collections are even more valuable than calendars because they make source material available to scholars who cannot afford to visit Africa and Europe. The publication of historical documents in the original or in translation forms the last stage in the archival process that started with the gathering and organizing of material and the production of lists, guides and calendars. During the 1820s German scholars initiated a historical revolution when they began to publish the *Monumenta Germaniae Historica*, a mammoth work which found imitators all over the world, giving a tremendous impetus to 'scientific' history. By the end of the nineteenth century South Africa had begun to participate in the systematic collection and publication of original sources, the first African country to do so. South Africa's historical pioneer was George McCall Theal, a Native Department official turned historian and archivist. Theal put out major series such as *Records of the Cape Colony* (Cape Town, Government Printer, 1897–1905, 36 v.). Rhodesia followed the South African example. Work began there when Professor J. P. R. Wallis joined the Archives as editor during World War II. With financial help from the late Sir Ernest Oppenheimer, a South African mining magnate, he produced the *Oppenheimer series* (1945–), which were mainly edited by himself and which contained journals and letters derived from European missionaries, explorers, traders and empire-builders – men such as the Reverend Robert Moffat, David Livingstone, Thomas Leask – covering European penetration into Central Africa during the nineteenth century. An additional series, the *Robin series* (1960–), later continued this work. The Rhodesian archives also sponsored a major scheme for the publication of Portuguese documents bearing on Portuguese penetration into what is now northern Mozambique, eastern Zambia, Malawi and Rhodesia. This collection was published in English and Portuguese under the English title *Documents on the Portuguese in Mozambique and Central Africa, 1497–1840* (National Archives of Rhodesia and Nyasaland, Salisbury, and Centro de Estudos Históricos Ultramarinos, Lisbon, 1962–).

In many other parts of Africa this kind of work is still left to individual scholars unsponsored by governments. From among the score of valuable collections, reference should be made to the Hakluyt Society founded in England in 1846 for the purpose of printing rare and valuable records concerning exploration and discovery from the Middle Ages to the nineteenth century. A good many of these publications deal with African travels. Other examples may be cited: G. S. P. Freeman-Grenville, ed., *The East African coast : Select docu-*

ments from the first to the earlier 19th century (London, Oxford University Press, 1962, 314 p.); G. E. Metcalfe, *Great Britain and Ghana: Documents of Ghana history, 1807–1957* (London, T. Nelson, 1965, 779 p.); C. W. Newbury, ed., *British policy towards West Africa: Select documents, 1786–1874* (London, Oxford University Press, 1965, 655 p.); and John D. Hargreaves, ed., *France and West Africa: An anthology* (New York, St. Martin's Press, 1969, 278 p.).

The International Council on Archives (ICA) is currently sponsoring a multivolume series called *Guide to the sources of the history of Africa*. These guides will be made up of surveys of the holdings in various individual countries outside of Africa. Another important series is *Guides to materials for West African history in European archives* (London, Athlone Press, University of London, 1962–). A great deal of material exists in the United States as well. This has been surveyed in Peter Duignan, *Handbook of American resources for African studies* (Hoover Institution, Stanford University, Calif., 1967, 218 p.). At the time of writing, Morris Rieger of the National Archives of the United States was engaged in putting together a guide of Africa-related materials in the United States, a project intended to form part of the ICA series.

The Colonial Records Project of the Oxford Committee for Commonwealth Studies has, since 1963, been trying to collect papers of people who have lived and worked in Africa in any capacity, be it missionary, merchant, government official or traveller. This effort has succeeded in gathering in thousands of collections of individuals and groups. But no similar program exists for any other colonial power.[8]

RESEARCH UNDERTAKEN BY INDIVIDUAL POWERS

During the colonial era, the imperial powers created the intellectual infrastructure of modern Africa. Research on Africa is impossible without reference to the vast mass of printed publications produced by various European bodies. We shall only list some of the more representative groups, even though such accounts necessarily make dry reading. For convenience, moreover, we have grouped these various bodies according to the countries which produced them. Further reference to these various organizations appear in the body of the text.

GREAT BRITAIN

In the development of African research, the British for a long time held a commanding lead, derived in part from a long history of exploration and commerce, evangelization and conquest. Until the end of the nineteenth century British research depended largely on the private enterprise of bodies such as the Royal Geographical Society (formed in 1830), which supported the exploratory work carried out by travellers and missionaries (though the government might assist such individuals as David Livingstone). Another important body was the Colonial Society, founded in 1868. The Colonial Society's original object was to

---

[8] For a detailed description of finding guides and descriptions of archives and library collections and of programs under way to retrieve the records of Africa's past, see Part I of the guide.

oppose sceptics who believed that Britain's white settlement colonies would inevitably cut adrift from the motherland, to promote the unity of the empire, and to spread knowledge concerning the different parts of the empire. The society built up an important library, published a journal of its own called *United Empire*, and created local branches in Britain as well as in the British empire. In addition the society held regular meetings for discussions, lectures and addresses; it also maintained a full Residential Club that provided a convenient meeting-ground for members on leave or on a visit in Great Britain. The Royal Empire Society later found imitators on the continent, where many colonial enthusiasts had a curious respect for the real or supposed abilities of British empire-builders, no matter whether they liked or detested the British as a people.[9]

The 'New Imperialism' also introduced many journals along with some changes in the organization of research. Following on Queen Victoria's Golden Jubilee, the British, in 1887, founded the Imperial Institute for the purpose of disseminating information and promoting research concerning the empire. This scientific endeavour, much of which centred on problems of tropical medicine and agriculture, was supported by the Royal Botanical Gardens at Kew and the natural history section of the British Museum. Interest in research received an additional impetus from the appointment of Joseph Chamberlain to the Colonial Office in 1895. Government money helped to set up the Liverpool School of Tropical Medicine (1898) and the London School of Tropical Medicine (1899). Another British institution of considerable importance was the Bureau of Hygiene and Tropical Diseases which was established in 1912 and published two monthly journals, the *Tropical Diseases Bulletin* and the *Bulletin of Hygiene*.[10]

The Great War and its aftermath stimulated interest in the real or assumed economic potential of the colonies and led to the creation of such bodies as the Empire Cotton Growing Organisation, established in 1921, the Commonwealth Forestry Institute, set up at Oxford in 1924, and a number of others.[11] During the 1920s the Colonial Research Committee provided some funds for study purposes, but not until the passing of the Colonial Development Act of 1929 did larger sums become available. In 1929 the British set up a whole group of Imperial Agricultural Bureaux. These in turn expanded into highly specialized institutions concerned with problems as varied as entomology, mycology, biological control, animal breeding, veterinary science, animal nutrition, dairy products, forestry, helminthology, horticulture, pastures, plant breeding and soils. In addition, the Economic Advisory Committee, a body appointed to report to the cabinet, set up separate committees to deal with specific problems of applied scientific research, for instance, tsetse control. The British were also the first to initiate ecological surveys in tropical Africa. (In 1935 they sponsored detailed investigations in Uganda.) These combined a close examination of the social life of the people with studies concerning their agricultural practices, the peculiarities of the soil, nutrition, and so forth. The surveys were designed, among other things, to provide information required for resettling people from areas where the soil had become exhausted.

The British promoted a host of other research schemes as well. In 1936, for example, they set up the Colonial Forest Resources Development Department.

[9] See T. R. Reese, *The history of the Royal Commonwealth Society, 1868–1968* (London, 1968), 280 p.
[10] An important journal of political opinion was *The Round Table : A Quarterly Review of the Politics of the British Commonwealth* (1910– , London).
[11] The British Cotton Growing Association was founded in the 1890s by A. L. Jones, who was active economically in West Africa and Uganda.

Research undertaken by individual powers

This was financed by the Colonial Office and worked in close collaboration with the Forest Products Research Laboratory at Princes Risborough and with other bodies. The Empire Forestry Conferences, held every five years, served to disseminate information and to provide a valuable link between forestry officers in different territories. Similarly, the Colonial Empire Marketing Board, set up in 1937, provided officials with guidance on a vast range of economic problems.

Essentially, however, the bulk of British research effort was much less centralized than that of France or Portugal. Government bodies in Great Britain itself did only a limited amount of research of their own. The British preferred instead to make grants to governmental agencies or to semi-official bodies in the various colonies that dealt with scientific problems as they occurred. The British likewise were slow in providing formal training to their proconsuls, preferring the cultured amateur to the specialist. Colonial administrators learned their craft for the most part on the job, under the supervision of their seniors. More theoretical courses tended to operate on an ad hoc basis. Nevertheless, by 1900 the British government had made arrangements for training candidates for the Indian Civil Service at Oxford and Cambridge and at University College, London. Language courses in Hausa and Swahili were taught to Colonial Service officers at King's College in London.

Colonial governments, recognizing early in this century the need to know more about the people they governed, employed anthropologists or encouraged colonial officers to act as anthropologists. In 1908 the British appointed a government anthropologist for Southern Nigeria, and in 1909 Dr. C. G. Seligman went to the Sudan to conduct an ethnographic survey. After 1920 British colonial governments increasingly used anthropologists to help them formulate and execute policy.[12] There was a great need for information about traditional societies, and governments felt an increased sense of social responsibility to modernize traditional life. Thus they called on the anthropologist to sketch in the habits, thoughts and patterns of behaviour of the colonized people. Men like Charles K. Meek, R. S. Rattray and Hans Cory prepared studies for the British colonial governments on tribal customs and institutions.[13]

Each colony undertook some studies of the people of its area. To illustrate, the Native Affairs Department of the Gold Coast published a concise account of the history and constitution of the state of Peki. This study was intended as one in a projected series on the 'native states of the Gold Coast'. At least one other state survey was published, that of Ahanta in 1930.[14] The International African Institute (IAI) founded in 1926 likewise contributed a great deal to the study of Africa. The Institute acted as an information centre on African ethnology, linguistics and social study. It conducted research programs, seminars and conferences; it also maintained a library. Its publications included

[12] Daryll Forde, 'Applied anthropology in government: British Africa', in A. L. Kroeber, ed., *Anthropology to-day* (Chicago, 1953).

[13] See the following works of Charles K. Meek: *The northern tribes of Nigeria: An ethnographic account of the Northern Province of Nigeria, together with a report on the 1921 decennial census* (London, 1925), 2 v.; *A Sudanese kingdom: An ethnographical study of the Jukun-speaking peoples of Nigeria* (London, 1931); *Tribal studies in Northern Nigeria* (London, 1931), 2 v.; *Law and authority in a Nigerian tribe ...* (London, 1937); and *Land tenure and land administration in Nigeria and the Cameroons* (London, 1957); also the following works of Robert Sutherland Rattray: *Ashanti* (Oxford, 1923); *Religion and art in Ashanti* (Oxford, 1927); *Ashanti law and constitution* (Oxford, 1929); and *Tribes of the Ashanti hinterland* (Oxford, 1932), 2 v.

[14] See C. W. Welman, *The native states of the Gold Coast: History and constitution, Part I Peki, Part II Ahanta* (London, 1925 and 1930).

19

Africa (1928–), an important journal, *African Abstracts* (1950–), and numerous monographs.

The creation of the International African Institute itself gave evidence of the increasing importance now attained by anthropology. Anthropologists perfected methods of field work based on the assumption that investigators familiar with a native language and living among the people whom they studied were much more likely to understand African society than scissors-and-paste scholars who compiled their books by using the accounts of ship-captains, explorers and missionaries. The use of field work in anthropology and the emphasis on minute studies in depth of small communities amounted to an intellectual revolution comparable to the methodological shift in history brought about when historians began to utilize original correspondence files in addition to secondary works. Anthropology gradually came to be included in training courses for colonial administrators. In fact, governments themselves began to appoint anthropologists, and government presses began to publish anthropological accounts. British, and to a lesser extent French and Belgian, scholars became increasingly interested in work on African institutions and tribal governance. Colonial theoreticians tried to use indigenous institutions for two related but often contradictory purposes. In the first place, they wished to maintain surviving African states and statelets for the purpose of providing law and order with a minimum of social disruption and financial expenditure. They desired also to transform traditional society in a humane and organic fashion, thereby facilitating the development of cash economies. Many policy makers believed that the work of the International African Institute, through promoting the study of African kinship systems, marriage, politics, religion, etc., and through its detailed linguistic and ethnographic surveys of specific peoples throughout Africa, would be helpful in this task.[15] The Rhodes-Livingstone Institute, established in 1937, carried out similar studies but only for Central Africa. Its main series were *Communications* (1943–65), *Rhodes-Livingstone Papers* (1938–65), and the *Rhodes-Livingstone Journal* (1944–65).

The study of traditional African institutions played a predominant part in British academic work during this period. But the British also maintained their interest in more practical problems, such as those connected with labour. British officials such as Major G. St. J. Orde Browne, head of the Labour Department of Tanganyika, produced an important comparative study, *The African labourer* (London, Oxford University Press, 1933). Godfrey Wilson, the first director of the Rhodes-Livingstone Institute, compiled his *Essay on the economics of detribalization in Northern Rhodesia* (Livingstone, Northern Rhodesia, Rhodes-Livingstone Institute, 1941–42, 2 v.), which in fact amounted to a harsh critique of Northern Rhodesia's colonial economy.

World War II, the aftermath of war, and the attendant social and political problems, all encouraged additional research connected with economic matters. The fall of France for a time threw Great Britain largely on her own resources and on those of the empire. The Colonial Development and Welfare Act first passed onto the statute book in 1929 and then again in 1940. This new legislation provided funds (£500,000) for investigations into ethnography, sociology, medicine, forestry, agronomy, entomology, and so forth. The Colonial Office had supported some anthropological studies with its own funds; but these were greatly increased after 1944 with the setting up of the Colonial Social Science Research Council. This body helped raise money for establishing the East

---

[15] Lugard was one of the founders of IAI and was perhaps instrumental in getting certain kinds of research done.

Research undertaken by individual powers

African Institute of Social Research at Makerere in 1948, and the West African Institute of Social and Economic Research at Ibadan in 1951. The Colonial Office formed its own research department, and in 1949 a separate Colonial Research Service came into being.[16]

At the same time the British tried to co-ordinate research by regions. The East African High Commission established a whole range of research institutes in 1948 to oversee scientific investigations in agriculture, forestry, veterinary science, fishing and medical research. One such group was the East African Bureau of Research in Medicine and Hygiene in Nairobi. Other bodies included the East African Agriculture and Forest Research Organisation, the East African Agricultural and Fisheries Research Council, the East African Inland Fisheries Research Station, the East African Industrial Research Organization, the East African Leprosy Research Centre, the East African Meteorological Department, the East African Veterinary Research Organization and many others.

In Central Africa, the lead in applied sciences was taken by Southern Rhodesia, scientifically as well as economically the most developed part of the region. It was here that government-sponsored research into such subjects as demography, statistics and meteorology was first undertaken. The Central African Council, established in 1945, in some ways the precursor of the short-lived Federation of Rhodesia and Nyasaland, co-ordinated research among the three Central African territories. Later on (1953–63), the Federal Government became responsible for a substantial number of research services. By the 1950s, local bodies centred on Salisbury included groups as varied as the Agricultural Research Council of Rhodesia and Nyasaland, the National Archives of Rhodesia and Nyasaland and the Central African Statistical Office, which for a time ministered to the needs of all three Central African territories. In addition, the separate territorial governments continued to operate their own services, including agricultural stations and geological surveys. Investigations into human problems were supported by the National Museum of Southern Rhodesia at Bulawayo, founded in 1901, the Commission for the Preservation of Natural and Historical Monuments and Relics, set up in Southern Rhodesia in 1936, and the Rhodes-Livingstone Museum of Northern Rhodesia, opened in 1934. Later, in 1937, the Rhodes-Livingstone Institute carried on extensive research on human problems in Central Africa.

In British West Africa, the colonial authorities likewise encouraged inter-territorial co-operation, even though the various territories were not contiguous. Regional research institutes included the West African Council for Medical Research, the West African Institute for Trypanosomiasis Research, the West African Institute for Oil Palm Research, and the West African Institute of Social and Economic Research. Various ministries carried out studies on specialized problems connected with agronomy, forestry, demography, veterinary research and antiquities. The creation of autonomous university colleges associated with London University such as at Ibadan, Nigeria, in 1947 and the University College, Legon, Gold Coast, in 1948 lent further impetus for research into a great variety of topics.

British expatriates as well as British-trained Africans also set up a whole range of private organizations that produced historical journals, reviews concerning ethnography and geography and similar publications. Such scholarly or semi-

---

[16] See Sir Charles Jeffries, ed., *A review of colonial research* (London, H.M. Stationery Office, 1964), 238 p. For a more general description of British governmental research, see D. N. Chester and F. M. G. Willson, eds., *The organization of British central government . . .* (London, Allen and Unwin, 1957), p. 249–273.

scholarly journals included the Uganda Society's *Uganda Journal*, founded in 1923, *Tanganyika Notes and Records* (1936–65), the *Northern Rhodesia Journal* (1950–65), and many others. The format of these journals, whose readers were interested in the history, literature, cultures and scientific study of the colony and its peoples, was basically the same: all contained articles, notes, correspondence, book reviews and bibliographies. Tables, maps and photos were often included as well. These publications remain primary sources for the study of African history and ethnography. Other societies specialized in economics, or flora and fauna. For example, *Nigerian Field* (organ of the Nigerian Field Society, 1931–) concerned itself with plant and animal life, as well as with history and culture in Nigeria.

GERMANY

The Germans were among the last Europeans to appear on the colonial scene and the first to leave in the twentieth century. The first twenty years of German governance saw warfare on an extensive scale, and it was not until the first decade of the present century that major reforms were brought about. During the short period of their effective colonization, however, the Germans did accomplish a great deal. Earlier, of course, German scholars like Barth had worked for the British government or had undertaken missions for learned associations and had produced works of great erudition. As it happened, Germans acquired their African empire at a time when German scholarship held a leading place in the world of learning, especially in fields such as linguistics, geography and tropical medicine. In the German colonies, missionaries such as Jakob Spieth, with his classic studies of the Ewe, or Heinrich Vedder, with his investigations into the history and ethnology of South-West Africa, took the initiative. In time the German Kolonialamt produced a massive series of *Veröffentlichungen*, which dealt with a broad range of economic and scientific questions and formed part of a wider effort to make colonization at the same time more enlightened and more profitable. The Germans also promoted governmental research through more specialized institutions set up in Africa. For instance, the Biologisch-Landwirtschaftliches Institut Amani, established in 1902 in East Africa, aimed at promoting agricultural research as well as giving instruction for European settlers and African peasants, and represented a major pioneering effort in colonial agronomy.

The Deutsche Kolonialgesellschaft came into being in 1887. It derived from a merger of the Deutsche Kolonialverein (1882) and the Gesellschaft für deutsche Kolonisation (1884). The Gesellschaft claimed to be 'above parties and religious creeds', but in fact collaborated closely with other nationalist and right-wing organizations for the purpose of popularizing colonialism. The organization issued a wide variety of publications ranging from academic studies to popular brochures. The Gesellschaft was organized into local sections centring on the various German towns. The sections in turn were grouped into provincial units (Gauverbände), with a central directory in Berlin. The political influence of the Gesellschaft was considerably greater than, say, that of the Royal Empire Society in Great Britain.

Germany's scientific efforts in Africa were supported by numerous academic institutions at home. By 1914 a German student interested in African affairs had several options. He might, for instance, attend the Seminar für Orientalische Sprachen at the University of Berlin, founded in 1887 for the purpose of training interpreters as well as colonial civil servants. The Seminar became an important teaching institution where a young man might learn African languages such as Amharic, Swahili, Yaounde and Ewe, as well as concern himself with more general problems of colonial administration, geography and ecology. The Seminar, like others of its kind, produced a prestigious series of *Lehrbücher* and *Mitteilungen*, as well as the *Archiv für das Studium deutscher Kolonialsprachen.* Alternatively, a student might register at the Hamburgisches Kolonialinstitut, set up in 1908. Here he could study various African languages, anthropology and allied subjects. The Kolonialinstitut also issued a prestigious series of *Abhandlungen* on a great variety of colonial topics. A medical doctor or missionary would be able to learn about tropical diseases at the Seemannskrankenhaus und Institut für Schiffs und Tropenkrankheiten at Hamburg, at the Robert Koch Institut für Infektionskrankheiten at Berlin, or the Deutsches Institut für ärtzliche Mission at Tübingen. A jurist would be able to obtain information concerning African law through learned bodies such as the Internationale Vereinigung für vergleichende Rechtswissenschaft und Volkswirtschaftslehre. A would-be agronomist might attend the Kolonialschule Witzenhausen, founded in 1899, or the Kolonialakademie Halle, where he would have available the facilities of an institute of natural science.

German colonialism derived ideological support from the Deutsche Kolonialgesellschaft, a body that combined imperial propaganda with more specialized investigations. The Kolonialgesellschaft had a special committee concerned with economic questions known as the Kolonial-Wirtschaftliches Komitee. This body was responsible for issuing a considerable number of specialized publications, including monographs on various commodities, as well as an agricultural publication entitled *Der Tropenpflanzer.* This research effort was supported also by an extensive number of learned journals, many of which published articles directly or indirectly concerned with African questions. These comprised serials as varied as the *Zeitschrift für Ethnologie* (1869–), the *Zeitschrift für Kolonialpolitik*, the *Zeitschrift für Volkskunde* (1891–), *Globus* and others whose back numbers remain of great value to researchers. The Zentralstelle of the Kolonialinstitut in Hamburg served as the co-ordinating body for German economic and scientific work on Africa.

FRANCE

French scholarship played an essential part in the 'opening up' of Africa. As early as the 1850s the French governor of Senegal, Faidherbe, encouraged studies in the history of the peoples of the Senegambia. He wrote histories and he started three government publications – *Moniteur du Sénégal, Annales Sénégalaises* and the *Annuaire du Sénégal.* Articles in these journals are basic sources of information not only about French colonial rule but also about the customs and history of the people of the area.

During the nineteenth century the French, like their neighbours, also set up a network of learned institutions for the purpose of promoting overseas research. These bodies centred in Paris, the intellectual as well as the political hub of France, and included societies such as the Société de Géographie de Paris (1821) and the Société d'Anthropologie de Paris founded in 1859. Other societies dealt with agronomy, geology and botany, and their members might also make individual efforts to study Africa.

A most influential body was L'Aurore Coloniale Française, which from 1897 to 1937 published an important review, *La Quinzaine Coloniale.* This journal was dominated by the views of the leading French colonial theorist, J. Chailley-Bert, and provided a kind of clearing-house for information on colonial matters. A very important newspaper for colonial and economic matters was *La Dépêche*

Coloniale, published in Paris from 1896 as a daily with an illustrated monthly edition.

By and large, however, the French cultural and scientific effort in Africa, like French administration at large, was much more highly centralized than its British equivalent and at least after World War II spent far more money on research. During the late nineteenth century, the world-famous Institut Pasteur, established in Paris in 1888, sent out missions to various colonies. These missions would sometimes establish local research groups of the institute, for instance at St Louis in 1896 and at Brazzaville in 1910. The medical work of the Institut Pasteur was paralleled by the labours of a whole series of other technical institutes with branches in various French colonies. These bodies included the Laboratoire Central de Recherches Vétérinaires des Pays Tropicaux (1903) and other more specialized institutions established later, such as the Institut de Recherches du Coton et des Textiles Exotiques, the Institut Français des Recherches Fruitières Outre-Mer, with branches in Mauritania, the Ivory Coast, the Congo, Madagascar, Guinea and elsewhere, and the Institut de Recherches pour les Huiles et Oléagineux (1942). These and other scientific research centres were integrated into a larger organization, the Centre National de la Recherche Scientifique (CNRS) founded in 1939 at Paris. The CNRS was controlled by the Comité National de la Recherche Scientifique and directed a whole range of sections concerned with the natural sciences and the humanities. It was designed to promote and co-ordinate scientific investigations, to make grants-in-aid to suitable bodies, and to subsidize or establish laboratories for scientific research. The CNRS thus acquired a key position in French research. Even the apparent independence of the *facultés* was diminished by the financial control exercised by CNRS over specialized investigations and by the assistance it rendered to students working for their Doctorat ès Lettres. The CNRS also created its own centre of documentation, with its own library. Its publications were concerned primarily with scientific subjects but also included serials such as the *Bibliographie annuelle de l'histoire de France*.

During the same period colonial studies, properly speaking, were integrated into the highly systematized network of academies centred in Paris that played such an important part in French intellectual life. In France, as in Great Britain, interest in colonial history originally focused on the doings of the colonizers themselves. In 1913 French scholars set up the Société d'Histoire des Colonies Françaises (later Société Française d'Histoire d'Outre-Mer), which published the *Revue d'Histoire des Colonies*. In 1922 French scholars founded the Académie des Sciences Coloniales (later called the Académie des Sciences d'Outre-Mer). The Académie had separate sections on geography, politics, administration, law, economics, sociology, medicine and education. It issued besides a valuable series entitled *Comptes-Rendus Mensuels des Séances*, which dealt with all branches of the natural and social sciences. During the inter-war period, however, the study of African institutions came increasingly into its own. In 1931, French Africanists created the Société des Africanistes at the Musée de l'Homme to study anthropology; this body, like others of its kind, issued its own publication, the *Journal de la Société des Africanistes*. Also important was the Institut d'Ethnologie (founded in 1926) attached to the University of Paris and financed by the Overseas Ministry.

In West Africa the Comité d'Etudes Historiques et Scientifiques de l'Afrique Occidentale Française published monographs and its own *Bulletin* from 1918 to 1938. Most of the research effort in French Africa, however, became concentrated at the Institut Français d'Afrique Noire (IFAN), founded in 1938 at

Research undertaken by individual powers

Dakar, the main intellectual, commercial, and administrative centre of French West Africa. This institution issued a *Bulletin* (1939–53) that was succeeded by *Bulletin, Série A, Sciences Naturelles* (1954–), *Bulletin, Série B, Sciences Humaines* (1954–), several monographic series: *Catalogues et documents* (1947–), *Mémoires* (1947–), *Initiations et études africaines* (1950–) and a general cultural review for West African ethnology, history and linguistics, *Notes Africaines* (1939–). Subsidiary centres were established over the years in all the colonies forming the French West Africa Federation: Centre Cameroun (1948–58), Centre de Mauritanie (1948–), Centre du Niger (1953–), Centre du Soudan, Centre Haute-Volta (1950–), Centre Sénégal (1949–). These centres issued monographic series irregularly, usually under the title of the research institute, for example, *Etudes nigériennes*. In addition, IFAN maintained a number of museums which specialized for the most part in history and ethnography.

From 1943 onward, the Office de la Recherche Scientifique d'Outre-Mer (ORSOM), part of the Ministry for Overseas France, became responsible for organizing basic research in the colonies. This institution (now ORSTOM) established research centres and also directed the Institut d'Etudes Centrafricaines (1947) at Brazzaville and the Institut de Recherches Scientifiques du Cameroun (1953) at Yaoundé for example. In addition it trained scientists and laboratory personnel and published numerous monographs.[17]

The framework of French colonial research had been laid before the end of World War II. The post-war period, however, saw considerable expansion. The scope of CNRS was enlarged by the creation of new bodies such as the Institut National d'Etudes Démographiques (1945), the Institut d'Elevage de Médecine Vétérinaire des Pays Tropicaux (1958), and the Institut de Recherches Agronomiques Tropicales (1960). In the humanities, the French made further advances in African history, archaeology and anthropology. They also expanded academic teaching in university centres located respectively at Strasbourg, Aix-en-Provence, Montpellier and Bordeaux. Paris, however, remained the intellectual nerve cell of France, and most of the important work continued to be done in the capital. Studies were pursued at institutions such as the Centre de Recherches Africaines, administratively part of the Faculty of Letters and Humanities at the Université de Paris à la Sorbonne, and at the Centre de Hautes Etudes Administratives sur l'Afrique et l'Asie Modernes (originally set up in 1936 as Centre de Hautes Etudes d'Administration Musulmane to train colonial personnel). The Centre put out a whole range of publications, including *L'Afrique et l'Asie* (1948–). The Ecole Pratique des Hautes Etudes at Paris maintained its own Centre d'Etudes Africaines, which issued publications such as *Cahiers d'Etudes Africaines* (1960–).

BELGIUM

The intellectual and organizational history of Belgium bore considerable similarity to that of France. The Belgians, like the French, were inclined to centralize their research, a policy made easier both by the relatively small size of the motherland and the centralized system of governance employed in the Congo, itself a single territorial bloc. One of the first major institutions specifically designed to deal with colonial affairs was the Musée Royal de l'Afrique Centrale, formerly Musée Royal du Congo Belge, founded in 1897 at Tervuren,

[17] Office de la Recherche Scientifique et Technique Outre-Mer (ORSTOM), *Office de la Recherche Scientifique et Technique Outre-Mer: Organization, activités, 1944–1955* (Paris, 1955), 182 p.

Introduction : colonial research on Africa

near Brussels. The Museum carried out research into a wide variety of human problems and built up extensive collections in pre-history, ethnography and African art, as well as geology, mineralogy, palaeontology, zoology, and other subjects. From 1898 onward, the Museum launched an extensive publications program, with series such as the *Annales de Zoologie* (1898), the *Annales d'Ethnographie* (1899), the *Revue de Zoologie et de Botanique Africaines* (1911). In 1910 the Belgians established the Ecole de Médecine Tropicale at Brussels, transferred to Antwerp in 1931 under the name Institut Prince Léopold. The Union Royale Belge pour le Congo et les Pays d'Outremer (founded in 1910 as the Union Royale Coloniale Belge) dates from the same period.

In Belgium, as in France and Great Britain, the years following World War I saw a considerable expansion in colonial studies. In 1920, for instance, the Belgians founded the Université Coloniale de Belgique at Antwerp, with faculties for political, administrative and commercial sciences. Eight years later, in 1928, the Académie Royale des Sciences d'Outre-Mer (ARSOM, originally known as Institut Royal Colonial Belge) opened its doors at Brussels. Its object was to develop overseas research and to disseminate information through Belgian universities and scientific bodies. The Academy issued an outstanding series of publications such as its *Bulletin* and *Mémoires* (*Classe des sciences morales et politiques, Classe des sciences naturelles et médicales, Classe des sciences techniques*) and similar works. Another specialized institution was the Ecole de Médecine Vétérinaire de l'Etat, which dated back to 1832, and which played an important part in the history of Belgian veterinary research. Investigations into agricultural problems were undertaken first of all by the State Botanical Gardens at Brussels, by the Botanical Department at the Musée du Congo Belge at Tervuren, and by the University of Louvain. In 1931 Louvain University initiated its own research centres in the Congo for the purpose of improving African agriculture. The new organization became known as CADULAC (Centres Agronomiques de l'Université de Louvain au Congo). In 1933 the Belgians established the Institut National pour l'Etude Agronomique du Congo (INEAC), which maintained a network of stations in the Congo where agronomists studied problems concerning the cultivation of oil-palms, coffee, rubber, cotton and indigenous food crops. In addition, INEAC concerned itself with veterinary questions and the improvement of African-bred cattle.

The aftermath of World War II witnessed scientific expansion on a large scale. In addition to undertaking more 'practical' work, the Belgians became increasingly concerned with sociological issues. In 1946 Belgian scholars founded the Centre d'Etude des Problèmes Sociaux Indigènes (CEPSI) at Elizabethville (Lumumbashi). A year later they set up the Centre d'Etudes Sociales Africaines (CESA) at Léopoldville (Kinshasa), as well as the Institut pour la Recherche Scientifique en Afrique Centrale (IRSAC), which centred at Brussels but maintained separate research stations at Lwiro, at Astrida in Ruanda-Urundi, at Uvira at Lake Tanganyika, at Mabali at Lake Tumba and at Elizabethville in Katanga. Its researches extended over numerous disciplines, including biology, physics and the humanities. Like INEAC, IRSAC had several important series to its credit, including reports, journals and monographs, such as the *Folia Scientifica Africa Centralis*; (INEAC, the *Série scientifique*, the *Série technique*, 1935–).[18] Other bodies of post-war provenance included the Institut Royal des Relations Internationales, set up in 1947 at Brussels, which published material dealing with colonial as well as international studies, and the Centre de Docu-

---

[18] See *Encyclopédie du Congo Belge* (Bruxelles, Editions Bieleveld, 1949–52), for a full survey of educational and scientific institutions of the Belgian Congo.

26

mentation Economique et Sociale Africaine (CEDESA, established in 1957 at Brussels). This last-named body co-ordinated documentation concerning the social and economic development of Central Africa. In 1958 a group of Belgian scholars, journalists and economists founded the Centre de Recherche et d'Information Socio-Politiques (CRISP) to provide information on the background to current developments in the Congo. Finally in 1959, just before the breakdown of Belgian rule, the Belgians created the Conseil National de la Politique Scientifique (CNPS) for the purpose of co-ordinating advanced research and higher education in the Congo.

PORTUGAL

Portugal's colonial empire is the oldest in Africa, and yet in some respects the most recent. Portuguese discoverers were the first Europeans to provide accounts of sub-Saharan Africa. Portuguese missionaries and travellers, as well as scholar-administrators (such as Governor F. J. M. Lacerda e Almeida, an eighteenth-century explorer of Brazilian origin), did much of the early scientific pioneering work in Africa. But unable to sustain her colonial position, Portugal found herself by the middle of the nineteenth century with her African empire reduced to little more than a few enclaves while the motherland languished. Between 1836 and 1852, however, the Portuguese founded or reorganized their Escola Médico-Cirurgia, the Escola Polytéchnica, and the Instituto de Agronomia Veterinária at Lisbon. These institutions supplied the small country with a relatively large number of qualified men, some of whom sought careers in Portugal's overseas possessions. Much colonial and ethno-history material appeared in the *Boletim Oficial* of Angola and of Mozambique. In 1875 Portuguese scholars founded the Sociedade de Geografia de Lisboa, which published a *Boletim* and many other works and exercised considerable influence on the history of colonial expansion. (See Sociedade de Geografia de Lisboa, *75 Anos de actividades ao serviço da ciência e da Nação : 1875–1950*, Lisbon, 1950.) In 1885 the Instituto de Antropologia came into existence at the University of Coimbra. In 1902 the Portuguese founded their own School of Tropical Medicine; and the Jardim e Museu Agricola do Ultramar, which opened its doors at Lisbon in 1906, made an important contribution to the study of colonial plants and agricultural products. It published an *Index Seminum* as well as other series of considerable value.

During the same period the Portuguese, determined to hold onto their empire despite foreign threats, founded the Escola Colonial (raised to the level of the Escola Superior Colonial in 1927). The Escola Superior (later known as the Instituto Superior de Estudos Ultramarinos) was run by the Ministério das Colonias for the purpose of training administrators and promoting research. Graduates might acquire a doctorate in colonial sciences. The Institute also published works on linguistic, ethnographic and related themes. Its series included *Anuários* (from 1919) and *Estudos Ultramarinos* (from 1948). (The Escola Superior in turn developed into the Instituto Superior de Ciências Sociais e Política Ultramarina, which offers courses at both the undergraduate and the graduate levels.)

In 1936 the Portuguese further reorganized their system of colonial studies. The Junta das Missões Geográficas e de Investigacões do Ultramar, which was rigidly centralized, was set up to co-ordinate and expand existing research. Twenty years later, the Junta comprised more than forty different institutes, centres and ' missions ', which between them dealt with a vast range of studies that included such natural science subjects as geology, pharmacology and biology, as well as the humanities. The most important of these institutions included the Centro de Geografia do Ultramar (founded in 1946), the Centro de Estudos Históricos Ultramarinos (1955), the Centro de Estudos Políticos e Sociais (1956), the Centro de Estudos Missionários (1959), the Centro de Estudos de Servicio Social (1960) and the Centro de Estudos de Antropologia Cultural (1962). Documentation was provided by the Centro de Documentação Ciêntífica Ultramarina (1957). Other bodies dealt with specialized problems such as the treatment of coffee diseases. The Junta as a whole sustained an extensive publications program (including an annual since 1946, *Anais*, and monographic series entitled *Estudos de ciências políticas e sociais*, begun in 1956, *Estudos ensaios e documentos*, and others). In addition, the Agência Geral do Ultramar, Lisbon, issued a vast array of works on all aspects of African affairs, works designed to put the Portuguese case for colonialism, as well as to publicize the results of scholarly investigations. It also published an important journal *Boletim Geral do Ultramar* (1925–).

Finally, the Portuguese set up a number of research institutes based in the colonies themselves. The earliest of these were concerned with meteorological studies and included the Observatório Meteorológico e Magnetico João Capelo, founded at Luanda in 1875, and the Observatório Astronómico e Meteorológico Campos Rodrigues, established at Lourenço Marques. By the 1930s, moreover, the Portuguese maintained a central laboratory for veterinary pathology as well as experimental farms both in Angola and in Mozambique. Work on the breeding of cattle and sheep for export from Angola proved of particular value.

The 1930s and 1940s also saw the creation of some additional bodies like the Museu de Angola at Luanda (1938) and the Missão Geográfica de Angola (1941). Expansion on a large scale did not occur until the 1950s, when there was a major increase in the development of Portugal's scientific resources, designed at the same time to legitimize the Portuguese position overseas, to expand knowledge, and to use more effectively the human and physical potential of Portugal's overseas provinces. Newly founded bodies included the Instituto de Angola at Luanda (1952, concerned with science, art and literature), the Centro do Investigação Ciêntífica Algodeira (concerned with the development of cotton), the Instituto de Investigação Agronómica de Angola, the Instituto de Investigação Ciêntífica de Angola, the Instituto de Investigação Médica de Angola, and corresponding bodies in Mozambique. Local publications included the *Boletim* of the Sociedade de Estudos de Moçambique (1931–) at Lourenço Marques and the *Arquivos de Angola* (1933–) at Luanda. Working in collaboration with the Centro de Estudos Históricos Ultramarinos at Lisbon, the Instituto de Investigação Ciêntífica de Angola put out a major series known as *Angolana* (*Documentação sobre Angola*), which covered the development of Angola from 1783 onward. A corresponding publication for Mozambique and the adjoining parts of what later became British territory in Central Africa was *Documentos sobre os Portugueses em Moçambique e na Africa Central 1497–1840* (1962–), published in Portuguese and English, in collaboration with the National Archives of Rhodesia. Portugal also produced an extensive missionary and military literature in journals such as *García de Orta* (1953–), *Portugal em Africa : Revista de Cultura Missionária* (1894–), *Revista Militar* (1849–) and others.

ITALY

Italian travellers were among the earliest explorers in Africa, and Italian soldiers, missionaries, engineers and merchants had an important part in the opening up of the continent. Modern Italian colonialism, however, dates only from the unification of Italy. In Italy, as in France and Portugal, geographical studies played a major role as a precursor of colonial expansion. In 1867 Cesare Correnti founded the Società Geografica Italiana, which originally had its headquarters at Florence but soon shifted its location to Rome, where it acquired a semi-official character. The society issued a *Bollettino* (1868–), *Memorie* (1878–), and other publications.[19] Whereas the Società Geografica was concerned primarily with theoretical studies tinged with humanitarian concern, the *Esploratore, Giornale di Geografia Commerciale*, founded at Milan in 1877, was more practical in its orientation. This journal, because it received considerable support from the Northern Italian bourgeoisie, was able to subsidize expeditions to Africa. In 1879 supporters of the journal set up the Società d'Esplorazioni Commerciali in Africa, whose committee contained many of the best known industrialists and merchants of Lombardy. Other bodies included the Società Africana d'Italia, which was established in 1880 at Naples and issued a periodical called *Africa*, later known as *Africa Italiana* (1888–). The Società di Studi Geografici e Coloniali at Florence was started in 1884 and was responsible for putting out the *Rivista Geografica Italiana* (1893–). The Istituto Italiano di Antropologia (known earlier on as the Società Romana di Antropologia), set up in 1893, also played its part in Italian scholarship through the journal *Rivista di Antropologia*.

Another body, founded in 1906 at the behest of private individuals, was the Istituto Coloniale Italiano (later known as the Istituto Coloniale Fascista). The Istituto had its origins in the Congress of Asmara, assembled in 1905 for the specific purpose of combating 'colonial defeatism'. The Istituto aimed at co-ordinating the work of all 'patriotic' bodies interested in colonial matters, including organizations such as the Lega Navale, the Istituto la Società Dante Alighieri, the Società Geografica, and others. The Istituto did propaganda work in favour of Italian expansion. In addition, it published numerous works of an academic or semi-academic nature. Particularly noteworthy are the *Annuario delle Colonie Italiane e dei Paesi Vicini* (1926–) and the *Rivista Coloniale* (1906–27) followed by *L'Oltremare* (1927–34). Students of colonialism should consult also the works published under the auspices of the Biblioteca di Studi Coloniali, which put out monographs on the Italian colonies and on 'semi-colonial' countries such as Venezuela and Siam, as well as on problems concerning Italian emigration overseas.

Italian universities likewise developed colonial research. A few institutions require special mention, for example the Istituto Agricolo Coloniale Italiano in Florence, which was organized in 1903 and which published *L'Agricoltura Coloniale* (1907–44), monographs and other works. The Scuola di Lingue Slavi ed Orientali Viventi, initiated at Rome University in 1918, began to offer courses in the languages and cultures of various African peoples; so did the Istituto Universitario Orientale at Naples. Other academic bodies at other universities performed work of direct or indirect interest to Africa, including departments such as forestry and veterinary science. In this connexion the Istituto Superiore

---

[19] See Enrico de Agostini, *La Reale Società Geografica Italiana e la sua opera dalla fondazione ad oggi 1887–1936* (Rome, Reale Società Geografica Italiana, 1937).

di Sanità, founded at Rome in 1935, with courses in epidemiology, parasitology, therapeutic chemistry and related fields, assumed special importance.

Italian official publications were numerous and their provenance deserves some explanation. The central direction of Italy's colonial empire was at first entrusted to the Ministry of Foreign Affairs. Following the occupation of Assab in 1882, a special section within the Ministero degli Affari Esteri took charge of colonial matters, a practice that corresponded to the German pattern. When the Italians embarked on an expansionist policy, the colonial bureau became increasingly important. This department was reorganized in 1908 as the Direzione Centrale degli Affari Coloniali within the Ministero degli Affari Esteri. In 1912, after the occupation of Libya, colonial affairs were entrusted to a separate Ministero delle Colonie. From 1913 this ministry issued its own *Bollettino* under varying titles, known from 1927 as the *Rivista delle Colonie*. During the fascist regime, in 1937, the ministry was renamed Ministero dell'Africa Italiana. Like its predecessor, this ministry published an extensive amount of material, including the *Annali* (1938–41). After the breakdown of the Italian empire, the archives of the colonial ministry were returned to the Ministero degli Affari Esteri, which set up the Comitato per la Documentazione dell'Opera dell'Italia in Africa. The Comitato published *L'Italia in Africa*, a major series with specialized subdivisions, including a *Serie Storica* (1958–), *Scoperte Archaeologiche* (1960–), *Serie Civile* (1965–), *Serie Giuridico-amministrativa* (1963–), *Serie Storica-militare* (1959–), *Serie Scientifico-culturale* (1963–), as well as monographs such as one on the *Servizio veterinario nell'Africa*.

The more specialized forms of research were directed by the Consiglio Nazionale delle Ricerche (CNR), founded in 1923 under fascist auspices. The Consiglio's object was to promote and co-ordinate scientific investigations into the mathematical, physical and natural sciences, both pure and applied (including engineering and medicine), to make grants-in-aid to scientific institutions and to individuals, and also to advise ministries on technical matters. The Consiglio controlled a considerable number of centres and institutes, some of which were directly concerned with African problems.

The Italians also built up a considerable number of research centres that were locally based in the colonies. These included the Museo della Garese at Moga-discio, with ethnographic and natural history collections, veterinary institutions at Asmara, Merca and Addis Ababa, and hydro-biological observatories. The Italians likewise created a network of agricultural offices and experimental farms for the purpose of investigating zoological, botanical, climatological, eco-logical and related problems. Agricultural experts provided advice both to Italian settlers and to indigenous farmers. Furthermore the government dis-patched a number of specialized commissions to East Africa for the purpose of investigating particular products such as wool, oil seeds, etc.

After the collapse of the Italian empire, research into the history of the empire reverted to the Ministero degli Affari Esteri, which we have already mentioned. Italian scholars set up a number of other bodies to study Africa, which included the Istituto Italiano per l'Africa at Rome. The institute's publication was called *Africa* (1946–).

SPAIN

The main thrust of Spanish colonization was directed toward South America; and though the country's stake in sub-Saharan Africa remained minimal, its contribution to research in Africa was by no means negligible. A number of learned societies were concerned with African studies in one way or another, for instance, the Instituto de Estudios Políticos (set up in 1939), which among many publications issued an index to the laws of Guinea.

Research in Spain was highly centralized. In 1940 the government set up the Consejo Superior de Investigaciones Científicas (CSIC), whose purpose was the co-ordination of research among existing institutions. In addition, the Consejo aimed at sponsoring studies in fields of scholarship previously neglected. The Consejo embraced a number of separate *patronatos* covering the various branches of knowledge. Thus the Patronato 'Santiago Ramón y Cajal' comprised such bodies as the Instituto 'Bernardino de Sahagún' de Antropología y Etnología, the Museo Etnológico and the Instituto Español de Medicina Tropical. The Patronato 'Diego Saavedra Fajardo' directed the Instituto 'Juan Sebastián Elcano' de Geografía, some of whose work was of African interest. Other *patronatos* concerned themselves with agricultural, veterinary, hydrological and similar studies. Another body controlled by the CSIC was the Museo Canario in the Canary Islands, with major sections on ethnography and archaeology, and a noteworthy local library. In 1945 the Spaniards founded the Instituto de Estudios Africanos, whose publications included *Africa* and *Archivos* and numerous monographs.

INTERNATIONAL BODIES

In addition to building up these national bodies, the colonial powers and their allies made some attempts at international co-operation. The publications of the League of Nations in connexion with bodies such as the mandates or the Temporary Slavery Commission, set up in 1925, are well worthy of mention. They include studies such as the 'Report of the International Committee of Experts on Native Labor', submitted at the nineteenth session of the International Labor Conference in 1935, a document of particular value to the socio-economic history of modern Africa. The annual reports from the mandates were of course valuable documents as well.[20]

The League undertook a considerable amount of work in the medical field as well. The earliest international organization in this field was the Office International d'Hygiène Publique, set up in 1907 at Paris with support from numerous governments. Its primary object was to prevent by international sanitary conventions the spread of infectious diseases. Later on, the League of Nations created a Health Section under the League Secretariat. The work carried out under this section on subjects such as sleeping-sickness, malaria, and leprosy proved of considerable benefit to Africa. So did the labours undertaken by the Permanent Commission on Biological Standardization also appointed by the Health Organization of the League.

The work of the League depended on technical co-operation between governments. In addition, the colonial powers created various institutions of a nonofficial kind, one of the earliest of which was the International Colonial Institute, created in 1894. This body, which was based in Brussels, called conferences, commissioned reports and published valuable monographs on political, social and economic aspects of colonialism. Africa was well covered in the group's various publications.[21] It also published a *Compte rendu* (1895–) and numerous

[20] See Hans Aufricht, *Guide to League of Nations publications: A bibliographical survey of the work of the League, 1920–1947* (New York, 1951), 682 p. The United Nations in later years carried on a similar series of publications and added many others.

[21] See, for example, *Le régime et l'organisation du travail des indigènes dans les colonies tropicales* (Brussels, 1929), 326 p.

valuable monographs on political, social and economic aspects of colonialism around the world. In 1949, the institute became the Institut International des Civilisations Différentes (INCIDI), with headquarters at Brussels. It publishes a journal called *Civilisations* (1951–) and reports on the international conferences it sponsors on social science topics. Perhaps the most important of these multi-national organizations was the International African Institute, set up in 1926 at London for the purpose of promoting research into the culture, language and social institutions of the African peoples. This institute issued a journal, as well as numerous books and pamphlets concerned with anthropology, linguistics and related subjects.

After World War II the colonial powers extended their co-operation to a number of more technical fields. Conferences were held on subjects such as diseases of animals and humans, locust control, etc. A permanent advisory body to co-ordinate scientific research for all Africa south of the Sahara was established in 1950, the Commission for Technical Cooperation in Africa South of the Sahara (CCTA); and an advisory group with expert advisers, the Scientific Council for Africa South of the Sahara (CSA). The CCTA was able to set up institutes, spread information and speed up liaison through many organizations on problems of mutual concern. Some of these groups were the Bureau Permanent Inter-africain de la Tsétsé et de la Trypanosomiase at Léopoldville; the Inter-African Bureau for Soils and Rural Economy, Paris; the Inter-African Bureau of Epizootic Diseases, Muguga, Kenya; and the Inter-African Labour Institute at Bamako, Mali (see its *Bulletin*, 1953–). The CCTA also sponsored valuable conferences on problems of medicine and health, labour, rural economies, soil science, statistics, fisheries, etc. The CSA had its headquarters at Bukavu in the former Belgian Congo. It performed a valuable service by having specialists make recommendations to the CCTA concerning topics for conferences or for research.

Scholarly international groups also met to discuss African history, ethnography or languages. For example, the Pan-African Congress on Prehistory first convened in 1947, then in 1952, 1955, 1959, 1963. *Proceedings* or *Acts* were usually published following these congresses.

Within two generations scholarship in Africa has undergone revolutionary changes. Colonialism occasioned an unprecedented transfer of administrative, literary, scientific and technological skills. The colonizers laid the foundations on the continent for modern research in medicine and science. They created an array of research centres, institutions, archives, government departments and related agencies. These in turn produced masses of data and records and new tools of communicating and storing knowledge. The colonial government printing-presses alone published formidable collections of gazettes, proceedings, annual reports, transactions, and blue books that no student of Africa can afford to neglect. As Ndabaningi Sithole, an African nationalist from Rhodesia, noted, for all the ills occasioned by imperialism, it also had a profound impact for good. For instance, ' The exchange of ideas has been greatly accelerated. . . . The dissemination of all kinds of information has been unprecedented in African history.' [22] No previous imperialists in the history of the world – not Egyptian, Greek, Roman or Russian, not Mongol, Arab, Chinese or Norman – wrote so much about the people they conquered or knew so much about the languages, laws, customs and traditions of the people they ruled.

[22] Ndabaningi Sithole, *African nationalism* (Cape Town, Oxford University Press, 1959), p. 70.

PART I

GUIDE TO
REFERENCE MATERIALS

CENTRES, INSTITUTIONS AND
RECORDS OF RESEARCH

Note In recent years there has been a substantial growth of institutions concerned with African studies and research. No comprehensive directory has been published, and new bodies come into existence so fast that no published record can for long be up to date. A few lists of institutions of specifically African interest have been issued, and some general world directories include groups relating to Africa. The names of those organizations that publish periodicals, as most do, usually appear in the indexes of lists of serials. Some large study centres maintain card files of organizational names to which constant additions are made as new institutions come to notice. Information about newly formed organizations is carried regularly in the ' News and Notes ' sections of the leading Africanist journals. These same journals are also among the best sources for accounts of research in progress or completed. In this section we indicate available lists of organizations concerned with African studies, guides to research on Africa, and registers of individual researchers.

1 *Africa : Journal of the International African Institute.* 1928– . London, Oxford University Press. Quarterly.

The ' News and Notes ' section is indispensable for reports on new institutions, conferences, programs of universities, and research and foundation activities. It is now available as an offprint (as is the ' Bibliography of Current Publications ').

2 *African Social Research.* 1966– . Manchester, Eng. Publ. on behalf of the Institute for Social Research, University of Zambia, by Manchester University Press (distributed in the United States by Humanities Press, New York 10010). Biannual.

Formerly the *Rhodes-Livingstone Journal : Human Problems in Central Africa.* In its scholarly articles and book reviews the journal plans to widen its scope to cover social research in all Africa and even work being done elsewhere when the findings appear to be applicable to Africa, especially in sociology and social anthropology, psychology, economics, human geography and demography, history and political science. An index is to be issued every five years.

3 African Studies Association, New York. *African Studies Bulletin.* 1958– . Publ. for the ASA by Hoover Institution, Stanford, Calif., 1965–66; by African Studies Center, Boston, 1967– . 3 times a year.

The African Studies Association was formed in March 1957 at a conference in New York at which 35 Africanists were present. In 1967 membership had grown to more than 1,400, almost 700 of them fellows. The first number of the *African Studies Bulletin* made its appearance in April 1958. The Association has reported in its pages on advances in African studies, for example, efforts to foster teaching and research in the African field, to promote courses and programs in colleges and universities (the *Bulletin* includes an annual list of American universities together with the courses they offer, e.g., ' African studies in the United States ', by Norman R. Bennett, v. 11, no. 1, April 1968: 83–127), to widen the scope of studies across disciplines, and to improve American library and archival resources. Reports of many conferences have been included, among them those under the auspices of the African Research Committee. A 24-page *Index* covering

35

v. 1–10 (1958–67) was issued in 1968. The Association also issues each year a *Roster of Fellows*. In 1970 the name of the bulletin was changed to *African Studies Review*. Henceforth substantive articles will be published. The Research Liaison Committee was established by the Association in 1966 to serve as a central agency for information on the planning and conduct of research with regard to Africa and for issuance of further information through the ASA *Bulletin* and through special reports (e.g., *A directory of studies centers and research institutes abroad : Africa*, New York (1967 ?), 63 1.). A grant by the Ford Foundation was crucial in the formation of this committee. A supplement was issued in 1968.

The Association's Libraries-Archives Committee has been important in encouraging compilation of descriptions of archives and manuscript collections and guides and bibliographies on holdings. Many of these lists and descriptions in the *Bulletin* are referred to in the following pages of this guide.

4 African Studies Association, New York. *African Studies Newsletter*. v. 1, no. 1– , 1968– . New York. 6 or 9 times a year.

Experimental issues of this leaflet were published in 1967 by the Washington Liaison Committee, and the Research Liaison Committee began issuing the *Newsletter* regularly in 1968. It is sent automatically to the membership of the Association and is devoted to announcements of interest to Africanists, including the news and notes section formerly published in the *African Studies Bulletin*. Among the items are data on institutions, conferences, meetings, seminars, U.S. Government action in connexion with Africa, foundation grants for study and research, positions available for teaching in or about Africa, African visitors in the United States, and new or forthcoming publications of special import. Beginning with the third issue, May–June 1968, the *Newsletter* has been publishing the record of research in progress previously issued by the U.S. Office of External Research.

5 African Studies Association of the United Kingdom. *Bulletin*. 1964– . Birmingham. 3 nos. a year.

Like the American *African Studies Bulletin* and the *Newsletter*, this journal is a prime source of information regarding institutions, centres of research and activities relating to African studies in the United Kingdom.

6 *Bulletin of Information on Current Research on Human Sciences Concerning Africa. Bulletin d'Information sur les Recherches dans les Sciences Humaines Concernant l'Afrique*. no. 1– , 1963– . Bruxelles, Centre International de Documentation Economique et Sociale Africaine (CIDESA).

Annotated list of research in progress, irregularly issued. Almost every issue begins with a list of works published prior to the current date, theses completed, works scheduled for publication, etc. There are indexes of institutions, authors, topics (by title words), and geographic distribution. The studies recorded are from universities and centres of learning in England, Germany, France, Belgium, Australia, Africa, and, in a few cases, the United States, etc.; there seems to be no attempt at complete coverage.

In Jozef Bogaert's *Sciences humaines en Afrique noire : Guide bibliographique, 1945–1965* (CIDESA, Enquêtes bibliographiques, no. 15, 1966), there are lists of organizations characterized as ' Répertoires d'institutions scientifiques, de bibliothèques et de chercheurs ', and ' Répertoire de sociétés et d'organismes commerciaux, politiques, économiques et sociaux '.

Centres, institutions and records of research

7 Centre d'Analyse et de Recherche Documentaires pour l'Afrique Noire (CARDAN). *Recherche Enseignement Documentation Africanistes Francophones, Bulletin d'Information et de Liaison*, v. 1, no. 1– , 1969– . Paris. Quarterly.

A francophone publication covering African studies in French-speaking Africa, Belgium, France, Switzerland and Canada. Format will be in ' fiches ' which can be cut up for filing. A bristol paper edition will be produced if there is sufficient demand. Future issues will carry lists of *thèses* and *diplômes*, annotations of Africanist periodicals, reports of research projects and trips, and studies of documentary methods. The social sciences and humanities are the disciplines covered.

The first issue, ' Inventaire des ressources documentaires africanistes à Paris ', by Joanne Coyle Dauphin, Agnès Rosset and Brigitta Rupp, comprises a directory of 129 organizations (libraries, research institutes, information centres) in Paris. Data given are sponsoring organization, address, amount and types of material in collection (maps, photographs, records, etc.), areas of specialty, publications, current projects, history of facilities, services and access. There are indexes of abbreviations used, of series, and of periodicals cited, with separate lists for bibliographical bulletins, acquisitions lists, publications lists, and annual reports of organizations. There is also a subject and geographic index.

8 Dauphin, Joanne Coyle. ' Belgian centers of documentation and research on Africa '. *African Studies Bulletin*, v. 8, no. 3, Dec. 1965: 21–39.

Signalling the many changes in ' orientation and in nomenclature ' of Belgian institutions concerned with Africa, this welcome list gives information on about 50 bodies.

9 ——— ' French provincial centers of documentation and research on Africa '. *African Studies Bulletin*, v. 9, no. 3, Dec. 1966: 48–65.

A checklist of more than 40 French institutions outside Paris.

10 Desai, Ram. ' The explosion of African studies in the Soviet Union '. *African Studies Bulletin*, v. 11, no. 3, Dec. 1968: 248–257.

The most important centres for African studies are described on p. 249–251. The major part of the article is devoted to a review of Soviet publications in the African field.

11 German Africa Society. *Museums in Africa: A directory*. New York, Africana Publishing Corp., 1970. 594 p.

12 Gessain, Monique. ' Liste des chercheurs dans les états francophones de l'Afrique noire et Madagascar; Séminaire des Sciences Humaines, Département d'Afrique Noire, Musée de l'Homme '. *Journal de la Société des Africanistes*, v. 32, fasc. 1, 1962: 179–205.

In this listing as of July 1962, 25 institutes and 700–800 researchers were named.

13 Hewitt, Arthur R. *Guide to resources for Commonwealth studies in London, Oxford, and Cambridge, with bibliographical and other information*. London, published for the Institute of Commonwealth Studies, University of London, by Athlone Press, 1957. 219 p.

Prepared by the then secretary of the Institute and its librarian, this guide describes in detail the resources of the chief British centres for African studies. (For full description see no. 74.) The third part (p. 183–203) names universities, research and advisory organizations, and other official and unofficial institutions and organizations. There is a comprehensive index. Although designed for students of British Commonwealth matters, some of the resources described furnish material for studies of all parts of Africa.

Part I : guide to reference materials

For further and current information on scholarly institutions relating to Africa, see issues of the *Bulletin of the African Studies Association of the United Kingdom* (no. 9) and *SCOLMA directory of libraries and special collections on Africa* (no. 83).

14 Institut Africain de Genève. *Répertoire des principales institutions s'intéressant à l'Afrique noire.* Genève, 1963. 1 v. unpaged. loose-leaf.

Survey of the leading European and American institutes, research centres, universities, publishing and documentation centres, libraries, archives and museums interested in African affairs. Particular emphasis is given to institutions specializing in history, economics, political science, etc. Over 180 centres are surveyed, and information includes name and address of the institution, its director, and a résumé of the organization's activities, library facilities and publication program. The loose-leaf format permits easy addition of data on new institutions or revision to bring information up to date. As of 1967, this work provided the most complete source available for description of the chief learned bodies (outside of those within Africa) concerned with African studies. It is inevitable that there are certain inaccuracies.

15 International African Institute. *International register of organisations undertaking Africanist research in the social sciences and humanities, 1970.* London, 1971. 65 1.

This register lists the major libraries, universities and research institutes of 43 African countries and 28 countries in Europe, Asia, and the Americas. Gives for most organizations the address, date of establishment, name of director, research units, regional focus within Africa and titles of publications. The information will be regularly supplemented in the new serial *International Bulletin of Current Africanist Research.*

16 International Conference on African Bibliography, Nairobi, Dec. 1967. *Survey of current bibliographical services on Africa.* London, International African Institute, 1967. 1 v. various pagings.

A working document for the International African Institute conference, the results of questionnaires answered by directors of bibliographical services dealing with Africa. Information given includes address of organization, bibliographies issued, compiler, frequency, subscription cost, circulation figures, number of items, promptness of service (date of entries in current issue), scope of bibliography, and whether abstracts or annotations are provided. There are over 60 organizations listed.

17 *Journal of Modern African Studies.* 1963– . Cambridge, Eng., and New York, Cambridge University Press. Quarterly.

For description see no. 244. Section on Africana provides descriptions of new African institutes and programs and surveys individual country programs.

18 Rupp, Brigitta. *Inventaire des registres de la recherche en cours dans le domaine des sciences sociales et humaines en Afrique noire.* Paris, CARDAN (Centre d'Analyse et de Recherche Documentaires pour l'Afrique Noire), Dec. 1966. 32 p.

19 Smith, Dorothy, comp. 'Scientific research centres in Africa', *African Studies Bulletin*, v. 10, no. 3, Dec. 1967: 20–47.

Contains recommendations for scientific research, traces research development under the colonial powers, and discusses the current status of some of the major African research centres, including a listing by country of research establishments (South Africa is not included). There is a bibliography and an abbreviations list.

Centres, institutions and records of research

20 Société des Africanistes. Centre de Documentation et d'Information. *Bulletin d'Information*. no. 1– , June 1964– . Paris. Quarterly.

The Society maintains in its documentation centre card files of scientific institutions in Africa, of courses relating to Africa in French-speaking institutions, and of research in progress, as well as calendars of congresses and conferences, exhibitions and other events of scholarly interest. These are recorded in the quarterly bulletin in sections of 'Thèses et diplômes', 'Fichier des chercheurs', and under other rubrics.

21 Tropical African Studies Conference, Ibadan, 1964. *A preliminary register of African studies at universities, research centres and other institutions*. [London ?] International African Institute, 1964. 33 p. 33 cm. mimeo.

The register, prepared for the conference and compiled from a questionnaire sent out at the end of 1963, was intended to provide an outline of the organization and scope of teaching and research in African studies. Data provided by the institutions answering the inquiry include name, address, and status, committees, centres, institutes, etc., concerned with African studies and, also, the scope of teaching and research, indicated by abbreviations. A good many institutions that failed to reply are given with name and address only. Entries are by country, in alphabetical order within continents, beginning with Africa; institutions from 28 countries of Africa south of the Sahara are listed.

22 U.S. Congress. House. Committee on Foreign Affairs. Subcommittee on International Organizations and Movements. *Overseas programs of private non-profit organizations*. Washington, U.S. Government Printing Office, 1965. 565 p. (89th Cong., 1st sess.)

Description of the work of welfare organizations, colleges, universities, etc.

23 U.S. Department of State. Bureau of Intelligence and Research. External Research Staff. *African programs of U.S. organizations: A selective directory*. Comp. by Jacqueline S. Mithun. Washington, May 1965. 132 p.

Earlier reports were issued in 1958, 1960 and 1961. Here are listed: American colleges and universities (42) having (*a*) area studies and language training programs and (*b*) operational programs; foundations (30); religious and missionary organizations (224); business organizations (266); and private nonprofit organizations and institutions specifically concerned with African culture, education and training (162). Also helpful are an index by African countries and a general index of organizational names. The comprehensiveness of this directory makes it mandatory for information on American interests in Africa.

24 Walraet, Marcel. *Documentation belge et tiers monde*. Bruxelles, Bibliothèque Royale de Belgique, 1965. 71 p.

Outlines chief Belgian sources of information in the form of printed materials regarding the developing countries of Asia, Africa and Latin America. Among collections described are those of official scientific and administrative organizations, international bodies, universities and private learned societies. The first appendix is a list of groups, with bibliographical references for each, and the second appendix gives periodicals in Belgium concerned in whole or in part with the Third World. See also, by the same author, *Les études africaines dans le monde: Hier, aujourd'hui, demain*. Bruxelles, Centre de Documentation Economique et Sociale Africaine, 1971. 104 p.

25 *Wissenschaft in Afrika*. Bonn, Deutsche Afrika-Gesellschaft, 1962. 168 p.

List of principal research centres and scientific organizations in Africa, arranged by country. Although by the time it was published additions were needed, the brochure is useful. Many of the institutions named are government departments and offices, which have changed names and increased in number since independence.

LIBRARIES AND ARCHIVES

Note Information on African libraries and archives and American and European holdings of published and manuscript African material dealing with the colonial period is scattered through scores of journals and specialist publications. Some of the most important sources are *African Studies Review* (formerly *African Studies Bulletin*, African Studies Association, New York); *Africana Library Journal* (formerly *Africana Catalogues*, New York); *Bulletin of the African Studies Association of the United Kingdom* (Birmingham); *American Archivist* (Menasha, Wis.); *Archives, Bibliothèques et Musées de Belgique* (Bruxelles); *Archives* (journal of the British Records Association, London); *Archivum : Revue Internationale des Archives* (Paris); *Gazette des Archives* (Paris); *Library Literature* (New York); and *Library Science Abstracts* (London). The Standing Conference on Library Materials on Africa (SCOLMA, London) produces a newsletter, *Library Materials on Africa* (see no. 82), which has information on library and archival holdings and acquisitions. Also useful are *SCAUL Newsletter* (Dar es Salaam); *African Libraries* (Pretoria); *UNESCO Bulletin for Libraries* (Paris); the former *WALA News* (see no. 117), bulletin of the West African Library Association, and its successors in 1964, the bulletins of the Ghana Library Association and the Nigerian Library Association, respectively.

The following section will list first general reference works and then works for specific regions and countries – i.e., library and archive collections in Western Europe and in the United States and then those in Africa (by region and country).

WESTERN EUROPE

General reference works

26 *Les grands dépots d'archives du monde : Notices sur les archives les plus importantes....* Paris, Presses Universitaires de France, 1969. 374 p.
Reviews many major national archives, their organization, holdings, publications, and other relevant information.

27 *Guide to the diplomatic archives of Western Europe.* Ed. by Daniel H. Thomas and Lynn M. Case. Philadelphia, University of Pennsylvania Press, 1959. 389 p.
Chapters by specialists on Western European archives provide history of principal depositories, chronological scope, arrangements, organization and condition of materials, and administration and use of records. Attention is called to valuable collections on Africa in Belgium, France, Germany, Great Britain, Italy, Portugal, Spain and the Vatican.

28 *Guides to materials for West African history in European archives* [series]. London, Athlone Press, University of London, 1962– .
The following in this series have been published :

no. 1 *Materials for West African history in the archives of Belgium and Holland.* By Patricia Carson. 1962. 86 p. (1,258 items)
Additions to this work are provided by H. M. Feinberg in *African Studies Bulletin* (v. 10, no. 3, Dec. 1967; and v. 12, no. 1, 1969).

no. 2 *Materials for West African history in Portuguese archives.* By A. F. C. Ryder. 1965. 92 p. (997 items)

no. 3 *Materials for West African history in Italian archives.* By Richard Gray and David Chambers. 1965. 164 p. (1,480 items)
Part 1 covers the Vatican archives and other archives in Rome, Part 2 the archives and libraries outside Rome.

no. 4 *Materials for West African history in French archives.* By Patricia Carson. 1968. 170 p. (2,723 items)
Basic surveys of governmental, institutional and private collections. Lists of finding aids are included. These will not be repeated here.

29 International Council on Archives. *Guide to the sources of the history of Africa.* Zug, Switzerland, Inter Documentation Co., 1970– .
Beginning in 1963, the International Council on Archives, supported by UNESCO, has been preparing a multi-volume series covering European and American sources for the history of Africa. The first eight volumes are designed to cover, respectively, the holdings in the German Federal Republic, Spain, France, Italy, the Vatican and the Scandinavian countries. Additional volumes on Belgium, the United Kingdom and the United States will be published separately.

The purpose of these guides is to provide access to the whole body of sources – not just to the archival holdings of the colonial governments. While the guides will be primarily concerned with public and private archives, they will also take account of material in libraries and museums.

Sources are described by repository and, within each repository, by archival groups and series. The work as a whole was co-ordinated by an international committee of specialists, headed originally by Etienne Sabbe, Archivist-General of Belgium.

By 1971, the following works had appeared: *Quellen zur Geschichte Afrikas südlich der Sahara in den Archiven der Bundesrepublik Deutschland* (1970, 126 p.); *Sources de l'histoire de l'Afrique au sud du Sahara dans les archives et bibliothèques françaises, 1 – Archives* (1971, 959 p.); *Guide to . . . Scandinavia. Sources in Denmark, Norway and Sweden* (1971, 101 p.); and *España. Guía de Fuentes para la historia de Africa Subsahariana* (1971, 210 p.).

30 Leopard, Donald D. 'Africa-related materials in European missionary archives'. *African Studies Bulletin*, v. 10, no. 2, Sept. 1967: 1–5.
The article describes the type of material to be found in three archives in London (London Missionary Society, United Society for the Propagation of the Gospel, and Friends Foreign Missionary Association) and one in France (Société des Missions Evangéliques de Paris).

31 McCall, Daniel F. *A report on African materials and activities in some European institutions.* Boston, Boston University, 1967. 59 p. (Boston University Papers on Africa, no. 1)
Description of holdings, and finding aids on Africa, of archives and museums in Austria, Denmark, France, Germany, Italy, Sweden and Switzerland.

Part I : guide to reference materials

Belgium

Note Archival development within the Belgian colonies was beset with many difficulties. As early as 1888 Leopold II created an archival service for his Congo Free State that operated as part of the Département de l'Intérieur at Brussels. The king established the archives as his personal property, however; and in 1906 the major part of the administrative records of the Congo Free State were systematically destroyed. When the Free State was annexed by Belgium in 1908, the newly founded Ministère des Colonies was thus almost completely lacking in earlier files. To some extent, however, the history of the Congo Free State can still be documented by reference to the papers of missionary societies, humanitarian bodies, commercial firms and private individuals.

After World War I there arose a renewed interest in Belgian colonial history, and in 1929 the Commission d'Histoire du Congo was set up within the newly founded Institut Royal Colonial Belge. The Commission encountered many difficulties, however. In 1940 Belgium was overrun by Germany, for the second time within a quarter of a century, and little was achieved. No systematic attempts were made during this period to preserve the records produced within the Congo itself.

It was only in 1947 that a section called ' Archives-Bibliothèques ' was created within the Secrétariat Général du Gouvernement Général in the Congo. A year later an archival service came into being as part of the Ministère des Colonies in Brussels. Private collections were sent to the Musée Royal du Congo Belge. Searchers today can consult the material at Archives Générales du Royaume at 78 Galerie Ravenstein, Brussels 1. In addition there is relevant material in the Ministère des Affaires Etrangères, Dépôt Central des Archives, 56, Avenue des Arts at Brussels; in the Ministère des Affaires Africaines, Place Royale, Brussels; and also in the Musée Royal de l'Afrique Centrale at Tervuren, in museums, in town archives and in other institutions.

The Congolese archives, later called Archives du Congo Belge, at Léopold-ville, began to operate from 1949 onward, and worked in close co-operation with the administrative and legal departments of the Congo. It comprised the archives derived from the departments of the Gouverneur-Général, those of provincial, district, municipal, native and related administrations. It is now known as the Archives de la République Démocratique de Zaïre at Kinshasa.

In 1919 Belgium also became responsible for the administration of Rwanda and Burundi which had previously formed part of German East Africa, and which became independent in 1962. At the time of writing, the International Council on Archives was preparing a comprehensive guide on Belgian sources for the former Belgian territories, as part of a wider series. (See no. 29.)

32 Académie Royale des Sciences d'Outre-Mer (formerly Institut Royal Colonial Belge and Académie Royale des Sciences Coloniales). *Bulletin des Séances.* v. 1–25, 1930–54; n.s. v. 1– , 1955– . Bruxelles, illus., ports., maps.
In the *Bulletin* and in the *Mémoires* of the Académie there have been frequent articles having to do with archives of Congolese history and administration. It is the best source for such information.

33 Anstey, Roger. 'Earlier and later Congo '. *Journal of African History*, v. 2, no. 2, 1961: 324–326.
Anstey discusses other papers on Congo documentary material that appear in the *Bulletin des Séances.*

Libraries and archives: Western Europe

34 Belgium. Archives Générales du Royaume. *Inventaire des archives relatives au développement extérieur de la Belgique sous le règne de Léopold II.* Comp. by Emile Vandewoude. Bruxelles, 1965. 293 p.

35 —— Ministère des Affaires Africaines. Bibliothèque. *Catalogue de la bibliothèque.* By Th. Simar. Bruxelles, Vromant, 1922– .

36 —— Ministère du Congo Belge et du Ruanda-Urundi. *Document Notte : Stanley au Congo, 1879–1884.* Bruxelles, 1960. 206 p.

Facsimile report prepared by C. Notte, archivist of the Independent State of the Congo, from the administrative records of Stanley's two expeditions into the Congo.

37 Carson, Patricia. *Materials for West African history in the archives of Belgium and Holland.* London, University of London, 1962. 86 p.

A pioneer study of material in Belgian and Dutch repositories, including relevant records in the Algemeen Rijksarchief, the National Archives of the Netherlands. This information was supplemented by H. M. Feinberg, who has perused the material in the Archives of the Second West India Company and the Archives of the Netherlands Settlement on the Guinea Coast. See his ' Additions to *Materials for West African history in the archives of Belgium and Holland* by Patricia Carson, London, 1962 ', *African Studies Bulletin* (v. 10, no. 3, Dec. 1967: 48–53), and ' Further additions to *Materials for West African history in the archives of Belgium and Holland* ', *African Studies Bulletin* (v. 12, no. 1, Apr. 1969: 80–89).

38 Fonds National de la Recherche Scientifique. *Inventaire des microfilms de papiers privés relatifs à l'histoire du Congo conservés à la 'School of Oriental and African Studies' de l'Université de Londres et au 'British Museum'.* Bruxelles, 1959 ? 18 l. 30 cm.

At the School of Oriental and African Studies letters microfilmed were from the Mackinnon Papers (Jules Devaux, J. Hutton, Sir John Kirk, L. Lambert, H. M. Stanley and Colonel Strauch). The British Museum material consists of some pages of the Gladstone Papers and the Dilke Papers.

39 —— *Inventaire des microfilms des documents relatifs à l'histoire de la Belgique et du Congo conservés au 'Public Records Office' à Londres, 1866–1903.* Bruxelles, 1959 ? 57 l. 30 cm.

The documents are mostly correspondence between the Foreign Office and British ministers abroad.

40 —— *Inventaire des microfilms des papiers Morel, Séries A, B, E, F, G, H, I, se rapportant à l'histoire du Congo et conservés à la British Library of Political and Economic Science, London School of Economics and Political Science.* Bruxelles, 1961 ? 115 l. 32 cm.

The E. D. Morel Papers (he is famous for organizing the Congo Reform Association) were assembled at the suggestion of Jean Stengers and on the advice of the organization's Commission Interuniversitaire du Microfilm. The two preceding inventories were also suggested by the Commission.

41 Grieken, Emile van. *La bibliothèque du Ministère des Affaires Africaines : Son rôle, ses collections et ses ouvrages précieux.* Bruxelles, 1962. p. 186–201. (Académie Royale des Sciences d'Outre-Mer, Commission d'Histoire, fasc. 82)

Extract from the *Bulletin des Séances* of the Académie Royale des Sciences d'Outre-Mer, n.s. v. 8, no. 2, 1962. The most valuable works in the library of the Ministry of African Affairs are listed.

Part I : guide to reference materials

In this entry and the three following, the name of the institution is that given as of the publication date. Former names are Institut Royal Colonial Belge and Académie Royale des Sciences Coloniales.

42 —— and Madeleine van Grieken-Taverniers. *Les archives inventoriées au Ministère des Colonies.* [Bruxelles, 1958] 69 p. (Académie Royale des Sciences d'Outre-Mer, Classe des sciences morales et politiques, Mémoires in-8°, n.s. v. 12, fasc. 2) Bibliography: p. 66–69.
' Les archives de l'Etat indépandant du Congo ' is by E. van Grieken, ' La Commission d'Histoire du Congo et les archives historiques de l'Institut Royal Colonial Belge ' by M. van Grieken-Taverniers.

43 Grieken-Taverniers, Madeleine van. ' L'histoire de l'état indépendant du Congo et les archives du Ministère du Congo Belge et du Ruanda-Urundi'. *Archives, Bibliothèques et Musées de Belgique,* v. 30, no. 1, 1959.

44 —— *Inventaire des archives des affaires étrangères de l'Etat indépendant du Congo et du Ministère des Colonies, 1885–1914.* Bruxelles, 1955. 125 p. (Académie Royale des Sciences Coloniales, Classe des sciences morales et politiques, Mémoires in-8°, n.s. v. 2, fasc. 2)

45 Heyse, Théodore. ' L'Academie Royale des Sciences Coloniales et l'ancien Congo '. *Archives, Bibliothèques et Musée de Belgique,* v. 29, no. 1, 1958.
On sources for history of the Congo.

46 —— ' A propos d'un inventaire des archives des territoires du Congo et du Ruanda-Urundi'. Académie Royale des Sciences Coloniales. *Bulletin des Séances,* n.s. v. 4, no. 2, 1958: 271–286.

47 Luwel, Marcel. ' Inventaire des archives historiques du Musée Royal du Congo Belge à Tervuren '. Institut Royal Colonial Belge. *Bulletin des Séances,* v. 25, no. 2, 1954: 799–821.

48 —— *Inventaire : Papiers Jules Cornet, géologue (1865–1929).* Tervuren, Musée Royal de l'Afrique Centrale, 1961. 100 p. polycopie. (Inventaire des archives historiques, no. 1)

49 Vandewoude, E. ' Les archives du personnel d'Afrique de 1877 à 1918 '. Institut Royal Colonial Belge. *Bulletin des Séances,* v. 25, no. 2, 1954: 615–651.

50 Walraet, Marcel. ' Inventaires d'archives et publications de textes '. Académie Royale des Sciences Coloniales. *Bulletin des Séances,* n.s. v. 3, no. 2, 1957: 359–373.
Account of four years of activity of the Commission d'Histoire du Congo to produce an inventory of archives.
See also *Materials for West African history in the archives of Belgium and Holland,* no. 28.

France

Note Students of French colonial history are fortunate in having at their disposal a major archival reference work by the International Council on Archives, *Sources de l'histoire de l'Afrique au sud du Sahara dans les archives et bibliothèques françaises. 1 – Archives* (Zug, Switzerland, Inter Documentation Company, 1971, 959 p.). This guide is so extensive that it would be pointless to summarize the information it contains except in the briefest fashion.

The greater part of the modern French colonial archives is now lodged at the Dépôt des Archives d'Outre-Mer at Aix-en-Provence, which was opened in 1966.

When the French gave independence to their African territories, they left to the African successor states the so-called *archives de gestion*, that is to say, all records of immediate relevance to the work of day-to-day administration. The French retained for themselves what they styled *archives de souveraineté*, that is to say, political, diplomatic, military or private archives, derived from officials to whom the French state had directly delegated its authority. Archives preserved in France include material derived from the offices of governors and of prefects (in Algeria), and also some local administrative archives. The French also brought back all files of an international and diplomatic nature, dossiers on French officials and civil registers. Files bearing on subjects such as finances, public works, education, local personnel and public health were not deposited at Aix, except when the subject matter was of sufficient importance to reach the governor's office of the council.

There is a wealth of older material at the Archives Nationales, 60, rue des Francs-Bourgeois, Paris 3e. Neither the so-called Section Ancienne nor the Section Moderne contains series specially concerned with Africa; but both hold many files of African interest. There are also various private papers, fully described in the *Sources de l'histoire de l'Afrique* ... The Archives Nationales also administers a variety of *Fonds Ministériels*, including part of the archives of the Ministère de la Marine (which historically had played an important part in colonial affairs) as well as the older Fonds des Colonies. Generally speaking, the material produced before 1815 is housed at the Palais Soubise at Paris. The records dating after 1815 are mostly at the Section Outre-Mer of the Archives Nationales, 27, rue Oudinot, Paris 7e. The Section Outre-Mer was formed in 1961. It took over the archives of the Ministère des Colonies (later known as the Ministère de la France d'Outre-Mer). Its holdings are extremely varied, but special reference should be made to the *Séries géographiques : Afrique*, which deal with particular territories. There is also a film library, a map collection and many other noteworthy collections. The Fonds Vieillard is of particular interest for French West Africa. (The administration of the archives is exceptionally efficient.) Interested readers are referred to a pamphlet produced at Aix entitled *Présentation des Archives d'Outre-Mer d'Aix-en-Provence*. Within six pages this publication provides a short description of the material available for each major geographical region and related sources.

Searchers should also consult other relevant material at the Archives Nationales, for instance material derived from the Ministère des Travaux Publics from the French legislature and from the Commissions Parlementaires (set up to investigate specific questions such as colonial army recruitments and colonial budgets). A vast amount of information is also to be found in the archives of the Ministère des Affaires Etrangères, Direction des Archives Diplomatiques et de la Documentation, 37, Quai d'Orsay, Paris 7e. This material includes commercial reports, correspondence with foreign powers, private papers and similar documents. The Service Historique de l'Armée, Château de Vincennes, 94, Valde-Marne, administers a great collection of military archives for the period before 1920, which are open to the public. Finally, there is a wealth of material in French departmental and municipal archives, all of which are described in detail in *Sources de l'histoire de l'Afrique*. . . There are also private collections belonging to commercial firms and to missionary bodies, such as the Archives de la Congré-gation du Saint Esprit at Paris, the Paris Evangelical Mission Society, and many others. Students should of course consult also the holdings in the former French states of Africa, especially the major holdings now at Dakar, as well as the material collected by other learned institutions in Africa. See also Vincent

45

Confer, 'The dépôt in Aix and archival sources for France Outre-Mer', *French Historical Studies*, v. 6, no. 1, Spring 1969: 120–126.

Confer's article provides an indispensable introduction to the organization of the holdings at Aix, to the existing reference books on French colonial archives, and to the relation of Aix archives to other French holdings that bear on the colonies.

By 1971 the great majority of French archives up to 1921 could be consulted. Arrangements were being made at that time to make more material accessible. French archivists hoped to apply the 'thirty-year rule' in the near future.

51　*Annuaire international des archives. International directory on archives.* Paris, Presses Universitaires de France, 1956. 253 p.

52　Boyer, Pierre. 'Présentation des archives d'Outre-Mer d'Aix-en-Provence'. *Bulletin d'Histoire des Pays d'Outre-Mer*, v. 5, 1968–69: 10–19.

53　France. Armée. Etat-major. Service Historique. *Guide bibliographique sommaire d'histoire militaire et coloniale française.* Paris, Impr. Nationale, 1969– .

54　—— Direction des Bibliothèques de France. *Répertoire des bibliothèques d'étude et organismes de documentation.* Publié sous l'égide de la Délégation Générale à la Recherche Scientifique et Technique. Paris, Bibliothèque Nationale, 1963. 3 v.

This edition of a useful reference tool lists 2,382 research collections and libraries in France in two volumes. Volume III contains a small supplement and an extensive subject index that includes special collections by name and enables the user to find quickly the research libraries of special interest to him. Under the general heading of Africa are listed more than 30 research collections.

55　—— Ministère de la France d'Outre-Mer. Service des Archives, de la Bibliothèque et de l'Etat Civil. *Afrique.* Paris [1962]. 1 v. unnumbered leaves.

This large volume, inventory of the Africa holdings of the Archives of the Overseas Ministry of France, is organized first for Africa in general by subjects, i.e., explorations, diplomacy, personnel, with the date and contents of each file given; then there are breakdowns for the major regions (French West Africa, French Equatorial Africa) and for the countries within each region. The contents of each dossier are described briefly and the inclusive dates provided. Copies are held by Carlo Laroche in Paris and J. F. Maurel in Dakar. A few xerographic copies are also in existence.

56　International Council on Archives. *Sources de l'histoire de l'Afrique au sud du Sahara dans les archives et bibliothèques françaises. 1 – Archives.* Zug, Switzerland, Inter Documentation Company, 1971. 959 p. (Guide to the sources of the history of Africa, v. 3)

The series is prepared by the International Council on Archives with help from UNESCO. The material is grouped according to archival repositories, which are themselves arranged in alphabetical order. Holdings are described according to their respective archival groups.

Work on this *Guide* was initiated in 1964 under the auspices of a commission headed by André Chamson, Director-General of the Archives of France. The guide covers French Africa from the period of the discoveries in the fifteenth century to the year 1920. The authors stress that theirs is not a complete inventory but only a general description. It is nevertheless one of the most complete guides in existence, a model of its kind, and an indispensable aid to archival research on French colonial history. The appendix, modestly but somewhat misleadingly entitled *Chronologie des secrétaires et ministres de la France d'Outre-Mer*, alone covers nearly a hundred pages. It lists all French ministers concerned with colonial issues, the most senior civil servants in France and in the colonies, and itself forms an important research tool. (See also no. 439, Henige, for list of colonial servants.) The authors also provide the full address of each archival repository which they cover, general guidance for the use of the material and bibliographical information concerning the principal finding aids.

The *Guide's* first part covers the Archives Nationales in Paris. This part is subdivided into Section Ancienne, the Section Moderne, Fonds Ministériels (including Fonds de la Marine, Fonds des Colonies, Fonds des Affaires Etrangères), Section Outre-Mer (subdivided by classes, geographical regions, and special institutions). The next major section deals with the Dépôt des Archives d'Outre-Mer at Aix-en-Provence. This material is subdivided in archives derived from French West Africa, French Equatorial Africa, Madagascar and Somaliland. A further section describes the various departmental and municipal archives.

The second part describes the French ministerial archives, first of all the records of the Ministère des Affaires Etrangères, then the Ministère d'Etat chargé de la Défense Nationale, including army and naval archives. The compilers then pass to the material produced by the French Assemblée Nationale and the Sénat; printed material; private archives (including missionary archives, archives derived from chambers of commerce, from individual commercial firms and from private persons).

57 Laroche, Carlo. ' Les archives d'outre-mer et l'histoire coloniale française '. *Revue Historique*, no. 206, Oct.–Dec. 1951: 213–253.

58 Laroche, Charles. ' Les archives de l'expansion française outre-mer conservées en Métropole '. *Gazette des Archives*, n.s. no. 55, 1966: 235–252.
The author is chief conservator of the Section Outre-Mer des Archives Nationales, having previously been chief archivist of the former Archives du Ministère de la France d'Outre-Mer. In addition to these two analytical articles, he has written a number of brief descriptions of the current state of the archives which have appeared in the *Gazette des Archives* (n.s. no. 4, 1948: 14–20; no. 23, Jan. 1958: 77–79; no. 28, 1960: 32–33).

59 Taillemite, Etienne. ' Les archives de la France d'Outre-Mer '. *Gazette des Archives*, n.s. no. 22, 1957: 6–22.

Germany

Note Articles on German African holdings occasionally appear in *Archivalische Zeitschrift, Der Archivar* and *Archivmitteilungen*. The German material of metropolitan origin is found mainly in the Deutsche Zentralarchiv in the German Democratic Republic. The Zentralarchiv has a Historische Abteilung at 15 Potsdam, Berliner Str. 98–101, and another at 42 Merseburg, Weisse Mauer 48. The Potsdam archives contain a wealth of material derived from the Reichskolonialamt, the Deutsche Kolonialgesellschaft, the administration of South-West Africa, and from various ministries. The Merseburg archives concentrate on Brandenburg-Prussia, but also yield some source material on colonial problems. (Owing to the nature of the federal constitution of Imperial Germany, searchers should keep in mind that relevant material may be found in the archives of Land governments which, during the period 1871–1918, had some say in matters concerning the Reich.)

Part I : guide to reference materials

The material now available in the Federal German Republic has been described by the International Council on Archives, *Quellen zur Geschichte Afrikas südlich der Sahara in den Archiven der Bundesrepublik Deutschland* (Zug, Switzerland, Inter Documentation Company, 1970, 126 p.). This work also reviews finding aids and published accounts of West German archives. Bundesarchiv of the German Federal Republic, 54 Koblenz, Am Wöllershof 12, has fairly substantial holdings, including material from the Reichskanzlei, the Reichsfinanzministerium, the Reichswirtschaftsministerium and other agencies. Researchers should also consult the Politische Archiv of the Auswärtige Amt, Bonn, Wörth Str. This contains the records of the Auswärtige Amt, from the formation of the North German Confederacy in 1867 to 1945. Much of the material created during World War II has, however, been lost. The holdings comprise material derived from the Politische Abteilungen of the Ministry, as well as from German embassies and consulates abroad.

There are also many records of colonial interest in municipal and Land archives, especially in the Staatsarchiv der Freien und Hansestadt Hamburg, Hamburg 1, Rathaus, in the Generaldirektion der staatlichen Archive Bayerns, Munich, Arcisstr. 12, and so forth. Searchers finally have to consult missionary archives, for instance the holdings of the Rheinische Missionsgesellschaft at Wuppertal-Barmen, business archives such as the Historische Archiv der Firma Friedrich Krupp at Essen and the archives of scholarly bodies.

In addition to the archival descriptions listed in the subsequent entries, scholars should consult the description of the various German archival holdings in the essay by Hartmut Pogge von Strandmann and Alison Smith, 'The German Empire in Africa and British perspectives: A historiographical essay', especially p. 757–765, in *Britain and Germany in Africa.* . . . See no. 436 for description. In addition, researchers will find material in such basic works as J. Lepsius, A. Mendelssohn-Bartholdy, F. Thimme, *Die grosse Politik der europäischen Kabinette, 1871–1914 : Sammlung der diplomatischen Akten des Auswärtigen Amtes* (Berlin, Deutsche Verlagsgesellschaft für Politik und Geschichte, 1922–27, 40 v.).

Archival material produced by the German colonial authorities is also found in various parts of Africa. The Archives Depot of South-West Africa at Windhoek is administered by the South African archival service. It contains holdings of the Zentral-Bureau, of various other departments such as the Bergbauamt (mining department), of different *Bezirksämter* (districts), as well as private and semi-official papers of German and of indigenous leaders, etc. Material relating to German colonialism is also found in the Cape Archives Depot and the Transvaal Archives Depot. These records are partially described in the appendix to J. H. Esterhuyse, *South West Africa 1880–1894 : The establishment of German authority in South West Africa* (Cape Town, C. Struik, 1968, p. 246–251), which also has an extensive bibliography concerning South-West Africa.

The records of the German East African government are to be found in Dar es Salaam, Tanzania, but at the time of writing would have required a good deal of additional work to make them fully usable. They have been partially described in Eckhart Franz, ' Die Deutsch-Ostafrika-Akten im Nationalarchiv Dar es Salaam ', *Der Archivar*, November 1970, p. 329–42. West African material is found, for instance, in the Bibliothèque Nationale at Lomé, Togo, and in various other locations. Much of this material still needs to be retrieved and properly processed.

Material of value to students of German colonialism is available in the British Public Record Office, the National Archives of France and of the United States (for instance, consular reports). Students should also consult sources of private provenance. These include, among others, mission societies, political organizations and so forth, to which more detailed reference is made in Pogge von Strandmann's essay cited above. American material of value in the investigation of German colonialism is also mentioned in Peter Duignan, *Handbook of American resources for African studies* (see no. 99).

For an up-to-date account of East German archives, see Deutsche Demokratische Republic. Staatliche Archivsverwaltung des Ministerium des Inneren. *Taschenbuch Archivswesen der DDR* (East Berlin, Staatsverlag der Deutschen Demokratischen Republik, 1971, 304 p.).

60 American Historical Association. Committee for the Study of War Documents. *Catalogue of German Foreign Ministry files and microfilms, 1867–1920*. Washington, 1959. xliv, 1,290 cols.

Continued by:

61 U.S. Department of State. Historical Office. *A catalog of files and microfilms of the German Foreign Ministry Archives, 1920–1945*. Compiled and edited by George O. Kent. Stanford, Calif., Hoover Institution, Stanford University, 1962–66. 3 v. (Hoover Institution Publications)

The defeat of Germany in 1945 has made available to scholars archival collections of the greatest importance. Most of the captured collections were shipped to England or the United States, where they were microfilmed and indexed before the new German government could request their return. Among the materials are the archives of the German Foreign Ministry (Auswärtiges Amt), to which these two guides refer. For those specializing in African affairs, the first-named catalogue has almost a hundred columns (cols. 726–812) of primary sources.

Reference should be made also to other guides listing African material. The *Guide to captured German documents*, edited by Fritz T. Epstein (Air University, 1952), cites an I. G. Farben report on the foreign trade of the Congo, dated June 1940 (p. 41). During World War II the German Foreign Ministry published a volume of *Völkerrechtliche Dokumente über Afrika* (1942), using papers from the Belgian and French foreign ministry archives. An *Index of microfilmed records of the German Foreign Ministry and the Reichs Chancellery covering the Weimar period*, prepared by Ernst Schwandt for the Committee on War Documents of the American Historical Association and published by the National Archives and Records Service (Washington, 1958), contains some files about Africa.

62 Facius, Friedrich, ed. *Das Bundesarchiv und seine Bestände: Übersicht bearbeitet von Friedrich Facius, Hans Boom und Heinz Boberach*. Boppard am Rhein, H. Bold. 1961. xvi, 211 p. facsims. (Schriften des Bundesarchivs, no. 10)

The archives of the Federal German Republic are not as rich in German colonial archival material as those of East Germany, but they do contain a good deal of material, especially derived from consular sources. Some of this has been microfilmed and is available abroad. See no. 436, Pogge von Strandmann's essay, p. 757, footnote 32; the same work also mentions various private German sources in Western Germany.

63 International Council on Archives. *Quellen zur Geschichte Afrikas südlich der Sahara in den Archiven der Bundesrepublik Deutschland*. Zug, Switzerland, 1970, 126 p. (*Guide to the sources of the history of Africa*, no. 1)

The series is prepared by the International Council on Archives with aid from UNESCO. The material is grouped according to the archival repositories, which are themselves arranged in alphabetical order. Holdings are described according to their respective archival groups and series, including serial numbers.

The records described in this volume include archives in the Bundesarchiv in Bonn, in the archives of the Auswärtige Amt at Bonn, material in *Land* archives, in various municipal archives, archives of private commercial companies, such as the Deutsche Afrika Linien in Hamburg, the firm of Friedrich Krupp in Essen, or Firma W. M. O'Swald und Compagnie, archives of missionary societies such as the Bethel-Mission, material kept in ethnographic museums, and similar documents. The guide provides the full address of every archival institution listed. There is an appended list of the leading officials in the German colonial administration.

The compilers did not include film archives, phonographic records, manuscripts concerning religious and philosophical themes, and so forth. The compilers stress that their guide is illustrative rather than exhaustive. It is nevertheless an indispensable research guide to the study of German colonial history, though a perusal of its contents must be supplemented by study of the material in East Germany, especially in the German *Zentralarchiv* at Potsdam.

64 Lötzke, Helmut, and Hans Stephan Brather, eds. *Übersicht über die Bestände des Deutschen Zentralarchivs, Potsdam.* Berlin, Rütten und Loening, 1957. 232 p. illus. (Schriftenreihe des Deutschen Zentralarchivs, no. 1) Includes bibliography.

The main holdings concerning German colonial activities are to be found in the Central Archives of the German Democratic Republic (East Germany) in Potsdam and Merseburg. The survey gives information concerning files dealing with the colonies, but there is as yet no similar guide for the archives in Merseburg. The files concerning the Kolonialrat (a central advisory body on which economic interest groups were also represented) have been microfilmed. The material in question covers the period 1890–1906, and microfilms are available at Hoover Institution, Stanford University, and Rhodes House, Oxford.

65 Markov, P. 'West African history in German archives'. *Journal of the Historical Society of Nigeria,* v. 2, no. 4, Dec. 1963: 602–605.

Outlines the holdings in the German Federal Republic (the Bundesarchiv at Koblenz and the local archives of Hamburg, Bremen and Emden) and in the German Democratic Republic (the archives at Merseburg, the Geographische Gesellschaft in Gotha and the second central archives at Potsdam).

66 Mommsen, Wolfgang A., ed. *Die Nachlässe in den deutschen Archiven (mit Ergänzungen aus anderen Beständen). Teil 1 : Einleitung und Verzeichnis.* Boppard, Harald Boldt Verlag, 1971. 582 p.

Lists private papers held in the Bundesarchiv, and in the archives of the German Democratic Republic. Each entry indicates the name, dates, occupation and location of the papers listed. See also Ludwig Denecke, ed., *Die Nachlässe in den Bibliotheken der Bundesrepublik Deutschland.* Band 2, *Verzeichnis der schriftlichen Nachlässe in den deutschen Archiven und Bibliotheken* (Boppard, Harald Boldt Verlag, 1969, 268 p.). Private papers (soldiers and administrators) held in East Germany are listed in Berlin Universität, Institut für Bibliothekswissenschaft. *Gelehrten und Schriftstellernachlässe in den Bibliotheken der Deutschen Demokratischen Republik* (Berlin, 1959–1972), 3 v.

Great Britain

Note The British official records are collected in the Public Record Office, London, which has issued several valuable guides. The most recent statement concerning access to records and future disposition among the depository at Chancery Lane, London, present temporary branch repositories and a future repository to be built at Ruskin Avenue, Kew, is set forth in Lord Chancellor's Office, *The twelfth annual report of the keeper of public records on the work of the Public Record Office ... 1970* (London, H.M. Stationery Office, 1971), especially p. 16–18 and p. 38–40.

The British have recently modified their existing ' thirty-year rule ' by opening their official archives, including the highly confidential Cabinet records up to 1945. This decision makes Great Britain the most ' open ' country from the archival point of view in so far as the former colonial powers are concerned.

Excellent guides to British (and German) archives, unpublished and published sources, books and monographs have appeared also in the following works: *The Cambridge history of the British Empire*, v. 3 (1959, p. 769–904), no. 664; Prosser Gifford and Wm. Roger Louis, eds., *Britain and Germany in Africa* (p. 709–795), no. 436; and Vincent Harlow and E. M. Chilver, eds., *History of East Africa*, v. 2 (p. 700–736), no. 1035.

The Cambridge history of the British Empire, v. 3, is especially useful in surveying official records and parliamentary papers. The *History of East Africa*, v. 2, no. 1035, provides data on collections in Great Britain, Kenya, Uganda, Tanganyika and Zanzibar. Both studies list titles of parliamentary papers on Africa.

67 *The Cambridge history of the British Empire*, v. 3. Cambridge, 1959.
See pages 767–907, particularly Part I, ' Collections of manuscripts and public and private archives, and official papers and publications '.

68 Church Missionary Society, London. Archives. *Index lists*. microfilm ed. [1960 ?]
Listed are papers of the West Africa (Sierra Leone) Mission, 1803–1914, the Yoruba Mission, the Niger Mission, and the Nyanza Mission, as well as those of other missions, e.g., Tanganyika, Northern Nigeria, Ruanda, East Africa and South Africa. Entries cover letters and journals from missionaries and government officials, minutes of committee meetings, correspondence, treaties, petitions, proclamations and ordinances. Included are papers of Samuel Crowther, Thomas B. Macaulay, William Balfour Baikie and Alexander M. Mackey. Xerographic copies of this material are available from the Center for Research Libraries, Cooperative African Microfilm Project (CAMP).

69 Great Britain. Foreign Office. *Index to the correspondence of the Foreign Office of Great Britain for the years 1920–1938*. London, Public Record Office. 77 v.
The confidential period for the archives of the Foreign Office was amended in 1969 from 50 years to 30 years, thus opening to scholars significant material covering the inter-war years. The actual documents exist only in the Public Record Office in London, but photocopies can be ordered provided the index number is quoted.

A list of the archives of the Foreign Office from 1782 (the date of the establishment of the office as a separate department of state) to 1878 had been published previously in the Public Record Office's *Lists and indexes*, No. LII. A supplementary list covering 1879 to 1905 had been published in 1964 in the Public Record Office's *Lists and indexes*, Supplementary Series, No. XIII. The total period for indexes to British Foreign Office correspondence now in print is 1879–1905, 1920–1938. Publication plans are being formulated for an index of the period 1906 to 1919. As the open date for the confidential period is advanced annually, indexes subsequent to 1938 will be published.

Part I : guide to reference materials

70 ───── Public Record Office. *Guide to the contents of the Public Record Office*. v. 1, *Legal records, etc.*, v. 2, *State papers and departmental records*. Revised and extended to 1960 from the Guide by the late M. S. Giuseppi. London, H.M. Stationery Office, 1963. 249, 410 p.

Africa-related materials are found almost entirely in v. 2, in the records of the Colonial Office (p. 52–92), the Commonwealth Relations Office (p. 93–97) and the Foreign Office (p. 123–164). All records are arranged by region or country, with separate classes for each. The Colonial Office and the Commonwealth Relations Office material is classed by Original Correspondence, Registers of Correspondence, Entry Books, Colonial Acts, Sessional Papers (of colonial assemblies or councils), Government Gazettes and Miscellanea. The Foreign Office records are classed under General Correspondence, Treaties, Embassy and Consular Archives, Archives of Commissioners, Confidential Prints, and Private Collections. Each volume has two indexes, one for persons and places, another for subjects.

71 ───── ───── *List of Colonial Office confidential print to 1916*. London, H.M. Stationery Office, 1965. 179 p. (PRO Handbooks, no. 8)

The section on Africa (p. 5–85) has over a thousand numbered items in 116 volumes of selected correspondence, memoranda, reports, and other documents which range from a single page to several hundred pages.

72 ───── ───── *Lists and indexes* [series]. London.

The Public Record Office has available various Search Room lists – (a) Colonial Office, (b) Foreign Office – and xerographic copies of these and other Search Room finding lists can be supplied on request. The following volumes in the *Lists and indexes* series are essential for Africa:

    no. 36 *List of Colonial Office records*. 1911.

    no. 52 *List of Foreign Office records to 1878*. 1929.

    no. 53 *Alphabetical guide to War Office and other military records preserved in the P.R.O*. 1931.

    no. 13 in the *Supplementary lists and indexes. List of Foreign Office records (1879–1913 ?)*. 1966 ? 8 v. v. 1–4, General correspondence; v. 5, Various classes; v. 6–8 (?), Embassy and consular archives.

Other lists are in preparation, including those for the Board of Trade, War Office, Admiralty and State papers.

73 *A handbook of library holdings of Commonwealth literature*. Comp. by Gail Wilson. Commonwealth Institute, London, 1971. 41 p.

A survey of libraries in Great Britain that have large collections of Commonwealth literature – fiction, poetry, drama – written in English by nationals of any Commonwealth country except Great Britain. The type of material held and the facilities available are described.

74 Hewitt, Arthur R. *Guide to resources for Commonwealth studies in London, Oxford, and Cambridge, with bibliographical and other information*. London. Published for the Institute of Commonwealth Studies, University of London, by Athlone Press, 1957. 219 p.

This guide, prepared by the then secretary of the Institute and its librarian, describes in detail the resources of the chief British centres for African studies. In the first part Hewitt covers public and private archives, papers of chartered companies and other companies, parliamentary papers and official publications, periodicals and newspaper holdings in libraries, theses and research in progress, bibliographies and works of reference. A second part describes individual collections, and the third part (p. 183–203) names universities, research and advisory organizations, and other official and unofficial institutions and organizations. There is a comprehensive index. Although designed for students of British Commonwealth matters, some of the resources described furnish material for studies of all parts of Africa. Hewitt cites existing guides, registers and inventories to collections. Hewitt's volume remains one of the most useful descriptions of Africa-related material of any country yet produced.

75 Hill, Richard. 'The Sudan Archive, School of Oriental Studies, University of Durham, England'. *Africana Newsletter*, v. 1, no. 4, 1963: 40–41.

76 Keen, Rosemary. *A survey of the archives of selected missionary societies.* London, Historical Manuscripts Commission, 1968. 1 v.

Indexes for countries and persons. Arrangement is alphabetical by name of society. Under each section for a society it lists broad categories of mss held with dates of coverage. Some of the societies described are Africa Evangelical Fellowship, Baptist Missionary Society, Conference of Missionary Societies in Great Britain and Ireland, Congregational Council for World Mission, the Leprosy Mission, Methodist Missionary Society, Sudan United Mission and the United Society for the Propagation of the Gospel.

77 Matthews, N., and M. D. Wainwright, comps. *A guide to manuscripts and documents in the British Isles relating to Africa.* London, Oxford University Press, 1971. 321 p.

The United Kingdom volume for the International Council on Archives series 'Guide to sources for the history of the nations'. Some 240 depositories are listed. A major guide to British resources. J. D. Pearson, librarian of the School of Oriental and African Studies, is the editor. See also Addenda.

78 Oxford University. Committee for Commonwealth Studies. Colonial Records Project. *Annual report.*

Since 1963, the Colonial Records Project has been trying to collect the diaries, papers, correspondence, etc., of people who have lived and worked in Africa in any capacity, be it as missionary, merchant, government official, or traveller. In 1965 the Project had approached 3,200 possible contributors, and 6,000 additional names still remained. The 1966 report listed more than 400 additions to the Rhodes House Library at Oxford. Notes on acquisitions are issued irregularly and are listed at the end of each annual report. The Project is producing name lists, lists of papers received, and inventories or registers of papers and collections. Mr. Louis Frewer is combining these individual registers to bring out a descriptive catalogue of all the archival and manuscript materials held at Rhodes House Library. Meanwhile he has produced a checklist of 1,300 collections, entitled *Manuscript collections of Africana in Rhodes House Library* (Oxford, 1968, 100 p.).

79 Oxford University. Rhodes House Library. *Accessions of note received.* These lists, irregularly issued, of manuscripts or copies of manuscripts received, provide a most important bibliographic source of information.

80 Pugh, Ralph B. *The records of the Colonial and Dominions Offices.* London, H.M. Stationery Office, 1964. 118 p. (Public Record Office Handbooks, no. 3)

Valuable material is also found in the *List of Cabinet papers, 1880–1914* (London, 1964; PRO Handbooks, no. 4), and *List of papers of the Committee of Imperial Defence, 1888–1914* (London, 1964; PRO Handbooks, no. 6).

81 Scotland. Record Office. *Material relating to Africa in the Scottish Record Office.* Edinburgh, 1965. 7 l. Typescript.
Arranged alphabetically by collections. Provides information on Scottish mission churches, as well as individuals.

82 Standing Conference on Library Materials on Africa (SCOLMA). *Library Materials on Africa : Newsletter.* 1962– . London. Irregularly issued.
This bulletin is concerned largely with descriptions of library and archival collections on Africa. Among individual holdings described in the first several volumes are the following:

> Colonial Office and Commonwealth Office Library, v. 1, no. 2, 1963: 2–6.
> Good account of these two offices whose collections represent perhaps the most important source for official material on the parts of Africa formerly under British control.

> Rhodes House Library, Oxford, v. 1, no. 4, 1964: 3–6.
> This survey of African archival and manuscript collections shows the richness and variety of the holdings of Rhodes House and indicates the wide scope of materials dealing with the British Empire, i.e., films of private collections in South Africa or the United States.

83 Standing Conference on Library Materials on Africa (SCOLMA). *The SCOLMA directory of libraries and special collections on Africa.* 2d ed. Comp. by Robert Collison. London, Crosby Lockwood; Hamden, Conn., Shoe String Press, 1967. 92 p.
Expanding on the information in the 1963 edition and listing some 15 additional libraries, this very useful directory now includes about 155 libraries, archives, institutes, government depositories, etc., in the United Kingdom that hold Africa-related materials. It supplements no. 74, Hewitt's *Guide to resources for Commonwealth studies* (1957), but analyses, except in a few cases, are not as informative as Hewitt's. (Still, one could wish for such directories for each country of Europe and Africa.) Arrangement is alphabetical by towns. Data for each collection are generally confined to address, telephone number, name of director and/or librarian, hours, brief description of holdings, conditions of access to materials, and relevant publications issued. An index is included.

Portugal

Note The archives for Portugal's overseas territories – Arquivo Histórico Ultramarino, Palácio da Ega, Calçada da Boa Hora, 30, Lisbon 3 (formerly known as the Arquivo Histórico Colonial) – contains the papers of the important overseas council from 1643 to 1833, as well as the papers of the colonial offices that succeeded the council. For the history of Portuguese diplomatic affairs and involvement with other nations in Africa, these archives are indispensable. Officially there is a 50-year rule, but foreigners do not appear to be able to see documents later than 1903. So little is known about Portuguese archives that we have here provided more details than for the other colonial powers.

84 The following archives, in addition to the Arquivo Histórico Ultramarino, contain pertinent material:

> (a) Arquivo e Biblioteca do Ministério dos Negócios Estrangeiros, Largo do Rilvas, Lisbon.
> For the period since 1851 the Foreign Office keeps its own archives.

Material is classified chronologically by origin and stored in classified sections: correspondence of the Portuguese and foreign diplomatic missions and of Portuguese consulates and ministries; correspondence on the Lourenço Marques railway and on boundary questions; correspondence of overseas province governors; and documents on Portuguese Guinea, Portuguese sovereignty in Zambezia, and the Boer War.

(b) Arquivo Histórico Militar, Museu Militar, Largo dos Caminhos de Ferro, Lisbon.

One section of the archives deals with overseas expeditions, campaigns and colonial wars. The material is organized chronologically by subject.

(c) Arquivo Nacional da Torre do Tombo (the National Archive of Portugal), Palácio de São Bento, Lisbon.

The Torre do Tombo is the most important archive in Portugal. It holds millions of records, many of which have not been fully inventoried. For the diplomatic history of Portugal in Africa the most valuable source is the Historical Archives of the Portuguese Foreign Office now housed in the Torre do Tombo.

Among the 717 boxes of materials (from approximately 1756 to 1851) are correspondence of Portuguese and foreign diplomatic missions and consulates (Correspondência das Caixas); internal records of the Foreign Office; letters of cardinals and princes; records relating to slavery, the slave-trade and the suppression of the slave-trade; miscellaneous petitions, investigating commissions and international treaties and conventions.

Diplomatic correspondence and instructions from 1641 to 1705 are also preserved in the National Archives.

(d) Biblioteca da Acadêmia das Ciências, Rua da Acadêmia das Ciências, 19, Lisbon.

Contains papers of religious orders and of diplomatic affairs. Especially valuable are the letter books dealing with Africa.

(e) Biblioteca da Ajuda, Palácio Nacional da Ajuda, Lisbon.

Valuable library for diplomatic history of Portugal; for example, it has the correspondence of the governors of India and Africa from 1500 on.

(f) Biblioteca e Arquivo da Assembleia Nacional, Lisbon.

Contains government records of the proceedings of the National Assembly.

(g) Biblioteca Geral da Universidade de Coimbra, Coimbra.

Contains manuscripts and letter books dealing with Africa.

(h) Biblioteca Nacional, Rua Ocidental ao Campo Grande, Lisbon.

The National Library has large amounts of materials (books, manuscripts and documents) dealing with diplomatic affairs of the Portuguese in Africa. A catalogue of the collection has been printed.

(i) Biblioteca Pública Municipal, Oporto.

One of the best libraries in Portugal; valuable for documents relating to Africa and diplomatic history. A catalogue has been printed.

(j) Biblioteca da Sociedade de Geografia de Lisboa, Lisbon.

Excellent library resources for overseas expansion. Several catalogues have been issued.

Part I : guide to reference materials

85 'Documenting Portuguese Africa: Archives, libraries, and institutes'. *Africana Newsletter*, v. 1, no. 3, 1963 : 19–24.

A brief description of the main archives, libraries and institutes – fourteen in Lisbon and two in other cities of Portugal, six in Angola, Mozambique and Portuguese Guinea. Also cited are sources in Rhodesia, England, Germany and the United States. See also no. 89, *Materials for West African history in Portuguese archives.*

86 Ferrao, António. *Os arquivos e as bibliotecas em Portugal.* Coimbra, Imprensa da Universidade, 1920. 314 p.

The introduction reviews administrative history and basic legislation during the period 1913 to 1918. The author then deals with the libraries and archives of the various universities, learned societies, ministries, and so forth, including the archives of the Ministério da Guerra (p. 158–164), the Ministério dos Estrangeiros (p. 169–177), the Ministério da Marinha (p. 234), and the Ministério das Colónias (p. 235–236). He ends with a series of technical recommendations and a general exhortation.

87 Portugal. Biblioteca Nacional. *A Secção Ultramarina da Biblioteca Nacional : Inventários.* Lisbon, Oficinas Gráficas da Biblioteca Nacional, 1928. 333 p. (Publicações da Biblioteca Nacional)

Owing to lack of space in the Arquivo Nacional, the Biblioteca Nacional came to house a considerable body of archives collected in Mozambique by António Ennes in the 1890s. The Biblioteca Nacional also became a repository for material derived from the Arquivos da Direcção Geral da Marinha, of the Comando Geral da Armada and of various papers derived from individual men-of-war. This material was grouped into the Secção Ultramarina da Biblioteca Nacional.

The present guide lists main titles, dates covered, and numbers of volumes. The first part, put together by Hedwig Fitzler, describes the records of the former Conselho Ultramarino from the 17th to the early 19th century. The second portion describes the Mozambique material in the Biblioteca Nacional. The third part deals with the Arquivo da Direcção Geral da Marinha. These archives derive mainly from the 18th and early 19th centuries, but a few go to the latter part of the 19th century.

88 Portugal. Ministério dos Negócios Estrangeiros. *Dez anos de política externa (1936–1947).* Lisbon, 1961– .

The Portuguese have recently begun to print some of their more recent material derived from Foreign Office archives. The Portuguese diplomatic documents appear to contain a good deal of material on the colonial question and Germany, and on foreign relations with the allies and axis powers.

89 Ryder, A. F. C. *Materials for West African history in Portuguese archives.* London, Athlone Press, 1965. 92 p. (997 items)

Gives useful descriptions of archives and information on how to use them, but for the most part describes material before the nineteenth century.

Note There is also relevant material in England and in Germany.

90 British Museum, London.

Contains miscellaneous maps and manuscripts, large book and government document collection dealing with the Portuguese in Africa. For example, British Consular and Diplomatic Reports from 1855 are excellent sources of information on Portuguese Africa.

91 Government Records, Public Record Office, Colonial Office and Foreign Office Libraries, London.

92 King's College, University of London, Strand, London, W.C.2.
Houses a Portuguese library containing extensive material on colonial history.

93 American Historical Association, Committee for the Study of War Documents. *Catalogue of German Foreign Ministry files and microfilms, 1867–1920.* London, Oxford University Press, 1959.
Has a good deal of material on Portuguese Africa.

94 Germany, Democratic Republic of. Deutsches Zentralarchiv, Potsdam. *Übersicht über die Bestände des Deutschen Zentralarchivs Potsdam.* Berlin, Rütten & Loening, 1957. (Schriftenreihe des Deutschen Zentralarchivs, no. 1)

     p. 53–55, *Reichskolonialamt—Portugiesische Besitzungen* in Afrika (1870–1921, 22 v.).

95 Hinsley, F. H., and M. H. Ehrmann. *A catalogue of selected files of the German Naval Archives.* London, The Admiralty, 1957. Microfilmed at the Admiralty for the University of Cambridge and the University of Michigan.

     p. 20, *Portugal, Ganz geheime Nachrichten* (Aug. 1896–Jan. 1913, 1 v.). *Operationspläne gegen Portugal* (Nov. 1892–Feb. 1908, 1 v.).

     p. 26, *Portugal, Kolonien in Westafrika* (Nov. 1904–Aug. 1914, 2 v.). *Portugal, Kolonien in Ostafrika* (Jan. 1909–Mar. 1914, 1 v.).

96 Kent, George O., ed. *A catalog of files and microfilms of the German Foreign Ministry Archives, 1920–1945.* v. 1–4. Stanford, Calif., Hoover Institution, Stanford University, 1962–1972.

Spain

Note The main Spanish archives are described in the International Council on Archives, *España: Guía de Fuentes para la historia de Africa subsahariana* (Zug, Switzerland, Inter Documentation Company, 1971, 210 p.). The most important collection concerning Spanish Africa in modern times is to be found in the Archivo de la Dirección General de Promoción de Sahara, Castellana núm. 5, Madrid. This serves both as a library and as an archival institution. It contains material derived from the former Ministério de Ultramar, whose records were later on taken over by the Presidencia del Consejo de Ministros, and then for a time by the Sección Colonial del Ministério de Estado. In 1925 a new Dirección General de Marruecos y Colonias was formed within the Presidencia del Consejo. This office (later renamed Dirección General de Promoción de Sahara) came to administer all colonial archives, including the records dealing with Guinea. At the time of writing these files were still closed to the public.

The files on Guinea consist of material from the Consejo del Estado (1846–1899) and from the Dirección General de Marruecos y Colonias (1851–1936). The former includes the files of Gobernación, which are of a general administrative character, as well as series dealing with particular subjects, such as justice, war, etc. The material taken over from the Dirección General de Marruecos y Colonias embraces files from the Administración General (1887–1924) and from the Administración Colonial (1876–1923); correspondence concerning particular topics, such as security and public order (1885–1910); and justice and religion (1859–1924), public health (1865–1936), commerce (1859–1912), etc. In addition there is a considerable body of miscellaneous records, subdivided by topics, such as customs, forestry, fauna and flora, education, etc.

The Archivo Histórico Nacional in Madrid contains scattered references to early nineteenth-century Africa. These are to be found mainly in files of the Ministério de Estado and of the Consejo de Estado. There is no special division dealing solely with Africa. The Archivo del Ministério de Asuntos Exteriores in Madrid contains material concerning the slave-trade, as well as negotiations with foreign powers during the nineteenth century. The records kept in the Archivo de las Cortes Españolas comprise session papers and similar material bearing on Africa during the nineteenth century. Records in the Archivo General de Indias go up to the eighteenth century.

The Guide lists also material contained in other libraries and archives, as well as the holdings of missionary societies, such as the Carmelitas Misioneras, the Congregación de Hermanos de la Sagrada Familia, the Congregación de Misioneras Domínicas, etc. Spanish missionaries were also active outside the Spanish possessions. Information concerning their work is to be found, for instance, in the Archivo del Seminario Nacional de Misiones – Procura Central.

Italy

Note From 1882 to 1912, Italian colonial affairs were handled by a special section within the Ministero degli Affari Esteri. In 1912 the Ministero delle Colonie came into existence as a separate body (renamed Ministero dell'Africa Italiana in 1937). After the Second World War, African affairs once more reverted to the Ministero degli Affari Esteri. In 1952 this body instituted a separate commission for the study of Italy's colonial past, known as the Comitato per la Documentazione dell'Opera dell'Italia in Africa (recently changed to delle attivita Italiane). From 1958 this body put out a major series of publications based on Italian archives.

At the time of writing, the Archivio Centrale dello Stato at Rome officially permitted access to documents when they were more than fifty years old. But permission was sometimes granted to scholars to consult material up to 1930, and sometimes even up to 1943. A much more rigorous rule, however, applied to the archives of the Ministero degli Affari Esteri. Generally speaking, these could be consulted only up to 1896. There was apparently a vast collection in the Archivio Storico dell'ex-Ministero dell'Africa Italiana (ASMAI), however.

Professor Robert L. Hess, *Italian colonialism in Somalia* (University of Chicago Press, 1966), p. 214–215, explains that ASMAI contains some 80,000 documents dealing with all phases of Italian interest and administration. During the Second World War, however, a good deal of material was lost in the course of repeated evacuations; and the sources of the Fascist era in Somalia are sparse. Certain documents are still classified as ' confidential ', ' highly confidential ', or ' secret '. The sources include the correspondence of colonial governors and officials with metropolitan authorities; confidential correspondence of trading companies and exploration societies; reports of travellers and government investigators; copies of diplomatic correspondence; minutes of cabinet meetings and a great deal of related material.

The colonial archives of Somalia were not available to the author. He states that during the British occupation from 1941 to 1950, all documents not destroyed by the Italian authorities were methodically confiscated and shipped to London, where they are not yet available to scholars.

See also no. 28, Gray and Chambers, *Materials for West African history in Italian archives.*

UNITED STATES

Note United States links with Africa have been close not only because of the slave-trade but also because Americans as explorers and missionaries, frontiersmen and soldiers, tobacco farmers and mining engineers played a role in the history of the continent. Because of the extent of American commercial, missionary, philanthropic, scientific and governmental contacts with Africa since 1619, the resources are many.

97 ' ASA guide to archival and manuscript materials relating to Africa in the United States '. *African Studies Bulletin*, v. 7, no. 2, May 1964: 1–2.
Announcement of the program for production of a guide to cover the broad range of Africa-related archives and manuscript materials in the United States being undertaken by the African Studies Association with a Ford Foundation grant over a three-year period. The National Archives and Records Service will assume joint responsibility with ASA for the conduct of the project, which is to be directed by Morris Rieger of the NARS staff. The guide will become the U.S. national volume of the project Guide to the Sources of African History outside Africa, sponsored by the UNESCO-affiliated International Council on Archives. An article by Mr. Rieger, ' Africa-related papers of persons and organizations in the United States ', appears in the *Africa Studies Bulletin*, v. 8, no. 3, Dec. 1965: 1–11; it illustrates preliminary findings of the project in the area of private (i.e., nongovernmental) papers and emphasizes their wide variety and distribution.

98 Hamer, Philip M., ed. *A guide to archives and manuscripts in the United States*. New Haven, Conn., Yale University Press, 1961. xxxii, 775 p.
Useful for locating African material in the United States, though unfortunately entries do not always indicate an African relationship.

99 *Handbook of American resources for African studies*. Ed. by Peter Duignan. Stanford, Calif., Hoover Institution, Stanford University, 1967. 218 p. (Hoover Institution, Bibliographical Series, no. 29)
This compilation, brought closely up to date as of early 1966, supersedes *Americans in Africa : A preliminary guide to American missionary archives and library manuscript collections on Africa*, by Robert Collins and Peter Duignan (1963), and articles in the former *Africana Newsletter* and the *African Studies Bulletin* describing library collections and archives in America. Descriptions of African holdings are given for 95 library and manuscript collections, 108 church and missionary libraries and archives, 95 art and ethnographic collections, and 4 business archives. A long article describes material in the National Archives dealing with Africa. While this handbook offers the fullest description yet produced of American holdings on Africa, the individual entries necessarily differ in quality and quantity because of varied responses to the author's questionnaire. An index is included.

100 King, Kenneth J. ' Africa-related material in black American colleges and the Phelps-Stokes Fund of New York '. *African Historical Studies*, v. 3, no. 2, 1970: 419–426.
A brief inventory of material held at Tuskegee Institute, Hampton Institute, Morehouse College, Howard University, Livingstone College, Stewart Missionary Foundation and the Phelps-Stokes Fund of New York. Of especial value to black Americans involved with colonial Africa as missionaries and educators.

101 Macmillan, Gary D. *An informal index to documents in the U.S. National Archives (U.S. Dept. of State records), pertaining to Liberia 1852–1906, 1910–1929*. Monrovia, 1968.

102 *The national union catalog of manuscript collections, 1959–1961.* Ann Arbor, Mich., J. W. Edwards, 1962. 1,061 p.

1962. Hamden, Conn., Shoe String Press, 1964. 532 p.

Index, 1959–1962. Hamden, Conn., Shoe String Press, 1964. 732 p.

1963–1964. Washington, Library of Congress, 1965. 500 p.

1965 [and] Index, 1963–1965. Washington, Library of Congress, 1966. 701 p.

Compiled by the Library of Congress from reports provided by American repositories. Many American collections containing African material are cited. Indexes are complete, including names, places, subjects and historical periods.

103 Newberry Library, Chicago. *A catalog of the William B. Greenlee collection of Portuguese history and literature and the Portuguese materials in the Newberry Library.* Comp. by Doris V. Welsh. Chicago, Newberry Library, 1953. 342 p.

The library is excellent with respect to Portuguese diplomatic and colonial affairs. Probably the best collection of literature in the United States concerning Portuguese overseas expansion.

AFRICA

General reference works

104 ' African archival directory '. *Africana Newsletter*, v. 1, no. 1, 1962: 16–18. Lists name, address, director, and founding date of 26 archives in Africa. It brought the Baxter survey (see below) up to date.

105 Baxter, T. W. *Archival facilities in sub-Saharan Africa.* Report prepared for CCTA. London, Commission for Technical Co-operation in Africa, 1959. 68 p. (Scientific Council for Africa South of the Sahara, Publication no. 78)

This report, prepared by the director of the former National Archives of Rhodesia and Nyasaland (now the National Archives of Rhodesia), begins with a list of 27 governmental archives in Africa south of the Sahara and then continues with the replies of these archives to a questionnaire regarding their control, scope of holdings, techniques and available finding aids, etc. It ends with an outline of prospects for further interarchival co-operation and the recommendations of the Inter-African Conference on Social Science at Bukavu in 1955 regarding conservation of archives. Due to difficulties over organization and personnel, the recommendations on interarchival co-operation were never carried out.

106 Curtin, Philip D. ' The archives of tropical Africa: A reconnaissance '. *Journal of African History*, v. 1, no. 1, 1960: 129–147.

Brief description of organization, problems, and holdings of archives in former French West Africa, Senegal, Mauritania, Ivory Coast, Cameroun, Guinea, Soudan, Togoland, Niger, Dahomey, former French Equatorial Africa, Nigeria, Ghana, Sierra Leone, Gambia, Zanzibar, Kenya, Tanganyika, Uganda, Sudan, Congo (Kinshasa, Zaïre), Portuguese Guinea, Ethiopia and Ruanda-Urundi.

107 *Directory of archives, libraries, and schools of librarianship in Africa. Répertoire des archives, bibliothèques et écoles de bibliothéconomie d'Afrique.* By E. W. Dadzie and J. T. Strickland. Paris, UNESCO, 1965. 112 p.

Systematic information on each of 508 responding institutions gives all the necessary detail – address, constitution, scope, special interest and collections, etc. Each section is arranged by country; in the first, 36 archives are described. The section on libraries (464) is subdivided by character of institution: national libraries, educational establishments, special libraries and documentation centres, public libraries. Archival data include foundation, staff, subjects covered, and date of oldest record and series of records held. Details concerning the existence of catalogues, inventories, guides, registers, etc., as well as publication data and availability are provided. At least 23 archives indicated that they had some guides or inventories, though most of these finding aids were for internal use only.

108 Jenkins, William, and Frederick Kirk, Jr. *A preliminary report on a survey of the public records depositories of Africa, the Levant and Western Europe, 1963.* Chapel Hill, Bureau of Public Records, University of North Carolina, 1966. 139 p.
Included are reports about archives and libraries in Morocco, Senegal, Nigeria, Rhodesia and South Africa.

109 U.S. Library of Congress. General Reference and Bibliography Division. *African libraries, book production, and archives: A list of references.* Comp. by Helen F. Conover, African Section. Washington, 1962. 64 p.
Divided into three sections, each beginning with general tools, and then subdivided by region.

Note This short selection of books, papers and articles must be considered as no more than illustrative of material that can be found regarding the libraries and particularly the archives of the individual countries of Africa. It is arranged by region, with subgrouping by country. Leads to further research are often given in the bibliographical references included in authoritative country studies.

110 *The bibliography of Africa: Proceedings and papers of the International Conference on African Bibliography, Nairobi, 4–8 Dec. 1967.* London, Cass, 1970.
A recently published major work containing essays on libraries, archives, acquisition programs and bibliographic projects.

West Africa

General

111 Alagoa, E. J. 'Preliminary inventory of the records of the United States diplomatic and consular posts in West Africa, 1856–1935'. *Journal of the Historical Society of Nigeria* (Ibadan), v. 2, no. 1, Dec. 1960: 78–104.
Records described are from Record Group 84 in the U.S. National Archives, Records of the Foreign Service Posts of the Department of State; they are papers from consular offices in Liberia (legation records at Monrovia also), the Gold Coast, Sierra Leone, Senegal, Gambia, and Lagos, Nigeria. The book concludes with a 'Select list of significant documents'. This article also appears in *Handbook of American resources for African studies* (see no. 99). For West African material in Europe, see no. 28.

112 Destaing, E. 'Notes sur les manuscrits arabes de l'Afrique occidentale'. *Revue Africaine,* v. 55, 1911: 64–99, 216–248, 484–522; v. 56, 1912: 267–300, 447–469; v. 57, 1913: 139–162.

113 Hiskett, M. 'Material relating to the state of learning among the Fulani before their jihād '. *Bulletin of the School of Oriental and African Studies,* v. 19, pt. 3, 1957: 551–578.

This article, a large part of which consists of the text and translation of a century-old Arabic manuscript, contains excellent bibliographic information on Arabic manuscripts of West Africa.

114 Ibadan. University. Institute of African Studies. Centre of Arabic Documentation. *Research Bulletin,* v. 1, no. 1– , July 1964– . Ibadan, Nigeria. semi-annual (v. 1, 3 issues).

A leading source for information on Arabic manuscripts, texts and archives dealing with West Africa, including data on private library collections and location of Arabic manuscripts in Europe and Africa.

115 Institut Fondamental d'Afrique Noire, Dakar. *Catalogue des manuscrits de l'I.F.A.N.* By Thierno Diallo et al. Dakar, IFAN, 1966. 155 p. (Catalogues et Documents, no. 20)

A catalogue of six collections of documents on peoples and regions of West Africa. The manuscripts are in the Arabic, Peul, and Voltaic languages, but most have been translated into French.

116 Monteil, V. 'Les manuscrits historiques arabo-africaines (bilan provisoire) '. *Bulletin de l'I.F.A.N.,* v. 27, ser. B, nos. 3–4, July–Oct. 1965: 531–542; 'Les manuscrits historiques arabo-africaines (II) ', v. 28, ser. B, nos. 3–4, July–Oct. 1966: 668–675.

The first article deals with Ghana, Nigeria, East Africa and French-speaking Africa; the second with Nigeria, Cameroun, Chad, Senegal, Mali and Niger. The articles were continued in nos. 3–4, July–Oct. 1967: 599–603, which dealt with Mali, Niger and Nigeria.

117 *WALA News.* Ibadan, West African Library Association, 1953–64. semi-annual.

The West African Library Association, an organization of the librarians of English-speaking West Africa, was formed in 1953 and published two issues of a journal, *West African Libraries.* The Association held an inaugural conference in Lagos in September 1954, at which John Harris of the Ibadan University College Library was elected president and the name of the journal was changed to *WALA News.* It appeared regularly twice a year until 1964, when the regional character of the organization had so declined that it split into separate bodies, and *WALA News* was superseded by the *Ghana Library Journal* and *Nigerian Libraries,* bulletin of the Nigerian Library Association. *Nigerian Libraries,* edited in the beginning by John Harris, augments three issues a year with supplementary mimeographed newsletters.

French West Africa

118 Charpy, Jacques. 'Les archives de l'Afrique occidentale française'. *ABCD—Archives, Bibliothèques, Collections, Documentation,* no. 12, Nov.–Dec. 1953: 317–322.

The writer, director of the Service des Archives of French West Africa, also published a volume of documents in 1958 titled *La fondation de Dakar, 1845–1857–1869* (see no. 1628).

119 Faure, Claude. *Les archives du Gouvernement Général de l'Afrique occidentale française.* Paris, Larose, 1922. 57 p.
Publication of the Comité d'Etudes Historiques et Scientifiques du Gouvernement Général de l'AOF, the predecessor of IFAN.

120 French West Africa. Service des Archives. *Les archives du Gouvernement Général de l'A.O.F. en 1954 : Organisation et fonctionnement du dépôt d'archives et de la bibliothèque administrative. Rapport annuel, 1954.* Dakar, 1955. 67 p. plans. mimeo.

121 —————— *Répertoire des archives.* Sér. A– , 1954– . Rufisque.
Prepared under the direction of Jacques Charpy.

> Sér. A, E, H à T, issued by the Haut Commissariat de la République en Afrique occidentale française; Sér. B, D, F and G, by the Gouvernement Général de l'Afrique occidentale française.
>
> Sér. A–B, by Claude Faure and Jacques Charpy. 2 v.
> Sér. A. *Actes officiels, 1817–1895.* 1958. 18 p.
> Sér. B. *Correspondance générale, 1779–1895.* 1955. 70 p.
>
> Sér. C. [Not published in 1968.]
>
> Sér. D. *Affaires militaires, 1763–1920.* 1956. 90 p.
>
> Sér. E. *Conseils et assemblés, 1819–1920.* 1958. 37 p.
>
> Sér. F. *Affaires étrangères, 1809–1921.* 1955. 57 p.
>
> Sér. G. *Politique et administration générale, 1782–1920.* 1954–55. 9 pts. in 1 v.
>
> Sér. H–T. *Affaires sociales, judiciaires, économiques et financières, 1782–1920.* 1958. 213 p.

122 Johnson, G. Wesley, Jr. 'The archival system of former French West Africa'. *African Studies Bulletin*, v. 8, no. 1, Apr. 1965: 48–58.
Account of the central archives of AOF in Dakar as well as other archives and associated research institutes in Senegal, Mauritania, Mali, Upper Volta, Niger, Dahomey, Ivory Coast and Guinea, based on visits made by the writer in late 1964.

123 Verdat, Marguerite. *Brèves instructions à l'usage des bibliothécaires-archivistes dans les cercles de l'A.O.F., suivies du cadre de classement des archives de l'A.O.F.* Rufisque, Impr. du Gouvernement Général [n.d.]. 29 p. (Publication of the Institut Française d'Afrique Noire)
The official archives of former French Africa formed the Section Outre-Mer of the Service des Archives Nationales located at the former Colonial Ministry (27 rue Oudinot, Paris 7e).

Western Sudan

124 Hunwick, J. O. 'Arabic manuscript material bearing on the history of the Western Sudan'. Supplement to *Bulletin of News of the Historical Society of Nigeria*, v. 7, no. 2, Sept. 1962. 9 p.

125 Smith, H. F. C. 'Arabic manuscript material bearing on the history of the Western Sudan: A list (published in the 1950's) of books written by the Khalifa Muhammad Bello'. Supplement to *Bulletin of News of the Historical Society of Nigeria*, v. 3, no. 4, Mar. 1959. 4 p.

Part I: guide to reference materials

126 Smith, H. F. C. 'Source material for the history of the Western Sudan'. *Journal of the Historical Society of Nigeria*, v. 1, no. 3, 1958: 238–247.

Both the *Journal* and the *Bulletin of News* of the Historical Society of Nigeria provide interim publication of material such as that above which is to be integrated into an eventual *Handlist of Arabic manuscripts bearing on the history of the Western Sudan*, a project of the Department of History of the University of Ibadan in co-operation with the Nigerian National Archives.

Gambia

127 'African archives: Gambia'. *Africana Newsletter*, v. 1, no. 3, 1963: 38–39.

See also 'A note on the Gambian archives' by Harry A. Gailey in *African Studies Bulletin*, v. 11, no. 3, Dec. 1968.

128 Gambia. *Report on the public records of the Gambia, April 1966*. By J. M. Smyth. Bathurst, 1966. 8 p. (Sessional Paper, no. 10 of 1966)

Gambia organized a Public Record Office in 1965, and this report details progress in collecting and organizing the PRO. The largest group of records consists of those of the Colonial Secretary – routine, confidential and secret. Numerous departmental records were uncovered but have not been transferred. Handlists of records (approximately 50) have been prepared.

Ghana

129 Boyo, (al-Hajj) Osmanu Eshaka, Thomas Hodgkin, and Ivor Wilks, comps. *Check list of Arabic works from Ghana*. Legon, Institute of African Studies, University of Ghana, Dec. 1962. 12 l.

A provisional list of material (originals, photographic reproductions, or microfilms) held by the Institute of African Studies. Revised lists, with additional acquisitions, are issued periodically and may be obtained from the Institute upon request.

130 Ghana. National Archives. *Report*. 1950– . Accra, Government Printer. Annual.

Begun as the Gold Coast National Archives report. Now one of the most well-organized archives in Africa. Lists of finding aids are in preparation.

131 Rieger, Morris. 'Gold Coast: Archives reports, 1950–57'. *American Archivist*, v. 22, Apr. 1959: 243–245.

Account and description of the National Archives of Ghana (formerly Gold Coast) established in 1950.

132 Wolfson, Freda. 'Historical records on the Gold Coast'. *Bulletin* (Institute of Historical Research, University of London), v. 24, no. 70, 1951: 121–240.

Guinea

133 Guinea. Institut National de Recherches et de Documentation. *Premier répertoire des archives nationales de Guinée*. Sér. A à Sér. N, 1720–1935. By Damien d'Almeida. Conakry, 1962. 224 p. (Mémoires, no. 1)

This is the first calendar of part of the archives, covering Sér. A, *Actes officiels, 1720–1935*; Sér. B, *Correspondance générale, 1890–1935*; Sér. D, *Administration générale, 1907–1932*; Sér. E, *Affaires politiques, 1896–1936*; Sér. N, *Affaires militaires, 1907–1919*. Other parts will follow.

Liberia

134 Foley, David M. 'Liberia's archival collection'. *African Studies Bulletin*, v. 11, no. 2, Sept. 1968: 217–220.
A brief survey of Liberia's rich store of archival materials. The author stresses that with persistence the serious researcher can gain access, despite occasional government discouragement, to this virtually unrecognized collection. Since France and Great Britain both sought territorial gains at the expense of Liberia, this archive may have useful information on colonial expansion and diplomatic affairs.

Mali

135 Smith, H. F. C. 'Arabic manuscript material bearing on the history of the Western Sudan: The archives of Segu'. Supplement to *Bulletin of News of the Historical Society of Nigeria*, v. 4, no. 2, 1959.

Mauritania

136 Heymowski, Adam. 'Organizing the National Library of Mauritania in Nouakchott'. *UNESCO Bulletin for Libraries*, v. 20, no. 2, Mar.–Apr. 1966: 98–99.
Describes holdings. A preliminary list has been compiled of all manuscripts by Mauritanian authors in private collections.

Nigeria

Note WALA News (no. 117) in 1964 became *Nigerian Libraries*, bulletin of the Nigerian Library Association and chief organ for information about libraries and manuscript collections in Nigeria.

137 Arif, Aida S., and Ahmad M. Abu Hakima. *Descriptive catalogue of Arabic manuscripts in Nigeria [in the] Jos Museum and Lugard Hall Library, Kaduna*. London, Luzac and Co., 1965. 216 p.
A briefly annotated title listing of more than 1,000 manuscripts, with names of authors supplied wherever possible. Dates are omitted. Some of the subjects covered are history, religion, language, poetry, folklore, prose, geography, education, sociology and law. Presumably material on colonial period is included.

138 Bivar, A. D. H. 'Arabic documents of Northern Nigeria'. *Bulletin of the School of Oriental and African Studies*, v. 22, pt. 2, 1959: 324–349. plates.
The first article, based on photographs of 19th-century Arabic official letters, emphasizes the importance of distinguishing between original official documents and various transcripts made from them.

139 Dike, Kenneth Onwuka. *Report on the preservation and administration of historical records and the establishment of a Public Record Office in Nigeria*. Lagos, Government Printer, 1954. 27 p.
Following this report by Nigeria's leading historian, the Record Office was established. It has been superseded by the National Archives (see no. 147).

Part I : guide to reference materials

140 Gwam, L. C. *A bibliography of the National Archives Library, Ibadan.* Part 1, *Africana*; Part 2, *General works.* Ibadan, 1964. 2 v. 94 l., 165 l.

141 —— 'First permanent building of the Nigerian National Archives '. *American Archivist*, v. 26, Jan. 1963: 67–74.

142 —— *A handlist of foreign official publications in the National Archives Library.* Ibadan, 1964. unpaged.

143 —— *A handlist of Nigerian official publications in the National Archives Headquarters, Ibadan.* Ibadan, 1964. 188 l. mimeo.

Supersedes two provisional volumes published in 1961. Part I covers occasional publications, including reports of commissions, committees, tribunals, etc.; anonymous series; speeches; dissertations; petitions; addresses; specialist publications; constitutional material; etc. Part II deals with periodical publications, including minutes of legislative bodies and departmental reports. Part III is an index of personal names and references.

144 —— 'Introduction to the Nigerian National Archives '. *WALA News*, v. 4, Dec. 1961: 59–69.

The author was until his untimely death in 1965 director of the National Archives of Nigeria. In his charge was the extensive project of recording the voluminous archival material held in Ibadan and in other official archives (Enugu, Kaduna, Lagos, etc.). For titles of individual records, see under Nigeria, National Archives (no. 147).

145 Kensdale, W. E. N. 'The Arabic manuscripts collection of the library of the University College of Ibadan, Nigeria '. *WALA News*, v. 2, June 1955: 21–25.

146 Kirk-Green, A. H. 'A preliminary note on the sources for Nigerian military history '. *Journal of the Historical Society of Nigeria*, v. 3, no. 1, 1964: 129–147.

147 Nigeria. National Archives. *Report.* 1954/55– . Lagos, Ibadan. Annual.

The Nigerian Record Office was established in Lagos in 1954, and the first three reports were issued under its name. In 1961, the fourth annual report (for 1959–60) appeared, the first under independence and considered a landmark. *The seventh report of the work of the National Archives of Nigeria, 1962–63* was published by the Federal Ministry of Information, Lagos, in 1964. The National Archives Headquarters was eventually located in Ibadan, with L. C. Gwam as director until his death in 1965. Work is continuing on lists and inventories of several of the archival record groups. A handlist of finding aids is available. By 1967, some 35 lists and inventories had been published in mimeographed form. These are listed here merely to illustrate the various kinds of documents inventoried by archival finding aids.

> Adedipe, G. A. K. *A special list of records on land and survey, Nigerian Secretariat record group.* Ibadan, 1963. 23 l.
>
> —— *A special list of records on international affairs, Nigerian Secretariat record group.* Ibadan, 1965. 22 l.
>
> —— *A special list of records on inter-state affairs in the Nigerian Secretariat record group.* Ibadan, 1965. 99 l.
>
> —— *A special list of records on the army, in the Nigerian Secretariat record group.* Ibadan, 1965. 79 p.
>
> —— *A special list of records on the police force, from the Nigerian Secretariat record group.* Lagos, 1965. 22 l.

Derived from Chief Secretary, Lagos.

Akinfemiwa, Akintunde. *A special list of records on ' the origins and development of the Nigerian medical and sanitary services', 1861–1960, from the Nigerian Secretariat record group.* Ibadan, 1964. 123 l.

A valuable guide concerning source material for Nigerian medical history. Arranged according to records dealing respectively with general administration, establishment and personnel, finance, legislation, outbreaks of diseases, hospitals, etc.; voluntary health organizations.

—— *A special list of records on the subject of public works, from the Nigerian Secretariat record group.* Lagos, 1965. 106 l.

Alagoa, E. J. *Series inventory of the records of the Provincial Office, Onitsha – ' Onprof ', 1896–1955.* Enugu. 1961. 19 l.

The material is described according to ' filed papers ', ' bound volumes ', each divided by archival classes. The appendices contain a class list of Provincial Office records at Onitsha, a list of officers in charge of the province, and a list of miscellaneous reports.

·—— *Special list of materials concerned with tribal and related studies among Kaduna Secretariat record groups.* Kaduna, 1962. 84 l.

An important finding aid. Listed in the original order of the depositing agencies. The records deal with the social organization of Nigerian communities and with the white impact. The *List* contains a variety of records, including intelligence reports, reports on organization, anthropological and special reports, notes, study papers, monographs, and so forth. Name of author, date of production, and other data are provided where possible.

—— *Special list of records related to historical, anthropological and social studies among provincial administration record groups at National Archives, Kaduna.* Kaduna, 1962. 71 p.

Supplements the information contained in the above documents.

Anyimbu, A. *Index of routine administrative reports in the National Archives, Enugu.* v. 1, *A preliminary index to the routine administrative reports in Enugu Secretariat record group.* Enugu, 1963. 26 l.

—— *A special list of records on land among the Enugu Secretariat record group.* Enugu, 1964.

—— *A special list of records on the subject of agriculture in record series CSO.26.* Ibadan, 1962. 126 l.

Ashikodi, L. N. *A special list of annual, half yearly and quarterly reports among Kaduna Secretariat record group.* Kaduna, 1962. 73 l.

Enwere, J. C. *An inventory of the Secretariat, Northern Province.* Kaduna, 1963. 47 p.

—— *A preliminary index to organisation and reorganisation reports in record group CSO.26.* Ibadan, 1961. 13 l.

—— *A provisional guide to official publications at the National Archives, Kaduna.* Kaduna, 1962. 78 l.

Part I : guide to reference materials

Enwere, J. C. *A special list of annual, half yearly and quarterly reports among the Nigerian Secretariat record group.* 1963. 58 1.

——— *A special list of records on chieftaincy matters, Nigerian Secretariat record group.* Ibadan, 1962. 43 1.

Gwam, L. C. *An inventory of the administrative records assembled from Benin Province.* Ibadan, 1961. 109 1.

Covers the years 1897 to 1956. The records described cover the material from the Provincial Office, Benin City; records of Divisional Office, Benin City; records of the Local Government Adviser, Benin City; records of the Asaba Divisional Office, Ogwashi-Uku; records of the Sub-District Office, Agbor; records of the Ishan Divisional Office, Ubiaja; records from Kukuruku Divisional Office, Auchi. The first part deals with administrative changes in the evolution of Benin Province; the second is titled 'Record description and arrangement'. In this section the various classes of records are analysed. The third part consists of appendices illustrating local administrative history.

——— *An inventory of the administrative records assembled from the Colony Province.* Ibadan, 1961. 123 1.

The Colony Province records contain a representative collection of record groups illustrating the work of a province. Part I is an essay entitled 'Landmarks in the administrative organization of the Colony Province, 1861–1956'. Part II covers record description and arrangement. Part III contains 23 appendices, including class lists, summaries of record groups, extracts of treaties relating to the making of the colony, letters patent, and tables of administrators.

——— *A preliminary index to the assessment and reassessment reports among the Nigerian Secretariat record group.* Ibadan, 1961. 23 1.

A preliminary description of material derived from the old Nigerian Secretariat, Lagos, registered as CSO 26. The introductory chapter furnishes a general description of the reports. Part I provides an index of reports; Part II contains an index of authors; Part III furnishes an index of provinces. These intelligence reports, which are among the series of records most sought after by researchers, merit special study.

——— *A preliminary index to the intelligence reports in the Nigerian Secretariat record group.* Ibadan, 1961. 39 1.

Another collection of major importance.

——— *A preliminary inventory of the administrative records assembled from Ondo Province.* 1963. 64 1.

——— *A preliminary inventory of the archives of the Nigerian Secretariat, Lagos.*

——— *A special list of records on the subject of education in record series CSO 26.* 1961. 56 1.

Mbah, V. C. J. *A preliminary index to the intelligence reports in the Enugu Secretariat record group.* Enugu, 1962. 15 1.

Supplements L. C. Gwam, *Preliminary index to the intelligence reports in the Nigerian Secretariat record group.* Contains a general description of the reports; a summary description of each report, including the author and year of compilation; an index of authors; and an index of provinces.

Nwaguru, J. E. N. *An inventory of the administrative records from the old Calabar Province.* Lagos, 1965. 102 l.

Supplements the information provided by Mrs. R. E. Nwoye, *Inventory of the administrative records from Ogoja Province* [not available for inspection]. The *Inventory* contains a general administrative history; a detailed description of the records, arranged by depositing agency; and appendices.

Nwaobi, J. O. *A special list of records on agriculture, fishery and veterinary [science] in the Kaduna Secretariat record group.* 1964.

Ododo, Kate. *A special list of records on forestry from the Nigerian Secretariat record group.* Ibadan, 1963. 87 l.

—— *A special list of records on veterinary [science] and the fish industry in the Nigerian Secretariat record group CSO.9–CSO.26.* Ibadan, 1963. 49 l.

Onuoha, Kate. *A special list of records on the Nigerian railway in the CSO record group 11–21.* Ibadan, 1964. 3 v.

—— and A. O. Evborokhai. *A special list of records on land cases in the Oyo provincial record group.* 1964.

Waniko, S. S. *A descriptive catalogue of the early papers of the Secretariat, Northern Provinces, Kaduna: National Archives record group S.N.P., series 10.* Kaduna, 1961. 57 l.

—— and M. S. D. Ilyasu. *A descriptive catalogue of early Lugard-Sultan of Sokoto correspondence including a description of 131 Arabic letters found in Sokoto in 1903.* Kaduna, 1961. 24 l.

148 Nigeria. National Archives Headquarters. Ibadan. *A subject catalog of the National Archives Library, Ibadan.* pt. 1– , no. 1– , 1964–65– .

See also *A descriptive catalogue of the early papers of the Secretariat, Northern Provinces, Kaduna* (Kaduna, 1961, 57 l.; National Archives record group, S.N.P. series 10).

149 Northern Region of Nigeria. Library. [Catalogue of] *Holdings.* Kaduna, 196– . 55 l. 33 cm.

Author list of holdings. Official documents of the Northern Region are heavily represented.

150 Waniko, S. S. *Arrangement and classification of Nigerian archives.* Lagos, Nigerian Archives Service, 1958. 21 p.

Senegal

151 Diallo, Thierno, and others. *Catalogue des manuscrits de l'I.F.A.N. Fonds Vieillard, Gaden, Brévié, Figaret, Shaykh Moussa Kamara et Cremer, en langues arabe, peule et voltaïques.* Dakar, I.F.A.N., 1966. 156 p. (Catalogues et Documents, 20)

152 Johnson, G. Wesley. ' Archival materials of Senegal '. *Africana Newsletter*, v. 2, no. 1, 1964: 74–76.

153 Saint-Martin, Y., ed. *Les rapports de situation politique, 1874–1891; une source de l'histoire coloniale du Sénégal.* Dakar, 1966. 168 p.

Extracts from and commentary on a series of six important registers in the archives of Senegal (2B/73–2B/78).

154 Senegal. Archives Nationales. Centre de Documentation. *Bulletin Bibliographique des Archives du Sénégal.* no. 1– , Jan. 1963– . Dakar. Irregular.

155 ——— ——— ——— *Eléments de bibliographie sénégalaise : 1959–1963.* Dakar, 1964. 140 p.
Covers reports concerning the economy, the seven regions of Senegal, and the main commercial and industrial companies. Details regarding full title, provenance and archival location are provided. Highly confidential reports have been excluded.

156 ——— ——— ——— *Répertoire des archives.* By J. F. Maurel.
The archival collections of the former colony of Senegal have now been transferred from Saint-Louis to Dakar, and M. Maurel is preparing an index for them.

Sierra Leone

157 Gailey, Harry. ' African archives: Sierra Leone '. *Africana Newsletter,* v. 1, no. 3, 1963 : 39.

158 Sierra Leone. *Catalogue of archives, the property of the government of Sierra Leone, deposited at Fourah Bay College, Sierra Leone, West Africa.* [Freetown ? 1952 ?] 33 p.
A typescript inventory of the holdings of the archives has also been prepared by Mrs. Gladys Sheriff.

Equatorial Africa

French Equatorial Africa

159 Glénisson, Jean. ' Les archives de l'A.E.F.: Lettre de Brazzaville '. *Gazette des Archives,* n.s. no. 22, July 1957 : 23–30.
By the former chief archivist of the Gouvernement Général de l'AEF. A reference is made, in the bibliography accompanying Guy Lasserre's study, *Libreville : La ville et sa région (Gabon, A.E.F.); étude de géographie humaine* (Paris, A. Colin, 1958; Cahiers de la Fondation Nationale des Sciences Politiques, no. 98), to a mimeographed inventory of documents by Jean Glénisson, *Les sources de l'histoire d'A.E.F.: Inventaire sommaire des archives du Ministère de la France d'Outre-Mer concernant l'A.E.F.* (Brazzaville, 1953, 96 p.).

160 Institut d'Etudes Centrafricaines, Brazzaville. Bibliothèque. *Catalogue de la bibliothèque de l'I.E.C.* By Jeanine Lambert. Montpellier, Impr. Charité, 1951. 152 p. (Mémoires, no. 4.) Supplement no. 1, 1953. 232 p.
About 5,000 entries are listed.

161 Ledoux, Daniel. Archives du Gouvernement-Général de l'A.E.F. Série B: *Correspondance ancienne (Enregistrement in-extenso de la correspondance) 1848–1912.* 1970. 59 p. mimeo.

162 Ledoux, Daniel. Archives du Gouvernement-Général de l'A.E.F. Série D: Politique et Administration Générale. Sous-séries 4D à 21D. 1971. 207 p. mimeo.

> 4D. *Rapports politiques 1889–1954,* p. 1.
>
> 5D. *Dossiers divers des affaires politiques (1891–1958),* p. 63.
>
> 6D–13D. *Conseils de gouvernement et d'administration antérieur au Grand Conseil de l'A.E.F. (1888–1954),* p. 112.

14D–20D. *Grand Conseil de l'A.E.F. et Assemblées locales : Généralites, élections (1946–1958)*, p. 168.

21D. *Elections aux différentes Assemblées métropolitaines (1945–1958)*, p. 203.

Cameroun

163 Gardinier, David E. 'African archives: Cameroun'. *Africana Newsletter*, v. 1, no. 3, 1963: 37–38.

Belgian Congo (Zaïre)

164 Congo, Belgian. Force Publique. *Catalogue de la bibliothèque de Léopoldville*. Léopoldville, Force Publique, 1953. 488 p.

165 Depasse, Charles. *Les bibliothèques publiques au Congo*. Bruxelles, Editions Universitaires, 1948. 32 p. illus. Extracts from *Zaïre*, v. 2, Mar. 1948: 277–302.

Short historical account beginning with legislation in 1898. Included are statistics of public libraries for Europeans and Congolese and data on research and mission libraries.

East Africa

Note See also Gifford and Louis, eds., *Britain and Germany in Africa*; and Harlow and Chilver, eds., *History of East Africa*, v. 2 (nos. 438 and 1035, respectively), for information on archives and library collections in this region.

166 Belton, E. J. *Directory of East African libraries*. Kampala, Uganda, Makerere College Library, 1961. 76 p. (Makerere Library Publications, no. 1)

A thorough survey of all libraries existing in East Africa at the time. It contains entries of more than 90 specialized and larger general libraries.

167 Charman, D., and M. Cook. 'The archive services of East Africa'. *Archives : The Journal of the British Records Association*, v. 8, 1967: 70–80.

168 *East African Library Association Bulletin*. no. 1– . Jan. 1962– . Kampala, Uganda, published for the Association by Makerere College Library. Quarterly.

An organ for information on East African libraries. Some information regarding manuscript and archival collections is provided.

Kenya

169 Kenya. Government Archives. *Archives microfilming programme*. Sec. I. Nairobi, Mar. 1964. 75 l. fold. map. 33 cm. mimeographed.

An inventory of provincial and district annual and quarterly reports held in the Kenya Government Archives – the first section of a projected program to make records from the beginning of colonial rule to 1962 available on film. Two other syllabi which list the political record books of provinces and districts, and miscellaneous early records and diaries will be published; but these will cover only the years to 1939. Each section is to be preceded by an introduction dealing with the form and content of the documents. The general introduction in

Part I : guide to reference materials

Section I is by Derek Charman, government archivist seconded from England as technical adviser on archives to the Kenya government.

170 Soff, Harvey G. *A guide to the Coast Province microfilm collection, Kenya National Archives, Kenya Seyidie (Coast) Province. Correspondence and reports, 1891–1962.* Syracuse, 1971. 191 p. (Syracuse University, Program of Eastern African Studies. Occasional Bibliography, no. 18)

171 Syracuse University. Maxwell Graduate School for Citizenship and Public Affairs. Program of Eastern African Studies. *A catalogue of the Kenya National Archive collection on microfilm at Syracuse University.* Comp. by Nathan W. Fedha and John B. Webster. Syracuse, N.Y., 1967. 1 v. (Occasional Bibliography, no. 6)

172 —————— —————— —————— *A guide to the Kenya National Archives, to the microfilms of the provincial and district annual reports, record books, and handing-over reports : Miscellaneous correspondence; and intelligence reports.* Comp. by Robert C. Gregory, Robert M. Maxon and Leon P. Spencer. Syracuse, N.Y., 1968. 452 p. (Eastern African Bibliographical Series, no. 3)

A detailed annotated guide to the 157 reels of microfilm which Syracuse University purchased from the Kenya National Archives. Coverage includes Secretariat circulars and debates of the Legislative Council and the National Assembly. Also given are accounts of administrative reorganizations, a list of ethnic groups, and indexes for province and district, personalities and organizations, and miscellaneous correspondence (subject index). The work concerns mainly the period 1900 to 1965, but the period covered varies with the type of material, some of which goes back as far as the 1880s.

Tanganyika and Zanzibar (Tanzania)

173 Dar es Salaam. University College. Library. *Library Bulletin and Accessions List.* 1961– . Dar es Salaam. Monthly, 1961–Feb. 1965; fortnightly (irregular), Mar. 1965– . stencilled.

Bulletin sometimes carries inventories of MSS. collections; for example, that of the Hans Cory Collection appeared in 1969.

174 —————— —————— —————— *List of manuscripts in the East African Swahili Committee Collection.* Dar es Salaam, Mar. 1964. 25 p. (Library Bulletin, no. 24)

Annotated list, mainly of Swahili texts but including also some historical and bibliographical works in European languages. A similar list appeared in *Swahili* (v. 35, no. 1, Mar. 1965: 99–115).

175 —————— —————— —————— *The papers of Hans Cory in the library of the University College, Dar es Salaam.* Dar es Salaam, 1968. 53 p.

A government sociologist and linguist, Cory wrote and collected much valuable material on all aspects of traditional life.

176 Hill, Patricia J. *Shelf list and index to secretariat archives (early series), 1919–1927.* Dar es Salaam, National Archives of Tanzania, 1966. 104 p.

Covers 1,539 files and contains provincial, district and departmental annual reports; information on medical, economic, political, military, legal and educational matters.

177 Tanzania. National Archives. *Annual report of the National Archives of Tanzania for the year 1964–1965.* Dar es Salaam, Government Printer, 1966. 19 p.

This first annual report lists surveys of archives and gives a summary of archive holdings available for study.

178 Wright, Marcia. 'The Tanganyika Archives'. *American Archivist*, v. 28, no. 4, Oct. 1965: 511–520.

An article on the National Archives, which, since its formation in June 1962 at Dar es Salaam, has been collecting a wide variety of historical records – official (including both German and British colonial periods), missionary and commercial – as well as the private papers of important persons or families. Walter T. Brown, 'German records in the National Archives of Tanzania', *African Studies Bulletin* (v. 12, 1969, no. 2: 147–151), gives a short review of German material that was reorganized by a West German archivist who was attached for a period to the Tanzanian Archives (See also Germany, p. 48.)

179 Zanzibar. Archives and Museum Department. *Report.* 1956– . Zanzibar, Government Printer. Annual.

The Zanzibar Archives was approved in 1955 and combined with Peace Memorial Museum.

Uganda

180 English, Patrick T. 'Archives of Uganda'. *American Archivist*, v. 18, July 1955: 225–230.

181 Teso, Uganda (District). Office of the District Commissioner. *Index list to the archives of the Office of the District Commissioner, Teso District.* Soroti, 1960. 106 p.

182 Trowell, Kathleen M., comp. *A handbook of the museums and libraries of Uganda.* Kampala, Uganda Museum, 1957. 16 p. (Uganda Museum, Occasional Paper, no. 3)

The Horn

Ethiopia

183 Eldon, Rita. 'The National Library of Ethiopia'. *Ethiopian Observer*, v. 1, Oct. 1957: 369–370.

A description of the first public library in Ethiopia, founded shortly after the liberation.

184 Wright, Stephen. 'Book and manuscript collection in Ethiopia'. *Journal of Ethiopian Studies*, v. 2, no. 1, Jan. 1964: 11–24.

An interesting article on the Ethiopian attitude towards books, the development of printing and publishing and the history and current status of book and manuscript collection.

The author, in collaboration with Stephen G. Wright, has compiled a *Catalogue of Ethiopian manuscripts in the Cambridge University Library* (Cambridge, Eng., University Press, 1961, 75 p.). Many registers of early Ethiopian manuscripts have been published. Since these do not deal with the period from 1870 to 1960, however, they have been omitted.

Sudan

185 Holt, Peter M. 'Mahdist archives and related documents'. *Archives* (London), v. 5, no. 28, Sept. 1962: 193–200.
A brief historical account of Mahdist manuscripts and a survey of their scope and present distribution. Some of these materials or copies of them are to be found outside the Sudan, as, for example, those described by Richard Hill in 'The Sudan Archive, School of Oriental Studies, University of Durham, England', *Africana Newsletter*, v. 1, no. 4, 1963: 40–41.

South Central Africa

The Rhodesias and Nyasaland (Rhodesia, Zambia and Malawi)

186 Baxter, T. W., and L. H. Gann. 'The National Archives of Rhodesia and Nyasaland'. *Africana Newsletter*, v. 1, no. 4, 1963: 31–40.
The first archival institution in the former states of British Central Africa was created in Southern Rhodesia, where a Government Archivist was appointed in 1935. Southern Rhodesia took the lead in archival development in the area, and in 1946 the functions of the Government Archivist were extended to Northern Rhodesia and Nyasaland. The archives, which continued to centre on Salisbury, became known as the Central African Archives, with separate depots in the northern territories. In 1954 the department was renamed the National Archives of Rhodesia and Nyasaland. The archival resources of the three territories continued to be administered jointly, until the dissolution of the Federation of Rhodesia and Nyasaland in 1963. The three successor archival institutions became known respectively as the National Archives of Malawi at Zomba, the National Archives of Rhodesia at Salisbury and the National Archives of Zambia at Lusaka.

187 Graham, I. M., and B. C. Halwinde. *Guide to the public archives of Zambia.* v. 1, *1895–1940.* Lusaka, National Archives, 1970. 153 p.
Not available for annotation.

188 Rhodesia. National Archives. *Guide to the historical manuscripts in the National Archives of Rhodesia.* By T. W. Baxter and E. E. Burke. Salisbury, National Archives, 1970. 527 p.
The Historical Manuscripts Collection consists of material of non-official provenance – political papers, records of commercial companies, missionary material, papers of clerical organizations, African associations and other private bodies and papers of individual settlers and Africans. Entries for each group of papers contain either a biographical sketch of the person or a historical note on the institution, whichever is appropriate; a general description of the papers (origins, dates covered, approximate volume, etc.); a selective calendar of the material in question and editorial notes. This is a shortened version of a six-volume typescript guide in the possession of the National Archives of Rhodesia.

189 Rhodesia, Southern. Central African Archives. *Report by the chief archivist.* Aug. 31, 1947–June 30, 1954. Salisbury. illus.
Included are the following:

> *Central African Archives in retrospect and prospect : A report ... for the twelve years ending 31 August 1947.* 1947. 118 p.

Libraries and archives: Africa

A report... for the period 1 September 1947 to 31 December 1948. 1949. 102 p.

Archives in a new era: A report... for the period 1 January 1949 to 30 June 1954. 1955. 81 p.

On July 1, 1954, the Central African Archives became a body of the Federation of Rhodesia and Nyasaland. After the dissolution of the Federation in 1963, the Archives split up into the National Archives of Malawi, the National Archives of Rhodesia and the National Archives of Zambia. See the following entries.

190 Rhodesia and Nyasaland. Central African Archives. *The coming of age of the Central African Archives.* [Glasgow] 1956. 40 p. illus.

191 —————— *A guide to the public records of Southern Rhodesia under the regime of the British South Africa Company, 1890–1923.* Salisbury, Central African Archives, 1956. xxxviii, 282 p. illus.

A most comprehensive publication which arranges the records according to their archival groups as determined by their departmental provenance. The groups are further subdivided into classes, and these into series of related materials. The guide is supplemented by detailed historical notes on the history and functions of the various departments and public bodies. It is fully indexed. The information given in the guide is supplemented by an even more detailed typescript inventory, which is locally available and which covers each single archival unit. Between them, they provide the most detailed description of any large group of records in Africa.

A revised edition by T. W. Baxter appeared as *A guide to the public archives of Rhodesia,* v. 1, *1898–1923* (Salisbury, 1969, 262 p.). Volume 2 will cover the archives from 1923 to 1940. The great majority of the archives are open for public inspection when they are 30 years old.

192 —————— National Archives. *Archives in a growing society: A report by the Director for the period 1 July 1954 to 30 June 1962.* Salisbury, 1963. 105 p. illus.

193 Zambia. National Archives. *Annual report.* 1964– . Lusaka.

Angola

194 Angola. Arquivo Histórico. *Boletim do Arquivo Histórico e de Biblioteca do Museu de Angola.* Luanda.

Most issues contain texts of documents; indexed in *Archivum.* V. Salvadorini has surveyed the archive in ' Biblioteche e archivi d'Angola ', *Bolletino della Associazone degli Africanisti Italiani* (see no. 197).

195 *Arquivos de Angola: Publicação trimestral.* 1933– . Luanda.

Published by the Museu de Angola. Frequent collections of texts from documents appear. Also inventories and finding aids are described. Indexed in *Archivum.*

196 Instituto de Investigação Científica de Angola. Arquivo Histórico de Angola. *Roteiro topográfico dos Codices: Núcleo antigo da Secretaria Geral; núcleo do Governo de Benguela; núcleo geral.* Luanda, Imprensa Nacional de Angola, 1966. 183 p.

A major archival tool to locate and describe the government records of Angola. The period from 1600 to 1920 is covered, but most entries are from 1800 on.

Part I: guide to reference materials

A chronological index and subject and geographical indexes are included. The work is part of a continuing program to prepare inventories of the records held at the Arquivo Histórico de Angola. Many of these inventories appear in *Arquivos de Angola* (see, for example, the issue of July–Dec. 1959). See also M. A. Samuels, 'Report of historical research in Angola', *African Studies Bulletin*, v. 11, no. 3, 1968, 245–247, for descriptions of archives in Luanda and elsewhere in Angola. See also *Boletim cultural do Luanda*, 1933– , which carries inventories of private and municipal records.

197 Salvadorini, Vittorio. 'Biblioteche e archivi d'Angola'. *Bolletino della Associazone degli Africanisti Italiani*, v. 2, nos. 3-4, July–Dec. 1969: 16–30.

Mozambique

Note The Arquivo Histórico de Moçambique, Lourenço Marques, under the Direcção dos Serviços de Instrução of Mozambique, contains some historical archives and has a library of over 8,000 volumes.

198 Montez, Caetano. 'Inventário de fundo do século XVIII do Arquivo Histórico de Moçambique'. *Moçambique, Documentário Trimestral*, nos. 72–79, 1952–54; no. 81, 1955: 135–150.

199 Pinto, Frederico da Silva. *Roteiro histórico-biográfico da cidade de Lourenço Marques*. Lourenço Marques, 1965. 204 p.

Note See also Portugal, pp. 54–57.

Southern Africa

Basutoland (Lesotho)

200 *Catalogue of the Basutoland Government Archives.* Nov. 1962. 74 p. Available from the Bursar, Pius XII College, P.O. Roma, Basutoland.
The Archives contain such valuable material as census reports from 1891; papers, letters and circulars of the Resident Commissioner's office, 1884–1917; correspondence of the Governor's agents from 1871 to 1884, of the High Commissioner from 1884 to 1917, and general from 1917 to 1931; council proceedings; district correspondence; diaries, letter books, Pitso books, police correspondence, etc.

South Africa

Note South Africa has the most extensive and the most widely used archival system in Africa. The South African archival system is administered as an organic whole. The State Archives in Pretoria administers the bulk of the records since the creation of the Union of South Africa in 1910. The Transvaal Archives are likewise in Pretoria; the Cape Archives are in Cape Town, the Natal Archives in Pietermaritzburg and the Orange Free State Archives in Bloemfontein. The archives of South-West Africa are located at Windhoek; they are administered separately, but come under the authority of the South African Chief Archivist. The material cited here is intended to be illustrative rather than exhaustive. See also under Great Britain and Germany.

201 Botha, Carol. *A catalogue of manuscripts and papers in the Killie Campbell Africana Collection.* . . . Johannesburg, Department of Bibliography, Librarianship and Typography, University of Witwatersrand, 1967. 85 p.

202 Botha, Colin Graham. *Cape archives and records.* v. 3, *Collected works.* Cape Town, C. Struik, 1962. 331 p.

This has a useful historical account, especially chapter five, ' The public archives of South Africa, 1652–1910 ', p. 113–211. Appendix five (p. 205–207) of this chapter gives a list of publications relating to documents in the Cape Archives; appendix six (p. 208–209) contains another useful list, ' Transcripts of documents in Europe in the Cape Archives '. An earlier publication of this chapter appeared in 1928 with the same title (Cape Town, Cape Times, Ltd., 108 p.).

203 Cape of Good Hope. Archives. *Lists and inventories available in the Cape Depot.* Cape Town, n.d. 9 p.

A brief mimeographed checklist of material housed in the Archives. Similar lists exist for the other Archives Depots as well.

204 Johannesburg. University of Witwatersrand. Library. *Guide to the archives and papers.* Johannesburg. 1967. 60 p.

205 Long, Una. *An index to authors of unofficial, privately owned manuscripts relating to the history of South Africa, 1812–1920, being the result of two years' research.* Cape Town, University of Cape Town, 1947.

Edition limited to 200 copies; very unusual and important work.

206 Musiker, Reuben. *Guide to sources of information in the humanities.* Potchefstroom, Potchefstroom University, in collaboration with the South African Library Association, 1962. 100 p.

A directory of libraries and special collections in non-scientific and non-technical fields. Special attention has been paid to libraries of Africana. The material is alphabetically arranged, with subject and geographical indexes.

207 Quinn, Gerald D., and Otto H. Spohr, comps. *Handlist of manuscripts in the University of Cape Town Libraries.* Ed. by R. F. M. Immelman. Cape Town, University of Cape Town Libraries, 1968. 81 p. ports., facsims.

Contains articles in Afrikaans and English on the history and development of archival agencies and work in South Africa. No. 2 and subsequent issues appear as the official organ of the newly organized South African Association of Archivists.

208 South Africa. Archives. *Annual report of the director of archives.* Pretoria, The Archives.

These annual reports are very comprehensive. They give detailed information about Archives staff, work performed, preparation of documents for binding and microfilms, research and supply service, public use of the Archives, the Archives Depots, publications, and schedule of fees. *A list of finding aids in archives depots,* published in 1969, is also useful.

209 —————— *Argief – jaarboek vir die Suid-Afrikaanse geskiedenis. Archives year book for South African history.* Cape Town, 1938– .

A major series containing archival material, monographs and theses on South African history, with contributions in Afrikaans, English and Dutch. By 1967 a total of 53 volumes had been published. The volumes are indexed, provided with maps, bibliographies, and a detailed description of the archival material used for the various publications.

210 —————— *List of archives publications published officially after 1925.* Pretoria, The Archives, 1964. 9 p. mimeo.

This is a full list of archives publications giving author, title and price of each publication. It includes a full contents list of *Archives year book for South Africa*, v. 1 (1938) to v. 26 (1963), and has details of South African archival records for each province.

211 *South African Archival Records. Suid-Afrikaanse Argief-Stukke.* Parow, Cape; later Cape Town, 1952– .

Issued under the supervision of the Archives Commission by the Publications Section of the South African Archives. An important series containing reprints of original documents such as the complete *Notule van die Volksraad van die Suid-Afrikaanse Republiek.*

212 *South African Archives Journal. Suid-Afrikaanse Argiefblad.* 1959– , Pretoria, South African Society of Archivists. Annual.

Contains articles on sources, such as F. J. Steytler, ' Bronnenavorsing in Groot-Brittanje, 1951–1954 ', no. 8, 1962: 7–17; and on archival administration, such as J. H. Davies, 'The organisational development of the Government Archives of the Union of South Africa ', no. 2, 1960: 7–19.

213 *South African Libraries.* 1933– . Pretoria, South African Library Association. Quarterly.

Ed. by P. A. Coetzee, Department of Library Science, University of Pretoria. The chief organ for news of libraries in South Africa, this quarterly includes articles and notes, bibliographical notices and book reviews. Cumulative indexes are issued every two years.

214 South African Public Library, Cape Town. *Quarterly Bulletin. Kwartaalblad.* v. 1– , Sept. 1946– . Cape Town. illus.

In this journal (title has varied), which is a major source for bibliographies of South African publications (see also in area section), there are also news notes and articles of library and archival interest.

Madagascar (Malagasy Republic) and the Mascarenes

Madagascar

215 ' Les archives de Madagascar '. *Bulletin de Madagascar*, no. 150, Nov. 1958: 973–974.

216 Decary, Raymond. ' Chronique de l'histoire coloniale: Madagascar (1950–1955) '. *Revue d'Histoire des Colonies*, v. 43, no. 150, 1956: 82–119.

In the first chapter the author lists many documents of special importance preserved in the Archives of the Gouvernement Général in Tananarive.

217 Deschamps, Hubert J. ' Conceptions, problèmes et sources de l'histoire de Madagascar '. *Journal of African History*, v. 1, no. 2, 1960: 249–256.

Includes account of existing archives.

218 Molet, Louis. ' Les manuscrits arabico-malgaches '. *Revue de Madagascar*, v. 30, Jan. 1957: 53–61.

219 Sicard, Fernand. ' Les archives de Madagascar '. *Comptes Rendus Mensuels des Séances de l'Académie des Sciences d'Outre-Mer*, v. 25, no. 8, 1965: 420–431.

A report, followed by a panel discussion, on how the archives of the Malagasy Republic have been and are being collected, classified, and utilized.

220 ' Tananarive, Madagascar '. *Bulletin des Bibliothèques de France*, v. 6, Apr. 1961: 190.

Note on the Bibliothèque Universitaire de Tananarive, which on the occasion of a visit by French statesmen, February 10, 1961, published a mimeographed brochure describing its development since its opening in January 1960.

221 Valette, Jean. *Guide des sources de l'histoire religieuse antérieures à 1896: Inventaire de la série HH (Cultes).* Tananarive, Malagasy Republic, Service des Archives et de la Documentation, 1962. 31 p.

Prepared by the archivist of the Malagasy Republic, this guide is an inventory of material on Protestant and Catholic missions up to 1896. Included is the correspondence addressed by the missionaries to the government, with an indication of the number of pieces and the dates. The Protestant missions concerned are the London Missionary Society, the Society of the Propagation of the Gospel, the Friends' Foreign Mission Association, and the Norske Mission or Mission Norvégienne. The Catholic missions are the Société de Jésus, Frères des Ecoles Chrétiennes, and Soeurs de St. Joseph Cluny.

222 Valette, Jean. 'Les instruments de travail aux archives de la République malgache'. *Africana Newsletter*, v. 2, no. 1, 1964: 70–72.

Lists the various typed summaries and inventories available on January 1, 1964, for material (some of it going back to the 1820s) deposited at the Archives.

223 Valette, Jean. *Inventaire de la Série Mi des archives de la République malgache.* Tananarive, Impr. Nationale, 1963. 16 p. Reprinted from the *Bulletin de Madagascar*, no. 201, Feb. 1963: 163–176.

Useful guide to the recently microfilmed collections deposited at the National Archives of the Malagasy Republic after an intensive search for foreign source materials conducted by the archivist Jean Valette. The inventory contains such items as photocopies from archives in Mauritius pertaining to Madagascar, 1767–1848; microfilms of the correspondence of General Gallieni deposited at the Bibliothèque Nationale in Paris; microfilms of documents on Madagascar preserved at the Bibliothèque Centrale des Archives du Ministère de la Marine de France; microfilms of documents relating to Madagascar before 1789 deposited at the Archives du Ministère des Affaires Etrangères de France, as well as certain political correspondence for the period 1816–85 from the same collections. In addition to these sources, the guide lists manuscripts from the British Museum and the National Archives of the United States of America concerning Madagascar.

224 Valette, Jean. 'La Série C des archives de la République malgache'. *Bulletin de Madagascar*, no. 232, Sept. 1965: 804–806.

Mascarenes

225 Lartin, U. 'Archives de la Réunion'. *Africana Newsletter*, v. 2, no. 1, 1964: 72–74.

Inventories, some published, of the archival holdings are listed, as are a few other publications of the Archives. Journals and reviews of the 19th and 20th centuries are also held.

226 Mauritius. Archives Department. *Bibliography of Mauritius, 1502–1954, covering the printed records, manuscripts, archivalia and cartographic material.* By A. Toussaint, Chief Archivist. Port Louis, Esclapon, 1956. xvii, 884 p.

The active interest of Mr. Toussaint has resulted in exceptionally complete recordings of Mauritian archives, as shown in this work.

227 Mauritius. Archives Department. *Report.* 1893– . Port Louis, Government Printer. Annual.
Previously issued as *Report* of the Archives Branch. See also its *Bulletin,* 1948– . Issued irregularly.

228 Pérotin, Yves. 'The archives of Réunion: A workshop opened for historical research '. *American Archivist,* v. 17, July 1954: 257–261.

229 Toussaint, Auguste. 'The Mauritius Archives'. *Indian Archives,* v. 6, Jan.–Dec. 1952: 13–20.

BIBLIOGRAPHIES FOR AFRICA IN GENERAL

BIBLIOGRAPHIES OF BIBLIOGRAPHIES

Note The Grey bibliography mentioned below (no. 233) is unique in its completeness and has stood for many years as the standard work. African bibliographies are included with bibliographical work in all other fields in several well-known guides, all fully described by Winchell, for example:

230 Besterman, Theodore. *A world bibliography of bibliographies and of bibliographical catalogues, calendars, abstracts, digests, indexes, and the like.* 4th ed., rev. and greatly enl. throughout. Lausanne, Societas Bibliographica, 1965–66. 5 v.
Earlier editions: 1939–40, 1947–49, 1955–56. The fourth edition includes more than 117,000 bibliographies, classified under almost 16,000 headings and sub-headings. Over 55,000 are in English and 70 in Afrikaans. V. 5 is the index.

231 Bogaert, Jozef. *Sciences humaines en Afrique noire: Guide bibliographique (1945–1965).* Bruxelles, Centre de Documentation Economique et Sociale Africaine (CEDESA), 1966. 226 p. (Enquêtes bibliographiques, no. 15)
The compiler has brought together what he considers the most important sources and reference works dealing with black Africa – over 1,500 entries. Books, monographs, journals, articles and government publications are included.

232 Cambridge University. African Studies Centre. *Bibliography of African bibliographies.* Comp. by Anthea Garling. Cambridge, Eng., 1968. 138 p. mimeo. (Occasional Papers, no. 1)
This compact bibliography, covering references from the earliest times to 1966, is derived from relevant titles in Besterman's work (see no. 230), the Centre's own current bibliographical catalogue and bibliographical cards provided by CARDAN. Arrangement is by country under regional headings and alphabetical by author within each country. Though the work contains some misinformation and suffers from a high proportion of typographical errors, it nevertheless constitutes a valuable reference tool.

233 South African Public Library, Cape Town. *A bibliography of African bibliographies covering territories south of the Sahara.* 4th ed., rev. to Nov. 1960. Cape Town, 1961. 79 p. (Grey Bibliographies, no. 7)
The standard guide to bibliographical publications on Africa. This was first published as a reprint from the quarterly *South African Libraries,* October 1942 and January 1943, at which time it covered all Africa; with the third edition in 1955 it was limited to Africa south of the Sahara. It is supplemented regularly

in the *Quarterly Bulletin* of the Library. The fourth edition contains well over a thousand items, both monographic bibliographies and works including significant reading lists. These are classified according to the Universal Decimal Classification; they include most of the important older bibliographies as well as recent material. A new edition was in preparation in 1969.

CURRENT BIBLIOGRAPHIC SOURCES

Note Sources for current and continuing information on new writings about colonial Africa are almost inexhaustible. There are a few serial bibliographies devoted to Africa, and practically all significant reviews and journals in the African field give more or less space to book reviews and notices. The numerous general bibliographical and book-reviewing organs are often more ready library tools than the Africanist serials, and in view of the quantity of writing now appearing on Africa, they reward attention. Abstracting services are few except in special fields where the approach is usually by discipline, e.g., agriculture, economic aid, library science, etc. Most tools of this nature are not specifically for Africa, but cover the tropics, underdeveloped countries, or the world scene. In this section only the most useful serials covering the whole field of African studies are named.

234 *Africa: Journal of the International African Institute.* 1928– . London, Oxford University Press. Quarterly.

'Bibliography of current publications', a classified list of several hundred titles of books and pamphlets, periodical articles and documents, fills about 10 or more pages of each issue. Among the classes are ethnography, anthropology and sociology, history, religion, language and linguistics, economic development, government, law, the arts and literature, and education. Each issue of *Africa* carries around 20 book reviews, often signed or initialed by specialists. These usually relate to the Institute's special interests of ethnology, which involves a broad area of social anthropology, and linguistics. The French equivalent is the journal of the Société des Africanistes. An index for v. 1–35 (1931–1965) of the journal appeared in 1966.

235 *Africa Report.* v. 1, no. 1– , July 5, 1965– . Washington, D.C., African-American Institute. Monthly, 11 numbers a year; from 1966– , 9 numbers a year, Oct.–June, and annual index.

Leading American journal devoted to African affairs. The bibliographical sections vary from issue to issue, but during the year most major American books on Africa are noticed, with some reviewed at length by specialists and others appearing in the 'Received' lists.

236 *African Abstracts: Quarterly Review of Articles Appearing in Current Periodicals.* 1950– . London. Quarterly.

Published by the International African Institute with the assistance of UNESCO. The Ford Foundation also gave support from 1956 to 1966. With the January 1967 issue the name *Bulletin Analytique Africaniste* was dropped, and *African Abstracts* is now entirely English. A separate French edition, *Analyses Africanistes*, is published by the Centre d'Analyse et de Recherche Documentaires pour l'Afrique Noire (CARDAN). Both editions contain exactly the same material. Around 200 abstracts appear in each issue in geographical arrangement. The subject of each is indicated by a number of brackets, according to a key given at the front. The serials abstracted are listed on the inside back cover. A separate index is issued each year.

Part I : guide to reference materials

237 *African Affairs : Journal of the Royal African Society.* 1901– . London.
Book review section, with signed or initialed comment, and current bibliography of books and documents are arranged by geographical location. Most works cited are in English. Many publications of African countries are included.

238 *Afrique Contemporaine : Documents d'Afrique Noire et de Madagascar.* 1962– . Paris, La Documentation Française. 6 times a year.
Prepared at the Centre d'Etudes et de Documentation sur l'Afrique et l'Outre-Mer. This journal includes reviews or notices of a broad selection of books.

239 Cambridge University. African Studies Centre. [Index of current publications on Africa] 1961– . Cambridge, Eng.
The card file prepared by this centre covered author and title entries for books, government documents, theses, conference proceedings, unpublished material, and articles selected from several hundred periodicals. The cards, classed according to the Universal Decimal Classification, were sent on exchange to interested institutions in Europe and elsewhere; subsequently these institutions provided titles. In 1966 this service was merged with that of CARDAN (see next entry).

A comparable card file service is carried on by the Fondation Nationale des Sciences Politiques, 27 rue Guillaume, Paris 7e. Their photo-reproduced cards, also in decimal classification, carry brief annotations describing content and have reportedly been supplied periodically since the early 1960s. Hitherto they have not been readily available in the United States.

240 Centre d'Analyse et de Recherche Documentaires pour l'Afrique Noire (CARDAN). *Fiches Analytiques/Fiches Signalétiques : Sciences Humaines Africanistes.* 1965– . Paris. Quarterly; from 1967– , 3 times a year. Processed.
Fiches Analytiques : Sciences Sociales et Humaines was originally an abstracting service issued quarterly that provided around 2,000 filing cards a year on the principal new books and on articles in periodicals on sub-Saharan Africa in the social sciences. The cards carried summaries of the items analysed. Indexes (geographical, ethnic-linguistic, author) and lists of works analysed and of periodicals covered were usually provided in each issue. An annual subject index was also available.

In 1966 the *Fiches Analytiques* and the bibliographical cards of the Cambridge African Studies Centre (CAS) were consolidated into one joint service, to become the *Fiches Analytiques/Fiches Signalétiques : Sciences Humaines Africanistes*, with several thousand cards issued annually. The cards with bibliographical information only are published separately. The cards having abstracts are numbered in the CARDAN-F.A. sequence; and for each issue there are author, ethnic-linguistic, geographical, and subject indexes as well as lists of periodicals covered and of work analysed. In all, CARDAN and CAS between them probably encompass some 800 periodicals. There are separate annual subject indexes, for the *Fiches Signalétiques* on green stock and the *Fiches Analytiques* on white stock. Because of the complicated classification system that is used, a 24-leaf pamphlet *Keywords used by C.A.R.D.A.N. and C.A.S.* was issued in February 1966.

Another CARDAN-CAS publication began in 1966 with *Fiches d'Ouvrages, 1964 : Sciences Humaines Africanistes* (on green stock), in which book-length works are listed alphabetically; there are subject, geographical, and ethnic-linguistic indexes. CARDAN also publishes an annual list of French writings on Africa, *Bibliographie française sur l'Afrique au sud du Sahara* (1968–).

82

241 ———— *Bibliographie française sur l'Afrique au sud du Sahara, 1968.* Paris, 1969. 143 p. (v. 1, no. 4)

Modelled after the annual list of publications on Africa published in the United States (see no. 251). This French-language list makes the fourth such national survey. Like the other annuals it is valuable both as a reference tool and as an acquisitions tool for books and articles published in French on Africa south of the Sahara. The 584 entries are annotated. An annex lists Africanist periodicals published in France (86).

242 Deutsche Afrika-Gesellschaft. Wissenschaftlicher Ausschuss. *Afrika-Bibliographie: Verzeichnis des wissenschaftlichen Schrifttums in deutscher Sprache aus den Jahren 1960/1961.* Comp. by Rudolf Thoden. Bonn, Kurt Schroeder, 1963–64. 2 pts. 83, 182 p.

1962. Comp. by Rudolf Thoden. 1964. 148 p.

1963. Comp. by Rudolf Thoden. 1965. 134 p.

1964. Comp. by Elisabeth Greschat. 1966. 131 p.

These annual lists, showing the greatly increased German interest in Africa, are issued by the leading study centre in West Germany. They catalogue books and periodical articles in all major fields relating to Africa as published in the German language for each year. The 1965 issue appeared in 1969 and had 246 p., the 1966 issue appeared in 1970 and had 188 p.

243 *Genève-Afrique: Acta Africana.* 1962– . Geneva. Quarterly. Contains numerous short book reviews.

244 *Journal of Modern African Studies: A Quarterly Survey of Politics, Economics and Related Topics in Contemporary Africa.* Ed. by David and Helen Kimble. 1963– . New York and Cambridge, Eng., Cambridge University Press.

A distinguished periodical, with contributions by leading Africanists and specialists in many fields. Good book review section. News and notes, 'Africana', carries in each issue informal statements on the work of a few institutes and centres of African studies, 'brief reports on recent conferences; occasional accounts of important research in progress; information about a wide variety of groups and associations existing in or concerned with Africa; and any other items of professional interest to students of Africa'. In addition, some issues carry a 'review article' – a bibliographical essay on a particular theme.

245 *Kroniek van Afrika.* 1961– . Assen, Van Gorcum Co. Quarterly.

Published on behalf of the Afrika-Studiecentrum at Leiden. Contains articles (including essays in English), reviews and communications concerning scholarly activities regarding Africa, especially those carried out in the Netherlands.

246 *Middle East Journal.* 1947– . Washington, D.C., Middle East Institute. Quarterly.

This scholarly journal carries regular sections of chronology, book reviews, and a 'Bibliography of periodical literature', which is also issued separately. The coverage includes Sudan, Ethiopia and Somalia.

247 Royal Anthropological Institute. *Index to current periodicals received in the library.* 1963– . London.

This index contained over 5,000 entries in the first volume. Each issue is arranged under the rubrics of general works, Africa, America, Asia, East India, Oceania and Australia, and Europe. Under each major heading entries are further sub-divided under general works, physical anthropology, archaeology, cultural anthropology and ethnology, and linguistics.

248 Société des Africanistes. *Journal.* 1931– . Paris. 2 issues a year.

An extensive bibliographical section (around 50 pages) in this important journal, which is in many respects comparable to that of the International African Institute's *Africa*, is included annually in one of the two issues each year. It is classified according to disciplines and takes in more fields of interest than does *Africa.* Also included are references to European writings that have not always reached the Institute in London. It is sometimes one or even two years behind *Africa* in its citations. An index to volumes 1–35 (1931–1965) of the *Journal* appeared in v. 36, no. 2, 1966.

249 *Soviet periodical abstracts : Asia, Africa, and Latin America.* no. 1– , May 1961– . New York, Soviet Society. Quarterly.

Formerly titled *Selective Soviet annotated bibliographies.* The purpose of these abstracts of Soviet literature is to give an idea of Soviet ideology regarding social and political development in the underdeveloped countries. The content is therefore heavily weighted with statements of anti-imperialist dogma. The articles abstracted are from current issues of *Narody Azii i Afrika* and occasional other journals and daily press. The section on Africa, arranged under general and country headings, is substantial.

250 Standing Conference on Library Materials on Africa (SCOLMA). *United Kingdom publications and theses on Africa, 1963.* Cambridge, Eng., Heffer, 1966. 94 p.

    1964. Cambridge, Eng., Heffer, 1966. 89 p.

    1965. Cambridge, Eng., Heffer, 1967. 92 p.

    1966. Cambridge, Eng., Heffer, 1967. 96 p.

This annual listing was begun by SCOLMA as a record of theses only (see no. 307). It has now been enlarged to include published books and articles. The general section is divided into subject headings (from agriculture to wildlife and hunting); the second section is arranged by country and region (for 1965, entries are listed first by region and thereunder by country). Both sections utilize book and article subdivisions. Each volume contains a section called ' References to Africa in Hansard ', compiled by Malcolm McKee, a supplement to *Theses on Africa*, and an index to authors. The 1965 issue also includes lists as well as maps and an appendix consisting of corrections and additions to *Theses on Africa.*

251 *United States and Canadian publications on Africa in 1960.* Washington, D.C., African Section, General Reference and Bibliography Division, Library of Congress, 1962. 98 p.

    1961. Ed. by Peter Duignan. Stanford, Calif., Hoover Institution, Stanford University, 1963. 114 p. (Hoover Institution Biblio-graphical Series, no. 14)

    1966 retitled *United States and Canadian publications and theses on Africa . . .* Comp. by Liselotte Hofmann. Stanford, Calif., Hoover Institution, Stanford University, 1970. 300 p. (Hoover Institution Bibliographical Series, no. 38)

An annual of books, pamphlets, documents, essays in collective works, periodical articles of more than news value, and (beginning with the volume for 1965) doctoral theses on Africa south of the Sahara. (Morocco, Algeria, Tunisia, Libya and Egypt are not covered.) Arrangement is first by subject and then by

region and country, with further division into books and articles. An index of
authors is also included. Publication of the series was suspended after the 1966
edition.

RETROSPECTIVE BIBLIOGRAPHIES

General

Note This group represents monographic bibliographies for Africa in general,
covering diversified subject fields. Several of them include, or because of date
are limited to, the older literature of the 19th and early 20th centuries (Gay,
Paulitschke, Royal Commonwealth Society Catalogue, and Work); the others
emphasize more recent writing. There is, of course, much duplication in all. See
also the excellent listings of books on the colonial period in nos. 436, 664, 1035 –
Cambridge history of the British empire, v. 3 and 8; *Britain and Germany in
Africa*; and *History of East Africa*, v. 1 and 2.

252 Africa Bibliography Series: Ethnography, Sociology, Linguistics, and
Related Subjects. (Based on the bibliographical card index of the Inter-
national African Institute.) Comp. by Ruth Jones. London, International
African Institute, 1958– . (Series A)

Volumes are *West Africa* (1958, 116 l.); *North-east Africa* (1959, 51 l.); *East
Africa* (1960, 62 l.); and *South-east Central Africa and Madagascar* (1961, 53 l.).
See also under regions. These lists, which analyse periodical holdings of the
International African Institute as well as books and documents, relate primarily
to anthropological studies but in so broad a sense that they deserve reference as
general sources for the colonial period.

253 *Afrika Schrifttum: Bibliographie deutschsprachiger wissenschaftlicher
Veröffentlichungen über Afrika südlich der Sahara.* [Title also in English
and French.] v. 1. Ed. by George T. Mary. Wiesbaden, Franz Steiner
Verlag GmbH, 1966. 688 p.

An excellent catalogue of German scholarly works (books, articles, and dissertations) on sub-Saharan Africa from the 1870s to 1962. The subjects covered are
geography, ethnology, linguistics, theology, education, tropical medicine,
zoology, and botany. Arrangement is alphabetical by author under each topic,
and essential keywords in English and French are appended as marginal notes
alongside each entry (except in the section on theology and education). A second
volume comprising an index has apparently been prepared but not yet published.

254 American Historical Association. *Guide to historical literature.* New York,
Macmillan, 1961. 962 p.

'Africa', by Vernon McKay, p. 745–769. Annotated selection of 545 fundamental works for a study of African history, by the former head of the African
studies program of the Johns Hopkins University School of Advanced International Studies. Dr. McKay's interpretation of history is broad, including geography, anthropology and the social sciences. The volume of which the Africa
chapter forms a part is successor to the well-known handbook of the same title
edited by G. M. Dutcher and others in 1931 (see Winchell, *Guide to reference
books*, for description).

255 American Universities Field Staff. *A select bibliography: Asia, Africa,
Eastern Europe, Latin America.* New York, 1960. 534 p. Supplement, 1961,
75 p.; 1963, 66 p.; 1965, 80 p.

'Africa', comp. by L. Gray Cowan and Edwin S. Munger, p. 193–253. This
chapter is arranged in regional sections, subdivided in part by subject. It

comprises around 750 items, most of them with brief descriptive annotations. The work has author and title indexes. Supplements are being issued at two-year intervals.

256 Cartry, Michel, and Bernard Charles. *L'Afrique au sud du Sahara : Guide de recherches.* Paris, Fondation Nationale des Sciences Politiques, Centre d'Etude des Relations Internationales, 1962. 85 l. processed. (Sér. D, Textes et documents, no. 3, Apr. 1962)

This guide for advanced study is in four parts: (1) Généralités (introduction and reference works, geography, demography, economics, history, societies, and civilization); (2) Contexte traditionnel et changements sociaux (ethnology and sociology); (3) La vie politique (general problems, including documentary sources, political forces, organizations, and political influence); (4) Idéologies. The selection of 700–800 references to books and articles is broken down into numerous sections and subsections, explained in a detailed table of contents (there is no index). Within the groupings, works – sometimes only one or two – are apparently listed according to the compilers' judgement of significance.

257 Fontán Lobé, Juan. *Bibliografía colonial : Contribución a un índice de publicaciones africanas.* Madrid, Dirección General de Marruecos y Colonías, 1946. 669 p.

This sizeable bibliography of books, documents, and periodical articles arranged alphabetically by author represents the 17,000 cards assembled for his own library by Sr. Fontán Lobé, former director of the Spanish colonial service and at one time Governor-General of Guinea, for many years an authority on Africa. His collection included almost all the notable works in European languages, with many volumes of the 19th century, and a larger representation of Spanish and Portuguese writings than most of the other standard bibliographies of Africana. An index includes geographical names and subjects.

258 Gay, Jean. *Bibliographie des ouvrages relatifs à l'Afrique et à l'Arabie : Catalogue méthodique de tous les ouvrages français et des principaux en langues étrangères traitant de la géographie, de l'histoire, du commerce, des lettres et des arts de l'Afrique et de l'Arabie.* Amsterdam, Meridian Publishing Co., 1961. 312 p.

Reprint of a celebrated bibliography first published at San Remo in 1875. Coverage is of writings before that date.

259 *Index Islamicus, 1906–1955 : A catalogue of articles on Islamic subjects in periodicals and other collective publications.* Comp. by J. D. Pearson. Cambridge, Eng., Heffer, 1958. 897 p.

Supplement, 1956–1960. 1962. 316 p.

Supplement, 1961–1965. 1967. 342 p.

Indexes more than 26,000 articles devoted to all aspects of Islamic studies. Classification is by subject, some with geographical breakdown, and by region. Included are a significant number of entries dealing with Islam in Africa south of the Sahara; this catalogue should therefore not be ignored by Africanists. It is especially valuable because before the 1930s there were few good surveys of African periodical literature. Further supplements at five-year intervals are planned.

260 International African Institute. *Select annotated bibliography of tropical Africa.* Comp. under the direction of Daryll Forde. New York, Twentieth Century Fund, 1956. various pagings (about 490 p.). mimeo.

Some 20 specialists were involved in the preparation of this extensive research bibliography. Within the topical sections arrangement is by major geographical areas, with subject subheadings. References are to books and periodical articles, with considerable variation in standards of choice and in treatment by the individual compilers. Annotations are scanty, though a good many headings have introductory notes. Material includes some writings of the 19th and early 20th centuries as well as more recent studies. There are unfortunately no indexes.

261 Mylius, Norbert. *Afrika Bibliographie, 1943–1951.* Vienna, Verein Freunde der Völkerkunde, 1952. 237 p. processed.

A huge title list, containing 2,700 references to books and documents. Periodical articles are not included, but 250-odd periodicals are named in the introductory section, together with some 100 titles of bibliographies. The references, which were selected as a supplement to Wieschhoff (no. 266), are arranged by geographical regions and subdivided by subject – handbooks, travel, history and biography, arts, sociology, law, culture, economics, colonies, politics, missions, etc. Works cited are in Western European languages. There is no index.

262 Royal Commonwealth Society, London. Library. *Subject catalogue of the library of the Royal Empire Society, formerly Royal Colonial Institute.* By Evans Lewin. London, The Society, 1930–37. 4 v.

      v. 1. *The British empire generally and Africa.* Africa, 582 p. separately paged. (Reprint: Dawson of Pall Mall, 1967.)

The Royal Colonial Institute was established in the 1860s, and publication of its proceedings began in 1869. (The name was changed in the 1920s to Royal Empire Society; still later it became the Royal Commonwealth Society, the present style.) Its outstanding library collections – particularly rich in papers of the chartered companies and British colonial documents – include most writings in English over nearly a century, as well as notable works of other metropolitan powers. This important catalogue was compiled by the librarian, Percy Evans Lewin. The arrangement is geographical by country, with subject classes, and entries are arranged chronologically. Besides books and pamphlets, the catalogue includes articles in reviews and journals, papers read before learned and other societies, and, in spite of Mr. Lewin's apology, a mass of official documentation. There is an author index. This is a prime source for any historical study of British Africa.

A new edition of the *Subject Catalogue* was issued by G. K. Hall of Boston in 1971 (7 v.). This 1971 work contains all additions to the library since publication of the catalogue in 1930–1937.

263 U.S. Library of Congress. African Section. *Africa south of the Sahara: Index to periodical literature, 1900–1970.* Boston, G. K. Hall, 1971. 4 v.

The result of interfiling many bibliographic indexing services (*Africa, African Abstracts*, CARDAN, CIDESA, FNSP/CDC, etc.). Most entries are for the past 10 years but some date from 1900 on. Over 1500 periodicals (cited in the index) are listed in volume 1. The alphabetical coverage is as follows: v. 1, Africa – General – Central Africa; v. 2, Central Africa – Ivory Coast; v. 3, Kenya – Somalia; v. 4, South Africa – Zambia.

264 U.S. Library of Congress. General Reference and Bibliography Division. *Africa south of the Sahara: A selected, annotated list of writings.* Comp.

      by Helen F. Conover, African Section. Washington, 1963 [i.e., 1964]. 354 p.

This substantial compilation, designed as a basic guide for advanced research, was selected from the entire body of writing on Africa south of the Sahara identifiable through reference sources in the Library of Congress as well as in its large collections. The items (2,173 numbered, 600–700 more titles in notes) are classified under 30-odd subjects for Africa in general, and then by region and country, with smaller subject subdivisions. There is a combined author-subject index, with detailed geographical breakdown under major subjects. A special effort was made to stress available bibliographies in each category, particularly those in serial form, in the hope that the study would extend the range of source material well beyond the limitations of one compilation and thus not become obsolete too quickly.

Note One out-of-print bibliography is the following:

265 U.S. Library of Congress. General Reference and Bibliography Division. *North and northeast Africa: A selected, annotated list of writings, 1951– 1957.* Comp. by Helen F. Conover. Washington, 1957. 182 p. processed.

266 Wieschhoff, Heinrich A. *Anthropological bibliography of Negro Africa.* New Haven, Conn., American Oriental Society, 1948. xi, 461 p. (American Oriental Series, no. 23)

Prepared from a working card catalogue. Was to be followed by a second subject bibliography, even more comprehensive, which was never issued. Works cited are in all fields related to anthropology, including travelers' accounts, history, geography, etc., and are broken down as they apply to individual tribes. Besides books and pamphlets, articles are selected from over 200 scholarly periodicals and journals of learned societies, which are listed at the beginning (p. vii–xi).

267 Work, Monroe N. *Bibliography of the Negro in Africa and America.* New York, H. W. Wilson, 1928. xxi, 698 p.

Reprint: New York, Octagon Books, 1965.

Part 1, The Negro in Africa, p. 1–247.

Comprehensive bibliography of the older literature on Negro Africa arranged in 19 classes, covering history, ethnology and linguistics, slavery, governments and colonization, race problems, Christian missions, etc. The last grouping (p. 242–247) is composed of bibliographies. References include titles of books, pamphlets, and periodical articles in English and other Western European languages.

Library catalogues

Note The card files of the major libraries holding African collections, which constitute a continuing source for colonial bibliography, are the first recourse of anyone studying in a large centre. Several libraries have recently issued catalogues of their Africana collections, which differ from the monographic publications cited above in that, whether classed by subject or not, they are inclusive rather than representative of a studied selection. The catalogues published by G. K. Hall in Boston consist of photographic reproductions of card files.

268 American Geographical Society of New York. *Research catalogue.* Boston, G. K. Hall, 1962. 15 v.

Map supplement. 1962. 16 p.

Parts pertinent to African studies are the following: v. 1–2, General (topics 1–9); v. 9, Africa (regional nos. 25–35); v. 15, Tropics (regional no. 52).

In 1923 the library began a classified catalogue with regional and systematic classification based on geographical regions and individual countries. Subjects other than geography are covered. In addition to references to books, government documents, and pamphlets there are cards for essays in books and articles in journals received by the library. Since 1938 this most valuable retrospective bibliography source has been kept up to date by the Society's *Current Geographical Publications*. An *Index to maps in books and periodicals* was issued in 1968 by G. K. Hall, in 10 volumes.

269 Great Britain. Colonial Office. Library. *Catalogue of the Colonial Office Library, London*. Boston, G. K. Hall, 1964. 15 v. 37 cm.

Books, pamphlets, reports, some official publications, and periodical titles and articles, with imprints from the mid-17th century, are covered. It is a union catalogue and therefore has material on Commonwealth countries after independence and on some non-Commonwealth countries. Pre-1950 accessions are given first, then post-1950 accessions. Volumes 1–6 are by author or title, v. 7–13 by subject, and v. 14–15 in classified order (post-1950 only, in the Library of Congress system). African material may be found under Africa and the country name; many subjects (as agriculture, education) have subdivisions for Africa.

270 Harvard University. Library. *Africa: Classification schedule, classified listing by call number, alphabetical listing by author or title, chronological listing*. Cambridge, Mass., Harvard University Press, 1965. 1 v. in 4 pts. Classification schedule unpaged [82], 302, 204, 196 p. (Widener Library Shelf-list, no. 2)

The classification schedule is essentially geographical, with subject subdivisions, except for African literatures, which are arranged according to languages.

271 —— Peabody Museum of Archaeology and Ethnology. Library. *Catalogue ... authors*. Boston, G. K. Hall, 1963. 26 v. *Catalogue ... subjects*. Boston, G. K. Hall, 1963. 27 v.

In the Authors volumes, reference to the many works relating to Africa must be made by individual name. In the Subjects set, v. 1 begins with some place names (these are *see* references) and then come Abyssinia, Africa (p. 4–356), Algeria (p. 424–455), etc.

272 Howard University. Library. The Moorland Foundation. *A catalogue of the African collection*. Comp. by students in the Program of African Studies; ed. by Dorothy B. Porter. Washington, D.C., Howard University Press, 1958. 398 p.

Classified list of 4,865 books and pamphlets, with supplementary lists of periodicals and newspapers (Howard has a notable collection of newspapers). There is an author index.

273 London. University. Institute of Education. *Catalogue of the collection of education in tropical areas*. Boston, G. K. Hall, 1964. 3 v.

A large proportion of the works cited relate to Africa.

274 —— —— School of Oriental and African Studies. Library. *Library catalog*. Boston, G. K. Hall, 1963. 28 v.

In v. 1–8 the library holdings are listed by author, in v. 9–14 by title. Volume 14 is entitled *Subjects: General*; and v. 15, *Subjects: Africa*.

275 New York. Public Library. Schomburg Collection. *Dictionary catalog of the Schomburg collection of Negro literature and history*. Boston, G. K. Hall, 1962. 9 v. 8,473 p. 37 cm.

Supplement. 1967. 2 v.

The catalogue includes books, pamphlets, and periodicals concerning the Negro in Africa, America, and elsewhere. Authors, titles, and subjects are entered in a single alphabet.

276 Northwestern University. Library. *Catalogue of the African collection.* Boston, G. K. Hall, 1962. 2 v.

Author-title catalogue of over 20,000 works. Especially strong on languages, linguistics and ethnography.

277 Paris. Musée de l'Homme. Bibliothèque. *Catalogue systématique de la Section Afrique, Bibliothèque du Musée de l'Homme, Paris.* Boston, G. K. Hall, 1970. 2 v.

Catalogue of a major library for African ethnographic materials (over 8,000 items).

278 Royal Commonwealth Society. *Subject catalogue...* See no. 262 for annotation.

Special bibliographies

Note The kinds of bibliographies that may be described as special are many and diverse. One consists of bibliographies on Africa written in particular languages, such as Russian or German, or emanating from countries of communist ideology. Another kind appears in the steady flow of general reading lists on Africa compiled for special audiences – staff use, special study groups (see above, at beginning of Current Bibliographies). The following titles are given as a sampling of such special material.

279 African Bibliographic Center, Washington, D.C. *African affairs for the general reader : A selected and introductory bibliographical guide, 1960– 1967.* Comp. for the Council of the African-American Institute; prepared under the general editorship of Daniel G. Matthews. New York, Council of the African-American Institute, 1967. 210 p. loose-leaf. (Special Bibliographic Series, v. 5, no. 4)

A basic checklist of current resources for elementary, secondary, college, and public libraries. Emphasis is on English-language materials, and a significant number of selections published in Africa are listed.

280 Akademiia Nauk SSSR. Institut Afriki. *Bibliografiia Afriki.* Moscow, Nauka, 1964, 276 p.

The standard Russian bibliography covering works in the Russian language, original and translations, from the second half of the eighteenth century up to and including 1961. The work is divided into six parts. The first covers documents and 'brochures', concerned respectively with history, geography, economics, ethnography, culture, languages and colonialism. The remaining sections bear on particular geographical regions. These are subdivided according to countries, and then again according to topics. The compilers are S. I. Miliavskaiia and I. E. Sinitsyna.

281 Central Asian Research Centre, London. *Soviet writing on Africa, 1959– 1961 : An annotated bibliography.* London, distributed for the Royal Institute of International Affairs by Oxford University Press, 1963. 93 p.

Less extensively annotated than the earlier work, this list contains 433 references to books and articles, similarly in classed arrangement. Most of the Russian titles are followed by an English translation. The coverage includes works of 1959 not cited by Holdsworth and writings of 1960 and 1961.

Further references are carried in the Central Asian Research Centre's *Mizan Newsletter* (1959–), a monthly bulletin including book notes and bibliography. The proportion on Africa is small compared to that for Asia.

282 Higham, Robin, ed. *Official histories: Essays and bibliographies from around the world*. Manhattan, Kansas State University Library, 1970. 644 p. Contains bibliographical essays as well as full bibliographies concerning the military history of many nations, including the Union of South Africa, the Rhodesias, and the various metropolitan powers during the two world wars.

283 Holdsworth, Mary. *Soviet African studies, 1918–1959: An annotated bibliography*. Oxford, distributed for the Royal Institute of International Affairs by the Oxford University Press, 1961. 2 pts. in 1 v. 80, 76 p. mimeo. (Chatham House memoranda)

This work, by a specialist in Soviet studies, is practically an essay on Soviet writing regarding Africa, arranged in classed bibliographical form. Some 500 items, books, articles, reports, etc., are commented on, many of them to the extent of a page or more. There are author and subject indexes.

Miss Holdsworth's bibliography was supplemented two years later in the following work: Central Asian Research Centre, see no. 281.

284 Ragatz, Lowell, and Janet Evans Ragatz, comps. *A bibliography of articles, descriptive, historical, and scientific, on colonies and other dependent territories, appearing in American geographical and kindred journals. V. 1, Through 1934*, comp. by Lowell Ragatz; v. 2, *1935 through 1950*, comp. by Janet Evans Ragatz. 2d ed. Washington, D.C., Education Research Bureau, 1951. 2 v. 214, 149 p.

Lists articles published from the 1870s through 1950. References relevant to Africa appear in a general section, in a section devoted to Africa, in sections on the Belgian, British, French, former German, Italian, Portuguese, and Spanish empires, and in sections on U.S. spheres of influence (Liberia) and on jointly held regions (Anglo-Egyptian Sudan).

285 Simpson, Donald H., ed. *Biography catalogue of the library of the Royal Commonwealth Society*. London, Royal Commonwealth Society, 1961. 511 p.

The first section lists biographical writings on individual men and women born in, or actively connected with, countries of the Commonwealth and on Britons concerned with colonial affairs. Full names, dates of birth and death, and a brief description are given for as many names as possible, with titles of books and articles of a biographical nature and bibliographies. The second section (register) – collective biography and country indexes – is by area and country. Each begins with works of collective biography, both biographical dictionaries and collections of articles by one or more writers. The arrangement of these entries is chronological by date of publication, with continuing series at the end. These details are followed by lists of the names relating to the country or region. There is an extensive section on Africa. The author index includes editors, translators, writers of introductions, etc.

286 Venys, Ladislav, comp. *A select bibliography of Soviet publications on Africa in general and eastern Africa in particular, 1962–1966*. Syracuse, N.Y., Maxwell School of Citizenship and Public Affairs, Syracuse University, 1968. 125 l.

  Supplement 1, 1967–68. 1968.
  Supplement 2, 1968–69. 1969.

Serials lists

Note Checklists of serials are a most valuable source for determining what journals and newspapers and series were published during and after the colonial period. The number of important government annual reports, publications of research institutes, missionary and learned journals, etc. on Africa is staggering. A major need is to prepare indexes to these serials so that scholars can more readily have access to the materials. Only lists of African serials are cited here.

287 de Benko, Eugene, and Patricia Butts. *Research sources for African studies : A checklist of relevant serial publications based on library collections at Michigan State University.* East Lansing, African Studies Center, Michigan State University, 1969. 384 p.

A list of over 2,000 serial titles, most of them covering the colonial period by listing government serials, missionary and scholarly journals. Complements no. 294, *Serials for African studies,* comp. by Helen Conover, and *A checklist of serials for African studies, based on the libraries of the Hoover Institution and Stanford University* (Stanford, Calif., Hoover Institution, Stanford University, 1963, 104 p.), comp. by Peter Duignan and Kenneth Glazier, which is especially strong on serials of the colonial period.

288 Hewitt, Arthur R. *Union list of Commonwealth newspapers in London, Oxford, and Cambridge.* London, published for the Institute of Commonwealth Studies, University of London, by Athlone Press, 1960. 101 p. offset. legal size.

See no. 618 for annotation.

289 Institut Français d'Afrique Noire. *Catalogue des périodiques d'Afrique noire francophone (1858–1962) conservés à IFAN.* Comp. by Marguerite Thomassery. Dakar, IFAN, 1965. 117 p. (Catalogues et documents, no. 19)

A valuable list of almost 600 serials and government document series held by IFAN at Dakar. Included are files of rare newspapers produced by Africans since 1900. There are four indexes: geographic and analytical; chronological; organizations; directors, editors and authors.

290 Institut Royal des Sciences Naturelles de Belgique. *Liste des périodiques africains de la bibliothèque.* [Title also in Flemish.] Bruxelles, 1960. 48 p.

List of 223 serials, mostly bulletins, memoirs, and other series issued by universities and learned societies or other institutions, official and unofficial, in Africa. The emphasis is on publications relating to the natural sciences, but enough are of general coverage to warrant mention here.

291 Ruth Sloan Associates, Washington, D.C. *The press in Africa.* Ed. by Helen Kitchen. Washington, 1956. 96 p.

Analytical tables of the principal newspapers and periodicals, country by country, with accompanying comment on the state of the press. Included are publications in the vernacular. The work is now out of date, but contains useful historical data.

292 Standing Conference on Library Materials on Africa. *Periodicals published in Africa.* London, 1965– . 6 pts.

Country-by-country survey of periodicals published in Africa. Daily newspapers and government department reports are excluded, but government periodicals and annuals are listed. A most useful record of what was published in colonial Africa and of what is still being published in independent Africa.

293 United Nations. Economic Commission for Africa. Library. *Periodicals received in the UNECA library.* Addis Ababa, Oct. 1961. 113 p. mimeo. (E/CN.14/LIB/SER.A/1)

The UNECA library listed 829 periodicals received, a large proportion of which were African in origin, with many others relating primarily to African interests.

The entries are arranged in three parts: Nongovernmental (415 items), Governmental (292 items), UN and specialized agencies (122 items). Part 2, Governmental, is arranged by country (77; of these, 52 are African entries) and includes most official gazettes, statistical bulletins, etc. There is a title index to the first two parts as well as a detailed subject index. The first supplement was issued in 1962.

294 U.S. Library of Congress. General Reference and Bibliography Division. *Serials for African studies.* Comp. by Helen F. Conover, African Section. Washington, 1961. 163 p. offset print.

This list, which has 2,080 numbered entries of serial titles, was designed to record as many as possible of the world-wide periodical publications relating to Africa and having more than ephemeral interest. A revised list of more than 4,600 titles was published in 1970 by the Library of Congress: *Sub-Saharan Africa: A guide to serials.*

295 U.S. Library of Congress. Serial Division. *African newspapers in selected American libraries.* 3d ed. Comp. by Rozanne M. Barry. Washington, 1965. 135 p.

List of current and retrospective holdings of African newspapers in 33 selected American libraries as of the spring of 1964. Lists 708 African newspapers, and includes both hard copy and positive microfilms.

Official publications

Note In many African countries reports of government agencies, legislative papers, and other documents were mimeographed in very limited editions, and copies were often extremely hard to come by. Sometimes the government printer issued a list of documents in stock. More often the chief source of information regarding current publications was the country's official gazette, in which documents were sometimes announced as they appeared and in which from time to time there were lists of material available from the government printer. In these lists documents are difficult to identify because their titles are not set down in strict conformity with library rules.

General library tools for official documents include (besides the entries under names of countries) such comprehensive works as the *National union catalog*; *New serial titles*; etc.; and *Serial publications of foreign governments, 1815–1931*, ed. by Winifred Gregory (New York, H. W. Wilson Co., 1932, 720 p.). (See also under individual African countries.)

296 *Bibliographie de la France.* Supplément F, *Publications Officielles.* Paris, Au Cercle de la Librairie. Irregular. 5 to 7 numbers a year.

This list of official French documents included those of the overseas possessions (in alphabetical arrangement by country). Like the British Ministry of Overseas Development's *Technical Co-operation* (successor to the Colonial Office's *Monthly List*), the entries have greatly diminished in number, with a few appearing only occasionally for Outre-Mer.

Another listing, more prompt but less complete, is the semi-monthly, *Bibliographie Sélective des Publications Officielles Françaises*, 1952– , published by La Documentation Française, which is the publishing arm of the official Direction de la Documentation. This bibliography includes a listing of the various series put out by La Documentation Française, e.g., the *Notes et études documentaires*, in which there are valuable background surveys of individual African countries or questions. These are not limited to former French Africa.

297 Boston University. Libraries. *Catalog of African government documents and African area index.* 2d ed., rev. and enl. Comp. by Mary Darrah Herrick. Boston, G. K. Hall, 1964. 471 p.

One of the photoprinted reproductions of library cards published by G. K. Hall, this shows the large collections in the Boston University libraries of official publications of African governments. The program of African studies at Boston University has been slanted towards politico-economic and administrative affairs, and great efforts have been made to acquire the documents of the African countries on the largest possible scale. A set of cards for these documents is kept closely up to date. The second part of this publication lists the subject headings under which African materials are to be found in the libraries. A preliminary edition of 124 pages was published in 1960.

298 Great Britain. Colonial Office. Library. *Monthly List of Official Colonial Publications.* v. 1, no. 1–v. 16, no. 12. June 1948–Dec. 1963. London. 33 cm. mimeo.

Until the 1960s the *Monthly List* was the fullest available record of official publications for a large part of Africa and for other overseas possessions of the United Kingdom, and it is now an indispensable source for retrospective study of the countries of Africa formerly British. In several sections, the listing is alphabetical by countries. Part 1A cites typescripts and other papers prepared in the colonies but not for sale; Part 1B lists colonial government publications, and 1C colonial legislation. Part 2 includes publications of H.M. Stationery Office and the intelligence services of the Commonwealth Economic Committee. Part 3 lists government gazettes, and a maps section includes those listed in the Directorate of Overseas Surveys supplement.

The Ministry of Overseas Development took over some of the functions of the Colonial Office; and its publication, *Technical Co-operation : A Monthly Bibliography* with an irregular supplement, covers much of the material formerly in the *Monthly List*. The Colonial Office as such ceased to exist in August 1966, when it was merged with the Commonwealth Relations Office to form the Commonwealth Office.

299 U.S. Library of Congress. General Reference and Bibliography Division. [Official publications of the countries of Africa.] 1959– .

The African Section of the Library of Congress began a series of lists of the official publications of African countries in 1959 with *Nigerian official publications, 1869–1959 : A guide.* This has been followed by listings of government documents of many other countries of Africa south of the Sahara, a number of which were in print by 1968 (see under Region and Country section). In general, they are restricted to publications on the national (also federated states) or regional level. Arrangement is usually by issuing agency. All have author and subject indexes.

Dissertations

Note The most important American general library tool to be consulted is *Dissertation Abstracts* (Ann Arbor, Mich., 1952– , monthly), which since July 1961 has had author and subject indexes in each issue. The issues from 1961 only are worth consulting, since the Library of Congress list (see below, no. 309) covered the earlier numbers and predecessors, *Microfilm Abstracts* (1938–51) and *Doctoral Dissertations Accepted by American Universities* (1933–55). For continuing references to French dissertations, the extensive lists in the *Biblio-*

graphie de la France, Supplément D, *Thèses*, are a helpful source. In 1966 the Faculté de Droit et des Sciences Economiques of the Université de Paris issued unpaged lists of theses and memoirs (in preparation, defended, or on file) on African subjects in the fields of law, political science, and economics for 1964, 1965, and 1966. The Faculté is continuing this listing on an annual basis.

300 Amosu, Margaret, comp. *Nigerian theses : A list of theses on Nigerian subjects and of theses by Nigerians.* Ibadan, Ibadan University Press, 1965. 36 p.

This is a West African first with respect to thesis lists. There are almost 500 entries, as well as author and subject indexes.

301 Centre d'Analyse et de Recherche Documentaires pour l'Afrique Noire (CARDAN). *Inventaire de thèses et mémoires africanistes de langue française soutenus depuis 1966 : Première série.* By Brigitta Rupp and Agnès Rosset. v. 1, no. 2, 1969 : 93 l.

Covers 464 theses and memoirs registered from January 1, 1966, through May 1969, including those from Belgium, Switzerland and Senegal. It continues the listing through 1965 which appeared in the Société des Africanistes, *Bulletin d'Information*, no. 5, June 1965, and no. 6, Sept. 1965. Arrangement is by the geographical area covered by the thesis. The work is in ' fiche ' form which may also be arranged by subject. There are separate indexes for author and subject.

Also issued by CARDAN are *Inventaire de thèses et mémoires africanistes de langue française en cours : Deuxieme série : Thèses de 3e cycle*, v. 1, no. 3, 1969, 124 p., and *Inventaire . . . : Première série : Thèses d'état et d'université*, v. 2, no. 1, 1969, 104 p., both by Brigitta Rupp and Agnès Rosset. The CARDAN publications appeared in *Bulletin Information et Liaison*, Paris.

302 Deutsche Afrika-Gesellschaft. *Deutsche Dissertationen über Afrika : Ein Verzeichnis für die Jahre 1918–1959.* Comp. by Jochen Köhler. Bonn, K. Schroeder, 1962. 1 v. unpaged. (Deutsche Afrika-Gesellschaft, Bonn, Veröftlichungen)

This list comprises 795 numbered entries, arranged by geographical area, with a separate section of linguistic studies. Indexes by author and subject are included.

303 Dinstel, Marion, comp. *List of French doctoral dissertations on Africa, 1884–1961.* Boston, G. K. Hall for Boston University Libraries, 1966. 336 p.

This work contains almost 3,000 listings; author, area, and subject indexes are by Mary Darrah Herrick.

304 London. University. Institute of Historical Research. *Historical theses on African subjects completed in the universities of Great Britain.* London, 1961. 20 l.

There are 169 entries, arranged by region.

305 Paris. Université. Faculté de Droit et des Sciences Economiques. *Thèses et mémoires africanistes soutenus et déposés. Année 1967.* [1968] 33 l.

306 Potchefstroom University for Christian Higher Education. Department of Librarianship. *Union catalogue of theses and dissertations of the South African universities, 1942–1958.* Comp. by S. I. Malan. Potchefstroom, The University, 1959. xii, 216 p. tables. (2 fold.)

Annual supplement, 1959– .

The work is arranged systematically under broad subject headings, with an author index. Locations are given, and published theses are indicated.

The period before 1942 is covered in A. M. L. Robinson, *Catalogue of theses and dissertations accepted for degrees by the South African universities, 1918–1941* (Cape Town, The Author, 1943, 155 p.; available from Potchefstroom University Library).

307 Standing Conference on Library Materials on Africa. *Theses on Africa accepted by universities in the United Kingdom and Ireland.* Cambridge, Eng., Heffer, 1964. 74 p.

The second study by SCOLMA on African material in British institutions, this supplements the *Directory of libraries and special collections on Africa*, issued in 1963. There are listed 1,142 theses and dissertations prepared for advanced degrees at 22 major British and Irish universities between 1920 and 1962 (coverage for 1962 is incomplete). Entries are arranged by region or country and by field of study; and there are separate indexes to authors and ' tribes and peoples '. Information on the availability of theses and dissertations at each institution is included. Coverage for 1963 and 1964 was published in 1966 as *United Kingdom publications and theses on Africa* (see no. 250).

308 United Nations Educational, Scientific and Cultural Organization. *Thèses de sciences sociales : Catalogue analytique international de thèses inédites de doctoral, 1940–1950.* Paris, 1952. 236 p.

Many theses having to do with Africa, from many countries and in various subject fields, are included in this long listing of titles supplied by representatives in member states. The tables and index include the broad subject classification by which entries are arranged, an alphabetical index of detailed subject matter, and a geographical index through which the items relating to Africa may be identified.

309 U.S. Library of Congress. General Reference and Bibliography Division. *A list of American doctoral dissertations on Africa.* Prepared by the African Section. Washington, U.S. Government Printing Office, 1962. 69 p.

This alphabetical listing of doctoral dissertations on Africa presented in universities of the United States and Canada attempted a comprehensive record from the late 19th century through the academic year 1960–61.

The list has been supplemented in the following work compiled by Doris M. Cruger: *A list of American doctoral dissertations on Africa, covering 1961/62 through 1964/65; France, covering 1933/34 through 1964/65; Italy, covering 1933/34 through 1964/65* (Ann Arbor, Mich., University Microfilms Library Services, 1967, 36 p., xerography).

A bibliography of theses derived from v. 26 of *Dissertation Abstracts* (1965–66) is presented by B. C. Bloomfield in ' American theses on Africa ', *Library Materials on Africa*, v. 4, no. 3, Apr. 1967, p. 13–19. Organization is alphabetical by author under a general section and under sections on North, West, Central, East, and Southern Africa. Dates of theses range from the late 1950s to 1966, but the majority of entries are dated 1965.

United States and Canadian doctoral dissertations have been listed since 1965 in the annual *United States and Canadian publications and theses on Africa* (see no. 251).

Atlases and maps

Note General bibliographic sources that include sections listing maps of Africa are as follows:

310 *Bibliographie cartographique internationale.* 1950– . Paris, A. Colin. Annual.

Compiled by the Comité National Français de Géographie with the co-operation of the International Geographical Union, UNESCO, and the Centre National de la Recherche Scientifique. The 12th annual volume, 1960 (1962, 687 p.), cites 2,566 maps, 141 for Africa.

311 British Museum. *Catalogue of printed maps, charts and plans.* London, 1967. 15 v.

This updates the *Catalogue of printed maps,* first published in two volumes in 1885, to the end of 1964.

312 *Current Geographical Publications.* 1938– . New York, American Geographical Society. Monthly, except July and August.

Continuation of the *Research Catalogue* of the Society (see no. 268). Maps in books and individual maps are cited as well as writings on cartography. The British version is called *New Geographical Literature and Maps,* published by the Royal Geographical Society.

313 U.S. Library of Congress. Copyright Office. *Catalog of copyright entries.* Part 6, *Maps and Atlases.* Washington. Semi-annual.

The arrangement of this list of maps published in America is by name of copyright claimant, but there is a geographical index.

Note The following bibliographic sources contain extensive lists of maps on Africa:

314 Dahlberg, Richard E., and Benjamin E. Thomas. ' An analysis and bibliography of recent African atlases '. *African Studies Bulletin,* v. 5, no. 3, Oct. 1962: 23–33.

The bibliography cites 92 atlases examined by the authors at the Library of Congress, the American Geographical Society and the University of California at Los Angeles.

315 ——— ' Map resources on Africa ', *African Studies Bulletin,* v. 5, no. 1, Mar. 1962: 1–8.

The authors describe the common types of maps (political, topographic, aerial, resources-inventory, nautical, etc.), indicate their availability, and conclude with 24 references that will provide further information.

316 U.S. Library of Congress. Map Division. *A list of geographical atlases in the Library of Congress.* v. 6. Comp. by Clara Egli LeGear. Washington, U.S. Government Printing Office, 1963. lxxii, 681 p.

The section on Africa appears on p. 426–475 (titles 10085–10169).

The atlases of Africa and accompanying annotations cited in this comprehensive work relate to regions rather than to the general picture of Africa.

PART II

SUBJECT GUIDE
FOR AFRICA IN GENERAL

Note This part covers a few of the more important titles on various subjects dealing with Africa primarily during the colonial period. An effort was made to include representative and basic titles of important older books and journals produced under European colonial rule as well as more recent scholarly works.

GENERAL REFERENCE WORKS

Note See also Part III, Area Guide, for additional references to specific colonial powers, regions and countries.

317 Buell, Raymond Leslie. *The native problem in Africa.* New York, Macmillan, 1928. 2 v. maps, tables.

Reprint: London, Frank Cass, 1965. Bibliography: v. 2, p. 983–1049. This monumental work by an American expert on foreign affairs has served as a basis for all subsequent investigations. It was prepared following 15 months of field work and study of all available documents, which are listed by region in a 67-page bibliography. For each of the British, French and Belgian territories south of the Sahara and for Liberia, Dr. Buell surveyed analytically history, government, labour conditions, racial questions and the colonial policy, with the aim of determining how and to what extent the governments concerned were solving the problems raised by the impact of industrial civilization on preliterate peoples.

318 Hailey, William Malcolm Hailey, 1st baron. *An African survey : A study of problems arising in Africa south of the Sahara.* Issued under the auspices of the Royal Institute of International Affairs. Revised in 1956. London and New York, Oxford University Press, 1957. 1,676 p.

An encyclopaedic reference book, the most comprehensive of its kind regarding Africa south of the Sahara. For a full description of this work, which covers most fields of modern knowledge, see *Africa south of the Sahara*, compiled by Helen Conover (1963), p. 4; or see Winchell. Hailey, a senior British civil servant with extensive experience of high office in India and of academic life, produced the first version of his book in 1938 with the help of a distinguished group of researchers. This pioneer work was also described at length by Lord Harlech and various collaborators in *Lord Hailey's African survey surveyed for the Royal African Society by the Right Hon. Lord Harlech . . . edited for the Society by F. H. Melland and published as a supplement to the Society's journal for January, 1939* (London, Macmillan and Co., 70 p.).

319 Hailey, William Malcolm Hailey, 1st baron. *Native administration in the British African territories.* London, H.M. Stationery Office, 1950–53. 5 v.

An encyclopaedic survey compiled under the auspices of the British Colonial Office and the Commonwealth Relations Office. Part 1 covers Uganda, Kenya, Tanganyika. Part 2 deals with Zanzibar, Nyasaland and Northern Rhodesia. Part 3 surveys Nigeria, Gold Coast, Sierra Leone and Gambia. Part 4 provides a general review of British colonial administration. And Part 5 concerns Basutoland, the Bechuanaland Protectorate and Swaziland.

In 1941 Lord Hailey reported on journeys in the British colonies during the two previous years, examining administration under wartime conditions. After an inspection in 1947–48 he found the situation so changed that he rewrote his report, the first four volumes of which (East Africa, Central Africa, West Africa, General Survey) appeared in 1950–51; the fifth, on the High Commission

Territories, appeared in 1953. The work is little concerned with political or constitutional development but is a detailed statement of administrative systems in the colonies under review, including the administration of justice through native tribunals and changes in land law and customary law – the whole forming a handbook for administrative officers in the Colonial Office.

320 Junod, Violaine I., ed., assisted by Idrian N. Resnick. *The handbook of Africa*. New York, New York University Press, 1963. 472 p. illus., appendix, map.

Gives information on each of the 50-odd political units of Africa. The format is that of fact sheets: short geographical and historical sketches, followed by data on government, population, society (education, health, social welfare, etc.) and economy. Long bibliographical notes are chiefly of official sources from which data are taken. Five appendices summarize colonial policies in Africa, list regional groupings as of 1961, analyse British and French aid to African development and the trade and marketing systems of the metropolitan powers with dependencies, and give tables of measures and currencies.

321 Kimble, George H. T. *Tropical Africa*. New York, Twentieth Century Fund, 1960. 2 v. illus., port., maps (1 fold. col.). Bibliographical footnotes.

A broad geographical study of Africa, in which many scholars collaborated. The list of 46 contributors of working papers is given opposite the title page. Dr. Kimble, the geographer, served as director and put together the final text, which though massive in its assemblage of facts, is eminently readable. The first volume covers the continent in terms of physical and economic geography. The second opens with an account of the ' Old Order ' and goes through the factors of social and political change to the ' Price of Growth ' and the ' Shape of Things '. In general, the Africa reflected is that of the mid-1950s.

A pamphlet by Dr. Kimble in the Foreign Policy Association Headline Series, *Tropical Africa : Problems and promises* (New York, 1961, 62 p.; no. 147), serves in part as a précis of the full-length work.

322 *The statesman's year-book*. 1864– . London, Macmillan and Co.; New York, St. Martin's Press. Annual.

1972–73 ed. 1,575 p.

The concise volume of concentrated historical and statistical information about the colonies and countries of the world was quite up to date regarding government and politics of all nations. The useful index includes place-names for practically all important regions and cities. A most useful general statistical and historical yearbook with a good bibliography of statistical and reference books for each country from 1864 on.

ANTHROPOLOGY AND LINGUISTICS

Note Bibliographical sources for the study of African languages and linguistics are numerous and extensive, particularly for the early period, when missionaries and colonial officers, making contacts for the first time with unstudied tribes, were prolific in their written attempts at grammar and vocabularies and in their translations of Scripture. Long bibliographies are included in such important linguistic studies as Cust's in 1883 or Sir H. H. Johnston's in 1919–22. *The catalogue of Bantu, Khoisan and Malagasy in the Strange collection of Africana* in the Johannesburg Public Library (ed. by Anna H. Smith, Johannesburg, 1942, 232 p.) contains 1,671 numbered entries.

Among the most useful sources are the various publications of the International African Institute, which was founded in 1926 under the name International Institute of African Languages and Cultures. The quarterlies *Africa* and *African Abstracts* are in part bibliographical, with language a major concern. The Africa Bibliography Series based on the bibliographical card index of the Institute has linguistics as one of its three subject classifications. *Bibliographie linguistique de l'année* [–] (English title also; 1949– , Utrecht, Spectrum, annual) includes a section on the languages of Negro Africa. It is published by the Permanent International Committee of Linguists with financial assistance from UNESCO. The volumes of the Handbook of African Languages series contain long bibliographies of the languages covered, and the references in a good many of the volumes of the Ethnographic Survey of Africa include linguistics.

The recently established *Journal of African Languages* is an important source. Other scholarly journals which, both in articles and in bibliographical sections, count linguistics among their primary interests are *African Studies* (formerly *Bantu Studies*, published at the University of the Witwatersrand); *Afrika und Übersee : Sprachen, Kulturen*; and the *Journal* of the Société des Africanistes (Paris, 1931–).

Notable regional institutions devoted to language studies are the Institute of Swahili Research and the West African Language Committee. Such regional bodies as the East African Literature Bureau and the Bureau of Ghana Languages, which are publishing texts in the vernacular in increasing numbers, issue occasional lists of their stock. Lists from government information services include their publications in the vernacular. The current bibliography, *Nigerian Publications*, has a separate listing of works in African languages, as does the South African bibliography, *Africana Nova*.

See also Part III for works pertaining to specific regions and peoples.

MAPS

323 Froelich, Jean-Claude. *Carte des populations de l'Afrique noire.* Paris, La Documentation Française, 1955. col. map. 76×11 cm., fold. (Carte no. 71) Scale: about 1 : 5,000,000.

324 Froelich, Jean-Claude. *Notice et catalogue.* Paris, La Documentation Française, 1955. xxx, 113 p. Bibliography: p. xiii–xxvii.

A valuable tribal map. The accompanying text (*Notice et catalogue*) explains the map and contains a ' répertoire alphabétique des populations ' and listings of peoples in big cities and along important watercourses. The tribes are entered according to the best-known names, with indication of other names, and locations on the map (1,540 peoples numbered and located). The coverage takes in all West Africa from Mauritania to Angola, including Rwanda and Burundi as well as the former Belgian Congo. A long bibliography gives basic reference works and works consulted. See also George Peter Murdock, *Africa : Its peoples and their culture history* (New York, 1959), for an excellent tribal map of the entire continent.

BIBLIOGRAPHIES

Note See also nos. 234, 236, 248, 266, 267, 332, 336 and 528.

325 *African Abstracts: Bulletin Analytique Africaniste.* 1950– . London. Quarterly.

Provides reviews and abstracts of ethnological, social and linguistic studies appearing in current periodicals.

326 Andor, L. E. *Aptitudes and abilities of the black man in sub-Saharan Africa, 1784–1963: An annotated bibliography.* With an introduction by W. Hudson. Johannesburg, National Institute for Personnel Research, South African Council for Scientific and Industrial Research, 1966. 174 p.

A nonselective catalogue of books, pamphlets, monographs, confidential reports and articles concerned mainly with the Bantu-speaking African. Annotations are in the form of abstracts. The 486 references in Part 1, on intellectual functions, are given in chronological units (1784 to 1963). The 35 entries in Part 2, on personality characteristics, cover the period 1950 to 1963. Author and subject indexes are given for Part 1 only.

327 *Bibliographie ethnographique de l'Afrique sud-saharienne.* 1932– . Tervuren, Belgium, Musée Royal de l'Afrique Centrale. Annual.

Extensive annotated bibliography of books and periodical articles in ethnological fields relating not only to the Congo but to most of sub-Saharan Africa. The first volume covers literature from 1925 to 1930; the volumes issued after 1930 usually cover a single year (except after World War II). The title was originally *Bibliographie ethnographique du Congo belge et des régions avoisinantes*; the adjective *belge* was dropped with the volume for 1959, published in 1961; and the new title was adopted with the volume for 1960, appearing in 1962. Earlier names of the Museum are Musée du Congo Belge and Musée Royal du Congo Belge. For some years the bibliography has been edited by Olga Boone. The arrangement is alphabetical by author, with an index of subjects, names of peoples and countries. Increasingly over the years attention has been given to writings on the 'neighbouring regions', and subjects have been widened to include art, geography, law, literature, history and philosophy.

328 International African Institute. *Africa bibliography series: Ethnography, sociology, linguistics, and related subjects.* London, 1958– .

See no. 252 for description.

329 *International bibliography of social and cultural anthropology. Bibliographie internationale d'anthropologie sociale et culturelle.* v. 1– , 1955– . Paris, UNESCO, 1958–61; London, Stevens & Sons, 1962–63; London, Tavistock Publications, 1963– . Annual. (International Bibliography of the Social Sciences)

Prepared by the International Committee for Social Sciences Documentation with the financial support of UNESCO. V. 10, appearing in 1966, covers the works of 1964. V. 1–5, published by UNESCO, were in the Documentation in Social Sciences series. Articles – from an international roster of more than a thousand periodicals – are arranged in a detailed scheme of subject classification. There are author and subject indexes. Some subjects are geo-archaeology, cultural anthropology, ethnography, and linguistics. A separate annual index is to be published. In the first three issues of 1963 almost 600 references relate to Africa.

Anthropology and linguistics

330 Knappert, J. *Un siècle de classification des langues bantoues 1844–1945.* Brussels, Centre de recherche et d'information socio-politiques. 1971.

331 Royal Anthropological Institute. *Index to Current Periodicals Received in the Library.* v. 1, no. 1– , May 1963– . London. Quarterly.

Classed listing of articles in the periodicals received during the quarter (400–500). The sections – general, Africa, America, Asia, Europe, East Indies, Oceania, Australia – are subdivided into physical anthropology, archaeology, cultural anthropology, ethnography, and linguistics. A separate annual index is to be published. In the first three issues of 1963 almost 600 references relate to Africa.

REFERENCE WORKS

332 Brokensha, David. *Applied anthropology in English-speaking Africa.* Lexington, University of Kentucky, 1966. 31 p. (Society for Applied Anthropology Monographs, no. 8)

Most useful survey of the theory and practice of applied anthropology. Part 1 is a bibliographical essay reviewing the major works by regions and subjects. Part 2 is a bibliography of important books and articles classed by subjects, i.e., health, labour. For an earlier survey see Daryll Forde, ' Applied anthropology in government: British Africa ', in A. L. Kroeber, ed., *Anthropology to-day* (Chicago, 1953).

333 *Ethnographic survey of Africa* [series]. Ed. by Daryll Forde. London, International African Institute, 1950– .

The French series, *Monographies ethnologiques africaines,* is published for the Institute by Presses Universitaires de France, Paris. The Belgian series was published by the Musée Royal du Congo Belge under the title *Monographies ethnographiques.*

The volumes in this survey are generally considered the most comprehensive sources of information on the peoples of Africa, based on extensive research in published material as well as on original field studies. Each volume presents a concise summary of an African people or group of peoples, covering location, natural environment, economy, crafts, social structure, political organization and religious beliefs and cults. Each contains a bibliography and a specially drawn map. A number of the individual volumes are now out of print, and there are plans to make revisions in some of them before the proposed reprinting.

Subseries are Western Africa (English and French series); East Central Africa; West Central Africa; Belgian Congo (prepared with the co-operation of the Musée Royal du Congo Belge, now the Musée Royal de l'Afrique Centrale; and also published in the series *Monographies ethnographiques*); Southern Africa; and Madagascar.

The full list of surveys published in English or French in the various subseries is given in a list of publications issued each year by the International African Institute. Many individual volumes are cited in regional sections of the present guide. See also the excellent volumes in the general series: African ethnography, sociology, history, etc.; and *African systems of kinship and marriage* under no. 342.

334 Hambly, Wilfrid D. *Source book for African anthropology.* Chicago, Field Museum of Natural History, 1937. 953 p. maps, figs. (Anthropological Series, nos. 394 and 396) Bibliography: p. 728–866.

This huge volume by the curator of African ethnology of the Field Museum is an attempt ' to bring together a summary of all the most important facts that are known about Africa ', on the basis of significant anthropological publications,

Part 1, a synthesis of studies, covers outlines of physiography and nature, history, prehistory, physical anthropology, dress and ornament, psychology, languages and literature, and the culture area concept. Part 2 comprises basic elements of Negro culture, social organization, religion, and economic life and the European period. There is a long bibliography of the authors and works quoted, as well as a large, general index and a bibliographical index. So ambitious a work naturally evoked much criticism. Since it has in addition been outdated, in specific areas, by later research, its chief value is probably as a bibliography.

A supplemental work, *Bibliography of African anthropology, 1937–1949*, was published by the Museum in 1952 (*Fieldiana : Anthropology*, v. 37, no. 2, p. 155–292). A long list of periodicals from which references have been cited begins the bibliography (p. 161–173).

335 International African Institute. *African worlds: Studies in the cosmo-logical ideas and social values of African peoples.* Ed. by Daryll Forde. London and New York, Oxford University Press, 1954. xvii, 234 p. diagrs., tables. Reprint, 1960; paperback reprint, 1963.

This set of concise studies of the relationship of religious myth and social practice as exemplified by typical African peoples is one of the best-known works on African religion. The introduction by Professor Forde, director of the Institute, explains the general frame of reference – analysis of the world outlook of each people as expressed in beliefs, ritual and secular practice. The nine separate essays are by distinguished ethnologists and social anthropologists who have studied at first hand the societies of which they write. All are provided with scholarly footnotes and reading lists.

A later significant contribution on this theme was made at the Third International African Seminar, held in Salisbury, December 1960. The studies presented were published in 1965: Meyer Fortes and G. Dieterlen, eds., *African systems of thought* (London, published for the International African Institute by Oxford University Press, 392 p.).

336 Malinowski, Bronislaw. *The dynamics of culture change : An inquiry into race relations in Africa.* Ed., with a new introd., by Phyllis M. Kaberry. New Haven, Yale University Press, 1961. 171 p.

Originally published in 1945 and edited by a former student, this work embodies much of Malinowski's doctrines concerning practical anthropology, especially during the colonial period. His functional approach exercised a profound influence on the study of anthropology, particularly in the British Commonwealth. Malinowski's approach was subjected to far-reaching criticism in Max Gluckman, *Malinowski's sociological theories* (Oxford University Press, 1949, Rhodes-Livingstone Paper, no. 16, 28 p.). Gluckman deals exhaustively with Malinowski's 'functional' analysis, as well as with the major contribution that Malinowski made to the study of social anthropology and to the development of anthropological field work, depending on the systematic and exhaustive collection of social data by trained observers working on the spot. See also Arthur Tuden, ed., *Social stratification in Africa* (New York, Free Press, 1970, 392 p.).

337 Murdock, George P. *Africa : Its peoples and their culture history.* New York, McGraw-Hill, 1959. xiii, 456 p. illus., maps (1 fold. in pocket). Includes bibliographies.

A compendium of African ethnological data. In the first few chapters Professor Murdock summarizes the general topics of geography, race, language, economy, society, government and history for the whole continent. Then he presents systematic surveys by cultural areas. Each regional section begins with a numbered list of the tribes in groups of essentially identical language and culture, and each chapter ends with a selective reading list. There is an index of about 5,000 tribal names, and, in a pocket inside the back cover, a large folded map of the chief culture areas.

Professor Murdock of Yale University had been associated with the large project of Human Relations Area Files (HRAF) that brought together in card form systematic data on all peoples of the world. The material for Africa was a main source for this work. In 1959 a collection was made available by Yale University, *African cultural summaries* – a box containing reproductions of about 2,000 5×8 cards of data on African tribes. The collection is held by a limited number of libraries. For a description of Africa-related work of HRAF see ' News and Notes ', *Africa*, July 1968, p. 341–343.

338 Ottenberg, Simon, and Phoebe Ottenberg, eds. *Cultures and societies of Africa.* With a general introduction, commentaries and notes. New York, Random House, 1960. 614 p. plates. Bibliography: p. 565–598.
Selections chosen to fill the need for a collection of readings on Africa suitable for use in courses in anthropology. The articles, all by well-known specialists, date from 1940 to 1960. They follow an introductory survey of Africa and its peoples by the editors. There are six groups of papers, some general, some relating to individual areas or tribes. Most of the essays are followed by references for further reading, and there is a long classified bibliography.

339 Parrinder, Edward Geoffrey. *African traditional religion.* 2d rev. ed. London, SPCK, 1962. 156 p. illus. (Seraph)
First published in 1954 in Hutchinson's University Library, World Religions.
A general account of the old beliefs of the ' incurably religious ' people of Africa which are said to be still held by the majority of Africans and underlie the veneer of new faiths accepted by the educated. The author, a former missionary and professor of religious studies in Ibadan University, is a recognized authority on African religious beliefs (see his *West African religion*, no. 735). An interesting study, *Witchcraft*, by Dr. Parrinder, was brought out by Penguin Books, Harmondsworth, in 1950 (208 p.; Pelican Books, A409; new ed., 1963). In it he compares African witchcraft to the witch lore of Europe, finding major similarities.

340 Paulme, Denise, ed. *Women of tropical Africa.* Trans. by H. M. Wright. London, Routledge and Kegan Paul, 1963. 308 p. Bibliography: p. 231–293.
Six exceptionally interesting essays, by women ethnologists, are based on field experience of the last 10 years. The introduction, generalizing on the theme of the work, the status, and ways of life of women in Africa, is by the editor, a well-known anthropologist now with the Ecole Pratique des Hautes Etudes. The analytical bibliography is classified by subject. *Femmes d'Afrique noire*, the French original, was published by Mouton, Paris, in 1960 (280 p.; Le monde d'outre-mer passé et présent, 1st ser., Etudes, no. 9).

341 Phillips, Arthur, ed. *Survey of African marriage and family life.* London and New York, published for the International African Institute by Oxford University Press, 1953. xli, 462 p. fold. map. Includes bibliographies.
The survey came to fruition through a suggestion made to the International Missionary Council by Lord Hailey in 1946. The editor, then reader in administration of colonial law at the University of London, wrote the introductory essay. Part 1, ' African marriage and social change ', is by Dr. Lucy P. Mair; Part 2, ' Marriage laws in Africa ', by Dr. Phillips; Part 3, ' Christian marriage in African society ', by the Rev. Lyndon Harries, now at the University of

Wisconsin. Each part has its own scholarly footnotes, bibliography, and index. Included also are a list of tribes referred to (Part 1) and tables of statutes and cases (Part 2).

A short summary of the *Survey of African marriage and family life* was published by the International Missionary Council as no. 1 of their series of Research Pamphlets: *African marriage*, by Thomas Price (London, SCM Press, 1954, 56 p.). The conflicts of Christian practices and principles with the tribal marriage customs – particularly with polygamy and bride price – are the main points of discussion.

342 Radcliffe-Brown, Alfred R., and Daryll Forde, eds. *African systems of kinship and marriage.* London and New York, published for the International African Institute by the Oxford University Press, 1950. 399 p. illus., maps. Reprint in paperback edition, 1960.

Symposium by nine eminent anthropologists who illustrate, through study of a representative selection of native tribes in Africa south of the Sahara, the main varieties of kinship organization. The long introduction by Professor Radcliffe-Brown is a definitive essay on existing knowledge and theory regarding kinship systems.

343 Smith, Edwin W., ed. *African ideas of God : A symposium.* 2d ed. Revised and re-edited by E. G. Parrinder. London, Edinburgh House Press, 1961. 308 p. map.

The introductory essay by the late Dr. Smith, a general survey of the subject, is followed by a group of analyses of the religious beliefs of the tribes with which the writers have worked. The contributors are well-known missionary anthropologists of South-West Africa, the Belgian Congo, and East and West Africa. The essay on the Luo peoples of Uganda is by H. B. Thomas, formerly of the Civil Service, the only layman of the group. The peoples studied are Bantu and Negro tribes (except Bushmen) and the writing is nonacademic. The first edition was published in 1950.

344 Tempels, Placide. *Bantu philosophy.* Trans. into English from *La philosophie bantoue*, the French version by A. Rubbens of Fr. Tempels's original work. Colin King, trans. Paris, Présence Africaine, 1959. 123 p. illus. (Collection Présence Africaine) First French edition, 1949.

This celebrated monograph by a Catholic missionary priest in the Belgian Congo is described as a 'revolutionary' study of the soul of the Bantu. It tries to prove that the Bantu's religious creed is not sheer incoherent animism but is based on a solidly built set of abstract ideas which constitute a complete philosophical system. Father Tempels argued that a new approach is needed for the European missionaries and ethnologists if their '*mission civilisatrice*' is to produce *évolués* 'in the noble sense of the word' – something which the civilization of money values has failed to do.

DEMOGRAPHY

Note See also Part III, Area Guide, for references dealing with specific colonial powers, regions or countries.

BIBLIOGRAPHIES

345 France. Institut National de la Statistique et des Etudes Economiques. Service de Coopération. *Bibliographie démographique, 1945–1964 : Travaux publiés par l'I.N.S.E.E. (Service de Coopération), les Services de Statistique des Etats Africains d'Expression Française et de Madagascar et le Ministère de la Coopération.* Paris, 1965. 36 l. Processed.

The first part lists handbooks, studies, and bibliographies; the second covers the former French African territories and regions and includes entries on non-indigenous populations; and the last part is arranged by country.

346 ———— ———— ———— *Bibliographie des études démographiques relatives au pays en voie de développement : Ouvrages parus depuis 1945, mise à jour le 1er juillet 1961.* Paris, 1961. 110 p.

Most useful for French-speaking countries but includes a certain amount of material for ' pays d'expression anglaise '. Arrangement is by country.

347 *Population Index.* v. 1– , 1935– . Princeton, N.J., School of Public Affairs, Princeton University and the Population Association of America. Quarterly.

Annotated bibliography of book and periodical literature on all phases of population problems, world-wide. The arrangement is by class, but annual cumulated indexes by author and country provide guidance to the literature of African demography.

348 Texas. University. Population Research Center. *International population census bibliography : Africa.* Austin, Bureau of Business Research, College of Business Administration, University of Texas, 1965– . loose-leaf. (Census Bibliography, no. 2)

Part of a project of the Population Research Center to compile a universal bibliography of census reports. It is arranged alphabetically by country, and thereunder entries are in chronological order. Title is given and then English translation of title. Coverage is limited to population censuses, but other types of census reports are given if they were included in the population census.

349 U.S. Library of Congress. Census Library Project. *Population censuses and other official demographic statistics of Africa (not including British Africa) : An annotated bibliography.* Prepared by Henry J. Dubester. Washington, U.S. Government Printing Office, 1950. 53 p.

350 U.S. Library of Congress. Census Library Project. *Population censuses and other official demographic statistics of British Africa : An annotated bibliography.* Prepared by Henry J. Dubester. Washington, U.S. Government Printing Office, 1950. 78 p.

Full coverage of published official material to 1949. For supplementary census reports see the Library of Congress series on Official Publications of African Countries.

See also Frank Lorimer, no. 353 below.

REFERENCE WORKS

351 Blanc, Robert. *Handbook of demographic research in under-developed countries.* n.p., n.d. 115 p. diagrs. (Scientific Council for Africa South of the Sahara, no. 36)
Translation of a paper in French, issued in a limited mimeographed edition as publication no. 36 of CSA in 1958 or 1959. The English handbook was given out to participants at the Seminar on Population Problems held in Cairo (see below).

352 Kuczynski, Robert René. *Demographic survey of the British colonial empire.* v. 1, *West Africa*; v. 2, *East Africa*; v. 3, *West Indian and American territories.* London and New York, Oxford University Press, 1948–53. 3 v.
A comprehensive survey of demographic statistics before the Second World War, prepared under the auspices of the Royal Institute of International Affairs. The author was an adviser to the British Colonial Office and the most distinguished expert in his field. The writer's study provides detailed material concerning censuses, fertility, mortality, population growth and related problems. There is detailed information concerning the value and limitations of the available census material, and a wealth of other relevant data. The author also wrote *The Cameroons and Togoland : A demographic study* (London and New York, Oxford University Press, 1939, 579 p.), as well as studies concerned with subjects as varied as colonial populations in general, international banking, housing, and Franco-German economic relations.

353 Lorimer, Frank. *Demographic information on Tropical Africa.* Boston, Boston University Press, 1961. 207 p. map. Includes bibliographies.
The result of a study carried out under the auspices of the African Studies Program at Boston University and the Population Council of New York.

ECONOMICS

Note See also Part III, Area Guide, for works pertaining to specific colonial powers, regions or countries.

ATLAS

354 *Oxford regional economic atlas : Africa.* Prepared by P. H. Ady and the Cartographic Department of the Clarendon Press, with the assistance of A. H. Hazlewood. Oxford, Clarendon Press, 1965. 60, 164 p. maps, tables.
This impressive volume edited by two British specialists in African economics is in three parts: economic commentary; maps, thematic and regional; and gazetteer. The first part consists of concentrated notes grouped under population, agriculture, minerals and mines, manufacturing industries, sources of energy and power, transport and foreign trade.

Economics

BIBLIOGRAPHIES

355 Commission for Technical Co-operation in Africa South of the Sahara [CCTA/CSA]. *Inventory of economic studies concerning Africa south of the Sahara : An annotated reading list of books, articles and official publications.* [Title also in French] Contendo uma relação de títulos em português. London, 1960. xi, 301 p. (Publication no. 30; Joint Project, no. 4) *Supplement 1.* 1962. 150 p.

A useful bibliography, edited by Miss Peter Ady of St. Anne's College, Oxford, with the aid of national correspondents. The period covered is largely from 1945 through 1956, though there are a few references of 1957 and 1958. Nearly all the 1,377 entries are annotated (in French or English). A section for general works is followed by works arranged by area or country with subdivision by country where appropriate and with subject subclassifications for all. Supplement 1, also edited by Miss Ady, follows the same general format, but not all the areas are subdivided by country. All of the 896 entries are annotated except those pertaining to Portuguese Africa. Each of these two volumes contains an author index.

356 Commonwealth Bureau of Agricultural Economics, Oxford. *Aspects of agricultural policy and rural development in Africa : An annotated bibliography.* Oxford, 1971. 5 v.

357 Hazlewood, Arthur, comp. *The economics of ' under-developed' areas : An annotated reading list of books, articles, and official publications.* 2d enl. ed. London, published for the Institute of Commonwealth Studies by Oxford University Press, 1959. xii, 156 p.

Reprint of the first edition (1954, p. 1–89) with an additional section of 67 pages, including separate indexes. Classifications are by subject – national income, consumption, and investment, population and labour, etc. For references to parts of Africa, the indexes of places must be consulted, where, under each place name, there is a subject breakdown.

A succinct overall study by Mr. Hazlewood, *The economy of Africa* (London, Oxford University Press, 1961, 90 p. ; New African Library), is a helpful introduction in this field.

358 Lefèvre, P. C. *Alimentation des populations africaines au sud du Sahara.* Bruxelles, CEDESA, 1965. xiv, 221 p. (Enquêtes bibliographiques, no. 13)

359 —— *Les paysannats en Afrique au sud du Sahara.* Bruxelles, CEDESA, 1965. 215 p. (Enquêtes bibliographiques, no. 12)

Both of these books are based on the library collections of the Institut National pour l'Etude Agronomique du Congo (INEAC) in Brussels. Arrangement is alphabetical by author and most of the entries are for periodical articles, although a few books are included, and most are annotated. The first book lists 985 entries on the food of African populations south of the Sahara. The 844 references in the second book concern farming in sub-Saharan Africa, covering such topics as agricultural systems, social and economic improvements, mechanization of farming, agricultural credit, and crop diseases. Each book contains subject and geographic indexes as well as a list of periodicals analysed.

360 Smet, Guy. *Contribution à l'étude de la progression économique de l'Afrique.* Bruxelles, Centre de Documentation Economique et Sociale Africaine, 1960. 217 p. (Enquêtes bibliographiques, no. 5)

Over 1,500 lightly annotated references to books, pamphlets, official documents, and articles chosen from a four-page list of periodicals. Arrangement is alphabetical by author, with a complicated plan of analytical and geographic classification by number referring to the entries. Material analysed runs through the first half of 1959.

361 United Nations. Dag Hammarskjöld Library. *United Nations Documents Index.* v. 1– , Jan. 1950– . New York. Monthly, with annual cumulated index.
Comprehensive current list of all documents and publications of the United Nations and specialized agencies except restricted materials and internal papers. Arrangement each month is by issuing agency, and entries give full titles, document numbers, dates and paging. A general index on coloured stock is included in each issue and cumulated at the end of the year, furnishing complete coverage of references to persons, places, agencies and subjects. The number of references on Africa has increased a hundredfold since 1950. During the first five years they were almost entirely limited to documents relating to the trust territories. These can be identified in the UN Department of Public Information volume *Ten years of United Nations publications, 1945 to 1955 : A complete catalogue* (New York, 1955, 217 p.). For the publications of the League of Nations relating to Africa, Hans Aufricht, *Guide to League of Nations publications : A bibliographical survey of the work of the League, 1920–1947* (New York, Columbia University Press, 1951, 682 p.), may be consulted.

For those lost in the intricacies of United Nations documentation, a helpful general work is that by Brenda Brimmer, L. R. Wall, Waldo Chamberlin and Thomas Hovet, *A guide to the use of U.N. documents* (Dobbs Ferry, N.Y.. Oceana Publications, 1962, 272 p.; New York University Library, Occasional Paper, no. 3).

362 United Nations. Dag Hammarskjöld Library. *United Nations documents index : Cumulative checklist.* v. 1– , 1950– . New York. Annual.
The 14th edition of the *Cumulative checklist*, covering publications of late 1962 and 1963, was issued in 1964 (245 p.). Unlike the *Index*, the volume omits the specialized agencies and is arranged for the full year by the issuing agency. It has no general index. The material on Africa most readily identifiable is that emanating from the Economic and Social Council, Economic Commission for Africa (p. 185–205). Here several thousand entries appear. They include, for instance, General series; Information series; Limited series; Meeting records; Economic Committee, Social Committee; Committee on Programme of Works and Priorities; Committee of Nine on the Establishment of an African Development Bank; Seminar on Population Problems (Cairo, 1962); Conference of African Statisticians (3d session).

363 United Nations. Economic Commission for Africa. *Bibliography of African statistical publications, 1950–1965.* [Title also in French] [Addis Ababa ?] Dec. 1966. 256 p. processed. (E/Cn.14/LIB/SER.C/2)
The second issue (the first was published in April 1962) of this valuable listing of official documents, serials and reports from African countries, including a few significant unofficial publications on African statistics on all subjects. Entries are listed by region and by country (Algeria to Zambia). Each publication is given a broad subject classification and reference number.

364 U.S. Library of Congress. General Reference and Bibliography Division. *Agricultural development schemes in sub-Saharan Africa : A bibliography.* Comp. by Ruth S. Freitag. Washington, U.S. Government Printing Office, 1963. xii, 189 p.
An extensively annotated bibliography, prepared for the African Section with the assistance of a panel of consultants. The introduction, by Miss Freitag and Dr. Walter Deshler, gives a full outline of the subject, which is broad enough

to cover most general writings on agriculture in Africa. This work has been commended as a model of a subject bibliography.

REFERENCE WORKS

365 Bauer, P. T. *West African trade : A study of competition, oligopoly and monopoly in a changing economy.* Cambridge University Press, 1954. xvi, 450 p. map, tables, diagrs.
A major work by a leading free enterprise economist. Among other matters, the writer stresses the importance of independent peasant producers, the value of small traders in a developing economy, the disadvantages of compulsory marketing arrangements which, in practice, impose a discriminatory form of taxation on peasant producers. The author also wrote *The economic analysis and policy in under-developed countries* (London, Routledge and Kegan Paul, [1965]), and other works.

366 Bohannan, Paul J., and George Dalton, eds. *Markets in Africa.* Evanston, Ill., Northwestern University Press, 1962. 762 p. maps, tables, diagrs. (African Studies, no. 9) Bibliography: p. 739–753.
Papers written by professional anthropologists, economists and geographers on the role of markets, money uses and external trade in the nonindustrial economies of 28 societies south of the Sahara.

367 Clark, Grover. *The balance sheets of imperialism : Facts and figures on colonies.* New York, Columbia University Press, 1936. 136 p., tables.
An attempt to assess the profitability of imperialism. The author writing at a time when German and Italian revisionists put forward claims to a larger share of colonial legacy, argued that colonialism entailed heavy financial expense, and that colonial trade accounted for only a limited share of metropolitan commerce.

368 Du Jonchay, Ivan. *L'industrialisation de l'Afrique : Historique, énergie, matières premières, industries, transports, main-d'oeuvre et infrastructure, finances.* Paris, Payot, 1953. 344 p. illus., maps. (Bibliothèque géographique)
Encyclopaedic treatment, by subject, heavily reinforced by tables of statistics and maps at the end of the volume. The lack of an index is somewhat compensated for by a full table of contents.

A previous French survey of economic development of all Africa by René Laure, *Le continent africain au milieu du siècle : Perspectives et problèmes de la mise en valeur économique* (Paris, Charles-Lavauzelle, 1952, xv, 433 p., maps, tables), is in the form of sections on general factors, followed by paragraph résumés of the situation in individual territories.

369 The Economist Intelligence Unit, London. *Three-monthly Economic Review.* 1952– . London.
Title varies; also appears as *Quarterly Economic Review.* These are series of statistical surveys of individual countries, summarizing latest data in large pamphlets which conclude with tables of economic activity.

370 Ewing, A. E. *Industry in Africa.* New York, Oxford University Press, 1968. 189 p.
The author considers the history of industrial development in Africa and the difficulties in the way. He describes the past and present pattern of industry, the prospects of industrial growth, the possible African groupings, the problems of international trade, and the instruments of industrial development. Ewing is an economist with the U.N. Commission for Africa.

Part II : subject guide for Africa in general

371   *Food Research Institute Studies.* v. 1, no. 1– , Feb. 1960– . Stanford, Calif., Food Research Institute, Stanford University. 3 times a year.

In 1968, the title was changed to *Food Research Institute Studies in Agricultural Economics, Trade, and Development.*

The Food Research Institute, established in 1921, has been engaged in studies of African food and agricultural economics since 1953 and has issued numerous books and pamphlets. Its journal of scholarly research frequently carries monograph-length articles (also available as reprints) on economic aspects of food in Africa. Among them are the following:

> v. 2, no. 1, Feb. 1961: 3–20. ' Food and agricultural economies of Tropical Africa: A summary view '. By William O. Jones.

> v. 3, no. 2, May 1962: 87–124. ' Agricultural change in Uganda, 1945–1960 '. By G. B. Masefield.

> v. 4, no. 1, Feb. 1963: 39–89. ' Agricultural change in Ruanda-Urundi, 1945–1960 '. By Philippe R. Leurquin.

> v. 4, no. 2, 1963–64: 165–223. ' African agricultural development in Southern Rhodesia, 1945–1960 '. By R. W. M. Johnson.

> v. 5, no. 2, 1965: 137–200. ' Agricultural change in the Belgian Congo: 1945–1960 '. By V. Drachoussoff.

> v. 5, no. 3, 1965: 220–285. ' Agricultural change in Nyasaland: 1945–1960 '. By R. W. Kettlewell.

> v. 6, no. 2, 1966: 195–247. ' Agricultural change in Northern Rhodesia/ Zambia: 1945–1965 '. By S. M. Makings.

> v. 7, no. 2, 1967: 177–203. ' The Nigerian palm oil industry '. By Peter Kilby.

> v. 8, no. 1, 1968: 33–90. ' Agricultural change in Kenya: 1945–1960 '. By L. H. Brown.

372   Frankel, Sally Herbert. *Capital investment in Africa : Its course and effects.* London, Oxford University Press, 1938. xvi, 486 p. maps, tables, diagrs. Bibliography: p. 435–462.

An encyclopaedic work which examines foreign capital investments and their impact on Africa. It was written originally as a research memorandum to Lord Hailey's *African survey*, but was subsequently vastly expanded. It places special emphasis on mining and railway finance. The author then wrote *Investment and the return to equity capital in the South African mining industry, 1887–1965 : An international comparison* (Cambridge, Mass., Harvard University Press, 1967, 131 p.). He also worked on South African railway finance, general problems of colonization, and related matters.

373   Gaudy, M. *Manuel d'agriculture tropicale (Afrique tropicale et équatoriale).* Paris, Maison Rustique, 1959. 443 p. illus., map, diagrs.

Handbook for students in African agricultural schools and for officials of the agricultural services. The work covers systems and possible improvements in African agriculture, problems of soil conservation, irrigation and drainage, mechanization, and rural economy.

374   Harroy, Jean Paul. *Afrique, terre qui meurt : La dégradation des sols africains sous l'influence de la colonisation.* 2d ed. Bruxelles, M. Hayez, 1949. 557 p. fold. map. ' Principaux ouvrages cités ': p. 549–557.

Among important older studies of soil exhaustion and erosion in Africa is this brilliant work by the Belgian director of a foundation promoting scientific study of the national parks of the Belgian Congo, later Governor of Ruanda-Urundi and director of IRSAC (Institut pour la Recherche Scientifique en Afrique Centrale). Of his seven lucidly presented sections, two are devoted to the transformation of African life and agriculture under colonization and two to possible remedial measures and their application through science, education and government direction.

375 Herskovits, Melville J., and Mitchell Harwitz, eds. *Economic transition in Africa*. Evanston, Ill., Northwestern University Press, 1964. xviii, 444 p. (Northwestern University African Studies, no. 12) Bibliography: p. 409–425.

Papers of a Conference on Indigenous and Induced Elements in the Economics of Sub-Saharan Africa held at Northwestern University in November 1961.

376 Inter-African Conference on Statistics. [Publications] London, CCTA/CSA, 195?

The first meeting of the Inter-African Conference on Statistics was held in Salisbury in 1951, the second in Lourenço Marques in 1957. A semi-annual *Bulletin* was begun in 1955, published in Lisbon.

377 Jucker-Fleetwood, Erin Elver. *Money and finance in Africa : The experience of Ghana, Morocco, Nigeria, the Rhodesias and Nyasaland, the Sudan, and Tunisia from the establishment of their central banks until 1962.* London, Allen & Unwin; New York, Praeger, 1964. 335 p. illus., tables, graphs, map. Bibliography: p. [322]–330.

A detailed study of the monetary and financial problems of emerging African countries. The author begins with an analysis of conditions for economic growth, considers the African social, political and economic background, and then examines the central banks, various other financial intermediaries, monetary policy, and modern development plans. There are several appendices and an index.

378 Newlyn, Walter Tessier, and D. C. Rowan. *Money and banking systems of eight British African territories.* Oxford, Clarendon Press, 1954. xiv, 301 p. diagrs., tables.

A detailed survey of banking and currency questions.

379 Neumark, S. Daniel. *Foreign trade and economic development in Africa : A historical perspective.* Stanford, Calif., Food Research Institute, Stanford University, 1964. 222 p. maps. (Miscellaneous Publications, no. 14) Bibliographic references are given at the end of each chapter.

Well-balanced summary of historic aspects – early contacts, European settlement, slave-trade, colonial development of transportation, mining, agricultural exports, etc. – and of international trade and economic development at present.

380 *Sols Africains. African Soils.* v. 1– , 1951– . Paris, Inter-African Bureau for Soils and Rural Economy. 3 times a year.

This affiliate of CCTA/CSA has an extensive library, containing over 100,000 subject index cards. Since the early 1950s it has issued *Index cards : Selected current bibliography*, a biweekly series of 32 index cards for the principal articles received. Besides the scientific journal *Sols Africains*, the Bureau published a *Monthly Analytical Bulletin* (v. 1– , 1951), with alternate title *Bibliographical Bulletin*; this carries abstracts and accessions lists.

The Inter-African Soils Conference, sponsored by this bureau and by CCTA/CSA, held meetings at Goma, Belgian Congo, in 1948; Leopoldville in 1954; and Dalaba, Guinea, in 1959. The *Comptes rendus* of the third conference has been published by CSA (1959, 924 p.; CSA publication no. 50).

Related to the Inter-African Bureau for Soils and Rural Economy is the Inter-African Pedological Service, with headquarters at Yangambi, Republic of the Congo (Zaïre). It is working on a map of soils of Africa.

381 Tempany, Harold A., and D. H. Grist. *An introduction to tropical agriculture.* London and New York, Longmans, Green, 1958. 347 p. illus.

The late Sir Harold Tempany was agricultural adviser to the Secretary of State for the Colonies. This book, written in collaboration with a former agricultural economist of Malaya, is a general account of tropical regions. It is in three parts, the first on the tropical background of climate, soils, types of vegetation, etc., the second on agricultural practices, and the third on economic conditions of marketing and transport, land tenure and use, and finance and credit.

382 Thomas, M. F., and G. W. Whittington, eds. *Environment and land use in Africa.* London, Methuen, 1969. 554 p.

Has much useful information covering the colonial period. See especially J. A. Hellen, 'Colonial administrative policies and agricultural patterns in tropical Africa', p. 321–53.

383 United Nations. Statistical Office. *Statistical yearbook. Annuaire statistique.* 1948– . New York, 1949– .
17th issue, for 1965. 1966. 747 p.

Summary of international statistics covering population, agriculture, mining, manufacturing, trade, finance, social statistics, education, etc., with tables as closely up to date as possible and some that include pre-war figures. Sources are given for the information if other than the Statistical Office. The tabulated figures are in subject classes, with country breakdown for most. There is a separate country index. See also the Economic Commission for Africa, *Economic survey of Africa since 1950* (1959).

Note For mineral resources, see nos. 513 and 514.

EDUCATION

Note See also Part III, Area Guide, for other references to specific regions, countries and colonial powers.

BIBLIOGRAPHIES

384 Brembeck, Cole S., and John P. Keith. *Education in emerging Africa : A select and annotated bibliography.* East Lansing, College of Education, Michigan State University [1962 ?]. 153 p. (Education in Africa Series, no. 1)

Classified by subject: administration and control; education and change; educational planning; fundamental and adult education; teachers, teaching and students; vocational, technical and special education; bibliographies in African education. Under each heading there are only a few references chosen to cover all aspects of the topic. An annotation so extensive as to form an abstract of the book or article accompanies each reference.

Education

385 Couch, Margaret. *Education in Africa: A select bibliography.* London, Institute of Education, University of London.

> Part 1, *British and former British territories in Africa.* 1962. 121 p. (Education Libraries Bulletin, Supplement 5)

> Part 2, *French-speaking territories (former French and Belgian colonies); Portuguese and Spanish territories; Ethiopia and Eritrea; Liberia; and general African references, 1962–1964.* 1965. xii, 116 p. (Education Libraries Bulletin, Supplement 9)

The first part is taken from the catalogue of the Department of Education in Tropical Areas Library and includes material to the end of 1961 (it does not include South Africa). Arrangement is by country with subdivisions for bibliography, general, primary, etc. Part 2 lists books, articles and reports available in the United Kingdom, arranged by country and then chronologically.

386 Drake, Howard. *A bibliography of African education south of the Sahara.* Aberdeen, University Press, 1942. 97 p. (University of Aberdeen Anthropological Museum, no. 2)

Standard work providing extensive coverage of pre-war material on the subject.

387 Hanson, John W., and Geoffrey W. Gibson. *African education and development since 1960: A select and annotated bibliography.* East Lansing, Institute for International Studies in Education and African Studies Center, Michigan State University, 1966. 325 p.

The 1,587 items listed cover books and articles in English, French and German. Entries are arranged by subject and thereunder by country and include works not specifically on education. Some helpful cross-referencing has been included, and there is an author index. Addresses of serials and journals frequently cited are given in an appendix.

388 Leyder, Jean. *L'enseignement supérieur et la recherche scientifique en Afrique intertropicale.* Bruxelles, CEDESA, 1959–60. 2 v. 67, 220 p. (Enquêtes bibliographiques, no. 2)

One of the bibliographical series issued by the CEDESA (see no. 589). The bibliography contains 1,025 entries.

389 London. University. Institute of Education. *Catalogue of the collection of education in tropical areas.* Boston, G. K. Hall, 1964. 3 v.

Many of the works cited relate to Africa.

390 Nussbaum, Mary Johnston, comp. *A selected bibliography for literacy workers (with special reference to Africa).* Rev. and enl. Hartford, Conn., Hartford Seminary Foundation, 1965. 133 l. (Hartford Studies in Linguistics, no. 16)

Useful for literacy teachers everywhere. Entries are arranged under headings such as teaching adults, teaching reading, writing for new literates, and literacy campaigns and programs. Some entries are annotated. There are author, title, and country indexes, a periodical list, and a list of agencies and organizations.

391 Parker, Franklin, comp. *African education: A bibliography of 121 U.S.A. doctoral dissertations.* Washington, D.C., World Confederation of Organizations of the Teaching Profession, 1965. 48 p.

Some of the dissertations listed are followed by abstracts taken from *Dissertation abstracts.* Many entries concern studies undertaken in Egypt. Arrangement is by author, and there is a subject index.

117

392 Yates, Barbara A. ' A bibliography on special problems in education in Tropical Africa '. *Comparative Education Review*, v. 8, Dec. 1964: 307–319.

393 ——— ' Educational policy and practice in Tropical Africa: A general bibliography '. *Comparative Education Review*, v. 8, Oct. 1964: 215–228. Useful, up-to-date bibliographical articles in the journal published at Teachers College, Columbia University, and simultaneously at Oxford. The *Comparative Education Review* is significant as a source for information on African education.

REFERENCE WORKS

394 African Education Commission. *Education in Africa: A study of West, South and Equatorial Africa.* Conducted by the African Education Commission under the auspices of the Phelps-Stokes Fund and foreign mission societies of North America and Europe; Report prepared by Thomas Jesse Jones, chairman. New York, Phelps-Stokes Fund, 1922. xxviii, 323 p. illus., maps, plates. Abridged ed., 1962.

395 African Education Commission. *Education in East Africa....* Prepared by Thomas Jesse Jones, chairman. New York, Phelps-Stokes Fund, 1925. xxviii, 416 p. illus. Abridged ed., 1962.

The Phelps-Stokes Commission on African Education sent representatives in the early 1920s to study the entire field of education in Africa south of the Sahara. The reports marked an important step in American interest in African development. As a direct result, the Jeanes schools were begun in East and Central Africa in 1925. Named after a Philadelphia philanthropist who left a fund for such purposes, these institutions trained African teachers and their wives to take charge of village schools and community improvement. An abridged edition of the two Phelps-Stokes reports, with introduction by Leonard J. Lewis, was published by the Oxford University Press in London, September 1962 (5,213 p.). The volumes are the best surveys of African education ever done.

396 Ashby, Eric, in association with Mary Anderson. *Universities: British, Indian, African: A study in the ecology of higher education.* Cambridge, Mass., Harvard University Press, 1966. 558 p. References and Notes: p. [377]–448; Bibliography: p. 527–540.

A valuable history and analysis of the ' export ' of British university models overseas from the early 19th century to 1965. In Parts 1 and 2 Sir Eric establishes the historical background of European universities and discusses the founding of universities in Ireland, Australia and India. Part 3 (almost two-thirds of the text) is confined to educational strategy in tropical Africa and to the founding of universities there. Included is a section on the development of academic freedom and autonomy in Britain and Africa and a section comparing non-British patterns of higher education in Africa, i.e., the ' Bantu ' colleges in South Africa, Haile Selassie I University, Lovanium University, and the universities in French-speaking Africa. Appended are 75 pages of documentary material. There is an analytical index.

An excellent essay on higher education in Africa by Sir Eric Ashby, based on a lecture series at Harvard in April 1964, was published with the title *African universities and Western tradition* (Cambridge, Mass., 1964, 113 p.).

397 Conference of African States on the Development of Education in Africa, Addis Ababa, May 15–25, 1961. *Final report.* Paris, UNESCO and UN Economic Commission for Africa, 1961. 64, 27, 127 p.

Organized and convened by the UN Economic Commission for Africa and UNESCO, this conference brought together representatives of 63 governments (39 participating, 24 as observers, including the United States) and delegates from UN and international nongovernmental agencies.

398 Ruth Sloan Associates, Washington, D.C. *The educated African: A country-by-country survey of educational development in Africa.* Ed. by Helen Kitchen. New York, Praeger, 1962. xvii, 542 p. illus., maps. (Books That Matter) Bibliographical footnotes.

A ' functional reference survey ', a source-book of lasting value. It represents a notable accomplishment of collecting and synthesizing factual and statistical information on all phases of education in almost 50 countries of Africa, presented to the editors in working papers by about 30 area specialists. The arrangement is ordered by region and country. For each country there are thumbnail statistics, historical background, an outline of the history of education, a statement (with statistics) of the present situation, and plans and prospects for the future. It supersedes a compilation of 1955, *Resources and needs for training facilities for Africans in British Africa, Ethiopia and Liberia* (Washington, D.C., 1955, 250 l., diagrs.).

GEOGRAPHY

ATLAS

Note See also Part I, Atlases and Maps, and Part II, History.

399 The Times, London. *The Times atlas of the world.* Ed. by John Bartholomew. Mid-century ed. v. 4, *Southern Europe and Africa . . . with an index-gazetteer.* London, The Times Publishing Co., 1956. plates (96 col.); 50-page index. 49 cm.

One of the best general atlases of Africa.

BIBLIOGRAPHIES

Note In most geographical works no clear distinction is made between physical, human and economic geography; and for geographical studies nearly all non-specialized bibliographies are applicable. The two bibliographies mentioned below are designed primarily for the use of geographers. They include African material within a wider framework. Journals of the geographical institutions of the West are also largely pertinent for African material relating to many areas. Institutions within Africa are predominantly regional. In the Library of Congress list *Serials for African studies* (see no. 294), over 40 periodicals are indexed under geography.

400 Bederman, Sanford H. *A bibliographic aid to the study of the geography of Africa: A selected listing of recent literature published in the English language.* Atlanta, School of Business Administration, Georgia State University, 1970. 212 p.

Part II : subject guide for Africa in general

401 *Current Geographical Publications.* 1938– . New York, American Geographical Society. Monthly, except July and Aug.

A continuation of the Society's *Research catalogue* (see no. 268). Each issue of this valuable publication contains a section on Africa – general and by region and country – listing references to books, pamphlets, government documents, periodical articles and essays in composite works. African maps are noted in a separate section on atlases. A cumulative annual index has a subject section and an author and regional section.

402 International Geographical Union. Special Commission on the Humid Tropics. *A select annotated bibliography of the humid tropics.* [Title also in French] Comp. by Theo L. Hills. Montreal, Geography Department, McGill University, 1960. xiii, 238 p.

A substantial part of this bibliography is concerned with Africa (p. 69–144). Arrangement is by region and country, with subdivisions by discipline. The selection, though covering general aspects, is slanted towards the use of the geographer.

403 Sommer, John W. *Bibliography of African geography, 1940–1964.* Hanover, N.H., Geography Department, Dartmouth College, 1965. 139 p. (Geography Publications at Dartmouth, no. 3)

The 1,724 numbered items are divided into four parts: human, economic, and physical geography, each with a number of subdivisions, and general Africana. References are derived from English and French periodical literature (primarily scholarly geographical journals). There is an author index.

404 Val, María Asunción del. *Catálogo de la exposición de libros españoles sobre geografía y viajes en Africa.* Madrid, Consejo Superior de Investigaciones Científicas, Instituto de Estudios Africanos, 1948. 120 p.

There are 575 numbered entries covering works in Spanish on geography, travels, and explorations in Africa. A list of general works is followed by regional subdivisions. Also included are sections on Spanish explorers in the 19th century, expeditions to Guinea, periodicals which frequently have material on geography and voyages in Africa, and bibliographies consulted. There is an alphabetical index of authors and anonymous works.

REFERENCE WORKS

405 American Geographical Society. *Index to maps in books and periodicals.* Boston, G. K. Hall, 1968. 10 v. 35 cm.

A commendable reference work, especially useful because maps that appear in monographic or serial publications are rarely entered in other cartobibliographies. Making up the large volumes are photoreproductions of some 160,000 cards from the catalogue maintained by the Society's map department. Arrangement is alphabetical by subject and geographical-political division, with entries listed chronologically under each geographical division.

406 Fitzgerald, Walter. *Africa : A social, economic, and political geography of its major regions.* 10th ed., rev. by W. C. Brice. London, Methuen, 1967. xii, 503 p. maps, tables. Includes bibliographies.

Standard advanced manual of the geography of Africa, originally published in 1934. The 10th edition, revised by a former student of the late Professor Fitzgerald, is updated, rather unevenly, to about 1963. The physical environment, history, and societies of Africa as a whole are discussed first. More than three-fourths of the book is then devoted to regional studies – South Africa, East

Geography

Africa, Madagascar, Central Africa, West Africa, the Barbary States, the Nile Valley and Abyssinia and its borderlands. While the treatment of physical geography and history stands up well, as a text on social, economic, and political geography the work suffers by comparison with a number of recent African geography texts. The extensive bibliographies include mostly older British and French works and apparently have not been updated since the 9th edition of 1961.

407 *Geographical abstracts.* London, London School of Economics. 1960– . The computer-produced *Geographical abstracts : Index 1966* has approximately 40,000 entries. A valuable new abstracting service to call attention to articles dealing with developments during the colonial period as well as recent times.

408 Hance, William A. *The geography of modern Africa.* New York, Columbia University Press, 1964. xiv, 653 p. illus., charts, maps, tables.

A comprehensive survey of the economic development of Africa. After introductory chapters giving the background of physical setting, population and peoples, and describing the present political scene, treatment is by regions and countries, varied in accordance with the particular features important to the economy of each. A good survey of economic development and changes during the colonial period. See also Kimble, *Tropical Africa* (no. 321).

409 Kirchherr, Eugene C. *Abyssinia to Zona Al Sur Del Draa : An index to the political units of Africa in the period 1951–1967; a listing of former and current place names with supplementary notes and maps.* Kalamazoo, Institute of International and Area Studies and School of Graduate Studies, Western Michigan University, 1968. 32 p. maps (1 fold.). (Monographic Series on Cultural Changes, no. 2)

This convenient reference work is of considerable help in disentangling the toponymic confusion generated by political transitions in Africa in the post-1950 period. A systematic and comprehensive guide to countries, territories, and regions is provided by the alphabetical index. Supplementing this are notes and maps clarifying the sequence of the changing names on the contemporary map of Africa.

410 Meyer, Hans H., ed. *Das Deutsche Kolonialreich : Eine Länderkunde der Deutschen Schutzgebiete.* Leipzig, Verlag des Bibliographischen Instituts, 1909–10. 2 v. plates, maps.

The standard geography of the German colonial empire, treated in great detail by individual colonies: v. 1, East Africa, Cameroon; v. 2, Togo, German South-West Africa, and the South Seas. The many photographs, colour plates, and maps are a significant feature of this impressive older work.

411 Migliorini, Elio. *L'Africa.* Torino, Unione Tipografico-Editrice Torinese, 1955. 821 p. illus., plates, maps. Includes bibliographies.

An impressive volume covering all Africa in terms of physical, social, and politico-economic geography. Arrangement, after a general section, is by region. The folded, coloured maps, supplemented generously by subject sketch maps, are of high quality and value. The author is director of the Institute of Geography at the University of Naples.

While American and British geographers now tend to treat regions or continents in independent studies of moderate length, continental writers continue the tradition of multivolume sets of world geography. The great French *Géographie universelle* edited by P. Vidal de la Blache and L. Gallois reached its 15th and final volume after the war (Paris, A. Colin, 1927–48), though those devoted to Africa south of the Sahara – v. 9, Part 2, *Afrique occidentale*, by

Augustin Bernard (p. 285–529), and v. 12, *Afrique équatoriale, orientale et australe*, by Fernand Maurette (398 p.) – appeared in 1939 and 1938 respectively. Little attention is paid in these to political and economic factors, the stress being on physical and human geography. An even more lavish publishing venture is the *Geografia universale illustrata : La fisionomia attuale del mondo considerata nell'aspetto fisico, antropico ed economico*, ed. by Roberto Almagià (Torino, Unione Tipografico-Editrice Torinese). Volume 5, *L'Africa*, by Elio Migliorini, was announced in 1960. Volume 2 of the *Géographie universelle Larousse*, ed. by Pierre Deffontaines, is titled *Afrique, Asie péninsulaire, Océanie* (Paris, Larousse, 1959, 391 p.).

HISTORY

Note See also Part III for references pertaining to specific colonial powers, regions or countries.

ATLASES AND MAPS

412 Boyd, Andrew, and Patrick van Rensburg. *An atlas of African affairs.* With maps by W. H. Bromage. New York, Praeger, 1962. 133 p. maps.
Provides the background and an explanation of the fast-changing map of Africa, prepared with 'the plain newspaper reader' in mind. The 50 sketch maps are 'general' (population, regions and barriers, a few relating to history, the new political scene as of late 1962, United Nations activity, Pan-Africanism and regional unity, education, health, minerals, transport, power development) and 'sectional'. They are explained succinctly on facing pages. Available in hard-cover and paperback editions.

413 Fage, J. D. *An atlas of African history.* London, E. Arnold, 1958. 64 p. 62 maps.
          Reprint: 1962.
The first work of its kind for Africa, with 62 sketch maps in diagrammatic form illustrating stages of African history from the eve of the Muslim Arab invasions to the present. Captions vary from thumbnail sketches of the historic situation to keys to symbols that are used to indicate, for example, the spread of Christian missions. See also Harry Gailey, *The history of Africa in maps* (Chicago, 1967, 96 p.).

414 Healy, Allan M., and E. R. Vere-Hodge. *The map approach to African history.* London, University Tutorial Press, 1959. 64 p. 28 maps.
Prepared by two secondary-school teachers, this study is a much simplified presentation of African history in 28 sketch maps with facing explanatory text.

History

BIBLIOGRAPHIES

Note Most good bibliographies concerning the history of colonialism appear as part of larger general bibliographies. A large amount of this work deals with the history of one particular colonial power (see Part III and nos. 252–267, 436 and 437). The following works are, however, noteworthy:

415 Frank, Z., and S. Stancioff. ' Bibliographie sur l'histoire de l'Afrique et la colonisation européenne de sources principalement soviétiques '. *Bulletin des Séances* (Académie Royale des Sciences d'Outre-Mer), v. 8, no. 4, 1962: 658–691; v. 9, no. 2, 1963: 265–302; no. 4, 1963: 751–790; no. 5, 1963: 1017–1050; v. 10, no. 2, 1964: 186–220.

A classified title list of works, mostly in Russian, prepared by two specialists at the Centre d'Etudes des Pays de l'Est in Brussels. It is currently appearing in three issues a year of the ARSOM *Bulletin*, presented by M. M. Walraet.

416 Griffin, Appleton Prentiss Clark. *List of books, with references to periodicals, relating to the theory of colonization, government of dependencies, protectorates, and related topics.* 2d ed. Washington, Library of Congress, 1900. 156 p.

417 Hess, Robert L., and Dalvan M. Coger. *Semper ex Africa : A bibliography of primary sources for nineteenth-century tropical Africa as recorded by explorers, missionaries, traders, travelers, administrators, military men, adventurers and others.* Stanford, Hoover Institution Press, 1972. 800 p.

A major source-book covering articles and other publications from a great variety of printed sources in English, French, German, Italian, Portuguese, etc. Secondary sources have been ignored. The work is divided by geographic regions. North and south Africa have been excluded. There is an index of authors, a select list of bibliographies and an extensive list of periodicals consulted.

418 Kayser, Gabriel. *Bibliographie d'ouvrages ayant trait à l'Afrique en général dans ses rapports avec l'exploration et la civilisation de ces contrées.* Bruxelles, 1887. 176 p.

419 Martineau, Alfred, ed. *Bibliographie d'histoire coloniale (1900–1930).* Paris, Société de l'Histoire des Colonies Françaises, 1932. 667 p.

This massive bibliography, which cites the chief sources relating to acquisition and administration of colonial possessions throughout the world – British, Belgian, Dutch, German, Italian, Portuguese, and Spanish, as well as French – has for each colony an introductory essay on the sources of bibliography and then a reading list of several pages. The collaborators were specialists in their respective fields.

420 Ragatz, Lowell. *A bibliography for the study of African history in the nineteenth and twentieth centuries.* Washington, D.C., Paul Pearlman, 1943. 47 p.

A good selection, arranged by region and country, and including books, documents, and significant periodical material. See also no. 285 and bibliographies in nos. 436 and 437.

Part II : subject guide for Africa in general

REFERENCE WORKS

421 *African Historical Studies.* Ed. by Norman R. Bennett. v. 1, no. 1– , 1968– . Brookline, Mass., African Studies Center, Boston University. Twice a year.
This new journal presents about five essays in each issue. In addition, there is a solid section of book reviews and a ' News and Notes ' section.

422 Beer, George Louis. *African questions at the Paris Peace Conference. With papers on Egypt, Mesopotamia, and the Colonial Settlement, by George Louis Beer . . . edited with introduction, annexes and additional notes by Louis Herbert Gray. . . .* New York, Macmillan, 1923. 628 p. illus., maps, diagr.
This is the standard work on the subject.

423 Bell, J. Bowyer. *The myth of the guerrilla: Revolutionary theory and malpractice.* New York, A. Knopf, 1971. 273 p. Bibliography: p. 275–285.
A general study of guerrilla warfare which contains, among other case studies, an account of guerrilla warfare in South Africa, Rhodesia and the Portuguese colonies. The author tries to counteract what he regards as a romantic view of guerrilla warfare and is sceptical of its chances for success in southern Africa. Much of the Winter 1972 issue of *Africa Today* (v. 19, no. 1) is taken up with critiques of Bowyer Bell's book, written from an African nationalist standpoint. As regards more general interpretations of guerrilla warfare, Lewis H. Gann, *Guerrillas in History* (Stanford, Hoover Institution Press, 1971, 99 p.), also touches on Africa. The writer argues that guerrilla warfare is neither new in history, nor necessarily progressive in political orientation, nor a sure road to victory.

424 Brunschwig, Henri. *L'avènement de l'Afrique noire.* Paris, Librairie Armand Colin, 1963. 248 p.
An intelligent survey of African history, especially good on the period of the partition and in comparing the varying results of British and French colonialism.

425 Butler, Jeffrey, ed. *Boston University papers in African history.* 2 v. Boston, Boston University Press, 1964–1967.
Following publication of the first volume, the title of this series was modified in v. 2 to reflect the wider scope of future volumes, i.e., not only history but also political affairs and interdisciplinary subjects. Both volumes derive largely from faculty seminars held by the African Studies Center at Boston University.
The 10 papers in v. 1 are concerned mainly with the colonial period in specific areas of Africa, but include also such articles as 'Historical inferences from linguistic research in sub-Saharan Africa ', by Joseph Greenberg, and 'European sources for tropical African history ', by Graham Irwin.
Volume 2 consists of eight papers devoted wholly or in part to activities of non-African groups and individuals in Africa during the colonial period and three papers concerned with earlier periods. The new series entitled ' Boston University Papers on Africa ' began in 1967 and has produced several volumes.

426 *Cahiers d'Etudes Africaines.* 1960– . Paris. Quarterly.
This distinguished review is the French counterpart of the *Journal of Modern African Studies,* and like that periodical presents essay-length articles on all the so-called ' human sciences '. It is published by Mouton for the Ecole Pratique des Hautes Etudes, Université de Paris, 6e Section: Sciences Economiques et Sociales. Concern is primarily – but far from exclusively – with French-speaking Africa.

History

427 Callwell, C. E. *Small wars : Their principles and practice.* London. Printed for His Majesty's Stationery Office by Harrison and Sons, 1906. 559 p., maps. 2d ed.

A classic on colonial warfare. The author, a British colonel, deals with 'the broad rules which govern the conduct of operations in hostilities against adversaries of whom modern works on the military seldom take account'. The writer goes into all aspects of warfare where 'tactics favour the regular troops while strategy favours the enemy'. Many examples are drawn from African campaigns against opponents as varied as the Ashanti and the Boers. Account is also taken of German and French campaigns. Arrangement is by topic, such as the nature and strategy of small wars, the employment of the various arms, hill and bush fighting, etc. All general propositions are illustrated by case studies from particular campaigns. This work, which was originally issued in 1899 and later brought up to date, sums up a century of experience in colonial conquests.

428 Collins, Robert O., ed. *Problems in the history of colonial Africa 1860–1960.* Englewood Cliffs, N.J., Prentice-Hall, Inc., 1970. 389 p.

A collection of readings with good introductions for each of the seven sections organized around a theme or problem: 'The partition of Africa', 'Collaboration or resistance to European rule in Africa', 'Indirect rule in theory and practice', 'Assimilation and association in French colonial rule in Africa', 'White settlers in tropical Africa', 'Exploitation and development in colonial Africa', 'The élites, the masses and African nationalism'. See also his book of readings, *The partition of Africa : Illusion or necessity?* (New York, John Wiley and Sons, Inc., 1969, 239 p.).

429 Cornevin, Robert, and Marianne Cornevin. *Histoire de l'Afrique, des origines à la deuxième guerre mondiale.* 3d ed. Paris, Petite Bibliothèque Payot, 1970. 437 p. maps. Bibliography: p. 393–404.

A revised edition of a work first published in 1964. A second volume will continue the story from 1940 to the end of empire in Africa. The present edition embodies a number of changes designed to keep pace with more recent research.

Robert Cornevin has also written various regional histories, including *Le Dahomey* (Paris, Presses Universitaires de France, 1965); *Histoire du Congo, Léopoldville-Kinshasa, des origines préhistoriques à la République Démocratique du Congo . . .* (Paris, Berger-Levrault, 1966); and *Histoire du Togo . . .* (Paris, Berger-Levrault, 1969).

430 Deschamps, Hubert Jules. *L'Europe découvre l'Afrique: Afrique Occidentale 1794–1900.* Paris, Editions Berger-Levrault, 1967. 287 p. maps, illus., ports.

A short history of European exploration which traces the story from the Age of Enlightenment down to the end of the nineteenth century when the age of the great discoveries came to an end.

Another recent study bearing on the age of discoveries is Robert I. Rotberg, ed., *Africa and its explorers : Motives, methods and impact* (Cambridge, Mass., Harvard University Press, 1970. 351 p., illus., maps, bibliography: p. 323–332).

431 Edinburgh. University. Centre of African Studies. *The theory of imperialism and the European partition of Africa : Proceedings of a seminar held in the Centre of African Studies, University of Edinburgh, 3rd and 4th November, 1967.* Edinburgh, 1968. 187 p.

A series of papers dealing with the background of imperialism and subjects as varied as the imperial idea and English fiction, the origins of the Congo Free State, French militarism and the Western Sudan, the search for an Anglo-German understanding before the years immediately preceding World War I, opposition to slavery and its impact on the partition, the role of the 'man on the spot', and Victorian views about Africa and imperialism. An historiographical essay by Eric Stokes, *Imperialism and the scramble for Africa* (Salisbury, Historical Association of Rhodesia and Nyasaland, 1963, 15 p.), is also useful.

432 Fieldhouse, D. K. *The colonial empires : A comparative survey from the eighteenth century.* New York, Dell Publishing Company, 1971. 450 p., illus., maps.

An English paperback edition of a work which originally appeared in German as an integrated volume within the multi-volume Fischer *Weltgeschichte.* The author examines the activities of the European colonial powers in all parts of the world. His view is avowedly Eurocentric; in his own words he ignored related aspects of imperial history such as the role of Christian missions and the cultural and social impact of alien powers on dependent peoples. Only a limited space is allotted to African problems, but African colonization is placed in its wider context. While Fieldhouse takes a generally positive attitude towards imperial expansion, the paperback compiled by Roland Oliver and Anthony Atmore, *Africa since 1800* (Cambridge, Eng., The University Press, 1967, 304 p., maps), is more concerned with local African developments, and altogether more critical of the imperial impact.

433 Ganiage, Jean, Hubert Deschamps, and Odette Guitard, with the collaboration of André Martel. *L'Afrique au XXe siècle.* Paris, Sirey, 1966. 908 p. maps (part fold. col.), tables. (L'histoire du XXe siècle) Bibliography: p. 863–867.

This massive volume includes in its broad scope not only major historical events but also the geographic, sociological, demographic, political, economic and cultural framework of developments on the African continent from 1900 to 1965. Ganiage's study of North Africa takes up roughly a third of the book, with Martel contributing some 30 pages on the Saharan region. The next section (p. 303–517), by Deschamps, covers West, Central, and northeastern Africa, and the last section (p. 521–867), by Guitard, is devoted to southern and East Africa and includes the volume's only bibliography. There is an index.

434 Gann, Lewis H., and Peter Duignan. *Burden of empire : An appraisal of Western colonialism in Africa south of the Sahara.* New York, published for the Hoover Institution by Praeger, 1967. xii, 434 p. maps. (Hoover Institution Publications) Reprinted in paperback, 1971. Bibliography: p. 399–417.

The authors discuss different theories of imperialism and their application to the realities of Africa. They seek to evaluate the impact of colonial rule on the indigenous people and to reinterpret the process of decolonization. They believe that despite its many failings colonial empire in Africa was one of the most 'efficacious engines of cultural diffusion in world history'. Their work is based on extensive reading in both African and European history and also has a comparative dimension. See also their *White settlers in tropical Africa* (Penguin Books, 1962. 170 p.).

435 Gann, L. H., and Peter Duignan, eds. *Colonialism in Africa 1870–1960.* Cambridge, Eng., The University Press, 1969. maps, tables. 5 v.

A major series designed to re-evaluate the impact of colonialism on Africa south of the Sahara. The first two volumes, edited by L. H. Gann and Peter Duignan, are entitled *The history and politics of colonialism 1870–1960.* The first volume deals with the era 1870 to 1914, and contains articles written, respectively, by Elizabeth Colson, Colin W. Newbury, Henri Brunschwig, Catherine Coquery-Vidrovitch, John D. Hargreaves, John E. Flint, Jean Stengers, T. O. Ranger,

D. W. Krüger, Richard J. Hammond, Robert Cornevin, Harold G. Marcus, Charles Pelham Groves, the editors, and a conclusion by J. F. A. Ajayi. The second volume deals with the period 1914 to 1960, that is to say, from the Great War to decolonization. It contains contributions by K. W. J. Post, George Bennett, James Duffy, Roger Anstey, Hubert Deschamps, Robert Delavignette, William E. Gutteridge, Michael Crowder, Martin Kilson, Immanuel Wallerstein, C. G. Baëta, Crawford Young, the editors, and a conclusion by A. Adu Boahen. Both volumes are designed to present differing and contrasting viewpoints. They summarize some of the available knowledge in major fields concerned with the impact of imperialism on Africa and break new ground by presenting hitherto unpublished material based on original research. Each article has a separate bibliography.

The third volume in the series is edited by Victor Turner and is entitled *Profiles of change : African society and colonial rule* (1971). The contributors are mainly anthropologists and sociologists, including John Middleton, Martin Klein, Ronald Cohen, Max Gluckman, Lucy Mair, Elizabeth Colson, Aidan Southall, Michael Banton, Hilda Kuper, F. B. Welbourn, Margaret Read and Peter Rigby. At the time of writing, Peter Duignan and L. H. Gann were engaged in producing a fourth volume designed to deal with the economics of colonialism. The present *Bibliographical guide* is the fifth and final volume in the series.

436 Gifford, Prosser, and Wm. Roger Louis, eds., assisted by Alison Smith. *Britain and Germany in Africa : Imperial rivalry and colonial rule.* New Haven and London, Yale University Press, 1967. xvii, 825 p. maps. Bibliography: p. 707–795.

The most up-to-date work in English on British and German colonial policy. It is distinguished by the high standard of the majority of the 24 contributions, by the comparative dimension introduced through a juxtaposition of British and German colonial theory and practice and by the original research that went into many of the essays. The first part, entitled 'Imperial rivalry', deals with Germany's role in the scramble, Anglo-German rivalry and Anglo-German collaboration in the colonial field, and the 'repartition' of Africa occasioned by World War I. The second part, entitled 'Colonial rule', comprises essays on various aspects of colonial administration, missionary policy, African responses to European rule, the policies of trusteeship and of indirect rule, and related topics. The third part is an excellent historiographical essay on the German empire in Africa and British perspectives, with detailed notes on archival sources (p. 709–774), an extensive listing of works (p. 775–795), lists of senior British and German officials, and other relevant information. There is an index and five maps.

437 Gifford, Prosser, and Wm. Roger Louis, eds. *France and Britain in Africa : Imperial rivalry and colonial rule.* New Haven, Conn., Yale University Press, 1971. 989 p., maps, plates, tables. 'Bibliographical essay': p. 782–902.

A major work which corresponds to the previous study published by the editors, *Britain and Germany in Africa*. . . The volume is divided into three parts: Part I on imperial rivalry (10 essays) and a conclusion by Henri Brunschwig; Part II on colonial rule (10 essays) and a conclusion by Leonard Thompson; and Part III a bibliographical essay by David Gardinier, a major effort which provides excellent coverage of the literature on French Africa during the colonial period.

438 Hallett, Robin. *Africa to 1875 : A modern history.* Ann Arbor, University of Michigan Press, 1970. xii, 503 p. maps. Bibliography: p. 429–483.

Covers the entire continent, including Islamic Africa. The first portion deals with general problems of African historiography. The second portion concentrates on the various regions of Africa and traces their past from early times to about 1850. The last part tries to assess the inner dynamics of Africa up to 1875, the beginning of the 'New Imperialism'. The section entitled 'Suggested Readings' is itself a bibliographical essay of major importance. A second volume is in preparation.

439 Henige, David. *Colonial governors from the fifteenth century to the present: A comprehensive list.* Madison, University of Wisconsin Press, 1970. 461 p.

All colonies of Africa are covered fully for each colonial power.

440 Hertslet, Sir Edward. *The map of Africa by treaty : A reprint of the third edition, revised and completed to the end of 1908 by R. W. Bryant and H. L. Sherwood.* 3d ed. London, F. Cass, 1967. 3 v. 1,404 p.

The author was librarian of the British Foreign Office. His classic work traces the changes in the political frontiers imposed by the European powers from the late 18th century to 1908. It concentrates on the period covered by the scramble, and approaches the subject primarily from the British point of view. The study contains geographical tables and detailed maps, as well as the texts of relevant treaties, conventions, proclamations and other relevant documents. The first volume deals with the various British possessions in Africa, which are arranged by territory. The second and third volumes cover the relations between Britain and foreign countries, which are placed in alphabetical order. There is an index to the three volumes. Hertslet also wrote an equally impressive work on *The map of Europe by treaty* . . . (London, Butterworths, 1875–1891, 4 v.).

441 Institute of Race Relations. *Newsletter.* no. 1– , Jan. 1961– . London. Monthly.

A monthly booklet summarizing events in race relations throughout the world, and particularly in Africa and Britain. The Institute also publishes a quarterly journal, *Race* (v. 1, no. 1– , Nov. 1959– , printed by Oxford University Press), and occasional pamphlets on race questions.

442 *Journal of African History.* v. 1, no. 1– , May 1960– . London, Cambridge University Press.

Edited by R. A. Oliver and J. D. Fage. Two issues a year appeared in 1960 and 1961, and thereafter three each year. The journal is designed to represent the highest scholarly standards in its contributions to the broad field of African history. A major source, valuable both for its articles and its reviews.

443 *Journal of Modern African Studies: A Quarterly Survey of Politics, Economics and Related Topics in Contemporary Africa.* v. 1, no. 1– , Mar. 1963– . Cambridge, Eng., Cambridge University Press.

Edited by David and Helen Kimble. This significant scholarly journal, of 100–150 pages per issue, carries authoritative articles on the present scene and recent past in Africa, a 'review article', which is a critique of writings in some special field, substantial reviews of 10 or more new books, and an interesting section on 'Africana'.

444 July, Robert W. *A history of the African people.* New York, Charles Scribner's Sons, 1970. xxii, 650 p. illus., maps. Bibliography: p. 607–611.

A readable textbook which concentrates on sub-Saharan Africa. More than two-thirds of the book is concerned with Africa since about 1800. The story is continued to independence and its aftermath. Each chapter is provided with a separate section containing 'suggestions for further reading'.

445 Lucas, Sir Charles. *The partition and colonization of Africa*. Oxford, Clarendon Press, 1922. 228 p. fold. map.

A set of lectures by a noted Oxford historian of the British empire who had formerly been head of the Dominions Department of the Colonial Office. The first two chapters give pre-19th-century background; then nine talks expound with exemplary clarity the phases of the European penetration, rivalries, and wars in Africa. The last chapter assesses the results of World War I on the map of Africa and speculates on problems of the future, as 'millions of natives [become] year by year less unsophisticated and possessed of more race consciousness and more self-respect'.

The 19th-century standard history is Sir John Scott Keltie's *Partition of Africa* (1st ed., 1893; 2d ed., rev., 1895). It was further revised and edited by Professor Albert Galloway Keller of Yale and published with the title *Africa* in the History of Nations series edited by Henry Cabot Lodge (Memorial ed., New York, P. F. Collier & Son, 1928, 335 p.).

Documentation on the diplomatic aspects of the European take-over of Africa is provided in one of the Peace Handbooks series prepared by the Historical Section of the British Foreign Office, *Partition of Africa* (London, H.M. Stationery Office, 1920, 82 p.; Handbooks, no. 89). The appendix gives texts of the bilateral agreements and treaties of Great Britain with the other European powers concerning African colonies, 1890–1904.

The involvement of the European powers in Africa was treated importantly later in William L. Langer's basic works on European diplomatic history, *European alliances and alignments, 1871–1920* (1931; 2d ed., New York, Alfred Knopf, 1950; reprinted 1960, 510 p.); and *The diplomacy of imperialism, 1890–1902* (1935; 2d ed., New York, Alfred Knopf, 1950; reprinted 1962, 797 p.).

446 McEwan, P. J. M., ed. *Readings in African history* [*series*]. New York, Oxford University Press, 1968. 3 v.

> v. 1, *Africa from early times to 1800*. xxiv, 436 p. 14 maps.

> v. 2, *Nineteenth-century Africa*. xxiv, 488 p. 8 maps.

> v. 3, *Twentieth-century Africa*. xxiv, 517 p. 3 maps.

The volumes in this series present documents on African history. The editor has selected contrasting passages from recognized authorities on the most significant events and movements in the history of the continent. Volume 1 contains 41 selections, while v. 2 and 3 contain 45 and 50 selections respectively. Each volume includes an editorial introduction, maps, a chronological table and an index.

447 Mair, Lucy Philip. *Native policies in Africa*. London, George Routledge and Sons, 1936. Reprinted New York, Negro University Press, 1969, xi. 303 p., maps. Bibliography: p. 295–298.

The writer, a prominent British anthropologist, gives a general introduction on 'Europe's task in Africa'. She then traces the African policies in force, respectively, in 'the white man's countries' of South Africa, Southern Rhodesia and Kenya; in the various 'black' colonies under British rule; and in the French, Belgian and Portuguese territories. She concludes with a chapter on science and the future of Africa. There are statistical appendices with information on subjects such as wages, labour dues, number of Africans in employment, etc., in various parts of Africa. The author also produced a wealth of other studies, including *Welfare in the British colonies* (London, Royal Institute of International Affairs, 1944, 115 p.); *Primitive government* (Baltimore, Md., Penguin Books, 1962, v. 288 p., bibliography: p. 279–281), and *The New Africa* (London, Watts, 1967, 226 p.).

Another well-known work on African policy in the 1930s is Ifor Leslie Evans, *Native policy in Southern Africa: An outline* (Cambridge, Eng., The University Press, 1934, vi, 177 p., maps, notes and sources: p. 155–172).

448 Neill, Stephen Charles. *Colonialism and Christian missions.* New York, McGraw-Hill, 1966. 445 p. Bibliography: 426–429.

There are chapters on the history of slavery in Africa, the colonial policies of Portugal, Britain, France, Belgium and Germany in Africa and the effects on missions under their jurisdiction. An excellent anthropological analysis is Monica Hunter Wilson's *Reaction to conquest: Effects of contact with Europeans on the Pondo of South Africa* (London, 1961, 582 p.).

449 Oliver, Roland A. *Sir Harry Johnston and the scramble for Africa.* New York, St. Martin's Press, 1958 [c. 1957]. 368 p. illus.

A satisfactory telling of history through the medium of biography. In 10 years of intensive study of African history, says Mr. Oliver, 'no one personality has more constantly crossed my path' than Johnston, whose career as naturalist, explorer, civil servant, administrator, and historian extended to most parts of black Africa. Johnston's own works, including *The colonization of Africa* (1899) and *The opening up of Africa* (1911), as well as regional histories, linguistics, and zoological writings, are among the most important source works of his period.

Note Other biographies, which are of less continent-wide application, are noted in regional or topical sections of the present work.

450 Perreau Pradier, Pierre. *L'effort colonial des alliés.* Nancy, Paris, Berger-Levrault, 1919. 184 p. (Les grands problèmes coloniaux)

Part 1 is entitled 'La guerre dans les colonies'; Part 2, 'L'entr'aide coloniale des alliés'; and Part 3, 'La politique coloniale des alliés'.

451 Price, A. Grenfell. *White settlers in the tropics.* New York, American Geographical Society, 1939. (Special Publication, no. 23)

Valuable monograph appraising the experiences of tropical colonization.

452 Robinson, Ronald, and John Gallagher, with Alice Denny. *Africa and the Victorians: The official mind of imperialism.* London, Macmillan and Co., 1965. xii, 491 p. plates, maps, tables.

A major reassessment of British policy during the scramble. Specially emphasizes the importance of strategic motives, the role of the maritime route to India and the effects of British involvement in Egypt and the Cape. Based on a wide range of archival sources.

453 Rotberg, Robert, ed. *Africa and its explorers: Motives, methods, and impact.* Cambridge, Mass., Harvard University Press, 1970. 351 p. Bibliography: p. 323–32.

A series of interpretative essays investigating the careers of men who, 'by any European-derived standards, played a significant part in the opening up of Africa to the Western world'. Anthony Kirk-Greene writes on Heinrich Barth, Norman R. Bennett on David Livingstone, Caroline Oliver on Richard Burton, Roy C. Bridges on John Hanning Speke, Robert Collins on Samuel White Baker, Wolfe W. Schmokel on Gerhard Rohlfs, Eric Halliday on Henry Morton Stanley, James R. Hooker on Verney Lovett Cameron, and Robert Rotberg on Joseph Thomson.

454 Rotberg, Robert I., and Ali A. Mazrui, eds. *Protest and power in black Africa.* New York, Oxford University Press, 1970. xxx, 1,274 p. maps.

Each contributor provides a case study to illustrate the subject. The various sections cover successively particular instances of resistance to colonial conquest by African peoples, rebellions against alien rule, religious expressions of discontent, the emergence of pressure groups and political parties, the economic expression of discontent, the literary forms of protest, revolutions and coups, as well as problems of sovereignty and diplomacy in post-independent Africa.

455 U.S.S.R. Academy of Sciences. Institute of Africa. *A history of Africa 1918–1967.* Moscow, 'Nauka' Publishing House, Central Department of Oriental Literature, 1968. 540 p.

This is a translation of the second Russian edition of a work which first came out in 1964. The volume covers the whole of the continent, including Islamic Africa. The various countries of Africa are each covered by one contributor. This is the first comprehensive work on modern Africa compiled by Soviet writers. The framework is rigidly Marxist-Leninist. The work was compiled under the supervision of an editorial board composed of A. B. Davidson, M. Y. Frenkel, G. A. Nersesov and S. R. Smirnov (the editor-in-chief).

456 *West Africa.* 1917– . London, illus. Weekly.

Although the title indicates a limited geographic coverage, this long-established weekly magazine touches on most events in the continent south of the Sahara. For any study of the west coast from Mauritania to Angola it is indispensable. Among regular features, there appears in each issue a full-page biographical 'profile' of a prominent person, usually an African. There are three or four reviews of new books each week.

457 Zimmermann, Alfred. *Die europäischen Kolonien. Schilderung ihrer Entstehung, Entwicklung, Erfolge und Aussichten.* Berlin, E. S. Mittler und Sohn, 1896–1903. 5 v. Bibliography at the end of each volume.

Contents includes: 1 Bd., Die Kolonialpolitik Portugals und Spaniens; 2–3 Bd., Die Kolonialpolitik Grossbritanniens; 4 Bd., Die Kolonialpolitik Frankreichs; 5 Bd., Die Kolonialpolitik der Niederlande.

An important historical work.

LABOUR

Note See also Part III for works dealing with specific colonial powers, regions or countries.

BIBLIOGRAPHIES

458 African Bibliographic Center, Washington, D.C. *Le tiers monde : A select and preliminary bibliographic survey of manpower in developing countries, 1960–1964.* Comp. by Daniel G. Matthews. Washington, 1965. 30 p. processed. (Special Bibliographic Series, v. 3, no. 5)

459 African Bibliographic Center, Washington, D.C. *Trade unions in Africa : A select bibliography, 1960–1962.* Washington, 1962. 7 p. processed. (Special Bibliographic Series, Labor in Africa, v. 1, no. 1)

460 Friedland, William H. *Unions, labor and industrial relations in Africa : An annotated bibliography.* Ithaca, N.Y., Center for International Studies, Cornell University, 1965. 159 p. (Cornell Research Papers in International Studies, no. 4)

This excellent bibliography begins in unorthodox fashion with subject and geographic indexes (p. 7–16) and continues with 683 numbered and descriptively annotated entries in alphabetical order by author or title. The subject index has about 40 headings covering general surveys, bibliography, child labour, collective bargaining, conditions of work, conventions of the ILO, diet, disputes and strikes, etc. The compiler explains the chief sources in his introduction.

461 Panofsky, Hans E. *A bibliography of labor migration in Africa south of the Sahara.* Evanston, Ill., University Library, Northwestern University, 1961. 28 l.

Compiled by the curator of Africana of the Northwestern University Library and focused on a limited phase of the labour question, although a number of general works on labour in Africa are included. The arrangement is by region and includes an author index. The work provides extensive coverage of books and periodical materials in English and European languages up to mid-1961 and includes slight annotations and indication of reviews or précis in *African abstracts*. This bibliography was reproduced in the Inter-African Labour Institute report cited below (no. 464).

REFERENCE WORKS

462 Davies, Ioan. *African trade unions.* Middlesex, Eng., Baltimore, Md., Penguin Books, 1966. 256 p. (Penguin African Library, AP19) Bibliography: p. 233–244.

Davies, a lecturer in sociology at the University of Essex, covers labour policies of Britain, France and Belgium, industrialization and racial policies in South Africa and the growth of trade unions in Africa. A glossary and an index are included.

463 Inter-African Labour Institute. *Bulletin.* v. 1– , 1953– . London, Commission for Technical Cooperation in Africa. Quarterly.

The text is in English and in French.

The Institute was set up in 1948 as the permanent organ of the Inter-African Labour Conference, which operated under the aegis of CCTA. The *Bulletin* provides broad coverage of important aspects of African labour in its articles and also has bibliographical notes that include texts of labour legislation. It reports on the sessions of the Inter-African Labour Conference (see below, sixth, 1961) and regional conferences (first, Lagos, Dec. 1960).

464 Inter-African Labour Institute. *Migrant labour in Africa south of the Sahara : Proceedings under Item II of the agenda of the sixth Inter-African Labour Conference, Abidjan, 1961, and other relevant papers.* London, CCTA, 1962. 338 p. (Scientific Council for Africa South of the Sahara, no. 79)

Contains the report, conclusions and recommendations of the sixth session of the Inter-African Labour Conference; the questionnaire issued to the member governments and the answers received; six important articles published in the years 1959–61 in the Inter-African Labour Institute's *Bulletin*; and a bibliography compiled by Hans E. Panofsky. There is an index of authors and editors.

The Institute also prepares monographic studies of varying extent – e.g., *The human factors of productivity in Africa : A preliminary survey* (2d ed., Brazzaville, 1960, 156 p., diagrs.) – announcement of which may be found in the *Bulletin*.

Labour

465 International Labour Office. *African labour survey.* Geneva, 1958. xiv, 712 p. map, tables. (Studies and Reports, n.s. no. 48) Bibliography: p. 695–707.

The drafts of this survey, which had been authorized by the ILO in 1956, were examined by its Committee of Experts on Social Policy in Non-metropolitan Territories in late 1957. The final text was prepared under supervision of the director general, its primary purpose to provide a point of departure for future work in Africa south of the Sahara. All possible aspects bearing on labour are covered. Each chapter ends with a summary of conclusions, and the final chapter gives the general conclusions of the Committee of Experts, which in 1958 was replaced by a separate ILO African Field Office for liaison with the Economic Commission for Africa and an African Advisory Committee. Appendices are texts of ILO documents of standards and recommendations, citation of principal labour legislation of the countries of Africa, miscellaneous tables of statistics and a bibliography.

466 Meynaud, Jean, and Anisse Salah Bey. *Trade unionism in Africa : A study of its growth and orientation.* Trans. by Angela Brench. London, Methuen, 1967. 242 p. Bibliography: p. 161–163.

Survey of the evolution of African trade unionism to the mid-1960s, with emphasis on its political significance. Part 1 analyses socio-economic conditions and outside influences which led to establishment of the first trade unions in the primarily agricultural African countries. Part 2 examines the rise of the unions under colonial administration and their role in the national liberation movements. Part 3 discusses the development of Pan-African trade unionism and the participation of the African unions in the International Labour Organization. A glossary gives brief descriptions of the situation in each country and of the major trade-union organizations. The book concludes with a biographical section on seven African trade-union leaders, a 54-page documentary appendix and an index.

The work was originally published as *Le syndicalisme africain : Evolution et perspectives* (Paris, Payot, 1963, 260 p.; Etudes et documents Payot).

467 Noon, John A. *Labor problems of Africa.* Philadelphia, University of Pennsylvania Press, 1944. 144 p.

A useful account of the development of a wage class during World War II.

468 Orde-Browne, G. St. J. *The African labourer.* London, published for the International Institute of African Languages and Cultures by Oxford University Press, H. Milford, 1933. 240 p. map. Reprint: New York, Cass, 1968.

Pioneer study of the problems of African labour, by a former labour commissioner in Tanganyika who was subsequently a representative in the International Labor Organization and an adviser on colonial labour to the British Colonial Office. Part 1 is concerned with the background of African society and the first impact of foreign influences, the incentives offered the African for wage earning, forced labour, methods and conditions of recruiting and labour contracts, living and social conditions of labourers, etc. Part 2 contains a country-by-country summary of labour legislation, and Part 3 cites international draft conventions relative to African labour.

LAW

Note See also Part III for references to specific colonial powers, regions or countries.

BIBLIOGRAPHIES

469 African Law Association in America, Inc. *Bibliography of African Law.* Comp. by A. Arthur Schiller. New York, 1965– .
Various issues of the Association's *News Letter* were used to publish preliminary drafts of the African law bibliography. French Africa appeared first in 1965, then South Africa, Italian Africa, German Africa, Portuguese and Spanish Africa, then sections on individual countries. The bibliography is a most useful and full listing of all aspects of African law, especially valuable for the colonial period. There are usually sections on bibliographies, legislative enactments, compilations of law, treatises and monographs, gazettes and government reports.

470 *African law bibliography, 1947–1966.* Addis Ababa, Centre for African Legal Development, Faculty of Law, Haile Selassie I University; Bruxelles, Centre pour le Développement Juridique Africain, Institut de Sociologie, Université Libre de Bruxelles [1968].
This bibliography, which consists of titles of all books and articles on African law available at the Law Library of Haile Selassie I University, is being issued in two forms: separate cardboard sheets holding four perforated cards, with an entry on each card; and book form (at the end of 1968). There are an estimated 6,000 entries, titles being listed first by subject and thereunder by country.

471 Gilissen, John. *Introduction bibliographique à l'histoire du droit et à l'ethnologie juridique. Bibliographical introduction to legal history and ethnology.* Bruxelles, Ministère de l'Education Nationale et de la Culture, 1963– .
Three volumes had appeared by 1969. They cover South Africa, Ethiopia-Eritrea, Somaliland, and Madagascar.

472 *Index to Periodical Articles Related to Law.* v. 1– . 1958– . Stanford, Calif., Law Library, Stanford University. Quarterly.
Surveys periodicals containing articles on African law, excluding titles covered by the *Index to Legal Periodicals* and the *Index to Foreign Legal Periodicals.* A one-volume, six-year cumulation (1958–1964) has been issued.

473 Karal, Gulgan. *African legal and constitutional materials : An annotated bibliography.* Los Angeles, University of California, 1969. 125 p.
Bibliography on constitutional developments in Africa.

474 *A legal bibliography of the British Commonwealth of Nations.* v. 7, *The British Commonwealth excluding the United Kingdom, Australia, New Zealand, Canada, India and Pakistan.* Comp. by Leslie F. Maxwell. 2d ed. London, Sweet & Maxwell, 1964. 459 p.
    African section: p. 1–188.
New edition of a volume first published in 1949 (*British colonies, protectorates and mandate territories*). It has a large general section and is then broken down by regions, islands and countries (and by provinces, territories, or regions within specific countries). Articles, books, gazettes, reports, collections of statutes, ordinances, sessional papers, subsidiary legislation, etc., are covered, and there is a full index. An additional source for details of reports and periodicals is to be

found in *A complete list of British and colonial law reports and legal periodicals* by W. H. Maxwell and C. R. Brown (3d ed., 1937, with supplements thereafter).

475 Meek, Charles K. *Colonial law : A bibliography with special reference to native African systems of law and land tenure.* London, published for Nuffield College by Oxford University Press, 1948. xiii, 58 p.

Old standard bibliography by a leading British authority on land law and tenure in the colonies.

476 Schiller, A. Arthur. *African law.* South Hackensack, N.J., Fred B. Rothman & Co., 1970. xi, 175 p. (Association of American Law Schools, Law Books Recommended for Libraries, no. 39)

This volume includes books on the law of the territories in French Africa, German Africa, Italian Africa, Portuguese Africa, and Spanish Africa, and in the geographical regions and individual countries within North Africa (including Algeria, Morocco, Tunisia), northeast Africa (including Afars and Issas, Ethiopia, Somalia, Sudan), West Africa (including French West Africa and all the individual states of West Africa), and of South Africa, within the region of southern Africa. In the second volume, to be published in 1971, in addition to supplemental entries, law books devoted to all Africa, to the regions of West Central Africa, East Africa, and the remainder of southern Africa will be covered. The attempt has been made to be as complete as possible in those spheres and areas where bibliographies are virtually nonexistent (e.g., the law of the former colonies of Germany and Italy, or of many of the French and British possessions and their successor states, such as Dahomey, the Gambia, Guinea, Mali, etc.). The bibliography is more selective where comprehensive bibliographies already exist. In most cases the bibliographic entry is accompanied by an annotation by the author. An index of authors is included.

477 United Nations Educational, Scientific, and Cultural Organization. *Catalogue des sources de documentation juridique dans le monde : A register of legal documentation in the world.* Paris, 1953. 362 p.

An excellent guide to legal documentation in all countries. The index of places includes the names of many African countries but as dependencies under Great Britain, France, and the other metropolitan powers of pre-independence. For each country there are summarized legislation, the constitution, principal laws, collections of laws, jurisprudence, centres of legal activities and libraries, and periodicals and reviews.

REFERENCE WORKS

478 Afrika-Instituut (Netherlands). *The future of customary law in Africa. L'avenir du droit coutumier en Afrique.* Symposium-colloque, Amsterdam, 1955. Organized by the Afrika-Instituut, Studiecentrum, Leiden, in collaboration with the Royal Tropical Institute, Amsterdam. Leiden, Universitaire Pers Leiden, 1956. xvii, 305 p. Bibliography: p. 273–305.

Papers on the law of indigenous societies in Africa as exercised through the native courts and local jurisdictions in the former Belgian, British and French territories. Past development, present conditions and future possibilities under spreading detribalization were discussed.

479 Allott, Antony N., ed. *Judicial and legal systems in Africa.* London, Butterworth, 1962. xiii, 226 p. diagrs. (Butterworth's African Law Series, no. 4)

A thorough compilation, covering systems of the entire continent in digest form. For the most part, the institutions reported are little changed from those of pre-independence days; consequently the study is valuable for an understanding of the colonial period.

480 Anderson, James N. D. *Islamic law in Africa*. London, H.M. Stationery Office, 1954. 409 p. (Colonial Research Publication, no. 16) Bibliographical footnotes.

Survey prepared for the Colonial Office by the professor of Oriental laws in the University of London. His interest was in the interaction of Islamic law – the Shari'a – and the customary law of the various Muslim societies of British Africa and of the native law and Islamic law and institutions. Appendices include surveys of the Sudan and of the law as affecting immigrant Muslims, tables of ordinances and cases, and a glossary. There is a full index.

481 Butterworth's African Law Series. London, Butterworth, 1960– .

Excellent surveys of the legal system of individual African countries. Each volume includes a good historical survey. (See also the Sweet and Maxwell Series.)

482 *Journal of African Law*. v. 1, no. 1– , Spring 1957– . Ed. by Antony N. Allott. London, Butterworth. 3 times a year.

Designed as an organ for the discussion of general principles that might emerge from objective study, criticism and comparison of the diverse legal systems operative in Africa – the heterogeneous tribal laws, the variant forms of Islamic law, the British common law, the codes imported from France, Belgium and the other colonial powers.

483 Kuper, Hilda, and Leo Kuper, eds. *African law : Adaptation and development*. Pub. under the auspices of the African Studies Center, University of California, Los Angeles. Berkeley and Los Angeles, University of California Press, 1965. 275 p. Bibliography: p. 261–266.

An introduction by the editors is followed by 10 studies: 'The sociological framework of law ', by M. G. Smith; 'Land law in the making ', by Philip and Iona Mayer; 'Justice and judgment among the southern Ibo under colonial rule ', by Daryll Forde; 'A traditional legal system: The Kuba ', by Jan Vansina; 'Reasonableness and responsibility in the law of segmentary societies ', by Max Gluckman; 'The adaptation of Muslim law in sub-Saharan Africa ', by J. N. D. Anderson; 'L'évolution de la législation dans les pays africains d'expression française et à Madagascar ', by Gabriel d'Arboussier; 'The evolution of law and government in modern Africa ', by T. O. Elias; 'The adaptation of customary family law in South Africa ', by Leslie Rubin; and 'The future of African law ', by Antony N. Allott.

LITERATURE

Note See also Part III for references to specific countries and regions.

BIBLIOGRAPHIES

484 Abrash, Barbara. *Black African literature in English since 1952 : Works and criticism*. New York, Johnson Reprint Corp., 1967. xiv, 92 p.

A worthy contribution to African literature studies. Listed first are bibliographies and works of criticism (books and journal articles, the latter arranged by subject). Mrs. Abrash then lists the major African authors alphabetically, citing their full-length works, reviews of these works, short stories, anthologies in which the author's work appears, and critical articles on his work.

485 Jahn, Janheinz. *A bibliography of neo-African literature from Africa, America, and the Caribbean.* New York, Praeger, 1965. xxxv, 359 p.
Editorial matter in English, French and German. (A revised and expanded edition appeared in 1971.)

The African material (p. 4–129) is arranged by region following the listing of anthologies on Africa as a whole: western, central, eastern, and southern Africa. The German edition is titled *Die neoafrikanische Literatur : Gesamtbibliographie von den Anfängen bis zur Gegenwart* (Düsseldorf, Diederichs, 1965, xxxv, 359 p.). See also Bernth Lindfors, ' Additions and corrections to Janheinz Jahn's *Bibliography of neo-African literature* (1965) ', *African Studies Bulletin*, v. 11, no. 2, Sept. 1968, p. 129–148. A useful guide to African publications during the colonial period.

REFERENCE WORKS

486 Cartey, Wilfred, and Martin Kilson, eds. *The African reader.* New York, Random House, 1970. 2 v.
Volume 1 covers colonial Africa. See also Cartey's *Whispers from a continent : The literature of contemporary black Africa* (New York, Random House, 1969. 397 p.).

487 Congrès International des Ecrivains et Artistes Noirs, 1st, Paris, Sept. 1956. *Contributions.* Paris, Présence Africaine, 1958. 363 p. ports. (*Présence Africaine*, n.s. no. 14–15, June–Sept. 1957)

488 ———— 2d, Rome, Mar.–Apr. 1959. *Responsabilités des hommes de culture.* Paris, Présence Africaine, 1959. 368 p. (*Présence Africaine*, n.s. no. 27–28, Aug.–Nov. 1959)
The first International Congress of Negro Writers and Artists was called by Alioune Diop, founder and editor of the journal *Présence Africaine*, which is the chief organ of French-speaking African intellectuals. It was well attended by Negro writers from many parts of Africa and from the United States. The second Congress, three years later, was given still more attention. Papers contributed at both sessions were concerned with the manifestations of African culture: in 1956, with literature, art, theatre, dance, etc., but also with political expression, particularly the expression of race and culture conflicts; in 1959, with the concept of négritude, with the recreation of African history, African philosophy, and, in general, the assertion of the African personality in the arts and social sciences.

The influence of African art and music on the Western world was the main theme of a conference, the International Congress of African Culture, held in Salisbury, Rhodesia, in August 1962. About 70 delegates from Africa, the Americas, Europe and the West Indies were invited to give papers.

489 Eliet, Edouard. *Panorama de la littérature négro-africaine, 1921–1962.* Paris, Présence Africaine, 1965. 263 p.
A sensitive study of 40 years of Negro-African literary developments. The introduction includes a discussion of Etienne Lero and of the concept of négritude. Part 1 covers poetry, specifically that of Rabearivelo, Senghor, Césaire, Fodéba, Rabemananjara, and Diop. Part 2 deals with the novel and the works of Maran, Dadié, Oyono, Beti, Roumain, Alexis, and Laye. The concluding Part 3 covers essays and critiques and the writings of Césaire and Fanon. Eliet uses

a literary approach to African writings in contrast to Kesteloot's more historical approach (see no. 491).

490 Gleason, Judith Illsley. *This Africa : Novels by West Africans in English and French*. Evanston, Ill., Northwestern University Press, 1965. xix, 186 p. illus. (Northwestern University African Studies, no. 14) Bibliography: p. 178–186.

A discussion of the influence of colonial rule precedes consideration of some 25 novels, 17 originally of French expression, 8 in English, mainly West African. These are grouped into novels of the African past, novels about village life, novels of the cities, and finally novels of psychic conflict in which traditional Africa and imperial Europe play symbolic parts. See also no. 725.

491 Kesteloot, Lilyan. *Les écrivains noirs de langue française : Naissance d'une littérature*. Bruxelles, Institut de Sociologie, Université Libre de Bruxelles, 1963. 340 p. (Etudes Africaines) Bibliography: p. 331–340.

A detailed, well-documented history and analysis of the origins, evolution, and present state of the works of French-speaking black writers in Africa, the West Indies, and the United States. Interwoven throughout the book are the cultural, sociological, and political factors influencing these writers. Special attention is given to the works of Léon Damas, Aimé Césaire, and Léopold Senghor, and to the origins and influence of the journal *Présence Africaine*. There is an index of authors and journals.

492 Killam, G. D. *Africa in English fiction*. Ibadan, 1968. 200 p.

Excellent study of the myths and attitudes of English authors about Africa. A good, selective bibliography. See also no. 490. For a good overview of the press in Africa, see William A. Hachten, *Muffled drums : The news media in Africa* (Iowa State University Press, 1971, 314 p.).

493 Pageard, Robert. *Littérature négro-africaine : Le mouvement littéraire contemporain dans l'Afrique noire d'expression française*. Paris, Le Livre Africain, 1966. 138 p. Bibliography: p. 119–120; Bio-bibliography: p. 121–128.

A literary history of African writers in French-speaking black Africa during the colonial period, 1920–46, the period of the French Union, 1946–58, and the early era of independence, 1958–64. The second part of the book covers African literature by type, including chapters on political and social works, theories of African personality, oral tradition and ethno-history, modern histories, the novel, the short story, theatre and poetry. Biographical sketches are given, and there are both author and title indexes.

494 Ramsaran, J. A. *New Approach to African literature : A guide to Negro-African writing and related studies*. Ibadan, Ibadan University, 1965. 177 p.

Essays on oral and traditional literature in the various regions of Africa, on modern writing in Western languages and vernaculars, and on Caribbean and American literature. Each essay is followed by a book list.

495 Senghor, Léopold Sédar, ed. *Anthologie de la nouvelle poésie nègre et malgache de langue française, précédée de ' Orphée noir ' par Jean-Paul Sartre*. Paris, Presses Universitaires de France, 1948, xliv, 227 p. (Colonies et empires, 5e sér., Art et littérature)

By the celebrated French African poet and apostle of négritude – also political leader up to independence for Senegal and currently President of that country – this anthology includes the most famous poems by blacks and Malagasy brought up in the French culture, with bio-bibliographical sketches of the authors. The volume has as its introduction the essay by Jean-Paul Sartre, ' Orphée noir ' (black Orpheus), which introduced the concept of négritude to the French literary world.

Among the more recent anthologies and biographical studies are two volumes by Armand Guibert, *Léopold Sédar Senghor* (Paris, Seghers, 1961, 215 p., ports.; Poètes d'aujourd'hui, no. 82; bibliography, p. 205–211), and *Léopold Sédar Senghor: L'homme et l'oeuvre* (Paris, Présence Africaine, 1962, 175 p., illus.); an anthology with commentary by Robert Mercier and Monique and Simon Battestini, *L. S. Senghor, poète sénégalais* (Paris, F. Nathan, 1965, 63 p.; Classiques du monde, Littérature africaine, no 3); and a volume of Senghor's works selected and translated by John Reed and Clive Wake, *Prose and poetry* (London, Oxford University Press, 1965, 181 p.; bibliography, p. 173–182).

496 Wauthier, Claude. *The literature and thought of modern Africa: A survey.* Trans. by Shirley Kay. London, Pall Mall Press, 1966; New York, Praeger, 1967. 323 p. (Library of African Affairs) Bibliography: p. 286–295.

This revised version of the original French edition, *L'Afrique des africains: Inventaire de la négritude* (Paris, Editions du Seuil, 1964, 314 p.; Collection 'L'histoire immédiate'), is updated to 1966 with regard to major political events. Wauthier, a correspondent of Agence France Presse specializing in African affairs, discusses the works of some 150 African writers and intellectuals as he traces the parallel development of cultural revival and the demand for independence. The main substance of the book covers the literature up to May 1963 and is confined to former colonial Africa. Part 1 is concerned with writings in the *linguae francae* (pidgin, creole, etc.) and with African folklorists and historians. In Part 2 the literature of revolt against colonialism is considered, and in Part 3 themes of the new Africa. The bibliography cites over 300 works, mostly by Africans. There is a name index and a subject and title index.

MEDICINE AND HEALTH

Note See also Part III for works dealing with specific countries and regions.

BIBLIOGRAPHIES

497 Frank, M. K., comp. *Bibliography of East African literature on bilharziasis (including that of Malawi, Rhodesia, Sudan and Zambia) presents material published between 1933 and 1964.* Mwanza, Tanzania, East African Institute for Medical Research, 1965. 16 p. 35 cm.

Selected list of references to books, reports, and articles on bilharziasis in various African countries, with the first of two parts devoted to East Africa. Under each country, arrangement is alphabetical by author. An expanded edition is planned.

498 Klingelhofer, E. L. *A bibliography of psychological research and writings on Africa.* Dar es Salaam, University College, University of East Africa, 1967. 31 p. mimeo.

Lists mainly articles but also includes books, conference proceedings, dissertations, and mimeographed papers covering the period from as early as 1895 to 1966. Arrangement is by subject, and most entries are in English. The work updates J. Hopkins's 'Bibliographie des recherches psychologiques conduites en Afrique', *Revue de Psychologie Appliquée*, v. 12, no. 3, 1962, p. 201–213.

499 Langlands, B. W., comp. *Bibliography of the distribution of disease in East Africa (complete to 1963).* Kampala, Makerere University College, 1965. 184 p. (Makerere Library Publication, no. 3)
Chiefly a listing of medical geographic articles and papers. References under each geographical entity – East Africa, Kenya, Uganda, Tanganyika, Zanzibar, and Ruanda-Urundi – are first listed in a general section and according to type of disease (alphabetically arranged). Except for the East African section, entries are then further broken down into administrative subsections. An index of diseases and an author index are included.

500 *Liste des périodiques africains de la bibliothèque.* [Title also in Flemish] Bruxelles, Service de Documentation des Sciences Naturelles, Institut Royal des Sciences Naturelles de Belgique, 1960. unpaged.
Practically all 223 African periodicals received by the library of the Institut Royal des Sciences Naturelles in Brussels are publications of learned institutions devoted to the natural sciences.

REFERENCE WORKS

501 *Bulletin of Hygiene.* 1926– . London, Bureau of Hygiene and Tropical Diseases. Monthly.
This has superseded the Sanitation supplements of the *Tropical Diseases Bulletin.* Both journals give considerable emphasis to Africa.

502 Carothers, John C. *The African mind in health and disease : A study in ethnopsychiatry.* Geneva, World Health Organization, 1953. 177 p. diagr. (World Health Organization Monograph Series, no. 17) Bibliography: p. 173–177.
By a former colonial medical officer and consultant in mental health to WHO. This technical study, full of statistics, draws on the author's own experience and that of many other authorities to examine African psychology against the background of the environment, physical anthropology and other factors. Dr. Carothers includes comparative consideration of the psychology and psychiatry of the Negro in the United States.

503 Colbourne, Michael James. *Malaria in Africa.* London, Ibadan, etc., Oxford University Press, 1966. 115 p. map, tables, diagrs. (Students' Library)
A survey for medical students and laymen which discusses the causes and effects of malaria, its treatment and eradication. The author, a WHO adviser on malaria eradication, was Government Malariologist in Ghana from 1952 to 1955 and is now head of the Department of Social Medicine and Public Health, University of Singapore.
    For a history of malaria in 19th-century Africa and its effects on European exploration, see Michael Gelfand, *Rivers of death in Africa* (London, Oxford University Press, 1964, 100 p., maps). See also R. Mansell Prothero, *Migrants and malaria* (no. 508), and, for a technical, specialized study, David F. Clyde, *Malaria in Tanzania* (London, Oxford University Press, 1967).

504 Commission for Technical Co-operation in Africa South of the Sahara. *Inter-African scientific and technical co-operation, 1948–1955.* London, Commission for Technical Co-operation in Africa South of the Sahara [CCTA] and Scientific Council for Africa South of the Sahara [CSA], 1956 ? xv, 294 p. maps.
This comprehensive report was issued after eight years' work by the inter-African organizations that were formed to provide long-term programs of technical and

scientific conferences and exchanges of technical and research information and specialists.

The report details conferences held, projects, and recommendations of the bodies from 1948, when the idea was first proposed, to 1955. The first chapters describe the organization of CCTA/CSA (established in 1950) and the scope and accomplishment of the bureaux set up under it, which represent 'a network of technical co-operation covering practically every field of technical activity in Africa south of the Sahara'. The list of bureaux and committees is followed by an index of technical conferences held, in five groups: natural resources, health, organization of production, social welfare, and statistics. The final page gives the list of CSA publications. A bi-monthly information bulletin, *Science-Afrique*, was issued by CCTA/CSA from 1956 to 1961.

505 Gelfand, Michael. *The sick African : A clinical study.* 3d ed. Cape Town, Juta, 1957. 866 p. illus. Bibliography: p. 793–842.

A handbook on diseases most common to the people of Africa – 'destined', said a reviewer *in African Affairs* at the time of its first publication (1944), 'to lie upon the table of doctors, nuns, priests, medical missionaries, colonial administrators, in fact, every white man and woman working in Equatorial Africa who has to treat the sick African'. The preliminary chapters discuss popular fallacies regarding tropical diseases and African psychology: the African's fear of hospitals and his conviction that some illnesses are caused by witchcraft. Succeeding chapters describe and analyse individual diseases and give directions for their treatment, in a non-technical style. Most of Dr. Gelfand's other studies relate specifically to the Rhodesias and Nyasaland, although a 1964 book is entitled *Medicine and custom in Africa* (Edinburgh, E. and S. Livingstone, 174 p.). The author holds the Chair of African Medicine at the University of Rhodesia.

506 Harley, George Way. *Native African medicine : With special reference to its practice in the Mano tribe of Liberia.* Cambridge, Mass., Harvard University Press, 1941. xvi, 294 p. Bibliography: p. 255–263.

An ethnographic study by a famous missionary of West Africa. A supplement treats of African medical practices throughout Africa.

507 New York. Missionary Research Library. *Directory of Protestant medical missions.* Comp. by Arthur W. March. New York, 1959. 134 p.

In this long list there is first a statistical survey by continent and country, Africa leading, with the name of each mission followed by figures of size, number of patients, doctors, nurses, and other pertinent data. Next a separate index of leprosy missions in Africa and Asia is given.

508 Prothero, R. Mansell. *Migrants and malaria.* London, Longmans, 1965. 142 p. illus., maps. Includes bibliographies.

This book on medical geography, by a sometime consultant to the World Health Organization, is concerned with the influence of all human factors on malaria and its eradication in Africa. Prothero describes malaria at some length and explains the significance of population mobility in Africa. The bulk of the book deals with the situation in the Sudan, Horn of Africa, east and south-central Africa, West Africa, and Morocco. An index is included.

509 *Tropical Diseases Bulletin.* 1912– . London, Bureau of Hygiene and Tropical Diseases. Monthly.

This abstracting/indexing journal is very useful for African material.

Part II: subject guide for Africa in general

510 Trowell, Hubert C. *Non-infective disease in Africa: The peculiarities of medical non-infective diseases in the indigenous inhabitants of Africa south of the Sahara.* London, E. Arnold [on cover: Baltimore, Williams & Wilkins], 1960. 481 p. illus. Includes bibliography.

Technical study of diseases common among Africans but seldom found elsewhere. 'Examples are endomyocardial fibrosis, idiopathic cardiomyopathy, siderosis, porphyria, primary carcinoma of the liver, kwashiorkor and some of the haemoglobinopathies'. The author is a clinician with 29 years' experience in East Africa as well as work in other parts of Africa south of the Sahara.

NATURAL SCIENCES

Note In this section, the chief stress is on works involving nature and the physical sciences, with much lesser emphasis upon man's part in the development of nature. For material on agriculture and mining, for example, see under Economics. See also Part III for references to specific countries and regions.

BIBLIOGRAPHIES

Note Bibliographies of all-African coverage in the general field of natural sciences are those included in the reference works named below, notably in the UNESCO review of natural resources (no. 519) and in the two volumes by Worthington (nos. 520 and 521). Organizations of intercontinental scope are the CCTA/CSA and its affiliates, now merged in the Organization of African Unity (OAU).

Although 40 serials are indexed under science in the Library of Congress *Serials for African studies*, only the now-discontinued bulletin of CCTA/CSA, *Science-Afrique*, applies to all Africa. Others are regional, though often of broad extent, like *Bulletin A, Sciences Naturelles* of the Institut Fondamental d'Afrique Noire or the scientific publications series *Science-Afrique*.

REFERENCE WORKS

511 Bannerman, David Armitage. *The birds of West and Equatorial Africa.* Edinburgh, Oliver & Boyd, 1953. 2 v. xiii, 1,526 p.

Handbook with full descriptions in clear, simple language and with technical data; illustrated with drawings and colour plates of all species. The two-volume edition is condensed from an eight-volume work by this leading British ornithologist, *Birds of tropical west Africa* (London, Crown Agents for the Colonies, 1930–51). A portion of the handbook has been further condensed for a popular audience in a volume of the Penguin Books series, *Larger birds of West Africa* (Harmondsworth, Middlesex; Baltimore, Md., 1958, 195 p.).

512 Copley, Hugh. *The game fishes of Africa.* London, H. F. & G. Witherby, 1952. 276 p. illus.

Designed as a standard reference book, a companion volume to the time-honoured work of Richard Lydekker, *The game animals of Africa* (2d ed., rev. by J. G. Dollman, London, Ward, 1926, 483 p.).

Natural sciences

A good series of illustrated handbooks on animals by Charles T. Astley Maberly has been published by H. Timmins in Cape Town, *Animals of Rhodesia* (1959, 211 p.), *Animals of southern Africa* (1959, 211 p.), and *Animals of East Africa* (1960, 211 p), as well as a more recent volume from Nelson in Johannesburg, *The game animals of southern Africa* (1963, 292 p.).

513 De Kun, N. A. *The mineral resources of Africa.* Amsterdam, Elsevier, 1965. 740 p. illus., maps. Bibliography: p. 683–697.

A large, important study. The first part is on industrial development and mineral economics (African production value and distribution by groups of minerals, history and development of mining, in general and by regions); Part 2 is economic geology, broken down by mineral groups. The first appendix gives conversion factors, the second a list of companies, individuals, and organizations engaged in mineral and related industries, many of which go back to the colonial period.

514 Furon, Raymond. *Les ressources minérales de l'Afrique: Géologie et mines, la production africaine dans le monde, la production régionale, les nouveaux problèmes.* 2d ed. Paris, Payot, 1961. 284 p. maps, diagrs. (Bibliothèque économique)

The first edition of Professor Furon's survey of mineral resources came out in 1944. The second edition is extensively revised and modernized, with a general and historical introduction, a classification and allocation of individual mineral products, discussion of their regional importance, and a concluding section on prospects and problems for the future.

515 Hutchinson, John, and J. M. Dalziel. *Flora of west tropical Africa, the British west African colonies, British Cameroon, the French and Portuguese colonies south of the Tropic of Cancer to Lake Chad, and Fernando Po.* Prepared at the Herbarium, Royal Botanic Gardens, Kew, under the supervision of the Director. London, Crown Agents for Overseas Governments and Administrations, 1954–63. 2 v. in 4. illus. Includes bibliographies.

An earlier issue of this work was supplemented by J. M. Dalziel, *The useful plants of west tropical Africa, being an appendix to the flora of west tropical Africa* (London. Published under the authority of the Secretary of State for the Colonies by the Crown Agents for the Colonies, 1948 [c. 1937], xii, 612 p.).

516 Irvine, Frederick Robert. *West African botany.* 2d ed., rev. London, Oxford University Press, 1956. 203 p. illus.

A standard work.

517 Mackworth-Praed, Cyril W., and Claude H. B. Grant. *Birds of eastern and north eastern Africa.* 2d ed. London, New York, Longmans, Green, 1957–60. 2 v. (African Handbook of Birds, ser. 1, v. 1–2)

A reprint, with additions, of the first edition of this authoritative ornithological handbook which was published in 1952–55. The various species of birds are catalogued with brief descriptions and diagrams and illustrated in black-and-white drawings and colour plates. The two large volumes have, respectively, 806 and 1,113 pages, with full unpaged indexes of scientific and popular names.

518 Skaife, Sydney H. *African insect life.* London and New York, Longmans, Green, 1953. 387 p. illus.

By a South African entomologist, this book is written ' in language as simple as is consistent with scientific accuracy'. Arrangement is systematic by orders, from lowest to highest – primitive insects, cockroaches, to bees and wasps, ants. Illustrated with drawings and photographs. The few colour plates are mostly of the more amiable insects, moths and butterflies.

519 United Nations Educational, Scientific and Cultural Organization. *Review of geology and mineral investigation in Africa.* By Frank Dixey; Prepared for the Economic Commission for Africa. Paris, UNESCO, 1959. 77, 6, 25 p. (E/CN.14/30, Dec. 10, 1959)

Published by UNESCO in a series of surveys of resources, this report is the work of a distinguished British scientist, for many years director of geological research in Nyasaland. It provides a résumé of current geological knowledge in general, covering geological surveys, departments of mines, governmental interest in prospecting and mining, mining companies, universities, scientific societies and research organizations, international collaboration, interterritorial and foreign technical aid, etc. The author outlines the present state of mineral investigation and development, as well as the search for new mineral deposits. The report ends with recommendations. A list of geological research organizations and a bibliography of geological maps make up two appendices.

An earlier work of somewhat the same nature by Mr. Dixey was *Colonial geological surveys, 1947–56: A review of progress* (London, H.M. Stationery Office, 1957, 129 p., illus., maps).

520 Worthington, Edgar B. *Science in Africa: A review of scientific research relating to tropical and southern Africa.* London and New York, Oxford University Press, 1938. xiii, 746 p. maps., diagrs. Bibliography: p. 626–691.

The bibliography in this pioneer work is arranged by chapters: surveys and maps, geology, meteorology, soil science, botany, forestry, zoology, fisheries, entomology, agriculture, health and medicine, and anthropology. A list of authorities who assisted is included.

521 ——— *Science in the development of Africa: A review of the contribution of physical and biological knowledge south of the Sahara.* London, Commission for Technical Co-operation in Africa South of the Sahara, 1958. xix, 462 p. illus., maps (1 fold. col.). Bibliography: p. 421–435.

Survey by the first secretary-general of CCTA/CSA, 1950–55. It covers research for all Africa recorded in Dr. Worthington's earlier book, *Science in Africa*, and work accomplished or projected under the aegis of CCTA and affiliated international organizations. The appendices give lists of abbreviations, of the principal inter-African meetings from 1948 to 1956, and of scientific bodies and services. See also Dorothy Smith, 'Scientific research centers in Africa', *African Studies Bulletin*, v. 10, no. 3, 1967, p. 20–47; and CCTA, *Directory of scientific institutes, organizations and services in Africa* (Publication no. 14 of CCTA, 1954).

POLITICS

Note See also Part III, Area Guide, for references to specific countries, regions and colonial powers.

BIBLIOGRAPHIES

522 Alderfer, Harold F. *A bibliography of African government, 1950–1966.* 2d and rev. ed. Lincoln University, Pa., Lincoln University Press, 1967. 163 p.

Entries, in English or French, cover the entire continent. Following a general section, arrangement is by region and then by country, with book and article subdivisions. Under ' books ' are included unpublished manuscripts, government documents, pamphlets, conference proceedings, doctoral dissertations and chapters from larger works. There is an author index. The Institute of African Government of Lincoln University plans to update this bibliography with supplements. See also Francis Carnell, *The politics of the new states* . . . (London, 1961, 171 p.).

523 Boston University. African Studies Program. Development Research Center. *Bibliographie sélective d'ouvrages de langue française sur les problèmes gouvernementaux et administratifs (notamment en Afrique). Select bibliography of French-speaking works on governmental and administrative problems (with special attention to Africa).* Ed. by Edouard Bustin. Boston, Nov. 1963. 36 p.

This bibliography, which is more or less preliminary to *A selective bibliography of books, articles and documents on the subject of African administrative problems* (see no. 524 below), was prepared specifically for the needs of institutions in French-speaking Africa. It includes much material on governmental and administrative problems in general as well as those with special reference to Africa. Arrangement is by technical subject headings, e.g., ' Personnel management and training '.

524 Boston University. African Studies Program. Development Research Center. *A selective bibliography of books, articles and documents on the subject of African administrative problems.* [Title also in French] Prepared under contract for the Agency of International Development. Boston, 1964. 51 p.

This bibliography, prepared by Dr. Wilbert J. Le Melle, follows the same pattern as *Select bibliography of French-speaking works* . . . (see no. 523 above), though it includes works in English as well as in French and applies more widely to the new African nations. See also the *Catalog of African government documents and African area index*, published by G. K. Hall for Boston University in 1961 (no. 297).

525 Conover, Helen F., comp. *Non self-governing areas with special emphasis on mandates and trusteeships : A selected list of references.* Washington, D.C., Library of Congress, 1947. 2 v. Africa section: p. 280–333.

A most valuable source for books, articles, government documents dealing with African mandates.

526 Engelborghs-Bertels, Marie. *Les pays de l'Est et la décolonisation particulièrement en Afrique : Bibliographie.* Bruxelles, 1962. 62 p. (Académie Royale des Sciences d'Outre-Mer, Classe des sciences morales et politiques, Mémoires in-8°, n.s. v. 28, fasc. 2, Histoire).

Annotated list of articles in journals of the Soviet bloc countries regarding colonialism, anti-colonialism, and national liberation. Arrangement is by countries of publication, with subdivision by African countries. Titles in Eastern European languages and Chinese are given in French translation. The annotations in many cases are essentially abstracts.

527 Hanna, William John, and Judith Lynne Hanna. *Politics in black Africa : A selective bibliography of relevant periodical literature.* East Lansing, African Studies Center, Michigan State University, 1964. 139 p. offset print.

The list of articles in English and French is arranged in categories. There are 17 in all: tradition and change, communication, towns and urbanization, economy, etc. Items total 1,283, with index of names.

Part II: subject guide for Africa in general

528 Hertefelt, Marcel. *African governmental systems in static and changing conditions: A bibliographic contribution to political anthropology.* Tervuren, Musée Royal de l'Afrique Centrale, 1968. 178 p.
A listing of 1,269 entries (books and articles).

529 McGowan, Patrick J. *African politics, a guide to research sources, methods, and literature.* Syracuse, New York, 1970. 130 p. (Syracuse University, Program of Eastern African Studies, Occasional Paper, no. 55)
A most valuable bibliographical reference book for students of African politics. There are two main parts. The first cites references and guides, handbooks, bibliographies – both of general and of African interest; the second lists a select number of items on political change in Africa. Although the annotations are brief, McGowan comes close to providing a Winchell for African studies. He describes many bibliographies, bibliographic tools and provides information on libraries, catalogues, special collections, and various lists for locating material. Since it is a draft edition there are many misprints.

530 Perham, Margery. *Colonial government: Annotated reading list on British colonial government, with some general and comparative material upon foreign empires, etc., with an introduction.* London. Published for Nuffield College by Oxford University Press, 1950. xvii, 80 p. (Nuffield College Colonial Reading Lists, no. 1)
The author has been director of the Institute of Colonial Studies as well as a long-time Fellow of Nuffield College. She is among the best-known writers on government of developing countries. As the title indicates, this list is not limited to British colonial administration but includes references on French, Belgian and other colonial systems.

REFERENCE WORKS

531 Carter, Gwendolen M., ed. *National unity and regionalism in eight African states: Nigeria, Niger, the Congo, Gabon, Central African Republic, Chad, Uganda, Ethiopia.* Ithaca, N.Y., Cornell University Press, 1966. xiii, 565 p. maps. Includes bibliographies.
The third and final volume of essays on individual African states edited by Miss Carter. Her introduction is followed by essays which give a broad political, economic and historical account of the country concerned. Richard L. Sklar, C. S. Whitaker, Jr., Virginia Thompson, John A. Ballard, Donald Rothchild, Michael Rogin, and Robert L. Hess contribute essays. The essays on the four equatorial states (the 'Congo' refers to Congo-Brazzaville) and that on Niger are especially useful since they survey countries about which there is a paucity of material in English. See also Carter, ed., *African one-party states* (Cornell Univ. Press, 1962, 501 p.). Covers Senegal, Guinea, Ivory Coast, Tanganyika and Liberia. See also *Five African states*, edited by Gwendolen M. Carter (Ithaca, N.Y., Cornell University Press, 1963; London, Pall Mall Press, 1964).

532 Cohn, Helen Desfosses. *Soviet policy towards black Africa: The focus on national integration.* New York, Praeger, 1972. 316 p. Bibliography: p. 273–316.
An exhaustive inquiry concerning Soviet theories of modern nation-building in Africa, the process of social stratification and the prospects of socialism. The bibliography is particularly valuable for its detailed listing of modern Russian books and articles. It is divided into 'communist' and 'non-communist sources'.
David Morison, *The U.S.S.R. and Africa* (London, Oxford University Press,

Politics

1964, 124 p.), provides a brief discussion of Soviet aims, attitudes and the state of African studies. The appendix contains a country-by-country survey of Soviet attitudes with source references. Arthur Jay Klinghoffer, *Soviet perspectives on African socialism* (Rutherford, Fairleigh Dickenson University Press, 1969), should also be consulted for Soviet views concerning decolonization. It likewise contains a good bibliography of Soviet material (p. 249–268). A recent study by V. G. Solodovnikov, A. B Letnev, and P. Manchka entitled *Politicheskyiye Partii Afriki* (Moscow, 1970) has been put out in English in mimeographed form: United States Department of Commerce, Joint Publications Research Service, *Political parties of Africa [A Soviet Study]* (Arlington, Virginia, 1971, 340 p.).

533 Coleman, James S. 'Politics of sub-Saharan Africa', in Almond, Gabriel A., and James S. Coleman, eds., *The politics of the developing areas*, p. 247–368. Princeton, N.J., Princeton University Press, 1960.

Professor Coleman focuses his discussion on the great diversity of African traditional and evolving political systems and on the racial and tribal pluralism which complicates the establishment of new governments. He includes tables of population, degree of commercialization, political groups, types of élites, etc.

534 Coleman, James S., and Belmont Brice, Jr. 'The role of the military in sub-Saharan Africa', in Johnson, John J., ed., *The role of the military in underdeveloped countries*, p. 359–405. Princeton, N.J., Princeton University Press, 1962.

The authors examine the military legacy of the colonial powers and the national military situation, buildup, and policies in the new nations.

535 Decraene, Philippe. *Tableau des partis politiques de l'Afrique au sud du Sahara*. Paris, Fondation Nationale des Sciences Politiques, Centre d'Etude des Relations Internationales, 1963. 137 l. (Sér. C, Recherches, no. 8, May 1963)

A valuable brochure, in two parts, the first an analysis of the development and role of political parties in sub-Saharan Africa, the second a country-by-country inventory of the principal parties. In the latter, data on each party include an outline and dates of history, present status, program, and names of leaders. The index, p. 124–135, lists the parties by their initials. See also his *Le panafricanisme* (Paris, 1970, 128 p.).

536 Fortes, Meyer, and E. E. Evans-Pritchard. *African political systems.* London, published for the International Institute of African Languages and Cultures by Oxford University Press, H. Milford, 1940. xxiii, 301 p. maps, geneal. tables, diagrs. Reprint in paperback ed.: Oxford University Press, 1961.

A group of short surveys by prominent anthropologists, a number of the essays being taken from longer works by the same writers. The peoples studied are representative of the major political groupings of Africa. The writers vary in treatment, some concentrating on traditional patterns, others on the changes made under European rule.

A complementary work, *Tribes without rulers : Studies in African segmentary systems*, ed. by John Middleton and David Tait (London, Routledge & Kegan Paul, 1958, 234 p.), relates largely to tribes of the southern Sudan and East Africa.

537 Geiss, Imanuel. *Panafrikanismus : Zur Geschichte der Dekolonisation.* Frankfurt am Main, Europäische Verlagsanstalt, 1968. 489 p. maps. Bibliography: p. 457–474.

A major work by a student of the German historian Fritz Fischer, who has

147

previously worked on trade unionism in Africa as well as on German history. Geiss first of all defines Pan-Africanism, and links it to the 'triangle of trade' in the Atlantic and to American slavery. He subsequently discusses what he calls 'proto-Panafricanism'; the settlements of Liberia and Sierra Leone; Methodism and early nationalism on the Gold Coast; emigration from the United States; and early demands for equal rights, as well as independent African churches. The second section of the book relates to the formulation of Pan-African thought between 1900 and 1945 both in the New World and in Africa. It covers, among other subjects, the role played by men such as Garvey and Du Bois; Pan-African thought in France and the French colonies; Pan-Africanism in Great Britain; the impact of the Second World War and of the Fifth Pan-African Congress in Manchester, 1945. The writer concludes with a general appraisal of Pan-Africanism between 1945 and 1966, as well as the role of Pan-Africanism in history. There is a detailed bibliography covering archival sources, private collections and published works. The work, by its thorough coverage, supersedes valuable previous accounts such as Thomas Hodgkin's or Colin Legum's.

538 Hodgkin, Thomas. *Nationalism in colonial Africa.* London, F. Muller, 1956. 216 p. illus.

539 ——— *African political parties : An introductory guide.* Harmondsworth, Middlesex, Penguin Books, [1962, c. 1961]. 217 p. (Penguin African Series, WA 12)

Two works widely hailed as authoritative surveys of the politics of the developing countries in Africa. The author made extensive use of sources on African politics, sociology, and history in French and other languages as well as English. In *Nationalism in colonial Africa* he compared in tabular form the self-contradictions of French, British and Belgian policies, examined the institutions of African nationalism and the ideologies behind them and foresaw accurately what would be the results of the chain reactions of nationalism in the territories then considered calm in their colonial status.

African political parties, issued in a paperback edition, is a concise and valuable guide that sketches the setting, origins, types of political parties, party organizations, activities and objectives, with a conclusion of generalized 'hypotheses' regarding them. A bibliography of sources is followed by an appendix listing the major parties from 1945 to 1960.

540 Institut Colonial International, Brussels. *Compte-rendu.* Bruxelles, 1894– . Irregular.

From 1894 to 1949 the organization was known as the Institut Colonial International; after 1949 the name was changed to International Institute of Differing Civilizations. The early group called conferences, commissioned reports and published valuable monographs on political, social, and economic aspects of colonialism around the world. Each volume covers a specific problem. Africa is well covered in these publications. See, for example: *La crise et les colonies* (Bruxelles, 1933), which discusses economic conditions in the colonies between 1918 and 1933.

> Institut Colonial International, Brussels. *Organisation politique et administrative des colonies.* Bruxelles, Etablissements Généraux d'Imprimerie, 1936. 533 p.
> Contents: Les institutions politiques et administratives des pays africains soumis à l'autorité de la Belgique, par Michel Halewyk de Heusch; Le régime politique et administratif des colonies françaises, par Pierre Dareste; Organisation politique et administrative des

Politics

colonies italiennes, par A. Malvezzi de Medidi; Organisation politique et administrative de l'empire colonial portugais, par José de Penha Garcia; Le régime politique et administratif de l'empire britannique et spécialement des colonies de la couronne; Organisation politique et administrative de l'empire britannique, par J. Coatman; Les gouvernements de l'empire britannique, by A. Berriedale Keith; Addendum; Bibliographie (p. 529–533).

Institut Colonial International, Brussels. *Le régime et l'organisation du travail des indigènes dans les colonies tropicales.* Bruxelles, Etablissements Généraux d'Imprimerie, 1929. 326 p. (Bibliothèque Coloniale Internationale)
Report on South Africa, Belgian Congo, French African colonies, Netherlands Indies, Indo-China, Eritrea, Portuguese colonies.

Institut Colonial International, Brussels. *Le régime foncier aux colonies.* Bruxelles, 1898–1905. 6 v. (Bibliothèque Coloniale Internationale, Sér. 3)
V. 1: Documents officiels.
V. 2–6: Documents officiels précédés des notices historiques.
Covers French, German, British and Belgian colonies in Africa.

541 League of Nations. Permanent Mandates Commission. *Minutes.* 1st Oct. 1921– . Geneva.
Minutes of the 8th–10th, 12th– sessions were issued as Series of League of Nations Publications VI. A. Mandates. Minutes for the 8th session include Report of the Commission to the Council. Indexes to the *Minutes* were issued at five 5- and 10-year intervals as: 1st–5th session. 1925. VI; 6th–10th session. 1927. VI; 11th–20th session. 1931. VI; 21st–30th session. 1937. VI.

The League was a far more useful source of information in its time than its successor, the United Nations, is today. The annual reports submitted by mandate powers were valuable records, as were the minutes of the Permanent Mandates Commission.

542 Lee, John Michael. *African armies and civil order.* New York, published for the London Institute for Strategic Studies by Praeger, 1969. 198 p. map. Bibliography: p. 302–309.
Probably the best existing work concerning the impact of armies on African society, a relatively neglected subject. The book deals with the colonial inheritance, problems of independence, and the wider role of the military within the political community. The author covers police as well as military problems. He provides unusual material concerning the ethnic composition of the army, the changing nature of the officer corps, military training, etc.

Lee has previously written *Colonial development and good government: A study of the ideas expressed by the British official classes in planning decolonization 1939–1964* (no. 685) (Oxford, Clarendon Press, 1967, vii, 311 p., tables, diagrs.).

543 Mackenzie, William J. M., and Kenneth Robinson, eds. *Five elections in Africa: A group of electoral studies.* Oxford, Clarendon Press, 1960. 496 p. illus., maps. Bibliographic footnotes.
Papers examining the pioneer elections in which the characteristically Western device of the electoral system was used in African society: the Western Region of Nigeria in 1956, the Eastern Region in 1957, Sierra Leone in 1957, Senegal in 1957, Kenya in March 1957.

The same theme and the same elections were treated within a broader context

149

by T. E. Smith in his *Elections in developing countries: A study of electoral procedures used in tropical Africa, south-east Asia, and the British Caribbean* (London, Macmillan and Co.; New York, St. Martin's Press, 1960, 278 p.).

544 Macmillan, William M. *The road to self-rule: A study in colonial evolution.* London, Faber & Faber, 1959. 296 p. illus. Includes bibliography.

A historical study of the process of change from colonial rule to independent government. The author, a South African historian, had been director of colonial studies at the University of St. Andrews from 1947 to 1954. His examination of African evolution is limited to British Africa.

545 Padmore, George. *Pan-Africanism or Communism? The coming struggle for Africa.* London, Dobson; New York, Roy Publishers, 1956. 463 p. illus., ports. Bibliographical footnotes.

Standard work on the history of Pan-Africanism by a foremost spokesman. The late author has given a straightforward account of nationalist movements in West Africa, in East and Central Africa, and in Liberia and of the Pan-African movement, of its launching by the Afro-American leader W. E. B. Du Bois, of its international congresses, and of leaders in the individual countries who follow its aims. In his review of communist attempts to influence African movements, Padmore describes the policy of communism as false and cynical.

A more recent survey of this subject is by Philippe Decraene, a French Africanist – *Le Panafricanisme* (Paris, Presses Universitaires de France, 1959, 126 p., maps; 4th ed., rev. and corr., 1970, 128 p., maps). There is also a pamphlet issued by the British Central Office of Information in 1964, *Pan-Africanism* (53 p.; R.5512/64). Another general survey is Colin Legum, *Pan-Africanism: a short political guide* (New York, Frederick Praeger, 1965, 326 p.). The German standard work is no. 537, Imanuel Geiss, *Panafrikanismus: Zur Geschichte der Dekolonisation.*

546 Rotberg, Robert I., and Ali A. Mazrui, eds. *Protest and power in black Africa.* New York, Oxford University Press, 1970. 1,274 p. maps. Bibliography: p. 1197–1213.

A most comprehensive anthology. The editors, assisted by 31 contributors, cover the most variegated forms of resistance to colonial conquest and rebellions against imperial governance, as well as a large number of political, economic and literary expressions of discontent, all of which are interpreted as forms of anti-colonial resistance. The book deals also with post-colonial rebellions against African rule, with problems of plural societies, socialism and Pan-Africanism as forms of protest, and so forth. A 'postlude' attempts to formulate a theory of protest. The book concentrates on factors making for change rather than on those making for stability.

547 Segal, Ronald, in collaboration with Catherine Hoskyns and Rosalynde Ainslie. *Political Africa: A who's who of personalities and parties.* New York, Praeger, 1961. 475 p. map. (Books That Matter)

The most useful and comprehensive biographical directory as yet available in English. The author, formerly editor of the now defunct *Africa South in Exile*, states in the preface that his information is more complete for South Africa, Kenya and Nigeria than for former French Africa and other territories where contacts were scanty. Part 1 consists of biographical sketches of political figures in alphabetical order, varying in length from a short paragraph to two or three pages. Part 2, p. 291–475, is a country-by-country report on political parties, their actions and their status. In some cases information is given for 1961. A condensed version, *African profiles*, was published in the paperback Penguin African Library (Baltimore, Penguin Books, 1962, 352 p.).

548 Senghor, Léopold Sédar. *On African socialism*. Trans. and with an introduction by Mercer Cook. New York, Praeger, 1964. xv, 173 p.

Speeches enunciating the special socialistic theory of President Senghor, a combination of Marxism and Christianity with strongly romantic, spiritual and
African nationalist overtones. They include his exposition of négritude. A
French edition of Senghor's speeches was published by Présence Africaine in
1961, *Nation et voie africaine du socialisme* (138 p.; Collection 'Leaders
politiques africains').

549 Sithole, Ndabaningi. *African nationalism*. 2d ed. London, Oxford University Press, 1968. 196 p. frontis.

A greatly revised version of the first edition of 1959. The earlier version had
been intended as a 'justification' of African nationalism. In the new edition
the author, a black Rhodesian clergyman, treats the subject somewhat
differently – because he feels that nationalism has 'justified itself by its own
achievements'. Since writing the original version he has become president of
the militant Zimbabwe African National Union. The first of the work's four
parts is largely autobiographical, the second deals with factors contributing to
the rise of African nationalism, the third concerns the nature of white
supremacy, and the fourth discusses nationalism's problems consequent upon
Africa's sovereign independence. Sithole also edited *Obed Mutezo: The
Mudzimu Christian nationalist* (Nairobi, Oxford University Press, 1970. 210 p.).

550 Widstrand, Carl G., ed. *African boundary problems*. Uppsala, Scandinavian Institute of African Studies, 1969. 202 p.

A collection of essays on various aspects of African boundary problems, for
example, 'Colonialism and territorial conflicts'.

RELIGION AND MISSIONS

Note See also Part III, Area Guide, for works dealing with specific countries,
regions and colonial powers. See also nos. 336–344.

BIBLIOGRAPHIES

551 *Bibliografia Missionaria* v. 1– , 1933– . Comp. by Giovanni Rommers-
kirchen and Giovanni Dindinger. Roma, Unione Missionaria del Clero in
Italia. Annual.

A classified bibliography of books and periodical material on Catholic missions
throughout the world, with author and subject indexes. The regional arrangement includes a long section on Africa.

552 *Index Islamicus, 1906–1955: A catalogue of articles on Islamic subjects in
periodicals and other collective publications*. Comp. by J. D. Pearson.
Cambridge, Eng., Heffer, 1958. 897 p.
    Supplement, 1956–1960. 1962. 316 p.
    Supplement, 1961–1965. 1967. 342 p.

See no. 259 in Part I for annotation.

553 *International Review of Missions*. v. 1, no. 1– , Jan. 1912– . Geneva and
New York. Quarterly.

Formerly the organ of the International Missionary Council, the review is now published by the Commission on World Mission and Evangelism of the World Council of Churches. Each issue has a ' Bibliography on World Mission and Evangelism ', in eight sections, which include a number of works on Africa.

554 Mitchell, Robert Cameron, and Harold W. Turner, comps., with the assistance of Hans-Jürgen Greschat. *A comprehensive bibliography of modern African religious movements.* Evanston, Ill., Northwestern University Press, 1966. 132 p.

A bibliographical survey of non-Islamic African religious movements which arose in connexion with the West's impact on African societies. Items in various languages are listed (English, French and German predominate). The 1,313 entries, most of which are annotated and some of which extend into 1966, include periodical articles, books, dissertations, and sections of books. Arrangement is by the following categories: theory, Africa general, west Africa, central Africa, middle Africa, and southern Africa (each region is subdivided by country). There is an index of authors and one of ethnic groups.

555 New York. Missionary Research Library. *Cumulative list of doctoral dissertations and master's theses in foreign missions and related subjects.* As reported by the Missionary Research Library in the *Occasional Bulletin,* 1950–60; comp. by Laura Person. New York, Missionary Research Library, 1961.

Although this classed list has no regional breakdown, the subject index, which occupies only a few pages (39–46), shows which items are of import for Africa.

The irregular *Occasional Bulletin* of the Missionary Research Library often contained listings or other data of interest for studies of the mission field in Africa. See also the library's *Dictionary Catalog* (Boston, G. K. Hall, 1968, 17 v.).

556 New York. Missionary Research Library. *Current periodicals in the Missionary Research Library : Alphabetical list and indexes.* Comp. by John T. Ma. 2d and rev. ed. New York, 1961. 38 l.

Published as an issue of the *Occasional Bulletin,* which should be watched for revisions.

557 New York. Missionary Research Library. *Missionary biography : An initial bibliography.* New York, 1965. 151 p. processed.

A guide to biographical information on missionaries to all parts of the world. The 2,155 entries derive from books, pamphlets, articles and obituaries. Arrangement is alphabetical by title, and there is an index of authors, editors and compilers.

558 Streit, Robert, and Johannes Dindinger. *Bibliotheca missionum.* Münster i. W., Aachen, 1916–63. 22 v.

Tremendous bibliographical enterprise covering the literature of Catholic missions throughout the world from earliest times to the present day. The volumes have been issued by various publishing concerns. The literature is set down by continents and periods. Volumes 15–20 cover writings on African missions to 1940. See also Streit, no. 2022.

559 Vriens, Livinus. *Critical bibliography of missiology.* Nijmegen, Bestelcentrale du V. S. K. B. Publ., 1960. 118 p.

560 Walls, A. F., ed. *Bibliography of the Society for African Church History, 1.* 94 p. (Reprint from the *Journal of Religion in Africa,* v. 1, 1967)

Listed are 425 works related to African church history which have appeared since 1961. General arrangement is alphabetical by country, with a special section on biography.

Religion and missions

561 Zaretsky, Irving I., comp. *Bibliography on spirit possession and spirit mediumship.* Berkeley, Department of Anthropology, University of California, 1966. xvi, 106 p. processed.

A valuable listing of ethnographic sources (books, monographs, and articles) on spirit mediums in Africa, with focus primarily on sub-Saharan Africa. Most of the entries are annotated. Arrangement is alphabetical by author, and an ethnic group index is included.

REFERENCE WORKS

562 Barrett, David B. *Schism and renewal in Africa: An analysis of six thousand contemporary religious movements.* Nairobi, Oxford University Press, 1968. 363 p.

Begins with a detailed examination of the Luo tribe of Kenya, and then continues with a survey of 300 African tribes. This study probes the movements of renewal, protest and dissidence that have been taking place in Africa within the Protestant and Catholic churches in 34 nations over the last hundred years. By means of a new type of cross-cultural methodology, it is shown that movements of renewal and independence emerge spontaneously from a well-defined background of social and religious tension the strength of which can be assessed.

563 Beetham, Thomas Allan. *Christianity and the new Africa.* London, Pall Mall Press; New York, Praeger, 1967. 206 p. maps. (Library of African Affairs) Bibliography: p. 183–186.

A discussion of the future role of Christianity in Africa by a Methodist minister who was with Wesley College in Kumasi, Ghana, from 1928 to 1948. His emphases are on English-speaking Africa and the Protestant religions. The author traces the coming of Christianity, evaluates the weaknesses and strengths of the Church at national independence, and weighs the challenges facing the Church and the Christian community, e.g., nationalism, Islam, traditional religion, secularism, and communism. Appendix III is a brief history of the all-Africa Conference of Churches. For coverage of French-speaking Africa, see Robert L. Delavignette, *Christianisme et colonialisme* (Paris, Fayard, 1960, 127 p.).

564 Burridge, William. *Destiny Africa: Cardinal Lavigerie and the making of the White Fathers.* London and Dublin, G. Chapman, 1966. 195 p.

The author, a White Father, recounts the life and work of Cardinal Lavigerie, who founded the White Fathers and the White Sisters and opened Catholic missions in East, Central and West Africa (after the Holy Ghost Fathers). Emphasizing religious rather than historical aspects, the book discusses the Cardinal's religious principles, his concept of missionary spirituality and of his role as spiritual director to individuals, and his method of conversion and of missionary training.

565 Colloque sur les religions, Abidjan, Ivory Coast, 1961. *Colloque sur les religions, Abidjan, 5/12 avril, 1961.* Paris, Présence Africaine, 1962. 240 p.

Eighteen studies by Africanists and clergymen on ' The contribution of religions to the cultural expression of the African personality ', presented at a conference sponsored by the Société Africaine de Culture. The studies comprise four main sections – animism, Islam, Protestantism and Catholicism – each of which is accompanied by a panel discussion in summary. Representative topics are the structure of African religions, by Melville J. Herskovits; Islam and black Africa, by Hampate Ba; Quakerism and the African personality, by Olumbe Bassir; and the Bantu and Christ, by Placide Tempels.

566 De Mestral, Claude. *Christian literature in Africa*. London, distributed by the Christian Literature Council, 1959. 84 p.

Useful survey of fundamentals (the readers, the literature), administrative matters (church leaders and missionary boards), and matters of production and distribution (literature committees, Christian bookshops, Christian presses). The last three sections contain lists of addresses; the bookshops and presses are of Protestant sects only.

567 Froelich, Jean-Claude. *Les musulmans d'Afrique noire*. Paris, Editions de l'Orante, 1962. 406 p. maps, tables. (Lumière et nations) Bibliography: p. 361–366.

Impressive overall study of Islam in sub-Saharan Africa by a former administrator of France Overseas, a distinguished ethnologist who is now director of studies at the Centre des Hautes Etudes sur l'Afrique et l'Asie Modernes (CHEAM; earlier name, Centre des Hautes Etudes d'Administration Musulmane). He covers comprehensively and succinctly the Islamization of black Africa, east and west, in ancient and recent times and the colonial period. He then describes the character of Islam – its aspect of conciliation of pagan and Christian, its appeal to the animist, the ignorant, the learned, its mysticism, and the Brotherhoods. He concludes with an analysis of modern tendencies of laicism and reform and prospects for the future. Appendices include various doctrinal creeds; a lexicon of vernacular terms; tables on numbers of Muslims, Christians, and pagans by country (p. 360); and a chronology of Islamization in black Africa (p. 371–389). See regional sections for studies of Islam by countries.

568 Groves, Charles Pelham. *The planting of Christianity in Africa*. London, Butterworth, 1948–58. 4 v. maps. (Butterworth Library, v. 26, Missionary Research Series, no. 12) Bibliographical footnotes.

Published under the auspices of the Department of Missions, Selly Oak Colleges, Birmingham, this is the definitive history in English of Christian missionary work in Africa, Protestant and Catholic, written by a professor of missions in the Selly Oak Colleges. V. 1 goes to 1840; v. 2, 1840–78; v. 3, 1878–1914; v. 4, 1914–54. An excellent older work is J. Du Plessis, *The evangelisation of pagan Africa* . . . (Cape Town, 1930, 408 p.). See also Neill, no. 448.

569 International African Seminar, 5th, Zaria, Nigeria, 1964. *Islam in tropical Africa: Studies presented and discussed at the fifth International African Seminar, Ahmadu Bello University, Zaria, January 1964*. Edited with an introduction by I. M. Lewis. London, published for the International African Institute by Oxford University Press, 1966. 470 p. front., maps. Includes bibliographies.

Contributions on the history and sociology of the Muslim communities of sub-Saharan Africa from the seventh century to the present by leading experts in the field. Four of the selections are in French, the remainder in English; each is accompanied by a summary in the other language. In Part 1 the editor reviews the penetration of Islam into tropical Africa and sociological aspects of the interaction between Islamic and non-Islamic institutions; a five-page bibliography is included. Part 2 consists of 19 special studies on the subjects of expansion of Islam and Islamic belief and practice in Senegal, Mali, the Ivory Coast, Ghana, Nigeria, Sudan, the Somali Republic, Kenya and Tanzania. There is an index.

Religion and missions

570 International African Seminar, 7th, Accra, 1965. *Christianity in tropical Africa : Studies presented and discussed at the seventh International African Seminar, University of Ghana, April 1965,* Edited by C. G. Baëta. London, published for the International African Institute by Oxford University Press, 1968. xiii, 449 p. Bibliographical footnotes.

Eighteen wide-ranging studies (in English or French, with summary in the other language) on the general theme of issues and problems most directly relevant to Christianity in tropical Africa. Arrangement is in three parts: 'Historical perspective', 'The analytical perspective', and 'Trends and prospects in African Christianity'. The Rev. Professor Baëta has provided an introduction to each part, summing up the salient points of the discussions elicited by the papers. An index is included.

571 *Journal of Religion in Africa/Religion en Afrique.* 1967- . Leiden, E. J. Brill. 3 times a year.

This journal is devoted to the study of the forms and history of religion within the African continent, especially south of the Sahara. Bibliographical material and *instrumenta studiorum* are regular features. For example, v. 1, fasc. 3, 1968, carried 'Supplement I, Bibliography of modern African religious movements'.

See also *Bulletin of the Scottish Institute of Missionary Studies* (v. 1, no. 1- , 1968- , Edinburgh, University of Edinburgh, 3 times a year), which gives good coverage of Africa, geographically and historically.

572 Richter, Julius D. *Geschichte der evangelischen Mission in Afrika.* v. 3. *Missionsgeschichte Afrikas.* Gütersloh, C. Bertelsman, 1922. 813 p.

A standard history, written from the missionary standpoint, dedicated to J. Du Plessis. Covers African mission history by regions, including West Africa, South Africa, East Africa and North Africa. The author also supplies some data on Catholic missions. There is no bibliography, but there are numerous notes, and also sections dealing with topics such as the part played by missions in African linguistic studies, and a list of Bible translations into African tongues (p. 706–711).

573 Scanlon, David G., ed. *Church, state, and education in Africa.* New York, Teachers College Press, Teachers College, Columbia University, 1966. 313 p.

Seven essays on the past, present and future status of church-state relations with regard to education in Ethiopia, the two Congos (Zaïre and Brazzaville), Uganda, Ghana, Nigeria and South Africa. The authors are, respectively, Richard Pankhurst, Richard Dodson, Gerard Lucas, Roland Hindmarsh, Nicholas O. Amin, David B. Abernethy, and A. P. Hunter, with commentary by J. J. Fourie. See also David G. Scanlon, ed., *Traditions of African education* (New York, Columbia University, 1964, 184 p.).

574 Sundkler, Bengt. *The Christian ministry in Africa.* Uppsala, Swedish Institute of Missionary Research, 1960. 346 p. illus. (Studia missionalia Upsaliensia, no. 2) Includes bibliographical footnotes.

This extensive general study of the native African ministry was written at the request of the International Missionary Council. The author is a Swedish scholar and missionary who, after experience in Zululand and Tanganyika, was named research secretary of the Council. He travelled widely in Africa gathering the material for his survey. He examines the development, mostly recent, of African leadership in both Protestant and Catholic churches, the role of the pastor in the new Africa, and his relations with his co-workers. Almost half the text describes the training of ministers, including the patterns and trends of African theological thought. In an appendix is a list of the theological schools, other than Roman Catholic, in the whole of Africa. See also his outstanding *Bantu prophets in South Africa* (London, 1948, 344 p.), a pioneering work on African reactions to Christianity.

575 Schlosser, Katesa. *Propheten in Afrika*. Braunschweig, A. Limbach Verlag, 1949. 426 p. map. (Kulturgeschichtliche Forschungen, v. 3) Bibliography: p. 410–422.

An ambitious work, identifying leaders of the dissident sects which have arisen widely both among Christian converts and in Islamic Africa. The list of prophets recorded, each through citation of published sources of information, begins with the eighth century when the first wave of Islam brought forth opposing prophets of the old indigenous religions of Africa. These are followed through northwest Africa, the Sahara, Gambia, south and east Africa, and the Upper Nile. Then come Islamic prophets, from the eighth century through the time of the 'Mad Mullah' in Somaliland. Last are discussed the prophets leading splinter movements from the Christian missions, who often represented nationalistic as well as religious dissension, like Harris in Guinea and Kimbangu in the Congo.

Studies on individual prophets and sects are noticed in the regional sections of the present guide. Dr. Schlosser has herself written a notable book on indigenous churches in South Africa, *Eingeborenenkirchen in Süd- und Südwestafrika* (Kiel, Mühlau, 1958, 355 p.).

576 Silva Rego, António da. *Curso de Missionologia*. Lisboa, Agência Geral do Ultramar, 1956. xlv, 700 p. fold. maps. Bibliography: p. xxvii–xlv.

A history of Catholic missions in general and Portuguese missions in particular. Included is a chapter on comparative religions with 10 pages devoted to Bantu religion. Among the chapters on Portuguese missions are seven on Africa – North Africa, São Tomé and Príncipe, Portuguese Guinea, Cape Verde Islands, Congo, Angola, Mozambique, and Ethiopia. There are several appendices, a chronology (1455–1955), and an index of proper names and place-names.

577 Society for African Church History. *Bulletin*. v. 1, no. 1– , Apr. 1963– . Nsukka, Nigeria. Semi-annual, 1963–64; annual, 1965– .

The Society for African Church History was founded in 1962 in Freetown, Sierra Leone, as an international and interdenominational organization. The president is Professor Groves, and vice-presidents are Professors Baëta and Dike, Dr. M'Tinkulu and Bishop Sundkler. The *Bulletin* carries articles on church history (e.g., 'Foreign missions in Ethiopia, 1828–1868', 'Christian African participation in the 1906 Zulu rebellion'), news of recent publications, and other relevant data.

578 Trimingham, John Spencer. *Islam in the Sudan*. London and New York, Oxford University Press, 1949. 280 p. maps (1 fold. col.). Reissue: New York, Barnes & Noble, 1965.

579 ———— *Islam in Ethiopia*. London and New York, Oxford University Press, 1952. xv, 299 p. maps (part fold. col.). (Reissue: New York, Barnes & Noble, 1965)

580 ———— *Islam in West Africa*. Oxford, Clarendon Press, 1961. 262 p. map, diagr.

581 ———— *A history of Islam in West Africa*. London, Glasgow and New York, published for the University of Glasgow by Oxford University Press, 1962. 262 p. maps, tables.

582 ———— *Islam in East Africa*. Oxford, Clarendon Press, 1964. 198 p. maps (1 fold.).

Religion and missions

583 —— *The influence of Islam upon Africa.* New York, Praeger, 1968. 170 p. maps. (Arab Background Series) (Includes bibliography)

The best-known English studies of Islam in Africa are by a clergyman who is also a sociologist and Arabic scholar. Dr. Trimingham was in the Sudan as secretary of the Church Missionary Society in the late 1940s. He published his first booklet, *The Christian approach to Islam in the Sudan*, in 1948 (Oxford University Press, 73 p.). The following year came his full-length study of Islam in the Sudan. In this he analysed the conflict between the dogmatic conception of religion, the Shari'a, and the mystic Sufistic interpretation that had inspired the Mahdist movement. In the same work he examined the present-day impact of the West upon the Islamic way of life. Dr. Trimingham then turned to Ethiopia. A short pamphlet, *The Christian church and missions in Ethiopia*, was published in a survey series by the World Dominion Press. *Islam in Ethiopia* continues the author's main work, a definitive study of Islam in Africa south of the so-called Middle East. This work was carried farther in *Islam in West Africa*, which similarly deals with the present age and the effects of cultural change. The second volume on West Africa is a historical study of Islam, going back to the mediaeval states of the Sudan before, during and after the Mohammedan invasion. The chronological tables in the appendix run from the Soninke state of Wagadu in A.D. 750–800 to the French conquest of Guinea in 1902.

Note An important source providing information on the missionary culture, the work of specific mission-sending societies and individual missionaries is the biographies and memories of individual missionaries. See, for example:

584 Bentley, H. Margo. *W. Holman Bentley, D.D., University of Glasgow : The life and labours of a Congo pioneer.* London, The Religious Tract Society, 1907, x, 446 p., photos.

A biography written by his widow, based on diaries, personal reminiscences and information furnished by the Rev. H. E. Crugington, one of Bentley's early co-workers. Mrs. Bentley wrote the book so that it might serve as 'a stimulus to others to be followers of Holman Bentley'. Missionary literature is full of works of this kind, for instance, Catherine Winkworth Mackintosh, *Coillard of the Zambezi : The lives of François and Christina Coillard of the Paris Missionary Society in South and Central Africa, 1858–1904* (London, T. F. Unwin, 1909, 484 p.), comp. by Coillard's niece. Despite their obvious bias, many of these works, such as Mackintosh's book, have considerable scholarly value.

585 Du Plessis, Johannes. *Life of Andrew Murray of South Africa.* London, Marshall Brothers, 1920. 553 p. maps, illus., ports. Bibliography of Murray's works: p. 526–535.

Andrew Murray was one of the great Dutch Reformed missionary statesmen in Central Africa. This is a pro-missionary account written by a South African church historian. Murray's own account of missionary work was furnished in A. C. Murray, *Nyasaland en mijne ondervindingen aldaar* (Amsterdam, Hollandsch-Afrikaansche Uitgevers, 1898, 313 p.). See also W. E. F. Ward, *Fraser of Trinity and Achimota* (London, University Press, 1965, 328 p.).

Note Marxist historians have written critically of Christian missions. Among the many studies only a few can be mentioned here:

586 Loth, Heinrich. *Die christliche Mission in Südwestafrika. Zur destruktiven Rolle der Rheinischen Missionsgesellschaft beim Prozess der Staatsbildung in Südwestafrika, 1842–1893.* East Berlin, Akademie-Verlag, 1963. 180 p. (Studien zur Kolonialgeschichte und Geschichte der nationalen und Befreiungsbewegung, v. 9)

A negative appraisal of the role played by the Rhenish Mission Society which is depicted as an ally of German imperialism. The author made his name with a Ph.D. thesis submitted at the University of Rostock, published as *Kolonialismus und 'Humanitäts intervention': Kritische Untersuchung der Politik Deutschlands gegenüber dem Kongostaat (1884–1908)* (East Berlin, Akademie-Verlag, 1966, 117 p.). A very different interpretation of Rhenish Missionary Society history is to be found in Elfriede Strassberger, *The Rhenish Mission Society in South Africa* (Cape Town, C. Struik, 1969, 109 p.), based on missionary archives and compiled by a missionary's daughter with a historical training.

Another example of a neo-Marxist interpretation of missionary history, similar to Loth's, is Hubert Mohr, *Katholische Orden und deutscher Imperialismus* (East Berlin, Akademie-Verlag, 1965, 359 p.). These studies have in common a fairly favourable appraisal of tribalism and early feudalism in the precolonial era; this is linked to a militant critique of capitalism which is not credited with having played any kind of a progressive role in African colonial history. For an assessment of Marx and Engels's own views concerning the historical role of colonialism, see Shlomo Avineri, ed., *Karl Marx on colonialism and modernization* . . . (New York, Doubleday, 1968, 464 p.).

Note There are numerous standard histories of individual mission societies. The following are cited only as representative samples.

587 Anderson-Morshead, A. E. M. *The history of the Universities Mission to Central Africa*. London, Universities Mission to Central Africa, 1955–1962. 3 v.

A narrative history, written wholly from the missionary standpoint. The first volume covers the years 1898–1906, the second 1907–1932, the third 1933–1957. Each volume is furnished with a chronological table and a separate index. The third volume contains a list of all European mission members. The history is designed to serve inspirational as well as historical needs. Others of the kind are the following: Elizabeth Glendinning Kirkwood Hewat, *Vision and achievement, 1796–1956: A history of the foreign mission of the Churches United in the Church of Scotland* (London, Nelson, 1960, 380 p.); Richard Lovett, *The history of the London Missionary Society, 1795–1895* (London, H. Frowde, 1899, 2 v.); Karl Müller, *200 Jahre Brüdermission* (Herrenhut, Verlag der Missionsbuchhandlung, 1931, 2 v.); C. F. Pascoe, *Two hundred years of the S.P.G.: An historical account of the Society for the Propagation of the Gospel in Foreign Parts 1701–1900* (London, The Society, 1901, 2 v.); and William Ellsworth Strong, *The story of the American Board* (New York, Arno Press and New York Times, 1969, 523 p.).

SOCIOLOGY

Note See also Part III for works pertaining to specific countries, regions and colonial powers.

BIBLIOGRAPHIES

588 *African urbanization: A reading list of selected books, articles and reports.* Comp. by the Department of Social Anthropology, University of Edinburgh. London, International African Institute, 1965. 27 p. (Africa Bibliography, Series B)

This guide to research on urban problems and urbanization in Africa south of the Sahara lists almost a thousand works with scope mainly demographic, economic and sociological. Main sections are bibliographies, Africa in general, and west, central, southern, and east Africa. Each region has a general category followed by component countries and further subdivision into cities and towns (alphabetical index to the last also included).

589 Centre de Documentation Economique et Sociale Africaine (CEDESA). Enquêtes bibliographiques [series]. Bruxelles, 1959– .

CEDESA, Belgian centre for documentary services relating to economic and social studies of Africa, was created in December 1957 and in 1958 began an extensive distribution of file cards with annotated entries in classed decimal arrangement. As a result of the co-operation of scholars and libraries abroad, the Centre International de Documentation Economique et Sociale Africaine (CIDESA) came into being in 1961 and thereafter issued the file cards; CEDESA also produces the *Bulletin d'Information sur les Recherches dans les Sciences Humaines Concernant l'Afrique* (1963–). The CEDESA Enquêtes bibliographiques series is usually the work of individual compilers and deals with special subjects of social or economic significance. Among those in the field of sociology are the following:

> no. 1 *Le problème de la délinquance juvénile.* By M. L. Kerremans-Ramioulle. 1959. 63 p. (1,027 entries)

> no. 3 *Le problème de l'habitat rural en Afrique noire.* By Paul Verhaegen. 1960. 73 p. (433 entries)

> no. 7 *Bibliographie de la condition de l'Africaine en Afrique noire.* By F. Plisnier-Ladame. 1961. 241 p. (1,418 entries)

> no. 8 *Aspects économiques et sociaux de l'industrialisation en Afrique.* By P. Dethine. 1961. 136 p. (726 entries)

> no. 9 *L'urbanisation de l'Afrique noire : Son cadre, ses causes et ses conséquences économiques, sociales et culturelles.* By Paul Verhaegen. 1962. xiii, 387 p. (2,544 entries)

> no. 15 *Sciences humaines en Afrique noire : Guide bibliographique (1945–1965).* By Jozef Bogaert. 1966. 226 p. (1,494 entries)

590 Centre de Recherche et d'Information Socio-Politiques. *Bibliographie sur les classes sociales en Afrique.* Comp. by B. Verhaegen. Bruxelles, 1965. 70 l. processed. (Travaux africains, Dossier documentaire, no. 2)

An annotated list of 364 articles and books dealing with various aspects and problems of social classes in Africa. Most citations are of material published since 1960. Following an introduction and eight chapters on general literature about social classes are separate chapters on Algeria, Egypt, Guinea and the former Belgian Congo. There is an author index.

591 Comhaire, J. L. L., comp. *Urban conditions in Africa : Select reading list on urban problems in Africa.* New and rev. ed. London, published for the Institute of Colonial Studies by Oxford University Press, 1952. xi, 48 p.

The first edition of this list, edited by Dr. Margery Perham, was issued in 1947. It was revised to reflect the great increase in literature on the subject in five years, and the new list is no. 3 of the distinguished series of reading lists upon colonial questions prepared for the Institute of Colonial Studies. Like the others of the series, it might be cited as a model for a subject bibliography relating to Africa.

REFERENCE WORKS

592 *African Urban Notes.* v. 1, no. 1– , Apr. 1966– . Milwaukee, Department of
Political Science, University of Wisconsin-Milwaukee, Apr. 1966–Mar. 1967;
Los Angeles, Department of Political Science, University of California, Apr.
1967– . Irregular.

An informal newsletter on conferences, research, courses, dissertations, and
publications of interest to students and scholars concerned with African urbanization. George Jenkins is the issue editor, with Ruth Simms Hamilton and Ed Soja
(replacing Remi Clignet) as co-editors in late 1967. Occasionally an issue is
devoted to a specific topic, e.g., a special issue on Nigeria (Apr. 1967) and one on
geography (May 1967). By June 1968 seven bibliographical supplements had
appeared, among them *A historical bibliography of the city of Durban*, by M. W.
Swanson (no. 1, Nov. 1966, 12 p.); *Unemployment*, by Peter C. W. Gutkind (nos.
2 and 5, Feb. and Dec. 1967, 5 and 4 p.; no. 6, Apr. 1968, 4 p.); *A preliminary
checklist of Nigerian biographical and autobiographical chapbooks in English*,
by Bernth Lindfors (no. 4, Nov. 1967, 13 p.); and *Elisabethville*, by Bruce Fetter
(no. 7, June 1968, 33 p.), which includes commentative notes.

593 Banton, Michael. *Race relations.* London, Tavistock, 1967. 434 p. Bibliography: p. 394–415.

A timely sociological study of race relations the world over, but with emphasis on
Africa and the United States. Banton discusses the history of thinking on race
from the time of Aristotle, race as a role determinant, cultural symbiosis, caste
and conquest, the concept and roots of prejudice, ethnic differences, slavery in
the new world, growth of African prophetic movements, tribal relations in Africa
with particular reference to British Africa, stereotypes, and social distance. Three
of the chapters are produced from the author's *White and coloured* (London,
Jonathan Cape, 1959).

594 *L'enfant africain : L'éducation de l'enfant africain en fonction de son
milieu de base et de son orientation d'avenir.* Paris, Editions Fleurus, 1960.
484 p. (Bureau International Catholique de l'Enfance, Collection Etudes et
Documents) Bibliography: p. 464–484.

The report of a conference on child welfare held under the auspices of the Bureau
at Yaoundé, Cameroun, in 1957 and attended by 400 European and African
missionaries, priests, nuns, doctors and teachers. Twelve chapters summarize the
material gathered from responses to a preliminary questionnaire and from papers
and discussions upon various aspects of the life, education and well-being of the
African child. The text of the questionnaire, a synthesis of 800 pages of documentation, and a bibliography of about 1,500 references are given as appendices.

595 Hunter, Guy. *The new societies of tropical Africa : A selective study.* Issued
under the auspices of the Institute of Race Relations, London. London and
New York, Oxford University Press, 1962. xviii, 376 p. illus., fold. maps,
tables. Bibliography: p. 348–360.

The result of a project undertaken in 1959 and placed under the direction of Mr.
Hunter, who travelled widely in Africa and interviewed over a thousand people.
Although he alone was responsible for the final text, it was based on the work
of many writers and on papers done especially for this purpose by local study
groups in Africa. The chapters cover the historical growth of modern economies
and changing culture, present rural and urban society, growth of industry, labour
problems, education and manpower, evolving political systems, and, last, ' The
quality of African society '.

Sociology

596 Inter-African Conference on Housing and Urbanization, 2d session, Nairobi, Jan. 1959. *Report.* London, CCTA, 1959 ? 267 p. diagrs. (Scientific Council for Africa South of the Sahara, no. 47)

Report of a conference under CSA auspices, including summaries of papers. More important for research purposes is an accompanying paper, *Directory of research and other organizations providing information on housing in Africa south of the Sahara* (London, 1960; CSA, no. 72).

597 International African Institute. *Social implications of industrialization and urbanization in Africa south of the Sahara.* Paris, UNESCO, 1956. 743 p. illus., maps, tables, diagrs. (Tensions and Technology Series)

Under the auspices of UNESCO an International Conference on the Social Impact of Industrialization and Urban Conditions in Africa South of the Sahara was organized by the International African Institute and held at Abidjan in September–October 1954. This volume represents the results. The first two parts comprise an introduction by the director of the Institute, Professor Daryll Forde, explaining the conference and its field of study, and a survey by Miss Merran McCulloch of about 30 recent and current field studies on the social effects of economic developments in tropical Africa, ending with a chapter of comparisons and conclusions. Part 3 is the report of a sample study made by a field research team on social effects of urbanization in Stanleyville, Belgian Congo (preliminary report by V. G. Pons, N. Xydias, and P. Clément). Part 4 contains papers presented at the conference, five on West Africa, five on East Africa, three on the Belgian Congo, and three on southern Africa.

598 International African Seminar, 1st, Makerere College, 1959. *Social change in modern Africa : Studies presented and discussed.* Ed. by Aidan Southall. London and New York, published for the International African Institute by Oxford University Press, 1961. xi, 337 p. Reprint: 1965. Includes bibliographies.

The great increase in research on African contemporary social and cultural life has been accompanied by the establishment of a number of research centres and frequent meetings held under the auspices of various organizations. In the notable seminar of which the present volume is the report, leading scholars from most countries of black Africa took part. There were papers on general themes—e.g., anthropological problems arising from the African industrial revolution and papers relating to specific issues or areas.

599 International African Seminar, 6th, University of Ibadan, 1964. *The new élites in tropical Africa : Studies presented and discussed.* Ed. with an introduction by P. C. Lloyd. London, published for the International African Institute by Oxford University Press, 1966. 390 p. tables, diagrs. Includes bibliographies.

Participants who contributed papers and took part in discussions were 18 social anthropologists. Their topics included description and history, educational systems and social mobility, the structure of élite families, modern and traditional associations, and concepts in relation to the contemporary situation. Lloyd has written a book on a related subject, *Africa in social change : Changing traditional societies in the modern world* (Baltimore, Penguin Books, 1967, 362 p.; Penguin African Library).

600 International Children's Centre, Paris. *Etude des conditions de vie de l'enfant africain en milieu urbain et de leur influence sur la délinquance juvénile : Enquête entreprise à Madagascar, au Cameroun et en Côte d'Ivoire de 1954 à 1957.* Paris, 1959. 175 p. (Travaux et documents, no. 12) Includes bibliography on juvenile delinquency in Africa and other underdeveloped areas (p. 165–173).

Thorough sociological study presented statistically with many tables, graphic charts, maps and case histories.

601 International Institute of Differing Civilizations. *Women's role in the development of tropical and sub-tropical countries.* Brussels, 1959. 543 p.

Report of the 31st meeting, Brussels, September 17–20, 1958. At this session of the influential organization known as INCIDI, representatives from 18 countries were present, and papers were on a high level of authoritativeness. After the opening speeches, the first 254 pages are given over to reports from Africa, beginning with that by Sister Marie André du Sacré Coeur on French West Africa. Then follow reports by spokesmen for the Ivory Coast, Liberia, Nigeria, Somalia, the Portuguese provinces in Africa, the Belgian Congo, Ruanda, Rhodesia and Nyasaland, Uganda, Madagascar, the Union of South Africa (by Muriel Horrell of the S.A. Institute of Race Relations), Egypt and the Sudan. The remainder of the volume is taken up with reports from Asia and Latin America.

602 Miner, Horace, ed. *The city in modern Africa.* London, Pall Mall Press, 1967. xi, 364 p. maps, tables. Bibliography: p. 337–352.

Based on papers presented by distinguished American and British social scientists at the Conference on Methods and Objectives of Urban Research in Africa, held in Warrenton, Virginia, April 1965. Representative essays are: 'Africa and the theory of optimum city size', by Joseph J. Spengler; 'Urbanisation and economic growth: The cases of two white settler territories', by William J. Barber; 'Father-child relationships and changing life-styles in Ibadan, Nigeria', by Robert A. Levine, Nancy H. Klein, and Constance R. Owen; and 'Kampala-Mengo', by Aidan Southall. An index is included.

603 New York. Missionary Research Library. *Directory of Protestant medical missions.* Comp. by Arthur W. March. New York, 1959. 134 p.

In this long list there is first a statistical survey by continent and country, Africa leading, with the name of each mission followed by figures of size, number of patients, doctors, nurses, and other pertinent data. Next is given a separate index of leprosy missions in Africa and Asia.

604 Phillips, Arthur, ed. *Survey of African marriage and family life.* London and New York, published for the International African Institute by Oxford University Press, 1953. xli, 462 p. fold. map. Includes bibliographies.

The survey came to fruition through a suggestion made to the International Missionary Council by Lord Hailey in 1946. The editor, then reader in administration of colonial law at the University of London, wrote the introductory essay. Part 1, 'African marriage and social change', is by Dr. Lucy P. Mair; Part 2, 'Marriage laws in Africa', by Dr. Phillips; Part 3, 'Christian marriage in African society', by Rev. Lyndon Harries, now at the University of Wisconsin, formerly of the Universities' Mission to Central Africa. Each part has its own scholarly footnotes, bibliography, and index; included also are a list of tribes referred to (Part 1) and tables of statutes and cases (Part 2).

A short summary of the *Survey of African marriage and family life* was published by the International Missionary Council as no. 1 of their series of Research Pamphlets, *African marriage*, by Thomas Price (London, SCM Press, 1954, 56 p.).

The conflicts of Christian practices and principles with the tribal marriage customs—particularly with polygamy and bride price—are the main points of discussion. See also A. R. Radcliffe-Brown and Daryll Forde, *African systems of kinship and marriage* (London, International African Institute, 1950, 339 p.).

605 United Nations. Secretariat. *Progress of the non-self-governing territories under the Charter.* v. 3, *Social conditions.* New York, 1961. 251 p. (ST/TRI/ Ser. A/15/v. 3)

Review of general developments in social conditions of dependent territories throughout the world, covering race relations, social welfare, social security legislation, community development, freedom of association and industrial relations, co-operative societies, demographic conditions and population trends, health services and activities, nutrition. This is one of five volumes: the first a general review; v. 2 on economic conditions; v. 4 on educational developments; v. 5 a summary of individual territories. A cumulative index is to be published separately. The progress report covers the period from 1946 to 1957, and thus most of Africa south of the Sahara (former British colonies except Ghana, former French territories, the Belgian Congo, Portuguese and Spanish territories) is included. Official sources are given for almost all the data.

606 Wallerstein, Immanuel. *Social change : The colonial situation.* New York, Wiley, 1966. 674 p.

Book of readings (articles or chapters from books by specialists) on various social, political, and economic phenomena evolving out of the interaction of colonial rule and African societies. Covers subjects such as nationalism, labour migration and changes in traditional authority.

PART III

AREA GUIDE
(by colonial power, region and colony)

British Africa

Note In this part of the guide we suggest atlases, bibliographies, serials and reference works by colonial powers, regions and countries. A few titles from the earlier sections are sometimes repeated if especially meaningful, but in general the references for Africa as a whole or by subjects must be consulted for their application to individual regions. In the case of official documents, for instance, it has seemed unnecessary to name for each country the gazettes, statistical publications, development plans, legislative debates, etc., which are recorded not only in the Library of Congress series of official documents now published for many countries but also in the inclusive lists cited in the bibliographies of Part II, under Official Publications. But we have listed some government serials for illustrative purposes. Similarly, newspapers and journals of individual countries are for the most part omitted here, since they are named by country in the various bibliographies in Part II, Lists of Serials. Information on libraries, archives and manuscript collections dealing with each colonial power and specific regions and countries will be found in Part I.

Following the headings under colonial power, region and colony, we give numbers of some items in other parts of the bibliography that have specific reference to the region, colony or country in question. See, for example, no. 476, Schiller's bibliographies of African law, which cover each colonial power and most colonies.

BRITISH AFRICA

Note The most useful single reference tool for the study of former British Africa is perhaps A. R. Hewitt, *Guide to resources for Commonwealth studies* (see no. 74). See also, in earlier sections: *The SCOLMA directory of libraries and special collections on* Africa (no. 83); Royal Commonwealth Society, *Subject catalogue* (no. 262); Great Britain, Colonial Office, *Catalogue* (no. 269); London, University, School of Oriental and African Studies, *Catalogue* (no. 274); London, University, Institute of Historical Research, *Historical theses on African subjects* (no. 304); [Archives in Britain] (nos. 67–83).

Other useful works are the two following: Albert J. Walford, *Guide to reference material* (London, Library Association, 1959, 543 p.; Supplement, 1963, 370 p.); and Francis Carnell, *The politics of the new states: A select annotated bibliography with special reference to the Commonwealth* (London, published for the Institute of Commonwealth Studies by Oxford University Press, 1961, 171 p.).

Official gazettes of the countries formerly under British administration are primary sources for any research. In general, legislation went into effect only when the text of the law, ordinance, decree, proclamation, etc., was published in the gazette. Gazettes also carried news items of governmental action, announcements of official publications, and other information regarding administration. The supplements were often long reports on particular questions of economic and social conditions and developments.

Since the gazette and government series for the English-speaking countries are fully recorded in a number of bibliographies – the *Monthly List* cited below (no. 611) and the Library of Congress lists of official publications of each country – mention of them is omitted in the following country-sections except in a few cases where they are listed as examples of the kind of government series and publications that developed in each colony. Likewise omitted are the annual

167

reports, statistical bulletins, and budgets that were regular publications of each government before independence, and the proceedings of the various legislative bodies found in the colonies. Again, a few such titles are listed only as illustrations of the structure and scope of government documents produced in the colonies.

The Library of Congress lists are invaluable not only for their bibliographic citations but also for the administrative histories and government organizational changes they describe. The information that follows is summarized from the L.C. surveys.

Each colony produced an official gazette and supplements. The gazette was the official organ of the government. No enacted law or regulatory notice was binding until it had been published in the gazette or its accompanying supplements. The gazette carried notices of ordinances and regulations, appointments and vacancies in the civil service, lists of licensees in businesses and professions, tenders (advertisements for bids), trade and customs notices, statistics. The longer texts of ordinances, bills, schedules, statistics, and other public matters were published in the supplements or in extraordinary numbers.

In addition to creating numerous technical departments concerned with agriculture, health, treasury, statistics, etc., each colony passed through stages from legislative council to legislative assembly to a parliament. The legislative council and assembly produced debates of their meeting and sessional papers. The sessional papers usually consisted of some departmental reports, committee reports, memoranda, correspondence, and other miscellaneous papers that were 'laid on the table' at the start of the sessions of the legislative council. For a guide to the whole body of British government publications, see John E. Pemberton, *British official publications* (Oxford, Pergamon Press, 1971. 315 p.).

Bibliographies

607 Brokensha, David. *Applied anthropology in English-speaking Africa.* Lexington, Society for Applied Anthropology, University of Kentucky, 1966. 31 p. (Monograph, no. 8)

A compact survey, with emphasis on the application of social anthropology to government planning. The main part of the text is in four sections—regional surveys, topics of study, other applications, and conclusion. The bibliography, which is divided into 18 subject headings, lists mainly works published from 1955 to 1966. See also Forde, no. 332n.

608 Coleman, James S. ' A survey of selected literature on the government and politics of British West Africa '. *American Political Science Review*, v. 49, Dec. 1955: 1130–1150.

Coleman's bibliographical essay is useful in its indications of methodology of research. Many of the sources he mentions apply to East and southern Africa as well as to West Africa.

609 Couch, Margaret, ed. *Education in Africa : A select bibliography.* Part 1, *British and former British territories in Africa.* London, Institute of Education, University of London, 1962. 121 p. (*Education Libraries Bulletin*, Supplement 5)

Bibliography on education in the British and former British territories in Africa, excluding the Republic of South Africa. Selected from the catalogue of one of the Institute of Education libraries, it contains material listed to the end of 1961. Entries of both books and articles are arranged by country and subdivided by subject headings. There is an author index.

610 Frewer, L. B., ed. *Bibliography of historical writings published in Great Britain and the Empire, 1940–1945.* Ed. for the British National Committee of the International Committee of Historical Sciences. Oxford, Blackwell, 1947. 346 p.

611 Great Britain. Colonial Office. Library Reference and Research Section. *Monthly List of Official Colonial Publications.* June 1948– . London. 33 cm. mimeo.

Until the 1960s the *Monthly List* was the fullest available record of official publications for a large part of Africa and for other overseas possessions of the United Kingdom, and it is now an important source for retrospective study of the formerly British countries of Africa. In several sections, the listing is alphabetical by countries.

612 ——————— ——— *Bibliography of published sources relating to African land tenure.* London, 1950. 156 p. (*Its* Colonial, no. 258)
Each part begins with a brief introductory survey of land tenure in the country, then has systematic sections on: A, Statutory and legal sources (laws, orders in council, ordinances, case law); B, Legislative debates; C, Official statements and investigations; D, Special studies and monographs; E, General literature.

613 ——————— ——— *Dominions and Colonial Office List . . .* London, 1862–1966.
A comprehensive annual reference book, essential for a study of the organization and personnel of British colonial administration. Title varies; sometimes called *Colonial Office List . . .* Continued after 1966 as *Commonwealth Office Yearbook.*

614 ——— Ministry of Overseas Development. *Public administration: A select bibliography.* London, 1964. *2d supplement, 1966.*

615 ——— Parliament. House of Commons. *General index to the accounts and papers . . . 1852–1899.* London, H.M. Stationery Office, 1909.
——— ——— ——— *General index to the bills, reports and papers printed by order of the House of Commons and to the reports and papers presented by command, 1900–1948/49.* London, 1960. 893 p.
In these general 50-year indexes there are subject headings for Africa, with cross-references to individual countries. Very few appear in the first 50 years, but the indexes from 1852 to 1948/49 indicate rich sources for historical studies of the British African territories. These and other indexes to British official publications are described in the general guides to reference tools by Walford and Winchell. For those of particular usefulness in African studies, see Hewitt, no. 74.

616 ——— ——— House of Lords. *A general index to the sessional papers printed by order of the House of Lords or presented by special command, 1801–1859.* London, H.M. Stationery Office, 1938. 992 p. (1st ed., 1860)
1858–1870. London, Eyre and Spottiswoode, 1872. 368 p.
1871–1884/85. London, Hansard, 1890. 544 p.
Headings include African colonies, African states, slave-trade, and individual place-names. The general indexes for 1858–70 and 1871–85 have not so far been reissued.

Note To find one's way in the maze of British parliamentary papers, there is a *vade mecum* by Percy and Grace Ford, *A guide to parliamentary papers: What they are, how to find them, how to use them* (Oxford, B. Blackwell, 1955, 79 p.). Part 1 describes papers relating to Parliament's business and proceedings (procedure papers, journals, debates, standing committee debates) and papers giving Parliament information for consideration (bills, reports of committees, royal commissions, departmental papers, command and non-Parliamentary papers). Part 2 explains indexes, collections, sets, consolidated lists, and other aids in finding material. Part 3 discusses use of reports, etc.

617 Great Britain. Stationery Office. *Government Publications.* 1936– . London. Monthly, with annual cumulations and five-year indexes.

The systematic listing of official British publications from H.M. Stationery Office began with a *Monthly List of Parliamentary Papers* in 1881, to which was added a *Quarterly List* in 1894; there were also *Monthly* and *Quarterly Lists of Official and Parliamentary Publications* (more inclusive) from 1897 to 1921. In 1922 these were superseded by the *Monthly List of Government Publications*, with semi-annual cumulations, and the annual *Consolidated list of Parliamentary and Stationery Office publications.* In January 1936 these two were combined with the *Monthly Circular : A Selection from Recent Publications* to form the present catalogue. Arrangement in all is by issuing agency, with numbered listing of command papers, etc. The monthly catalogues have no indexes, and items of interest for Africa must be looked for by agency. In the annual volume and the five-year indexes, entries are by subject, including place-names.

H.M. Stationery Office also has a set of *Sectional lists* for separate agencies or groups of agencies. Number 34 is titled *Colonial Office*, containing a list of papers by subject, etc., from 1925– complete lists in the colonial numbered series, the Colonial Research Studies, the Colonial Research Publications, the Colonial Advisory Council of Agriculture, Animal Health and Forestry publications, and Fishery publications. This list has presumably been revised and updated.

Note In addition, students should consult Great Britain, Public Record Office, *List of Cabinet papers, 1880–1914* (London, 1964); and also Great Britain, Public Record Office, *The records of the Colonial and Dominions Offices*, Handbook no. 3, by Ralph Bernard Pugh (London, 1964). See archives section in Part I.

618 Hewitt, Arthur R. *Union list of Commonwealth newspapers.* London, published for the Institute of Commonwealth Studies, University of London, by Athlone Press, 1960. 101 p. offset. legal size.

Listing of newspapers of Commonwealth countries in London, Oxford, Cambridge, and other centres. The arrangement is geographical, with title index; and the table of contents lists 18 African countries. Holdings of the receiving libraries are given.

619 Horne, A. J. *The Commonwealth today : A select bibliography on the Commonwealth and its constituent countries.* London, Library Association, 1965. 107 p. (Library Association Special Subject List, no. 45)

Listing of 720 books published in recent years and still in print. Works on Britain are not included. Arrangement is geographical by continent and country, with subclassification by subject. See also *A legal bibliography of the British Commonwealth of Nations* (no. 474).

620 Meek, Charles K. *Colonial law : A bibliography with special reference to native African systems of law and land tenure.* London, published for Nuffield College by Oxford University Press, 1948. xiii, 58 p.

This reading list, compiled by a leading British authority on African land law, is restricted to the territories under U.K. administration in 1948.

621 *Overseas Official Publications... Quarterly Bulletin of Official Publications Received by the Royal Empire Society and Issued in the Overseas British Empire Relating Thereto.* v. 1–5, Apr. 1927–32. London, Royal Empire Society.

Unofficial listing of official documents of the British Empire, most of which came

into the library of the Society, now the Royal Commonwealth Society. See also
T. R. Reese, *The history of the Royal Commonwealth Society, 1868–1968*
(London, Oxford University Press, 1968, 280 p.).

622 Oxford University. Institute of Colonial Studies. Nuffield College Colonial
Reading Lists.

> *Colonial administration : General.* By Margery Perham. 1947. Rev. ed.,
> with title *Colonial government : Annotated reading list on British
> colonial government, with some general and comparative material
> upon foreign empires, etc.* 1950. 80 p.

> *Colonial economics.* By Penelope A. Bower. With a supplementary list
> added in July 1949 by Professor Frankel. 1949. 42 p.

> *Urban conditions in Africa : Select reading list on urban problems in
> Africa.* New and rev. ed. By J. L. L. Comhaire. 1952. 48 p.

These three lists were prepared in 1947–48 before the Nuffield College program of
colonial studies headed by Dame Perham was replaced by the Institute of Colonial
Studies; they are focused on the British colonial system.

623 Temperley, W. V. Harold, and Lillian M. Penson. *A century of diplomatic
blue books, 1814–1914.* Cambridge, Eng., University Press, 1938. xvi, 600 p.
A record, by year, of bills, sessional papers and command papers, covering the
entire published diplomatic activity of the British government. The index is by
country with which the diplomatic arrangement was made, and by subject, including place-names (Africa and individual countries). It was succeeded by Vogel
(no. 625, below).

624 *Union list of Commonwealth and South African law : A location guide to
Commonwealth and South African legislation, law reports and digests held
by libraries in the United Kingdom, May 1963.* London, Institute of
Advanced Legal Studies, 1963. xi, 129 p.
Publication nos. 1 and 2 of the Institute cover earlier lists: *A survey of legal
periodicals held in British libraries* (London, 1949, 52 p.) and *Union list of
Commonwealth law literature in libraries in Oxford, Cambridge and London*
(London, 1952, various pagings; South Africa E.1–17, Colonies G.1–49, including
East Africa, Kenya, etc.).

625 Vogel, Robert. *A breviate of British diplomatic blue books, 1919–1939.*
Montreal, McGill University, 1963. xxxv, 474 p.
A successor to Temperley and Penson; follows the same arrangement but is con-
siderably fuller with regard to Africa. In the subject index there appears at once
Abyssinia, shortly thereafter Africa, and then other individual countries by name.

626 Winks, Robin W., ed. *The historiography of the British Empire-Commonwealth : Trends, interpretations and resources.* Durham, N.C., Duke University Press, 1966. xiv, 596 p.
Contains a series of distinguished bibliographical essays. The following are
particularly relevant to Africa: Leonard M. Thompson, ' South Africa '; George
Shepperson, ' British Central Africa '; Harrison M. Wright, ' British West Africa ';
Robert O. Collins, ' Egypt and the Sudan '; William Roger Louis, ' Great Britain
and the International Trusteeship System '.

Serials

Note So many serials published in Great Britain dealt with Africa that only a
few can be mentioned here. The various lists mentioned at the beginning provide

full coverage; and for current titles see Part I. Furthermore, the British established a network of government and non-government serials in every colony. Some of these titles appear in the region and country sections.

Empire was much in the news for the English-speaking world. Newspapers most concerned with empire and imperial affairs were *The Times*, the *Standard*, the *Daily Telegraph*, the *Daily Chronicle*, the *Daily Mail*, the *Financial Times*, the *Pall Mall Gazette*, the *Manchester Guardian*, the *Glasgow Herald*, the weekly *Sunday Times*, and *The Observer*.

A few of the more important periodicals that regularly covered the overseas empire were the following:

627 *African Affairs: Journal of the Royal African Society.* v. 1, no. 1– . Oct. 1901– . London. plates, ports., maps. Quarterly.

Published until July 1944 as *Journal of the Royal African Society*; v. 1–55 published in London and New York by Macmillan, 1901–46. Separately paged supplements accompany some numbers. There are sections of book reviews and a bibliography of new books and documents.

Membership of the Society includes Britain's leading Africanists and former colonial administrators. Many of the articles are addresses on current conditions in African countries presented before the Society and are followed by highly informed discussion. Until recently an introductory section by the editor formed a commentary on events of the quarter. Contributions are largely concerned with the former British territories.

628 *The Anti-Slavery Reporter and Aborigines' Friend.* 1840– . London, published under the auspices of the Anti-Slavery and Aborigines Protection Society. Frequency varies.

Most important journal for criticism of colonial rule and for exposing abuses against Africans as well as conditions of slavery and forced labour.

629 *Baptist Magazine* (later *Missionary Herald*). 1809–1904. London.

630 *Blackwood's Magazine.* 1817– . Edinburgh and London. Monthly.

631 *Bulletin of the School of Oriental and African Studies.* 1917– . London. 3 times a year.

632 *Cambridge Historical Journal.* 1923–57. Cambridge and London. Continued as *Historical Journal.* 1958– . London and New York. 4 times a year.

633 *Chronicle of the London Missionary Society.* 1836– . London.

634 Church Missionary Society (for Africa and the East).

A variety of publications were issued by the CMS:

> *Church Missionary Review.* 1849–1927. London. (Also *Church Missionary Outlook* and *Church Missionary Gleaner*)
>
> *Missionary Leaves.* 1868– . London.
>
> *Proceedings.* 1801– . London.

635 *Colonial Office Journal.* 1907–10. London. Continued as *Colonial Journal.* 1907–20. London.

636 *Commonwealth and Empire Review.* 1901–44. London.

637 *Cornhill Magazine.* 1860– . London. 4 times a year.

638 *Corona: The Journal of Her Majesty's Overseas Service.* 1949–62. London, H.M. Stationery Office. Monthly.

639 *Edinburgh Review.* 1802–1929. Edinburgh and London.

640 *Empire.* 1938–49. London, Fabian Society. Superseded by *Venture.* 1949– . London. Monthly.

641 *Fortnightly Review.* 1865–1934. London. Absorbed by *Contemporary Review.* 1934– . Monthly.

642 *Geographical Journal.* 1893– . London, Royal Geographical Society. 4 times a year.

643 *Geographical Magazine* (supersedes *Ocean Highways*). Superseded by Royal Geographical Society, *Proceedings*, ns. 1874–78. London.

644 *Imperial Institute Journal.* 1895–1902. London. Superseded by Imperial Institute, *Bulletin.* 1903–48. London.

645 *International Review of Missions.* 1912– . Edinburgh and London. Quarterly.

646 *Journal of African History.* See no. 442 for annotation.

647 *Journal of Administration Overseas.* v. 1– . Jan. 1949– . London, H.M. Stationery Office. Quarterly.
This journal, concerned with practical problems of government in Africa, primarily English-speaking Africa, was earlier titled the *Digest of African Local Administration*, then the *Journal of African Administration*, and was formerly edited in the African Studies Branch of the Colonial Office. It was taken over by the Department of Technical Co-operation (now Ministry of Overseas Development) in 1962.

648 *Journal of Modern African Studies.* See no. 244 for annotation.

649 *Missionary Review of All Nations.* 1912– . London.

650 *New Statesman.* 1913– . London. Weekly.

651 *Nineteenth Century, a Monthly Review.* 1877–1900. Superseded by *Nineteenth Century and After.* 1901–50. London.

652 *Presbyterian Messenger.* 1848– . London. Monthly.

653 *Proceedings of the Royal Colonial Institute.* 1869–1909. London. Continued in *United Empire.*

654 *Proceedings of the Royal Geographical Society* (supersedes *Geographical Magazine*). 1855–78. London. n.s. 1879–92. Superseded by *Geographical Journal.* 1893– .

655 *Proceedings of the Royal Society of Edinburgh.* 1832–1939/40. Irregular.

656 *Race : The Journal of the Institute of Race Relations.* 1959– . London. Quarterly.

657 *The Round Table. A Quarterly Review of the Politics of the British Commonwealth.* 1910– . London, Macmillan and Co.

658 *Scottish Geographical Magazine.* 1885– . Edinburgh. 3 times a year.

659 *Spectator.* 1828– . London. Weekly.

660 United Africa Company, Ltd. *Statistical and Economic Review.* 1948–63. London. Semi-annual.

661 *United Empire.* 1910–58. London. Superseded *Journal* and *Proceedings of the Royal Colonial Institute.* 1869–1909.

Part III: area guide (by colonial power, region and colony)

662 *West African Review.* 1922–62. London. Monthly.

663 *Zambesi Mission Record.* 1898–1934. London.
Important journal of Jesuit missionaries to Central Africa.

Reference Works

664 *The Cambridge history of the British Empire.* Ed. by J. Holland Rose, A. P. Newton, and E. A. Benians. Cambridge, Eng., University Press, 1929– .

> v. 2, *The growth of the new empire, 1783–1870.* 1940. (Bibliography: p. 885–1004.)

> v. 3, *The Empire-Commonwealth, 1870–1919.* 1959. (Bibliography: p. 769–907.)

> v. 8, *South Africa, Rhodesia and the protectorates.* 1936. (2d ed., ed. by Eric A. Walker, 1963. Bibliography: p. 917–1017.)

In v. 2 and 3, the treatment of African history occupies only a small portion of the text. But the bibliographies are of outstanding importance. In v. 3, Part 1 surveys collections of manuscripts in public and private archives and official papers and publications. Select lists of parliamentary papers and parliamentary debates are included. Part 2 contains two sections – general bibliographies and special bibliographies. In the former are listed bibliographies and guides, periodicals, collected historical records, general histories and descriptive works, and biographies. Under special bibliographies are listed manuscripts as well as the above categories of material for each unit: colonial policy and administration in general, 1870–1921; the opening of tropical Africa, 1870–1914; imperial finance, trade, and communications, 1870–1914; international relations and colonial affairs, 1869–1914; the British Empire and the United States, 1870–1914; imperial defence, 1870–1914; the Empire at war, 1914–18; the British Empire and the peace treaties, 1918–19; international law and colonial questions, 1870–1914; and the Colonial Office. Volume 8 is equally good for southern Africa.

665 *Colonial Office List.* 1862–1940; 1946– . [1947, not published] London, H.M. Stationery Office. Annual.

This handbook, which has now been published for more than a full century (1966 ed., 334 p.), formerly had as its subtitle the words ' comprising historical and statistical information respecting the colonial empire, list of officers serving in the colonies, etc., and other information '. The first section gives history and functions of the Colonial Office in London, its staff, its subject departments, and associations, institutions, and committees concerned with colonial affairs. Next are sections on individual colonies, with information on area, population, history, the economic situation, etc., former governors, present cabinet, and civil establishment. These are followed by a directory of colonial officials, with biographical data and record of services. The volume ends with a bibliography, a list of ' Parliamentary and non-Parliamentary papers of colonial interest published during [the past year] ', as well as periodicals, in two groupings, by subject and by country.

A separate *Map supplement* was issued with the *Colonial Office List* of 1948, containing 38 maps, most of them folded to a size uniform with the list.

666 *The Commonwealth Relations Office Yearbook.* v. 1– . 1951– . London, H.M. Stationery Office.

> 1966 ed. 658 p.

This work largely replaces the *Colonial Office List* with respect to African countries. Until 1966 it was titled the *Commonwealth Relations Office List* and included biographical notes on staff members.

667 Conference on African Education, Cambridge, Eng., 1952. *African education : A study of educational policy and practice in British tropical Africa.* Ed. by W. E. F. Ward. Oxford, University Press, to be obtained from the Crown Agents for the Colonies, London, 1953. 187 p.

Significant publication resulting from the work of two study groups sponsored by the Nuffield Foundation and the Colonial Office, 1951–52, and an ensuing conference at Cambridge in September 1952. The reports were based on six months' visits by teams of three or four educational specialists, who examined thoroughly the entire educational systems of West Africa and of East and Central Africa. For an earlier survey see the Phelps-Stokes reports, nos. 394 and 395.

668 Cookey, S. J. S. *Britain and the Congo question, 1885–1913.* London, Longmans, 1968. 340 p.

A detailed account of the Congo Reform Movement, its relations with the British Foreign Office, and its role in getting Belgium to annex the Congo Free State. A good history of the Congo Free State and European diplomacy.

669 Elias, Taslim Olawale. *British colonial law : A comparative study of the interaction between English and local laws in British dependencies.* London, Stevens, 1962. 323 p.

670 —— *The nature of African customary law.* Manchester, Manchester University Press, 1956. 318 p.

The above two works, by the best-known African jurist, who rose to be attorney general of the Federation of Nigeria, are confined to the countries formerly under British control.

671 Goldsworthy, David. *Colonial issues in British politics, 1945–1961.* London, Oxford University Press, 1971. 425 p.

A review of the pressures that led to the changes in British colonial policies. The part played by the permanent Colonial Office officials is barely outlined, for most attention is given to parties and groups who pressed for change from outside the structure. The role of African nationalists is also largely ignored. Mainly shows the influence of pressure groups in London in producing changes in Britain's colonial policies.

672 Great Britain. Colonial Office. [Annual reports on the colonies.] London, H.M. Stationery Office.

The reports were begun in 1846 as the *Report made for the year . . . with a view to exhibit the past and present state of H.M.'s colonial possessions* and continued as *Papers relating to H.M.'s colonial possessions* through 1886. A new numbered series, Colonial Reports – Annual, assigning the same Command number to all reports issued in the same year, was started in 1887. This series was suspended in 1940, but publication of the reports was resumed in 1946 with the initiation of the above series.

They were published annually or, in some cases, biennially, in uniform booklets having about 50 to over 100 pages, with a few pages of photographs and a folded map. The arrangement of contents is systematic, with slight variations: Part 1, general review of the year's developments; Part 2, brief factual and statistical paragraphs on socioeconomic aspects; Part 3, geography, history, administration, etc., and various bibliographies. Appendices have texts of special documents and statistical tables.

The reports on the trust territories (Tanganyika, Togoland and British Cameroons) were submitted first to the League of Nations then to the General

Assembly of the United Nations and followed a rather different pattern, concentrating on social and economic advances.

673 ———— ———— *Colonial research.* 1944/45– . London. Annual.
Includes the overall report of the Colonial Research Council and individual reports of its branches. In 1959/60 these were the Committee for Colonial Agricultural, Animal Health and Forestry Research; Colonial Economic Research Committee; Colonial Fisheries Advisory Committee; Colonial Medical Research Council; Colonial Pesticides Committee, Colonial Road Research Committee; Colonial Social Science Research Council; Tsetse Fly and Trypanosomiasis Committee; and the report of the director, Anti-Locust Research Centre. A final section summarizes research matters not covered by the specialist advisory bodies. See no. 681n. for a review by Jeffries of colonial research.

674 ———— ———— *Digest of Colonial Statistics.* 1952– . London, H.M. Stationery Office. Bi-monthly.

675 ———— ———— Colonial Research Publications [series].

676 ———— ———— Colonial Research Studies [series]. no. 1– . 1950– .
Significant monographs on many aspects of colonial research. Titles will be found in the official bibliographies and in most listings of important works of each year.
The pamphlets now issued by the Central Office of Information (alternately British Information Services) are background surveys for the general public.

677 ———— ———— *An economic survey of the colonial territories.* 1932, 1933, 1935–37, 1951. London, H.M. Stationery Office. maps (part fold.). (Colonial) Begun as an annual review, this overall statistical report on British colonial possessions was published in one volume until 1938, when the war caused its suspension. The only post-war edition, 1951, appeared in 1952 in seven volumes of 100 to 200 legal-size pages each. Those relating to Africa are: v. 1, *The Central African and High Commission territories*; v. 2, *The East African territories*; v. 3, *The West African territories...with St. Helena.* The country sections give systematic coverage of economic life and conditions, with summarization of general background of geography and population, political structure, principal economic legislation, communications and transport, and then surveys of productive activities, finance and trade, and development. Many statistical tables and folded maps showing production areas are included. Volume 7, evenly divided into 100 pages of text and 100 pages of tables of exports, analyses principal products throughout the colonial territories.

Reports on the economics of anglophone Africa are issued by the British Central Office of Information, Reference Division. Also useful are the British Board of Trade's *Statistical abstract for the British Empire, 1889–1913* (11 v.; London, 1904–15), and *Statistical abstract for the several colonies and other possessions of the U.K.* (1850–), the latter also titled *Statistical abstract of British overseas dominions and protectorates* (1865–).

The Colonial Office was also responsible for conducting numerous specialized inquiries dealing either with particular topics such as labour or with the position of entire colonies. These studies include documents such as *Report of the commission appointed to enquire into the financial position and further development of Nyasaland* (Colonial no. 152, 1938, 345 p.) and *Report of the commission to enquire into the financial and economic position of Northern Rhodesia* (Colonial no. 145, 1938, 393 p.). These reports still form, as it happens, the best economic histories, respectively, of Malawi and Zambia under early colonial rule.

678 —— Foreign Office. *British and foreign state papers, with which is incorporated Hertslet's commercial treaties.* London, H.M. Stationery Office, 1841– .

These volumes contain texts of treaties, correspondence about foreign affairs, and many documents of historical interest, including texts of constitutions and organic laws of foreign countries. The Foreign Office handled many British territories in Africa from about 1885 to 1905, so that these years are of particular interest. The volumes of *Hertslet's commercial treaties*, each covering a number of years, were published for H.M. Stationery Office from 1827 to 1922, ceasing with the last index volume, v. 31 (London, Harrison & Sons, 1925). After 1922 the commercial treaty information was included with the *British and foreign state papers*, beginning with v. 116 of this publication in 1923. The *Papers* are well indexed, volume by volume, and there are several general indexes.

There is also the *Foreign Office treaty series* (London, H.M. Stationery Office, 1892–), numbered and indexed as a separate set. These and numerous other British official series of interest for Africa are fully described by Hewitt (see no. 74) and Pemberton (no. 691).

A companion work to *Hertslet's commercial treaties* and the *Foreign Office treaty series*, relating to the partition of Africa, is Sir Edward Hertslet's *The map of Africa by treaty* (3d ed., rev. and completed to the end of 1908, London, printed for H.M. Stationery Office by Harrison & Sons, 1909, 3 v. and portfolio of maps).

679 —— Overseas Development Ministry. *Colonial development and welfare acts 1929–70.* London, HMSO, 1971. 50 p. (Cmnd. 4677)

680 Holmberg, Ake. *African tribes and European agencies: Colonialism and humanitarianism in British South and East Africa 1870–1895.* Goteborg, Scandinavian University Books, 1966. 409 p.

Detailed studies of British expansion in Bechuanaland, Matabeleland, Nyasaland and East Africa and the role of local factors in determining how the areas fell under the Union Jack.

681 Jeffries, Sir Charles. *The Colonial Office.* London, Allen and Unwin, 1956. 222 p. (New Whitehall Series)

A standard work written by a former under-secretary in the Colonial Office. Jeffries served on numerous governmental and ecclesiastical committees, including the General Council of the British and Foreign Bible Society. He was also a most prolific writer. His administrative studies included *The colonial empire and its civil service* (Cambridge, Eng., The University Press, 1938, 259 p.); *The colonial police* (London, M. Parrish, 1952, 232 p.); and *A review of colonial research, 1940–1960* (London, H.M. Stationery Office, 1964, 238 p.).

682 Kirkman, W. P. *Unscrambling an empire: A critique of British colonial policy, 1956–1966.* London, Chatto & Windus, 1966. 214 p. maps.

Kirkman, a correspondent for the London *Times*, 1960–64, analyses what he regards as the British government's lack of a definite, well-conceived policy of disengagement. More than half of his book is devoted to Africa, with emphasis on Ghana, Nigeria, Kenya, Uganda, Rhodesia and Zambia, and on the failure of the Federation of Rhodesia and Nyasaland. An index is included.

683 Kirkwood, Kenneth. *Britain and Africa.* London, Chatto & Windus; Baltimore, Johns Hopkins Press, 1965. 235 p. (Britain in the World Today, no. 6)

Survey and analysis of the entire range of British connexions and relationships with African countries, from the earliest contacts to the present Commonwealth 'partnership'.

Part III: area guide (by colonial power, region and colony)

684 Kuczynski, Robert René. *Demographic survey of the British colonial empire.* London and New York, Oxford University Press, 1948. 4 v. tables.
See no. 352 for annotation.
See also Dubester, *Population censuses . . . of British Africa* (no. 350).

685 Lee, J. M. *Colonial development and good government : A study of the ideas expressed by the British official classes in planning decolonization, 1939–1964.* Oxford, Clarendon Press, 1967. 311 p. diagrs.
Bibliography: p. 286–290.
The author discusses successively the principles of good government as understood by the British governing classes; the framework for development in its social and political aspects; the foundations of good government, including education for social advance and democratic practice; Great Britain's rejection of international supervision; the transfer of power; and British commitments overseas in general, including the question of foreign aid and the lessons of colonial development. A bibliographical note gives data on the published works of British policy makers and administrators. Also included are diagrams illustrating the numbers of social scientists in British Africa in 1950, Colonial Service recruitment, 1920–60, Colonial Office organization in 1950, colonial development resources, 1955–60, and an analysis of the background, education, and careers of colonial governors between 1940 and 1960. See also his no. 542.

686 Lewis, Roy, and Y. Foy. *The British in Africa.* London, Weidenfeld and Nicolson, 1971. 238 p.
A social history of the British in Africa.

687 London. University. Institute of Commonwealth Studies. Commonwealth Papers [series]. London, Athlone Press, 1954– .
A series of which a number are devoted to Africa. Typical is no. 9, T. E. Smith and J. G. C. Blacker, *Population characteristics of the Commonwealth countries of tropical Africa* (1963, 72 p.; bibliographical footnotes).

688 Louis, William Roger. *Great Britain and Germany's lost colonies, 1914–1919.* Oxford, Clarendon Press, 1967. 168 p.
The story of Great Britain's efforts during the war to gain Germany's colonies not so much for economic reasons but for strategic and security reasons – as well as a belief that they, the British, were morally superior colonialists.

689 Lugard, Lord. *The dual mandate in British tropical Africa.* London, 1922. Reprint: Frank Cass, 1965. 619 p.
Basic work explaining the famous administrator's concepts on indirect rule in governing Africa. A classic of colonial apologetics. Lugard argues that Great Britain has incurred obligations of trusteeship with regard to her African subjects, and also the obligation to develop her imperial possessions for the benefit of the world at large. According to the author, British rule has been as beneficial in its long-term consequences in Africa as ancient Roman imperialism in Celtic Britain. His study covers colonialism in all its aspects, including history, administration, the machinery of government, and more specialized topics such as taxation, land tenure, settlement, labour, education, economic development and justice.

690 Parsons, H. Alexander. *The colonial coinages of British Africa : with the adjacent islands.* London, 1950. 94 p.
Not available for examination.

691 Pemberton, John F. *British official publications.* Oxford, Pergamon Press, 1971. 315 p.
All types of parliamentary publications are covered including concordance of

command papers, a list of Royal Commissions, a list of departmental committees, working parties, tribunals of inquiry for the period 1900–1969; non-parliamentary materials are also surveyed. There is a subject, author and title index.

692 Perham, Margery. *Lugard.* London, Collins, 1956–60. 2 v. illus., ports., maps, facsims. Circulated in America by Essential Books. Includes bibliographies.

These two volumes by one of England's foremost colonial scholars trace the career of the man who established the twentieth-century British concept of indirect rule in native administration.

British colonial policy during the second quarter of the twentieth century is discussed by Dame Perham in her recent contributions: *Colonial sequence, 1930 to 1949 : A chronological commentary upon British colonial policy especially in Africa* (London, Methuen, 1967, 351 p.); and the second part, *Colonial sequence, 1949 to 1969...* (London, Methuen, 1970, 377 p.).

693 Porter, Barnard. *Critics of empire : British radical attitudes to African colonialism.* New York, St. Martin's Press, 1968. 352 p. illus.

Analysis of activities of critics in the 1890s and their impact on imperial debate of the twentieth century. See also D. Hammond and A. Jablow, *The Africa that never was : Four centuries of British writing about Africa* (New York, Twayne Publ., 1970, 251 p.); and Christine Bolt, *Victorian attitudes to race* (London, Routledge & Kegan Paul, 1971, 245 p.). An attempt to depict late Victorian attitudes towards some races of men. Covers the period 1850–1900 and deals mostly with Africa.

694 Robinson, Kenneth. *The dilemmas of trusteeship : Aspects of British colonial policy between the wars.* London, Oxford University Press, 1965. 95 p.

A stimulating series of lectures by the then director of the Institute of Commonwealth Studies at the University of London. Lectures were 'The imperial context of trusteeship', 'The institutions of colonial policy', and 'The dilemmas of trusteeship'.

695 Robinson, Kenneth, and F. Madden, eds. *Essays in imperial government.* Oxford, Basil Blackwell, 1963. 293 p.

A tribute to the great imperial historian Margery Perham. Studies various aspects of colonial rule, the forces which that rule set in motion and the consequences of white governance. Includes a considerable number of life histories of officials, missionaries, settlers, historians and ethnographers.

696 Symonds, Richard. *The British and their successors : A study in the development of the government services in the new states.* London, Faber and Faber, 1966. 287 p.

Excellent comparative survey of British government administration overseas.

697 Synder, Louis L., ed. *The imperialism reader.* Princeton, Van Nostrand, 1962. 619 p.

A useful selection of documents covering a wide variety of topics relating to imperialism – that is, the concept of imperialism, the techniques, arguments for and against, and the decline of imperialism.

698 Younger, Kenneth. *The public service in new states.* London, Oxford University Press, 1960. 113 p.

An account of the phasing out of the British colonial service in Ghana, Nigeria and the Sudan. See also Robert Heussler, *Yesterday's rulers; the making of the British colonial service* (Syracuse, 1963, 260 p.).

Part III: area guide (by colonial power, region and colony)

WEST AFRICA

Note The entries below refer to English-speaking West Africa as a whole or in substantial part. Some items also cover French-speaking West Africa.

Bibliographies

699 Guides to materials for West African history in European archives [series]. London, University of London, Athlone Press, 1962– . See no. 28 for list of guides already published.

700 Fage, J. D. ' Continuity and change in the writing of West African history '. *African Affairs*, v. 70, no. 80, July 1971, p. 236–251.
A review article that examines the historiography of the formerly British and French parts of Africa from antiquity to the post-colonial era. It also provides interesting information on West African centres of learning and on changes of fashion in the writing of history. See also no. 626.

701 International African Institute. *West Africa : general, ethnography, sociology, linguistics.* Comp. by Ruth Jones, librarian, with the assistance of a panel of consultants. London, 1958. 116 l. 33 cm. (African Bibliography Series, Ethnography, Sociology, Linguistics and Related Subjects)
Based on the bibliographical card index of the International African Institute.

702 Rydings, H. A. *The bibliographies of West Africa.* Ibadan, Nigeria, published on behalf of the West African Library Association by Ibadan University Press, 1961. 36 p. tables.
Critically annotated bibliographical essay. The author comments comparatively on the chief general African bibliographies, on serial bibliographies and on selective lists, then on bibliographical sources for the individual countries of West Africa in English, French, and Portuguese. Besides bibliographical publications, he includes the valuable reading lists in leading country studies. He ends with a tabulated survey of the 50 items covered.

703 Simms, Ruth P. *Urbanization in West Africa : A review of current literature.* Evanston, Ill., Northwestern University Press, 1965. xv, 109 p. tables.
A concise survey of post-1950 publications, containing some 60 pages of text and 50 of slightly annotated bibliography. The bibliographical section contains more than 300 references to books and articles on African urbanization.

Serials

Note Numerous professional and learned society journals concerned with West Africa, particularly English-speaking West Africa, were published during the period of colonial rule. Only a few can be mentioned here. For a more complete listing see nos. 287–295, especially SCOLMA's *Periodicals published in Africa*, no. 292.

704 Bank of West Africa, London. *Annual report.*
Includes a notable review of the year's economic developments in the English-speaking countries of West Africa.
    See also the Economist Intelligence Unit digest *Three-Monthly Economic Review* for West African economic data.

705 Bank of West Africa, London. *Annual Review of Conditions in Gambia, Sierra Leone, Ghana and Nigeria.*

A booklet accompanying the annual report of the Bank, giving a detailed picture of conditions on the spot.

706 United Africa Company, Ltd. *Statistical and Economic Review*, v. 1, no. 1– . Mar. 1948– . London. illus. (part col.), maps, diagrs. Semi-annual.

This subsidiary of Unilever leads in the palm-oil and other industries of West Africa. Its journal is a useful source for articles of economic significance as well as for statistics and other data on West African trade.

707 *West Africa : A Weekly Newspaper.* v. 1– . Feb. 3, 1917– . London. illus.

West Africa, published by the West African Graphic Company, 9 New Fetter Lane, London, E.C.4, is an esssential source for continuing information about economic, political and social affairs in both British and French-speaking West Africa.

Reference Works

708 Behn, Hans Ulric. *Die Presse in Westafrika.* Hamburg, Deutsches Institut für Afrika-Forschung, 1968. 267 p. (Hamburger Beiträge zur Afrika-Kunde, v. 8)

Provides data for the various journals, their political affiliation, circulation, readership, advertising facilities, press agencies, and so forth.

709 Carney, David. *Government and economy in British West Africa : A study of the role of public agencies in the economic development of British West Africa in the period 1947–1955.* New York, 1961. 207 p.

A useful survey by an African economist.

710 Chukura, O. *A digest of decisions of Her Majesty's Privy Council in appeals from West Africa, 1841–1964.* Ibadan, Gillford and Co., 1969. 65 p.

711 Committee on Inter-African Relations. *Report on the press in West Africa.* Ibadan, Nigeria, distributed by Director, Department of Extra-mural Studies, University College, 1960. xi, 133 p. illus., fold. map, tables. 33 cm.

Prepared for an International Seminar on the Press and Progress in West Africa held at the University of Dakar, May 31 to June 4, 1960. Papers, which include lists and descriptions of newspapers, are ' Position of the press in French-speaking West Africa ', by Father J. de Benoist; ' Ghana press ', by K. B. Jones-Quartey; ' Press in Liberia ', by Henry B. Cole; and ' The Nigerian press, 1929–59 ', by Increase Coker.

712 Cowan, L. Gray. *Local government in West Africa.* New York, Columbia University Press, 1958. 292 p.

Authored by an American expert on African political questions. In this study of the representative institutions coming into operation, especially those in French territories under the *loi-cadre*, Professor Cowan focuses attention on the problems of getting the new local authorities accepted by the unprepared communities in which the traditional authority of the paramount chief still exists and is frequently in conflict with that of the government official. His data are of 1954–55.

713 Crowder, Michael. *West Africa under colonial rule.* London, Hutchinson, 1968. xv, 540 p. maps (1 fold.), tables. Bibliographical footnotes.

A massive survey of West Africa under British and French domination by a scholar who since January 1968 has been director of African Studies at the University of Ife. This study provides a comparative analysis of the differing impact of British and French colonial rule and of the reactions of the West Africans to that rule. Professor Crowder considers the history of the colonial period from both the European and the African point of view and is frankly critical of many aspects of the colonial administration. Discussion of Portuguese Guinea is excluded, and Togo is dealt with only fleetingly in this review of West Africa's diverse administrative, political, economic, and social histories. Appendices include chronologies of governors and governors-general. The substantial footnotes that follow each chapter give ample evidence of the author's effort to synthesize the more important sources available of the 1885–1945 period. A good analytical index is included. See also Bauer, *West Africa trade*, no. 365.

714 Crowder, Michael, ed. *West African resistance : The military response to colonial occupation.* New York, Africana Publishing Corp., 1971. 314 p. illus., maps.

A study conducted by nine historians concerning the African military response to colonial occupation in West Africa. Each case history deals with the African opposition to European forces by an organized army of a centralized state. The organization of the African armies, the weapons they used, the quality of their generalship, the strategy employed and the manner in which diplomacy was used to avoid warfare, all are treated in this study. Resistance groups covered are Ashante (Ghana), by J. T. Fynn; Tukolor (Mali), by A. S. Kanya-Forstner; Mahmadou Lamine (Senegambia), by B. O. Oloruntimehin; Samori (Guinea), by Yves Person; Dahomey, by David Ross; Iyebu (Nigeria), by Robert Smith; Ebroheini (Nigeria), by Obaro Ikime; Bai-Bureh (Sierra Leone), by La Ray Denzer; Sokoto Caliphate (Nigeria), by D. J. M. Muffett.

See also *West African chiefs : Their changing status under colonial rule and independence*, ed. by Michael Crowder and Obaro Ikime (New York, Africana Publishing Corp., 1970, 453 p.). This book consists of papers presented at a conference held by the Institute of African Studies of the University of Ife, December 17–21, 1968.

715 Daniels, W. C. Ekow. *The common law in West Africa.* London, Butterworth, 1964. lvi, 424 p. (Butterworth's African Law Series, no. 9)

716 Fage, J. D. *An introduction to the history of West Africa.* 3d ed. Cambridge, Eng., University Press, 1962. 232 p. illus. ' Further Reading ': p. 201–205.

The first edition of this authoritative story of West Africa from the earliest days of the trans-Saharan trade contacts to the present, now in its second updating revision, was published in 1955.

717 Forde, Daryll, and P. M. Kaberry, eds. *West African kingdoms in the nineteenth century.* London, published for the International African Institute by Oxford University Press, 1967. xiv, 289 p. front., maps, diagrs. Includes bibliographies.

An introduction by the editors is followed by 10 essays, each devoted to a West African kingdom. A bibliography and map accompany each study, and there is an index.

718 Hargreaves, John D. *Prelude to the partition of West Africa.* London, Macmillan and Co.; New York, St. Martin's Press, 1963. xi, 383 p. maps. Bibliography: p. 350–368.

In this well-written history of 19th-century Africa, the valuable bibliography includes main sources and authorities used, unpublished sources and published sources (official or semi-official documentary collections; works by contemporaries containing primary material; bibliographies, works of reference and general histories, modern studies of special topics). The unpublished sources mentioned are official British archives, archives of the government of Sierra Leone, official French archives, private collections of manuscripts in the United Kingdom, and unpublished theses.

The author also wrote a brief general history, *West Africa: the former French states* (Englewood Cliffs, N.J., Prentice-Hall, 1967, 183 p.). (The Modern Nations in Perspective Series)

719 Hill, Polly. *Studies in rural capitalism in West Africa.* New York, Cambridge University Press, 1970. 173 p.

A valuable collection of six empirical studies: on cocoa in Ghana, on Ewe fishermen, on cattle on the Accra Plains, on cattle-trading in northern Ghana, on tobacco trading in Katsina and on farming in Hausaland. The continuity of West African economic life is stressed.

720 Horton, James Africanus B. *West African countries and peoples : British and native, with the requirements necessary for establishing that self government recommended by the Committee of the House of Commons, 1865.* Reprinted with an introduction by George Shepperson. Edinburgh University Press, 1969. 281 p.

Horton was an African scholar, doctor and administrator who reached the rank of lieutenant-colonel in the British Army Medical Service. His present work, an African classic, seeks to ' disprove many of the fallacious doctrines and statements of anthropologists (detrimental to the African race) '. It considers that Great Britain should aim at creating new African nations. It elaborates on the benefits that West Africa has received from British rule, and finally discusses ' the requirements of the various colonies '.

721 Howard, Cecil, ed. *West African explorers.* London and New York, Oxford University Press, 1952. 598 p. (World's Classics, no. 523)

In his selections the editor has tried to cover each explorer's journey and achievement and to avoid repetition of routes travelled. Extracts are, among others, from the works of the famous 17th- and 18th-century travellers Richard Jobson and William Bosman and the 19th-century Mungo Park, Major Denham, Captain Clapperton, Richard Lander, Sir Richard Burton, William Balfour Baikie, Dr. Heinrich Barth and Mary Kingsley. The volume, printed on India paper, is pocket size, but its clear print is not hard to read. The list of sources, p. 26–27, cites the important original travel books.

The adventures and achievements of 19th-century West African explorers, along with excerpts from their writings, are related in Hubert Jules Deschamps's interesting narrative, *L'Europe découvre l'Afrique : Afrique occidentale, 1794–1900* (Paris, Berger-Levrault, 1967, 284 p., illus., maps; bibliography, p. 267–274).

722 International Seminar on Inter-University Co-operation in West Africa, Freetown, Sierra Leone, 1961. *The West African intellectual community : Papers and discussions.* Ibadan, published for the Congress for Cultural Freedom by Ibadan University Press, 1962. 356 p.

Leading figures in the intellectual community of West Africa include among their topics freedom of the universities, inter-university co-operation, liaison between governments in presenting needs to foreign organizations, planning, exchange of students and teachers and many other aspects of university education and exchanges.

723 International West African Conference. *Comptes rendus.* 1945– . illus., maps.

This international gathering of economists, sociologists, scientists, and other specialists from the countries of West Africa was begun at the instigation of the Institut Français d'Afrique Noire, and the first meeting was held in Dakar in

1945. The second session, 1947, was in Bissau, Portuguese Guinea; the third, 1949, in Ibadan, Nigeria; the fourth, 1951, in Santa Isabel, Spanish Guinea; the fifth, 1953, in Abidjan, Ivory Coast; the sixth, August 1956, in São Tomé, Portuguese West Africa; the seventh, April 1959, in Accra, Ghana. The papers are published by the hosts of the respective sessions, those of 1947 having appeared in five volumes, 1950–52, issued by the Ministério das Colónias in Lisbon. Contributions are in the languages in which the papers were delivered.

724 Jarrett, Harold Reginald. *A geography of West Africa.* New ed., completely rev. and corrected. London, Dent, 1966. 229 p. maps, diagrs.

An excellent compact text, especially suitable for school use. Another recently updated geography is the fifth edition, revised, of H. O. N. Oboli's *An outline geography of West Africa*, written with editorial assistance from R. J. Harrison Church (London, Harrap, 1967, 224 p., illus., maps, tables, diagrs.).

725 July, Robert W. *The origins of modern African thought : Its development in West Africa during the nineteenth and twentieth centuries.* New York, Praeger, 1967. 512 p. plates, map. Bibliography: p. 481–493.

A perceptive, well-written study of the confrontation of West Africa with Western Europe and America. Illustrations are provided from the lives of such West Africans as Africanus Horton, Olaudah Equiano, Gabriel Pellegrin, Bishop Samuel Ajayi Crowther, Edward W. Blyden, Bishop James Johnson, Blaise Diagne, and Casely Hayford. Westernization as reflected, for example, in the founding and development of Sierra Leone, Gorée and St. Louis, and Liberia is examined, and West African historians and nationalist journalism are discussed. See also Edith Holden, *Blyden of Liberia* (New York, Vantage Press, 1967, 1040 p.); and Hollis R. Lynch, *Edward Wilmot Blyden : Pan-Negro patriot 1832–1912* (London, Oxford University Press, 1967, 272 p.).

726 Kouassigan, Guy-Adjété. *L'homme et la terre : Droits fonciers coutumiers et droit de propriété en Afrique occidentale.* Paris, Office de la Recherche Scientifique et Technique Outre-Mer, Berger-Levrault, 1966. 248 p. (L'homme d'outre-mer, n.s. no. 8) Bibliography: p. [267]–277.

The work is in two main parts: customary land laws (the land as a collective, inalienable, sacred property and the complementary individual rights); and the rapid and profound transformation of traditional land laws and property rights induced by European contact during the 19th century.

727 Kuper, Hilda, ed. *Urbanization and migration in West Africa.* Published under the auspices of the African Studies Center, University of California, Los Angeles. Berkeley and Los Angeles, University of California Press, 1965. 227 p. maps. Bibliography: p. 203–214.

A collection of papers originally presented at an interdisciplinary seminar in 1962: ' The location and nature of West African cities ', by Benjamin E. Thomas; ' Some thoughts on migration and urban settlement ', by John D. Fage; ' Urbanism, migration, and language ', by Joseph H. Greenberg; ' Labor migration among the Mossi of the Upper Volta ', by Elliott P. Skinner; ' Oshogbo – an urban community? ' by William B. Schwab; ' Urban influences on the rural Hausa ', by Horace M. Miner; ' Social alignment and identity in a West African city [Freetown] ', by Michael Banton; ' Migration in West Africa: The political perspective ', by Immanuel Wallerstein; and ' The economics of the migrant labor system ', by Elliot J. Berg. An index is included.

728 Little, Kenneth Lindsay. *West African urbanization : A study of voluntary associations in social change.* London, Cambridge University Press, 1965. 187 p. maps. Bibliography: p. 167–172.

The author categorizes voluntary associations as 1) tribal unions and syncretist cults and 2) various groups concerned with mutual benefit and recreation, the Christian religion, and Western cultural or social pursuits. Using West Africa as an example of a former 'backward' area now undergoing considerable industrial and urban growth, he analyses the role played by these associations in adapting traditional institutions and in integrating the changing social system.

729 Lloyd, Peter C. *Africa in social change: Changing traditional society in the modern world.* Harmondsworth, Middlesex, and Baltimore, Md., Penguin Books, 1967. 363 p. maps. (Penguin African Library, AP22) Bibliography: p. 343–355.

Limiting his frame of reference to West Africa, the author focuses on the interaction between the new social groups (especially the Western-educated élites) and traditional society, the extent to which the patterns of Western industrial society are being reproduced, and the growth and present role of the new élites. The four parts of the work cover the historical background, the impact of the West, changing institutions, and, in conclusion, ideologies, tribalism, and conflicts. An appendix presents comparative data on the states discussed.

730 McPhee, Allan. *The economic revolution in West Africa.* London, Frank Cass, 1971 ed., 1971. 322 p., tables, maps.

McPhee's work was originally published in 1926 and reissued with an introduction by A. G. Hopkins. It stands out as a pioneer study, and ranks as a classic in African economic history. It is the author's aim to 'try and describe the recent economic changes in British West Africa . . . [and] to consider somewhat in detail the nature of . . . native policy'. The writer discusses successively the role of trade, transport, land policy, finance, currency, African policy and health. He emphasizes the role played by the British administration in revolutionizing the precolonial economies from the 1890s onward. McPhee devotes relatively little attention to the precolonial economies. These have been discussed in a much more recent work: Claude Meillassoux, *The development of indigenous trade and markets in West Africa* (London, Oxford University Press, 1971, 444 p.).

731 Morgan, W. B., and J. C. Pugh. *West Africa.* London, Methuen, 1969. xi, 788 p. illus., maps, charts.

A major study compiled by two British geographers. The first part deals with the peoples, their economies, and environmental factors. The second portion covers the impact of the modern economy, demographic changes, development of agriculture, fishing, mining, industry and commerce, and transport. For an excellent treatment of the shipping trade, see Charlotte Leubuscher, *The West African shipping trade, 1909–1959* (Leyden, A. W. Sythoff, 1963, 109 p.).

732 Newbury, Colin W., ed. *British policy towards West Africa: Select documents, 1786–1874.* Oxford, Clarendon Press, 1965. 656 p. illus., maps.

An indispensable collection, supplied with bibliographical footnotes. The author has also written *The western slave coast and its rulers: European trade and administration among the Yoruba and Adja-speaking peoples of south-western Nigeria, southern Dahomey and Togo* (Oxford, Clarendon Press, 1961), a basic text.

733 Newbury, C. W., ed. *British policy toward West Africa: Select documents 1875–1914. With statistical appendices, 1800–1914.* Oxford, Clarendon Press, 1971. 636 p.

The second volume of official documents covering British relations with African societies in West Africa. Organized into four groups of documents: Relations with African societies, Expansion and international partition, Jurisdiction and administration, Economic development.

Part III: area guide (by colonial power, region and colony)

734   Parrinder, Geoffrey. *West African psychology : A comparative study of psychological and religious thought*. London, Lutterworth Press, 1951. 229 p. (Lutterworth Library, v. 37; Missionary Research Series, no. 17)

735   —— *West African religion : A study of the beliefs and practices of Akan, Ewe, Yoruba, Ibo, and kindred peoples*. 2d ed., completely rewritten, rev. and enl. London, Epworth Press, 1961. xv, 203 p. map.

The writer of these two studies, a former missionary and a recognized authority on West African religious beliefs, spent ten years as lecturer in the Department of Religious Studies at Ibadan. The first edition of *West African religion* (1949) had been used as a doctoral thesis. The second edition brings the material up to date and includes coverage of the Ibo peoples as well as a final chapter on religious change. *West African psychology* is a comparative study of the concepts of the soul among West African tribes.

736   Pedler, F. J. *Economic geography of West Africa*. London and New York, Longmans, Green, 1955. xii, 232 p. illus., maps, tables.

Treats of ' the relationship of cause and effect in the work-a-day world of West Africa '. Pedler's coverage includes questions of land and its use, domestic production and export crops, mining, manufacturing, transport, commerce, and the economic aspects of government.

737   Price, Joseph H. *Political institutions of West Africa*. London, Hutchinson Educational, 1967. 266 p. fold. maps, tables, diagrs. Bibliography: p. [258]– 260.

Describes the political situation in English-speaking West Africa, including Liberia, to December 1966. Parts 1 and 2 consist of a political and constitutional history before and after 1945, with detailed examinations of the Ghana Constitution of 1960 and the Nigerian Constitution of 1960 and the Nigerian Constitution of 1963. The remainder of the book covers the judiciary, public services, public finance, and local government.

738   Trimingham, John Spencer. *The Christian church and Islam in West Africa*. London, S.C.M. Press, 1955. 56 p. illus., map. (International Missionary Council Research Pamphlets, no. 3)

738a   —— *A history of Islam in West Africa*. Oxford, Clarendon Press, 1962. 262 p. fold. map, diagr.

See nos. 578–583 for general comment on Dr. Trimingham's studies of Islam.

A recent scholarly analysis of the patterns of Islamization in the region now encompassing parts of Ghana, Upper Volta, Togo, and the Ivory Coast is presented in Nehemia Levtzion's *Muslims and chiefs in West Africa : A study of Islam in the middle Volta basin* (Oxford, 1968, 228 p.).

739   Westermann, Diedrich, and Margaret A. Bryan. *Languages of West Africa*. London, published for the International African Institute by Oxford University Press, 1952. 215 p. map (fold. col. in pocket). (Handbook of African Languages, pt. 2) Bibliography: p. 178–201.

740   Wilson, John. *Education and changing West African culture*. London, Oxford University Press, 1966. 113 p.

The author was a member of the Gold Coast Education Department, 1929–50, and later senior lecturer in the Department of Education in Tropical Areas of the Institute of Education, University of London. His topics include indigenous and early missionary education, education problems of new urban areas, quality in community education and in school education, and the implications for education of economic development. Illustrations are taken from Wilson's Ghanaian experience.

Gambia

Bibliographies

741 Gamble, David P. *Bibliography of the Gambia.* Bathurst, Government Printer, 1967. 154 p. 33 cm.

A mimeographed brochure revised and updated from his 1958 compilation by a scholar who formerly conducted research on the Gambia for the Colonial Office. Approximately 1,600 entries are classified and arranged in chronological order under subheadings. Books, articles and some theses and processed and typescript items are included. A section on government publications gives quite useful annotations on the background of departmental annual reports. There is an author index.

742 Kingdon, Donald. *A chronological table and index of the ordinances of the colony of the Gambia, 1901–1908 (inclusive), and of the rules, regulations and orders passed and made by the Governor-in-Council, and of the proclamations, acts of parliament, orders of the King-in-Council, treaties, etc. Published in the Gambia government gazettes, 1901–1908 (inclusive).* London, Waterlow, 1909. 103 p. (3,000 entries)

These tables and indexes were prepared for most British and Portuguese colonies. Useful reference book.

743 U.S. Library of Congress. General Reference and Bibliography Division. *Official publications of Sierra Leone and Gambia.* Comp. by Audrey A. Walker, African Section. Washington, 1963. xii, 92 p. Historical note on the Gambia: p. 58–61 (outline of political history); publications: p. 62–84.

One of the series of official publications of African states compiled at the Library of Congress (see no. 299). In the section on the Gambia, coverage is from the earliest British documents to within two years of the independence date, February 18, 1965.

Reference works

744 Deschamps, Hubert Jules. *Le Sénégal et la Gambie.* Paris, Presses Universitaires de France, 1964. 125 p. maps. (' Que sais-je? ' no. 597) Bibliography: p. [123]–125.

See no. 1631 for annotation.

745 Gailey, Harry A. *History of the Gambia.* London, Routledge and Kegan Paul, 1964. 244 p. fold. map. Bibliography and notes: p. 218–239.

Presentation of ' the political development of the area from a casual appendage of Britain, through the crucial period of the " scramble ", to the modern position of the tiny enclave on the verge of independence '. See also Frederick K. Ewart, *Some aspects of local government* (Bathhurst, 1946, 92 p.).

746 Gamble, David P. *The Wolof of Senegambia, together with notes on the Lebu and the Serer.* London, International African Institute, 1957. 110 p. illus., maps. (Ethnographic Survey of Africa, Western Africa, pt. 14) Includes bibliographies.

For a general description of the systematic ethnological surveys in this series, see no. 333. Mr. Gamble's study is notable for its extensive list of references on the Wolof (in the Colonial Office report, spelled ' Wollof '). This list is in three sections: linguistic material, religious literature, and general bibliography. The notes on the Lebu and the Serer are similarly followed by bibliography. In 1949

Mr. Gamble prepared for the Colonial Office an account of Wolof agriculture and money economy, *Contributions to a socio-economic survey of the Gambia.* A linguistic work by this author, *Gambian-Fula verb list,* was issued by the Research Department of the Colonial Office in 1958 (London, 43 p., processed).

The dominant tribe, the Mandingo, in Senegambia is treated in the French series Monographies ethnologiques africaines (see no. 333).

747 Gray, Sir John Milner. *A history of the Gambia.* Cambridge, Eng., University Press, 1940. 508 p. fold. map.

The standard scholarly history of the Gambia. The author, at that time Justice of the Supreme Court of the Gambia, made use of many early travel narratives that included references to the Gambia and of unpublished material in the Public Record Office and other university and mission archives. The book is documented with footnote references. See also Francis B. Archer, *The Gambia colony and protectorate : An official handbook* (London, 1906, 364 p.).

748 Great Britain. Colonial Office. *Annual report on. . .* See no. 672.

749 Hopkinson, Emilius. *Notes on the laws of the Gambia Protectorate, 1885–1923.* 1926. 41 p.

Contents: 1, Annotated list of the ordinances which are applicable to the Protectorate; 2, Notes on the Protectorate ordinance, its amending ordinance and regulations connected therewith; 3, A Mandingo translation of certain parts of the Protectorate ordinance and regulations.

750 *Ordinances of the settlement on the Gambia, passed in the years between the 10th August 1818 and [30th December 1885]; treaties of the Government of the Gambia with native chiefs; and a Convention with France.* Comp. by Algernon Montagu. London, Eyre and Spottiswoode, 1882–87. 3 v.

751 *A revised edition of the Ordinances of the Colony of the Gambia, including governor's orders and proclamations, Orders-in-Council, and rules and regulations made under ordinances; Letters Patent and Standing orders of Legislative Council; orders of the King in Council; and index and appendices.* Prepared by John Milner Gray. 1942. 3 v. illus.

752 *A revised edition of the Ordinances of the Colony of the Gambia, with an appendix containing governor's orders and proclamations, Orders-in-Council, and rules and regulations made under ordinances; Letters Patent and Standing orders of Legislative Council; various acts of Parliament in force in the Colony; orders of the King in Council. And an index prepared under the authority of the Statute law revision ordinance, 1916.* By Frederick Alan van der Meulen. London, printed by Waterlow, 1916–17. 2 v.

Such compilations are found for most colonies. Cited here just as illustrations.

Gold Coast (Ghana)

Bibliographies

753 Adams, Cynthia. *A study guide for Ghana.* Boston, African Studies Center, Boston University, 1967. 95 p.

Prepared for the Agency for International Development. Each section contains a general note drawing attention to the most important work on a particular topic, followed by a bibliography. The main headings are physical environment, early external influences, traditional societies, colonial rule and nationalism, politics, social change, and the economic system. There is also a general bibliography.

754 Agyei, Christiana Opokua. *References to the political history of Ghana, 1928–1957: A select introductory bibliography compiled in partial fulfilment of the requirements for the diploma in librarianship and archives.* Legon, Balme Library, University College, 1966. xxxiv, 125 p.

755 Amedekey, E. Y. *The culture of Ghana: A bibliography.* Accra, Ghana University Press, 1970. 215 p.

756 Brand, Richard R. *A selected bibliography on Accra, Ghana, a West African colonial city (1887–1960).* Monticello, Ill., Council of Planning Librarians, 1970. 27 p.

757 Cardinall, Allan W. *A bibliography of the Gold Coast.* Issued as a companion volume to the Census Report of 1931. Accra, Government Printer, 1932. xix, 384 p. Classified, with author index. Blank pages for ' Addenda ' at the end of each section.

This justly celebrated bibliography, covering all writing on the Gold Coast from 1496 to 1931 and much on West Africa in general, is described at length by Rydings in his *The bibliographies of West Africa.* The compiler was a British colonial official of long experience in West Africa and author of several semi-anthropological books on peoples on the Gold Coast and Togo.

758 Ghana. Ministry of Agriculture. Reference Library. *Ghana agriculture, 1890–1962 : A bibliography of crop and stock, co-operation and forestry, food and fishery.* By S. N. Tetteh. Accra, 1962. 315 p. (Ministry of Agriculture Bulletin, no. 3 [Draft])

Attempt at a full listing of all material published about Ghanaian agriculture from 1890 to 1962. Included are items written about other areas by Ghanaians or by people who came to Ghana. See also no. 799.

759 Ghana Library Board. *Ghana National Bibliography.* Accra, 1965– . Annual.

760 Johnson, Albert F. *A bibliography of Ghana, 1930–1961.* Evanston, Ill., published for the Ghana Library Board by Northwestern University Press, 1964. xiii, 210 p.

A continuation of A. W. Cardinall's *A bibliography of the Gold Coast,* listing titles of all monographic publications and selected periodical articles on the Gold Coast and Ghana during the formative years 1930–61. The list is intended to be comprehensive, including works of technical and scientific interest, translations and pure literature, but vernacular texts have been omitted. A few items have slight annotations. The 2,608 titles, among them 357 government publications, are classified in broad subject groupings, and an author index is provided.

The study entitled ' A bibliography of Ghana: 1958–1964 ', by David Brokensha and S. I. A. Kotei, *African Studies Bulletin,* v. 10, no. 2, Sept. 1967, p. 35–79, was designed as a continuation of Johnson's work.

A preliminary bibliography compiled by Mr. Johnson was issued by the Ghana Library Board in 1961, *Books about Ghana : A select reading list* (32 p.). This work contains about 300 titles covering the most significant and easily accessible works on the Gold Coast and Ghana, classified by subject, with an author index. A separate section names the chief official publications – commissions and special reports, documents on the constitution, etc.

761 Padmore Research Library on African Affairs. Bibliography Series. Accra, Ghana Library Board, 1962–65.

A set of special subject bibliographies prepared by this outstanding African library service. No. 3 is *The Akan of Ghana : A select bibliography* (1963, 17 p.).

Part III: area guide (by colonial power, region and colony)

No. 4, the subject of which is the father of Pan-Africanism, *Dr. W. E. B. Du Bois, 1868–1963* (1964, 39 l., mimeographed), lists Dr. Du Bois's own works and almost 50 books about him.

762 Pitcher, G. M. *Bibliography of Ghana, 1957–1959.* Kumasi, Kumasi College of Technology Library, 1960. 177 l.

Restricted to books, articles, pamphlets, etc., which appeared just before the transition to and during the first two years of Ghana's national independence. Entries are classified under broad headings; some have brief annotations.

763 Smalman Smith, Sir John. *Analytical index to the ordinances regulating the civil and criminal procedure of the Gold Coast Colony and the colony of Lagos.* London, Stevens, 1888. 119 p. (3,000 entries)

In addition to the many entries in this work, a later index of some 300 references appears in Stanley W. Morgan, *A chronological table and an alphabetical index of the ordinances of the Gold Coast Colony* (London, 1895, xxiv p.). See also no. 476 for Schiller's lists of indexes and collections of laws and ordinances.

764 Witherell, Julian W., and Sharon B. Lockwood, comps. *Ghana: A guide to research publications, 1872–1968.* Washington, General Reference and Bibliography Division, Reference Department, Library of Congress, 1969. 110 p.

This guide contains 1,283 entries, and covers material derived from the Gold Coast, modern Ghana, Great Britain, as well as publications of the League of Nations and the United Nations relating to British Togoland from 1920 to 1957.

Serials

765 *Economic Bulletin of Ghana.* v. 1– . 1957– . Accra, Economic Society of Ghana. Quarterly.

766 *Ghana Notes and Queries.* v. 1– . 1961– . Legon, Historical Society of Ghana.

767 *Ghana year book: A Daily Graphic publication.* 1957– . Accra, Ghana Graphic Co. illus. Annual.

Published by this leading newspaper office from 1953 to 1956 as *Gold Coast year book.* It includes general directory information of the government and organizations of Ghana, with a brief biographical section.

768 *Historical Society of Ghana: Transactions.* 1952– . Achimota. Twice a year.

Reference works

769 Apter, David E. *Ghana in transition.* Rev. ed. New York, Atheneum, 1963. 432 p. illus., ports., map.

Case study of political institutional transfer published first in 1955 with the title *The Gold Coast in transition* (Princeton, N.J., Princeton University Press, 355 p.). Much of the text, after a sketch of background, traditional system of politics, and the British policy of indirect rule, is devoted to the evolutionary changes between the constitution of 1950 and the Nkrumah constitution of 1954, which brought representative and responsible self-government, foreshadowing complete independence. In the new edition a chapter entitled 'Ghana as a new nation' has been added.

770 Austin, Dennis. *Politics in Ghana, 1946–1960.* London and New York, Oxford University Press, 1964. xiv, 459 p. maps, tables. Bibliography: p. [447]–451.

In describing the Gold Coast's progress from ' model colony ' to republic the author first provides an introductory preview, followed by chapters on early years (1946–51), the Convention People's Party in office (1951–54), the struggle for power (1954–56), and a concluding chapter on independence and succeeding years (1957–60). Appendices are included.

771 Bennion, Francis A. R. *The constitutional law of Ghana.* London, Butterworth, 1962. xxxvi, 527 p. (Butterworth's African Law Series, no. 5)

Discusses the legal history of the colony and the impact of English common law on African customary law.

772 Bourret, Florence M. *Ghana : The road to independence, 1919–1957.* 3d ed. Stanford, Calif., Stanford University Press, 1960. xiii, 246 p. map, tables. Bibliography: p. 221–231.

The third edition of an informative study by an American nun and history professor, first published with the title *The Gold Coast : A survey of the Gold Coast and British Togoland, 1919–1946* (Stanford, 1949, 231 p.). Mother Bourret planned her 20th-century political, economic, and social history of the colony as a case study of the ' day-by-day working out ' of British policy in bringing dependent territories into the modern world. An updated edition, *1919–1951*, was published in 1952; and the present volume completes the survey with a chapter detailing the political and constitutional changes of 1945–57 and Independence Day.

773 Braimah, J. A., and J. R. Goody. *Salaga : The struggle for power.* London, Longmans, Green and Company, 1967. 222 p.

A collection of material for a history of the scramble and the coming of British rule as experienced first hand by the eastern Gonja people (Kpembe division).

774 Claridge, William W. *A history of the Gold Coast and Ashanti from the earliest times to the commencement of the twentieth century.* 2d ed. London, Frank Cass; New York, Barnes & Noble, 1964. 2 v. 649, 638 p. maps (part fold. col.), geneal. table. Bibliography: v. 2, p. 577–581.

This famous work, known particularly for its full treatment of the Ashanti wars, first appeared in 1915. The second edition has a new introduction by W. E. F. Ward.

775 Dickson, Kwamina B. *A historical geography of Ghana.* London, Cambridge University Press, 1969. xiv, 379 p. illus., maps. Bibliography: p. 360–366.

Covers the development of Ghana from earliest times to the present. Describes the people, their social organization, migrations, manufactures, artifacts and history. Colonial period well covered, especially on economic developments, transport and communications.

776 Ethnographic Survey of Africa: Western Africa. London, International African Institute, 1950–52.

The volumes of the Ethnographic Survey relating to Ghana are by Madeline Manoukian, *Akan and Ga-Adangme peoples of the Gold Coast* (1950, 112 p.; Western Africa, pt. 1), *Tribes of the northern territories of the Gold Coast* (1951, 102 p.; pt. 5), and *The Ewe-speaking people of Togoland and the Gold Coast* (1952, 63 p.; pt. 6). Each has a bibliography of several pages.

The number of anthropological studies relating to Ghana is too large to permit mention of more than a few individual authors. Among the better known are David Brokensha, M. J. Field, Meyer Fortes, Robert Lystad, and J. R. Goody.

777 Fage, J. D. *Ghana: A historical interpretation.* Madison, University of Wisconsin Press, 1959. 122 p. illus., maps. Bibliography: p. 89–115 (notes). Short but valuable synthesis of Ghanaian history. See also no. 828, John E. Flint's *Nigeria and Ghana.* The standard modern text for the political history up to independence is William E. Ward, *A history of Ghana* (2d ed., rev., London, Allen & Unwin, 1958, 434 p.).

778 Gold Coast (Colony) Courts. *Reports, notes of cases and proceedings and judgments in appeals, etc., and references under rules, orders and ordinances relating to the Gold Coast Colony, and the colony of Nigeria from 1861 to 1914, and a few decisions given by H.M.'s Judicial Committee of the Privy Council affecting the aforesaid colonies.* Collected by Peter Awoonor Renner. London, Sweet & Maxwell [etc.], 1915. 2 v.
Most colonies issued this kind of reference work as well as compilation of laws, indexes to laws and law reports. See the Library of Congress lists, no. 271.

779 Great Britain. Colonial Office. *Annual report on...* See no. 672.

780 Harvey, William Burnett. *Law and social change in Ghana.* Princeton, N.J., Princeton University Press, 1966. xiii, 453 p. Bibliographical footnotes.
Professor Harvey, who was dean of the Faculty of Law at the University of Ghana from 1962 to 1964, presents a perceptive study of legal developments in Ghana, 1951–64, within the context of the social pressures impinging upon the contenders for political power. After providing a brief background, he traces the progress of independence from the constitutions of 1951 and 1957 through the constitution of 1960 and offers detailed analyses of relevant legislation and executive action.

781 Hayford, Joseph Ephraim Casely. *Ethiopia unbound: Studies in race emancipation.* New York, Humanities Press, 1969. 215 p. (Reissue of 1911 publication)
Hayford, a leading nationalist of the Gold Coast, was a lawyer, educator and journalist. His writings represent an important response to European colonial rule in West Africa and the incipient nationalist and Pan-African point of view expressed in novel form. See also his *Gold Coast land tenure and the forest bill* (London, C. M. Phillips, 1911); *The truth about the West African land question* (London, C. M. Phillips, 1913); and other works.

782 Hill, Polly. *The migrant cocoa-farmers of southern Ghana.* New York, Cambridge University Press, 1963. xv, 265 p. illus., ports., maps (3 fold.). Bibliography: p. 252–256.
A preliminary survey of this study was issued by Oxford University Press in 1956, *The Gold Coast cocoa farmer.* The new volume has been widely hailed as an authoritative work. The author does not follow the regular social-survey technique but instead what she calls ' hit-and-miss methods ', carried out in talks with many informants. She thus makes use to a considerable extent of history handed down by oral tradition. Each chapter of discussion and theorizing is followed by one or more appendices giving historical notes, statistics, case studies and other interesting data. See also no. 719, her *Studies in rural capitalism in West Africa* (Cambridge, Eng., University Press, 1970, xxiii, 172 p.).

For any study of the cocoa industry, reference should also be made to the annual reports of the Ghana Cocoa Marketing Board and to its quarterly magazine *C.M.B. Newsletter* (1957– , Accra). There are also reports of the West African Cacao Research Institute at Tafo.

783 Irvine, Frederick R. *The fishes and fisheries of the Gold Coast.* With illustrations and an account of the fishing industry by A. P. Brown and classification and keys for the identification of the fishes by J. R. Norman and E. Trewavas. London, published on behalf of the Government of the Gold Coast by the Crown Agents for the Colonies, 1947. 352 p. illus. Bibliography: 327–337.

There are three classification indexes, one of English and Latin names, one of Ga and Adangme names, and one of Fante, Ashanti and Twi names.

784 ———— *Woody plants of Ghana, with special reference to their uses.* London, Oxford University Press, 1961. xcv, 868 p. illus., plates (35 part col.). Bibliography: p. 790–793.

This was first published in 1930 under the title *Plants of the Gold Coast.* Another full-scale study of forestry in Ghana is by Charles J. Taylor, *Synecology and silviculture in Ghana* (Edinburgh, published on behalf of the University College of Ghana by Nelson, 1960, 418 p., illus., maps).

785 Kay, G. B. *The political economy of colonialism in Ghana: A collection of documents and statistics 1900–1960.* New York, Cambridge University Press, 1971. 448 p., 76 tables, 2 maps.

The main thrust of this work is that in Ghana the official British commitment to free trade and laissez-faire was not reflected in practice, rather that colonials were unwilling to foster trade that did not contribute directly to the accumulation of British capital or that threatened the social basis of British rule. An extraordinarily complete statistical abstract substantiates the author's conclusions on the political and economic expedience of British imperialism. The work is furnished with a bibliography.

786 Kimble, David. *A political history of Ghana: The rise of Gold Coast nationalism, 1850–1928.* Oxford, Clarendon Press, 1963. xviii, 587 p. ports., maps, tables.

The author, former director of the Institute of Extra-mural Studies at the University College of Ghana, is editor of the *Journal of Modern African Studies.* In this excellent, full-scale history of the origins of nationalism in the former Gold Coast, he gives sources in the footnotes. His thesis is that Gold Coast nationalism is of relatively early origin.

787 Metcalfe, G. E., ed. *Great Britain and Ghana: Documents of Ghana history, 1807–1957.* London, published on behalf of the University of Ghana by Nelson, 1964. xvii, 779 p. maps.

Documents were selected in order to illustrate the development of British policy in Ghana, but this should be understood in its West African and even global context. There are brief introductions to each period (age of experiment, 1807–52; of laissez-faire, 1852–86; of expansion, 1887–1918; of fulfillment, 1919–57). Appendices include lists of British governors and administrators and of Gold Coast government treaties, statistics on trade and revenue, and maps. There is an index. See also no. 1593.

788 Mobley, Harris W. *The Ghanaian's image of the missionary.* Leiden, E. J. Brill, 1970. 180 p.

An analysis of the published critiques of Christian missionaries by Ghanaians. Provides a brief outline of missions in Africa, biographical sketches of the main critics (Mensah Sarbah, Casely Hayford, Busia, Nketia and Baëta, for example) and then their critiques of missionary thought and activity.

789 Nkrumah, Kwame. *Ghana: The autobiography of Kwame Nkrumah.* New York, Nelson, 1957. 302 p. illus.

790 —— *I speak of freedom : A statement of African ideology.* New York, Praeger, 1961. 291 p. illus. (Books That Matter)

791 —— *Neo-colonialism : The last stage of imperialism.* London, Nelson, 1965. 280 p. Bibliography: p. 260–262.

All primary source material by a leading African politician in the struggle against colonialism, Nkrumah's work displays many of the misconceptions and dogmas that contributed to his downfall.

The biography by a West African newspaperman, Timothy Bankole, *Kwame Nkrumah : His rise to power* (Evanston, Ill., Northwestern University Press, 1963, 191 p.), was first published in 1955 and has been reprinted with three added chapters: ' Osagyefo ', ' Nkrumah the man ', and ' Nkrumah and the African personality '.

792 Rattray, Robert Sutherland. *Ashanti.* Oxford, Clarendon Press, 1923. 348 p. Reprint: Kumasi, Basel Mission Book Depot, 1954.

793 —— *Ashanti law and constitution.* Oxford, Clarendon Press, 1929. 420 p. Reprint: London, Oxford University Press, 1956.

794 —— *Religion and art in Ashanti.* Oxford, Clarendon Press, 1927. 414 p. Reprint: Kumasi, 1955.

795 —— *Tribes of the Ashanti hinterland.* Oxford, Clarendon Press, 1932. 2 v.

There are modern reprints of three of the justly famous works by this authority on native languages and customs who as head of a new Anthropology Department in Ashanti submitted, in 1921, as a confidential ' Intelligence Report ' to the administration, the detailed investigation of the beliefs and customs of that war-like people. From this report the British were led to realize one of the true causes of the Ashanti wars – the disposition of the Golden Stool, in which the Ashanti believed the soul of the nation resided. Of the three first-named books, which were published as a uniform series, *Religion and art in Ashanti* comes closest to popular style; all are definitely scholarly works, as is the later *Tribes of the Ashanti hinterland.*

796 Scott, David. *Epidemic disease in Ghana, 1901–1960.* London and New York, Oxford University Press, 1965. xviii, 208 p. (Oxford Medical Publications) Includes bibliographies.

Study by an epidemiologist formerly in the Ghana Ministry of Health, giving a full account of the development of public health services in the British colony and under the independent government. Data are from official statistics and reports, fortified by personal experience. The account of measures to combat plague, yellow fever, smallpox, cerebrospinal meningitis, relapsing fever, and African trypanosomiasis and influenza is of wide application to the health problems of the continent.

797 Szereszewski, R. *Structural changes in the economy of Ghana, 1891–1911.* London, Weidenfeld and Nicholson, 1965. 161 p.

The economy of the Gold Coast was radically transformed between 1891 and 1911, and the next fifty years' growth was made possible by the economic structure laid down in that period. A major work of economic history of developments in one colony.

798 Wight, Martin. *The Gold Coast legislative council.* London, published under the auspices of Nuffield College by Faber & Faber, 1947. 285 p. fold. map. (Studies in Colonial Legislatures, v. 2)

This is the second volume of the significant series edited by Margery Perham.

Mr. Wight, an authority on colonial constitutions, also wrote the first general volume, *Development of the legislative council, 1606–1945* (1946). His specialist study of the Gold Coast function of self-government began with a review of historical and political development and continued with an analysis of the constitution of 1925, the Council set up by it, and its workings. He examined the post-war political situation of the colony and concluded with a brief glance at the new constitution of 1946.

799 Wills, J. Brian, ed. *Agriculture and land use in Ghana.* London and New York, published for the Ghana Ministry of Food and Agriculture by Oxford University Press, 1962. xviii, 503 p. illus., maps, charts, tables. Bibliography: p. 445–494.

Compendium of information available on background, state, and problems of agriculture and land use in Ghana, in three parts. The first part is on general conditions and patterns of rural land use; the second on special aspects, with particular emphasis on cocoa crops; the third on forestry and plant and animal husbandry. The work, intended as a textbook for officials, teachers and research workers, was begun in 1954 and was finished by Ghanaian officials. Wills also compiled the valuable *Bibliography of agriculture, land use and surrounding conditions in Ghana and adjacent territories, 1930–1959.*

800 Wraith, R. E. *Guggisberg.* London, Oxford University Press, 1967. 342 p. A major biography of one of the ablest governors of British Africa. Guggisberg was governor of the Gold Coast from 1919 to 1927 and launched economic development and education schemes that laid the basis for the colony's rapid development.

Nigeria

Bibliographies

801 Dipeolu, J. O. *Bibliographical sources for Nigerian studies.* Evanston, Ill., Northwestern University, 1966. 26 p.

Most entries are annotated, some evaluatively. Arrangement proceeds from general to topical (geography, agriculture, history, anthropology, etc.). Excluded are bibliographies that have been superseded by more comprehensive or up-to-date ones.

802 Ibadan. University. Library. *Nigerian publications.* 1950/52– . Ibadan, Ibadan University Press. Annual.

Until recently the only national bibliography published in black Africa. This serial has continued annually since the 1950/52 volume, with quarterly processed supplements. Before 1962 the publication appeared under the university's earlier name, University College; beginning with the 1961 edition the subtitle has been *Current national bibliography* (early issues were subtitled *A list of works received under the publications ordinance*). Each issue carries a comprehensive listing of books, pamphlets and documents in English and African languages published in the Federation. Since 1955 the issues include a section of new and defunct serial titles supplementing a monograph titled *Nigerian periodicals and newspapers, 1950–1955 : A list of those received from April 1950 to June 1955 under the publications ordinance, 1950* (1956, 23 p.).

803 Ike, Adebimpe O. *Economic development of Nigeria, 1950–1964 : A bibliography.* Nsukka, Library, University of Nigeria, 1966. 129 p. Processed. (University of Nigeria Library Series, no. 1)

Entries, some of which are annotated, are arranged by subject according to the

Part III: area guide (by colonial power, region and colony)

Library of Congress classification scheme. Topics covered are population, economic conditions, economic planning, land, agriculture, industry, minerals, labour, transportation and communication, commerce and trade, and finance (including banking). For each topic publications on the whole country are given first, with regions following. Geographical divisions are further subdivided into two sections, books and pamphlets in one, periodical articles in another. Included are official publications as well as books that do not deal primarily with the subject but contain substantial sections on the Nigerian economy. There are author and title indexes. Recent data have been incorporated in Adetunji Akinyotu's compilation *A bibliography on development planning in Nigeria, 1955–1968* (Ibadan, Nigerian Institute of Social and Economic Research, 1968, 133 p.).

804 Oni-Orisan, B. A., comp. *A bibliography of Nigerian history.* Ibadan, University of Ibadan Library, 1968. unpaged. mimeo.
An attempt to list all known books, pamphlets and articles on Nigerian history. The work lists 1,502 items arranged under 12 headings. Supplements are to be issued. See also *Lagos past and present: An historical bibliography* (Lagos, National Library of Nigeria, 1970, 102 p.). The National Library Occasional Publications Series is most useful.

805 Perry, Ruth. *A preliminary bibliography of the literature of nationalism in Nigeria.* [London, International African Institute, 1956] 38 p. Processed.
This bibliography is limited to titles of works – mainly pamphlets – on politics, history, tribal laws and customs, biographies, and trade union publications printed by the private presses of Nigeria.

806 U.S. Library of Congress. General Reference and Bibliography Division. *Nigeria: A guide to official publications.* Comp. by Sharon Lockwood, African Section. Washington, 1966. xii, 166 p.
A very full bibliography, much of it based on archival records from Nigerian sources. Over 2,450 numbered titles are given; many of those dated before 1947 are unavailable in American libraries. There are four parts: (1) publications issued from 1861 to 1914; (2) publications of the federal and regional governments, 1914–65, and of the Southern Cameroons, 1954–61; (3) British publications relating to Nigeria; and (4) League of Nations publications relating to Nigeria and U.N. publications on the trusteeship territory of the Cameroons. This compilation supersedes an earlier list compiled in 1959.

Serials

807 Historical Society of Nigeria. *Journal.* 1956– . Ibadan. Annual.
Edited at the University of Ibadan, this scholarly journal contains significant contributions to historical research. It concentrates on but is by no means confined to Nigeria and West Africa.

A new historical magazine, *Tarikh*, began publication (by Longmans) in 1965, under the editorship of Dr. J. B. Webster of the History Department of Ibadan. Articles, Pan-African in content, are of general interest, 'pleasant and readable', addressed in particular to secondary school and undergraduate students. The articles derive from experts in their respective fields. The University of Ife also issues irregularly *African Historian*.

808 *Nigeria Magazine.* no. 1– . 1934– . Lagos, Federal Government. illus. Quarterly.
Government-sponsored periodical, begun by the Education Department with the title *Nigerian Teacher*, later changed to *Nigeria: A Quarterly Magazine of*

British Africa: West Africa

General Interest. This is a distinguished journal, handsomely illustrated, with issues often devoted to a single theme or a special publication.

809 *Nigeria Trade Journal.* v. 1– . Jan. 1953– . Lagos. illus. (part col.), maps. Quarterly.
Published by the Federal Department of Commerce and Industry.

810 *Nigeria Year Book.* 1952– . Lagos, Daily Times Publication. illus. Annual.
Directory and guide of the almanac type, including a political who's who, a trade directory, and a register of federal and regional governments (1967 ed., 308 p.).

811 *Nigerian Bar Journal.* v. 1– . 1958– . Lagos, Nigerian Bar Association. Annual.

812 *Nigerian Geographical Journal.* v. 1, no. 1– . Apr. 1957– . Ibadan. Irregular.
Organ of the Nigerian Geographical Association, which, like a number of other learned societies, has its headquarters at the University of Ibadan.

813 Nigerian Institute of Social and Economic Research. *Annual Conference Proceedings.* 1952– . Ibadan, The Institute, University of Ibadan.
The latest report of this institute, formerly the West African Institute of Social and Economic Research, appeared in 1963 (230 p.).

814 *Nigerian Journal of Economic and Social Studies.* no. 1– . May 1959– . Ibadan. 3 times a year.
Publication of the Nigerian Economic Society, edited at University College, Ibadan.

815 *West African Pilot.* Lagos. Daily.
This newspaper, founded by Nnamdi Azikiwe in November 1937 and serving as the leading organ in the long nationalist struggle, was perhaps the most influential of Nigerian newspapers. See also no. 707, *West Africa*; a valuable feature is 'Portraits', short biographies of important people. An 'Index to "Portraits" in *West Africa*, 1948–1966' was prepared by Karen Fung in *African Studies Bulletin*, v. 9, no. 3, Dec. 1966.

Reference works

816 Abernethy, David B. *The political dilemma of popular education : An African case.* Stanford, Stanford University Press, 1969. 357 p. Bibliography: p. 330–346.
An excellent survey of the politics of education in Southern Nigeria. Part I has a useful survey of education from 1842 to 1950. Part II charts the history of education and the political setting in the 1950s during the period of transition from colonial rule to independence.

817 Awolowo, Obafemi. *Awo : The autobiography of Chief Obafemi Awolowo.* Cambridge, Eng., University Press, 1960. xii, 315 p. illus.
The personal story of the former head of the Western Region's 'loyal opposition' Action Group, covering the pre-independence part of his chequered career, is a primary source for the history of Nigerian nationalism.

818 Ayandele, E. A. *The missionary impact on modern Nigeria, 1842–1914 : A political and social analysis.* London, Longmans, Green, 1966. 393 p. plates, map. Bibliography: p. 347–360.
See also J. F. Ade Ajayi, *Christian missions in Nigeria, 1841–1891 : The making of a new élite* (London, Longmans, Green, 1965, 317 p.). Both works are excellent examples of the new African history written by Africans.

Part III: area guide (by colonial power, region and colony)

819 Azikiwe, Nnamdi. *Zik : A selection from the speeches of Nnamdi Azikiwe.* Cambridge, Eng., University Press, 1961. 344 p. illus.

This selection of the speeches of the dynamic leader of Nigerian nationalism, formerly the Premier of Eastern Nigeria and Governor-General of the Federation of Nigeria from October 1960, begins with his lectures as a graduate student in America in 1927 and offers the most celebrated examples of Zik's oratory through 1959. Among the topics discussed are education, democracy, the colour bar, finance and banking, the press and broadcasting, Moral Re-Armament, local government, the Church Missionary Society, and many aspects of anti-colonial politics. See also K. A. B. Jones-Quartey, *A life of Azikiwe* (London, Penguin Books, 1965, 272 p.).

820 Burns, Sir Alan Cuthbert. *History of Nigeria.* 7th ed. London, Allen and Unwin, 1969. 366 p. ports., maps.

A standard history written by a former British colonial governor. The author's reminiscences are entitled *Colonial civil servant* (London, Allen and Unwin, 1949). He has also written on subjects as varied as colour prejudice and the history of the West Indies. Appendices (p. 312–343).

821 Coker, Increase Herbert Ebenezer. *Landmarks of the Nigerian press : An outline of the origins and development of the newspaper press in Nigeria, 1859 to 1965.* Apapa, 1968. 126 p. facsims. Includes bibliography.

History of the Nigerian press for a popular audience but with valuable summaries of people and newspapers. There are lists of newspapers from 1859 to 1965.

822 Coleman, James S. *Nigeria : Background to nationalism.* Berkeley, University of California Press, 1958. xiv, 510 p. illus., ports., maps. Bibliography: p. 481–496.

History of the emergence of the Nigerian nation from colony to full self-government, ending three years short of independence. The first part gives physical, cultural and historical background, the second an analysis of the factors in the Western impact that led to social and political change. With Part 3, p. 169, Dr. Coleman turns to a detailed account of the beginnings and the progress of the nationalist movement in the interwar years, and in the last part carries it to the post-war achievement of the new era of self-government.

823 Crowder, Michael. *A short history of Nigeria.* Rev. and enl. ed. New York, Praeger, 1966. 416 p. illus., ports., maps (1 fold.). (Books That Matter) Bibliography: p. 379–389.

A narrative of Nigerian history, based largely on modern research and written as a clear account for the general reader. Much important new material is provided in this new edition of a work originally published in 1962. Appendices include a summary of major events from independence to December 1964 and several dynastic lists. There are end-notes and an excellent analytical index.

See also J. C. Anene, *Southern Nigeria in transition, 1885–1906; theory and practice in a colonial protectorate* (Cambridge, Eng., Cambridge University Press, 1966, 360 p., port., map, tables; bibliography, p. 340–346); and Saburi O. Biobaku, *The Egba and their neighbours, 1842–1872* (Oxford, Clarendon Press, 1957, 128 p.; bibliography, p. 108–118).

824 Dike, Kenneth Onwuka. *Trade and politics in the Niger Delta, 1830–1885 : An introduction to the economic and political history of Nigeria.* Oxford, Clarendon Press, 1956. 250 p. map, tables. (Oxford Studies in African Affairs) Bibliographical references are in ' Notes on the sources ', p. 224–230.

This distinguished African historian, formerly professor at University College, Ibadan (which in 1962 became the University of Ibadan), is also on the editorial board of the *Journal of African History* and a leading figure in African scholarship. His book of 1956, based on his doctoral thesis at the University of London, is a thoroughly documented study of the gradual supplanting of the native governments of Nigeria by British Administration. See also G. I. Jones, *The trading states of the Oil Rivers: A study of political development in eastern Nigeria* (London, Oxford University Press, 1963, 263 p.).

825 Ethnographic Survey of Africa: Western Africa. London, International African Institute.

For the general note on this series, see no. 333. The following surveys relating to Nigeria summarize ethnological findings to the time of their publication, and each has tribal maps and three or four pages of bibliographical data.

> no. 3. *The Ibo and Ibibio-speaking peoples of south-eastern Nigeria.* By Daryll Forde and G. I. Jones. 1950. 80 p.

> no. 4. *The Yoruba-speaking peoples of south-western Nigeria.* By Daryll Forde. 1951. 102 p.

> no. 7. *The peoples of the plateau area of Northern Nigeria.* By Harold D. Gunn. 1953. 111 p.

> no. 8. *The Tiv of central Nigeria.* By Laura Bohannan and Paul Bohannan. 1953. 100 p.

> no. 10. *Peoples of the Niger-Benue confluence.* Nupe, by Daryll Forde; Igbira, by Paul Brown; Igala and Idoma-speaking peoples, by Robert G. Armstrong. 1955. 160 p.

> no. 12. *Pagan peoples of the central area of Northern Nigeria.* By Harold D. Gunn. 1956. 146 p.

> no. 13. *The Benin kingdom and the Edo-speaking peoples of south-western Nigeria.* By R. E. Bradbury. 1957. 212 p.

> no. 15. *Peoples of the middle Niger region of Northern Nigeria.* By Harold D. Gunn and F. P. Conant. 1960. 136 p.

826 Ezera, Kalu. *Constitutional developments in Nigeria : An analytical study of Nigeria's constitution-making developments and the historical and political factors that affected constitutional change.* 2d ed. Cambridge, Eng., University Press, 1964. xiv, 315 p. maps. Bibliography: p. 301–309.

Clear, factual analysis of the constitutional history of Nigeria.

827 Flint, John E. *Sir George Goldie and the making of Nigeria.* London, Oxford University Press, 1960. 340 p.

An excellent history of the Royal Niger Company and its dealings with the Liverpool traders and European imperialists, and the company's role in the diplomacy of the partition of Africa.

828 —— *Nigeria and Ghana.* Englewood Cliffs, N.J., Prentice-Hall, 1966. 176 p. (Modern Nations in Historical Perspective)

In a perceptive interpretation of the more recent impact of colonialism and African nationalism, the author explores the broader themes of society, politics, and culture in present-day Nigeria and Ghana. For a good, detailed study of the development of the multi-party system during British rule, see Richard Sklar, *Nigerian political parties* (Princeton, N.J., 1963, 578 p.).

829 Great Britain. Colonial Office. *Annual report on...* See no. 672.

830 Heussler, Robert. *The British in Northern Nigeria.* London, Oxford University Press, 1968. xxi, 210 p. Includes bibliography.

An historical survey of the men and methods of British indirect rule in Northern

Part III: area guide (by colonial power, region and colony)

Nigeria. Most valuable for the views and reminiscences of colonial officials Heussler interviewed. See also Sonia F. Graham, *Government and mission education in Northern Nigeria, 1900–1919, with special reference to the work of Hanns Vischer* (Ibadan University Press, 1966, 192 p.).

831 Hogben, Sidney John, and Anthony H. M. Kirk-Greene. *The emirates of Northern Nigeria: A preliminary survey of their historical traditions.* London, Oxford University Press, 1966. xxvii, 638 p. illus., maps (1 fold. col.), geneal. tables. Bibliography: p. 593–603.

A reorganized and extensively expanded version of Hogben's *The Muhammadan emirates of Nigeria* (1930). Part 1 (p. 3–146), by Hogben, presents a broad historical survey of the Western Sudan. Part 2, by both authors, is comprised of individual histories of 37 Northern Nigerian traditional states – the emirates deriving from the Hausa states and from the Bornu and Sokoto empires and those deriving independently. Included are a glossary, notes on European travellers in the Sudan and Sahara, 1875–80, and a list of Northern Nigerian chiefs.

832 Ikime, Obaro. *Niger Delta rivalry: Itsekiri-Urhobo relations and the European presence, 1884–1936.* New York, Humanities Press, 1969. 301 p.

A detailed history of two communities and their responses to colonial rule.

833 International Bank for Reconstruction and Development. *The economic development of Nigeria: Report of a mission organized by the International Bank for Reconstruction and Development at the request of the governments of Nigeria and the United Kingdom.* Baltimore, Md., Johns Hopkins Press, 1955. xxii, 686 p. maps, tables, diagrs.

An exhaustive study prepared in connexion with technical aid by a mission of experts on agriculture, money and banking, transportation, mineral resources, roads, and water resources.

834 Kilby, Peter. *Industrialization in an open economy: Nigeria, 1945–66.* London, Cambridge University Press, 1969. xiv, 399 p. Bibliography: p. 384–391.

A detailed study of how manufacturing and processing industries developed in Nigeria. Especially useful for its historical accounts of businesses, labour unions and government, and private enterprise activities after 1945. See also T. M. Yesufu, *An introduction to industrial relations in Nigeria* (Oxford University Press, 1962); and Margery Perham, ed., *Economics of a tropical dependency*, v. 1, *The native economies of Nigeria*; v. 2, *Mining, commerce and finance in Nigeria* (Faber & Faber, London, 1948). For the agricultural sector, see G. K. Helleiner, *Peasant agriculture, government and economic growth in Nigeria* (Homewood, Ill., 1966). Two important company histories are John Holt and Co., *Merchant Adventure*, and Charles Wilson, *The history of Unilever: A study in economic growth and social change* (London, Cassell and Company, 1954).

835 Kirk-Greene, Anthony H. M. *Adamawa, past and present: An historical approach to the development of a northern Cameroons province.* London, Oxford University Press, 1958. 320 p.

A valuable collection of documents. It supplies a gazetteer of Adamawa Province, an outline history of the emirates and of European contacts in the nineteenth century, and the development of British administration.

836 ——, ed. *The principles of native administration in Nigeria: Selected documents, 1900–1947.* London, Oxford University Press, 1965. 248 p.

There is a foreword by Margery Perham. Mr. Kirk-Greene, formerly a civil administrator, has provided a scholarly introduction (p. 1–42). Documents run from the first in 1903, the address at Sokoto by Lugard, to the last in 1947, the local government dispatch by Arthur Creech Jones, Colonial Secretary.

837 Lloyd, P. C., A. L. Mabogunje, and B. Awe. *The city of Ibadan.* Cambridge University Press, 1967. 280 p.

A symposium tracing the growth of Ibadan from a nineteenth-century Yoruba war camp through its development as a colonial administrative centre to the present.

838 Lugard, Lord. *Political memoranda : Revision of instructions to political officers on subjects chiefly political and administrative, 1913–1918.* 1st ed., 1906; 2d ed., 1919. Reprint: London, Frank Cass, 1970.

The single most important piece of writing for understanding indirect rule's administrative theory and philosophy. Called by Perham ' one of the most important and illuminating documents in the history of British native administration'. Issued by Lugard as High Commissioner of Northern Nigeria in 1906, as instructions and guidance for his political officers (the title was ' Instructions to political officers on subjects chiefly political and administrative '). A revised version of these instructions with all memoranda he issued between 1912 and 1918 appeared in 1919 as *Political memoranda.* . . . The second edition is larger (455 pages to 314 pages); some material was deleted from the 1906 edition and of course new material was added. Kirk-Greene's introduction is most valuable.

839 Mabogunje, Akin L. *Urbanization in Nigeria.* London, University of London Press, 1968. 353 p., maps, illus., tables.

A major study that seeks ' to provide for the first time a conspectus of traditional and modern urbanization in Nigeria '. The author, a Nigerian geographer, presents a theory of urbanization. An extensive section then deals with precolonial towns, their physical location, economic characteristics, and social structure. He discusses the British impact and consequent changes in the urban economic base, socio-demographic features, transport, utilities, trade, and so forth. Part 2 provides detailed data on types of urban development, including Ibadan, ' a traditional ', and on Lagos, a ' modern metropolis '. The conclusions concern general problems, such as ' over-urbanization ', ' primate, generative and parasitic ' cities. There are numerous appendices with a wealth of statistical information.

840 Mackay, Ian K. *Broadcasting in Nigeria.* Ibadan, Ibadan University Press, 1964. 159 p. illus., ports., maps, diagrs. Bibliography: p. 105–108.

A description and appraisal of broadcasting in Nigeria by the last expatriate director-general of the Nigerian Broadcasting Corporation (described as the largest broadcasting organization in Africa). Mr. Mackay points out the significant role of broadcasting as a social force in Nigeria, offers a plan for the future, and concludes his account with 50 pages of appendices.

841 Nicolson, I. F. *The administration of Nigeria, 1900 to 1960 : Men, methods and myths.* London, Oxford University Press, 1969.

A major critical reassessment of Lugard's work in Nigeria but also a fine survey of the administration of Nigeria as a whole by a man who served there. See also Sir Bryan Sharwood Smith, *Recollections of British administration in the Cameroons and Northern Nigeria, 1921–1957 : ' But always as friends '* (Durham, N.C., Duke University Press, 1969, 460 p.).

842 Nigeria. *Census of Nigeria, 1931.* London, published on behalf of the government of Nigeria by the Crown Agents for the Colonies, 1932–34. 7 v. Volume 2A has imprint: Lagos, printed and published by the Government Printer.

Contents: v. 1, *Nigeria,* by S. M. Jacob; v. 2, *Census of the Northern Provinces,* by N. J. Brooke; v. 2A, *Village directory, Northern Provinces, Nigeria*, by N. J. Brooke; v. 3, *Census of the Southern Provinces*, by H. B. Cox; v. 4, *Census of Lagos*, by H. N. G. Thompson; v. 5, *Medical census, Northern Provinces*, by Dr. R. C. Jones; v. 6, *Medical census, Southern Provinces*, by Dr. J. G. S. Turner.

843 ———— Federal Ministry of Commerce and Industry. *Handbook of Commerce and industry in Nigeria.* 5th ed. Lagos, 1962. 398 p.

Volume of useful information for businessmen, first issued in pamphlet form in 1952. It includes surveys and statistics of economic and governmental life, useful addresses, tables, maps, and miscellaneous commercial facts.

844 ———— *The laws of Nigeria, containing the ordinances of Nigeria and subsidiary legislation made thereunder, enacted on or before the 1st day of January 1948, and including imperial statutes, orders of His Majesty in Council, letters patent and royal instructions relating to Nigeria.* Rev. ed. prepared under the authority of the revised edition of the laws ordinance, 1947, by Neville John Brooke. 1948– . 12 v.

845 ———— *The laws of Nigeria, containing the ordinances of Nigeria, in force on the 1st day of January 1923, and the orders, proclamations, rules, regulations and bye-laws made thereunder, in force on the 1st day of May 1923, and the principal imperial statutes, orders in council, letters patent and royal instructions relating to Nigeria.* Rev. ed. Prepared under the authority of the revised edition of the laws ordinance, 1923, by Donald Kingdon. 1923. 4 v.

Superseded by the annual volume of the *Laws of Nigeria.*

846 ———— Legislative Council. *Debates.* 1923–51.

Superseded in 1952 by *Debates* issued by the House of Representatives.

847 ———— ———— *Sessional Papers.*

Sessional papers were issued in all British colonies. Basic source for all political acts of government.

848 ———— National Economic Council. Joint Planning Committee. *Economic survey of Nigeria, 1959.* Lagos, Government Printer, 1959. 132 p. plate, col. maps, tables.

Valuable assemblage of statistics and summary articles regarding the position and outlook of the economy of Nigeria as of mid-1958, with a review of economic development since 1945.

849 ———— *Nigeria Gazette.* 1914– . Weekly.

Apparently supersedes Protectorate of Southern Nigeria, *Government Gazette.* Title varies slightly. Separately paged supplements accompany most volumes. See note on p. 167–168 for explanation of the content of gazettes.

850 ———— *The Nigeria handbook.* London, published on behalf of the government of Nigeria by the Crown Agents for the Colonies, 1953. 339 p. illus. (part col.), maps (incl. 6 fold. col. in pocket), tables. Bibliography: p. 272–288.

This formerly indispensable work, containing essays, statistics, and tabular data on all aspects of the country and its life, is now useful mainly for historical research.

See also *A handbook of education, Nigeria, 1960* (ed. by J. E. Adetoro, issued as an independence year souvenir, Oshogbo, printed for the Schools and General Publication Services by Tanimehin-Ola Press, 1960, 280 p.). The handbook gives an outline of the history of educational development in southern and northern

Nigeria, and a directory, with catalogue information regarding institutions of learning.

851 —— *Nigeria Law Reports.* v. 1– , 1881 / 1911– .
A common publication for all British colonies. Valuable source for many aspects of social, legal and political history.

852 Orr, Sir Charles. *The making of Northern Nigeria.* London, Frank Cass and Company, 1965. 306 p.
Reissue of a classic history of Northern Nigeria with a useful introduction by Kirk-Greene. Best account still of Lugard's wars and campaigns against the emirates, as well as an original account of early British administration.

853 Schram, Ralph. *A history of the Nigerian health services.* Ibadan, Ibadan University Press, 1971. 480 p. Bibliography: p. 437–58.
A major survey of the health and medical history of Nigeria from 1460 to 1960. The work of early traders and explorers and missionaries is covered as well as that of government services and private organizations. There are useful tables and graphs on mortality rate, medical missionaries, growth of doctors and hospitals, etc.

854 Sklar, Richard L. *Nigerian political parties.* Princeton, N.J., Princeton University Press, 1963. xi, 578 p. Bibliography: p. 535–559.
A detailed study of the development of the multi-party system during the last years of British rule. The author has set his analysis in narrative form, beginning with the rise of political parties. Section 2 covers studies in power and conflict; Section 3, party structure and social structures. An appendix lists party officials and executive council members. The long and valuable bibliography is arranged by forms of material.

855 Smith, John. *Colonial cadet in Nigeria.* Durham, N.C., Duke University Press, 1968. 202 p.
An excellent critical account by one of the last generation of colonial administrators in the North (1951–1955), especially useful for its critique of early administrators. Should be read alongside an earlier hard-headed account by W. R. Crocker, *Nigeria: A critique of British colonial administration* (1936).

856 Tamuno, Takena N. *Nigeria and elective representation 1923–1947.* London, Heinemann, 1966. 136 p.
A survey of all elections for the Nigerian Legislative Council between 1923 and 1947. Includes an account of voter qualifications, registration and how elections were carried out. Early party organizations are also described. See also his *The police in modern Nigeria, 1861–1965* (Ibadan, Ibadan University Press, 1970, 332 p.).

857 Temple, O. *Notes on the tribes, provinces, emirates and states of the Northern Provinces of Nigeria.* 2d ed. Comp. from Official Reports. 1922. Reprint: London, Frank Cass, 1965. 595 p.
Classic study of the Northern Provinces. See also Murray Last, *The Sokoto caliphate* (London, Longmans, Green, 1967, 280 p.; bibliography, p. 236–262); and M. G. Smith, *Government in Zazzau, 1800 to 1950* (London, Oxford University Press, 1960, 371 p., maps; bibliography, p. 356–357).

858 *Who's Who in Nigeria: A biographical dictionary.* 1st ed. Lagos, Nigerian Printing and Publishing Co., 1956. 278 p. ports.
A *Daily Times* publication, with biographies of more than 1,500 prominent people.

Part III: area guide (by colonial power, region and colony)

From time to time the information services of the federal or regional governments published a Who's Who of legislative members, for example:

Who's Who of the federal House of Representatives. Lagos, 1958. 124 p. illus., ports.

Who's Who, Western Nigeria Legislature. Ibadan, Government Printer [1959 ?] 53 p.

Who's Who, Northern Region of Nigeria Legislature. Kaduna, 1961. 107 p. ports.

Who's Who in Midwestern Nigeria Legislature. 1st ed. Comp. by Peter M. Ayeni. Benin City, 1964. 81 p. ports.

Sierra Leone

Atlas

859 Clarke, John Innes, ed. *Sierra Leone in maps.* London, University of London Press, 1966. 119 p. maps, tables, diagrs. Bibliography: p. 115–119.
Fifty-one maps with brief accompanying texts illustrating the physical, social and economic geography of Sierra Leone. Among the subjects treated are economics, history, chiefdoms, ethnic groups, languages, education, transport and external trade. The result of a collaboration by past and present members of the Department of Geography, Fourah Bay College, University College of Sierra Leone, the volume is an outstanding piece of work.

Bibliographies

860 *A chronological table and an index of the ordinances of the Colony of the Gambia, 1901–1908 (inclusive), and of the rules, regulations and orders passed and made by the Governor-in-Council, and of the proclamations, acts of Parliament, orders of the King-in-Council, treaties, etc., published in the Gambia Government gazettes, 1901–1908 (inclusive).* By Donald Kingdon. London, printed by Waterlow, 1909. 103 p.

861 Luke, Harry C. *A bibliography of Sierra Leone, preceded by an essay on the origin, character and peoples of the colony and protectorate.* 2d, enl. ed. London, Oxford University Press, 1925. 230 p. port., plates, fold. map.
An authoritative bibliography, with wide coverage almost to date of publication, prefaced by an interesting essay that is one of the best introductions to Sierra Leone. The author was colonial secretary.

862 Pinkett, F. F. *Chronological and alphabetical index of the ordinances of Sierra Leone.* Rev. ed. London, 1900. 129 p. (3,000 entries)

863 U.S. Library of Congress. General Reference and Bibliography Division. *Official publications of Sierra Leone and Gambia.* Comp. by Audrey A. Walker, African Section. Washington, 1963. xii, 92 p.
Another excellent bibliography in the Library of Congress series of guides to the documents of African governments. Included are materials issued by the British government on the country in question. An introductory essay outlines governmental history for each. Entries are listed alphabetically by author and title, and there is an index to authors and subjects.

British Africa: West Africa

864 Williams, Geoffrey J. *A bibliography of Sierra Leone, 1925–1967.* New York, Africana Publishing Corp., 1971. 209 p.

The bibliography which supplements Luke is divided by subject, beginning with a general introduction concerning sources, followed by religion, social sciences, political sciences, economics, law, government, education, commerce, anthropology, philology, natural sciences, technology, agriculture, transport, industry, the arts, geography, biography, and history. Contains some 3,050 items – articles, books, theses, government documents, conference papers, etc.

865 Zell, Hans M., comp. and ed. *A bibliography of non-periodical literature on Sierra Leone, 1925–66.* Freetown, Fourah Bay College Bookshop, University College of Sierra Leone, 1966. 44, [2] p. processed.

Intended only as a provisional checklist, with a comprehensive annotated bibliography planned for later publication. The bibliography supplements Luke's bibliography and that issued by the U.S. Library of Congress (both cited above) as well as the bibliographies of the Sierra Leone Library Board. The 253 entries include books, chapters from comprehensive works, reports, and theses (British and American) but not Sierra Leone government publications. Arrangement is by subject. There is an author index.

Reference works

866 Cox-George, N. A. *Finance and development in West Africa : The Sierra Leone experience.* London, D. Dobson, 1961; New York, Humanities Press, 1962. 333 p. Bibliography: p. 317–321.

867 —— *Report on African participation in the commerce of Sierra Leone . . . and the government statement thereon.* Freetown, Government Printing Department, 1958. 64 p. tables, diagr.

An analysis of the economic and financial history of the former British dependency. The 1958 report, which is related to the drive for Africanization of the civil service, was prepared at the request of the Sierra Leone government while Mr. Cox-George was in the Department of Economics at Fourah Bay College.

An earlier work officially commissioned by the government of Sierra Leone was prepared by Professor Daniel T. Jack, an expert on international trade, and is titled *Economic survey of Sierra Leone* (Freetown, Government Printing Department, 1958, 75 p.).

868 Elias, Taslim Olawale. *Ghana and Sierra Leone : The development of their laws and constitutions.* London, Stevens, 1962. xii, 334 p. (The British Commonwealth, the Development of Its Laws and Constitution, v. 10)

For each country Elias surveys the origins of British rule, the development of central and local government, public corporations, the legal system. The appendix has a table of statutes from 1617 to 1961.

869 Fyfe, Christopher. *A history of Sierra Leone.* London, Oxford University Press, 1962. 773 p. fold. maps. ' Guide to Sources ': p. 621–639.

This impressive history has a brief introduction on the period from the 15th century to 1787, when the colony was founded; then it covers in great detail all affairs of Sierra Leone to about 1900. See also the author's documentary collection, arranged by topic, and entitled *Sierra Leone inheritance* (London, Oxford University Press, 1964, 352 p.).

870 Goddard, Thomas N. *A handbook of Sierra Leone.* London, G. Richards, 1925. 335 p. illus., map.

Prepared by the Colonial Secretary in Freetown, this handbook of governmental

Part III: area guide (by colonial power, region and colony)

information was sponsored by the Sierra Leone government. It is still useful for quick reference on the earlier history of the country and its administration.

871 Great Britain. Colonial Office. *Annual report on. . .* See no. 672.

872 Kilson, Martin. *Political change in a West African state : A study of the modernization process in Sierra Leone.* Cambridge, Mass., Harvard University Press, 1966. 301 p. illus., ports., maps. Bibliography: p. 293–296.

This excellent critical analysis of the political process in Sierra Leone puts the emphasis on the significance of groups and their interrelations. While Dr. Kilson traces developments in Sierra Leone over the whole period from 1863 to the present time, most of the book is taken up with the years between the Second World War and 1961, the year Sierra Leone achieved independence. A major analysis of modernization in Sierra Leone, but much of it applies to Africa in general. See also Kenneth L. Little, *The Mende of Sierra Leone : A West African people in transition* (rev. ed., London, Routledge and Kegan Paul; New York, Humanities Press, 1967, 307 p., illus., map; bibliography, p. 142–146). Also useful is Roy Lewis, *Sierra Leone: A modern portrait* (London, 1954, 263 p.). An important social study is Arthur T. Porter, *Creoledom : A study of the development of Freetown society* (London, Oxford University Press, 1963, 151 p.).

873 McCulloch, Merran. *The peoples of Sierra Leone Protectorate.* London, International African Institute, 1950. 102 p. (Ethnographic Survey of Africa, Western Africa, pt. 2) Reissue: *Peoples of Sierra Leone.* 1964. 102 p. fold. map. ('Supplementary Bibliography', 4 p., inserted.) Bibliography: p. 95–98.

Like other parts of the Ethnographic Survey, the study is intended as a basic reference source, bringing together scattered information regarding the tribes of the area in question and outlining their ethnic and cultural position.

874 *Sierra Leone Studies.* no. 1– . June 1918– . Irregular. n.s. no. 1– . Dec. 1953– . Freetown. Twice a year.

Reactivated in January 1966 under the editorship of Michael Crowder, after a lapse of more than two years. Early editors have been John Hargreaves, A. P. Kup and A. T. Porter. By arrangement with the government of Sierra Leone, it is now the journal of the Sierra Leone Society and is produced by the Institute of African Studies of Fourah Bay College, University College of Sierra Leone. Articles may be on any Sierra Leonean topic.

BRITISH CENTRAL AFRICA

Note This section covers the three countries referred to in the past as British Central Africa or, from 1953 to 1963, as the Federation of Rhodesia and Nyasaland. The region embraces the modern states of Malawi, Rhodesia and Zambia.

Bibliographies

875 Burke, E. E. 'Bibliography', in Central African Archives, *The story of Cecil John Rhodes : Set out in a series of historical pictures and objects to commemorate the centenary of his birth*, p. 131–192. Bulawayo, Central African Rhodes Centenary Exhibition, 1953.

This is the most complete bibliography on Rhodes now in existence. Its first part is subdivided by periodicals bearing on Rhodes, substantial biographies, shorter studies, and obituary notices. Its second part lists the various works with reference to the various periods in Rhodes's life, starting with his family history, his early career in South Africa, his struggle for the ' Road to the North ', and his impact on south and central Africa. The third part provides material concerning Rhodes the man and his various interests. The fourth part gives details concerning his speeches and writings. The fifth part records Rhodes in literature, and the last part shows ' Rhodes in Memory ', with details concerning such unusual media as films and memorabilia. The two appendices list manuscript sources and academic dissertations.

876 Cape Town. University. School of Librarianship. Bibliographical Series. Cape Town.

The bibliographical papers compiled as theses by students in the School of Librarianship are issued in stencilled form and contain a minimum of 150 titles; many are far longer. Microfilm copies are available from the University. The usual range of subjects relates to southern Africa.

The following are concerned with the Rhodesias and Nyasaland:

> *A bibliography of African education in the Federation of Rhodesia and Nyasaland, 1890–1958.* By M. H. Rousseau. 1958. 29 p.

> *A bibliography of the Federation of the Rhodesias and Nyasaland, up to June 30th, 1949.* By D. L. Cox. 1949. 23 l.

> *Cecil John Rhodes.* By Daphne W. Thomson. 1947. 29 l.

> *The Zambesi.* By Jill Sherlock. 1963. 20 p.

877 International African Institute. *South-east Central Africa and Madagascar : General, ethnography, sociology, linguistics.* Comp. by Ruth Jones. London, 1961. 53 l. (Africa Bibliography Series)

See note on series, no. 252. The section on Rhodesia and Nyasaland (p. 1–29) is an updated revision of R. M. S. Ng'ombe's *A selected bibliography of the Federation of Rhodesia and Nyasaland* (Lusaka, Rhodes-Livingstone Institute, 1957, 68 p.), which listed some 1,000 entries.

878 Shepperson, George. ' The literature of British Central Africa: A review article '. *Rhodes-Livingstone Journal*, no. 23, 1958: 12–46.

A detailed and discriminating account that stands out as a fine piece of historical writing in its own right. Additional bibliographical essays include no. 626, George Shepperson, ' British Central Africa ', in *The historiography of the British Empire-Commonwealth* (p. 237–247). See also Robert I. Rotberg, ' Colonialism and after: The political literature of Central Africa – a bibliographic essay ', *African Forum*, v. 2, no. 3, 1967, 66–73.

879 Taylor, A. R., and E. P. Dvorin. ' Political development in British Central Africa, 1890–1956: A select survey of the literature and background materials '. *Race*, v. 1, no. 1, Nov. 1959: 61–78.

Concentrates on the movement for closer association. *Race* is the quarterly journal of the Institute of Race Relations, London.

See also Leverhulme (no. 895, below).

880 U.S. Library of Congress. General Reference and Bibliography Division. *The Rhodesias and Nyasaland : A guide to official publications.* Compiled by Audrey A. Walker, African Section. Washington, 1965. 285 p.

The most extensive volume as yet prepared in the Library of Congress series of official publications of African governments, this study includes the record of all English-speaking Central Africa. Documents of the Federation of Rhodesia and Nyasaland and earlier joint Central African agencies take up p. 1–46; Northern Rhodesia, p. 47–117; Southern Rhodesia, p. 118–193; Nyasaland, p.

Part III: area guide (by colonial power, region and colony)

194–228; British government, p. 229–253; British South Africa Company, p. 254–258. Entries total 1,889, and there is an author and subject index. The coverage is from earliest records (1889) through 1963; material on the newly independent countries (1964) of Malawi and Zambia is not included.

Reference Works

881 Barber, William J. *The economy of British Central Africa : A case study of economic development in a dualistic society.* Stanford, Calif., Stanford University Press, 1961. 271 p.

Examination of the contrasting economic systems of European settlers, with their cash and money crops, and the subsistence agriculture of the African tribesmen. The writer argues that the meeting point of the two, in the labour market, has meant below-subsistence wages for African workers.

A number of other recent studies have centred on the same issue. Among them are Phyllis Deane, *Colonial social accounting* (Cambridge, Eng., University Press, 1953, 360 p.; National Institute of Economic and Social Research, Economic and Social Studies, no. 11); the U.N. Department of Economic and Social Affairs report, *Structure and growth of selected African economies* (New York, 1958, 201 p.); and a book, *Economic development in Rhodesia and Nyasaland* (London, Dobson, 1954, 205 p.), by Cecil H. Thompson and Harry W. Woodruff, government economists in Salisbury, who argued for long-term development through government finance in establishment of the Federation.

882 British South Africa Company. *Reports on the administration of Rhodesia. 1889/92. 1892/94. 1894/95. 1896/97. 1897/98. 1898/1900. 1900/1902.* London, 1892–1903. 8 v. in 4. maps (part fold.), plans, tables, diagrs.

Reports for 1889/92–1896/97 have the title: *Report on the Company's proceedings and the condition of the territories within the sphere of its operations.*

Contains reports of the administrative departments in both Northern and Southern Rhodesia. The company was both a commercial concern and the administering agent of the Rhodesias until 1923, when Southern Rhodesia became a self-governing colony, and in 1924, when Northern Rhodesia's administration was taken over by the British government.

Another series of reports was entitled *Reports on the Company proceedings and the condition of its territories within the sphere of its operations,* 1889–1907. A useful survey of the company's work was written by Dougal Malcolm, entitled *The British South Africa Company, 1889–1939* (London, 1939). The company also issued numerous reports on special topics.

883 Central African Historical Association. *Local Series.* 196? Salisbury. 3 times a year.

Valuable short pamphlets on historical subjects concerned primarily with Central Africa, but occasionally dealing with neighbouring territories. For example, see Douglas Wheeler, *Portuguese expansion in Angola since 1836.* The Association also publishes *Proceedings* of its conferences.

884 *Central African Journal of Medicine.* 1955– . Salisbury. Monthly.

Edited by Dr. Michael Gelfand, physician and medical anthropologist, this journal is a valuable source not only for medical matters, but also for wider social questions.

885 Central African Statistical Office. *Economic and Statistical Bulletin of Southern Rhodesia.* New ser. v. 1–21, 193(3)–54. Salisbury. 21 v. tables, diagrs. Semi-monthly.

One of the best colonial statistical services; many valuable series and reports.

886 Colson, Elizabeth, and Max Gluckman, eds. *Seven tribes of British Central Africa.* Reprinted with minor corrections. Manchester, Eng., published on behalf of the Rhodes-Livingstone Institute, Northern Rhodesia, by Manchester University Press, 1959. xix, 409 p. illus., maps, geneal. table. Includes bibliographies.

This symposium, an early result of the expanded research program of the Institute (see below), was published first in 1951 by the Oxford University Press. Dr. Colson, an American social anthropologist, edited it in conjunction with Dr. Gluckman, whom she had succeeded as director of the Institute in 1947 when Dr. Gluckman left to accept a lectureship at Oxford. The papers are studies of the leading tribes – Lozi, Tonga, Bemba, Ngoni, Nyakyusa, Yao, and Shona – by scholars whose field work was done under the auspices of the Institute. The studies are followed by short reading lists.

887 Dotson, Floyd, and Lillian O. Dotson. *The Indian minority of Zambia, Rhodesia, and Malawi.* New Haven, Conn., Yale University Press, 1968. 444 p. Bibliography: p. 410–426.

Concludes that while Indians are still in an intermediate economic position between Europeans and Africans, since independence they have become politically less influential and more insecure than either Europeans or Africans.

888 Gann, Lewis Henry. *Central Africa : the former British States.* Englewood Cliffs, New Jersey, 1971. x, 180 p., map, table. Bibliography: p. 169–176.

An interpretative study written by a former historian and archivist in Rhodesia. Covers the land, the people, ancient history, European colonization, the end of empire, and what the author calls the 'white counterrevolution'. The author states in his preface that, while he is conscious of the limitations that beset white Rhodesia, he sees 'no merit in the view, now widespread in many university departments, that denies the settlers' historical function, and looks upon them as parasites who led lives of lazy languor punctuated only by fits of energetic repression'. Gann is also the author of no. 964, *A history of Southern Rhodesia. . .*; and of no. 940, *A history of Northern Rhodesia. . .*

889 ———, and Michael Gelfand. *Huggins of Rhodesia : The man and his country.* London, Allen & Unwin, 1964. 285 p. plates, ports. Bibliography: p. 273–278.

A medico-political biography based on the private papers of Sir Godfrey Huggins (later Lord Malvern), Prime Minister of Southern Rhodesia, later of the Federation of Rhodesia and Nyasaland, 1933–56. An historical account of this period, seen from the European point of view.

890 Gray, Richard. *The two nations : Aspects of the development of race relations in the Rhodesias and Nyasaland.* Issued under the auspices of the Institute of Race Relations. London and New York, Oxford University Press, 1960. xvii, 373 p. maps. Bibliography: p. 356–361.

Study on the history of Central Africa concerning contacts of the British settlers and government with the African tribes and political development from the end of World War I to the beginning of the Federation in 1953. See also Edward Clegg, *Race and politics : partnership in the Federation of Rhodesia and Nyasaland* (London, Oxford University Press, 1960, 280 p., map), an astringent analysis written by a former soil scientist in the Colonial Research Service.

891 *Great Britain.* Colonial Office. Annual report on. . . See no. 672.

892 Hanna, Alexander John. *The beginnings of Nyasaland and north-eastern Rhodesia, 1859–95.* Oxford, Clarendon Press, 1956. 281 p. fold. maps. Bibliography: p. 270–273.

By a historian of Central and East Africa, this work is a carefully documented study of British interests and activities – missionary, chartered company, and official – in state building.

893 Hole, Hugh Marshall. *The making of Rhodesia.* London, Macmillan and Co., 1926. 402 p. illus., maps.

The early history of British colonization in Southern and Northern Rhodesia, written from the point of view of a senior official in the British South Africa Company's government, and based on both archival and unpublished sources. Hole's book emphasizes diplomatic and military events in the older ' imperial ' school of colonial history.

894 Johnston, Sir Harry H. *British Central Africa : An attempt to give some account of a portion of the territories under British influence north of the Zambesi.* With 6 maps and 223 illustrations reproduced from the author's drawings or from photographs. 2d ed. London, Methuen, 1898. xix, 544 p. illus., plates, maps.

This famous scholar-administrator who led the expeditions of the 1880s into Central Africa and helped to lay the foundations for British control in Nyasaland, Uganda and elsewhere, served as commissioner in British Central Africa (Nyasa-land and Northern Rhodesia) from 1891 to 1896. His book, the old standard work on the region, covers geography, history, botany, zoology, anthropology and languages. See also his *Handbook to British Central Africa* (1904).

895 Leverhulme Inter-Collegiate History Conference, University College of Rhodesia and Nyasaland, Salisbury, 1960. *Historians in tropical Africa : Proceedings of the Leverhulme Inter-Collegiate History Conference held at the University College of Rhodesia and Nyasaland, September 1960.* Salis-bury, University College of Rhodesia and Nyasaland, 1962. 425 p. 32 cm.

Thirty-one papers on various aspects of African history and ethno-history. Most of the contributions deal with 19th-century problems of Central and East Africa and with the European in Africa. An excellent bibliographic essay found on p. 387–400 is Alan Taylor's ' Recent trends in Central African historiography '.

896 Livingstone, David. *Livingstone's travels.* Ed. by James I. McNair, with geographical sections by Ronald Miller. London, Dent, 1954. xvi, 429 p. illus., ports., maps.

Generous extracts from Dr. Livingstone's three big books recording his explora-tions: *Missionary travels and researches in South Africa* (1857); *The Zambezi and its tributaries* (1865); and *Livingstone's last journal,* ed. by Horace Waller (1874, 2 v.), all published by John Murray, London. Four geographical sections are interspersed, explaining the African background, south and west central Africa, the lower Zambezi and Nyasaland, and the east African plateau. Brief appendices are in the nature of extended notes.

Another modern edition is *The Zambezi expedition of David Livingstone, 1858–1863,* edited by J. P. R. Wallis and published as no. 9 of the Central African Archives, Oppenheimer Series (London, Chatto & Windus, 1956, 2 v., col. plates, map). The first volume contains a part of the journals; the second continues the journals, with letters and dispatches therefrom. Among the many lives of Living-stone, a notable biography emphasizing his role as explorer is by the geographer Frank Debenham, *The way to Ilala : David Livingstone's pilgrimage* (London and New York, Longmans, Green, 1955, 336 p., illus., maps). See also Michael Gelfand, *Livingstone, the doctor : His life and travels* (Oxford, Basil Blackwell, 1957, 340 p.), for a medico-historical study.

897 Lockhart, John Gilbert, and C. M. Woodhouse. *Cecil Rhodes: The colossus of southern Africa.* New York, Macmillan, 1963. xiii, 525 p. illus., map. Includes bibliographies.

A recent biography of the Empire Builder, but a more valuable earlier portrait was by Basil Williams, *Cecil Rhodes* (London, Constable, 1938, 353 p., map; Makers of the Nineteenth Century).

898 Mason, Philip. *The birth of a dilemma : The conquest and settlement of Rhodesia.* Issued under the auspices of the Institute of Race Relations. London and New York, Oxford University Press, 1958. 366 p. illus.

899 —— *Year of decision : Rhodesia and Nyasaland in 1960.* Issued under the auspices of the Institute of Race Relations. London and New York, Oxford University Press, 1960. 282 p. illus.

The first of these two books is a readable and well-researched account of the period 1890 to 1923. Strongly critical of the British South Africa Company and white settlers. A critique of the soon-to-break-up Federation appears in the second book.

900 Ranger, T. O., ed. *Aspects of Central African history.* London, Heinemann Educational, 1968. 291 p. maps.

Papers prepared for a conference held at University College, Dar-es-Salaam, in 1967; specialist essays but most valuable.

901 Rhodesia and Nyasaland. Central African Archives. Oppenheimer Series. Ed. by J. P. R. Wallis [and others]. London, Chatto & Windus, 1945–56. illus., maps, plans.

A series of reprints of the manuscript journals and other primary source materials relating to the early missionaries and pioneers in Central Africa (primarily Southern Rhodesia). Unless otherwise specified, they are edited by Professor Wallis. An example is *Gold and the Gospel in Mashonaland, 1888, being the journals of: 1, The Mashonaland mission of Bishop Knight-Bruce; 2, The concession journey of Charles Dunnell Rudd,* edited respectively by Constance E. Fripp and V. W. Hiller (1949, 246 p.).

Another series based on the archives of the Rhodesian pioneers is the Robin Series, also published by Chatto & Windus. The first volume, edited by Edward C. Tabler, *Zambezia and Matabeleland in the seventies* (1960, 212 p., plates, ports., map), contains two narratives of 1875–78. Mr. Tabler in an earlier book, *The far interior : Chronicles of pioneering in the Matabele and Mashona countries, 1847–1879* (Cape Town, Balkema, 1955, 443 p.), gave a chronological account of the pioneers, including an 11-page bibliography of the printed and manuscript sources.

902 Rhodesia and Nyasaland. Federal Information Department. *Handbook to the Federation of Rhodesia and Nyasaland.* Ed. by W. V. Brelsford, Director of Information. London, Cassell, 1960. 803 p. plates (part col.), maps, charts, coat of arms, tables, diagrs. Includes bibliographies.

Chapters by recognized experts cover all phases of land, life and affairs of the three countries composing the Federation. Some are followed by short reading lists. Institutions and organizations are listed in the chapters on education, social welfare, culture, etc., and similarly useful data appear in those on administrative organization. Appendices include a chronology from 1498 to 1959, tables of statistics of population and income, lists of newspapers and periodicals, data on learned societies and other miscellaneous information.

903 *Rhodesiana.* no. 1– , 1956– . Salisbury. Annual.

Journal of the Rhodesiana Society, which began as the Rhodesian African

Society (1956–57). The articles are largely of historical and ethnological interest and relate to all Central Africa.

904 Rhodes-Livingstone Institute, Lusaka, Northern Rhodesia. Communications [series]. Nos. 1–29. Livingstone, Lusaka, 1943–65. Irregular. mimeo.
The Rhodes-Livingstone Institute in late 1964 became the Institute for Social Research of the new University of Zambia at Lusaka. The reconstituted institute issues a Communications series of preliminary reports.

905 ——— Rhodes-Livingstone Papers [series]. Nos. 1–37. Livingstone, Lusaka, 1938–65.
The Rhodes-Livingstone Institute from its beginnings in 1937 has been among the major centres of Africa for research in the social sciences, and in addition to the Papers, usually under 100 pages, 16 books of greater length have appeared. The original site of the Institute was at Livingstone in Northern Rhodesia, and from there it moved to Lusaka in 1953. The *Rhodes-Livingstone Journal*, also called *Human Problems in British Central Africa* (Manchester, Eng., Manchester University Press), totalled 38 numbers (1944–66); with no. 36 British was dropped from the title. The RLI also published, in mimeographed form, the proceedings of its annual conferences. Among them were the following: 13th Conference, Lusaka, 1959, *From tribal rule to modern government*, edited by Raymond Apthorpe (1959, 216 p.); 15th Conference, Lusaka, 1961, *Social research and community development*, edited by Raymond Apthorpe (1961, 173 p.); and 16th Conference, Lusaka, 1962, *The multitribal society*, edited by Allie Dubb (1962, 147 p., tables).
   In late 1964 the Rhodes-Livingstone Institute became the Institute for Social Research of the new University of Zambia at Lusaka. In the new setup a Communications series continues under the same name; the RLI Papers become the Zambian Papers; the journal *Human Problems in Central Africa* (1944–), has been renamed *African Social Research*; and the Conference Proceedings is replaced by a mimeographed *Bulletin*, to give news of the Institute and other information. *A complete list of the publications of the former Rhodes-Livingstone Institute* ([1966 ?] 12 unnumbered pages) has been issued by the Institute for Social Research.

906 Rolin, Henri. *Les lois et l'administration de la Rhodésie.* Bruxelles, E. Bruylant, 1913. xlvii, 532 p. illus., maps. Bibliography: p. vii–xix.
The standard work on administration in the two Rhodesias under the British South Africa Company's régime, written from a lawyer's point of view and yet to be superseded.

907 Rotberg, Robert I. *The rise of nationalism in Central Africa : The making of Malawi and Zambia, 1873–1964.* Cambridge, Mass., Harvard University Press, 1965. xv, 362 p. illus., maps. Bibliography: p. 329–340.
In this book the author, an historian, seeks to answer questions concerning the realities of colonial rule and the nature of the African response, the depth or shallowness of the roots of the expressions of then current African nationalism (whether these expressions indicated widespread grievances or merely manifested the aspirations of a few educated Africans). The study is also intended to portray the modern political history of the peoples of Malawi and Zambia and to place the achievement of independence within its immediate historical context. See also his *Christian missionaries and the creation of Northern Rhodesia, 1880–1924* (Princeton University Press, 1965), a dull, Eurocentric account; but it has a useful bibliography and biographical appendix.

908 Smith, Edwin W. *The way of the white fields in Rhodesia: A survey of Christian enterprise in Northern and Southern Rhodesia.* London, World Dominion Press, 1928. 172, 20 p. fold. maps, tables.

This volume in the World Dominion Survey series is of special interest because of the significant part played by missionary enterprise in the Rhodesias after the pioneer missionary of Bechuanaland, Robert Moffat (father-in-law of David Livingstone), went, in 1854, to visit the Matabele chieftains in what is now Rhodesia and in 1859 led the first party of white missionary settlers there. Dr. Smith devoted the first pages to a general account of the country and to a brief historical sketch, and then described each mission station and its work, ending with 20 pages of tabular statistics. The author also did important anthropological and historical work.

909 Sowelem, R. A. *Towards financial independence in a developing economy: An analysis of the monetary experience of the Federation of Rhodesia and Nyasaland, 1952–63.* London, Allen & Unwin, 1967. 329 p. tables, graphs. Bibliography: p. 324–327.

The short but significant account of the Bank of Rhodesia and Nyasaland is authoritatively analysed in this account of the Federation's adaptation and establishment of financial institutions in an area previously wholly dependent on an externally controlled monetary system.

910 Stokes, Eric, and Richard Brown, eds. *The Zambesian past: Studies in Central African history.* Manchester, Eng., Manchester University Press, 1966. xxxv, 427 p. illus., maps (1 fold.), diagrs. Includes bibliographies.

In their introduction the editors focus on the diverse responses of the Zambesian peoples to European influence. Only six of the papers deal with the pre-colonial period, the majority being devoted to the scramble and its immediate aftermath. There is an analytical index.

911 Welensky, Sir Roy. *Welensky's 4000 days: The life and death of the Federation of Rhodesia and Nyasaland.* London, Collins, 1964. 383 p. ports., map.

Memoir by the Rhodesian who was Prime Minister of the Federation of Rhodesia and Nyasaland from 1956 to its dissolution in 1963, and active in Northern Rhodesian politics and trade-union movements as a representative of white settler anti-imperialism.

912 Wills, A. J. *An introduction to the history of Central Africa.* 2d ed. London, Oxford University Press, 1967. 412 p. maps. Bibliography: p. 385–393.

A general history of the region comprising Malawi, Rhodesia and Zambia, written principally for students and teachers of history in Central Africa but deserving of a wide audience. Three chapters are devoted to the 19th century and include sections on the slave-trade, Livingstone, pioneer missions, and the European advance into and occupation of the area. In the final three chapters the narrative extends from the turn of the century to November 1965, describing the consequences of European occupation, the attempt at federation, and the end of the colonial phase. An analytical index is included.

913 *Year book and guide of the Rhodesias and Nyasaland, with biographies.* Salisbury, Rhodesian Publications, Ltd., 1937– . illus.

This was a handy volume covering all aspects of country and life; the 1962 edition, edited by Reginald Heath, had a hard cardboard cover and 350 pages, including advertising. There were no reading lists. Presumably publication has ceased.

914 Yudelman, Montague. *Africans on the land: Economic problems of African agricultural development in southern, central and east Africa, with special reference to Southern Rhodesia.* Prepared under the auspices of the Center for International Affairs, Harvard University. Cambridge, Mass., Harvard University Press, 1964. xiv, 288 p. maps, tables. Bibliographical footnotes.

The major problem of how to bring a predominantly agricultural society, producing largely for self-subsistence, into the market economy (with consequent increase in productivity) is the core of Dr. Yudelman's study. His emphasis is on Rhodesia, which, like South Africa and Kenya, comprises a ' dual ' society – one in which ' European agriculture ' and ' African agriculture ' coexist. Many of Dr. Yudelman's recommendations in this book (including the modification of certain strictures on allocation of land by race) were made to and endorsed by the government of Southern Rhodesia before the 1962 elections – in which the government party was rejected – and the dissolution of the Federation of Rhodesia and Nyasaland. An analytical index is included.

Nyasaland (Malawi)

Note Upon achieving independence July 6, 1964, the former British protectorate of Nyasaland took the name of Malawi.

Bibliographies

915 Syracuse University. Maxwell Graduate School of Citizenship and Public Affairs. Program of Eastern African Studies. *A bibliography of Malawi.* Comp. by Edward E. Brown and others. Syracuse, N.Y., 1965. 161 p. (Syracuse University, Eastern African Bibliographical Series, no. 1)

A title list, classed by subject, with author and title index. The most comprehensive available record of writing on the past and present of former Nyasaland. A supplement of 62 pages was issued in 1969.

916 Tangri, Roger K. ' Political change in colonial Malawi: A bibliographical essay '. *African Studies Bulletin,* v. 11, no. 3, Dec. 1968: 248–257. See also nos. 875–880.

Reference works

917 *The African law reports: Malawi series.* v. 1, *1923–1960 reports.* Dobbs Ferry, N.Y., Oceana Publications, 1968. 1,004 p.

918 Debenham, Frank. *Nyasaland, the land of the lake.* London, H.M. Stationery Office, 1955. xi, 239 p. illus., plates, fold. maps. (Corona Library, no. 3) ' Books consulted ': p. 231–232; ' Further reading ': p. 233–234.

One of a series sponsored by the Colonial Office, ' to be authoritative and readable, and to give a vivid yet accurate picture '. This descriptive survey of Nyasaland is by a noted Cambridge geographer who had previously prepared a report on the water resources of East and Central Africa.

919 Gelfand, Michael. *Lakeside pioneers: Socio-medical study of Nyasaland, 1875–1920.* Oxford, Basil Blackwell, 1964. 330 p. plates, ports., fold. map. Bibliography: p. 322–324.

This standard, but somewhat badly organized work (like Dr. Gelfand's comparable histories of the Rhodesias from the medical point of view), is valuable with regard to social conditions, labour housing and related aspects.

920 Great Britain. Colonial Office. *Annual report on. . .* See no. 672.

921 ———. *Report of the commission appointed to enquire into the financial position and further development of Nyasaland.* R. D. Bell, commissioner. London, H.M. Stationery Office, 1938, 340 p., maps, tables. (Colonial Office. Colonial no. 152)

One of a series of extensive inquiries carried out by special commissioners, comparable in importance to others completed by Sir Alan W. Pim. See, for instance, no. 944, *Report of the commission appointed to enquire into the financial and economic position of Northern Rhodesia.* The commission report remains the best economic and administrative history of Nyasaland under colonial rule.

922 Jones, Griffith B. *Britain and Nyasaland.* London, Allen & Unwin, 1964. 314 p. maps. Notes (by chapters): p. 266–303; references (classed): p. 304–307.

A study of the stages of relationships between Great Britain and the colony of Nyasaland, extending almost to the moment of independence of the new state of Malawi. The references cited include many command papers leading to the change of government.

923 Malawi. Department of Antiquities. *Johnston's administration, 1891–1897.* By C. A. Baker. Zomba, 1970. 134 p.

Not available for examination.

924 Moyse-Bartlett, Hubert. *The King's African Rifles : A study in the military history of East and Central Africa, 1890–1945.* Aldershot [Eng.], Gale and Polden, 1956. xix, 727 p. plates, maps, sketches.

The King's African Rifles comprised African troops from various British East African colonies. The regiment saw more or less continuous service from 1893 until the end of the First World War, and later on, during the Second World War. Colonel Moyse-Bartlett's work is far more than a regimental history of the conventional kind, but a work of much more far-reaching importance. The study has been assessed in detail by George Shepperson, 'The military history of British Central Africa: A review article', *Rhodes-Livingstone Journal*, no. 26, 1960, p. 23–33.

925 Murray, S. S. *The handbook of Nyasaland.* 4th ed. London, published for the government of Nyasaland by the Crown Agents for the Colonies, 1932. xxxvii (advertising), 436 p.

A general descriptive and economic guide to the country, issued first in 1908, with later editions in 1910 and 1922.

926 Nyasaland. Laws, statutes, etc. *The laws of Nyasaland in force on the 1st of January 1957.* Rev. ed., prepared . . . by Donald Kingdon. London, Waterlow, Government Printers, 1957. 6 v.

A common practice in British colonies was to publish periodically the laws and statutes of the colony.

927 *Nyasaland Journal.* v. 1– . 1948– . Blantyre, printed by the Church of Scotland Mission for the Nyasaland Society. Semi-annual.

The Nyasaland Society maintains a private library, promotes interest in literature, history, and scientific matters, and provides information about Nyasaland. The journal, the contents of which reflect these interests, includes in each issue a list of books received in the Society library. It is now called *Society of Malawi Journal.*

Part III: area guide (by colonial power, region and colony)

928 Pike, John G. *Malawi : A political and economic history.* New York, Praeger, 1968. 248 p. maps, charts. (Praeger Library of African Affairs) Bibliography: p. 225–232.

A review of physical factors serves as an introduction to a discussion of tribal migration into the area, the creation of a kingdom, the colonial situation, and the development of nationalism and independence. A basic introduction to Malawi by a former colonial official in that country.

929 Rhodesia and Nyasaland. Ministry of Economic Affairs. *Report on an economic survey of Nyasaland, 1958–1959.* Salisbury, 1959. 300 p. maps (part fold., part col.), charts, tables, diagrs. (Rhodesia and Nyasaland, C. Fed. 132)

Survey by a joint Federation and Nyasaland team under the British economist Daniel T. Jack with R. J. Randall acting as his deputy. The writers of this solid study found conclusive evidence that Nyasaland economic development was being aided by federation. Political considerations do not enter the report. A summary of its conclusions and recommendations was issued by the Nyasaland government (Zomba, 1960, 49 p.).

930 Tew, Mary. *Peoples of the Lake Nyasa region.* London and New York, published for the International African Institute by Oxford University Press, 1950. 131 p. maps. (Ethnographic Survey of Africa: East Central Africa, pt. 1) Bibliography: p. 118–131.

For a general note on the series, see no. 333.

Among other well-known anthropological studies of peoples of Nyasaland are two books by Margaret Read: *Children of their fathers : Growing up among the Ngoni of Nyasaland* (New Haven, Conn., Yale University Press, 1960, 176 p.), and *The Ngoni of Nyasaland* (London and New York, published for the International African Institute by Oxford University Press, 1956, 212 p.).

Northern Rhodesia (Zambia)

Bibliographies

931 Gifford, Prosser. 'An initial survey of the local archival and published materials for Zambian history (1895–Independence 1964) ', *African Social Research*, no. 1, June 1966: 59–84.

An informative bibliographic essay on Zambian source materials.

932 Parker, Franklin, comp. 'African education in Zambia (formerly Northern Rhodesia): A partial bibliography of magazine articles, 1925–1963 ', *African Studies Bulletin*, v. 10, no. 3, Dec. 1967: 6–15.

List of 148 articles, arranged chronologically.

Note See also under Central Africa nos. 875–880.

Reference works

933 Baldwin, Robert E. *Economic development and export growth : A study of Northern Rhodesia, 1920–1960.* Berkeley and Los Angeles, University of California Press, 1966. 254 p. tables, (Publications of the Bureau of Business and Economic Research, University of California, Los Angeles) Bibliography: p. 222–245.

An interesting analysis of the economic issues involved in the industrialization of Northern Rhodesia. This 'first economic history' of the country serves as a supplement to Lewis H. Gann, *History of Northern Rhodesia* (see no. 940). Baldwin discusses theories of development through export expansion, presents a survey of Rhodesian economic growth, and describes and appraises major aspects of the economy. He concludes that just as is the case with agriculture, significant industrial expansion must be directed at export markets and that a well-trained labour force, rather than the existence of any special natural resource, must form the basis for export growth. A good analytical index is included, and the bibliography is excellent.

934 Bancroft, Joseph A. *Mining in Northern Rhodesia : A chronicle of mineral exploration and mining development.* Arranged and prepared by T. D. Guernsey. Salisbury, British South Africa Co., 1961. 174 p. illus., ports., maps.

The author is a geologist who has carried out surveys for the Canadian government. This work is of considerable historical interest.

935 Brelsford, William V. *The story of the Northern Rhodesia regiment.* Lusaka, Government Printer, 1954. 134 p.

Regimental history written by a former colonial administrator.

936 —— *The tribes of Northern Rhodesia.* 2d ed. Lusaka, Government Printer, 1965. 157 p. illus., ports., map fold. col. Bibliography: p. 147–149.

The writer had formerly been a district commissioner in Northern Rhodesia. This guide was prepared to replace the long out-of-print *Memorandum on the native tribes and tribal areas of Northern Rhodesia* written in 1934 by J. Moffat Thomson, then Secretary of Native Affairs. Mr. Brelsford has made use of the extensive research and writing on many tribes since that time. His 22 chapters cover a great variety of tribes and tribal groups, treating briefly their history, ethnic composition and tribal origins. A large folded map in brilliant colours shows tribes and language groups. Mr. Brelsford has also written a number of studies of individual tribes, some appearing in the publications of the Rhodes-Livingstone Institute (since 1964 the Institute for Social Research of the University of Zambia, Lusaka). The most substantial is *Fishermen of the Bangweulu swamps : A study of the fishing activities of the Unga tribe* (Livingstone, 1946, 169 p., illus.; Rhodes-Livingstone Papers, no. 12). See also a work on the same area, Professor Frank Debenham, *Study of an African swamp : Report of the Cambridge University expedition to the Bangweulu swamps, Northern Rhodesia, 1949* (London, published for the government of Northern Rhodesia by H.M. Stationery Office, 1952, 88 p., illus.).

937 Ethnographic Survey of Africa [series]. Ed. by Daryll Forde. London, International African Institute, 1950– .

For the general note on this series, see no. 333.

The following relate to tribes of Northern Rhodesia: East Central Africa, Part 2, one volume (1951 [1950], 100 p.) made up of *Bemba and related peoples of Northern Rhodesia*, by Wilfred Whiteley, and *Peoples of the lower Luapula valley*, by J. Slaski; West Central Africa, Part 3, *The Lozi peoples of north-western Rhodesia* (1952, 62 p.), by V. W. Turner; and Part 4, *The Ila-Tonga peoples of north-western Rhodesia* (1953, 72 p.), by M. A. Jaspan. Because of the comparatively early date of these monographs, and particularly because of the important contributions to anthropological study of the territory made in publications of the Rhodes-Livingstone Institute (since 1964 the Institute for Social Research of the University of Zambia, Lusaka), there is later material available.

938 Epstein, Arnold L. *The administration of justice and the urban African : A study of urban native courts in Northern Rhodesia.* London, H.M. Sta. off., 1953. 124 p. (Colonial Research Studies, no. 7)
A most valuable analysis of urbanization and the problems it causes.

939 ——— *Politics in an urban African community.* Published for the Rhodes-Livingstone Institute by Manchester University Press, Manchester, 1958. 254 p.
Another valuable analysis of urbanization and its accompanying problems. Deals with the Copperbelt region but has relevance to much of Africa. Contains also a thorough analysis of African trade unionism on the Copperbelt and African political organization.

940 Gann, Lewis Henry. *A history of Northern Rhodesia: Early days to 1953.* London, Chatto & Windus, 1964. xiv, 478 p. maps (3 fold. col.). Bibliography: p. 461–471.
The standard history of Northern Rhodesia, compiled under the auspices of the National Archives of Rhodesia, based on ' open ' as well as ' closed ' government and private records in London, Lusaka and Salisbury. The writer concentrates on the political and social development of Northern Rhodesia under British rule. See also his earlier study, *The birth of a plural society : The development of Northern Rhodesia under the British South Africa Company, 1894–1914* (Manchester University Press, 1958, 230 p.).

941 Gelfand, Michael. *Northern Rhodesia in the days of the Charter: A medical and social study, 1878–1924.* Oxford, Basil Blackwell, 1961. xvii, 291 p. plates, ports., fold. maps. Bibliography: p. 278–283.
Written from a medical doctor's point of view but also valuable on early labour conditions and other related aspects.

942 Gluckman, Max. *The judicial process among the Barotse of Northern Rhodesia.* Manchester, published on behalf of the Rhodes-Livingstone Institute by Manchester University Press, 1955. 386 p. illus., port., fold. maps.
Classic study of the judicial process of an African people by an anthropologist with legal training. Emphasizes the concept of ' reasonable men ' in Lozi law.

943 Great Britain. Colonial Office. *Annual report on. . .* See no. 672.

944 ——— Commission on Financial and Economic Position of Northern Rhodesia. *Report of the commission appointed to enquire into the financial and economic position of Northern Rhodesia.* A. Pim and S. Milligan, commissioners. London, H.M. Stationery Office, 1938. xi, 394 p. maps, tables. (Colonial Office, Colonial no. 145)
During the 1930s extensive economic surveys of colonial territories were carried out by special commissions for the Colonial Office. Sir Alan W. Pim headed a number of these, including the surveys of Zanzibar and the High Commission Territories, Kenya, and, last, in 1937, Northern Rhodesia. The detailed report is basic to later British surveys, including the so-called Bledisloe Report (Great Britain, Rhodesia-Nyasaland Royal Commission, *Report*, London, 1939, 283 p.; Cmd. 5949),which examined the proposals for uniting the three territories. The recommendations of this commission, like those of an earlier commission in 1927, were against political union but for a larger measure of economic federation, with the creation of an Inter-territorial Council (set up in March 1945).

In 1938 Sir Alan Pim gave the Beit lecture series at Oxford, later published by the Clarendon Press, *The financial and economic history of the African tropical territories* (1940, 234 p.).

945 Hall, Richard. *Zambia.* London, Pall Mall Press, 1965; New York, Praeger, 1966. 357 p. maps. (Library of African Affairs) American ed. has subtitle *Story of the making of a nation.* Bibliography: p. 315–320.

A lively survey by the founder-editor of the *Central Daily Mail.* Hall first describes the geographic and cultural setting of Zambia's history and then discusses the period of colonial rule, the rise of nationalism, the 'genesis and exodus' of federation and the creation of the new state. A lengthy concluding section is devoted primarily to the economy and includes an analysis of the important role, economically and politically, of the Copperbelt. There are several appendices. An otherwise excellent account is marred by a number of factual and typographical errors.

946 Historical Association of Zambia. *History of Zambia.* 1970– . Lusaka. Twice a year.

A cyclostyled research bulletin that summarizes research in progress on all aspects of Zambian history. The first issue has a list of recent theses and publications on Zambia.

947 Kaunda, Kenneth. *Zambia shall be free: An autobiography.* New York, Praeger, 1963. 202 p. illus. (Books That Matter)

The leader of the United National Independence Party (UNIP) of Northern Rhodesia, since 1964 President of Zambia, followed the example of other African statesmen in writing his autobiography, which is also the history of the country's political and constitutional development to independence.

President Kaunda's recent views are recorded in *Zambia – independence and beyond: The speeches of Kenneth Kaunda,* edited by Colin Legum (London, Nelson, 1966, xiii, 265 p.), a collection that provides good source material on a type of African nationalism professedly directed towards nonviolence and practical politics.

948 Meebelo, Henry S. *Reaction to colonialism: A prelude to the politics of independence in Northern Zambia 1893–1939.* Manchester, England, published for the Institute for African Studies, University of Zambia, by Manchester University Press, 1971, 304 p., maps. Bibliography: p. 288–304.

A pioneer work based on extensive archival and secondary sources. Originally prepared as a doctoral dissertation for the University of London. Seeks to 'trace the development and assess the nature of African political consciousness under white rule in the Northern Province of modern Zambia'. The author seeks to redress what he considers the Eurocentric imbalance in much of Zambia's previous historiography. Through the use of the regional approach, it constitutes a new departure in Central African historiography: it represents a great step forward from Robert I. Rotberg, *The rise of nationalism in Central Africa: the making of Malawi and Zambia 1873–1964* (Cambridge, Mass., Harvard University Press, 1965, 362 p.).

949 Mulford, David C. *Zambia: The politics of independence, 1957–1964.* London, Oxford University Press, 1967. xii, 362 p. Bibliography: p. 344–352.

This scholarly study of Northern Rhodesia's transformation from a Central African state under white rule into an independent, African-governed Zambia is based on a notably rich, and heretofore unexploited, fund of documentary evidence. Concentration is on the nationalist political parties – especially on their evolution in relation to constitutional developments and elections and in relation to British administration of territorial politics.

Part III: area guide (by colonial power, region and colony)

950 *Northern Rhodesia Journal.* 1950–65. Livingstone, Northern Rhodesia Society. Semi-annual. Superseded by *Zambia Journal.*

A valuable journal on all aspects of Northern Rhodesian history and ethnology, geography and agriculture, mining and forestry. Book reviews were included. See L. H. Gann, 'The Northern Rhodesia Journal as an historical source book', *Rhodes-Livingstone Institute Journal* (no. 23), June 1958, p. 47–53. The last issue has a cumulative index.

951 Orde-Browne, Granville St. J. *Labour conditions in Northern Rhodesia: Report.* 1938. 99 p. maps (3 fold.), tables, diagrs. (Colonial no. 150)

Classical inquiry by a British labour expert into migrant labour conditions. The literature on labour conditions is extensive. For an account written from the standpoint of a Christian socialist, the first director of the Rhodes-Livingstone Institute, see Godfrey Wilson, *An essay on the economics of detribalization*, Rhodes-Livingstone Institute, Livingstone, 1941, 2 v. (Rhodes-Livingstone Papers nos. 5 and 6). Labour questions were discussed from the mining companies' point of view in Sir Ronald L. Prain, *Selected Papers 1953–1957* (London, Rhodesian Selection Trust, 1958, 203 p. maps, bibliographies). Prain was chairman of the Rhodesian Selection Trust.

952 Rhodes-Livingstone Institute, Lusaka, Northern Rhodesia. Communications [series]. nos. 1–29. Livingstone, Lusaka, 1943–65. Irregular. mimeo.

See no. 904 for annotation.

953 ——— Rhodes-Livingstone Papers [series]. nos. 1–37. Livingstone, Lusaka, 1938–65.

See no. 905 for annotation.

954 Rhodesia, Northern. *The Northern Rhodesia handbook.* Lusaka, Government Printer, 1953. 263 p. illus., maps. Bibliography: p. 256–261.

Useful reference book with historical, economic, geographic and political surveys. Provides basic data on people, trade and commerce, communications, and tourist facilities. Although it was superseded by the *Handbook to the Federation of Rhodesia and Nyasaland* (see no. 902), it remains valuable as a compilation of older facts and figures. Previous editions appeared in 1938 (144 p.), 1948 (98 p.) and 1950 (232 p.).

Southern Rhodesia (Rhodesia)

Note See preceding entries for bibliographic references, especially nos. 875–880.

Bibliographies

955 Bean, E. A. *Political development in Southern Rhodesia, 1890–1953 : A bibliography.* Cape Town, University School of Librarianship, 1969. 55 p.

956 Rhodesia. University College. *Catalogue of the parliamentary papers of Southern Rhodesia and Rhodesia, 1954–1970, and the Federation of Rhodesia and Nyasaland, 1954–1963.* Salisbury, The University College, 1970. 161 p. (Rhodesian University College, Political Science Department Source Books in Political Science, no. 6)

957 Rhodesia and Nyasaland. University College. Department of Government. *Catalogue of the parliamentary papers of Southern Rhodesia, 1899–1953.* By F. M. G. Willson and Gloria C. Passmore, assisted by Margaret T. Mitchell and Jean Willson. Salisbury, 1965. 484 p. (Source Book Series, no. 2)

British Africa: British Central Africa

Reference works

958 Barber, James. *Rhodesia : The road to rebellion.* London and New York, published for the Institute of Race Relations, London, by Oxford University Press, 1967. 338 p. illus., plates, map. Bibliography: p. 321–324.

The author was a temporary resident in Rhodesia during the year following the unilateral declaration of independence. In this book he offers a straightforward account and careful analysis of the political and constitutional developments during the early 1960s that led to the UDI. Included are four appendices and an analytical index.

959 Baxter, T. W., and R. W. S. Turner. *Rhodesian epic.* Cape Town, H. Timmins, 1966. 239 p. illus., ports., maps, facsims.

A pictorial history of Rhodesia from earliest times to the granting of self-government in 1923. The National Archives of Rhodesia, of which Mr. Baxter was director, provided most of the illustrations. The volume begins with maps of the 16th to 19th centuries, and after an excellent depiction of the drama of peoples and events, ends with a brief section on modern urban development. There is an index to illustrations.

960 Caton-Thompson, Gertrude. *The Zimbabwe culture : Ruins and reactions.* Oxford, Clarendon Press, 1931. xxiv, 299 p. illus., 63 plates on 48 l. (part fold.; incl. map, plans). Bibliography: p. xix–xxii.

A celebrated study that has set the standard for recent scholarship regarding Zimbabwe.

961 Crawford, J. R. *Witchcraft and sorcery in Rhodesia.* London, published for the International African Institute by Oxford University Press, 1967. xi, 312 p. plates, tables (1 fold.). Bibliography: p. 303–305.

The author, a lawyer and currently legal draftsman for the Botswana government, has written a thoughtful, carefully documented account of witchcraft in Rhodesia during the period 1956–62. He relied extensively on informants but used as his primary source the judicial records of the attorney-general of Rhodesia.

962 Day, John. *International nationalism : The extra-territorial relations of Southern Rhodesian African nationalists.* New York, Humanities Press, 1967. 143 p. (Library of Political Studies) Bibliography: p. 137–141.

The problem of Rhodesia is one of the most distinctive, complicated and publicized of all African problems. The Rhodesian Nationalist Movement has tried to combine internal with international pressure for self-government. This is a concise history of many aspects of the movement, and Day has attempted to estimate the relative importance of internal and international activity.

See also Nathan M. Shamuyarira, *Crisis in Rhodesia* (New York, A. Deutsch, 1965, 240 p.), a description of the nationalist movement in Rhodesia up to early 1965 by a ZANU leader, newspaper editor and university lecturer; and Ndabaningi Sithole, *African nationalism* (2d ed., London, Oxford University Press, 1968, 196 p.), an explanation of African nationalism in general by an active Rhodesian nationalist.

963 Gale, William Daniel. *The Rhodesian press : The story of the Rhodesian Printing and Publishing Company Ltd.* Salisbury, Rhodesia, 1962. 225 p., ports., facsims.

The Rhodesian Printing and Publishing Company dominated Rhodesian journalism. The author, a former information officer, wrote various popular works putting forward the European view of Rhodesian history, including *Heritage of Rhodes*, Cape Town, Oxford University Press, 1950. 158 p.

221

Part III: area guide (by colonial power, region and colony)

964 Gann, Lewis Henry. *A history of Southern Rhodesia : Early days to 1934.* London, Chatto & Windus, 1965. 354 p. fold. map. Notes on sources: p. 337–339; select bibliography: p. 341–348.

A standard work, compiled under the auspices of the National Archives of Rhodesia and based on both 'open' and 'closed' government and private records in Salisbury. Concentrating on European settlement and its political, social, and economic implications, the study supersedes the previous historical literature on the subject. The history ends with the consolidation of Sir Godfrey Huggins's rule in 1934.

965 Gelfand, Michael. *Tropical victory: An account of the influence of medicine on the history of Southern Rhodesia, 1890–1923.* Cape Town, Juta, 1953. 256 p. illus., plates, ports., map. Bibliography: p. 248–249.

A social as well as a medical history of the territory and its formative stage, written from a medical doctor's point of view; valuable on early labour conditions, housing and related aspects. The standard work on the subject.

966 Holleman, J. F. *Chief, council, commissioner; some problems of government in Rhodesia.* Assen, Netherlands, Royal Van Gorcum, on behalf of the Afrika-Studiecentrum, 1969. 391 p. Bibliography: p. 376–380.

A comprehensive study of Rhodesia's African policy by a Dutch anthropologist. Part 1, covering the background, investigates the history of African administration, as well as the controversial African Land Husbandry Act, 1951, and the African Councils Act, 1957. Part 2 presents a case study of the Mangwende people, including tribal structure, the relations between chiefs and followers, as well as those between chiefs and the white district officers. Part 3 deals with more recent changes in Rhodesia's African policy, including the 'rediscovery of the chief'.

967 Kuper, Hilda, and others. *The Shona and Ndebele of Southern Rhodesia.* The Shona, by Hilda Kuper; the Ndebele, by A. J. B. Hughes and J. van Velsen. London, International African Institute, 1954. 131 p. fold. map, tables. (Ethnographic Survey of Africa: Southern Africa, pt. 4) Bibliographies: Shona, p. 37–40; Ndebele, p. 110–117.

For general note on this series, see no. 333.

968 Leys, Colin. *European politics in Southern Rhodesia.* Oxford, Clarendon Press, 1959. xi, 323 p. maps, tables, diagrs. Bibliography: p. 313–316; bibliographical footnotes.

An examination of the foundations of European politics, structure of government, composition and living standards of the European population, interests and pressure groups, and the part played by political parties in Southern Rhodesia. The bibliography includes a listing of the more notable constitutional and political documents.

An excellent study measuring racial attitudes and behaviour patterns of whites as well as surveying the history of race relations is by Cyril Rogers and C. Frantz, *Racial themes in Southern Rhodesia : The attitudes and behaviour of the white population* (New Haven, Conn., Yale University Press, 1962, 427 p.).

969 Macdonald, John F. *The war history of Southern Rhodesia.* Salisbury, Government Printer, 1947–50. 2 v.

The official war history of Southern Rhodesia during World War II, based on Rhodesian military papers, written by an army officer.

970 Murphree, Marshall W. *Christianity and the Shona.* New York, Humanities Press, 1969. 200 p.

A careful study of the interactions of an African people and Christianity. Provides an excellent outline of the history of missionaries in Southern Rhodesia. While discussing Christianity and traditional religion the author does not ignore African politics.

971 *NADA*. nos. 1–40, 1923–63. n.s. no. 1– . 1964– . Salisbury. Annual.
This valuable magazine, originally subtitled *Southern Rhodesia Native Affairs Department Annual*, is being continued, with new numbering but with the same main title, by the Ministry of Internal Affairs. The annual carries a wide variety of articles relating to the work and experiences of the government agency and officials and their charges. Emphasis is largely on history and ethnology. A few book reviews are usually included.

972 *Outpost, Magazine of the British South Africa Police.* 1911– . Salisbury, published under the authority of the Commissioner of Police. Monthly.
The British South Africa Police began its career as a military police force in 1896. Its members took part in numerous campaigns, and *Outpost* is therefore of interest to the country's military, as well as for its administrative and general history. The official organ of the Rhodesian armed forces is now *Assegai: The Magazine of the Rhodesian Army* (1961– , Salisbury, monthly). The *Assegai* publishes information of local Rhodesian interest and also reprints from other journals concerning military problems.

973 Palley, Claire. *The constitutional history and law of Southern Rhodesia, 1888–1965, with special reference to imperial control.* Oxford, Clarendon Press, 1966. xxv, 827 p. tables, diagrs. Bibliography: p. 811–822.
A massive compilation, based on a great wealth of sources. It will remain the standard work on the subject for many years to come. The author first traces the constitutional history of Southern Rhodesia since the beginnings of British rule. Subsequently she analyses the country's constitutional law, with special reference to the limitations on Southern Rhodesia's sovereignty. She places considerable emphasis on the powers which – in her opinion – the British imperial government was traditionally able to wield in Southern Rhodesia. She pays special attention to what she considers to be the racially discriminatory character of Rhodesian rule. An addendum carries the story to the end of 1965 and deals with Rhodesia's unilateral declaration of independence. The book is furnished with numerous tables, a select bibliography, and a table of statutes and cases as well as an index. Written from the pro-imperial standpoint.

974 Parker, Franklin. *African development and education in Southern Rhodesia.* Columbus, Ohio State University Press, 1960. 165 p. (International Education Monographs, no. 2) Bibliographical notes.
By an American educationalist who studied at first hand conditions in Southern Rhodesia. He begins with a sketch of history focused on African development and then gives a historical review of African education.

975 *Rhodesia Agricultural Journal.* v. 1– . Aug. 1903– . Salisbury. illus., plans, fold. maps. Monthly.
The title varies, for example: from August 1903 to June 1910, the journal is called the *Rhodesian Agricultural Journal.*

Issued by the Southern Rhodesia Department of Agriculture and Lands under variant forms of that name until 1954, when publication was assumed by the Federal Ministry of Agriculture. Beginning with v. 61, no. 1, Jan./Feb. 1964, publication has been resumed by the Southern Rhodesia Ministry of Agriculture. See also no. 914.

976 Rhodesia and Nyasaland. University College. Department of Government. Source Book Series. no. 1– . Salisbury, Government Printer, 1963– . illus.

For the second work in this series of University College publications (the institution was renamed University College of Rhodesia in 1966), see no. 956, above. The first and third books in the series are as follows:

> no. 1. *Source book of parliamentary elections and referenda in Southern Rhodesia, 1898–1962*. Ed. by F. M. G. Willson, and written and compiled by Gloria C. Passmore and Margaret T. Mitchell, with the assistance of Jean Willson. Maps by R. F. Young. 1963. 255 p.

> no. 3. *Holders of administrative and ministerial office, 1894–1964, and members of the Legislative Council, 1899–1923, and the Legislative Assembly, 1924–1964*. By F. M. G. Willson and Gloria C. Passmore, assisted by Margaret T. Mitchell. 1966. 77, 10 p.

977 Rhodesia, Southern. *Official year book of the colony of Southern Rhodesia.* no. 1, 1924; no. 2, 1931; no. 3, 1932; no. 4, 1952. Salisbury, Rhodesian Printing and Publishing Co.

The 1952 edition (xvi, 792 p., illus., maps) gives population and other statistics, mainly up to 1950. There are full sections on physiography, geology, climate, population and migration (including figures for the 1948 sample census of the African population) agriculture, irrigation, forestry, and mining and mineral production.

978 —————— *Reports and decisions of the Court of Appeal for native civil cases, 1928–1962*. Salisbury, Government Printer, 1969.

A valuable source for legal relations between Africans and whites.

979 —————— Department of Agriculture and Lands. *Handbook for the use of prospective settlers on the land.* 6th ed. 1935. 101 p. illus.

Earlier editions of this work identified were published in 1924 (74 p.), 1925 (74 p.) and 1928 (99 p.).

980 —————— Department of Native Affairs. *Report of the Secretary for Native Affairs and Chief Native Commissioner.* 1913–61. illus., tables.

Continuation of the *Reports* of the Chief Native Commissioner, Mashonaland, and Chief Native Commissioner, Matabeleland.

Also includes the *Reports* of the Director of Native Development until 1926 and from 1935–58, of the Government Irrigation Engineer on water supplies in the native reserves, of the agriculturalist for instruction of natives, 1927–28, and most of the other government services affecting Africans, such as the following: Director of Native Education, Native Land Board and Native Area Administration, Township Officer, Chief Information Officer, Native Production and Marketing Branch, Chief Engineer Native Affairs, Forest Officer in Native Reserves.

981 —————— Department of Statistics. *Statistical year book of Southern Rhodesia: Official annual of the social and economic conditions of the colony.* Salisbury, Government Printer, 1924– . Irregular. tables.

Before the formation of the Federation, this statistical yearbook was issued in 1924, 1930, 1938, 1947 (covered years 1938–46) and 1950. (A *Statistical handbook* was also published in 1939 and 1945.) Well arranged and informative, it provided tabulated statistics on all phases of social and economic life. Under the Federation it was superseded by many publications issued by the Central African Statistical Office, notably the processed *Monthly Digest of Statistics of Rhodesia and Nyasaland.* For full details, see the Library of Congress list, no. 880.

982 ——— High Court. *Decisions of the High Court of Southern Rhodesia.*
  v. 1–45, 1911–55. Annual.
At the head of the title: v. 1–4, Juta reports of the High Court of Southern
Rhodesia; v. 5–24, Official reports of the High Court of Southern Rhodesia; v.
25–45, Southern Rhodesian law reports.
  Volumes 1–4 were published by J. C. Juta & Co., v. 5–14 by Argus Printing and
Publishing Co.
  Superseded in 1956 by the *Rhodesia and Nyasaland Law Reports.*
  Most colonies issued these compilations of decisions from the High Court of
the colony or region, for example East Africa. An important source too little
used by researchers. Annual volumes of the law or compilations of several years
also were a common publication in British Africa.

983 ——— Legislative Council. *Debates in the Legislative Council during the*
  years 1899 to 1923 (fourth session of the seventh Council, 25th to 31st May,
  11th to 14th June, 20th to 28th June, 23rd to 27th July, and during the
  special session of the seventh Council, 3rd to 11th October, 1923). Salisbury,
  Argus Printing and Publishing Co., 1904–23. 23 v. Reprint from the reports
  of the *Rhodesia Herald.*
Continued in October 1923, by the *Debates of the Legislative Assembly* (1923–).
Common publication for all colonies in British Africa.

984 ——— ——— *Minutes of the proceedings and ordinances (1st–7th*
  Council, May 15, 1889–October 11, 1923). Salisbury. 27 v.
The debates, votes and proceedings, and sessional papers were common for all
British colonies and represent basic material for the history of the individual
colonies.

985 *Rhodesian Journal of Economics.* v. 1, 1967, Salisbury. Quarterly.
Published by the Rhodesian Economic Society. Other journals concerned with
economic issues include no. 975, *Rhodesia Agricultural Journal*; *Rhodesian
Mining Journal*, v. 1, 1927, Johannesburg; *Rhodesian Tobacco Journal*, v. 1,
1951– , Salisbury.

986 Summers, Roger, and C. W. Pagden. *The Warriors.* Cape Town. Books of
  Africa, 1970. 181 p., maps, illus., tables.
Summers, a noted archaeologist renowned in Rhodesia for his researches on
Zimbabwe and other subjects, and Pagden, a local historian, have produced a
pioneer monograph, based on archival sources, secondary material and oral
tradition. *The Warriors* presents the development of Ndebele warfare primarily
from the Ndebele point of view. It thus differs from competent but Eurocentric
accounts such as R. S. S. Baden-Powell, *The Matabele campaign, 1896* (London,
Methuen, 1897).

987 Young, Kenneth. *Rhodesia and independence.* London, Eyre & Spottiswoode; New York, Heinemann, 1967. 567 p. maps.
British edition is subtitled *A study in British colonial policy.*
  A review of the events leading to the unilateral declaration of independence
and its aftermath. The material is partially based on unpublished documents and
private statements by leading participants in the Rhodesian episode. About half
the text is devoted to the years 1965 and 1966. An opening background chapter
and a sympathetic profile of Ian Smith are included. In a final section the author,
who is political adviser to the Beaverbrook newspapers and former editor of the
Yorkshire Post, offers some personal opinions, substantiating the pro-UDI viewpoint manifested in the book's preceding pages. Included are a chronology of
events, nine appendices and a select index.

EASTERN AFRICA

Note This section lists works relating to the region usually interpreted to comprise the four countries of what had been British East Africa, that is Kenya, Tanganyika, Uganda, and Zanzibar. It was decided that Somalia, the Sudan, Maritius, and the Seychelles would be included in this section as well. See also sections on German Africa and Italian Africa for references to the region and to individual countries.

Bibliographies

988 *Bibliography of African law*. Part I, *East Africa*. Ed. by Antony N. Allott. London, School of Oriental and African Studies, University of London, 1961. 83 p. mimeo.
The first part of the comprehensive bibliography is on customary law of former British Africa. It includes many references to unpublished documentary material in East African archives. See also Schiller, no. 476, for references to legal material for this region and individual colonies.

989 Butterfield, Harry R. F., comp. *Index digest of the reported cases determined by the Court of Appeal for Eastern Africa and on appeal therefrom by the Judicial Committee of the Privy Council, 1900–1952*. Nairobi, Government Printer, 1954. 135 p.

990 Durand, P. P. *Index to East African cases referred to, 1868–1969*. Nairobi, Legal Publishers, 1969.

991 East Africa High Commission. East African Agriculture and Forestry Research Organisation. *An East African forest bibliography*. Comp. by A. L. Griffith and B. E. St. L. Stuart. Nairobi, 1955. 118 p.
Includes many official papers and reports, articles from scientific journals, etc.
In 1962 the East Africa High Commission became the East African Common Services Organization.

992 —— East African Statistical Department. *Bibliography of economics in East Africa (Kenya, Tanganyika, Uganda and Zanzibar)*. Nairobi, 1958. 30 l.
The many official documents cited are covered in the Library of Congress bibliography described below, no. 1009.

993 East African Literature Bureau. *Catalogue*. Nairobi. Issued periodically.
List of books and pamphlets published by the Bureau in English, Swahili and vernaculars. The majority of the titles are for students. The bureau has a series on Early Travellers in East Africa, with short accounts of the first explorers, and also issues works on East African history, customs and languages.

994 East African Research Information Centre (EARIC). *Language problems in Africa, a bibliography (1946–1967) and summary of the present situation with special reference to Kenya, Tanzania and Uganda*. Comp. by Angela Molnos. Nairobi, Jan. 1969. 62 l. mimeo. (EARIC Information Circular, no. 2)
Part one explains the role of the EARIC, acknowledges the assistance of eminent socio-linguists and recounts to users the sources used, time periods covered, and tells how to obtain further information. Part two, 'Language problems in African development: A summary for the general reader', is a useful eight-page, single-space essay on language problems in Africa in general and East

Africa in particular. Part three contains the bibliography of 561 unannotated titles, alphabetically arranged by author. All foreign titles are translated into English. Part four contains three appendices on the mother tongues of the peoples of East Africa according to census data (Kenya, 1962; Tanzania without Zanzibar, 1957; and Uganda, 1959), a socio-linguistic glossary and seven pages of addresses of important research institutions. This is a most valuable document.

995 —— *Sources for the study of East African cultures and development: A bibliography of social scientific bibliographies, abstracts, reference works, catalogues, directories, writings on archives, bibliographies, book production, libraries, and museums; with special reference to Kenya, Tanzania, and Uganda, 1946–1966 (1967–1968).* Comp. by Angela Molnos. Nairobi, Sept. 1968. 54 p. 32 cm. mimeo. (EARIC Information Circular, no. 1)

The first publication of EARIC, a new centre sponsored by the East African Academy, is a comprehensive, unclassified listing that constitutes a substantially enlarged version of the fourth bibliography which appears in the appendix of the volume by Dr. Molnos described below (no. 1004). The 796 entries are arranged alphabetically by author. A list of selected addresses of organizations and agencies relevant to African studies concludes the bibliography.

996 Great Britain. Colonial Office. Pamphlet Series. *Inventory of materials dealing with East Africa.* Comp. by Cyril Ehrlich. 2 v. (Copies available from the Center for Research Libraries, Chicago, Illinois.)

This unique, valuable collection was gradually assembled by the Colonial Office from around 1890 to 1948 and includes reprints from journals, newspaper clippings, political ephemera, government documents, memoranda, committee reports, etc. There are series for West Africa and South Africa as well, but inventories for these collections are not yet available. This inventory covers Abyssinia, Somaliland, Belgian Congo, East Africa, Kenya, Uganda, Tanganyika, Zanzibar, the Rhodesias and Nyasaland.

997 International African Institute. *East Africa: General, ethnography, sociology, linguistics.* Comp. by Ruth Jones, librarian, with the assistance of a panel of consultants. London, 1960. 62 l. (Africa Bibliography Series, Ethnography, Sociology, Linguistics, and Related Subjects)

Covers ethnic groups of Kenya, Tanganyika, Uganda and Zanzibar.

998 Jacobs, Alan H. 'Bibliography of the Masai'. *African Studies Bulletin,* v. 8, no. 3, Dec. 1965: 40–60.

A useful list, revised from one compiled several years ago.

999 Langlands, B. W. *Research in geography at Makerere, 1947–1967.* Kampala, Makerere University College, 1967. 87 p. Includes bibliography.

Valuable for calling attention to little-known works.

1000 McLoughlin, Peter F. M. *Research on agricultural development in East Africa.* New York, Agricultural Development Council, 1967. 111 p.

Emphasis is on the economics of agricultural development in this monograph, which classifies and evaluates research on rural development and also indicates areas and priorities of future research in East Africa. The major portion of the volume consists of two bibliographies: Appendix 1 contains a bibliography of books, articles, government documents, reports, theses, dissertations, and research in progress on East Africa, Kenya, Tanzania, and Uganda; Appendix 2 consists of major bibliographies.

Part III: area guide (by colonial power, region and colony)

1001 Makerere University. Library. *Annotated list of theses submitted to the University of East Africa, and held by Makerere University Library.* Kampala, 1970. 52 p.

1002 Makerere Institute of Social Research. *Institute Publications. 1950–1970.* Kampala, 1971. 39 p.

Makerere University, later incorporated into the University of East Africa, played an important part in anthropological and sociological investigations through the East African Institute of Social Research, which conducted field work in Uganda, Kenya, Tanganyika and Zanzibar. The Institute was also interested in history, law, economics, linguistics, psychology, and other subjects. For publications of Dr. Audrey Richards, director from 1950 to 1956, see, for instance, no. 1047, *East African chiefs...*

1003 Mezger, Dorothea, and Eleonore Littich. *Wirtschaftswissenschaftliche Veröffentlichungen über Ostafrika in englischer Sprache: Eine Bibliographie des neueren englischsprachigen Schrifttums mit Inhaltsangaben.* München, IFO-Institut für Wirtschaftsforschung, 1967. 3 v.

Volumes 1 and 2 list 638 items including articles, monographs, government publications, unpublished papers, and chapters from books on East African economics (including Zanzibar). Arrangement is by subject, then alphabetical by author. Almost all items are annotated (in German). Subjects covered include population, development planning, finance, agriculture, land tenure, industry, trade and transport, labour, co-operatives, and inter-African trade. Volume 3 contains a bibliography of government publications and an author index.

1004 Molnos, Angela. *Die sozialwissenschaftliche Erforschung Ostafrikas 1954–1963 (Kenya, Tanganyika/Sansibar, Uganda).* Berlin and New York, Springer-Verlag, 1965. xv, 304 p. fold. maps, tables. (Afrika-Studien, no. 5)

A fine survey and bibliography of social and economic research in East Africa. Following a survey of research centres is a research review first by ethnic group and region and then by topic (history, politics, law, demography, health, economics, sociology and psychology, general works). A section on methodology concludes the survey material. A long appendix consists of four bibliographies and four lists: the bibliographies (p. 148–256) complement specific chapters and total 2,019 entries; the lists cover periodicals appearing in the bibliographies, group the tribes and districts of Kenya, Tanzania and Uganda, and include selected addresses of institutes and institutions. There is an insert in English on how to use the volume, with the table of contents annexed.

1005 Shields, James J., comp. *A selected bibliography on education in East Africa, 1941–1961.* Kampala, Makerere University College, 1962. 39 p. (Makerere Library Publications, no. 2)

Compiled by a research assistant to the American Teachers' East African Project, Columbia University, an effort to help provide teachers for East African secondary schools. The items in the bibliography are all in the Makerere Library with the exception of some of the older publications of the Education Department.

1006 Syracuse University. Maxwell Graduate School of Citizenship and Public Affairs. Program of Eastern African Studies. *A bibliography on anthropology and sociology in Tanzania and East Africa.* Comp. by Lucas Kuria and John Webster. Syracuse. N.Y., 1966. 91 l. (Occasional Bibliography, no. 4)

Arrangement is alphabetical by author; information is not always complete. German, French, Italian, and Portuguese entries are included, with coverage

228

from the late 19th century on. See also Barbara Skapa, *A select bibliography on urbanism in East Africa* (1967, 42 l.), and *A bibliography of Kenya* (no. 1057) – section A is devoted to East Africa in general and there are 141 entries containing significant bibliographies as well.

1007 —————————— *Occasional Bibliographies* [series]. Syracuse, N.Y., 1965– .

The Bibliographic Section of the Program of Eastern African Studies at Syracuse University is bringing out a series of bibliographies relating to East Africa and neighbouring areas. Although primarily for use in the Program, they are in a form to be made available to other libraries. These are extensive lists of books and articles, in straight author arrangement, prepared by John Webster and others of the Program's staff (see preceding entry). They are processed on loose-leaf pages, in a binder with bright red cover pages.

1008 U.S. Library of Congress. *Accessions List : Eastern Africa.* v. 1, no. 1– , Jan. 1968– . Nairobi, Library of Congress Office. Quarterly.

The first issue covers publications of Ethiopia, French Somaliland, Kenya, Malagasy, Malawi, Mauritius, Somalia, Sudan, Tanzania, Uganda and Zambia. Although it treats of current materials, many items refer to events during the colonial period.

1009 —————— General Reference and Bibliography Division. *Official publications of British East Africa.* Part 1, *The East Africa High Commission and other regional documents.* Comp. by Helen F. Conover, African Section. Washington, 1960. 67 p.

Covers as extensively as possible from printed sources the documents of the East African interterritorial official bodies. The East Africa High Commission, between the preparation of this guide and its appearance in print, had become the East African Common Services Organization. This list includes its documents from its inception and also those of several predecessors. The other three parts of the set of official publications of former British East Africa follow in the country sections.

1010 Vaughan, John H., and George H. Paterson. *Index-digest of the reported cases determined by the Court of Appeal for Eastern Africa and an appeal therefrom by the Judicial Committee of the Privy Council, 1900 to 1938.* Nairobi, 1939. 129, xv p. (200 entries)

1011 Whiteley, W. H., and A. E. Gutkind. *A linguistic bibliography of East Africa.* Rev. ed. Kampala, Uganda, East African Swahili Committee and East African Institute of Social Research, 1958. 1 v. loose-leaf. Supplement. no. 1– , Apr. 1960– .

The first edition attempted to bring together ' in one easily accessible publication a list of all that was known to have been written on the grammar and lexicon of the East African languages '. The revised edition incorporates the listings from the 1954 volume and its supplements with additional material: books, periodical articles and manuscripts. Sections are devoted to the languages of Tanganyika, Kenya and Uganda, with a special section for Swahili.

In 1930 the Arusha-based East African Inter-Territorial Language Committee issued its first report. Upon transfer to Makerere College in 1952, it was renamed East African Swahili Committee. In 1962 it was transferred to University College, Dar es Salaam, and renamed Institute of Swahili Research. The Institute sponsors numerous Swahili publications, including its journal, *Swahili*. The standard dictionaries of the Swahili language spoken by the mixed Arab-Bantu Swahilis of Zanzibar, now the lingua franca of the East African coast, are

Part III: area guide (by colonial power, region and colony)

those of the Inter-Territorial Language (Swahili) Committee, *Standard Swahili-English dictionary* and *Standard English-Swahili dictionary* (London, Oxford University Press, 1939, 2 v., 538, 635 p.). The old standard grammar was by Ethel O. Ashton: *Swahili grammar, including intonation* (London and New York, Longmans, Green, 1944, 398 p.).

Serials

1012 *East Africa and Rhodesia.* 1924– . London, published by East Africa, Ltd. (66 Great Russell St., W.C.1). Weekly.
The leading conservative organ for political and economic news. The editor, F. S. Joelson, is known for a number of books on East Africa. The chief daily of Nairobi, which formerly represented the white settlers' viewpoint, is the well-known *East African Standard* (1903–).

1013 East African Academy. *Proceedings of the...Symposium.* 1963– . Nairobi, Longmans, Green.

1014 *East African Agricultural Journal of Kenya, Tanganyika, Uganda and Zanzibar.* 1935– . Nairobi.

1015 *East African Economics Review.* 1954–63; n.s. 1964– . Nairobi, Oxford University Press. Semi-annual.

1016 *East African Geographical Review.* 1963– . Issued by Makerere University College. Irregular.

1017 *East African Medical Journal.* 1924– . Nairobi. Monthly.
Organ of the East African branches of the British Medical Association. Covers not only medical questions but also subjects related to medicine. This is an important source for the social, political and economic impact of Western medicine on East Africa.

1018 *East African Trade and Industry.* 1954– . Nairobi, D. A. Hawkins. Monthly.

1019 *Eastern Africa Law Review.* v. 1– , April 1968– . Dar es Salaam, Faculty of Law, University of East Africa.

Reference Works

1020 Beck, Ann. *A history of the British medical administration of East Africa, 1900–1950.* Cambridge, Mass., 1970. 271 p.
A useful survey of a somewhat neglected subject.

1021 Bennett, Norman R., ed. *Leadership in Eastern Africa: Six political biographies.* Boston, Boston University Press, 1968. 260 p.
A study of six African leaders of East and Central Africa and their relations with the incoming European invaders in the 19th and 20th centuries. The accounts deal with the political lives of Menelik II, Muhammad Abdullah Hassan, Sheikh Mbaruk bin Rashid bin Salim el Mazrui, Mwinyi Kheri, Gungunhana and Lobengula, and the impact of European colonialism on them.

1022 Commission on Administration of Justice in Kenya, Uganda and Tanganyika Territory in Criminal Affairs. *Report of the Commission of Inquiry into the Administration of Justice.* London, 1933. 160 p.

1023 Coupland, Sir Reginald. *The exploitation of East Africa, 1856–1890 :
The slave trade and the scramble.* Evanston, Ill., Northwestern University
Press, 1967. xiii, 507 p. plates, ports., map (fold. col.), geneal. table.
Bibliographical footnotes.

A classic study, first published in 1939, of East Africa and the European powers
in the 19th century. Coupland's work has not been tampered with; no attempt
has been made to update it, for, as Jack Simmons states in his introduction to
this edition, 'It stands, with its virtues and faults, as a work of its age, and it
will continue to be read: not only by students of East African history, but by
connoisseurs of good historical writing'. See also Coupland: *East Africa and
its invaders : From the earliest times to the death of Seyyid Said in 1856* (Oxford,
Clarendon Press, 1938).

1024 Cox, Richard. *Pan-Africanism in practice : An East African study,
PAFMECSA, 1958–1964.* Written under the auspices of the Institute of Race
Relations. London and New York, Oxford University Press, 1964. 95 p. map.

Summary history and analysis of the regional organization which began in 1958
as the Pan-African Freedom Movement of East and Central Africa and in 1962
became the Pan-African Freedom Movement of Eastern, Central and Southern
Africa. The hope of development into a working federation declined in 1963,
after the establishment of the OAU. By 1964, particularly in face of Ghana's
attacks on the idea of federation, PAFMECSA had ceased to function effectively.

1025 East Africa Central Legislative Assembly. *Proceedings : Official report.*
Nairobi, 1948–49– . Cited also as *Debates.*

The Assembly held three meetings a year, for each of which a volume
of Proceedings was published. See also *Interterritorial co-operation : Work of
the East Africa Central Legislative Assembly* (Nairobi, 1952, 107 p.), a review
of the work of the Assembly during its first term.

1026 *East African Annual.* 1941– . Nairobi, East African Standard. illus.
(part col.). Includes advertising.

Well-illustrated, slick-paper magazine published once a year by East Africa's
leading daily. Contents consists of articles on many phases of East African
countries and life.

1027 *East African Studies.* no. 1– . Kampala, Makerere Institute of Social
Research, Makerere University College, 1953– .

A series of valuable pamphlets and conference proceedings resulting from field
research carried out by the fellows of the Makerere Institute of Social Research
(formerly the East African Institute of Social Research). A typical study is no.
13, *Tribal maps of East Africa and Zanzibar,* by J. E. Goldthorpe and F. B.
Wilson (1960, 14 p., 8 l. of sketch maps). The Institute also issues an annual
bibliography, *Research and publications* (1967 ed., 67 p.), which describes
current projects of its members and lists publications of present and recent
members. Another valuable series published by the Institute is East African
Linguistic Studies.

1028 The Economist, London. *The economy of East Africa : A study of trends.*
Prepared by the Economist Intelligence Unit for the East African Railways
and Harbours Administration. Nairobi, East African Railways and
Harbours Administration, 1955. 237 p.

Requested as an independent opinion from skilled investigators to aid future
planning with regard to prospects for large capital investments. The report
reviews the activities of over a half-century of the Railways and Harbours
Administration and then studies likely trends in trade, agriculture and industry,

analysing them by specific products and aspects of development. See also quarterly surveys of East Africa by the Economist Intelligence Unit.

1029 Eliot, Sir Charles. *The East African Protectorate.* London, E. Arnold, 1905. 334 p. (Reprinted by Frank Cass.)

Eliot was commissioner for the East African Protectorate between 1900 and 1904. He gives a detailed account of the people of Kenya and Uganda, of their material way of life and of the problems faced by earlier British administrators.

1030 Ethnographic Survey of Africa: East Central Africa. London, International African Institute.

For the general note on this series, see no. 333. The following volumes relate to the peoples of Kenya, Tanganyika and Uganda.

Part 3. *The coastal tribes of the north-eastern Bantu (Pokomo, Nyika and Teita).* By A. H. J. Prins. 1952. 138 p. fold. map. (Bibliography: p. 133–134; Index of Tribes: p. 135–138.)

Part 4. *The Nilotes of the Anglo-Egyptian Sudan and Uganda.* By Audrey J. Butt. 1952. 198 p. fold. map. (Bibliography: p. 182–198.)

Part 5. *The Kikuyu and Kamba of Kenya.* By John Middleton. 1953. 107 p. fold. map. (Bibliography: p. 96–102.)

Part 6. *The northern Nilo-Hamites.* By G. W. B. Huntingford. 1953. 108 p. fold. map. (Bibliography: p. 99–102.)

Part 7. *The central Nilo-Hamites.* By Pamela Gulliver and P. H. Gulliver. 1953. 106 p. fold. map. (Bibliography: p. 100–101.)

Part 8. *The southern Nilo-Hamites.* By G. W. B. Huntingford. 1953. 152 p. fold. map. (Bibliography: p. 140–146.)

Part 10. *The Gisu of Uganda.* By J. S. La Fontaine. 1959. 68 p. fold. map. (Bibliography: p. 62–63.)

Part 11. *The eastern Lacustrine Bantu (Ganda, Soga [etc.]).* By Margaret Chave Fallers. 1960. 86 p. fold. map. (Bibliography: p. 74–81.)

Part 12. *The Swahili-speaking peoples of Zanzibar and the East African coast (Arabs, Shirazi and Swahili).* By A. H. J. Prins. 1961. 143 p. fold. map. (Bibliography: p. 116–138.)

Part 13. *The western Lacustrine Bantu (Nyoro, Toro [etc.]).* By Brian K. Taylor. 1962. 159 p. fold. map. (Bibliography: p. 149–152.)

Part 14. *Les anciens royaumes de la zone interlacustre méridionale (Rwanda, Burundi, Buha).* By Marcel d'Hertefelt, A. Trouwborst, and J. Scherer. 1962. 252 p. fold. map. (Bibliographies at end of sections; Buha of Tanganyika: p. 221–223.) Also issued as Musée Royal de l'Afrique Centrale, Monographies ethnographiques, no. 6.

1031 Ghai, Dharam P., ed. *Portrait of a minority : Asians in East Africa.* Nairobi and London, Oxford University Press, 1965 [i.e., 1966]. 154 p.

Consists of six essays of five prominent 'Asian' East Africans and an Austrian-born professor of Indian studies at Syracuse University. A chapter of historical background is followed by social, political, economic and educational surveys of the Asian community, with a concluding analysis of the future prospects of Asians in East Africa.

1032 Great Britain. East Africa Royal Commission. *Report [1953–55].* London, H.M. Stationery Office, 1955. xiv, 482 p. (Cmd. 9475) Chairman, Sir Hugh Dow.

Report of a commission appointed at the request of the Governors of East Africa to inquire into measures to increase national income and to raise the standards of living of the people of the East African territories, Africans, Europeans and Indians alike. Its central thesis was that restrictions to free competition of the races as to goods, services and land must be done away with, notably as regards rights of African landholders outside tribal areas. The commissioners recommended that barriers to the free exchange of land be progressively removed, and called for establishment of development boards to plan the use of land and the rehabilitation of overcrowded areas.

1033 *Handbook for East Africa, Uganda and Zanzibar.* Mombasa, Government Printing Press, 1903–4. 2 v.

Not available for examination.

1034 *Higher Education in East Africa.* Entebbe, Government Printer, 1958. 123 p.

A white paper issued jointly by Kenya, Tanganyika, Uganda and Zanzibar in which a University of East Africa was proposed, with the planned University Colleges in Kenya and Tanganyika as well as the then Royal Technical College of East Africa in Nairobi to be component parts of the new university. Included are the Carr-Saunders, Keir, Harlow, etc., report of the working party on Higher Education in East Africa, 1955, and the report by Giffen and Alexander on a visit to the Royal Technical College, 1956.

1035 *History of East Africa.* Oxford, Clarendon Press, 1963– .

v. 1, ed. by Roland A. Oliver and Gervase Mathew. 1963. 500 p. maps. (Bibliography: p. 457–480.)

v. 2, ed. by Vincent T. Harlow and E. M. Chilver, assisted by Alison Smith. 1965. li, 766 p. maps. (Bibliography: p. 700–736.)

The first two volumes of an authoritative history of East Africa, projected in three volumes. The editors have been joined by a group of specialist contributors for individual chapters. The first volume carries the history from the Stone Age to 1890; the second ends with the year 1945. Included in the appendices to v. 2 is a reprint of the British Mandate for East Africa. The select bibliographies cover published and unpublished materials, government documents and serials.

An earlier historical study by Dr. Oliver was *The missionary factor in East Africa*, first published in 1962 (2d ed., 1965, xv, 302 p., maps; bibliography, p. 293–297).

The Royal Commonwealth Society (London) maintains a dictionary file with over 5,000 names of East African biographies. The aim is to collect data on individuals who have played a significant part in the history of East Africa before 1900.

1036 Hoyle, B. S. *The seaports of East Africa : A geographical study.* Written under the auspices of the Makerere Institute of Social Research, Kampala, Uganda. Nairobi, East African Publishing House, 1967. 137 p. maps. (East African Studies, no. 26) Bibliography: p. 134–137.

A geographical analysis of the development of the ports of Mombasa, Tanga, Zanzibar, Dar es Salaam and Mtwara and of their role in the expanding economies of the countries of East Africa. Included are discussions of port facilities, port traffic, and the hinterlands of the ports.

Part III: area guide (by colonial power, region and colony)

1037 Ingham, Kenneth. *A history of East Africa*. London, Longmans, Green, 1962; New York, Praeger, 1963. xii, 456 p. illus., maps. Select bibliography: p. 443–448.

By the author of a notable study of Uganda, this is at present one of the better modern works covering the history of East Africa.

1038 King, Frank H. H. *Money in British East Africa*. London, 1957. 178 p. (Colonial Research Publication, no. 19)

1039 *Law reports containing decisions of the Court of Appeal for Eastern Africa and of the Judicial Committee of the Privy Council on appeal from that Court.* v. 1– , 1934– . Nairobi. Annual.

1040 Lugard, Frederick J. D. Lugard, baron. *The diaries of Lord Lugard*. Ed. by Margery Perham; assistant editor, Mary Bull. Evanston, Ill., Northwestern University Press, 1959–63. 4 v. ports., maps, facsims. (Northwestern University African Studies, no. 3)

The first three volumes cover the important career of Lugard in East Africa (especially in what was to become Uganda) from November 1889 to December 1890, December 1890 to December 1891, and January 1892 to August 1892, respectively; the fourth volume deals with the Nigerian area, in 1894–95 and again in 1897–98.

See also Dame Perham's two-volume biography, *Lugard*. Lord Lugard's own narrative of his campaigns as representative of the Imperial East African Company in suppression of the slave-trade, *The rise of our East African empire: Early efforts in Nyasaland and Uganda* (Edinburgh and London, W. Blackwood, 1893, 2 v., illus., maps, plans), is a primary source for the history of this period.

1041 Lury, D. A. *The trade statistics of the countries of East Africa, 1945– 1964, and population estimates: Back projections of recent census results.* Nairobi, Institute for Development Studies, University College, 1965. [5 p.] (Reprint Series, no. 13) Reprinted from East African Statistical Department, *Economic and Statistical Review*, March and September 1965.

The first part gives trade statistics for Uganda, Kenya, and Tanganyika; the second part contains population estimates for 1921, 1931, 1939, 1948 and 1963 for the three countries plus Zanzibar.

1042 Macpherson, Margaret. *They built for the future: A chronicle of Makerere University College, 1922–1962*. Cambridge, Eng., University Press, 1964. xiii, 212 p. illus. (1 col.), ports. Bibliographic references included in ' Notes ': p. 190–206.

Account of the chief centre for higher learning in East Africa.

1043 Mangat, J. S. *A history of the Asians in East Africa, c. 1886 to 1945*. Oxford, Clarendon Press, 1969. 216 p. Bibliography: p. 179–204.

The first detailed, historical survey on Asians in East Africa. Based on extensive research into original sources, the book examines fully the economic, political, and social implications of Asian immigration into East Africa during the colonial period.

1044 Matheson, J. K., and E. W. Bovill, eds. *East African agriculture: A short survey of the agriculture of Kenya, Uganda, Tanganyika, and Zanzibar and of its principal products.* London and New York, Oxford University Press, 1950. xvi, 332 p.

A collection of lucid and still useful descriptions by a number of specialists. The first 60 pages, by Mr. Matheson, give a general geographical introduction explaining land, population, land tenure, white settlement, indigenous labour, African welfare, soil conservation problems and agricultural research institutes. Part 2 describes in detail the agriculture of the European settlers, explaining practices and conditions regarding the chief crops. Part 3 is on African agriculture considered by territorial division. There are short lists of sources at the end of the sections. Appendices tabulate statistics.

1045 *Research services in East Africa.* Comp. for the East African Academy. Nairobi, East African Publishing House, 1966. 239 p.

A guide to research facilities in Kenya, Tanzania and Uganda up to the end of 1964. Field work for the survey was conducted by Marco Surveys, Ltd. Academic, commercial, private, and public services are described first by region and then by country in more than 30 fields of research, e.g., agriculture, antiquities, chemistry, economics, game, housing, library services, medicine, political science, religious studies and zoology. For each centre the data given are location, facilities, date established, staff, sources of finance, scope of research, and publications. There is an index. See also H. H. Story, *Basic research in agriculture : A brief history of research at Amani, 1928–1947 (East African Agriculture and Forestry Research Organization)*.

1046 *Report on the East Africa High Commission.* 1948– . London, H.M. Stationery Office. Annual. (*Its* Colonial no. 245)

1047 Richards, Audrey I., ed. *East African chiefs : A study of political development in some Uganda and Tanganyika tribes.* New York, Praeger, 1960. 419 p. illus. (Books That Matter) Bibliography: p. 398–409.

A comparative study of political development begun in 1952 under the auspices of the East African Institute of Social Research and carried out by anthropologists on the staff and other researchers, with the final writing by Dr. Richards, then head of the Institute. A collection was made of career histories of over 1,100 chiefs of varying types, kings, paramount chiefs, clan elders, and so on, with data about their age, education, religion, service, outstanding training, genealogy, and economic position within the community.

1048 Richards, Charles G., and James Place. *East African explorers.* London, Oxford University Press, 1960. 356 p. illus. (World's Classics, no. 572)

Compilation in a pocket-size volume of outstanding passages from the books and journals of the 19th-century explorers of East Africa: Krapf and Rebmann, Charles New, Livingstone and Stanley, Burton, Speke and Grant, Samuel W. Baker, Joseph Thomson, Gaetano Casati, Count Teleki and L. von Höhnel, J. W. Gregory, Lord Lugard, J. R. L. Macdonald, Herbert Austin. The works from which the extracts are taken are noted.

1049 Rosen, I., and F. de F. Stratton, eds. *A digest of East African criminal case law, 1897–1954; containing decisions of the Court of Appeal for Eastern Africa and the Judicial Committee of the Privy Council on Appeal from that Court.* Durban, Butterworth, 1957. 341 p.

1050 Trevelyan, Edward. *East African Court of Appeals, civil appeals digest, 1868–1956.* Dobbs Ferry, N.Y., Oceana Publications, Inc., 1967. 272 p.

The volume contains a complete table of subject headings, an index of cases and the main headings reference and a digest of each decision.

1051 Welbourn, Frederick B. *East African rebels : A study of some independent churches.* London, SCM Press, 1961. 258 p. maps. (World Mission Studies)

The author, a clergyman connected with Makerere University College, studies the movements of four separatist churches, three in Uganda and one in Kenya. His work, based on unpublished material as well as on printed sources, is at once church history, social psychology, and an analysis of the clash of cultures under the impact of changes brought by colonial rule. See also Welbourn, *East African Christians* (London, Oxford University Press, 1965, 226 p.).

1052 Wilson, C. J. *The story of the East African mounted rifles.* Nairobi, 1938. Not available for examination.

Kenya

Note For further specific references, see no. 169, and Eastern Africa, General section.

Atlases

1053 Kenya. Survey of Kenya. *National atlas of Kenya.* 3d ed. Nairobi, 1970. 103 p.
Previously published by the Survey of Kenya of Kenya Colony and Protectorate under title *Atlas of Kenya.* Scale of maps 1:3,000,000. Includes bibliographies.

1054 Kenya Colony and Protectorate. Survey of Kenya. *Atlas of Kenya: A comprehensive series of new and authentic maps prepared from the National Survey and other governmental sources, with gazetteer and notes on pronunciation and spelling.* Nairobi, printed by the Survey of Kenya, 1959. 44 l. of maps (part col.). page size, 20" x 18". Text on verso of a few maps.
Maps covering geology, physical features, soil, meteorology, agriculture, population, economy, administration, and history (scales, 1:1,000,000 to 1:3,000,000). Also included are a town plan of Mombasa and interesting reproductions of early maps. Some 1,500 to 2,000 names appear in the gazetteer.

Bibliographies

1055 DuPré, Carole E. *The Luo of Kenya: An annotated bibliography.* Washington, D.C., Institute for Cross-Cultural Research, 1968 164 p. (ICR Studies, no. 3)
The first section contains an introductory essay to Kenya and the Luo, with particular reference to contemporary problems in Luoland. This is followed by a bibliographic essay on Luo materials. The main bibliography is annotated and divided into three parts. Part 1 contains material on East Africa and Kenya. Part 2 covers references to the Luo, and Part 3 includes works containing information relevant to the Luo. Each part is further divided by subject. The over 130 references cited include documents, maps, articles, conference papers, theses and books. Some Luo language works are included.

1056 Hakes, Jay E. *A study guide for Kenya.* Boston, Development Program, African Studies Center, Boston University, 1969. 76 p.
Prepared for the Agency for International Development. Bibliographical information is presented under the following main headings: physical environment, traditional societies, pre-colonial history, colonial rule and nationalism, social change, political affairs, economic development. There is also a general bibliography.

1057 Syracuse University. Maxwell Graduate School of Citizenship and Public Affairs. Program of Eastern African Studies. *A bibliography of Kenya.* Comp. by John B. Webster and others. Syracuse, N.Y., 1967. xviii, 461 p. (Syracuse University, Eastern African Bibliographical Series, no. 2)
The 7,210 entries on Kenya and East Africa include books, articles, government

publications, dissertations, and conference papers in many European and East African languages. Arrangement is by subject. There is a large section on language and literature which lists works on and in Swahili and other East African languages. The bibliography, second in the series of national bibliographies by Syracuse University (the first is the 1965 *Bibliography of Malawi*), was originally compiled to aid development of the Kenya Institute of Administration and its library. It attempts to update the Library of Congress guide, which is described in the next entry.

1058 U.S. Library of Congress. General Reference and Bibliography Division. *Official publications of British East Africa.* Part 3, *Kenya and Zanzibar.* Comp. by Audrey A. Walker, African Section. Washington, 1963. 162 p.

Contains 994 entries (p. 1–120) for official publications of Kenya Colony and Protectorate and of the East African Common Services Organization and Great Britain relating to Kenya. The documents published by the colony under its earlier name, East Africa Protectorate (1899–1920), are included without differentiation. Many of the reports of the agencies are continued virtually unchanged under the independent government of Kenya.

Reference works

1059 *African Land Development in Kenya.* 1945/50– . Nairobi. illus., photos., fold. maps. Irregular.

Issued from 1945/50 to 1952 by the African Land Utilization and Settlement Board, with the title *African Land Utilization and Settlement Report*; to 1955/56, with the present title, by the African Land Development Board; and from 1956/57 by the Land Development Board (Non-scheduled Areas). The publication consists of progress reports on government-supported land reclamation and development schemes in the African areas of Kenya under British colonial administration. This basic source includes statistics.

1060 American University, Washington, D.C. Foreign Area Studies. *Area handbook for Kenya.* By Irving Kaplan and others. Washington, U.S. Government Printing Office, 1967. xii, 707 p. map, tables. (Department of the Army Pamphlet, no. 550–56) Bibliography: p. 663–689.

Similar to others of the series, this is a comprehensive survey of the country. The volume is composed of four main sections: social (including physical environment and historical setting), political, economic, and military. Arrangement of the bibliography is also by these four divisions. A glossary and an analytical index are included.

1061 Anderson, John. *The struggle for the school : The introduction of missionary, colonial government and nationalist enterprise in the development of formal education in Kenya.* London, Longmans, 1970, 192 p. Bibliography: p. 171–183.

History of education during the colonial period.

1062 Bennett, George. *Kenya, a political history : The colonial period.* London, Oxford University Press, 1963. 190 p. maps. (Students' Library)

Although hardly more than a rapid summary, this political history is perhaps the most useful single work on the British administration of Kenya. It contains broad coverage of political developments from 1900 – the Colonial Office take-over, the role of the European settlers, the development of racism and African nationalism, the Mau Mau 'emergency', changing multi-racial policies, and the last stages of the road to independence. Bibliographical notes refer chiefly to newspapers and official documents. For a more recent survey, see Marshall Archibald Macphee, *Kenya* (New York, F. A. Praeger, 1968, 238 p.).

1063   Corfield, F. D. *Historical survey of the origins and growth of Mau Mau.* London, H.M. Stationery Office, 1960. 321 p. (Cmnd. 1030)
The official study resulting from the trial of Kenyatta and presenting what appeared to be complete proof of his responsibility for the Mau Mau 'emergency'. According to most critics, by the time of publication the work was outdated, much of the evidence had been disproved, and Delf (below) speaks of it as 'history composed by the patient himself', though he admits that it was a reliable chronicle of government information at the time it was being written. For an opposite interpretation of the 'emergency', see Carl G. Rosberg Jr. and John Nottingham, *The myth of 'Mau Mau': Nationalism in Kenya* (New York, published for Hoover Institution by Praeger, 1966, 427 p.). Rosberg and Nottingham do not see 'Mau Mau' as primarily an atavistic Kikuyu movement but rather as part of the growth and development of Kenya African nationalism.

1064   Delf, George. *Jomo Kenyatta : Towards truth about 'the light of Kenya'.* London, Gollancz, 1961. 223 p. illus. U.S. ed. Garden City, N.Y., Doubleday, 1961. 215 p. Includes bibliography.
An attempt to trace Kenyatta's career as the future and logical leader of Kenya. The writer alludes to the widespread belief among Africans that the trial of Kenyatta for association with Mau Mau was 'rigged'. His argument is that Mau Mau was the 'inexorable product of a seriously distorted social system' and could have been prevented by a less weak British government. See Rosberg and Nottingham, above, for a more thoroughly researched book which offers other interpretations.

1065   Ghai, Y. P., and J. P. W. B. McAuslan. *Public law and political change in Kenya : A study of the legal framework of government from colonial times to the present.* Nairobi, Oxford University Press, 1970. 536 p.
A broadly conceived study covering the historical, administrative, political and economic interests which shaped public law. It does not, however, treat of local government or native administration. The first four chapters treat of the colonial period and the fifth chapter covers the transition from colonial to independent government.

1066   Great Britain. Colonial Office. *Annual report on...* See no. 672.

1067   Huxley, Elspeth. *White man's country : Lord Delamere and the making of Kenya.* London and New York, Macmillan, 1935. 2 v.
This biography of the leader who was largely responsible for attracting Europeans to the colony for permanent residence as farmers in the highlands is also a history of white settlement in Kenya. Its author is an expert on East Africa.

1068   Kenya. *A digest of the East African and Kenya law reports, 1897–1952.* Comp. by Kathleen Errington. 1953. 25 v.

1069   —— *East Africa Protectorate : Orders in Council, King's (Queen's) regulations, ordinances, rules, proclamations, and other official orders in force in the East Africa Protectorate on the 1st of January 1903. (1876–1902)* [n.p.], 1903. 242 p.

1070   —— *A handbook of the labour laws of the Colony and Protectorate of Kenya, consolidated and amended to 1st May 1945.* 1945. 241 p.

1071   —— *Kenya Gazette.* 1899– . Nairobi. illus. Weekly.
Began publication in 1899. Published until December 1956 as *Official Gazette.* Issued 1899–July 23, 1920, by East Africa Protectorate (1899–April 1, 1908, by

East Africa Protectorate and Uganda). Superseded in part in April 1908 by the *Official Gazette* of Uganda. Includes special issues, some with the title *Special Official Gazette.*

1072 —— African Affairs Department. *Report.* Nairobi, 1923– . Annual.
Reports for 1923–33 issued by the Native Affairs Department; 1934–47 by the Chief Native Commissioner as his *Report on native affairs*; 1948 and after by above department. Reports for 1939–45 were not published; instead they were summarized in *Report on Native Affairs* for 1939–45, which was published as one volume in 1947. Reports for 1951 and after consist of collected district and provincial accounts.

1073 —— —— *The work of an African chief in Kenya, being an edition of a chief's guide and handbook.* Nairobi, East African Literature Bureau, 1956. 48 p.

1074 —— Supreme Court. *Law reports of Kenya, containing cases determined by the Supreme Court, Kenya Colony and Protectorate, and by the Court of Appeal for Eastern Africa, and by the Judicial Committee of the Privy Council on appeal from that Court.* v. 1– . 1897– . 1906– .
Title varies: v. [1], *East Africa Protectorate : Law reports containing cases determined by the High Court of Mombasa, and by the Appeal Court at Zanzibar, and by the Judicial Committee of the Privy Council...*; v. [2], 4–8, pt. 1, *East Africa Protectorate : Law reports containing cases determined by the High Court of East Africa, and by the Court of Appeal for Eastern Africa, and by the Judicial Committee of the Privy Council...*; v. 8, pt. 2–v. 9, *Colony and Protectorate of Kenya : Law reports...*; v. 10 and after, *Law reports of Kenya.*
Volumes 1–4 and some of the later volumes have appendices containing notes on native customs, court rules, circulars to magistrates, etc.

1075 *Kenya Weekly News.* 1928– . Nakuru, Nakuru Press. Weekly.
Pro-settler journal; valuable for local whites' views and opinions.

1076 Kenyatta, Jomo. *Facing Mount Kenya: The tribal life of the Kikuyu.* London, Secker and Warburg, 1938. xxv, 339 p.
Detailed ethno-sociological study of the writer's people. As general secretary of the Kikuyu Central Association in the 1920s, Kenyatta had led the agitation against European settlement in the Kenya Highlands, which the Kikuyu claimed as their land. In this book, written after he studied under Professor Malinowski at the London School of Economics, Kenyatta attempted to show the evil effects of culture contact for the Kikuyu.

1077 Mungeam, G. H. *British rule in Kenya, 1895–1912 : The establishment of administration in the East Africa protectorate.* Oxford, Clarendon Press, 1966. xii, 329 p. plates, ports., maps. (Oxford Studies in African Affairs) Bibliography: p. 290–307.
A detailed introduction to Kenyan history in the 17 formative years of British administration. Emphasis is on the relationship between the district officer, the commissioner or governor, and the officials at Whitehall. The book ends at the point at which growing signs of African resentment and opposition began to appear. An analytical index is included.

1078 Sandford, George R. *An administrative and political history of the Masai Reserve.* London, Waterlow, 1919. 234 p.

1079 Singh, Makhan. *The history of Kenya's trade union movement to 1952.* Nairobi, East African Publishing House, 1969. 332 p.
A trade-union history by a left-wing participant. Singh himself was a leader of the

Part III: area guide (by colonial power, region and colony)

East African Trade Unions Congress. About half the book treats of post-World War II developments.

1080 Sorrenson, M. P. K. *Land reform in the Kikuyu country: A study in government policy.* Nairobi, Oxford University Press, 1967. 266 p. Bibliography: p. 253–256.

Thorough historical study based largely on official files of the Kenya government on the question of land policy. See also Hanfried Fliedner, *Die Bodenrechtsreform in Kenya: Studie über die Änderung der Bodenrechtsverhältnisse im Zuge der Agrarreform unter besonderer Berücksichtigung des Kikuyu-Stammesgebietes* (Berlin and New York, Springer-Verlag, 1965, 114 p.); and Hans Ruthenberg, *African agricultural production development policy in Kenya, 1952–1965* (Berlin, 1966, 164 p.).

1081 Wagner, Guenter. *Bantu of Western Kenya, with special reference to the Vugusu and Logoli.* London, Oxford University Press, 1970. 2 v.

A major study. Volume 1 was first published in 1949 and v. 2 in 1956.

Tanganyika (Tanzania)

Note On April 27, 1964, the two recently independent republics of Tanganyika (independence date, December 9, 1961; became a republic on December 9, 1962) and Zanzibar (independence date, December 10, 1963) merged to become a single United Republic of Tanganyika and Zanzibar, which in October 1964 changed its name to United Republic of Tanzania. The references in this section appear under the headings Tanganyika and Zanzibar below. See also German East Africa.

Atlases

1082 Jensen, S. *Regional economic atlas, mainland Tanzania.* Dar es Salaam, Bureau of Resource Assessment and Land Use Planning, University College, 1968. 70 p.

Eighteen maps illustrating population, employment, industrial location, trade, tax rates, cooperatives, schools, hospitals, crop production, etc. Each map is accompanied by a ' brief analysis, tabular material, references, and critical evaluation of the sources used '. The atlas is useful as a source to review growth and development during the colonial period.

1083 Tanganyika. Department of Lands and Mines. Survey Division. *Atlas of Tanganyika, East Africa.* 4th ed. Dar es Salaam, 1969. 29 col. plates of maps, tables, page size, 22″ x 23″.

Maps (uniformly 1:3,000,000) cover physical geography, biogeography, human geography, industry and commerce, and town plans. Appended are a statistical section and a gazetteer. A transparent population overlay is provided for use with the individual maps.

Bibliographies

Note See also German Africa section.

1084 Bates, Margaret L. *A study guide for Tanzania.* Boston, African Studies Center, Boston University, 1969. 83 p.

Prepared for the Agency for International Development. Each section has a general introduction drawing attention to the most important works on the

240

special subject treated, and a bibliography. The main topics are: physical environment, peoples, history, political development, Zanzibar, social change, economic system. There is a general bibliography.

1085 Langlands, Bryan W. 'Tanzania bibliography – 1965 publications – Part I '. *Tanzania Notes and Records*, no. 65, Mar. 1966: 113–122. Continued: ' 1965 publications – Part II; 1966 publications – Part I ', no. 66, Dec. 1966: 231–238; ' Tanzania bibliography – 1966, Part II ', no. 67, June 1967: 79–88; 'Tanzania bibliography – 1966–1967 ', no. 68, Feb. 1968: 117–124.

A continuing compilation of publications, including articles, appearing both in Tanzania and abroad. Following a general section, arrangement is by broad subject classification. The 1966–67 listing contains some 220 entries, a few of which refer to 1965. Langlands also compiles a Uganda bibliography for the *Uganda Journal*. ' A bibliography of Tanganyika, 1959–1964 ', by Andrew Roberts, appeared in *Tanganyika Notes and Records* (June 1967). The bibliography (209 entries) was confined to local and tribal studies and was intended to cover the period before an annual bibliography for Tanganyika started in 1965.

1086 Tanganyika Territory. Laws, statutes, etc. *Index to the laws of the Tanganyika Territory in force on the 31st day of December 1940, with a table showing the effect of amending legislation, 1929–40.* Comp. by G. M. Pillai. Dar es Salaam, Government Printer, 1941. xxv, 88 p. (3,000 entries).

An earlier edition, compiled by H. R. F. Butterfield, was published in 1935 (xii, 94 p.), with some 3,000 entries on laws in December 1933, with references to amending legislation enacted in 1934.

1087 U.S. Library of Congress. General Reference and Bibliography Division. *Official publications of British East Africa.* Part 2, Tanganyika. Comp. by Audrey A. Walker, African Section. Washington, 1962. 134 p.

List of 715 numbered entries and index of subjects and personal names. Arrangement is by name of issuing agency. The coverage is of former German East Africa, of Tanganyika Territory under British administration, and of British and UN documents relating to Tanganyika.

Reference works

1088 Chidzero, Bernard T. G. *Tanganyika and international trusteeship.* London and New York, Oxford University Press, 1961. 286 p. maps (2 fold. col. in pocket). Bibliography: p. 277–282.

History and analysis of the part played by the United Nations trusteeship in the progress of Tanganyika to independence. This scholarly and comprehensive study had been prepared by the Rhodesian author for his doctoral thesis at McGill University in 1958 and was subsequently worked on at Nuffield College, Oxford, for two years, being published just before the Tanganyika Constitutional Conference of March 1961.

1089 Clyde, D. F. *History of the medical services of Tanganyika.* Dar es Salaam, Government Press, 1962. 223 p. illus., ports., maps. Bibliography: p. 207–209.

Valuable history of medical services and public health problems.

1090 Cole, J. S. R., and W. N. Denison. *Tanganyika : The development of its laws and constitution.* London, Stevens, 1964. 339 p. (*The British Commonwealth : The development of its laws and constitutions*, v. 12)

Describes the constitutional structure of Tanganyika and gives an account of the laws by which the state regulates its internal affairs. It is for the general reader as well as the legal expert. Part 1 gives general background information on the country; Part 2, the laws of Tanganyika. Appendices carry the constitution and various agreements.

1091 De Blij, Harm. *Mombasa: An African city.* Evanston, Northwestern University Press, 1968. 168 p.

Provides a good historical survey of the development of the town during the colonial period.

1092 Great Britain. Colonial Office. *Annual report on . . .* See no. 672.

1093 *Handbook of Tanganyika.* 2d ed. Ed. by J. P. Moffett. Dar es Salaam, Government Printer, 1958. xi, 703 p. illus., plates, maps. Bibliography: p. 567–677.

Completely superseding a first edition of the *Handbook of Tanganyika* published in 1930, this work complements the 1955 *Tanganyika: A review of its resources and their development* (no. 1099); it is likewise edited by the Commissioner for Social Development, but is not an official publication. The first 150 pages are devoted to an outline of history from palaeolithic times to the mid-1950s. There follow detailed descriptions of the country province by province, and chapters on peoples, government, economic and social services, natural history, sport, and miscellaneous information for visitors. The long bibliography contains about 2,000 entries, including articles in periodicals. Arrangement is by topic.

1094 International Bank for Reconstruction and Development. *The economic development of Tanganyika: Report.* Baltimore, Md., Johns Hopkins Press, 1961. xxviii, 548 p. fold. maps, tables, diagrs.

This volume results from an Economic Survey Mission organized at the request of the Tanganyika and British governments. The field survey was carried out in the summer of 1959 and the study prepared during that winter, with additional data gathered in Tanganyika in the summer of 1960. The extended report begins with a general and budgetary examination of the Tanganyika economy and continues with analyses of specific economic aspects.

1095 Kimambo, I. N., and A. J. Temu, eds. *A history of Tanzania.* Nairobi, East African Publishing House, 1969. ix, 276 p. maps. Bibliography: p. 258–263.

Revised papers presented at a historical conference at the History Department, University College, Dar es Salaam. The subjects covered range from Tanzania's precolonial history, to the impact of Germany and Great Britain, the rise of nationalism, the problems of independence, and the revolution in Zanzibar.

1096 Morris-Hale, Walter. *British administration in Tanganyika from 1920 to 1945: With special references to the preparation of Africans for administrative positions.* Genève, Imprimo, 1969. 352 p. (Université de Genève, Institut Universitaire des Hautes Etudes Internationales, Thèse no. 192). Includes bibliography: p. 337–349.

A doctoral thesis presented at Geneva University, based on published works and on original sources in the Tanzania Archives. The first part deals with the historical background and the development of the country until the end of World War II. The second part discusses the political future of Tanganyika and the problem of African leadership. The third part, entitled 'the lost opportunity', censures the various British groups in Tanganyika on the grounds that 'they were misled by their belief in permanence and paternalism'.

1097 Nyerere, Julius Kambarage. *Freedom and unity – Uhuru Na Umoja : A selection from writings and speeches, 1952–65.* London, Oxford University Press, 1967. xii, 366 p. plates, ports.
By the President of Tanzania and one of Africa's more able leaders and political thinkers. His views are a blend of Catholicism, nationalism and socialism. See also TANU [Tanzania African National Union], *The Arusha declaration and TANU's policy on socialism and self-determination* (Government Printer, Dar es Salaam, 1967, 29 p.), which contains TANU's program, and a restatement of Nyerere's views on racialism and socialism.

1098 Stephens, Hugh W. *The political transformation of Tanganyika : 1920–67.* New York, Praeger, 1968. xii, 225 p. maps, charts, tables. (Praeger Special Studies in International Politics and Public Affairs) Bibliography: p. 217–225.
A delineation and analysis of the effects of basic social change upon politics in Tanganyika from the colonial era to the present. Following an introduction, the study is divided into six parts: background of political change; the 'mothball phase', 1920–40; the development phase, 1950–54; the nationalist phase, 1954–61; and the post-colonial quest for political stability. Included are a statistical appendix and an appendix presenting social mobilization indicators.

1099 Tanganyika. *Tanganyika : A review of its resources and their development.* Prepared under the direction of J. F. R. Hill; ed. by J. P. Moffett. Dar es Salaam, Government Printer, 1955. xviii, 924 p. maps, tables. Bibliography: p. 861–868.
Edited by the Commissioner for Social Development of Tanganyika, this big volume surveys resources and requirements of the territory in close detail. The various sections, covering widely the land, people, political structure, social services, communications, and all phases of production and economic life, were prepared largely by the heads of departments concerned. There are maps and tables throughout, a select bibliography (listing mainly documentary sources), and an extensive index.

1100 —— Department of Commerce and Industry. *Commerce and industry in Tanganyika.* Dar es Salaam, 1961. 106 p. illus.
Well-illustrated pamphlet prepared to coincide with independence, but also valuable as a survey of colonial economic growth.

1101 *Tanzania Notes and Records* (formerly *Tanganyika Notes and Records*). no. 1– . Mar. 1936– . Dar es Salaam. illus., ports., maps, diagrs.
The journal of the Tanzania (earlier Tanganyika) Society, published semi-annually except for a period in the 1950s. It is an organ for scholarly research in all disciplines relating to Tanzania. Issues carry a number of reviews of pertinent books and include bibliographical materials.

1102 Taylor, J. Clagett. *The political development of Tanganyika.* Stanford, Calif., Stanford University Press, 1963. 254 p. map. Bibliography: p. 243–248.
Readable political history of the period before and during the British mandate and trusteeship and the achievement of independence.

Zanzibar (now part of Tanzania)

Bibliographies

1103 Crossey, John M. D., and John A. Braswell. [Comprehensive bibliography of Zanzibar, Pemba, and adjacent islands.] New Haven, Conn., Yale University Library.
Classified bibliography now in course of compilation – to include books, articles, maps, manuscript collections. (Information from note in *African Studies Bulletin*, v. 8, no. 1, Apr. 1965, p. 90.)

1104 U.S. Library of Congress. General Reference and Bibliography Division. *Official publications of British East Africa*. Part 3, *Kenya and Zanzibar*. Compiled by Audrey A. Walker, African Section. Washington, 1963. 162 p.
The 254 official publications of Zanzibar and of Great Britain relating to Zanzibar here catalogued (p. 121–149) are put in a two-part bibliography together with Kenya because, as stated in the introduction, 'of the administrative tie held between Kenya and Zanzibar during the early years of British control and because of their mutual interest in the mainland strip'. The bibliography was published just before the announcement of the union of independent Zanzibar with Tanganyika.

1105 Zanzibar Protectorate. Laws, statutes, etc. *Chronological index of enactments issued 1863–1911, and text of enactments in force December 31, 1911*. Comp. by John H. Sinclair. [n.p.], 1912. 307 p.

1106 ——— ——— *Index to the laws of the Zanzibar Protectorate in force on the 1st day of March 1955*. Comp. by F. J. Jasavala. Zanzibar, 1955. 47 p.

1107 ——— ——— *List of Zanzibar decrees enacted up to . . . 1940*. Zanzibar, 1941. 8 p. (250 entries)

Reference works

1108 Ayany, T. G. *A history of Zanzibar*. Nairobi, East African Literature Bureau, 1970. 220 p.
A survey of economic and political developments in Zanzibar from 1934 to 1964.

1109 Coupland. *The exploitation of East Africa, 1856–1890*.
Much information in this book deals with Zanzibar. See no. 1023.

1110 ——— *East Africa and its invaders*.
Also provides extensive coverage of Zanzibar. See no. 1023.

1111 Crofton, Richard H. *Statistics of the Zanzibar Protectorate, 1893–1932*. 7th ed. 1933. 28 p.
     1893–1920. 1st ed. 36 p.

1112 Great Britain. Colonial Office. *Annual report on*... See no. 672.

1113 Ingrams, William Harold. *Zanzibar : Its history and people*. London, Witherby, 1931. 527 p. Bibliography: p. 515–519.
The most complete, authoritative history of Zanzibar, by a British expert on the Arab world, who was an official at Zanzibar from 1919 to 1927. The book begins with geography and people, covers the history from early times, and devotes its major part to ethnology, surveying the Arabs, the detribalized and mixed-blood Swahilis, and various African peoples, in a well-rounded anthropological study. See also Ingrams, *Chronology and genealogies of Zanzibar rulers* (1926, 10 p.).

1114 Lofchie, Michael F. *Zanzibar : Background to revolution.* Princeton, N.J., Princeton University Press, 1965. 316 p. maps, tables, Bibliography: p. 288–301.

The author goes back to the establishment of the Arab state and British colonial policy in his sketch of historical and social background and then examines the origins of the conflict between Arab and African in party politics. Incorporates extensive field research.

1115 Middleton, John, and Jane Campbell. *Zanzibar : Its society and its politics.* Issued under the auspices of the Institution of Race Relations, London. London, Oxford University Press, 1965. 71 p.

Describes historical and social conditions in Zanzibar before independence and relates these to recent events on the island.

1116 Prins, Adriaan H. J. *The Swahili-speaking peoples of Zanzibar and the East African coast (Arabs, Shirazi and Swahili).* London, International African Institute, 1961. 143 p. illus. (Ethnographic Survey of Africa, East Central Africa, pt. 12) Combined bibliography: p. 116–138.

See general note on this series (no. 333). In the exceptionally comprehensive bibliography, the author notes many historical and descriptive works and official documents in addition to ethnographical studies.

1117 Shelswell-White, Geoffrey H. *A guide to Zanzibar : A detailed account of Zanzibar, town and island, including general information about the Protectorate, and a description of itineraries for the use of visitors.* 1949. 190 p.

The first edition of this guide was compiled in 1932.

1118 Vaughan, John H. *The dual jurisdiction in Zanzibar.* London, Crown Agents for the Colonies, 1935. 124 p.

1119 Zanzibar. High Court. *Law reports containing cases determined by the High Court for Zanzibar and on appeal therefrom by the Court of Appeal for Eastern Africa and by the Privy Council.* v. 1– . 1868/1918– . 1919– .

Uganda

Note For further specific references, see nos. 180–182, and Eastern Africa, General section.

Atlas

1120 Uganda. Department of Lands and Surveys. *Atlas of Uganda.* 1st ed. Entebbe, 1962. 83 p. illus., col. maps. 48 cm.

Bibliographies

1121 Hopkins, Terence K. *A study guide for Uganda.* Boston, African Studies Center, Boston University, 1969. 162 p.

Prepared for the Agency for International Development. Each section provides a commentary on the principal works relating to that subject; the second consists of a bibliography. The information is presented under the following headings: physical environment, population, history, colonial society (c. 1910–1960), polity, economy, social structure, cultural dimensions. There is also a general bibliography.

Part III: area guide (by colonial power, region and colony)

1122 Langlands, Bryan W. 'Uganda bibliography, 1961–1962', *Uganda Journal*, v. 27, no. 2, Sept. 1963: 245–260.
Continued: '1962–1963', v. 28, no. 1, Mar. 1964: 115–124; '1963–1964', v. 28, no. 2, Sept. 1964: 233–242; '1964', v. 29, pt. 1, 1965: 115–132; '1965', v. 30, pt. 1, 1966: 119–136; '1965–1966', v. 30, pt. 2, 1966: 241–257; '1966', v. 31, pt. 1, 1967: 139–154; '1967', v. 32, pt. 1, 1968: 101–117.

This journal of the Uganda Society regularly carries a number of book reviews, and its scholarly articles are frequently followed by long subject reading lists. Langlands's record of current publishing regarding Uganda has been appearing as a regular feature of the journal. Many of the items are articles in scientific journals; references are in broad subject classification. Langlands also contributes a bibliography on Tanzania for the *Tanzania Notes and Records*.

1123 Manyangenda, Salome. *A selected and annotated bibliography of social science materials in English on Uganda from 1860 to the present.* Washington, D.C., 1966. 82 p.

In this master's dissertation (Catholic University of America), the entries are arranged by subject (anthropology, economics, geography, history, language, politics, sociology). There are author and title indexes.

1124 Syracuse University. Maxwell Graduate School of Citizenship and Public Affairs. Program of Eastern African Studies. *A bibliography on anthropology and sociology in Uganda.* Comp. by Robert Peckham, Isis Ragheb, and others. Syracuse, N.Y., 1965. 60 l. (Occasional Bibliography, no. 3)

Lists books, articles, conference papers, government documents, and a few dissertations alphabetically by author. Works are in German, English, Italian, and vernacular languages, from the late 19th century to 1965.

1125 —————— —————— —————— *A bibliography on politics and government in Uganda.* Comp. by Lucas Kuria and others. Syracuse, N.Y., 1965. 31 l. (Occasional Bibliography, no. 2)

1126 Uganda. Ministry of Lands and Mineral Development. *Bibliography of land tenure.* Entebbe, 1957. 57 p.

Many of the references cited are official documents which are covered in the Library of Congress bibliography, below.

1127 Uganda Protectorate. Laws, statutes, etc. *Chronological table and index to the laws of the Uganda Protectorate.* Entebbe, 1905. 38 p. (2,000 entries)
New. ed. 1909. xi, 61 p. (3,000 entries)

1128 —————— —————— *Index to the laws of the Uganda Protectorate in force on the 1st day of May 1947 : With a table of references to amending legislation enacted from 1936 to 1946.* Comp. by L. Mendonça. Entebbe, Government Printer, 1947. 92 p.

1129 U.S. Library of Congress. General Reference and Bibliography Division. *Official publications of British East Africa.* Part 4, *Uganda.* Comp. by Audrey A. Walker, African Section. Washington, 1963. 100 p.

Bibliography of documents of the Uganda government and of British governmental agencies concerned with Uganda, totalling 764 numbered items, with index of subjects and personal names. As in others of this series, arrangement is alphabetical by agency, with separate sections for publications of Uganda, the East African Common Services Organization, and Great Britain.

Reference works

1130 Fallers, Lloyd A. *Bantu bureaucracy : A study of integration and conflict in the political institutions of an East African people.* Cambridge, Eng., published for the East African Institute of Social Research by W. Heffer, 1956. xiv, 283 p. illus., maps, tables, diagrs.

1965. With new subtitle, *A century of political evolution among the Basoga of Uganda,* and ' Preface to the 1965 edition '. Chicago and London, University of Chicago Press. xix, 283 p. Bibliographical footnotes.

1131 ———, ed. *The king's men : Leadership and status in Buganda on the eve of independence.* London and New York, published on behalf of the East African Institute of Social Research by Oxford University Press, 1964. 414 p. illus., ports., fold. map. Bibliography: p. 401–409.

Professor Fallers, an American social anthropologist, had been director of the East African Institute of Social Research for some years after 1956. His *Bantu bureaucracy* is a highly professional analysis of the Soga people of Uganda. *The king's men* contains essays by Professor Fallers, Dr. Audrey I. Richards, C. C. Wrigley, Martin Southwold, Leonard W. Doob, and others, on traditional social structures and changing patterns in Buganda. It is one of a series of studies of political and economic leadership in East Africa resulting from field research carried out under the auspices of the East African Institute of Social Research. See also Lloyd A. Fallers, *Law without precedent : Legal ideas in action in the courts of colonial Busoga* (Chicago, University of Chicago Press, 1969, 365 p.).

1132 Foster, W. D. *The early history of scientific medicine in Uganda.* Nairobi, East African Literature Bureau, 1970. 112 p.

By a former professor of medical microbiology at Makerere. A key chapter is on the role of the Church Missionary Society in the development of Uganda's medical services.

1133 Great Britain. Admiralty. *A handbook of the Uganda Protectorate.* Prepared by the Geographical Section of the Naval Intelligence Division, Naval Staff, Admiralty. 1920. 447 p.

1134 ——— Colonial Office. *Annual report on . . .* See no. 672.

1135 Haydon, Edwin S. *Law and justice in Buganda.* London, Butterworth, 1960. 342 p. illus. (Butterworth's African Law Series, no. 2)

1136 Ingham, Kenneth. *The making of modern Uganda.* London, Allen & Unwin, 1958. 303 p. illus. Bibliography: p. 285–294.

Straightforward history of Uganda from the first European penetration in the 1860s to the present. The author has been a history professor at Makerere.

1137 Ingrams, William Harold. *Uganda : A crisis of nationhood.* London, H.M. Stationery Office, 1960. 365 p. illus. (Corona Library) Bibliography: p. 347–353.

One of a series prepared under Colonial Office auspices as authoritative popular presentations of specific countries. In addition to published and unpublished works, the author made use of oral source material gathered during long visits to the country.

1138 International Bank for Reconstruction and Development. *The economic development of Uganda.* Baltimore, Md., Johns Hopkins Press, 1962. xviii, 475 p. maps, charts, tables.

Report of an Economic Survey Mission, requested by the Uganda and British governments and organized by the World Bank, which surveyed and analysed the economy of Uganda, making recommendations for a five-year development program, 1961/62–1965/66, with particular attention to priorities for expenditure. The nine-man team was headed by Edward S. Mason of Harvard University and included expert advisers from five nations on economics, health, industry, transport, agriculture and education. Except for a 10-page introduction, the entire focus is on present economic conditions, priorities, and approaches for development. There are statistical annexes and a few footnotes indicating sources of statistics.

1139 Johnston, Sir Harry H. *The Uganda Protectorate: An attempt to give some description of the physical geography, botany, zoology, anthropology, languages, and history of the territories under British protection in East Central Africa, between the Congo Free State and the Rift Valley and between the first degree of south latitude and the fifth degree of north latitude.* 2d ed., with prefatory chapter giving additional matter. With 510 illustrations from drawings and photographs by the author and others, 48 full-page colored plates by the author, and 9 maps by J. G. Bartholomew and the author. New York, Dodd, Mead, 1904. 2 v. 1,018 p. col. front., illus., col. plates, ports., fold. maps.

Old standard work on Uganda by the explorer, naturalist, and empire-building administrator who served as Special Commissioner to the Uganda Protectorate from 1899 to 1902. Sir Harry Johnston negotiated the agreement of 1900 with Buganda which provided for the kingdom's administrative autonomy and helped to shape its land system under colonial rule.

1140 Morris, H. F., and James S. Read. *Uganda: The development of its laws and constitution.* London, Stevens, 1966. 448 p. map. (British Commonwealth: The Development of Its Laws and Constitutions, no. 13) Bibliography: p. 412–416.

Part 1 traces the development of the constitution from the tribal organizations of the second half of the 19th century through the colonial period to the year of independence, 1962. Part 2 deals with the constitution and its 'quasi-federal' structure, and includes a section on the prospect of an East African federation in the light of the functions of the East African Common Services Organization. In Part 3 the most important branches of law in Uganda are analysed. A table of legislation and one of cases are included.

1141 Morris, H. S. *The Indians in Uganda.* London, Wiedenfeld and Nicolson, 1968. 230 p.

An historical survey of Indians in Uganda up to 1955.

1142 Scott, Roger. *The development of trade unions in Uganda.* Nairobi, East African Publishing House, 1966. 200 p. fold. map. Bibliography: p. 182–187.

The early development of trade unions, effect of colonial labour policy on unions, international influences, and the role of unions in independent Uganda are among the subjects treated. Also included are case studies of individual unions such as the Railway African Union, National Union of Plantation Workers, and Uganda Public Employees Union. The appendices include a reprint of the Uganda Industrial Relations Charter and biographical notes on union-connected individuals.

1143 Taylor, John Vernon. *The growth of the Church in Buganda : An attempt at understanding.* London, SCM Press, 1958. Distributed by Friendship Press, N.Y. 288 p. illus. (World Mission Studies) Includes bibliographical references.
Important study of mission work.

1144 Thomas, Harold B., and A. E. Spencer. *A history of Uganda land and surveys and of the Uganda Land and Survey Department.* Kampala, 1938. 206 p.
Not available for examination.

1145 Thomas, Harold B., and Robert Scott. *Uganda.* London, Oxford University Press, H. Milford, 1935. xx, 559 p. plates, ports., fold. maps. Reprint, without change: 1949. Bibliography: p. 480–502.
Comprehensive reference work on Uganda by two administrative officers, published by authority of the government of the Protectorate. The historical chapter which opens the handbook is prefaced by a chronology of 50 guiding dates. There follow well-written sections on all aspects of the country, including its life, administration, and economy. A short final chapter on 19th-century writing about Uganda precedes a select list of references and statistical appendices.

1146 Tothill, John D., ed. *Agriculture in Uganda.* By the staff of the Department of Agriculture of Uganda. London, Oxford University Press, 1940. xvi, 551 p.
Officially sponsored specialist work that begins with an account of Uganda agriculture in general aspects and then covers climate, native agriculture and land tenure, crop rotation, ploughing, soils and soil erosion problems, fertilizers, experiment stations, native food crops, and (in a long analysis) the export crops – cotton, coffee, sugar, etc.

1147 Uganda. *The African local government ordinance and District Council proclamations and regulations, 1949.* Kampala, 65 p.

1148 —— Attorney-General. *Handbook on native courts for the guidance of administrative officers.* Kampala, 1941. 57 p.

1149 —— High Court. *Law reports, containing cases determined by the High Court of Uganda.* v. 1– , 1904/1910– . Kampala.

1150 —— —— *Notes of selected decisions of Her Majesty's High Court of Uganda on cases originated from the Buganda courts, 1940–1952.* Comp. by E. S. Hayden. Nairobi, E. A. Printers (Boyd's), 1958. 96 p.

1151 *Uganda Journal.* v. 1– , 1934– . Kampala, Uganda Society. Semi-annual.
A distinguished review, published for some years by Oxford University Press but now issued in Kampala. Contributors have been administrators, amateurs, researchers, and scholars, many of whom had worked in the British administration or had been connected with Makerere University College.

1152 Worthington, Stella, and E. B. Worthington. *Inland waters of Africa : The result of two expeditions to the great lakes of Kenya and Uganda, with accounts of their biology, native tribes and development.* London and New York, Macmillan and Co., 1933. xix, 259 p. Bibliography: p. 246–253.
Dr. E. B. Worthington, who was scientific secretary of CSA from 1951 to 1955, was scientific adviser for Lord Hailey's African Survey and in 1946 was development adviser for Uganda. This book records expeditions made with his wife to the African lakes from 1927 to 1931, with much geographical and biological information on fisheries. The bibliography refers to the publications arising from the various lake fishery expeditions.

Mauritius

Bibliographies

1153 Hahn, Lorna, with Robert Edison. *Mauritius: A study and annotated bibliography*. Washington, D.C., Center for Research in Social Systems, American University, 1969. 44 p.

A brief up-to-date study of the sociological, economic, and political conditions of Mauritius, to provide basic understanding of the country as it approached independence on March 12, 1968. It consists of an essay and a comprehensive annotated bibliography of books, periodicals, government documents, and other publications. See also *Madagascar and adjacent islands . . .*, no. 1807.

1154 Lalouette, Gérard. *The Mauritius digest: Being a digest of the reported decisions of the Supreme Court of Mauritius to the end of 1950*. Port Louis, Mauritius Printing Co. [195–]

Supplement, 1951–1955. Port Louis, 1957. xi, 191 p.

1155 Mauritius. Archives Department. *Memorandum of Books Printed in Mauritius and Registered in the Archives Office*. 1967– . Port Louis. Quarterly.

1156 —————— *Report*. 1950– . Port Louis, Government Printer. Annual. Previously issued as *Report* of the Archives Branch. It lists not only Mauritius publications but also works on Mauritius published abroad. The 1967 *Report* had a 23-page supplement of books on Mauritius.

1157 Toussaint, Auguste. *Bibliographie de Maurice, 1502–1954*. Port Louis, Esclapon, 1956. 884 p.

1158 —————— *Select bibliography of Mauritius*. Port Louis, printed by Henry, 1951. 60 p. (Société de l'Histoire de l'Ile Maurice Publication)

A large body of literature, mostly in French, has been recorded exhaustively by the chief archivist of Mauritius, M. Toussaint. His huge bibliography of 1956 (8,865 items) covers printed works, manuscripts, archivalia, and cartographic materials. Supplements appear in the *Annual report* of the Archives Department, which is presented by M. Toussaint. He collaborated earlier with Patrick J. Barnwell in *A short history of Mauritius* (London and New York, published for the government of Mauritius by Longmans, Green, 1949, 268 p., illus.).

Reference works

1159 Benedict, Burton. *Indians in a plural society: A report on Mauritius*. London, H.M. Stationery Office, 1961. 168 p. plates. (Colonial Research Studies, no. 34)

Socio-anthropological study of the Muslim and Hindu groups who came to Mauritius from 1835 to 1907 and who now form two-thirds of the population.

1160 Great Britain. Colonial Office. *Annual report on Mauritius*. London, H.M. Stationery Office, 1946– . illus., maps. (Colonial Annual Reports)

One of the very few Colonial Office annual reports still being published in the 1960s. The 1965 edition was published in 1967 (176 p., illus., maps, tables; reading list, classed: p. 166–176). See also *Blue book of the colony of Mauritius and its dependencies* (1858–1938, 1945– , annual), a review of all government activities in the colony. Many volumes include information on budgets, census reports, and trade statistics.

1161 *A handbook on the Constitution, practice and proceedings of the Council of Government of Mauritius.* Comp. by William Charles Rae, Clerk of the Council. Port Louis, 1896. 288 p.

1162 Mauritius. Archives Department. Mauritius Archives publications. A monographic series.

1163 —— Chamber of Agriculture. *The Mauritius Chamber of Agriculture, 1853–1953.* Port Louis, General Printing and Stationery Co., 1953. 377 p. illus., tables. Includes bibliography.

1164 —— Chamber of Commerce and Industry. *Mauritius guide, 1968–1969.* Port Louis, 1968. 87 p.
Useful surveys of past and present in Mauritius.

1165 Mauritius and Seychelles. *Statutory rules and orders and statutory instruments revised to December 31, 1948.* Port Louis, 1949. 732 p.
The major statutory instruments relating to constitutional changes in Mauritius and Seychelles are collected in this set. Statutory instruments on Mauritius for the period 1831–1948, including legislation on the powers of the governor, the Legislative Council, and the courts of justice, are collected in v. 13, p. 277–293. Legislation on Seychelles for the period 1903–48 is collected in v. 20, p. 683–731.

1166 Mauritius Institute. *Bulletin.* v. 1– , 1937– . Port Louis. Irregular.
Founded in 1880 ' for the purpose of promoting the general study and cultivation of various branches and departments of arts, sciences, literature, and philosophy '.

1167 Mauritius Sugar Industry Research Institute, Réduit. *Report.* 1953– . Réduit. Annual.
The primary place of the sugar industry in Mauritius is evidenced in the handsomely presented centenary volume of the Chamber of Agriculture, with text in English and French, and in the annual report of the Institute.

1168 Meade, James E., ed. *The economic and social structure of Mauritius : A report to the governor of Mauritius.* London, Methuen, 1961. xviii, 264 p. maps, tables, diagrs. (Mauritius, Legislative Council, Sessional Papers, no. 7, 1961)
These papers uniformly warn of critical conditions in the economy due to the rate of population increase. Included are studies on education and governmental structure. A short summary stresses that the only answer to the problems of Mauritius is birth control.

1169 Scott, Sir Robert. *Limuria : The lesser dependencies of Mauritius.* London and New York, Oxford University Press, 1961. 308 p. illus. ' Bibliographical note and selected bibliography ': p. 295–300.
The author was Governor of Mauritius from 1954 to 1959. He presents here a full account of the islands in the Indian Ocean to the north and northeast of Mauritius, from 245 to almost 1,200 miles away, which are known as the Lesser Dependencies: St. Brandon (a fishing-fleet island, where women are not allowed), Agalega, and the Chagos Archipelago. The book, one of the few full-length works on the region, is in two parts, first geography and history, then island-by-island description. See also no. 1158n.

1170 Société de l'Histoire de l'Ile Maurice. *Dictionnaire de biographie mauricienne. Dictionary of Mauritius biography.* Port Louis, 1941–52. 2 v.

1171 Titmuss, Richard Morris, Brian Abel-Smith, and Tony Lynes. *Social policies and population growth in Mauritius: A report to the Governor of Mauritius.* London, Methuen, 1961. xviii, 308 p. tables, diagrs.

The authors are British population experts. They warn that under present policies the island faces disaster from overpopulation and that the government must back a campaign for family planning, as well as economic programs for higher employment.

Seychelles

Bibliography

1172 U.S. Library of Congress. *Madagascar and adjacent islands.* . . . See no. 1807.

Reference works

1173 Benedict, Burton. *People of the Seychelles.* London, H.M. Stationery Office. 74 p. fold. map, tables. (Ministry of Overseas Development, Overseas Research Publication, no. 14)

Covers history, occupations, marriage and family relations, social status, religion, the domestic economy, and development problems.

1174 Bulpin, Thomas V. *Islands in a forgotten sea.* Cape Town, Howard Timmens, 1959. 435 p.

Popular account of Mauritius, Madagascar, the Seychelles and other Indian Ocean islands. See also William Travis, *Beyond the reefs* (London, Allen & Unwin, 1959, 221 p.).

1175 Great Britain. Colonial Office. *Report on Seychelles.* 1946– . London, H.M. Stationery Office.

See no. 672 for description.

1176 Hawtrey, S. H. C. *Handbook of Seychelles: Compiled from official and other reliable sources.* Mahé, 1928. 55 p.

1177 Tyack, Maurice. *Mauritius and its dependencies, the Seychelles: Treasures of the Indian Ocean.* Lausanne, L. A. M. Tyack, Frana Inter Presse, 1965. 191 p. illus., ports., maps.

Somalia

Note For further specific references, see Italian Africa section.

Material concerning Somalia can also be found in the records of the India Office in London. The correspondence between the British Resident, Aden, and the India Office, as well as the government of India, merit exploration. So do various holdings of the Public Record Office, especially Foreign Office material, sequence FO 78 (Turkey, Egypt, and the Red Sea).

Bibliographies

1178 African Bibliographic Center, Washington, D.C. *Somalian panoramas: A select bibliographical survey, 1960–1966.* Washington, 1967. 17 p. processed. (Special Bibliographical Series, v. 5, no. 3)

1179 International African Institute. *North-east Africa : General, ethnography, sociology, linguistics.* Comp. by Ruth Jones, librarian, with the assistance of a panel of consultants. London, 1959. 51 l. (Africa Bibliography Series, Ethnography, Sociology, Linguistics, and Related Subjects)
Included are ethnic groups of Ethiopia, Somalia, and the Sudan.

1180 *Middle East Journal.* v. 1– , Jan. 1947– . Washington, D.C., Middle East Institute. maps. Quarterly.
Good long articles. In the quarterly chronology, the book review section, and the 'Bibliography of Periodical Literature' (also issued as separate work), material is covered relating to the Arab world, including Ethiopia, the Sudan, and Somalia.

1181 Somalia. Laws, statutes, etc. *Index to the laws in force in the northern region on 15th August 1960.* Comp. by Iqbal Singha. Hargeisa, Government Printer, 1960. 56 l.

1182 U.S. Library of Congress. General Reference and Bibliography Division. *North and northeast Africa : A selected, annotated list of writings, 1951–1957.* Comp. by Helen F. Conover. Washington, 1957. 182 p.
The first annotated list on Africa prepared in the Library of Congress was the *Introduction to Africa*, compiled in 1951 and covering the whole continent. When revised in 1956, the extent of new writing necessitated division into two parts, and *North and northeast Africa* was interpreted to include Ethiopia and Eritrea, Somalia, and the Sudan, as well as the Mediterranean littoral. The sections on these countries occupy pages 124–173, with some 87 references, many of them annotated at considerable length.

1183 —————— *Official publications of Somaliland, 1941–1959 : A guide.* Comp. by Helen F. Conover. Washington, 1960. 41 p.
This bibliography will be useful for anyone doing serious research on Somalia and on the former British and French Somalilands. The first seven items, descriptively annotated, name published bibliographies in which unofficial literature in Italian and other languages regarding the Horn of Africa is exhaustively covered. The list gives detailed attention to UN documents relating to the trust territory of Somaliland under Italian administration.

1184 Viney, N. M. *A bibliography of British Somaliland.* Hargeisa, 1947. 36 p. mimeo.
Bibliography compiled under the military government by a former assistant director of the General Survey of British Somaliland and revised by John A. Hunt in his survey of the Somaliland Protectorate (see no. 1185). It is in classified arrangement by subjects and includes a scattering of material on both Italian and French Somaliland. See also no. 1189n.

Reference works

1185 Hunt, John A. *A general survey of the Somaliland Protectorate, 1944–1950 : Final report on 'an economic survey and reconnaissance of the British Somaliland Protectorate, 1944–1950', Colonial Development and Welfare Scheme D.484.* Hargeisa, to be purchased from the Chief Secretary, 1951. 203 p. maps, tables. Bibliography: p. 180–201.
Publication recording the results of the seven-year geographical survey carried out under a Colonial Development and Welfare scheme. Special attention is given to topography, meteorology, geology, and the ecology of the nomadic stock-herding tribesmen, and recommendations are made for various lines of

development. The text, printed on folio pages and illustrated with sketch maps, is divided between expository paragraphs and tables of many varieties, among which are a gazetteer of place-names, tables of road mileages, rainfall records, temperatures, genealogies, and summaries of the tribes. A long bibliography compiled by N. M. Viney in 1947 (see no. 1184) was revised by Mr. Hunt in 1950 and serves as the bibliography for this survey. See also Great Britain. Colonial Office. *Annual report on . . .* no. 672.

1186 International Bank for Reconstruction and Development. *The economy of the trust territory of Somaliland : Report of a mission organized at the request of the government of Italy.* Washington, D.C., 1957. 99 l. maps, tables, diagrs.
A report issued as ' a working paper . . . for those who will have to determine what has to be done ' in economic development to prepare Somalia for independence. The character of the economy, recent plans, prospects, and problems are analysed and conclusions presented stressing the need for continuing financial aid in the foreseeable future.

1187 Lewis, I. M. *The modern history of Somaliland : From nation to state.* New York, Praeger, 1965. xi, 234 p. plates, maps. (Praeger Asia-Africa Series) Bibliographical footnotes.
A well-written narrative of the historical events that led Somalia from cultural to political nationalism. The book is based in part on unpublished traditional source materials obtained by Dr. Lewis in Somalia during 1955–57 and 1962. Two brief opening chapters describe the physical and social framework and summarize Somalia's long history before partition. Next is an account of the European establishment in East Africa, the Italian East African empire, the restoration of colonial frontiers, and the period from trusteeship to independence. An analytical index is included.

1188 —— *A pastoral democracy : A study of pastoralism and politics among the northern Somali of the Horn of Africa.* London and New York, published for the International African Institute by Oxford University Press, 1961. 320 p. illus., maps. Bibliography: p. 307–312.
Study in ' pastoral habits and political institutions ' by one of the few English-speaking authorities on Somaliland. It is mostly confined to the northern Somali, the tribes of the former British protectorate – nomads with herds of camel, sheep and goats – whose political system ' lacks to a remarkable degree all the machinery of centralized government '. See also Saadia Touval, *Somali nationalism : International politics and the drive for unity in the Horn of Africa* (Cambridge, Mass., Harvard University Press, 1963, 241 p.; ' Notes ', p. 185–205).

1189 —— *Peoples of the Horn of Africa : Somali, Afar, and Saho.* London, International African Institute, 1955. 200 p. maps, tables. (Ethnographic Survey of Africa, North-eastern Africa, pt. 1) Bibliography: p. 177–194.
Summary of available information about the Somali, Afar (Danakil), and Saho, closely related nomadic peoples of camel culture and Mohammedan faith, who are spread through the three (former) countries of the Horn of Africa – Somalia (Italian Somaliland), the British Somaliland protectorate, and French Somaliland. The Afar and Saho are also distributed across the borders in Eritrea and Ethiopia, and the Somali in Ethiopia and northern Kenya. For his survey made from library sources the writer used many Italian and French works as well as English, which are listed in the bibliography.
Dr. Lewis supplemented the bibliography of this book with a bibliographical essay, ' Recent progress in Somali studies ', which was presented as a paper at

the Second International Conference of Ethiopian Studies at Manchester University in 1963 and published in *Ethiopian Studies* (Manchester, Eng., Manchester University Press, 1964, p. 122–134).

Sudan

Bibliographies

1190 Dagher, Joseph Assaad. *Sudanese bibliography, Arabic sources, 1875–1967*. Beyrouth, 1968. 1 v. In Arabic.
The contents include the following: periodicals list, bibliography-yearbooks-almanacs, religion, administration-government, literature, social science, education, history, geography, the Nile, economics-labour-finance, agriculture, health and hygiene, sports, journalism, and periodicals.
This is the first bibliography of Arabic language writings and translations by Sudanese writers. Contains approximately 2,000 entries of original works and translations. Covers books and articles. There is an author index.

1191 Hill, Richard L. *A bibliography of the Anglo-Egyptian Sudan, from the earliest times to 1937*. London, Oxford University Press, 1939. 213 p.
A justly celebrated area bibliography by an officer of the Sudan Civil Service. The list, covering books, periodical articles, and documents in Western languages and Arabic from Herodotus, ca. 457 B.C., to the year of its completion, is classified under disciplines and sub-disciplines according to a five-page table of contents. Within the subsections the entries, set down in the briefest identifiable form, are arranged in chronological order. There are indexes of persons and subjects.

1192 Ibrahim, Asma, and Abdel Rahman el-Nasri. ' Sudan bibliography, 1959–1963 '. *Sudan Notes and Records*, no. 46, 1965: 130–166.
A comprehensive ' Sudan bibliography ' was carried regularly (1921–56) in the semi-annual *Sudan Notes and Records*.

1193 Ibrahim-Hilmy, Prince. *The literature of Egypt and the Soudan from the earliest times to the year 1885 [i.e., 1887] inclusive : A bibliography : Comprising printed books, periodical writings, and papers of learned societies; maps and charts; ancient papyri, manuscripts, drawings, etc.* London, Trübner & Co., 1886–88. 2 v. 398, 459 p.
A massive compilation, this basic bibliography for the early period gives complete data for roughly 20,000 titles. Arrangement is by author, with some subject and form headings. In the second volume is an appendix of additional works to May 1887 (p. 371–459).

1194 International African Institute. *North-east Africa : General, ethnography, sociology, linguistics.* Comp. by Ruth Jones, librarian, with the assistance of a panel of consultants. London, 1959. 51 l. (Africa Bibliography Series. Ethnography, Sociology, Linguistics, and Related Subjects)
Included are ethnic groups of Ethiopia, Somalia and the Sudan.

1195 Khartoum. University. Library. *Theses on the Sudan and by Sudanese accepted for higher degrees.* no. 2. Comp. by Maymouna Mirghani Hamza, assisted by the library staff. Khartoum, 1966. 63 p.

1196 Knight, R. L., and B. M. Boyns. *Agricultural science in the Sudan : A bibliography with abstracts.* Arbroath, Scotland, T. Buncle, 1950. 251 p.
Survey of all publications in the field of agricultural science having direct relation to the Sudan, bringing together the research carried out in the country over

50 years under British administration. Many of the contributions had been previously published in obscure journals. Abstracts of the less readily accessible papers are included. The emphasis is largely on cotton growing, particularly the Gezira Scheme.

1197 el-Nasri, Abdel Rahman. *A bibliography of the Sudan, 1938–1958.* London, published on behalf of the University of Khartoum by Oxford University Press, Nov. 1962. 171 p.

Compiled by the librarian of the University of Khartoum. This bibliography, containing 2,763 numbered entries, updates Hill's work (no. 1191) and follows the same arrangement by subject: agriculture (general, by provinces and localities, crops, irrigation, soil conservation and rural water development, agricultural research); anthropology (general, by tribes); bibliography (items 630–651); biography, etc. There are subject and author indexes. See also essay on the Sudan in no. 626.

1198 Santandrea, Stefano. *Bibliografia di studi africani della missione dell'Africa centrale.* Verona, Istituto Missioni Africane, 1948. 167 p. (Museum combonianum, no. 1)

Most entries are annotated and are for works published from the middle 1800s, with Italian and German works predominating. Part 1 deals with archaeology, Mahdism, travels, agriculture, people and customs, religion, schools, slavery, music, art, and folklore. Part 2 covers ethnic groups arranged by area, and Part 3 traces the history of the Central African mission from 1840 to 1948. There is a name index.

1199 Twining, W. L., and others. ' Bibliography of Sudan law, 1 '. *Sudan Law Journal and Report,* 1960: 313–334.

Reference works

1200 Abd al-Rahim, Muddathir. *Imperialism and nationalism in the Sudan : A study of constitutional and political development, 1899–1956.* Oxford, Clarendon Press, 1969. 275 p.

The first full-scale study of the constitutional and political development of the Sudan under the Anglo-Egyptian condominium. The author used a great wealth of original sources in English and Arabic, including material in the Khartoum archives, the Milner Papers at New College, Oxford, and the Wingate Papers at Durham University. The author particularly stresses the impact of Anglo-Egyptian relations on administrative policy in the Sudan.

1201 American University, Washington, D.C. Special Operations Research Office. *Area handbook for the Republic of the Sudan.* 2d ed. By John A. Cookson and others. Washington, U.S. Government Printing Office, 1964. 473 p. map, tables. (Department of the Army Pamphlet, no. 550-27) Includes bibliographies.

Background study in the country series being prepared at American University. Bibliographies of sources follow comprehensive surveys of anthropological, sociological, political, economic, and military aspects.

1202 Barbour, Kenneth M. *The Republic of the Sudan : A regional geography.* London, University of London Press, 1961. 292 p. illus., maps. Bibliographical footnotes.

Physical and economic geography, emphasizing regional variation in agriculture and animal husbandry and the spread of the cash economy. The valuable study is by a geographer who taught at the University of Khartoum.

1203 Collins, Robert O. *The southern Sudan, 1883–1898 : A struggle for control.* New Haven, Conn., Yale University Press, 1962. 212 p. (Yale Historical Publications, Miscellany, no. 76) Bibliography: p. 192–198.

By an American scholar who has done exhaustive work in the Sudanese archives at Khartoum among the documents of the Mahdist state. He examines in detail all actions of the Mahdiya in the southern Sudan from the first appearance of the agents in the Bahr el Ghazal in 1882 to raise the tribes for the 'holy war' to the time of Kitchener's defeat of the Khalifa and the end of the era. The bibliography carries evaluative annotations of many items. See also Richard Gray, *A history of the southern Sudan, 1839–1889* (London, Oxford University Press, 1961, 219 p.). The story is continued in Robert O. Collins, *Land beyond the rivers : The southern Sudan, 1898–1918* (New Haven, Yale University Press, 368 p.).

1204 Collins, Robert O., and Robert L. Tignor. *Egypt and the Sudan.* Englewood Cliffs, N.J., Prentice-Hall, 1967. 180 p. (The Modern Nations in Historical Perspective) Bibliography: p. 165–171.

Covers the period from 1800 to the present and provides a background to contemporary Sudan and Egypt.

1205 Ethnographic Survey of Africa: East Central Africa. London, International African Institute.

For the general note on this series, see no. 333. The following volumes relate to tribes of the Sudan:

> Part 4. *The Nilotes of the Anglo-Egyptian Sudan and Uganda.* By Audrey J. Butt. 1952. 198 p.
>
> Part 6. *The northern Nilo-Hamites.* By G. W. B. Huntingford. 1953. 108 p.
>
> Part 9. *The Azande and related peoples of the Anglo-Egyptian Sudan and Belgian Congo.* By P. T. W. Baxter and Audrey J. Butt. 1953. 152 p.

All ethnological studies of the southern Sudan are indebted for their foundations to the pioneer work by Charles G. and Brenda Z. Seligman: *Pagan tribes of the Nilotic Sudan* (London, Routledge, 1932, xxiv, 565 p., illus., 60 plates, maps, fold. geneal. table; Ethnology of Africa).

1206 Evans-Pritchard, E. E. *The Nuer.* . . . Oxford, Clarendon Press, 1940. 271 p. illus., plates, maps, diagr.

1207 —— *Witchcraft, oracles and magic among the Azande.* Oxford, Clarendon Press, 1937. 558 p.

Outstanding works by the leading anthropologist of the Sudan.

1208 Gaitskell, Arthur. *Gezira : A story of development in the Sudan.* London, Faber & Faber, 1959. 372 p. illus., ports., maps. (Colonial and Comparative Studies) 'References': p. 358–363.

By the first chairman and managing director of the Sudan Gezira Board. This is the standard account of the great colonial irrigation scheme in the area called the Gezira, below the confluence of the Blue and the White Nile at Khartoum, by which a million acres of the long-staple cotton, Sudan's chief export crop, were brought into production.

1209 Great Britain. Colonial Office. *Annual report on* . . . See no. 672.

1210 Henderson, Kenneth D. D. *Sudan Republic*. London, E. Benn, 1965; New York, Praeger, 1966. 256 p. maps (1 fold.). (Nations of the Modern World) Bibliography: p. 229–233.

The author, who spent 36 years in the political service of the Sudan, offers 'a personal, but not, I hope, a subjective' account of the new Sudan. The opening chapters provide a geographic, ethnic, and historical framework for the core of the book, which deals with the political and administrative training period and preliminary trials. The text ends with a chapter on the problem of the South (several documents are included) and one on the October 1964 revolution. The bibliography is expository and there is an analytical index.

1211 Hill, Richard Leslie. *A biographical dictionary of the Sudan*. London, Frank Cass, 1967. 409 p.

This second edition includes a list of notes and corrections (p. 395–409). The first edition, entitled *A biographical dictionary of the Anglo-Egyptian Sudan*, appeared in 1951. There are over 1,900 biographies of people who died before 1948; inclusion has been based primarily on availability of information. Among them are the foreign-born who have played a significant part in Sudanese history. A glossary gives Arabic and Turkish ranks, titles, and other designations.

1212 ——— *Egypt in the Sudan, 1820–1881*. London and New York, Oxford University Press, 1959. xi, 188 p. fold. map. (Middle Eastern Monographs, no. 2) Bibliography: p. 171–177.

A concentrated history covering the period of Turco-Egyptian conquest and rule (or misrule) of the Sudan to the beginning of the Mahdist rebellion; issued under the auspices of the Royal Institute of International Affairs.

1213 ——— *Sudan transport: A history of railway, marine and river services in the Republic of the Sudan*. London, Oxford University Press, 1965. 188 p. illus., ports., maps. Bibliography: p. 173–182.

This study is a good historical survey of the transportation system of the Sudan.

1214 Holt, Peter M. *The Mahdist state in the Sudan, 1881–1898: A study of its origins, development, and overthrow*. Oxford, Clarendon Press, 1958. 264 p. illus. (Rev. ed. 1970, 295 p.) Bibliography: p. 248–252.

By a specialist in Sudanese studies who was archivist of the Sudanese government and then a professor at the University of Khartoum. In this study he examines the history of the Mahdiya less from the 'romantic' reporting on the European side than from the archives of the Mahdist state, to which he had access.

1215 ——— *A modern history of the Sudan, from the Funj Sultanate to the present day*. New York, Grove Press, 1961. 241 p., illus., maps. Bibliography: p. 221–227.

Dr. Holt's history, covering as it does the Turco-Egyptian period, the Mahdist revolution, the condominium, and the first years of the republic, is necessarily highly compressed. The theme is the interplay in the Sudan of Arab-African indigenous tradition and Egyptian and British influence. Sketch maps, notes, a select bibliography, and an index add to the usefulness of the work.

1216 MacMichael, Sir Harold A. *The Anglo-Egyptian Sudan*. London, Faber & Faber, 1934. 288 p.

Comprehensive standard work by a former colonial official in the Sudan (1905–34). This is an account of the country from Gordon's death – the Kitchener campaign, the final British conquest, the establishment of the condominium which gave Britain charge of government, and the development of the war-torn country into what the author considered a near model of peaceful administration and agricultural experimentation. Sources are cited in footnotes. See also his valuable *The tribes of northern and central Kordofan* (Cambridge, Eng., 1912, 259 p.).

1217 Sanderson, G. N. *England, Europe and the upper Nile.* Edinburgh, The University Press, 1965. 456 p.

A detailed analysis of the late nineteenth-century clash between Great Britain and France in the upper Nile Valley. Covers the roles of the Mahdist state and of Menelik II of Ethiopia as well.

1218 Santandrea, S. *Luci e ombre dell'amministrazione britannica nel Bahr el Ghazal (1898–1955).* Como, Istituto Italiano per l'Africa, 1967. 98 p.

Account by a scholar-missionary, Fr. Santandrea, of British administration of the Bahr al-Ghazal. While he praises them for bringing peace he criticizes them for doing little for the material development of the people they ruled.

1219 Shaw, D. J., ed. *Agricultural development in the Sudan.* Khartoum, 1966. 2 v.

The proceedings and papers delivered at the 13th annual conference of the Philosophical Society of the Sudan and the Sudan Agricultural Society.

1220 Squires, H. C. *The Sudan Medical Service: An experiment in social medicine.* London, Heinemann, 1958. 138 p. illus., maps.

The author was associated with the Sudan Medical Service for almost 43 years as doctor, teacher, and consultant. Provides a history of the medical services and training and a description of diseases endemic to the Sudan and of epidemics.

1221 Sudan. Southern Development Investigation Team. *Natural resources and development potential in the southern provinces of the Sudan: A preliminary report, 1954.* London, Sudan Government, 1955. xxii, 262 p. tables. Includes bibliographies.

This group, under the chairmanship of Dr. P. P. Howell of the Sudan Political Service and comprising officials of various branches of the service in the southern Sudan, functioned in the spring of 1954. Their report is wider in scope than that of the Jonglei Investigation Team, on which a number of the same specialists, including the chairman, had served; it covers the entire physical and economic picture, present and possible future, of the area.

1222 *Sudan almanac: An official handbook.* 1903– . Khartoum, Government Printing Press. Annual. 1967 ed. 312 p. fold. map, tables. Bibliography: p. 307–309.

Originally compiled by the Intelligence Department, Cairo, now by the Central Office of Information of the Republic of the Sudan. It contains a vast store of information about all aspects of administration, history, ethnology and religion, geology and climate (including data on the Nile water levels), agriculture, economy, health and welfare, and many other matters of interest.

1223 *Sudan directory.* Khartoum, 1920–? Annual.

Conventional trade directory published by Editions Fischer in Cairo, with text in English and Arabic.

1224 *Sudan law reports (civil cases).* Dobbs Ferry, N.Y., Oceana, 1969.

v. 1, *1900–1931 reports.* 533 p.

v. 2, *1932–1940 reports.* 440 p.

1225 *Sudan Notes and Records.* no. 1– , Apr. 1921– . Khartoum. Semi-annual. Journal of the Sudan Philosophical Society and important organ for the many scholars who participated in the British civil service in the Anglo-Egyptian Sudan. Contributions are in many disciplines – history, ethnography, and the social sciences.

1226 Tothill, John D., ed. *Agriculture in the Sudan : Being a handbook of agriculture as practised in the Anglo-Egyptian Sudan.* By numerous authors. London, Oxford University Press, 1948. xviii, 974 p. illus., maps. Includes bibliographies.

Articles by a group of high-ranking specialists, in a symposium edited by the former director of the Sudan Department of Agriculture and Forests. The chapters are on general and specific aspects of agriculture; many are followed by selective reading lists.

1227 Trimingham, J. Spencer. *Islam in the Sudan.* London and New York, Oxford University Press, 1949. 280 p. Reissue: New York, Barnes & Noble, 1965.

Useful background study of the entire country, its history and culture, by the former secretary of the Church Mission Society in the Sudan. The writer's aim was to give a composite picture of the people both as Moslems and as Sudanese, with emphasis on the role of Islam in shaping present-day society. In the same year, Mr. Trimingham published *The Christian church in the post-war Sudan* (London, World Dominion Press, 1949, 44 p.), a survey of the educational work of the Christian missions in this country of Moslems, a large section of whom are animated by Pan-Arabism.

1228 Tucker, A. N. *The eastern Sudanic languages.* v. 1. London, published for the International African Institute by Oxford University Press, 1940. 434 p.

Study of the Azande, Moru-Madi, Bongo-Baka-Bagirmi, and Ndogo-Sere groups of the Sudan and the Belgian Congo. It begins with a short section on ' distribution ' and history, to which three chapters (55 p.) are devoted. The second section contains intensive linguistic studies of these groups. There are two indexes, a ' Tribal and historical index ' (p. 419–427) and a ' Linguistic index ' (p. 428–434).

1229 Warburg, Gabriel. *The Sudan under Wingate : Administration in the Anglo-Egyptian Sudan 1889–1916.* London, Frank Cass, 1971. xi, 245 p., photos, maps. Bibliography: p. 229–236.

An important study based on archival material at the Public Record Office, London; the Sudan Archives at Durham University, England; missionary sources, and other material. Covers the period in which Sir Reginald Wingate and Slatin Pasha tried to restore the Sudan to viability and prosperity after fifteen years of governance by the Mahdi and the Khalifa.

SOUTHERN AFRICA

Republic of South Africa

Atlases

1230 South Africa. Department of Planning. *Ontwekkelingsatlas. Development atlas.* Pretoria, Government Printer, 1966– . illus., maps (part col.). 51 × 57 cm. Includes bibliographies.

Major new atlas, loose-leaf in form and issued in sections. Complemented by a brief but factual text in Afrikaans and English, it covers such topics as physical features, administration, water resources, and minerals.

1231 Talbot, A. M., and W. J. Talbot. *Atlas of the Union of South Africa.* Prepared in collaboration with the Trigonometrical Survey Office and under the aegis of the National Council for Social Research. Pretoria, Government Printer, 1960. [vii], lxiv, 177 p. maps (part col.), tables, diagrs.

A comprehensive atlas with maps showing relief, geology, mining, soils, vegetation, climate and water resources, population, agriculture, industries and occupations, transportation, and trade. The introduction has much useful descriptive and statistical information.

The National Advisory Survey Council has compiled a *Catalogue of maps published in the Republic of South Africa* (Pretoria, Government Printer, 1966, 23 p.). This catalogue includes maps produced by the Bureau of Census and Statistics, Water Affairs Department, Geological Survey and Natural Resources Development Council.

Bibliographies

1232 *Africana Nova : A Quarterly Bibliography of Books Currently Published in and about the Republic of South Africa, Based on the Accessions to the Africana Department . . . and Including Material Received by Legal Deposit.* 1958–1969. Cape Town, South African Public Library.

This current national bibliography, which was issued by South Africa's second national library (there are two), complements *S.A.N.B.* (see no. 1241, below), the major difference being that *Africana Nova* included material about South Africa published abroad, whereas *S.A.N.B.* is limited to South African imprints. Arranged under broad subject headings in the order of the Dewey decimal classification, with alphabetical author index in each quarterly issue and a cumulative annual index in the last number for each year. Included a list of publishers' names and addresses. From March 1962 on, included government and provincial publications.

1233 Both, Ellen Lisa Marianne. *Catalogue of books and pamphlets published in German relating to South Africa and South West Africa, as found in the South African Public Library, published between 1950–1964.* Cape Town, University of Cape Town Libraries, 1969. 132 p.

1234 *Index to South African periodicals.* 1940– . Johannesburg, Public Library. Annual.

An invaluable guide to the contents of more than 250 significant and useful periodicals. Two decennial cumulations covering 1940–49 (4 v.) and 1950–59 (3 v.) are available. Author entries are combined with Library of Congress subject entries in a single sequence. Particular attention has been paid to the selection of articles that may in the future contribute to the history of any aspect of South Africa. Among the periodicals indexed in the African studies sphere are *African Notes and News, African Music, African Studies, Bantu Education Journal, Journal of Racial Affairs, Optima,* and *South African Journal of Economics.* An index of similar scope for the period 1900–1939 is in preparation.

An index to Afrikaans periodical articles (which are also well covered in the *Index to South African Periodicals*) has also been published since 1949, P. J. Nienaber, *Bronnegids by die studie van die Afrikaanse taal en letterkunde* (Johannesburg, The Author, 1947–53, 3 v.; addenda, 2 v.), supplemented by annual reprints from *Tydskrif vir geesteswetenskappe,* in which journal this work is kept up to date.

Part III: area guide (by colonial power, region and colony)

1235 Mendelssohn, Sidney. *South African bibliography*. London, Kegan Paul, 1910, 2 v. Reprint: London, Holland Press, 1968. 2 v.

The standard and best-known retrospective South African bibliography covering the period before 1910. A revised edition is in preparation at the South African Public Library, Cape Town, and will cover the period to 1925.

The author, having accumulated a great fortune in the Kimberley diamond fields, became the country's most famous bibliophile and book collector. His study provided details concerning over 9,000 books, commencing with early Portuguese publications, and going on to the beginning of the present century. Mendelssohn died in 1917 and left his great library to the Parliament of the Union of South Africa, with additional funds to continue his work.

The entries are arranged alphabetically by author, with full bibliographical details and descriptive annotations for each item. It covers a great variety of subjects, including history, travels, linguistics, anthropology, poetry, ethnography, etc. The second volume also contains separate descriptions of the British Parliamentary Command Papers on Southern Africa. In addition there is a survey of magazines, divided by geographical areas and topics, a survey of 'autograph letters', and also a comprehensive 'chronological and topographical subject index', again subdivided by areas. The *Bibliography* covers mainly South Africa and the High Commission Territories, but there is also material on Rhodesia and on the Portuguese.

Another retrospective bibliography is the *South African catalogue of books*, edited by N. S. Coetzee, fourth edition, covering 1900–1950 (Johannesburg, The Editor, 1952, 2 v.). Volume 1 (A–K) of a projected fifth edition covering 1900–1954 was published by Technibooks, P.O. Box 1881, Johannesburg, in 1956. Volume 2 of this edition has not yet been published. This work is an author-title list of books published in South Africa, excluding government publications and mission presses.

1236 Muller, C. F. J., F. A. van Jaarsveld, and T. van Wyk, eds. *A select bibliography of South African history*. Pretoria, University of South Africa, 1966. xii, 215 p.

A useful, unannotated checklist of 2,521 items. It begins with general aids – bibliographies, periodicals, atlases, guides to archives, and general histories. The second part is arranged by periods, from prehistory to the present, and the third part by subject. An author index to persons is included. For legal material see no. 476, Schiller; also no. 623, Winks.

1237 Musiker, Reuben. *Guide to South African reference books*. 5th rev. ed. Cape Town, Balkema, 1971. 136 p.

Contains more than 500 entries of the more important works of reference on South African topics, limited to works published in South Africa. The first edition appeared in 1955. Arrangement is by subject headings in the sequence of the Dewey decimal classification and within sections alphabetically by author or title. English is used for collation, notes, and annotations. There is an index of authors, titles, and subjects.

1238 —— *South African bibliography*. London, Crosby Lockwood, 1970. 105 p.

A selective guide to 250 basic South African subject bibliographies, and a survey of national bibliography, archives, manuscripts and official publications.

1239 Niemandt, J. J. *Bibliografie van die Bantoetale in die Unie van Suid-Afrika*. v. 1–6. Pretoria, 1959–63.

> Volume 4 has title, *Bibliography of the Bantu languages in the Republic of South Africa*.

British Africa: Southern Africa

1240 Nienaber, Petrus Johannes. *Bibliografie van Afrikaanse Boeke*. Johannesburg, The Author [24 Kafue Road, Emmarentia, Johannesburg] 1943–67. 6 v.

A most important bibliography of books in the Afrikaans language, providing a record of books published in Afrikaans between 1861 and 1966. Full author, title, and subject lists are included in each volume, complemented by authors' and publishers' addresses.

A comprehensive bibliography of subject literature in the Afrikaans language was published in 1958: G. R. Morris, *Die Afrikaanse Vakliteratuur* (Pretoria, Transvaal Provincial Library, 1958). This is a classified list complemented by an alphabetical index of authors, titles, and subjects. The period since 1958 is well covered in the current national bibliographies.

1241 *S.A.N.B.: South African National Bibliography : Publications received in terms of Copyright Act No. 9 of 1916*. 1959– . Pretoria, State Library. Quarterly, with annual cumulations.

Formerly issued as an annual list: *Publications received in terms of Copyright Act No. 9 of 1916*, 1933–58.

Lists all publications received by this national library, including government and provincial publications, as well as new periodicals. The arrangement of entries is according to the Dewey decimal classification. Included are lists of publishers and authors writing under pseudonyms.

1242 Schapera, Isaac, comp. *Select bibliography of South African native life and problems*. Comp. for the Inter-university Committee for African Studies under the direction of I. Schapera. London, Oxford University Press, 1941. xii, 249 p.

A valuable bibliography, which includes government reports and periodical articles and is critically annotated. Contents cover physical anthropology, archaeology, ethnography, modern status and conditions, including administration, law, economics, education, religion, health and social services.

Three supplements to this work have been published by the University of Cape Town School of Librarianship in its Bibliographical Series: M. A. Holden and A. Jacoby, *First supplement, 1934–1949*; R. Giffen and J. Back, *Second supplement, 1950–1958*; and C. Solomon, *Third supplement, 1958–1963*. These three supplements cover only the section on modern status and conditions. The main work and the supplements have been reprinted by Kraus Periodicals, Inc.

1243 South Africa. Dept. of Statistics. *Bibliography of South African Government Publications, 1910–1968*. Pretoria, Government Printer, 1969. 123 p.

1244 South Africa (Republic). House of Assembly. *Index to the manuscript annexures and printed papers of the House of Assembly, including select committee reports and bills, and also to principal motions and resolutions and commission reports, including departmental committees, 1910–1961*. Cape Town, Government Printer, 1963. 631 p.

An invaluable index to government publications for the period 1910–61. Current lists of official publications are given in *Africana Nova* and *S.A.N.B.* (the two national bibliographies), in the *Government Gazette*, and in the monthly *List of Official Publications* (Pretoria, Government Printer).

1245 Spohr, Otto H., comp. *German Africana, German publications on South and South-West Africa*. Pretoria, State Library, 1968. 332 p. (Pretoria, State Library, Bibliographies, no. 14)

This bibliography, the most complete of its kind, covers 3,423 entries arranged in alphabetical order by author. There is also an index for personal names

Part III: area guide (by colonial power, region and colony)

(including joint authors, illustrators and editors), a subject index for South-West Africa and one for South Africa. Readers are also provided with an indication as to which South African library holds any particular book. The subjects covered include every conceivable topic – ethnography, history, geography, mining, agriculture, linguistic studies, and so forth. The entries are confined to published material; archival sources are not included. See also Gerhard Totemeyer, *Südafrika-Südwestafrika: Eine Bibliographie, 1945–1963* (Freiburg, Arnold-Bergsträsser-Institut für Kulturwissenschaftliche, Forschung, 1964, 285 p.).

1246 Turnbull, C. E. P., comp. *The work of the missionaries of die Nederduits Gereformeerde Kerk van Suid-Afrika up to the year 1910: An annotated bibliography of material in the Johannesburg Public and the University of the Witwatersrand Libraries.* Johannesburg, Department of Bibliography, Librarianship and Typography, University of the Witwatersrand, 1965. 85 p.

Lists some 850 books, pamphlets, and periodical articles dealing with missionaries of the Dutch Reformed Church and their work in Southern Africa. There are indexes for personal names, place-names, and subjects.

Serials

Note There are so many serial publications in South Africa that only a few can be mentioned here. See the preceding section on bibliographies for references to periodical lists, indexes to periodicals, etc.

1247 *African Studies.* 1942– . Johannesburg, Witwatersrand University Press. Quarterly. Formerly called *Bantu Studies*, 1921–1941.

1248 *Bulletin of the Africa Institute of South Africa.* 1964– . Pretoria, Africa Institute. 10 times a year.
　　See also: *Communications*, 1964– .
　　　　　　　Occasional Papers, 1964– .

1249 *Historia.* Amptelike Orgaan van die Historiese Genootskap van Suid-Afrika. Vereeniging. Quarterly.

1250 *Historiese Studies.* 1939– . Pretoria, University of Pretoria. Quarterly.

1251 *Imvo Zabantsundu.* 1884– . Johannesburg.
In English and Xhosa. The most important African newspaper in South Africa.

1252 *Militaria.* Periodical for military history. 1969– . Pretoria. 5 times a year.

1253 *South African Geographical Journal.* 1917– . Johannesburg. Annual.

1254 South African Institute of Race Relations, Johannesburg. *Fact Papers.* 1958– .
　　Survey of Race Relations. 1947– .
　　Race Relations Journal. 1933–62. Quarterly.

1255 *South African Journal of Economics: The Quarterly Journal of the Economic Society of South Africa.* 1933– . Johannesburg. Quarterly.

1256 *South African Law Journal.* 1900– . Cape Town.

1257 *Tydskrif vir rasse-aangeleentheide. Journal of Racial Affairs.* 1950– . Stellenbosch, South African Bureau of Racial Affairs. Monthly.

Reference works

1258 *The African who's who : An illustrated classified register and national biographical dictionary of the Africans in Transvaal.* 3rd ed. Johannesburg, Central News Agency, 1965. 373 p.
First published in the 1930s by T. D. MWeli Skota, a dealer of the A.N.C. Useful for facts and insights on African personalities and organizations and for all of South Africa.

1259 *Archives yearbook for South African history.* 1938– . Pretoria, Government Printer. illus., maps.
This important series consists of original contributions, some in English and some in Afrikaans, on various aspects of South African history.

1260 *Border regional survey.* 1961– . Cape Town, published for the Institute of Social and Economic Research, Rhodes University, by Oxford University Press. Irregular.
This series deals with economic and sociological problems in the Eastern Cape. The series includes a trilogy, *Xhosa in town*, the three volumes being as follows: (1) D. H. Reader, *The black man's portion : History, demography and living conditions in the native locations of East London, Cape Province* (1961, 180 p.); (2) P. Mayer, *Townsmen or tribesmen : Conservation and the process of urbanization in a South African city* (1961, 306 p.); (3) B. A. Pauw, *The second generation* (1963, 238 p.).
A basic work in this series is C. Board, *The border region : Natural environment and land use in the Eastern Cape* (1962, 2 v.), which presents the results of a land-use survey of the East London (Cape) and King William's Town districts.

1261 Brown, William Eric. *The Catholic Church in South Africa.* London, Burns and Oates, 1960. 384 p.
A history from 1837 to the present of the Catholic Church in South Africa. Based largely on archival material.

1262 De Kiewiet, C. W. *A history of South Africa : Social and economic.* Oxford, Clarendon Press, 1941, xii, 292 p. diagr. Reprint: University of California Press, 1971.
Though now partly out of date and mistaken in some of its forecasts, this is still one of the best economic histories of South Africa. For an account of the South African economy written from the standpoint of a free-enterprise economist, see Hobart Houghton, *The South African economy* (Cape Town, Oxford University Press, 1967, 280 p.). As regards the socioeconomic development of South Africa, there is a great mass of publications too voluminous to be summarized. An excellent older book is still L. C. A. Knowles and C. M. Knowles, *The economic development of the British overseas empire*, v. 3: *The Union of South Africa* (London, Routledge and Sons, 1936, 356 p.). A fully up-to-date economic history as yet remains to be written. The biographical approach to the problem is represented by Sir Theodor Gregory, *Ernest Oppenheimer and the economic development of southern Africa* (Cape Town, Oxford University Press, 1962. 637 p.).

1263 *Cambridge history of the British Empire.* Cambridge, Eng., University Press.
v. 8, *South Africa, Rhodesia and the High Commission territories.* 2d ed. General ed., Eric A. Walker. 1963. xxviii, 1,087 p.
The previous edition was published in 1936. This is a basic work covering

southern Africa from ancient times to date. Aspects covered include social, economic, and cultural development and native inhabitants. The bibliography (p. 917–1017) includes a detailed list of manuscripts, official sources, and other works.

1264 Carnegie Commission of Investigation on the Poor White Question in South Africa. *The poor white problem in South Africa: Report of the Carnegie Commission.* Stellenbosch, Pro-Ecclesia Drukkery, 1932. 5 v. plates, fold. maps, diagrs. Includes bibliography.

A comprehensive report by specialists on economic, psychological, educational, health, and sociological aspects of the problem.

1265 Carter, Gwendolen M. *The politics of inequality: South Africa since 1948.* Rev. ed. New York, Praeger, 1959. 541 p. maps, diagrs. 2d printing, 1962. Bibliography: p. 497–524.

A valuable contribution surveying the South African political scene, with an extensive annotated bibliography, including many official documents. This expanded edition includes a brief appendix (p. 491–495) on voting returns in the 1958 election and a reference to H. F. Verwoerd as Prime Minister following the death of J. G. Strijdom (p. 238).

Of equal importance is the sequel to this work: *Five African states*, edited by Gwendolen M. Carter (Ithaca, N.Y., Cornell University Press, 1963; London, Pall Mall Press, 1964); chap. vi, South Africa, by Thomas Karis. Has a valuable, critically annotated bibliography (p. 607–616) which includes official publications, newspapers and periodicals, pamphlets, and other material chiefly of a political nature.

1266 *Dictionary of South African biography.* v. 1. Editor-in-chief, W. J. de Kock. Cape Town, published for the National Council for Social Research, Department of Higher Education, by Nasionale Boekhandel Beperk, 1968– . 894 p.

The first volume in a main series which will contain biographies of persons who died before the end of 1950; succeeding series will cover persons who died after 1950. The second and each succeeding volume will have a cumulative index. Coverage includes individuals from the former High Commission territories and South-West Africa, those who either were born in South Africa or spent considerable time there and achieved distinction abroad, non-South Africans whose lives and activities have had a ' considerable influence ' on South Africa, and ' scoundrels ', and ' frauds '. The first volume contains 568 biographies, many quite lengthy, from A to Z. Each sketch is accompanied by a bibliography of books and articles about the biographee.

1267 Doxey, G. V. *The industrial colour bar in South Africa.* Cape Town, Oxford University Press, 1961. 205 p.

Discusses the origin and development of the segregated labour market.

1268 Duggan-Cronin, A. M. *Bantu tribes of South Africa: Reproductions of photographic studies.* Cambridge, Eng., Deighton, Bell, 1938–41. 4 v.

The excellent photographic studies are prefaced by introductions and bibliographies compiled by specialists. The peoples covered are the Bavenda, Bechuana, Bapedi, Basotho, Nguni, M'Pondo, M'Pondomise, Zulu, Swazi, Baca, Hlubi and Xesibe, Vathonga, and Vachopi, and those of the Ciskei and Southern Transkei.

British Africa: Southern Africa

1269 Du Plessis, Johannes. *A history of Christian missions in South Africa.* London, Longmans, Green, 1911. xx, 494 p. map. Bibliography: p. 466–479.

A well-documented historical account of missionary history in South Africa. It deals with the missions of the Dutch colonists, Dominican Fathers, Moravians, Wesleyans, Scottish, French, Rhenish, Dutch Reformed Church, Roman Catholics, and Scandinavians, as well as the early London missionaries, Berlin mission, Swiss Romane mission, American Zulu mission and Church of England mission.

1270 Hahlo, H. R., and Ellison Kahn. *South Africa : The development of its laws and constitution.* Cape Town, Juta, 1960. xxx, 900 p.

A compendium of the whole field of South African law, giving a general picture of the basic doctrines and institutions of South Africa's laws and constitution. Contents include the genesis of South African law, 17th to 18th centuries, constitutional development to 1910, administration of justice, criminal law, native law and native courts, mercantile law, economic and racial legislation. It has a very useful bibliography (p. 815–829). A supplement covering the transition of the country to a republic was published in 1962: E. Kahn, *The new constitution* (Cape Town, Juta).

The *Annual survey of South African law* (1947– , Cape Town, published for the Faculty of Law, University of the Witwatersrand, by Juta) is a valuable summary review covering numerous aspects of law, including administration of justice. *Acta Juridica* (Cape Town, published for the Faculty of Law, University of Cape Town, by Balkema), also published annually, has articles and reviews on various aspects of South African law. The 1960 volume was a special issue tracing the development of South African government and law from 1910 to 1960.

1271 Hattersley, Alan F. *An illustrated social history of South Africa.* Cape Town, Balkema, 1969. 261 p. illus.

The author has written extensively on the history of British settlement in Natal and on related subjects. His latest work covers the social history of South Africa from 1652 to 1910. The book is noteworthy for its illustrations. The writer emphasizes the social history of the Europeans rather than that of the Africans, and stresses the picturesque rather than the statistical element. For the Afrikaners see Pierre de Villers, ed. *Kultuurgekiedenis van die Afrikaner* (Cape Town, Nasionale Boekhandel, 1968, 419 p.), an abbreviated and revised edition of a compilation by M. van den Heever.

1272 Hellmann, Ellen, ed. *Handbook on race relations in South Africa.* Cape Town, published for the South African Institute of Race Relations by Oxford University Press, 1949. xii, 778 p. fold. map, tables (some fold.).

Although now dated, this is a useful historical survey. Contributions by 31 specialists on numerous aspects: population, government and administration, law, trade unions, land and agriculture in and outside the reserves, Indian land legislation and agriculture, pass laws, taxation, African education, health services, social welfare, African co-operative societies, African press, religion, literature of Africans, Indians, Cape Malays, race attitudes.

1273 Karis, Thomas, and Gwendolen M. Carter, eds. *From protest to challenge : A documentary history of African politics in South Africa, 1882–1964.* Stanford, Hoover Institution Press, 1972– . 3 v.

A major work of analysis and documentary history, making available rare and hard-to-find documents of black African movements. v. 1, *Protest and Hope*

Part III: area guide (by colonial power, region and colony)

1892–1934. Not yet published are the following: v. 2, *Hope and Challenge, 1935–1952*, and v. 3, *Challenge and Violence, 1953–1964*. There are introductions to each volume and to each part of each volume. Chronologies, bibliographies and a biographical index enhance the value of this collection.

1274 Le May, G. H. L. *The British supremacy in South Africa, 1899–1907.* Oxford, Clarendon Press, 1965. 229 p.

An interpretative essay on the future of British policy in South Africa. See also Dr. Jean van der Poel, *Jameson raid* (1951); J. S. Marais, *The fall of Kruger's republic* (1961); and L. M. Thompson, *The unification of South Africa* (Oxford, Clarendon Press, 1960, 549 p.).

1275 *Men of the times: Old colonists of the Cape Colony and Orange River Colony.* Johannesburg, Transvaal Publishing Co., 1906. 645 p. illus., plates.

An important biographical dictionary for retrospective biography. An index to this work was published by the University of Cape Town libraries in 1960. A companion work for the Transvaal province is *Men of the times: Pioneers of the Transvaal and glimpses of South Africa* (Johannesburg, Transvaal Publishing Co., 1905, 390 p., illus.). A dictionary of South African biography is now being published (see no. 1266, above).

The following are a few examples of outstanding biographies of some famous South Africans: Sir W. Keith Hancock, *Smuts* (Cambridge, Eng., University Press, 1962–68, 2 v.); John G. Lockhart and C. M. Woodhouse, *Rhodes* (London, Hodder & Stoughton, 1963, 511 p.); Albert J. Luthuli, *Let my people go: An autobiography* (New York, McGraw-Hill, 1962, 255 p.); M. Nathan, *Paul Kruger: His life and times* (Durban, Knox, 1941, 510 p.); A. Paton, *Hofmeyr* (Cape Town, Oxford University Press, 1964, 545 p.); and no. 1262, above, Sir Theodor Gregory, *Ernest Oppenheimer* . . .

1276 Natal Regional Survey [series]. 1951– . Cape Town and New York, published for the University of Natal by Oxford University Press. illus., maps, tables, diagrs.

General series edited by H. R. Burrows. The following volumes were among those in print in 1969:

Agriculture in Natal: Recent developments. 1957. 205 p.

Alsop, M. H. *The population of Natal.* 1953. 144 p.

Archæology and natural resources of Natal. 1951. 140 p.

Baumannville: A study of an urban African community. Ed. by the Institute for Social Research. 1959. 79 p.

Brookes, Edgar H., and Nathaniel Hurwitz. *The native reserves of Natal.* 1957. 195 p.

Electricity undertakings in Natal. 1954. 100 p.

Fair, J. D. *The distribution of population in Natal.* 1955. 99 p.

Hurwitz, Nathaniel. *Agriculture in Natal, 1860–1950.* 1957. 123 p.

Palmer, Mabel. *The history of the Indians in Natal.* 1958. 197 p.

The port of Durban. 1969. 150 p.

Studies of Indian employment in Natal. 1961. 167 p.

The Ungeri-Unbilo-Umlazi rivers catchment areas. Part 1. 1967. 179 p.

Woods, C. A. *The Indian community of Natal.* 1954. 102 p.

The Oxford University Press publishes also a series of numbered reports for various departments of the University of Natal, e.g.: Natal, University, Pietermaritzburg, Department of Economics, *The African factory worker: A sample study of the life and labour of the urban African worker* (1950, 221 p., illus., maps, tables; Durham Economic Research Committee, Report no. 2).

A four-volume research study of an African reserve in the same province was published in 1952: *The Keiskammahoek rural survey* (Pietermaritzburg, Shuter & Shooter).

1277 *The native tribes of South West Africa.* Cape Town, Cape Times, 1928. 211 p. plates.
The volume was prepared for submission to the League of Nations as a sketch of the tribes in the territory administered by South Africa as a C Mandate. The five main tribal divisions are briefly sketched as to history, customs, beliefs and manners. Mr. C. H. L. Hahn, representative of the administration in Ovamboland, wrote the first essay on the Ovambo. The Bushmen were analysed by Dr. L. Fourie, medical officer for South West Africa; the Berg Damara, the Nama, a branch of the Hottentots, and the Herero by Dr. Heinrich Vedder, a missionary who had lived among and was known as an authority on the Herero. Each section is followed by a bibliography.

The standard anthropological work on the Bushmen and the Hottentots of Cape province and Bechuanaland as well as on South West Africa is Dr. Isaac Schapera, *The Khoisan peoples of South Africa* (London, Routledge, 1930, xi, 450 p.; bibliography, p. 439–445).

1278 *Official South African municipal year book.* 1909– . Pretoria, South African Association of Municipal Employees.
    1967–68 ed. 443 p.
A comprehensive and important yearbook prefaced by a general statistical review of South African municipalities. Comparative statistics of municipalities (population, finance) followed by a directory of municipalities arranged alphabetically within each province and giving population statistics, ratable value, area, outline of development, brief description and features, members of town councils, and officials. Included is a separate section on the municipalities of South West Africa. There are also earlier editions.

1279 Plaatje, Solomon T. *Native life in South Africa, before and since the European war and the Boer rebellion.* 2d ed. London, P. S. King & Son, 1916. 352 p.
An important account by the first secretary-general of the A.N.C.

1280 Schapera, Isaac, ed. *The Bantu-speaking tribes of South Africa: An ethnographical survey.* London, Routledge, 1937. xv, 453 p. plate, map, tables. Reprint: 1953. Bibliography: p. 435–444.
A basic work by specialist contributors on African customs, languages and cultural life. Contents include racial origins, habitat, grouping and ethnic history, social organization, the native in the towns, the Bantu on European-owned farms, cultural changes in tribal life, traditional literature, religious beliefs and practice, magic and medicine, law and justice, political institutions, work and health, domestic and communal life.

1281 Simons, H. J. and R. E. *Class and colour in South Africa, 1850–1950.* Harmondsworth, Middlesex, Eng., Penguin Books, 1969.
A major work analysing the role of class and colour in South African history.

Part III: area guide (by colonial power, region and colony)

1282 South Africa (Republic). Bureau of Census and Statistics. *Official yearbook of the Republic and of Basutoland, Bechuanaland Protectorate and Swaziland.* 1910–60. Pretoria, Government Printer. Annual.

An important yearbook giving detailed statistical and descriptive information on numerous topics e.g., history, constitution and government, health, social conditions, labour and industrial conditions, education, justice, Bantu administration and development, state finance. Earlier volumes contain important source material not repeated in later volumes; e.g., no. 12, 1929/30, gives a bibliography of government reports since 1910; no. 30, 1960, has been greatly condensed and contains only descriptive material. A separate chapter on South West Africa is included.

Publication of the *Yearbook* was discontinued with the 1960 edition. Thereafter the statistical content was published as *Statistical year book* ([no. 1–] 1964–). A successor to the descriptive part of the *Official yearbook* is still awaited.

1283 —— Bureau of Census and Statistics. *Union statistics for fifty years.* Pretoria, Government Printer, pref. 1960. 1 v. various pagings. On cover: Jubilee issue, 1910–60.

More than 400 pages of statistical tables on all phases of the Republic's social and economic development, giving a résumé of the country's development over a 50-year period. Topics covered include population, health, education, crimes, labour, agriculture, mining, industry, trade, communications and finance.

The current official source of statistical information is the *Quarterly Bulletin of Statistics* (formerly *Monthly Bulletin of Statistics*) (Pretoria, Government Printer), compiled by the Bureau of Statistics. It contains data on demography, labour, agriculture, mining, manufacturing, construction, trade, transport and finance.

1284 —— Department of Bantu Administration and Development. Ethnological Publications Series. 1930– . Pretoria, Government Printer.

To date 49 monographs have been published, covering tribal studies in various parts of South Africa, e.g., 23, *Venda law* (1948–49, 4 v.); 27, *Language map of South Africa*, by N. J. van Warmelo (1952); 35, *Tribes of Umtata district* (1956). A full list of the series is given in the publications.

1285 —— Department of Customs and Excise. *Foreign trade statistics.* 1956– . Pretoria, Government Printer. Annual.

From 1906 to 1955 published as *Annual statement of trade and shipping*, with varying titles. Since 1956 issued in four volumes annually: v. 1, Imports; v. 2, Exports; v. 3, Supplementary trade statistics; v. 4, Standard internal trade classification and supplementary tables. These volumes show quantities and value of imports and exports by articles and countries of origin and destination. The trade statistics for Basutoland, Bechuanaland, Swaziland, and South West Africa are integrated in the South African tables and not shown separately. The current official trade statistical source is the *Monthly Abstract of Trade Statistics*, compiled by the Department of Customs and Excise (Pretoria, Government Printer). This gives monthly totals of imports and exports in value, imports by country of origin, and exports by country of destination.

1286 —— Statutes, laws, etc. *Union statutes: Classified and annotated reprint.* Durban, Butterworth, 1949. 13 v.

A consolidated compilation of South African law from 1910 to 1947, basic to any legal library. An annual cumulative supplement, giving references to new acts since 1948, is also published by Butterworth. The texts of new acts since

1948 are included in the annual volume of *Statutes of the Republic of South Africa* (Pretoria, Government Printer). The 1949 compilation is superseded by a new loose-leaf consolidated set, *Statutes of the Republic of South Africa, 1910–1967* (Durban, Butterworth, 19 v.), published in 1967–68 and revised continuously. The annual cumulative supplement to the 1949 publication and the annual volume of *Statutes* will no longer be published in their present form.

A useful index to statutes is C. H. Blaine, *New consolidated index to pre-Union and Union statutes and provincial ordinances and the regulations, etc., thereunder, up to 31st December 1936* (Durban, Prentice-Hall, 1937), supplemented annually by an alphabetical subject index, *Index of statute law and regulations.*

1287 South Africa (Union). Commission for the Socio-Economic Development of the Bantu Areas within the Union. *Summary of the report.* Pretoria, Government Printer, 1955. xviii, 213 p. maps, diagrs. (U.G. 61-1955)

In 1950 the South African government appointed a commission headed by Professor Frederik Rothman Tomlinson to inquire into South Africa's Bantu policy. The report of the commission's findings and recommendations constitutes one of the most comprehensive modern sources in existence for conditions in the African areas of South Africa. The full report of this basic statement of government policy was published in mimeographed form in 17 volumes and an atlas volume of 66 maps. The text, most of which is in Afrikaans, totaled 3,755 pages. The summary report is in English. The Tomlinson report was issued in a limited edition.

In 1956 the government published a white paper on the report called *Government decisions on the recommendations* (16 p.; W.P. F-56); and in the same year the South African Institute of Race Relations published its own summary, D. H. Houghton, *The Tomlinson report : A summary of the findings and recommendations* (Johannesburg, The Institute, 1956, 76 p.).

1288 *Southern African dictionary of national biography.* Comp. by Eric Rosenthal. London, Warne, 1966. xxxix, 430 p.

Contains over 2,000 biographies of notable persons, of whatever race, in South Africa, South West Africa, Rhodesia, Zambia, Malawi, Mozambique, Swaziland, Botswana, and Lesotho from the time of Bartholomew Diaz to the 20th century. No living person is included. The biographies attempt to ' assess [the individuals'] place in history and their achievements, be they soldiers, writers, statesmen, explorers, sportsmen, inventors, financiers – sometimes even criminals '. There is a classified list of personalities by field from ' Adventurers ' to those in ' Zoology and biology '.

1289 South African Institute of Race Relations. *Survey of race relations in South Africa.* 1951/52– . Johannesburg, The Institute. Annual.

Valuable summary review of developments and trends in legislation, government action, and opposition. The Institute also publishes a monthly periodical, *Race Relations News*, and a pamphlet series. Among important pamphlets published are D. H. Houghton, *Life in the Ciskei* (1955, 72 p.); and M. Horrell, *The new look in the African reserves* (1964, 45 p.), reprinted from the 1963 *Survey of race relations* and forming an excellent compendium of facts and figures about the Transkei.

1290 *Standard Encyclopaedia of Southern Africa.* Cape Town, Nasionale Opvoedskundige Uitgewery, 1970– .

Issued under the direction of D. J. Potgieter, editor-in-chief, and P. C. du Plessis, editor. This is the most comprehensive ' regional encyclopaedia ' of its kind. It centres on the Republic of South Africa and its immediate neighbours, but there is also material on other parts of Africa and related subjects. Work was first started in 1957. The editors drew on more than 1,000 contributors, all of them experts in their respective fields. Their pieces range from short entries to extensive contributions, some of them on subjects not previously covered. The editors state that ' in general it was policy to select authors who were not antagonistic or over-critical towards the religion, policy or group being described '. By 1971 four volumes had been published covering the letters AAN to FOR.

1291 *State of South Africa: Pictorial, social, economic, financial, statistical.* 1957– . Johannesburg, Da Gama Publications. Annual. 1968 ed. 396 p.
An up-to-date and useful annual, giving a comprehensive survey of the Republic's present state of development in numerous fields: constitution and government, defence, external affairs, population, education, housing, mineral resources, mining, agriculture, commerce, trade, industry. Title changed in 1964 from *State of South Africa yearbook: Economic, financial and statistical yearbook for the Republic of South Africa.*

1292 Sundkler, Bengt G. M. *Bantu prophets in South Africa.* 2d ed. London, published for the International African Institute by Oxford University Press, 1961. 381 p. illus., ports. Bibliography: p. 338–339.
A study of the Bantu separatist or independent churches in many aspects, e.g., leader and followers, worship, government policy.

1293 Tatz, C. M. *Shadow and substance in South Africa: A study in land and franchise policies affecting Africans, 1910–1960.* Pietermaritzburg, University of Natal Press, 1962. 238 p. Bibliography: p. 212–218.
A detailed survey of government policies towards African land ownership and political representation.

1294 Theal, George McCall. *History of South Africa, 1505–1884.* London, Allen and Unwin, 1919–26. 11 v. Reprint: Cape Town, Struik, 1964. 11 v. plates, maps. Editions earlier than that of Allen and Unwin were published by Swan Sonnenschein, London, 1888–93, 5 v., and 1907–10, 8 v.
This most comprehensive standard work on South African history is a valuable pioneering work based largely on original sources compiled by a senior administrator turned archivist and historian. Volume 1 covers ethnography and conditions of South Africa before 1505; v. 2–4, the history of South Africa before 1795; v. 5–9, the history of South Africa since 1795; and v. 10–11, the history of South Africa, 1873–1884.

Another important work which draws on Theal to a large extent but which is nevertheless invaluable for the Eastern Cape is Sir G. E. Cory, *The rise of South Africa* (London, Longmans, 1910–30, 5 v., fronts., plates, maps). A sixth volume was published in *Archives year book for South African history* (Part 1, 1939) (Reprint: Cape Town, Struik, 1965, 6 v.). The Eurocentric approach taken by pioneers such as Theal and Cory was revised in the first place by William M. Macmillan, whose classical studies concerning African policy and the Cape Coloureds – seen from the missionary-humanitarian standpoint – marked a new departure in South African historiography. The most general of his works is William M. Macmillan, *The road to self-rule: A study in colonial evolution.* (London, Faber and Faber, 1959, 296 p.); it compares events in South Africa with developments in other parts of the British empire, and with colonial North America. See also, by the same author, *Bantu, Boer, and Briton: The making of the South African native problem* (Oxford, 1963, 382 p.).

1295 Thompson, Leonard M. *The unification of South Africa, 1902–1910.*
Oxford, Clarendon Press, 1960. xv, 549 p. map. Bibliography: p. 513–527.
The standard work on the subject written from the standpoint of an English-
speaking South African liberal.

1296 Tylden, G. *The armed forces of South Africa.* Johannesburg, Africana
Museum, 1954. xvi, 239 p.
Gives a short account of the armed forces in South African history from 1659
to 1946. Armed forces are listed alphabetically by regiments or corps. Included
are a useful tabulation of wars waged in the four provinces and a bibliography.
Addenda and corrigenda have appeared in *Africana Notes and News,* Mar.
1955, Dec. 1958, and Sept. 1960.
A work that describes the campaigns and battle honors of the regiments is
Herbert Henry Curson, *Colours and honours in South Africa, 1783–1948*
(Pretoria, The Author, 1948, xv, 123 p., illus.).

1297 Van der Walt, A. J. H., J. A. Wiid and A. L. Geyer, eds. *Geskiedenis
van Suid-Afrika.* Cape Town, Balkema, 1951. 2 v. Bibliography: p. 705–
732.
A standard history, written in Afrikaans, with special emphasis on the
Afrikaners. The first volume, entitled 'The white man in South Africa', covers
South Africa from the Portuguese discoveries to 1939. The second volume deals
with special topics: the evolution of government; the country's economic
expansion, African and Coloured problems; the development of Afrikaner
culture, including language, literature and other aspects. The contributors
include the editors, as well as D. W. Krüger, N. J. J. Olivier, H. B. Thom,
P. J. van der Merwe, and others. The work is indispensable for the study of
South Africa up to the Second World War. Particularly noteworthy are the
contributions of P. J. van de Merwe, author of *Trek : Studies oor die Mobiliteit
van die Pioniersbevolking aan die Kaap* (Cape Town, Nasionale Pers Beperk,
1945) and of other studies that have greatly contributed to the study of the
trekker.

1298 Van Riebeeck Society. Publications. 1918– . Cape Town, The Society.
A series of great value for historical research. It contains mostly transcriptions
of manuscript records. A detailed list of the publications is given in each
volume and is available from The Society, c/o South African Public Library,
Queen Victoria Street, Cape Town.

1299 Walker, Eric Anderson. *A history of southern Africa.* 3d ed. London,
Longmans, 1957. xxiv, 973 p. maps. Bibliography: p. 925–945.
This is a well documented, standard work on South African history written from
the standpoint of British liberal imperialism. The bibliography draws on many
official sources, and there is a useful list of executive officers, from the earliest
times onward.

1300 Walshe, Peter. *The rise of African nationalism in South Africa: The
African National Congress 1912–1952.* Berkeley, University of California
Press, 1971. xv, 480 p. Bibliography: p. 422–455.
The standard history, based on a great array of published and unpublished
sources. The author discusses 'Congress policies, political attitudes and organisa-
tions, seen as a process of reaction to Native policy, as a response to the South
African industrial revolution, and the result of ideological factors generated
from within South Africa and abroad'. See also Edward Roux, *Time longer
than rope : A history of the Black man's struggle for freedom in South Africa*
(Madison, Wisconsin, University of Wisconsin Press, 1966, 469 p.), a history of

left-wing movements written by a former member of the South African Communist Party.

1301 Wellington, John Harold. *Southern Africa: A geographical study.* Cambridge, Eng., University Press, 1955. 2 v. plates, maps, tables, diagrs.

Standard work on South African geography. Volume 1 covers physical geography, climate, vegetation and soils, hydrography; v. 2, land utilization, minerals and other industries, the people. South West Africa is dealt with in many chapters.

1302 *Who's who of Southern Africa, including Mauritius and incorporating South African Who's Who and the Central African Who's Who: An illustrated biographical sketch book of personalities in Southern Africa.* 1907– Johannesburg, Wootton & Gibson, –1964; Johannesburg, Combined Publishers, 1965– . illus., ports. Irregular; then annual.

A major source of current biography. The 1968 volume (52d ed., 1,296 p.) includes roughly 8,000 entries. It has a directory of diplomatic, civil service, and university personnel and includes a separate section of some 250 entries on South West Africa. The title and incorporation of the publication have varied.

1303 Wilson, Monica, and Leonard Thompson, eds. *The Oxford history of South Africa.* V. 1, *South Africa to 1870.* Oxford, Clarendon Press, 1969. xiii, 502 p. illus., maps, tables. Bibliography: p. 447–472.

An important reappraisal that seeks to present the country's past in Afrocentric rather than Eurocentric terms. Draws heavily on anthropological material. Written in the British-South African liberal tradition. Traces the country's development from the Stone Ages to 1870. The contributors are R. H. Davenport, R. R. Inskeep, M. F. Katzen, Leonard Thompson and Monica Wilson.

At the time of writing, the second volume, covering the period 1870–1960, was being prepared. The contributors included Hobart Houghton, Leonard Thompson, René de Villiers, David Welsh, Francis Wilson and Monica Wilson. The subjects dealt with ranged widely, such as the growth of peasant communities; the development of farming, of towns; the subjection of African chieftainships; Afrikaner nationalism; economic history; the Boer War and the making of the Union. D. W. Krüger, in *The making of a nation: A history of the Union of South Africa 1910–1961* (Johannesburg, Macmillan, 1969, 348 p.), looks at the period from the standpoint of an Afrikaans-speaking historian.

South-West Africa

Note For further specific references, see preceding section and German Africa.

Bibliographies

1304 De Jager, Theo, comp. *South West Africa. Suidwes-Afrika.* Ed. by Brigitte Klaas. Pretoria, State Library, 1964. 216 p. (Bibliographies, no. 7)

About 2,000 references on South-West Africa, all to books or pamphlets; periodicals are included only when available in pamphlet reprints. The arrangement is alphabetical by author or title, with a detailed subject index. A second edition is planned; it will also include periodical articles, government publications, and books in the vernacular.

A consolidated bibliography of German Africana relating to South West

Africa and to South Africa as well, covering the period from the 17th century to 1965, compiled by O. H. Spohr, has been published by the State Library, Pretoria. (See entry no. 1245 in South African section for details.) It contains almost 4,000 titles and unites the entries at present scattered in some 25 other bibliographies.

1305 Roukens de Lange, E. J., comp. *South West Africa, 1946–1960: A selective bibliography.* Cape Town, School of Librarianship, University of Cape Town, 1961. 51 p. (Bibliographical Series)

This compilation of 332 references to books, pamphlets, and substantial periodical articles relating wholly or in major part to South West Africa complements an earlier publication of the University of Cape Town School of Librarianship, Floretta J. Welch, *South-West Africa: A bibliography* (Cape Town, 1946, 33 1.), which covers comparable literature from 1919 to 1946.

1306 Voigts, Barbara. *South West Africa imprints: A bibliography.* Cape Town, University of Cape Town, 1964. 58 p. (Bibliographical Series)

See also in this series L. S. E. Loening, *Bibliography of the status of South-West Africa up to June 30th, 1951.*

Reference works

1307 *Archives yearbook for South African history.* 1938– . Pretoria, Government Printer.

Several of the volumes in this series deal with South West African history.

1308 Goldblatt, I. *The mandated territory of South West Africa in relation to the United Nations.* Cape Town, Struik, 1961. 67 p.

Essay by a Windhoek lawyer, examining the question of South West Africa from 1919, when it was made a C Mandate of the League of Nations under the trusteeship of South Africa. He reviews South Africa's de facto annexation of the territory and refusal to submit reports to the Trusteeship Council, as well as United Nations action through the October–November session of 1959.

There now exists a great amount of polemical literature on the question. Attacks on the South African position are contained in Ruth First, *South West Africa* (Harmondsworth, Middlesex, 1963, 269 p., maps; Penguin African Library), written from the Marxist-Leninist standpoint, and Allard K. Lowenstein, *Brutal mandate: A journey to South West Africa* (New York, Macmillan, 1962, 257 p.).

1309 International Conference on South West Africa, Oxford, 1966. *South West Africa: Travesty of trust: The expert papers and findings of the International Conference on South West Africa, Oxford, 23–26 March, 1966, with a postscript by Iain MacGibbon on the 1966 judgement of the International Court of Justice.* Ed. by Ronald Segal and Ruth First. London, Deutsch, 1967. 352 p. tables.

Includes bibliographies. A harsh critique of the South African record.

1310 South Africa (Republic). *Reports presented by the Government of the Union of South Africa to the Council of the League of Nations concerning the administration of South West Africa.* 1918– . Pretoria, Government Printer. The title varies.

The Government Printer also publishes *United Nations, South West Africa: Proceedings at the United Nations* (Dec. 1949– , annual).

Part III: area guide (by colonial power, region and colony)

1311 ———— Commission of Enquiry into South West African Affairs, 1962–63. *Report*. Pretoria, Government Printer, 1964. li, 557 p. illus., 49 maps, tables, diagrs. Chairman: F. H. Odendaal. Bibliography: p. 552–557.

Text in English and Afrikaans. Includes much factual and statistical information on history, topography, natural resources, land utilization, population, government and administration, health services, social development and welfare services, education, agriculture, economic and industrial development.

An earlier government survey dealing with general conditions, administration, and policy is South Africa (Union), South West Africa Commission, *Report* (Pretoria, Government Printer, 1936, 104 p.; UG 26/36; chairman, H. S. van Zyl).

1312 ———— Department of Bantu Administration and Development. Ethnological Series. Pretoria, Government Printer, 1930– .

The following monographs in this series by O. Köhler deal with various parts of South West Africa: 40, *Karibib district* (1958, 116 p.); 42, *Gobabis district* (1959, 108 p.); 43, *Omaruru district* (1959, 113 p.); 44, *Otjiwarongo district* (1959, 98 p.); 45, *Grootfontein district* (1959, 85 p.).

1313 South-West Africa. Statutes. *Union legislation affecting South West Africa and proclamations, ordinances and principal government notices issued in South West Africa, 1915– . 1916– .* Windhoek, Administration of South West Africa.

The following annotated reprint covers the years 1915–28: *Law of South West Africa*, edited and prepared for publication by R. E. G. Rosenow (Parow, Cape Times, 1957, 3 v.). Further consolidated volumes of the laws have been issued by the administration of South-West Africa.

1314 *South West Africa annual*. 1946– . Windhoek, South West Africa Publications.

Does not give much statistical information but has articles of general interest on many South West African subjects.

1315 United Nations. General Assembly. Committee on South West Africa. *Report*. 1954– . New York. Issued as supplements to the Official Records of the General Assembly (GAOR).

Following discussions of the question of South West Africa, both in the Trusteeship Council and before the General Assembly from 1946 on, this seven-member committee was established in 1953 to study the question of the area considered by the United Nations a trusteeship but by South Africa a territory under its sole administration, 'until such time as an agreement is reached'. Annual reports have presented petitions and recommendations including the request that the case be referred to the International Court. For extended summaries of discussions and resolutions relating to South West Africa in the Fourth (Trusteeship) Committee and the General Assembly of the United Nations, see the annual volumes of the *United Nations year book*.

1316 Vedder, Heinrich. *South West Africa in early times: Being the story of South West Africa up to the date of Mahero's death in 1890*. Trans. and ed. by Cyril G. Hall. New York, Barnes & Noble, 1966. 525 p. maps. Bibliography: p. 508–510.

A modern edition of the author's classic *Das alte Südwestafrika*.

1317 Wellington, John H. *South West Africa and its human issues*. Oxford, Clarendon Press, 1967, xxiv, 461 p. plates, maps, tables. Bibliographical footnotes.

A full geographical survey of the area with good sections on history during the

German period and the mandate years under the League of Nations. Attempts to cover League of Nations and United Nations controversy with the government of South Africa.

High Commission Territories:
Bechuanaland, Basutoland and Swaziland
(Botswana, Lesotho and Swaziland)

Bibliographies

1318 Arnheim, Johanna. *Swaziland: A bibliography*. Cape Town, School of Librarianship, University of Cape Town, 1950. 20 p.
There are 150 entries arranged under subject headings, including administration, agriculture, botany, education, ethnology, geology, history, land and labour, language, medicine, and missions. A list of South African imperial blue books is given, and there is an author index. The bibliography is complemented and updated by the Wallace work described below (no. 1326).

1319 Botswana National Library Service. *The national bibliography of Botswana*. v. 1, no. 1. Gaberones, 1969. 10 p.
Lists current publications.

1320 Botswana National Library Service. *One hundred books on Botswana: An annotated list of books, articles and pamphlets*. Supplement to *Kutlwano*, Nov. 1969. Gaberones, 1969. 1 v.
The entries, most of which are annotated, are arranged by the following subjects: general works, missions and missionaries, travel and exploration, social anthropology, biography, administration and development, language, literature, natural history. Publications from 1842 through 1969 are covered.

1321 Groen, Juliette. *Bibliography of Basutoland*. Cape Town, School of Librarianship, University of Cape Town, 1946. 30 p.
The 288 entries are classified under broad subject headings, e.g., administration, agriculture, botany, Christian missions, crafts, education, geology, law, history, literature, medicine, music, and native races. An author index is included.
The list will be complemented by a bibliography for the period 1947 onwards being compiled by L. Gordon at the University of the Witwatersrand Department of Bibliography, Librarianship and Typography.

1322 Library of Congress. African Section. *Botswana, Lesotho and Swaziland: A guide to official publications, 1868–1968*. Washington D.C., 1971. 84 p.
See no. 299 for note on this series.

1323 Middleton, Coral. *Bechuanaland: A bibliography*. Cape Town, School of Librarianship, University of Cape Town, 1965. 37 p. (Bibliographical Series)
Complements and supplements the Stevens bibliography described in the next entry. Arranged by subject, the partially annotated list excludes periodical articles and works in vernacular languages but includes reprints from newspapers and periodicals. References cited were found in three African libraries, and the location of each work is indicated. There is an author index.

1324 Stevens, Pamela E. *Bibliography of Bechuanaland*. Cape Town, School of Librarianship, University of Cape Town, 1949. 27 p.
Consists of 305 entries including official publications, arranged under subject headings with an author index. Aspects covered include administration, botany,

boundaries, Christian missions, climate, education, geology, history, law, medicine, native races, railways, and zoology.

1325 Syracuse University. Maxwell Graduate School of Citizenship and Public Affairs. Program of Eastern African Studies. *A bibliography on Bechuanaland.* Comp. by Paulus Mohome and John B. Webster. Syracuse, N.Y., 1966. 58 l. (Occasional Bibliography, no. 5)

Books, articles, pamphlets, and some government publications are covered; emphasis is on social science topics. Entries are arranged by categories, e.g., general, bibliography, agriculture, education, politics, traditional religion.

1326 Wallace, Charles Stewart, comp. *Swaziland: A bibliography.* Johannesburg, Department of Bibliography, Librarianship and Typography, University of the Witwatersrand, 1967. 87 p. processed.

Adds to and continues the 1950 bibliography of Johanna Arnheim (see no. 1318, above) and brings coverage up to the end of 1965. The 1,191 entries are arranged by subjects and include all types of printed and unpublished materials.

Reference works

1327 Ashton, Hugh. *The Basuto.* London, published for the International African Institute by Oxford University Press, 1952. xi, 355 p. illus., tables. Bibliography: p. 346–349.

An important anthropological monograph on the Basuto peoples covering the following aspects: social background, education, religious beliefs, animal husbandry, land tenure, political and judicial organization, law, medicine, and magic and sorcery.

1328 *Basutoland Notes and Records.* 1959– . Maseru. Irregular.

Contains scholarly articles, news and notes and book reviews.

1329 Coates, Austin. *Basutoland.* London, H.M. Stationery Office, 1966. 135 p. (Corona Library)

Part of a series sponsored by the Colonial Office dealing with the United Kingdom dependent territories. The brief survey covers history, economic situation (including agricultural problems), traditional life, education, religion, and politics.

1330 Great Britain. *Basutoland, Bechuanaland Protectorate and Swaziland: Report of an economic survey mission.* London, H.M. Stationery Office, 1960. 2 v. Vol. 1, text, 555 p.; Vol. 2, maps. Chairman: Chandler Morse.

A comprehensive survey of the political, administrative, and fiscal background and the economic situation, including cattle, crops, water, minerals, power, communications, industry and commerce, and education. An appendix gives statistics of population, area, finance, and imports and exports.

One of several earlier surveys conducted in 1951: Great Britain, Colonial Office, *An economic survey of the colonial territories, 1951* (London, H.M. Stationery Office, 1952, 7 v.; Colonial, nos. 281–287). Volume 1 includes the High Commission Territories.

1331 —— Commonwealth Office. *Annual report on Basutoland.* 1891– 1964. London, H.M. Stationery Office. illus., map. (Colonial Annual Reports)

    1962. 126 p. Reading list: p. 124–126.

1332 ———— ———— *Annual report on Swaziland.* 1906–1967. London, H.M. Stationery Office. map. (Colonial Annual Reports) 1962. 125 p. Reading list: p. 119–122 (classed).

1333 ———— ———— *Annual report on the Bechuanaland Protectorate.* 1896–1965. London, H.M. Stationery Office. map. (Colonial Annual Reports) 1961 and 1962. 1964. 116 p. Reading list: p. 92–93.

Until December 1961 the annual reports of the three High Commission Territories were submitted to the Office of Commonwealth Relations (now the Commonwealth Office) by the High Commissioner, who was also High Commissioner of the Union of South Africa. After the Republic of South Africa withdrew from the Commonwealth, the office in South Africa was changed to that of Ambassador, responsible as High Commissioner of the Territories to the Colonial Office. The annual reports were then published by the Colonial Office until independence. They are in systematic style, containing short summaries of the chief events of the past year and handbook and statistical information on the territories. They include reading lists citing official publications as well as unofficial writings.

1334 ———— ———— *Basutoland, the Bechuanaland Protectorate and Swaziland : History of discussions with the Union of South Africa, 1909–1939.* London, H.M. Stationery Office, 1952. 135 p. map. (Cmd. 8707)

Historical review of the consistent and oft-repeated refusal of the United Kingdom to consider yielding its charge of the High Commission Territories for incorporation in South Africa, ' except with the full consent of the peoples concerned '.

1335 Hailey, William Malcolm Hailey, 1st baron. *Native administration in the British African territories.* Part 5, *The High Commission Territories : Basutoland, the Bechuanaland Protectorate and Swaziland.* London, H.M. Stationery Office, 1953. 447 p. tables.

For comment, see no. 319.

1336 Hailey, William Malcolm Hailey, 1st baron. *The Republic of South Africa and the High Commission Territories.* London and New York, Oxford University Press, 1963. 136 p.

Based on material collected from 1960 to bring the 1953 study up to date, but changed into a review and analysis of past and present aspects of the relations of the three territories with the Union and the Republic.

1337 *The High Commission Territories law reports: Decisions of the High Courts and special courts of Basutoland, the Bechuanaland Protectorate and Swaziland, 1926-1953.* Ed. by Sir Harold Willan. Maseru, High Court, 1955. xxiv, 328 p.
Annual volume, 1954– .

1338 Kuper, Hilda. *The uniform of colour, a study of white-black relationships in Swaziland.* Johannesburg, Witwatersrand University Press, 1947. 160 p. plates, maps.

A sociological classic. The author also wrote *The Swazi, a South African kingdom* (New York, 1963), and other works.

1339 Schapera, Isaac. *Handbook of Tswana law and custom.* London, published for the International African Institute by Oxford University Press, 1955, 328 p., maps, tables.

Professor Schapera, an anthropologist, has written extensively on many aspects of Botswana. Other works by the same author include *Married life in an*

African tribe (London, Faber and Faber, 1940, 364 p.); and *Migrant labour and tribal life, a study of conditions in the Bechuanaland Protectorate* (London, Oxford University Press, 1947, 248 p.).

1340 ⸻ *Tribal innovators : Tswana chiefs and social change, 1795–1940.* London, Athlone Press, 1970. 278 p.

A history of the role of chiefs as agents of change and innovators in the five largest chiefdoms in Botswana.

1341 ⸻ *The Tswana.* London, International African Institute, 1953. 80 p. map. (Ethnographic Survey of Africa, Southern Africa, pt. 3)

Professor Schapera is the recognized authority of the Tswana, Bakgatla, and other tribes of the former Bechuanaland Protectorate. This volume in the Ethnographic Survey Series is of the reference-guide nature, and its bibliography includes titles of many other books and articles by his hand.

1342 Sheddick, Vernon G. J. *The southern Sotho.* London, International African Institute, 1953. 87 p. map. (Ethnographic Survey of Africa, Southern Africa, pt. 2) Bibliography: p. 80–84.

Standard ethnographical survey. Another work by Dr. Sheddick, *Land tenure in Basutoland* (London, H.M. Stationery Office, 1954, 169 p., illus., fold. maps; Colonial Research Studies, no. 13), was a full field survey, analysing and suggesting remedies for land shortage in Basutoland.

1343 Silberbauer, George B. *Report to the government of Bechuanaland on the Bushman survey.* Gaberones, Bechuanaland Government, 1965. 138 p. illus., map.

An investigation into the present state of the Bushman population of the Bechuana Protectorate. It covers geographical disposition, interracial contacts, social structure and organization, law and justice, economics, material culture, and languages.

1344 Sillery, A. *The Bechuanaland Protectorate.* Cape Town, Oxford University Press, 1952. xii, 236 p. maps. Bibliography: p. 219–222.

An important general work covering history from the beginning to the 19th century, the traditions and history of the tribes, and an account of contemporary conditions – topography, the towns, lands and cattle posts, animal husbandry and agriculture, and migrant labour.

A more specialized work is the author's recent *Founding a protectorate : History of Bechuanaland, 1885–1895* (London, Mouton, 1965, 267 p., illus., maps; Studies in African History, Anthropology and Ethnology, no. 3), a very detailed account, much of it taken from the unpublished correspondence of the missionaries and traders who were the first Europeans in the region. The style of writing is easy and anyone concerned deeply with the period will find the book interesting reading. See also his *John Mackenzie of Bechuanaland, 1835–1899 : A study of humanitarian imperialism* (Cape Town, A. A. Balkema, 1971, 236 p.).

1345 South Africa (Republic). Bureau of Census and Statistics. *Official yearbook of the Republic of South Africa.* 1910– . Pretoria, Government Printer.

Each issue of the yearbook has separate chapters on Basutoland, Bechuanaland, and Swaziland, covering the following topics: history, description, game, administration, population, vital statistics, public health, education, labour, justice, land and agriculture, commerce, communications, public finance, and taxation.

1346 Spence, J. E. *Lesotho : The politics of dependence.* London, published for the Institute of Race Relations [by] Oxford University Press, 1968. 88 p. map.

By a political scientist who in 1965 visited what was then Basutoland. The historical background is established and developments are carried up to 1966 in this readable discussion of the country's economic and political difficulties, with particular reference to dependence on South Africa.

1347 Stevens, Richard P. *Lesotho, Botswana, and Swaziland : The former High Commission Territories in Southern Africa.* New York, Praeger, (Library of African Affairs) Bibliography: p. 277–285.

Account of political and constitutional development in the three countries. H. George Henry has contributed chapters on the economy of each.

1348 Theal, G. McCall. *Basutoland records.* Cape Town, W. A. Richard, 1883. 3 v. Reprint: Cape Town, Struik, 1964. 3 v. in 4. maps.

A pioneer work which includes 2,194 documents and letters (among them many missionary and official reports) relating to the history of Basutoland, printed in chronological order, and covering the period 1833–68. Three further volumes relating to 1868 and 1869 were never printed and exist only in manuscript form in the Cape Archives.

1349 Tylden, G. *The rise of the Basuto.* Cape Town, Juta, 1950. xi, 270 p. illus., ports., maps.

A concise history of Basutoland from 1824, well documented throughout the text, with a valuable bibliography (p. 241–246) which includes government publications and maps.

Two standard histories, especially good for the earlier period are D. F. Ellenberger and J. C. MacGregor, *History of the Basuto, ancient and modern* (London, Caxton, 1912); and Sir G. Lagden, *The Basutos* (London, Hutchinson, 1909, 2 v.).

FRENCH AFRICA

Note The only countries of the former vast empire of France in Africa still under French sovereignty are the overseas territories of former French Somaliland now called French Territory of the Afars and Issas, the Comoro Islands, and the overseas department of Réunion. For all francophone Africa, however, the great body of literature has been and still is in French and is published in Paris.

Because of the importance of official journals for any research and contrary to our practice for the English-speaking countries, the individual *journaux officiels* of some of the states of francophone Africa are cited in various sections that follow. See p. 468 for note on French Colonial Office.

Atlas

1350 Grandidier, Guillaume, ed. *Atlas des colonies françaises, protectorats et territoires sous mandat de la France.* Paris, Société d'Editions Géographiques, Maritimes et Coloniales, 1934. 236 p. illus., maps (159 col. maps on xxxix double plates), tables, diagrs. Large folio, loose-leaf, issued in parts; various pagings.

This monumental library atlas begins with an essay on the formation of the

Part III: area guide (by colonial power, region and colony)

colonial empire. Next are the maps, by region and country, with insets of geological, climatic, and other special maps, interspersed with text which is a full synopsis of physical geography, as well as detailed description of major cities, brief indications of ethnology, etc. North Africa has the first 48 pages and 13 folded maps, AOF 28 pages and 5 folded maps, AEF and Cameroun 20 pages and 5 folded maps, and Madagascar, Réunion and other islands 28 pages and 6 folded maps. The remainder covers French possessions outside Africa.

Bibliographies

Note These bibliographies, whose content covers all French-speaking Africa, are extensively supplemented in the regional bibliographies mentioned in the sections below. The comprehensive library guide to French writing is the *Bibliographie de la France* (Paris, Au Cercle de la Librairie, weekly, with annual indexes), Part 1, *Bibliographie Officielle*. Some bibliographies are included in the periodicals listed under the subsection Serials below. Best bibliographies of French colonialism are Roberts (no. 1367) and Gardinier (no. 1363). See also nos. 6, 18, 241, 277.

1351 Ballard, John A. ' Politics and government in former French West and Equatorial Africa: A critical bibliography '. *Journal of Modern African Studies*, v. 3, no. 4, Dec. 1965: 589–605.
An evaluation of major contributions, 1955–65, to the study of former French African territories during the colonial period and since independence.

1352 Baratte, Thérèse, comp. *Bibliographie : Auteurs africains et malgaches de langue française.* Paris, Office de Coopération Radiophonique (OCORA), 1965. 50 p.
A country-by-country listing of writers in French-speaking black Africa. Covers literature, education, politics, and economics.

1353 Boston University. Libraries. *List of French doctoral dissertations on Africa, 1884–1961.* Comp. by Marion Dinstel; with indexes by Mary Darrah Herrick. Boston, G. K. Hall, 1966. 336 p.
Reproduction of almost 3,000 cards, with author, area and subject indexes. The titles are for the most part studies of French African possessions, though occasional dissertations are concerned with other parts of Africa. See also no. 523.

1354 Centre d'Analyse et de Recherche Documentaires pour l'Afrique Noire and Club des Lecteurs d'Expression Française. *Afrique noire d'expression française : Sciences sociales et humaines; guide de lecture.* Ed. by M. C. Jacquey and F. Niellon. Paris, CARDAN, CLEF [1968 ?]. 301 p. maps.
A worthy contribution to reference material on French-speaking West and Equatorial Africa. Most references are annotated and many derive from publications of the Banque Centrale des Etats d'Afrique de l'Ouest, Musée Royal de l'Afrique Centrale, Centre d'Etude et de Documentation sur l'Afrique et l'Outre-Mer, Fondation Nationale des Sciences Politiques, etc. This is exclusively a guide to French-language publications (including many processed items), except where the basic character of a work or the absence of an equivalent publication in French warrants inclusion of a study in English or German. There are two main parts with many subdivisions: global studies and country studies. The former includes works on Africa as a whole and covers bibliographies, general works and various subjects. A very helpful inclusion in the second part is that of an ethnographic map for each country. There is an

French Africa

author index. There are some unnecessary duplications. More serious limitations, however, are the high number of typographical errors, the frequent lack of complete bibliographical data, and occasionally erroneous information. But even though it can be faulted, this is a highly recommended bibliography, invaluable for research on the areas treated.

1355 Favitski de Probobysz, Cmdt. de. *Répertoire bibliographique de la littérature militaire et coloniale française depuis cent ans.* Liège, Thone, 1935. 363 p.
Not available for examination.

1356 France. Direction de la Documentation. *L'Afrique à travers les publications de la Documentation Française: Bibliographie, 1945–1961.* [Etablie par Madame Coisel] Paris, La Documentation Française, 1961. 107 p. (Travaux et recherches, no. 14)
Listing of pamphlets, articles, maps, documents, etc., on Africa that have appeared in the several series of La Documentation Française, the more substantial of which are Notes et études documentaires, Documentation française illustrée, and Cahiers français. Arrangement is first by region or country (56 headings) and under that by year. There are perhaps 1,500 titles.

1357 ——— ——— *Bibliographie sélective des publications officielles françaises.* 1952– . Paris, La Documentation Française. Semi-monthly.
The most immediate record of French official publications, including those for France overseas and, since 1960, a few issued by the governments of French-speaking African states. Entries are by issuing offices, in Part 1. A separate enclosure, Part 2, is 'Bulletin des Sommaires'; this lists the contents of the various series of La Documentation Française, notably the Notes et études documentaires, which are background pamphlets, including country studies in which the French-speaking states of Africa are regularly covered.

1358 ——— Institut National de la Statistique et des Etudes Economiques. Service de coopération. *Bibliographie démographique, 1945–1962; liste des travaux démographiques publiés par le Service de coopération de l'I.N.S.E.E. et les services de statistiques des états africains d'expression française, ou réalisés avec leur collaboration.* Paris, 1963. 33 l.

1359 ——— ——— ——— *Bibliographie démographique (1945–1964). Travaux publiés par l'I.N.S.E.E. (Service de coopération), les services de statistiques des états africains d'expression française ou de Madagascar et le Ministère de la coopération.* Paris, 1965.

1360 ——— ——— *Bulletin Bibliographique.* Paris. Bi-monthly. (no. 124, Mar.–Apr. 1967)
An abstracting service, providing fairly full abstracts (500 words or more) of articles from the principal economic reviews and books in French and other languages regarding France and overseas.

1361 ——— Ministère des Affaires Culturelles. *Notice bibliographique des principaux ouvrages français récents intéressant les territoires français d'outre-mer, le Sahara, et les états africains d'expression française.* Paris, 1961. 61 p.
A listing of about 1,000 works, most of which were published since 1946.

1362 ——— Ministère des Armées. *Guide bibliographique sommaire d'histoire militaire et coloniale française.* Paris, Impr. nationale, 1969. 522 p.
A major guide covering general works, Ancien Régime, and the period from 1792 to 1940. Arrangement of index is by publications, periodicals and annuals.

Part III: area guide (by colonial power, region and colony)

1363 Gardinier, David E. 'French colonial rule in Africa: a bibliographical essay', in Prosser Gifford and Wm. Roger Louis, eds., *France and Britain in Africa: Imperial rivalry and colonial rule*, p. 787–902. New Haven, Conn., Yale University Press, 1971.

A major contribution which discusses not only sources, but also major issues in French colonial history since 1900. The author first deals with the North African territories, which occupy about one-third of his survey. He then discusses World War I and its aftermath, including military questions; the Mandates; administrative problems between the two World Wars; economic aspects of French rule; the missions, education and social change; as well as more general works. There is a guide to sources, including archival material, periodicals, academic dissertations, etc. The article concludes with a list of the most senior officials and politicians concerned with the French empire. See also no. 1367, Roberts, *History of French colonial policy*.

1364 Martineau, Alfred, ed. *Bibliographie d'histoire coloniale (1900–1930)*. Paris, Société de l'Histoire des Colonies Françaises, 1932. 667 p.

The following selections on French colonies in Africa are included in this work: 'Afrique occidentale française', by Georges Hardy (p. 331–341, including about 60 references); 'Afrique équatoriale française', by Georges Bruel (p. 311–332, 160–170 references); and 'Madagascar', by André You (p. 365–374, almost 150 references). See also A. Lebel, *L'Afrique occidentale dans la littérature française depuis 1870* (Paris, 1925, 279 p.).

1365 Mercier, Roger. 'Bibliographie africaine et malgache: Ecrivains noirs d'expression française'. *Revue de Littérature Comparée*, v. 37, no. 1, 1963: 145–171.

List of over 360 books and articles in French by Africans on Africa, covering anthologies, poetry, novels, the arts, legends, essays and history.

1366 Pasquier, Roger. 'Chronique de l'histoire coloniale: L'Afrique noire d'expression française'. *Revue Française d'Histoire d'Outre-Mer*. 1961: 438–57; 1963: 74–129, 382–535.

An important and detailed survey for the colonial period.

1367 Roberts, Stephen H. *History of French colonial policy*. See no. 1467.

In the appendices are listed the chief colonial officials and an excellent bibliography in four parts. Part 1 treats periodicals and official publications; part 2, general literature; part 3, special topics covering the empire, that is, political and economic affairs; and part 4 is a regional bibliography. Many items are annotated. A most important guide to the literature on French colonialism.

1368 Robinson, Kenneth E. 'Survey of the background material for the study of government in French tropical Africa'. *American Political Science Review*, v. 50, no. 1, Mar. 1956: 170–198.

Bibliographical article of lasting value for any serious research on former French Africa. The references are selected from the authoritative literature, largely in French, over the preceding quarter-century, with special emphasis on French legislative sources. Professor Robinson's evaluative analyses cover the chief bibliographical works, French official publications, specialized periodicals, books and articles on French Africa in general, and then in separate sections, French West Africa, French Equatorial Africa, and Madagascar.

1369 Société des Africanistes. *Journal*. 1931– Paris.

Outstanding bibliographic section carried once each year.

French Africa

1370 Thomassery, Marguerite. *Catalogue des périodiques d'Afrique noire francophone (1858-1962) conservés à l'IFAN.* Dakar, Institut Français d'Afrique Noire, 1965. 117 p. (Catalogues et documents, no. 14)
A listing of 584 serials and some series publications such as *Etudes sénégalaises* and *Etudes soudanaises* published in French-speaking Africa (excluding Madagascar) and held at the IFAN library in Dakar.

1371 U.S. Library of Congress. Division of Bibliography. *French colonies in Africa: A list of references.* Comp. by Helen F. Conover. Washington, 1942. 89 p.
A useful list of books and articles (1,265 items) for the period before 1942.

Serials

Note The following titles represent only a small selection among the many periodicals published. For more comprehensive bibliographic coverage, see Part I, ' Serials Lists ' and p. 25.

1372 Académie des Sciences Coloniales. *Comptes Rendus des Séances: Communications.* 1922/23-1941. Paris, Irregular. Continued in *Comptes Rendus des Séances,* 1941-46; *Comptes Rendus Mensuels des Séances,* 1947-57.
Continued under the Académie's new name (see next entry).

1373 Académie des Sciences d'Outre-Mer. *Comptes Rendus Mensuels des Séances.* 1957- . Paris.
See also preceding entry. Important for scholarly articles and reviews.

1374 *L'Afrique française: Bulletin du Comité de l'Afrique française et du Comité du Maroc.* 1891-1960. Paris, Comité de l'Afrique française. Bimonthly.
Most valuable journal. From time to time they printed supplements, *Renseignements Coloniaux.* These were reports of all kinds: reproduction of debates, missions of inquiry, travellers' accounts, speeches of local governors, etc.

1375 *Annales de Géographie.* 1891- . Paris, A. Colin. Quarterly.
From January 1941 onwards, issued as the *Bulletin* of the Société de Géographie.

1376 *Armée, marine, colonies.* Paris, 1899-1928. See also *L'armée coloniale.* Paris, 1891-1910.

1377 *Cahiers d'Etudes Africaines.* no. 1- . Jan. 1960- . Paris, Mouton. Quarterly.
This journal, edited by the Ecole Pratique des Hautes Etudes at the University of Paris (6e Section, Sciences Economiques et Sociales), is spoken of as the French counterpart of the *Journal of Modern African Studies.* Its essays and notes, on a high level of scholarship and authoritativeness, are concerned with the ethnology, sociology, history, and economic and cultural aspects of modern Africa, in particular with the French-speaking countries.

1378 *Cahiers d'Outre-Mer: Revue de géographie de Bordeaux et de l'Atlantique.* 1948- . Bordeaux. Quarterly.

1379 *Chroniques d'Outre-Mer; Études et Information.* 1951- . Paris, Editions de la Présidence du Conseil, La Documentation Française. illus., ports., maps. Monthly.

1380 *Communautés et Continents: Nouvelle Revue Française d'Outre-Mer.* n.s. v. 1- . 1909- . Paris. Quarterly.
The organ of the Comité Central Français pour l'Outre-Mer (41 rue de la

Part III: area guide (by colonial power, region and colony)

Bienfaisance, Paris 8e), published first (1909–50) as the *Bulletin* of the Comité, then from 1950 to 1958 (42 année–) as *La Nouvelle Revue Française d'Outre-Mer*. Its contents often include addresses made by members of the Comité.

1381 *La Dépêche Coloniale.* Paris. Daily and monthly illustrated edition. 1896– ?
Very important newspaper for colonial and economic matters.

1382 *Dossier on French Tropical Africa.* 1960– . By Raymond Lefèvre. Asinières (Seine). loose-leaf.
A serial consisting of groups of 'cards' (slips, 6 1/2"×8"), usually about 30 a month, giving biographical data regarding statesmen in the countries of French-speaking Africa, occasionally a few in English-speaking countries. The pink sheets, each with the name of an individual at the top, are interspersed with white cards showing government organizations. Provides important data for leaders during and after the colonial period.

1383 *Europe France Outremer.* 1923– . Paris. illus. Monthly.
This important monthly was published until 1958 with the title *France Outre-Mer*. Beginning as an illustrated feature magazine, the subject content has constantly increased in significance. Most issues are now devoted to a single theme or country, with a number of specialist articles. Since 1960, a spring issue – smaller in format than the regular review though thicker – has constituted a handbook of French-speaking Africa.

1384 France. Agence Générale des Colonies. *Bulletin.* 1908–34. Paris. Monthly.

1385 ——— Office de la Recherche Scientifique et Technique Outre-Mer [ORSTOM]. *Rapport d'activité de l'Office.* Paris. illus. Annual.
ORSTOM is an official research institution which sponsors technical and scientific research projects in the countries formerly part of overseas France. During its first few years (1949–54) it issued a helpful record of these researches, *Courrier des chercheurs* (1949– , Paris, 1956); in 1957 it began a serial *Sciences humaines outre-mer*. A new serial, *Cahiers O.R.S.T.O.M.: Sciences humaines*, was begun in 1963. The results of ORSTOM projects are published in part in mimeographed form, for limited distribution; one valuable series is printed for ORSTOM by Berger-Levrault, *L'homme d'outre-mer*. Important monographs on most former French African countries have been issued.
Some other major works include: *Bulletin scientifique* (no. 1– , 1951– , Nogent-sur-Marne – Seine); *Liste bibliographique des travaux, années 1958 à 1962* (Nogent-sur-Marne – Seine, 1964, 2 v.); *L'Office de la recherche scientifique et technique outre-mer et les recherches scientifiques et techniques en vue du développement économique et social en Afrique et à Madagascar* (Paris, 1962, 45 p.); *Organisation, activités, 1944–1955* (Paris, 1955, 182 p.).

1386 *Le Journal des Missions Evangéliques.* 1826– . Paris. Monthly.
Important missionary journal.

1387 *Marchés Tropicaux et Méditérranéens.* 1945– . Paris. Weekly.
This useful magazine reviewing commercial interests of France and French-speaking countries overseas was begun with the title *Marchés Coloniaux*; in 1956 it was changed to *Marchés Tropicaux du Monde* and in 1959 to the present form. The average issue runs from 40 to 50 pages, but each year there are several special issues, varying from some 150 to over 200 pages and each devoted to a single theme, country, or region.

1388 Marseille. Institut Colonial. *Etudes d'Outre-mer.* 1918– .
Roberts mentions this publication as an important one for basic statistics of

the colonies. See also Institut Colonial, *Le commerce et la production des colonies françaises*, 1896– .

1389 *Le Monde Colonial Illustré : Revue Mensuelle Commerciale, Économique, Financière et de Défense des Intérêts Coloniaux.* 1923–40. Paris. Monthly.
Superseded by *France Outre-Mer*. (1946–58).

1390 *Outre-Mer : Revue Générale de Colonisation.* 1929–37. Paris. Quarterly.

1391 *Penant : Recueil Général de Jurisprudence, de Doctrine et de Législation d'Outremer [coloniales et maritimes].* 1891– . Paris. Monthly.
A most valuable source for legal, political, and administrative matters.

1392 *Présence Africaine : Revue Culturelle du Monde Noir.* no. 1– . Nov.–Dec. 1947– . n.s. trimestrielle, 1953– . Paris.
The review *Présence Africaine*, edited by M. Alioune Diop, and the several series of books and pamphlets published under the auspices of *Présence Africaine* form the chief organs for the élites of French-speaking Africa. Contributions are largely by African writers, and the contributors during the decade of the 1950s included the foremost nationalist intellectuals. Typical books are Aimé Césaire, *Discours sur le colonialisme* (1955), and Albert Tevoedjre, *L'Afrique révoltée* (1958). Numbers of the review are often on a single theme, e.g., *Les étudiants noirs parlent* (Paris, 1953; Présence Africaine, no. 14). Catalogues of all publications are available from the Librairie Présence Africaine, 42 rue Descartes, Paris 5.

1393 *La Quinzaine Coloniale.* 1897–1939. Paris. Bi-weekly.
As the organ of the influential L'Union Coloniale Française, this review provided information on all the colonies and was a kind of clearing-house of information on colonial matters. *La Quinzaine* was developed by a leading French colonial theorist, J. Chailley-Bert.

1394 *Revue Française d'Histoire d'Outremer.* 1913– . Paris, Société de l'Histoire des Colonies Françaises. Quarterly, 1913–27; bi-monthly, 1928–33; quarterly, 1934– .
Title varies: 1913–31, *Revue de l'Histoire des Colonies Françaises*; 1932–58, *Revue d'Histoire des Colonies*.
Basic journal for all aspects of French colonialism. Authoritative articles by French officials and scholars. Indexes to the journal were published in 1933 (for 1913–32) and in 1958 (for 1933–58) by the Société. The Société also publishes books and pamphlets.

1395 *Revue Française d'Outre-Mer.* 1897– . 1914– . 1928– . Paris, Union Coloniale française. Frequency varies.

1396 *La Revue Indigène : Organe des Intérêts des Indigènes aux Colonies et pays de protectorat.* 1906–52. Paris. Monthly.

1397 *Revue Maritime. . . .* no. 1–636, 1861–1914; n.s. no. 1–236, 1920–39. Paris. Monthly.
Title varies: *Revue Maritime et Coloniale,* 1861–81, Apr. 1882–Mar. 1896. Superseded *Revue Algérienne et Coloniale*.

1398 Société de Géographie, Paris. *Bulletin.* 1822–99. Monthly.
Superseded by *La Géographie*, 1900–1939. Monthly.

1399 *Le Tour du Monde.* Paris, 1860–1914.
An important geographic and ethnographic journal with many articles on Africa, for example, Albeca, ' Au Dahomey ' (1894, 63 p.); Bertrand, ' Au pays des Ba-Rotsi (Haut-Zambèze) ' (1898, 47 p.).

Reference works

1400 Antonelli, E. *Manuel de législation coloniale*. Paris, Presses Universitaires de France. 1925. 420 p.
A summary handbook with a table of legislation in force in 1925.

1401 Augagneur, Victor. *Erreurs et brutalités coloniales*. Paris, Montaigne. 1927.
A book critical of colonial rule by a French politician and ex-governor-general of A.E.F.

1402 Blanchet, André. *L'itinéraire des partis africains depuis Bamako*. Paris, Plon, 1958. 209 p. (Tribune libre, no. 31)
This account of the pre-independence parties in French Africa has been rapidly outdated by events but remains a source for background study, especially for 1957–58. It includes a ' Petit bottin politique de l'Afrique noire ', with names and brief biographical notes on 30-odd leaders in early 1958. The author, a journalist, is *Le Monde's* expert on Africa.

Another reliable study, *Introduction à l'étude des partis politiques de l'Afrique française* (Paris, Librairie Générale de Droit et de Jurisprudence, 1959, 196 p.) by Léo Hamon, was reprinted from the authoritative journal, *Revue Juridique et Politique de l'Union Française*. A second part, by the same author, was published in 1961: *Les partis politiques africains* (Paris, 51 p.). Another important and complementary book is Ernest Milcent, *L'A.O.F. entre en scène* (Paris, Editions Témoignage Chrétien, 1958, 190 p.).

1403 Bouchaud, Joseph. *L'église en Afrique noire*. Paris, La Palatine, 1958. 189 p.
Treats of the effects of Africanization of the church after 1953. Also discusses the missionary encyclicals from 1919 on. See also Jean-Marie Sédès, *Le clergé indigène de l'empire français* (Paris, 1944). 2 v.

1404 Brench, A. C. *The novelist's inheritance in French Africa : Writers from Senegal to Cameroon*. London, Oxford University Press, 1967. 146 p. Bibliography: p. 135–146.

1405 —— *Writing in French from Senegal to Cameroon*. London, Oxford University Press, 1967. 153 p. Bibliography: p. 142–153.
Selections of untranslated extracts in the second volume complement essays in the first volume. Each volume has an introduction, a bibliography, and a biographical note for each author.

1406 Congrès Colonial National, 1889–1890. *Recueil des délibérations* ... Paris, Libraire des Annales Economiques 1890. 2 v.
The policy of assimilation emerged from this congress. Roberts, *History of French colonial policy* (no. 1367), gives the names of only the more important congresses, although they were held each year.

> Congrès Colonial International, Paris, 1889–1890. *Congrès colonial international de Paris*. Paris, A. Challamel, 1889. 382 p.
>
> Congrès Colonial International, 1900. No information on publisher.
>
> Congrès International de Sociologie Coloniale. *Rapports et procès-verbaux*. 2 v. No information on publisher.
> Valuable for discussions on labour questions and native policy.

Congrès Colonial, Marseille, 1906. *Compte rendu des travaux du Congrès colonial de Marseille*. Paris, A. Challamel, 1907–1908. 4 v.

The proceedings of the Congress provide material on a great variety of subjects connected with the French empire as a whole. Volume 1 dealt with the origins of the colonies, military questions and indigenous affairs; v. 2 covered economic matters; v. 3 provided data concerning public works and native administration; v. 4 centred on agriculture and forestry. This was the most important colonial congress after 1889 and represented a turning-point in colonial theory and the decline of assimilation as a policy.

Congrès d'Agriculture Coloniale Française, 1918. *Compte rendu*. 4 v. No information on publisher.

Provides full economic survey of the colonial empire.

Congrès du Régime Douanier Colonial, Marseille, 1925.

Compte rendu et rapports. Marseille, Institut Colonial, 1925. 566 p.

Valuable on tariff question and on the effects of assimilation in each colony.

1407 Culmann, Henri. *L'Union française*. Paris, Presses Universitaires de France, 1950. 135 p.

The best work on the French Union. For the evolution of the French Union see François Borella, *L'évolution politique et juridique de l'Union française depuis 1946* (Paris, R. Pichon et R. Durand-Auzais, 1958. 499 p.). Borella contends that changes in the French Union were intended to maintain colonial dependency, not to assist in decolonisation. The period 1946–1958 is also well covered by P. F. Gonidec, *L'évolution des territoires d'outre-mer depuis 1946* (1957–58). François Luchaire, in *Les institutions politiques et administratives des territoires d'outre-mer après la loi-cadre* (Paris, Librairie Générale de Droit et de Jurisprudence, 1958, 294 p.), analyses the new institutions created by the *loi-cadre* and contends that this was the beginning of some measure of self-government in each colony.

1408 Dareste de la Chavanne, Pierre. *Traité de droit coloniale*. Paris, 1931–32. 2 v.

Basic study of law and administration in the colonies. See also, by the same author, *Le régime de la propriété française en A.O.F.* (1908) for land policy.

1409 Decraene, Philippe. *Tableau des partis politiques de l'Afrique au sud du Sahara*. Paris, Fondation Nationale des Sciences Politiques, Centre d'Etude des Relations Internationales, 1963. 137 l. (Sér. C, Recherches, no. 8, May 1963)

Another work by Decraene is *Le panafricanisme* (Paris, Presses Universitaires de France, 1958).

1410 Delavignette, Robert. *L'Afrique noire française et son destin*. Paris, Gallimard, 1962. 207 p.

Discussion of evolution of black Africa from 1920 to 1962 and the problems of decolonization from 1946 to 1958 by one well qualified to speak. As a former Governor-General of French West Africa and from 1947 to 1951 Director of Political Affairs of the Ministry of France Overseas, Professor Delavignette has been among France's leading colonial thinkers. One of his important books is the 1948 *Service africain*, first published in English translation for the International African Institute as *Freedom and authority in French West Africa* (London and New York, Oxford University Press, 1950, 152 p.). See also his *Christianisme et colonialisme* (Paris, Fayard, 1960, 127 p.); and *Les vrais chefs de l'empire* (Paris, Gallimard, 1939).

1411 —— *Les paysans noirs.* Paris, 1931. New ed., 1946. 262 p.

A colonial novel by a then young commandant about the daily life of the African peasant. A most influential book for French colonialism – it inspired young men to enter the colonial administration and it directed the methods of administration of many commandants to promote the economic and social development of the people they ruled.

1412 Deschamps, Hubert J. *Les méthodes et les doctrines coloniales de la France, du XVIe siècle à nos jours.* Paris, A. Colin, 1953. 222 p. illus. (Collection Armand Colin, no. 281, Section d'histoire et sciences économiques) Bibliographie sommaire: p. 214–218.

By a former colonial governor and former professor of African history at the Sorbonne, who has written many books enunciating the enlightened views of liberal French thought. This short account includes in its chapters on the period from 1880 to 1940 comment on the foremost spokesmen of French colonial theory who foresaw an end to empire. A selected bibliography is arranged by period, the last covering the years 1940–50. See also Deschamps, *Les institutions politiques de l'Afrique noire* (Paris, Presses Universitaires de France, 1962, 126 p.; 'Que sais-je? ' no. 549).

1413 ——, ed. *Histoire générale de l'Afrique noire, de Madagascar, et des archipels.* Publiée sous la direction d'Hubert Deschamps. Paris, Presses Universitaires de France, 197– . 2 v., maps, illus., tables.

The editor tries to avoid both the ' heroic colonial hagiography of old, as well as anti-colonial stereotypes '. His contributors include distinguished Africanists from different countries, each of whom covers one section, each chapter being followed by a reading list. The first volume is entitled *Des origines à 1800*. At the time of writing, the second volume was being prepared. It was designed to go up from the early nineteenth century to the present, dealing successively with pre-conquest Africa, colonisation and decolonisation.

1414 Devèze, Michel. *La France d'outre-mer de l'empire colonial à l'union française, 1938–1947.* Paris, Hachette, 1948. 321 p.

Good interpretative historical account.

1415 Dislère, Paul. *Traité de législation coloniale.* Paris, P. Dupont, 3d ed. 1906–07. 3 vols.

Volume 1 gives a general account of colonial legislation. Volume 2 reproduces the documents. A standard account of colonial legal affairs.

1416 Duchêne, Albert. *Histoire des finances coloniales de la France.* Paris, Payot, 1938. 319 p.

Excellent account by a former colonial official of overseas finances. See also by Duchêne, *La politique coloniale de la France : Ministère des colonies depuis Richelieu* (Paris, Payot, 1928, 347 p.).

1417 Ehrhard, Jean. *Le destin du colonialisme.* Paris, Editions Eyrolles, 1958. 236 p.

A useful survey of post-war economic policies and developments in French Africa. The part played by public investments is treated in detail. See also Jean De la Roche and Jean Gottmann, *La fédération française* (Paris, 1945), for a study of the empire at war. De la Roche served with Governor-General Eboué. The text of Eboué's circular, 'La nouvelle politique indigène pour l'A.E.F. ', is reproduced.

French Africa

1418 *Encyclopédie coloniale et maritime.* Ed. by Eugène Guernier and G. Fromont-Guieysse. Paris, Encyclopédie de l'Empire Français, 1944–51. 15 v.
Basic reference work with separate folio volumes devoted to each of the French overseas territories, published in 15 parts during the between-war years. A revised post-war edition was begun in 1944 with v. 2, *Tunisie* (4th ed.). Parts relating to French sub-Saharan Africa are v. 4, *Afrique occidentale française* (1947, 2 v.); v. 5, *Afrique équatoriale française et Côte française des Somalis* (1950); v. 6, *Cameroun-Togo* (1951, 583 p.); and v. 7, *Madagascar et Réunion* (1947, 2 v.). Edited by two distinguished geographers and written by competent specialists, among them high-ranking colonial administrators, each volume presents a comprehensive set of essays on physical, economic, and human geography, history, administrative organization, and arts and culture of the territory in question, including statistics and extensive bibliographies. Volumes have been issued under various main titles, in addition to the above title: *Encyclopédie de l'Empire français*, *Encyclopédie de l'Union Française*, and *Encyclopédie de l'Afrique française*.

A new edition of this encyclopaedia, not available for examination, appeared under the title *Encyclopédie de l'Afrique française* (Paris, Editions de l'Union Française, 1952–53). Relevant volumes listed are *Afrique équatoriale française* (1953, 608 p.); *Afrique occidentale française* (1953, 2 v., 820 p.); *Cameroun-Togo* (1952, 550 p.); *Madagascar, Réunion* (1953, 2 v., 776 p.).

Another series of more popular surveys of the states formerly under French control, *Pays africains*, was published by the Société d'Editions Géographiques, Maritimes et Coloniales. Among the volumes in this series are the following: *La Côte d'Ivoire*, by Emmanuel Avice (1951, 94 p., illus., maps; bibliography, p. 93–94); *Le Dahomey*, by A. Akindélé and C. Aguessy (1955, 126 p., maps, tables; bibliography, p. 123–124); *La Guinée française*, by Maurice Houis (1953, 94 p., plates, maps; bibliography, p. 93–94); *Le Niger*, by E. Séré de Rivières (1952, 94 p., plates, maps; bibliography, p. 92–94); *Le Sénégal; Dakar*, by E. Séré de Rivières (1953, 127 p., plates, maps; bibliography, p. 126–127).

1419 *Etat actuel et perspectives de la recherche scientifique française en Afrique et à Madagascar (Colloque organisé par la 'Société Allemande pour l'Afrique' à Cologne les 2–4 Janvier 1964).* Paris, La Documentation Française, 1964. 84 p.
Includes papers by Raymond Mauny on French African historic research, Hubert Deschamps on the place of modern African history in French research, Marcel Merle on French research in African political science, Paul Pelissier on French geographical research in tropical Africa, General Vaucel on French medical research and the state of public health in tropical Africa, B. Gèze on geology, and G. Leduc on economic studies.

1420 France. *Journal Officiel.* Paris, Impr. des Journaux Officiels.
The highly centralized nature of French government is exemplified nowhere to better advantage than in the *Journal Officiel*, the component parts of which include practically all legislative material. Among these parts are *Débats Parlementaires* of the Assemblée Nationale, the Conseil de la République, and the former Assemblée de l'Union française (these all are daily during sessions); *Documents Parlementaires* of these bodies; *Lois et Décrets* (texts of laws, decrees, orders, etc. – daily), with monthly and annual tables; and *Textes d'Intérêt Général*, a selection from the *Lois et Décrets* published weekly and in special numbers. This is a primary source for historical study.

According to Roberts, *History of French colonial policy*, the *Journal Officiel* is the basic source for all questions on French colonialism of an official nature.

Part III: area guide (by colonial power, region and colony)

With all its components it is far more voluminous than the official journal of any other colonial power, since these include debates, parliamentary documents and outside reports in one publication with five parts published each day. The material to be found in the *Journal Officiel* includes:

(1) debates of both senate and house;
(2) budget reports—these were useful as an annual summary of events in each colony and as a statement of reforms on every subject. Some budget reports were of fundamental importance – for example, Herisse, 1906, on the Congo, and Violette, 1911, the major reform budget before World War I;
(3) reports and documents of parliamentary commissions with evidence;
(4) annual reports on each colony and reports of the governors;
(5) annual trade reports (for France and for each colony).

For supplemental information from the *Journal Officiel* see also *Recueil de Législation, de Doctrine, et de Jurisprudence Coloniales*. Paris. 1891– .

Among other tools relating to the French administration and useful in studies of former French Africa are the following: *Bottin administratif et documentaire* (Paris, Société Didot-Bottin, 166 année, 1963; Table alphabétique des noms); and *Encyclopédie permanente de l'administration française* (Paris, 30 nos. a year, loose-leaf), which includes *Les documents à jour* (current – replaced as they become outdated) and *Les documents périmés* (archives). The leaves are numbered 1–1400, and as one is withdrawn, it is replaced by another carrying the same number followed by a letter (e.g., 15, 15A, 15B). There are periodic *Tables de matières analytiques et alphabétiques*.

1421 ——— Bureau pour le Développement de la Production Agricole Outre-Mer. Publications. Paris.

Variety of studies on aspects of agriculture in African countries. Most valuable works.

1422 ——— Direction de la Documentation. Notes et études documentaires [series]. Paris, La Documentation Française.

This series includes valuable background surveys of individual African countries or questions. They are not entirely limited to former French Africa but occasionally include background material on other parts of Africa. The Notes et études are listed in the semi-monthly *Bibliographie Sélective des Publications Officielles Françaises*, along with the other series put out by La Documentation Française and the Direction de la Documentation.

1423 ——— Institut National de la Statistique et des Etudes Economiques. Publications. Paris.

A valuable service by the French government before and after independence which provided censuses, demographic and economic studies.

1424 ——— *Annuaire statistique des territoires d'outre-mer*. Paris.

1425 ——— *Bulletin mensuel de statistique d'outre-mer*. 1945– .

1426 ——— Ministère des colonies. *Annuaire*. 1899– . Paris, Charles-Lavauzelle.

1427 ——— ——— *Statistiques coloniales* . . . *1890–1914* (superseded by France, Office Colonial, *Statistiques du commerce des colonies françaises* . . . *1897–1914*).

See also France, Office Coloniale. *Statistiques décennales du commerce des colonies françaises (1896–1905)* . . ., ed. by P. Chemin Dupontés (Paris, 1910).

French Africa

1428 ‑‑‑‑‑‑ Ministère de la Coopération. Direction de la Coopération Culturelle et Technique. Division d'Information. *Guide pratique sur les républiques : Fédérale du Cameroun, Centralafricaine, du Congo, de Côte d'Ivoire, du Dahomey, Gabonaise, de Guinée, de Haute-Volta, Malgache, du Mali, Islamique de Mauritanie, du Niger, du Sénégal, du Tchad, du Togo, à l'usage des agents de la coopération.* Paris, 1964. 222 p. illus., col. maps. Includes bibliographies.

A guide-book to the geographic, social, economic, and political and administrative aspects of the French-speaking African nations. Brief data on education, medical services, the press, and communications are included. Each chapter concludes with tourist information and a short bibliography on the country concerned.

1429 ‑‑‑‑‑‑ Ministère d'Etat. *La politique de coopération avec les pays en voie de développement : Rapport de la commission d'étude instituée par le décret du 12 mars 1963.* Avec annexes. Paris, La Documentation Française, 1964. 136, 284 p.

Important report analysing the French policy of aid to developing countries and justifying its continuance. It was prepared under the direction of Professor Jeanneney and is generally cited as the Jeanneney Report. An English translation was published by the Overseas Development Institute in London. A balance sheet of FAC (Fonds de l'Aide et de Coopération), successor of FIDES (Fonds d'Investissement et de Développement Economique et Social), was issued in 1964 : Ministère de la Coopération, *Cinq ans de Fonds d'Aide et de Coopération, 1959-1964* (Paris, 1964, 71 p., tables), by Raymond Triboulet. Earlier a brief survey of FIDES appeared in an English edition by the French Embassy's Service de Presse et d'Information, *French Africa : A decade of progress, 1948-1958; achievements of FIDES, Investment Fund for Economic and Social Development in French West and Equatorial Africa* (New York, 1958, 40 p., col. maps, diagrs.). It includes a short bibliography giving titles of pertinent official documents. A very important book for understanding French aid policy is Teresa Hayter, *French aid* (Overseas Development Institute, London, 1966).

1430 ‑‑‑‑‑‑ Ministère de la France d'Outre-Mer. *Annuaire du Ministère de la France d'Outre-Mer et du Ministère d'État chargé des relations avec les états associés.* Paris.

1431 ‑‑‑‑‑‑ ‑‑‑‑‑‑ *Bulletin Officiel.* Paris. Monthly.

Published from 1887 by the Ministère des Colonies; from 1946–59 by the Ministère de la France d'Outre-Mer. See also Agence Générale des Colonies, *Bulletin* (1908–34 ? Paris, monthly – irregular), which superseded *Feuille de Renseignements*, also issued by the Office Coloniale.

1432 ‑‑‑‑‑‑ ‑‑‑‑‑‑ *Juris – classeur de la France d'outre-mer.* Paris, Editions techniques, 1940–59. 15 v.

Covers laws and regulations and appears to have been issued during the twentieth century.

1433 ‑‑‑‑‑‑ ‑‑‑‑‑‑ Service des Statistiques. *Annuaire statistique de l'Union française d'outre-mer.* 1938– . Paris, Impr. nationale.

Title varies slightly. Supersedes *Annuaire statistique des possessions françaises* issued by Service Coloniale des Statistiques. Issued in co-operation with Institut National de la Statistique et des Études Économiques.

1434 ‑‑‑‑‑‑ Ministère de la Guerre. *Mission d'études forestières envoyée dans les colonies françaises par les Ministères de la guerre, de l'armement et des colonies.* Paris. E. Larose, 1918–20. 5 v.

The chief of the mission was A. Bertin. Volume 1 was on the Ivory Coast, v. 2

on Gabon, v. 3 treats of the problems of colonial forestry in general, and v. 4 covers the Cameroun.

1435 —— Office de la Recherche Scientifique et Technique Outre-Mer (ORSTOM). *Office de la recherche scientifique et technique outre-mer : Organisation, activités, 1944–1955.* [Rapport présenté par Raoul Combes, directeur] Paris, 1955. 182 p. illus., maps (part fold.). Includes bibliography.

1436 —— Service des Statistiques d'Outre-Mer. *Outre-mer 1958 : Tableau économique et social des états et territoires d'outre-mer à la veille de la mise en place des nouvelles institutions.* Paris, 1959. 862 p. maps, charts, tables, diagrs.

Complete statistical handbook. Many of the tables include figures for the year 1957/58. Part 1 gives overseas territories in the world setting; Part 2, territories, plus Togo and Cameroun, 1947–58; Part 3, an analysis by subject as of about 1958, with tabular breakdown for individual countries.

Earlier works of the same character from this office were *L'économie de l'Union française d'outre-mer* (Paris, Sirey, 1952–54, 2 v.), a reprint from the professional journal *Revue d'Economie Politique*, and *Inventaire social et économique des territoires d'outre-mer, 1950 à 1955* (Paris, Impr. Nationale, 1957, 467 p., tables).

1437 Gaffarel, Paul. *Les colonies françaises.* 6th ed. Paris, F. Alcan, 1899. 564 p.

1438 —— *La conquête de l'Afrique.* 4th ed., Paris, Hachette, 1903. 318 p.

1439 —— *Histoire de l'éxpansion coloniale de la France depuis 1870 jusqu'en 1905.* Marseille, Baratier, 1906. 426 p. (Produced for the Exposition Coloniale de Marseille, 1906.)

1440 —— *Notre expansion en Afrique de 1870 à nos jours.* Paris, F. Alcan, 1918. 282 p.

Useful works by a French commentator, especially good on explorers and military.

1441 Gandolfi, Alain. *L'administration territoriale en Afrique noire de langue française.* Aix-en-Provence, La Pensée Universitaire, 1959. 199 p.

Good description of the structure of administration at the local and territorial level before the 1957 reforms.

1442 Girault, Arthur. *Principes de colonisation et de législation coloniale.* Paris, Société anonyme de Receuil Sirey, 1927–29. 5 v.

Three volumes deal with black Africa and provide a summary of events and colonial legislation as well as useful bibliographies. More analytical, interpretive works are by Louis Rolland and Pierre Lampué, *Précis de législation coloniale* (1931) and later under the title of *Précis de droit des pays d'outre-mer* (1949 and 1959). Both these volumes give a good historical account of the evolution of institutions and ideas. See also P. Leroy-Beaulieu, *De la colonisation chez les peuples modernes*, 2 v. classic work on France's need to colonize.

1443 Godfernaux, R. *Les chemins de fer coloniaux français.* Paris, 1911. 439 p. illus., map.

Standard work on railways in the French colonies in Africa. For information on land concession policy, see Robert Lenoir, *Les concessions foncières en A.O.F. et équatoriale* (Paris, 1936). For abuses of Africans by French companies, see Jules Saintoyant, *L'affaire du Congo, 1905* (Paris, 1906).

1444 Gonidec, P. F. *Constitutions des états de la communauté : Textes recueillis.* Paris, Sirey, 1959. 185 p.

Texts of the constitutions of the new states which had opted for the French Community in the referendum of September 1958. This specialist in the law of

France Overseas was responsible for two authoritative earlier works, both published by the Librairie Générale de Droit et de Jurisprudence: *Droit de travail des territoires d'outre-mer* (in collaboration with M. Kirsch, 1958, 743 p.; Bibliothèque de droit des territoires d'outre-mer, v. 1) and *L'évolution des territoires d'outre-mer depuis 1946* (1958, 126 p.). A more recent study, issued by the same publisher, is Gonidec's volume of 30 lectures on labour laws and legislation in the French Community and Madagascar, *Cours de droit du travail africain et malgache* (1966, 288 p.). See also his *Cours d'institutions publiques africaines et malgaches* (Paris, Les Cours de Droit, 1967, 406 p.).

A collection of 21 essays by Belgian, British, French, and Malagasy specialists, published under the direction of Jean Poirier, *Etudes de droit africain et de droit malgache* (Paris, Editions Cujas, 1965, 529 p., maps, bibliographies; Etudes malgaches, no. 16), offers diverse juridical, sociological, and ethnological studies and analyses. *Présence Africaine* in 1953 published a collection of articles on the labour question entitled *Le travail en Afrique noire*. See also Jean Poirier, *Les problèmes du travail en Afrique noire* (Geneva, 1958).

1445 —— *Droit d'outre mer.* Paris, Editions Montchrestien, 1959–1960. 2 v.
The first volume, entitled *De l'empire colonial de la France à la Communauté*, is primarily historical in approach. The second volume, called *les rapports actuels de la France métropolitaine et des pays d'outre-mer*, is devoted above all to the study of the *droit positif*. The author disclaims the intention of writing ' a learned work ', but aims above all at providing the more advanced doctoral student in law with a guide designed to put legal questions into a wider social, historical and political framework. Each chapter is prefaced with a reading list. François Borella, *L'évolution politique et juridique de l'Union Française depuis 1946* (Paris, R. Pichon et R. Durand-Auzias, 1958, 499 p.), is a much more technical work. For details of colonial laws and statutes during this period see France, Ministère de la France d'Outre-mer, *Juris-classeur de la France d'outre-mer* (Afrique du Nord excepté), Paris, Editions Techniques, 1948– , a multi-volume work in which laws were inserted in loose-leaf binders.

1446 Goyau, Georges. *La France missionnaire dans les cinq parties du monde.* Paris, Société de l'Histoire Nationale, 1948. 2 v.
In v. 2 the missions in Africa in the nineteenth and twentieth centuries are well covered. See also Bernard de Vaulx, *Histoire des missions catholiques françaises* (Paris, Fayard, 1951, 533 p.). Vaulx is especially good presenting the French domestic scene and in describing how African conditions determined mission work. See also for coverage of Protestant missions, Jean Bianqués, *Les origines de la Société des Missions Evangéliques* (1935). Also excellent for the Catholic missions of the Holy Ghost Fathers are Maurice Briault, *Le Vénérable Pére F.M.P. Libermann* (Paris, 1946, 580 p.); and Henry Koren, *The Spiritans* (Duquesne University Press, Pittsburgh, 1958, 641 p.). About half the Briault book treats the missions and places them within the context of French history and Catholic mission history.

1447 Hanotoux, Gabriel, and Alfred Martineau, eds. *Histoire des colonies françaises et de l'expansion de la France dans le monde.* Paris, Société de l'Histoire Nationale, 1929–33. 6 v. illus.
An illustrated semi-popular history designed to enlighten the reader concerning the creative achievements of France overseas. Volume 4 contains contributions, respectively, by Maurice Delafosse on Afrique Occidentale Française, by Auguste Terrier on Afrique Equatoriale Française, and by Martineau on Somaliland. The authors are concerned almost solely with the activities of the French from the beginnings of French colonisation. Volume 6, with numerous con-

tributed essays, deals with the French in the Indian Ocean and Southern Africa. The conclusion prophesies that France, which has already freed so many nations, will liberate all humanity.

1448 Hardy, Georges. *Histoire sociale de la colonisation française.* Paris, Larose, 1953. 268 p. Bibliography: p. 171–261.

Hardy, formerly director of the Ecole Coloniale at Paris, and previously an education inspector in Africa, played a major part in French colonial education by turning the Ecole Coloniale into the near-equivalent of the other *grandes écoles* at Paris. This survey covers colonization from the Ancien Régime to the end of World War II. His study covers all French colonies (including the former French possessions in North America) from the Francocentric standpoint. Hardy was an extraordinarily prolific writer who was interested in many aspects of colonial history. One of his best-known works was *Une conquête morale : L'enseignement en Afrique occidentale française* (Paris, A. Colin, 1917, xi, 356 p.).

1449 Harmand, Jules. *Domination et colonisation.* Paris, E. Flammarion, 1910. 370 p.

A critical attack on French assimilationist policy by a French colonial theorist.

1450 Haumant, Jean Camille. *Initiation aux finances publiques des territoires d'outre-mer.* Paris, Editions de l'Union française, 1952. 324 p. (Bibliothèque administrative de l'Union française, 1)

A thorough survey of financial arrangements in the overseas territories (the territorial budgets, the projects, material and personnel are also discussed).

1451 Leduc, Michel. *Les institutions monétaires africaines : Pays francophones.* Paris, Pedone, 1965. 397 p. (Collection du Centre de Recherches, d'Etudes et de Documentation sur les Institutions et les Législations Africaines, no. 6)

By a professor of economics at Dakar, this scholarly overall study gives a full account of the history of the ' banques d'émission ' and of the evolution of the franc zone, with changes in internal financial structures of the French-speaking states and the integration of the new institutions into world monetary systems. The second part reviews the monetary institutions of Equatorial Africa and Cameroun, French-speaking West Africa – with subsections on Mali and Guinea, which stand apart from the regional monetary union – and Madagascar. A short final chapter is on monetary institutions of the remaining French-controlled countries, the Comoro Islands, Réunion, and French Somaliland (now called the French Territory of the Afars and the Issas).

1452 Leroi-Gourhan, André, and Jean Poirier. *Ethnologie de l'Union française (territoires extérieurs).* Paris, Presses Universitaires de France, 1953. 2 v. 1,083 p. plates, maps. (Pays d'outre-mer, colonies, empires, pays autonomes, 6th sér., Peuples et civilisations d'outre-mer) Bibliography: v. 1, p. 441–468.

An encyclopaedic study, the first volume on Africa, the second on Asia, Oceania, and America. Volume 1, *Afrique*, begins with a general section, then treats the regions, and ends with an essay, ' Les sociétés négro-africaines '. There is a long bibliography as well as statistical appendices.

1453 Lombard, Jacques. *Autorités traditionnelles et pouvoirs européens en Afrique noire.* Paris, Armand Colin, 1967. 292 p.

An important political analysis of the main effects of colonialism on African political authorities. The author contends that most traditional rulers were undermined by colonial rule; by legislation which affected their power, by ideological changes which reduced their use of religious sanctions and by social and economic changes.

1454 Luchaire, François. *Droit d'outre-mer et de la coopération.* 2d ed. Paris, Presses Universitaires de France, 1966. 628 p. ('Themis': Manuels juridiques, économiques et politiques) Includes bibliographies.

An updated edition of a work published in 1959 under the title *Droit d'outre-mer.* An introductory analysis of colonialism, decolonization, and underdevelopment is followed by a study of the laws of the French territories. See also K. E. Robinson, *The public law of overseas France since the war* (London, 1954).

1455 Mangin, Charles Marie Emmanuel. *La force noire.* Paris, Hachette, 1910. 365 p., tables, diagrs., maps.

Mangin, at the time a lieutenant-colonel in the French army, later a general, wrote this influential book which proposed to strengthen the French armed forces against Germany by the creation of a great African army. The first part attempts to analyse the causes for the supposed decline of the French population. The second part gives a detailed account of Africans in the French army, their history, their contribution to French greatness, their special qualities, their present and future organization, etc. The author foresees the creation of an empire of 100,000,000 Frenchmen. The weaknesses in Mangin's project and the drain on metropolitan military resources occasioned by the French colonial army in the post-war period are discussed, for instance, in Judith M. Hughes, *To the Maginot line : The politics of the French military preparations in the 1920s* (Harvard University Press, 1971).

1456 Martin du Gard, Maurice. *La carte impériale : Histoire de la France outre-mer, 1940–1945.* Paris, A. Bonne, 1949. 464 p.

Account by a novelist of the French in Africa between June 1940 and September 1945. Each colony is covered. Good treatment of the personalities involved in the Free French movement (Eboué and Pleven, for example). Major work on the period, based on interviews.

1457 Méjan, François. *Le Vatican contre la France d'outre-mer ?* Paris, Librairie Fischbacher, 1957. 248 p.

Thesis is that the Vatican's policies in the 1950s were hostile to white rule in Africa in the hopes of maintaining Catholic influence in the non-white world. Richly documented work.

1458 Mercier, René. *Le travail obligatoire dans les colonies africaines.* Paris, Larose, 1933. 242 p.

Good account of forced labour in French Africa.

1459 Monographies ethnologiques africaines [series]. Paris, published for the International African Institute by Presses Universitaires de France, 1954– .

The French series of the Ethnographic Survey of Africa (see general note, no. 333). The individual volumes for peoples of French-speaking Africa are named under the separate regions and, where possible, countries.

1460 Mortimer, Edward. *France and the Africans, 1944–1960.* New York, Walker and Co., 1969. 390 p.

The history of French decolonization, written by a journalist with wide experience of France, and access to various unpublished papers.

1461 Moumouni, Abdou. *L'éducation en Afrique.* Paris, F. Maspero, 1964. 399 p.

Provides an historical sketch of education during the colonial period. A Marxist

Part III: area guide (by colonial power, region and colony)

view by an African. The book has been translated and published as *Education in Africa* (Praeger, 1968).

1462 Moussa, Pierre. *Les chances économiques de la communauté franco-africaine.* Paris, A. Colin, 1957. 271 p.

Good economic analysis showing among other things dependence of some sectors of the French economy on the African market. See also Jean Ehrhard, *Le destin du colonialisme* (1958), for an evaluation of post-World War II economic policy in Africa. Provides a good analysis of the impact of public investments. A communist interpretation of social change under colonial rule is Raymond Barbé, *Les classes sociales en Afrique noire* (Paris, 1964). Barbé is the French Communist Party's expert on Africa.

1463 Paris. Exposition Coloniale Internationale, 1931. [Publications]

Among the many publications prepared for the 1931 Exposition, the following are of lasting significance:

Exposition Coloniale Internationale de 1931. [Série géographique] Paris, Société des Editions Géographiques, Maritimes et Coloniales, 1931. 10 v.

Authoritative geographical studies. Those for Africa, sponsored by the Gouvernements Généraux, are *Le gouvernement général de l'Afrique occidentale française*; *La Côte d'Ivoire*; *Le Dahomey*; *La circonscription de Dakar dépendances*; *La Guinée*; *La Haute-Volta*; *La Mauritanie*; *Le Niger*; *Le Sénégal*; *Le Soudan*; *Territoires africains sous mandat de la France : Cameroun et Togo*; *Afrique équatoriale française*; and *Madagascar*.

France. Armée. Etat-major. *Les armées françaises d'outre-mer.* Paris, Impr. Nationale, 1931–32. 21 v. illus., plates (part col.), maps (including 5 portfolios of 63 fold. maps).

The contents include the following: v. 6, *Histoire militaire des colonies... Afrique occidentale française*; v. 7, *Afrique équatoriale française*; v. 8, *Madagascar*; v. 9, *La conquête du Cameroun et du Togo*; v. 10, *Les uniformes des troupes de la marine et des troupes coloniales et nord-africaines*, by Albert Depréaux (192 p., illus., col. plates).

This superlative multi-volume set gives the military history of the colonial possessions (9 v.), the service history of the colonial troops and their organizations, etc. (10 v.) and describes colonial leaders and heroes (2 v.).

An earlier Exposition Coloniale Nationale was held at Marseille in 1906. This was intended to publicize the development that had taken place in the French colonial empire since an earlier colonial exhibition held in 1900. The authorities in charge of the Exposition Coloniale Nationale of 1906 issued a 15-volume set of reports concerning the social and economic progress that had taken place 'since the age of conquest'. These reports are written by various authors and describe the natural features, the industries, the legal systems, and the administration of the French empire. The series culminates in a three-volume survey entitled *Les colonies françaises au début du XXe siècle*. The entire set was published by Baratier at Marseille between 1905 and 1906.

1464 Poquin, Jean J. *Les relations économiques extérieures des pays d'Afrique noire de l'Union française, 1925–1955.* Paris, Librairie A. Colin, 1957. 297 p. (Centre d'Etudes Economiques, Etudes et mémoires, no. 37) Bibliography: p. 289–291.

An economic analysis that deplores the nature of the dual economy in which

298

Europeans control the key positions. The author places his hope in rural Africa, and in what he regards as a balanced form of industrialization. The first part of the book deals with the commercial relations between French Africa and the world at large; the second part discusses the financial contacts between French Africa and the rest of the world. There is a wealth of statistical information.

1465 Priestley, Herbert Ingram. *France overseas: A study of modern imperialism.* New York, D. Appleton-Century Co., 1938. 463 p.

A good general history of French imperialism from 1800 to 1935.

1466 Régismanset, C. *Questions coloniales, 1900–1912.* 1 ser., *Questions coloniales, 1912–1919.* 2 v. Paris, E. Larose, 1912–23.

Useful summaries of changes and rationale of colonial policy by an official of the Ministry of Colonies.

1467 Roberts, Stephen H. *History of French colonial policy, 1870–1925.* London, P. S. King, 1929. 2 v. Reprint: New York, Archon Books, 1963. xvi, 741 p. Bibliography: p. 685–736.

Standard work on French administrative theory and practice in France's dependent territories, by an Australian historian. Appendices include a list of the chief colonial officers and an extensive bibliography.

1468 Rolland, Louis, et Pierre Lampué. *Droit d'outre-mer.* 3d ed. by Lampué. Paris, Dalloz, 1959. 459 p.

Good for all aspects of government and administration in French Africa. See also by Rolland, *Précis de droit administratif* (11th ed., Paris, Dalloz, 1957, 643 p.); Luchaire (no. 1454); Borella, *L'évolution politique* (no. 1445); and Gonidec (nos. 1444 and 1445).

1469 Rouard de Card, Edgard. *Traités de délimitation concernant l'Afrique française.* Paris, A. Pedone, 1910. 198 p.

1470 ——— *Supplément (1910–1913).* Paris, A. Pedone, 1913.

1471 ——— *Les traités de protectorat conclus par la France en Afrique, 1870–1895.* Paris, A. Pedone, 1897. 237 p.

Useful compilations of treaties; some are reproduced in appendices.

1472 Runner, Jean. *Les droits politiques des indigènes des colonies.* Paris, E. Larose, 1927. 158 p.

Useful account of impact of French rule on African political rights, especially under the *indigénat*.

1473 Saint-Maur, Thomas (pseud. Thomassin, Maurice). *Matho, soldat colonial 1892–1926.* Paris, Editions Witho, 1946. 2 v.

Interesting survey of the principal military campaigns in Africa.

1474 Salacuse, Jeswald W. *An introduction to law in French-speaking Africa.* v. 1, *Africa south of the Sahara.* Charlottesville, Va., Michie, 1969.

Useful for background on law and legal institutions during the colonial period.

1475 Sarraut, Albert. *La mise en valeur des colonies françaises.* Paris. Payot, 1923. 659 p.

Important book by a colonial official on the theory of the value of developing the colonies for France and world interests. It gives a detailed analysis of each colony and provides the documentation for the Sarraut Plan adopted by parliament. Excellent maps and useful as well as hard-to-come-by statistics.

1476 Soras, Alfred de. *Relations de l'Eglise et de l'Etat dans les pays d'Afrique francophone: Vues prospectives.* Tours, Mame, 1963. 156 p. (Esprit et mission)

A compact study of relations between the Catholic church and the state in

Part III: area guide (by colonial power, region and colony)

French-speaking Africa, along with a consideration of possible meeting-points between the two forces in independent black Africa. For an anti-clerical view of the topic, see no. 1457, François Méjan, *Le Vatican contre la France d'outre-mer?*

1477 Suret-Canale, Jean. *Afrique noire, occidentale et centrale.* Paris, Editions Sociales. 2 v. (La culture et les hommes)

> v. 1, *Géographie, civilisation, histoire.* 2d ed., rev. 1961. 321 p. illus., maps.

> v. 2, *L'ère coloniale (1900–1945).* 1964. 637 p. illus., maps, tables.

The writer, a geographer who had taught in Senegal, studied African history and problems from a Marxist point of view. Volume 1, first published in 1958, is an outline of physical and human geography and history up to 1900, heavily documented with footnotes and a long bibliography (2d ed., p. 273–313). Volume 2, published in 1964, brings the record up to 1945 and is centred on economic, social and political aspects. The bibliography, p. 601–616, does not repeat works listed in v. 1. Published in English as *The colonial era in French West and Central Africa* (London, Hurst, 1970, 550 p.).

1478 Union Coloniale Française. *Le domaine colonial français.* Paris, Editions du Cygne, 1929–1930, 4 v., illus., tables, maps.

A collaborative study with contributions from writers such as Sir Hesketh Bell, Georges Hardy, Jean Méniaud, and others. The book was produced under the joint auspices of the Union Coloniale and an official committee comprising numerous ministers and senior colonial officials. The first volume provides a general introduction concerning the history, administration and economic development of the colonies. The second volume covers North Africa and ' black ' Africa. The third volume deals with Madagascar, Somaliland, and the French Pacific colonies. The fourth volume provides data concerning economic development, indigenous art, medicine in the colonies, the colonial commerce, and the colonial administrative career structure. A conclusion written by Albert Sarraut lauds the French colonial achievements.

1479 Viard, René. *La fin de l'empire colonial français.* Paris, G. P. Maisonneuve et Larose, 1963. 160 p.

A good survey of the French Union from 1944 to the 1960s and independence.

FRENCH WEST AFRICA
(AFRIQUE OCCIDENTALE FRANÇAISE)

Note The colonies included in the Federation of French West Africa were Dahomey, Guinea, Ivory Coast, Mauritania, Niger, Senegal, Soudan, Togo, and Upper Volta.

Atlas

1480 Institut Français [Fondamental] d'Afrique Noire (IFAN). *International atlas of West Africa. Atlas international de l'Ouest africain.* Dakar, 1965– .
An impressive undertaking, which is appearing in separate folio sheets, to be bound in a book of maps opening to a size of 21×30 inches. It was begun in 1964 under the auspices of CSA (now absorbed by OAU/STRC – Organization of African Unity/Scientific, Technical and Research Commission) and will comprise about 48 separate maps, prepared by a team of experts directed by

Professor Théodore Monod. The basic scale is 1:5,000,000, though a few of the maps – notably those of relief and population – vary to 1:2,500,000. The first part will contain maps of environment, situation of West Africa in relation to the world, relief, geology, geomorphology, pedology, climate, and density of population. Part 2 will include maps of history, languages or civilization, industrial development, town planning, etc. Aerial photographs have been extensively utilized. See also *Cartes ethno-démographiques de l'Afrique occidentale*, prepared by G. Brasseur and G. Savonnet, respectively, for north and south (Dakar, 1960, 34 p., 4 maps).

For a description of IFAN, see no. 1506.

Bibliographies

Note The following bibliographies for French-speaking West Africa are with few exceptions the only general bibliographies available for the individual countries. Under the country headings from Dahomey to Upper Volta, cross-reference is indicated to this subsection. See also no. 1364n.

1481 Blaudin de Thé, Bernard, ed. *Essai de bibliographie du Sahara français et des régions avoisinantes.* 2d ed. Ed. with the assistance of the Organisation Commune des Régions Sahariennes. Paris, Arts et Métiers Graphiques, Librairie C. Klinksieck, 1960. 258 p.

For commentary on this work, see no. 1596 under Mauritania.

1482 Bovy, L., abbé. *Bibliographie du mouvement syndical ouest-africain d'expression française.* Bruxelles, CEDESA, 1965. 113 p. (Enquêtes bibliographiques, no. 14)

See no. 589 for note on the CEDESA series. The present work is an extensive examination of literature on all phases of the labour movement in French-speaking Africa. Most of the 518 entries are annotated. Arrangement is alphabetical by author; there is a classified subject index.

1483 Brasseur, Paule, and Jean-François Maurel. *Les sources bibliographiques de l'Afrique de l'Ouest d'expression française.* Dakar, 1967. 48 p. processed.

Although called a 'preliminary survey', this monograph is an essential bibliographical survey of the former French West African Federation and the states that once made up AOF. The authors (the distinguished bibliographer of Mali, Mme Brasseur, and the outstanding archivist, M. Maurel) survey first the federation-wide learned societies (their history, series published, etc.), government publications, and then essential sources by subject. Each country is treated in the same manner. Hundreds of entries are analysed and the starting dates and change of titles and structure for learned societies, journals, and government series are given. Articles as well as books and monographs are analysed. For a more recent and expanded version, see no. 1484.

1484 —— *Les sources bibliographiques de l'Afrique de l'ouest et de l'Afrique équatoriale d'expression française.* Dakar, Bibliothèque de l'Université de Dakar, 1970. 87 p.

The essential bibliographical survey of A.O.F. and A.E.F. The authors (Mme Brasseur, the distinguished bibliographer of Mali, and F. Maurel, the outstanding archivist of Senegal) survey first the federations and then each country in the federation. Each unit is treated in the same manner (by learned societies, government official gazettes, periodicals, bibliographies and essential sources by subject).

301

Part III: area guide (by colonial power, region and colony)

1485 Clozel, François. *Bibliographie des ouvrages relatifs à la Sénégambie et au Soudan occidental.* Paris, 1891. 60 p. (1,200 entries)
Appeared serially in the *Revue de Géographie* (July–Dec. 1890, Jan.–June 1891, July–Dec. 1891).

1486 Joucla, Edmond A. *Bibliographie de l'Afrique occidentale française.* Prepared with the assistance of the government of French West Africa and M. Maupoil. Paris, Société d'Editions Géographiques, Maritimes et Coloniales, 1937. 704 p. (Bibliographie générale des colonies françaises, by G. Grandidier and E. Joucla)
Basic to any study of French West Africa that involves background material, this huge bibliography appeared in an officially sponsored series begun shortly before World War II. Joucla cites almost 1,700 maps and charts of AOF. His references include books, papers, official documents (without distinction from unofficial material), and select periodical articles. The arrangement is alphabetical, with several subject indexes.

1487 Martonne, Edouard de. *Inventaire méthodique des cartes et croquis, imprimé et manuscrits, relatifs à l'Afrique occidentale existant au Gouvernement Général de l'A.O.F. à Dakar.* Laval, 1926. xvi, 138 p.
Valuable source containing 1,250 entries.

1488 Mauny, Raymond. 'Les recherches archéologiques et historiques en Afrique occidentale d'expression française de 1957 à 1961'. *Bulletin de l'IFAN*, ser. B, v. 24, nos. 1–2, Jan.–Apr. 1962: 279–298.
In this article the state of research is examined and a two-part bibliography is presented on tradition, legend, and history of the area within present French-speaking West Africa, including the Sahara.

1489 Paris-Leclerc, L. *Tables chronologiques et alphabétiques des actes métropolitains et locaux promulgés dans la colonie du Sénégal et dépendances, le Soudan français et les établissements français de la côte occidentale d'Afrique.* Melun, 1903. 872, lii p. (7,000 entries)

1490 —— *Compléments et continuation du premier jusqu'en 1902.* Goreé, Impr. du Gouv., 1926.

1491 —— *Compléments et continuation du 1903–1922.* Goreé, Impr. du Gouv., 1927.

1492 Société d'Etudes et de Réalisations Economiques et Sociales dans l'Agriculture. *Eléments de documentation sur l'Afrique occidentale.* Dakar, SERESA, 1959. 8 fasc. processed.
Eight partially annotated bibliographies on the rural economy of former French West Africa, each fascicle and its entries being allotted the code number employed by the Service Mécanigraphique de l'AOF. Each fascicle has two main sections – 'important documents' and 'other documents' – with several subdivisions, and references are to processed materials issued by various technical services of the administrations, to printed works, and to periodical articles. The eight fascicles are as follows: no. 1, *Sénégal* (60 l.; 281 entries); no. 2, *Mauritanie* (44 l.; 243 entries); no. 3, *Soudan* (65 l., 277 entries); no. 5, *Côte d'Ivoire* (76 l.; 250 entries); no. 6, *Haute-Volta* (15 l.; 87 entries); no. 7, *Dahomey* (48 l.; 238 entries); no. 8, *Niger* (21 l.; 84 entries); no. 9, *Afrique occidentale* (195 l.; 886 entries). There is no fascicle on Guinea.

1493 Tuaillon, Jean Louis Georges. *Bibliographie critique de l'Afrique occidentale française.* Paris, Lavauzelle, 1936. about 50 p.
Heavily annotated list prepared as a thesis by an artillery officer. Arrangement

302

is by subject – history, juridical works, geography and maps, etc., with further breakdown under history. The works, mostly of the 1920s and 1930s, are arranged chronologically in each section. Besides the hundred or so critically reviewed books there is a ' Bibliographie supplémentaire' in two parts: books and pamphlets (over 400 titles) and a short listing of important periodicals and articles in journals (p. 46–48).

1494 U.S. Library of Congress. General Reference and Bibliography Division. *French-speaking West Africa : A guide to official publications.* Comp. by Julian W. Witherell. Washington, 1967. xii, 201 p.

The guide is a greatly expanded revision of *Official publications of French West Africa, 1946–1958* (1960, 88 p.), compiled by Helen F. Conover, then also of the African Section. The new bibliography contains 2,431 entries listing published government records from the mid-19th century through early 1967. Following a listing of publications on French West Africa, arrangement is by country, and there are author and subject indexes. Included also are selected League of Nations and U.N. publications, and French documents on the area.

Serials

1495 *Afrique-Documents.* 1945– . Dakar. Bi-monthly.

Published from 1954 to February 1960 as *Savoir pour Agir : Bulletin du Centre Culturel Daniel Brottier.* It is a significant politico-social journal, including articles, texts of occasional documents, and a section of chronology, 'Ephémérides de l'Ouest africain'. A supplement, *Dossiers Africains*, is published irregularly, e.g., no. 1, *Médecine sociale au Sénégal*, by Drs. M. Sankalé and P. Pène.

1496 *Annales Africaines.* 1954– . Dakar, Faculté de Droit et des Sciences Economiques, Université de Dakar. Annual.

Although articles tend to be concentrated on West Africa, there is an attempt to cover all of Africa and a variety of subjects: the Organisation Commune Africaine et Malgache, the marriage rights of women in the Ivory Coast, monetary systems in West Africa, a social security system for Africans.

1497 *Afrique Nouvelle.* 1948– . Dakar. Weekly.

The leading newspaper of French-speaking West Africa after World War II.

1498 Banque Centrale des Etats de l'Afrique de l'Ouest. *Notes d'Information et Statistiques.* Paris. tables, graphs. Monthly.

This extremely useful serial publication comes in the form of separate leaflets in an overall cover. The fascicles are in part articles on specific financial and economic questions, in part bibliographic. The two bibliographical fascicles are printed in the form often used by French services – reproductions of catalogue cards adapted for clipping and filing. The first section contains cards for books and articles on general subjects, slanted towards economics; the second, ' Répertoire législatif ', has analytic cards for all important laws of the various states. The fascicles ' Indicateurs économiques' and ' Statistiques' have many graphs and tables.

The Banque Centrale also publishes occasional monographic studies, e.g., *Comptes économiques : Togo, 1956–1957–1958* (Paris, 1961, 278 p.), and *Sigles ouest africains d'hier et d'aujourd'hui : Contribution à l'entendement de l'Afrique de l'Ouest* (1959, 104 p.), outdated but useful, including acronyms for French and British institutions, companies, etc.

Part III: *area guide* (*by colonial power, region and colony*)

1499 ——— *Rapport d'activité.* Paris. illus., tables, charts. Annual.
Agriculture, mineral resources, foreign aid, exports of coffee, cocoa, cotton, etc., are among numerous topics discussed. There are numerous tables and charts.

1500 French West Africa. *Journal Officiel de l'Afrique Occidentale Française.* nos. 1–3049. 1905–59. Gorée, 1905–40; Rufisque, 1941–59. tables. Weekly.
The *journaux officiels* of the French-speaking states of Africa, like the French models, include all legislation in addition to official information in many fields. *Lois, décrets,* etc., do not go into effect until their publication in the *Journal Officiel.* For other official publications of the former AOF, see the Library of Congress bibliography above, no. 1494.

1501 *Guid'Ouest africain.* 1948– . Paris, Diloutremer; Dakar, Agence de Distribution de Presse. illus. Annual.
A sketchy and journalistic annual report, published from 1948 to 1955/56 with the title *Guid'A.O.F.*

1502 Institut Français [Fondamental] d'Afrique Noire, Dakar. *Bulletin.* v. 1–15, Jan. 1939–Oct. 1953. Quarterly.

1503 Institut Français [Fondamental] d'Afrique Noire, Dakar. Mémoires [monographic series]. 1939– . Irregular.

1504 Institut Français [Fondamental] d'Afrique Noire, Dakar. *Notes Africaines.* 1939– . Quarterly.

1505 Institut Français [Fondamental] d'Afrique Noire, Dakar. *Série A : Sciences Naturelles.* v. 16– , Jan. 1954– . Quarterly.

1506 Institut Français [Fondamental] d'Afrique Noire, Dakar. *Série B : Sciences Humaines.* v. 16– , Jan./Apr. 1954– . Semi-annual.
The renowned research institute of French West Africa was created in 1936 and activated in 1938 with the appointment of Dr. Théodore Monod as director. In 1960 it was incorporated as an institute in the University of Dakar. A sketch of IFAN's history for its 25th birthday was published in *Notes Africaines* (no. 90, Apr. 1961). Since 1966 the name has appeared as Institut Fondamental d'Afrique Noire, preserving the familiar acronym but discarding the colonial label. Over the years IFAN has undertaken learned studies in practically all disciplines relating to the region – botany, zoology, oceanography, ethnology, archaeology, anthropology, sociology, linguistics, geography; only geology, which comes within the province of the Direction des Mines, is excluded. The monographic series Mémoires, which was begun in 1939, has included distinguished contributions in all these fields. A few recent volumes in the human sciences are separately analysed in the present guide. Besides the Mémoires, there is the monographic series Initiations et études africaines (variant title, Initiations africaines), shorter papers usually in a more popular vein than the Mémoires; there is also the series Catalogues et documents (nos. 1–14 titled Catalogues), describing the various collections of natural and ethnological materials gathered by IFAN and preserved in its museums in Dakar and local branches. The *Bulletin* of IFAN, a journal of scholarly contributions in the various disciplines, often of monograph length, is now published in two sections, *Série A : Sciences Naturelles,* and *Série B : Sciences Humaines.* The full list of IFAN publications is given on the inside of the front and back covers of each issue. The bulletin of information and correspondence, *Notes Africaines,* is also published quarterly, and this too carries on its back-cover pages the full list of the Institut's publications.
Until independence the chief institutions in the states of French West Africa were the local Centres IFAN (or Centrifans) in the individual capitals. Most of

304

the centres began a series of studies – *Etudes camerounaises, Etudes daho-méennes*, etc. – some of which have continued since 1960 in the same or changed style. They are named in the country sections that follow.

Reference works

1507 *Afrique occidentale française [et le] Togo*. Paris, Hachette, 1958. ccxliv, 542 p. maps (part fold. col.). (Les guides bleus) Bibliography: p. ccxxiv–ccxxxi.

Still useful for most matters aside from politics is this Baedeker-like guide to the countries of the former AOF and Togo, with a preliminary section on airlines, shipping, railroads, and roads and detailed descriptions of localities. The introductory essays on West Africa, its geography, economy, history and pre-history, missions, peoples, arts and crafts, languages, and flora and fauna, are by prominent scholars, headed by Professor Théodore S. Monod of IFAN.

1508 Alis, Harry [Jules Hyppolyte Percher]. *A la conquête du Tchad*. Paris, Hachette, 1891. 296 p.

This account of the French conquest covers not only Chad, but much of French West Africa. The author provides a good deal of material on various French ' missions ', and also on Franco-British relations in West Africa.

1509 Amin, Samir. *L'Afrique de l'Ouest bloquée: L'économie politique de la colonisation, 1880–1970*. Paris, Les Editions de Minuit, 1971. 322 p., tables. Bibliography: p. 311–318.

' Not an economic history of West Africa ', but a critique of colonialism which supposedly retarded economic development by smashing the indigenous African states, and thereby preventing the emergence of an indigenous ' comprador bourgeoisie '. In the first part of the book, the author provides a series of case studies. He outlines the main features of the Senegalese ground-nut economy, 1830–1870, the plantation economies of Ghana and the Ivory Coast; then he gives instances of enclave-type mining economies, of colonies whose development was blocked by the colonial impact, or whose reserves were not properly exploited. The second part discusses what the writer calls the impasse of colonialism and the inability of the colonizers and of their successors to solve the financial and endemic balance-of-payment problems that beset the region. According to Amin, colonialism led to the balkanization of West Africa, and to the creation of tribal ' micro-nationalities '. Even after independence, economic development remained modest; between 1960 and 1970 the GNP on an average increased by no more than 4·3 per cent per annum as against an annual population growth of 2·3 per cent.

1510 ——— *Trois expériences africaines de développement: Le Mali, la Guinée et le Ghana*. Paris, Presses Universitaires de France, 1965. 236 p. tables. (Etudes ' Tiers-Monde ')

In this study of the development of three West African economies, Mali receives the most detailed treatment. A brief introduction to the geography, natural resources and political and social systems of the three countries sets the scene. The first three chapters (p. 21–129) are devoted to Mali – its structure and evolution during the colonial period of 1928–59, its decolonization, and its 1961–66 development plan. The author then describes the economic development of Guinea, 1959–63, and the recent and projected (to 1970) development of Ghana, and in a concluding section analyses the significance for West Africa of the experiences of the three countries. Amin follows a Marxist approach.

Part III: area guide (by colonial power, region and colony)

1511 *Annales africaines.* 1954– . Dakar, Université, Faculté de Droit et des Sciences Économiques de Dakar. Annual.

Although articles tend to be more on West Africa, there is an attempt to cover all of Africa and a variety of subjects: political organizations, the marriage rights of women in the Ivory Coast, monetary systems in West Africa, a social security system for Africans.

1512 Bouche, Denise. *Les villages de liberté en Afrique noire, 1887–1910.* Paris, Mouton, 1968. 282 p.

A study of free slave settlements set up by colonial administrators in French West Africa (to provide unskilled labour for porterage, railroad and road building) and by the French Anti-Slavery Society in French West and Equatorial Africa and British Nigeria.

1513 Bourcart, Robert. *Le Grand Conseil de l'Afrique occidentale française.* 2d ed. Paris, Encyclopédie d'Outre-Mer, 1956. 246 p. Bibliography: p. 227–229.

Discussion of the formation, functions, powers, and economic role of the assembly in French West Africa which gave many Africans their first political experience.

1514 Bovy, Lambert. *La nature du mouvement syndical ouest-africain d'expression française.* Bruxelles, Académie Royale des Sciences d'Outre-Mer, 1967. 194 p. (Académie Royale . . . Classe des sciences morales et politiques, n.s. 35, no. 2) Bibliography: p. 187–194.

In four sections. First part contains background on French-speaking West Africa, the major social, economic, political facts. The second part is a history of the trade-union movement in French-speaking West Africa from its origins on the eve of World War II up to 1963. Part three concerns labour legislation, national and international, before and after independence and the influence of the International Labor Organization. Part four considers the trade-union movement as revealed through statements of its leaders.

1515 Capet, Marcel. *Traité d'économie tropicale: Les économies d'A.O.F.* Paris, Librairie Générale de Droit et de Jurisprudence R. Pichon & R. Durand-Auzias, 1958. 348 p.

A thorough treatment of the economy of A.O.F. and the impact of the French introduction of new consumption and production methods. Money economy, cash crops, urbanization, investments and infrastructure are all covered. The lack of economic integration in A.O.F. is criticized and the social changes brought on by colonial rule are discussed.

1516 Chailley, Marcel. *Les grandes missions françaises en Afrique occidentale.* Dakar, IFAN, 1953. 145 p. illus., ports., maps, tables. (Initiations africaines, no. 10) Bibliography: p. 135–137.

Recital of French exploration in West Africa, from the first establishment in Senegal in 1636 (Saint-Louis in 1659, Gorée in 1677) to the 28,000-kilometre inspection by air, from the Sahara to Dakar, to Zinder and the AEF, by a 28-plane air squadron under General Vuillemin in 1933. There are indexes of geographical and personal names, illustrations and maps. The bibliography cites the original sources.

1517 —— *Histoire de l'Afrique occidentale française, 1638–1959.* Paris, Berger-Levrault, 1968. 580 p. (Mondes d'outre-mer, Série histoire)

The first section contains introductory material on geography, religion, the influence of the past on the present, the African 'life style', traditional political systems, arrival of the European.

The remaining six sections relate the history of French West Africa from the first French settlement in 1638 in Senegal to the dissolving of the A.O.F. in 1959. A useful chapter covers the inter-war period and discusses administrative organization and social and economic developments as well as the efforts at pacification of the territory.

1518 Cosnier, Henri Charles. *L'ouest africain français, ses ressources agricoles, son organisation economique.* Paris, L. Larose, 1921. 253 p.

A detailed survey of the agricultural and commercial potential of West Africa by a colonial official and senator.

1519 *Coutumiers juridiques de l'Afrique occidentale française.* Paris, Larose, 1939. 3 v. (Publications du Comité d'Etudes Historiques et Scientifiques de l'AOF, sér. A, nos. 8–10) Bibliography: v. 1, p. 43–54.

Comprehensive study on customary law of the French colonies of West Africa, the first volume devoted to Senegal, the second to the Sudan, the third to Niger, the Ivory Coast, Dahomey and French Guinea. The Committee preceded IFAN as a centre for scholarly research regarding the AOF.

1520 Cuvillier-Fleury, Robert. *La main-d'oeuvre dans les colonies françaises de l'Afrique occidentale et du Congo.* Paris, L. Larose and Forcel, 1907. 264 p. Bibliography: p. 259–64.

Good military account of the conquest of French West Africa.

1521 Dakar. Chambre de Commerce. *Synthèse de la situation économique de l'ex-Afrique occidentale française durant la période de 1948 à 1958.* Dakar, 1959. 7 v. 1,455 l. tables. mimeo.

The seven volumes cover numerous problems of the economy, its products, transportation and communications, investments, and important export markets. A particular subject often involves more than one volume.

1522 Davis, Shelby Cullum. *Reservoirs of men : A history of the black troops of French West Africa.* Geneva, Imprimeries Réunies, 1934. 205 p.

Surveys French use of troops from Africa during the nineteenth century up to and including World War I. Abdoulaye Ly covers recruitment during World Wars I and II in *Mercenaires noirs: Notes sur une forme d'exploitation des Africains* (Paris, Présence Africaine, 1957).

1523 Deherme, Georges. *L'Afrique occidentale française : Action politique, action économique, action sociale.* Paris, Bloud, 1908. 528 p.

Useful early survey of A.O.F.

1524 Deloncle, Pierre E. *L'Afrique occidentale française : Découverte, pacification, mise en valeur.* Paris, Leroux, 1934. 461 p.

General introduction to the conquest of West Africa by the French, published under the auspices of the Gouvernement Général of French West Africa.

1525 Dia, Mamadou. *Réflexions sur l'économie de l'Afrique noire.* 2d ed. Paris, Présence Africaine, 1961. 210 p. (Enquêtes et études)

The noted Senegalese economist Mamadou Dia was Prime Minister of the new state from 1958 to December 1962, when he was arrested and imprisoned after an abortive coup d'état. In this essay, first published in 1952, he advocated a co-ordinated socialist organization of African economy free from European pressures. The second edition reprints the original together with several later addresses.

In 1957 Dia published a second influential work on general economic theory, *L'économie africaine : Etudes et problèmes nouveaux* (Paris, Presses Universitaires de France, 119 p.), and in the next year a particularized study, *Contribu-*

tion à l'étude du mouvement coopératif en Afrique noire (Paris, Présence Africaine, 1958, 62 p.). A politico-economic study, stressing positive neutralism for Africa, was also published in an English translation by Mercer Cook, *African nations and world solidarity* (New York, Praeger, 1961, 145 p.).

1526 French West Africa. *Journal Officiel de l'Afrique Occidentale Française.* Rufisque. 1905–59. Weekly.

The *Journal Officiel* printed the laws and regulations for the entire federation, for Dakar and for Mauritania (1920–59), which did not have its own official journal. Included in the gazettes were the speeches of the governors-general, before first the Conseil de Gouvernement then the Grand Conseil. Statistics and lists of government publications were also carried. See no. 1494 for the numerous publications of A.O.F.

1527 French West Africa. Comité d'Études Historiques et Scientifiques. Publications. 1921– . Paris, Larose.

This group has produced a variety of valuable monographs. See, for example, *Coutumiers juridiques de l'Afrique occidentale française*, no. 1519, above.

1528 Gallieni, Joseph Simon. *Mission d'exploration du Haut-Niger : Voyage au Soudan français (Haut-Niger et pays de Segon) 1879–1881.* Paris, Hachette, 1885, 632 p.

1529 ——— *Gallieni pacificateur, écrits coloniaux de Gallieni.* Paris, Presses Universitaires de France, 1949. 342 p.

The first study covers Gallieni's activities during the exploration and pacification of the Sudan, and the second covers his writing on military and administrative duties in the French Sudan and Madagascar.

1530 Gautier, E. F. *L'Afrique noire occidentale : Esquisse des cadres géographiques.* Paris, 1935. 188 p.

This book is richly illustrated and contains numerous maps. Important study on the geography, ethnography, and history of former French West Africa. Published as part of the following series: Publications du Comité d'Etudes Historiques et Scientifiques de l'AOF (sér. A, no. 4).

1531 Gautier-Walter, A. *Afrique noire. Terre inconnue. La croisière noire de la santé. Récit de la Mission Ocem-Laforge à travers l'A.O.F. Chef de la Mission : Raymond Souques. Avec préface de M. L. S. Senghor, député du Sénégal.* Paris, 1951. 238 p.

Excellent study of the state of health and the numerous medical problems in former French West Africa. Richly illustrated. Important material for the study of African medicine and the general conditions of hygiene and health.

1532 Gouilly, Alphonse. *L'Islam dans l'Afrique occidentale française.* Paris, Larose, 1952. 318 p. fold. map. Bibliography: p. 285–287.

The author, a French authority on Islam, first describes the country and people of the semi-arid Sahelian zone where the Muslim nomads of the 'white' north have met, clashed and mingled with the sedentary animist 'blacks'. The work is then divided into four main parts: the history of Islamization in West Africa from the 11th through the 19th century; the religious brotherhoods; the effects of Islamization ('corruption' of the Muslim creed through animist accretions, influence of Islam on black African ways of life); and French policy towards Islam.

See also the work by Froelich in Part II, no. 567.

1533 Goyat, Michel. *Guide pratique de l'employeur et du travailleur en Afrique occidentale.* Dakar, Editions Clairafrique; Paris, Présence Africaine, 1960. 798 p. illus.
A treatise on labour legislation and practice.

1534 Great Britain. Naval Intelligence Division. *French West Africa.* v. 1, *The federation*; v. 2, *The colonies.* Oxford University Press, 1939–44. (Geographical Handbook Series, B.R. 512a)
Excellent summary of information available at that time.

1535 Hargreaves, John D., ed. *France and West Africa : An anthology of historical documents.* New York, St. Martin's Press, 1969. 278 p.
A collection of over sixty translated documents (10 unpublished archival ones) to illustrate important themes such as the colony of Senegal, the Muslim revival, the French conquest, French rule, and the African reaction.

1536 —— *West Africa : The former French states.* Englewood Cliffs, N.J., Prentice-Hall, 1967. 183 p. maps. (Spectrum Book: Modern Nations in Historical Perspective Series) Bibliography: p. 169–173.
The author, professor of history at the University of Aberdeen, has contributed the best survey of the area yet to appear. His book covers the early history to the post-independence period of Senegal, Mali, Guinea, Mauritania, Ivory Coast, Upper Volta, Dahomey, Niger, and Togo.

1537 Kanya-Forstner, A. S. *The conquest of the western Sudan : A study in French military imperialism.* London, Cambridge University Press, 1969. viii, 297 p. maps. Bibliography: p. 279–288.
A detailed study based on both official archives and numerous private papers; this archival material is fully described (p. 275–278). The author, a pupil of R. Robinson and J. Gallagher, investigates the mainsprings of French military expansion during the latter part of the 19th century. His work deals not only with the history of the French impact on the Niger and in the Sudan, but also with French military and domestic policy during the ' New Imperialism '.

1538 Lavergne de Tressan, Michel de. *Inventaire linguistique de l'Afrique occidentale française et du Togo.* Dakar, IFAN, 1953. 240 p. maps (9 fold.). (Mémoires, no. 30) Bibliography: p. 25–45.
Comprehensive reference work, with detailed information as to localities where the various languages of French West Africa are spoken and estimates of the number of speakers from the French census of 1950. The bibliography for each language or group of languages includes texts as well as ethnological books and articles. There is an index of languages, dialects, and tribes.

1539 Méniaud, Jacques. *Les pionniers du Soudan, avant, avec et après Archinard, 1879–1894.* Paris, Société des publications modernes, 1931. 2 v.
History of the French military conquest of the Soudan. A basic work.

1540 Monographies ethnologiques africaines [series]. Paris, published for the International African Institute by Presses Universitaires de France, 1954– .
In the French series of the Ethnographic Survey, the volumes studying tribes of the states of former French West Africa are particularly hard to place in the individual countries, where the Sudanic, Mande, and Voltaic peoples are mingled without respect to boundaries. The following numbers relate to some of these groups:

> no. 1. *Les Bambara.* By Viviana Paques. 1954. xiii, 131 p. illus., fold. map. (Bibliography: p. [113]–119.)

no. 2. *Les Songhay.* By Jean Rouch. 1954. 100 p. illus., fold. map. ('Essai de bibliographie analytique': p. [68]–95.)

no. 3. *Les Coniagui et les Bassari (Guinée française).* By Monique de Lestrange. 1955. 86 p. illus., maps (1 fold.), tables, diagrs. (Bibliography: p. [77]–82.)

no. 4. *Les Dogon.* By Montserrat Palau-Marti. 1957. xii, 122 p. illus., fold. maps. (Bibliography: p. [97]–109.)

no. 5. *Les Sénoufo (y compris les Minianka).* By Bohumil Holas. 1957; reissued 1966. 183 p. maps, tables. (Bibliography: p. 173–177.)

1541 Morgenthau, Ruth Schachter. *Political parties in French-speaking West Africa.* New York, Oxford University Press, 1964. xxii, 445 p. maps, tables. Reprint: 1967, with corrections. Bibliography: p. 359–376.

A detailed study of the growth of political parties in the states of the former French West Africa. The major emphasis is on politics, but the first chapter explains the African social setting, and there are long sections on the economy. The region as a whole is treated in an analysis of French policy and African institutions and of the part given to West Africans in the French Parliament; then long chapters discuss the political developments in Senegal, the Ivory Coast, Guinea, and Mali, with brief consideration of Upper Volta, Niger, Dahomey, and Mauritania. The last chapter examines the trend towards one-party states. Useful appendices detail administrators and politicians and tabulate other political, social and economic data. The bibliography includes much primary source material.

1542 Panis, J. C. *Le chemin de fer de la Méditerranée au Niger.* Bruxelles, Editions de Vischer, 1956. 138 p. fold. map. Bibliography: p. 131–134.

Dissertation by a Belgian colonial administrator reviewing and analysing the question of the trans-Saharan railway, at that time projected as the Mer-Niger, to run from Morocco into Algeria and south through Mauritania and the Sudan, to meet the West African transportation system now operating under the Office du Niger, from the dam at Sansanding to the railway line at Bamako. The bibliography lists papers, articles, speeches, etc. There are few books on the subject, though the proposal goes back to the late 19th century, well before the Chemin de Fer Transsaharien study group was set up under the French Ministry of Public Works in 1928.

For a lively, if brief, discussion of this subject and a full bibliographic survey, see Max Liniger-Goumaz, 'Transsaharien et transafricain: Essai bibliographique', *Genève-Afrique*, v. 7, no. 1, 1968, p. 70–84.

1543 Richard-Molard, Jacques. *Afrique occidentale française.* 3d ed., rev. Paris, Berger-Levrault, 1956. 252 p. illus. (L'Union française) Bibliography: p. 227–234.

A highly praised introductory survey by the late chief of the Geographical Section of IFAN; original edition, 1949. The preface by Professor Monod, director of IFAN, speaks of it as the most satisfactory up-to-date synthesis for the layman of the many special studies on French West Africa.

1544 Robert, André. *L'évolution des coutumes de l'ouest africain et la législation française.* Paris, Editions de l'Encyclopédie d'Outre-Mer, 1955. 255 p.

Discusses the causes of changes in customary law and the impact on African law of French legislation.

1545 Schefer, C. *Instructions générales données de 1763 à 1870 aux gouverneurs et ordonnateurs des établissements français en Afrique occidentale.* Paris, E. Champion, 1921. 2 v.

1546 Spitz, Georges. *L'Ouest africain français: A.O.F. et Togo.* Paris, Société d'Editions Géographiques, Maritimes et Coloniales, 1947. 508 p. illus. (Terres lointaines)

By a former colonial governor, this is an excellent survey intended for a general public as well as for students. It covers country and people, history, administrative and political structure, social welfare, economic development, and wartime history. The French West African countries are considered as a unit, and there is a separate section on Togo.

1547 Thompson, Virginia McLean, and Richard Adloff. *French West Africa.* Stanford, Calif., Stanford University Press, 1957. 626 p. illus., maps, tables. Bibliography: p. 599–614.

Detailed, analytical survey by two experts; indispensable resource material for any research on the French-speaking countries of West Africa. The useful bibliography includes books, pamphlets, documents and significant periodical material.

A concise pamphlet by Philip Neres summarizing the political history was published several years later under the auspices of the Institute of Race Relations: *French-speaking West Africa – from colonial status to independence* (London, Oxford University Press, 1962, 101 p., illus.).

1548 Traoré, Bakary, Mamadou Lô et Jean-Louis Alibert. *Forces politiques en Afrique noire.* Paris, Presses Universitaires, 1966. 312 p.

A survey of the political evolution of Guinea, Ivory Coast and Senegal between 1944–1959.

1549 Wade, Abdoulaye. *Economie de l'Ouest africain (zone franc): Unité et croissance.* Paris, Présence Africaine, 1964. 371 p. tables. (Enquêtes et études) Bibliography: p. 357–366.

By a scholar on the staff of the Faculty of Law and Economic Sciences at the University of Dakar. This work is developed from a thesis at Grenoble in 1959, and the data studied are largely pre-independence.

Dahomey

Bibliographies

Note See also nos. 1483 and 1484.

1550 Nzongola, Georges. *Essai sur le Dahomey.* Bruxelles, Centre d'Etude et Documentaire Africaine, 1971. 41 p. (Cat. du CEDAF, 5)
Bibliographical essay.

1551 Silva, Guillaume da. 'Contribution à la bibliographie du Dahomey'. *Etudes Dahoméennes*, n.s. v. 3, no. 12, Jan. 1969.

Entire issue consists of da Silva's article listing authors G–Z. The bibliography is based on the collection of the Institut de Recherches Appliquées du Dahomey, the former IFAN centre. Listed by author are articles, monographs, newspaper articles and government publications. There is an index of broad subjects such as agriculture, ethnology, history. Some 2,400 entries are given. Authors A–F appeared in v. 2, no. 12, but this issue was not available for examination.

Reference works

1552 Akindélé, Adolphe, and Cyrille Aguessy. *Contribution à l'étude de l'histoire de l'ancien royaume de Porto-Novo.* Dakar, IFAN, 1953. 168 p. (Mémoires, no. 25) ' Bibliographie sommaire ': p. 163–168.

Monograph by two African scholars relating to the general and particular history of the former kingdom of Porto-Novo, now the capital of Dahomey, including details on the selection and coronation of the king and other aspects of court and governmental life, as well as a list of kings and chiefs from 1688 to 1941, with notes on their reigns. It is based on a work written in Yoruba by Akindélé Akinsowon, father of one of the authors, and published in 1914 under the title IWE ITAN AJASE. The long section on family and religious customs contains poetic translations of funeral chants. Appendices give a list of native words and a select bibliography.

There is also a survey by these two writers in the Pays africains series, no. 6, *Le Dahomey* (Paris, Editions Maritimes et Coloniales, 1955, 126 p., plates, map, tables). This may be compared with the official survey of the colony at the beginning of the present century, issued by the Gouvernement Général de l'A.O.F. for the Colonial Exposition of Marseille, *Le Dahomey* (Corbeil, E. Crété, 1906, 351 p., illus.). See also the chapter on Dahomey by Virginia Thompson in Carter's *Five African states*, no. 531.

1553 Cornevin, Robert. *Histoire du Dahomey.* Paris, Berger-Levrault, 1962. 568 p. illus., ports., maps. (Mondes d'Outre-Mer, Série Histoire) Bibliography: p. 533–556.

A massive history, based on oral tradition as well as archives and published sources. The long bibliography is arranged by chapters.

A more recent work by Professor Cornevin is *Le Dahomey* (Paris, Presses Universitaires de France, 1965, 128 p., maps; ' Que sais-je? ' no. 1176), a compact survey of Dahomey's past and present. Part 1 deals with the natural environment and the peoples, Part 2 with the pre-colonial period. The third and longest part is devoted to the colonial period, the coming of independence, the economy, religion and social and cultural evolution.

1554 Dahomey. *Journal Officiel de la République du Dahomey.* 1958/59– . Porto-Novo. Semi-monthly.

In November 1958 the journal of the new republic superseded the former *Journal Officiel du Dahomey*, which had been published under various titles since 1890.

For government documents of the past, see the Library of Congress, *Official publications of French West Africa*, no. 1494.

1555 *Etudes dahoméennes.* v. 1– . 1948–58, n.s. 1959(?)– . Porto-Novo. illus., maps. Irregular.

The publication of the former Centre IFAN du Dahomey, a scholarly journal that is occasionally issued in monographic form. Since independence the Centre has become the Institut de Recherches Appliquées du Dahomey (IRAD) and is issuing the *Etudes dahoméennes* in a new series (latest, Apr. 1966). A new series of Mémoires brought out its first number in 1964. Valuable for historical and ethnographic articles.

1556 Glélé, Maurice A. *Naissance d'un état noir, l'évolution politique et con-stitutionnelle du Dahomey, de la colonisation à nos jours.* Paris, Librairie Générale de Droit et de Jurisprudence, 1969. 539 p.

A history of politics and parties in Dahomey from 1944 to 1965. Important and rare party and constitutional documents are published for the years 1944–1959.

See also Souru M. Apithy, *Au service de mon pays* (Montrouge, 1957), a collection of Apithy's speeches and reports when he was a territorial leader and a deputy in Paris. For earlier period, see Joseph F. Reste, *Le Dahomey: Réalisation et perspectives d'avenir* (Paris, 1934). Reste was a colonial official in Dahomey. See also H. De Santi, *Du Dahomé au Benin-Niger* (Paris, 1945). Account by a colonial official who served in Dahomey in the 1930s.

1557 Grivot, René. *Réactions dahoméennes.* Paris, Berger-Levrault, 1954. 180 p. Bibliography: p. 179–180.

The author, a senior colonial administrator, provides a general survey that deals with education, military affairs, economic development, justice, native administration, missionary problems, etc.

1558 Herskovits, Meville J. *Dahomey, an ancient West African kingdom.* New York, J. J. Augustin, 1938. 2 v. 402, 407 p. illus., plates (101 part col.). References: v. 2, p. [373]–376.

Standard anthropological study of Dahomey by the late Professor Herskovits, who was one of America's foremost Africanists. See also Adolphe Akindélé and Cyrille Aguessy, *Contribution à l'étude de l'histoire de l'ancien royaume de Porto-Novo* (Dakar, IFAN, 1953).

1559 Lombard, Jacques. *Structures de type 'féodal' en Afrique noire: Etude des dynamismes internes et des relations sociales chez les Bariba du Dahomey.* Paris and La Haye, Mouton, 1965. 544 p. illus., maps, geneal. tables. (Le monde d'outre-mer passé et présent, 1st ser., Etudes, no. 26) Bibliography: p. [535]–540.

An interesting study in which the author attempts to show that while colonization was the most important factor in the social transformation of an African society, it was neither the only nor the first to contribute to modifications. Lombard analyses the tribal hierarchy and its politico-social organization. Finally, he focuses on the reactions and adjustments of the Bariba to colonization and on the renewal of initiative and the birth of a ruling bourgeoisie, concluding with comments on conflicts and social cohesion in an old 'feudal' society.

1560 Marty, Paul. *Etudes sur l'Islam au Dahomey: Le bas Dahomey, le haut Dahomey.* Paris, E. Leroux, 1926. 295 p. illus., fold. map. (Collection de la *Revue du Monde Musulman*)

The first section, on lower Dahomey, reviews ethnic groups, beliefs and rites, and the Islamic community. In the second section, on upper Dahomey, focus is on ethnic groups, Islamic circles, unwritten law, social institutions, animism, and 'witch-doctoring'. There are 12 appendices. For note on Marty, see no. 1661.

1561 Pays africains [series].

Le Dahomey (Paris, Editions Maritimes et Coloniales, 1955, 126 p., plates, map, tables). This may be compared with the official survey of the colony at the beginning of the present century, issued by the Gouvernement Général de l'AOF for the Colonial Exposition of Marseille, *Le Dahomey* (Corbeil, Crété, 1906, 351 p., illus.). See also the chapter on Dahomey by Virginia Thompson in Carter's *Five African states*, no. 531.

1562 Polanyi, Karl, in collaboration with Abraham Rotstein. *Dahomey and the slave trade: An analysis of an archaic economy.* Seattle and London, University of Washington Press, 1966, xiii, 204 p. maps. (American Ethnological Society, Monograph, no. 42) Bibliography: p. 195–200.

The last scholarly work of the noted economic anthropologist and economic historian who died in 1964. Polanyi traces the origins and historical and geographical background of one of the great West African kingdoms, explains the patterns of an *étatiste* economy with due emphasis on the role of social institutions, and discusses the gold trade, colonialism, and, especially, the slave-trade and their impact on the economy. He includes an incisive analysis of the complexities of the Dahomeans' trade with the French and the British – complexities arising partly from the fact that only the Europeans had a fully monetized economy.

1563 Tardits, Claude. *Porto-Novo : Les nouvelles générations africaines entre leurs traditions et l'Occident.* Paris, Mouton, 1958. 128 p. (Le monde d'outre-mer, passé et présent, 1st ser., Etudes, no. 7)

Sociological study of the changes in Dahomean society in urbanized centres as contrasted with traditional mores. The writer based his research in part on replies to a questionnaire.

1564 Tevoedjré, Albert. *L'Afrique révoltée.* Paris, Présence Africaine, 1958. 157 p.

Attack on French colonial rule by a Catholic Dahomeyan. He denies any significant contributions by the French. See also René Grivot, *Réactions dahoméennes* (Paris, 1954) for reactions of post-war Dahomey to French efforts at reform and modernization.

Guinea

Note   For specific references in other sections, see nos. 133, 1463, 1465, 1483 and 1484.

Bibliographies

1565 Du Bois, Victor D. *Guinea : The years before World War II : An historical sketch and a bibliographic index of 112 titles.* New York, American Universities Field Staff, 1962. 20 p.

1566 Kake, B. *Bibliographie critique des sources imprimées d'histoire de la Guinée publiées avant 1914.* Dakar, Université Faculté des Lettres et Sciences Humaines, 1962.

A mimeographed thesis.

1567 Lalande-Isnard, Fanny. ' Ouvrages publiés en Guinée du 2 octobre 1958 au 31 décembre 1963 '. *Recherches Africaines* (Conakry), nos. 1–4, Jan.–Dec. 1964: 167–169.

Publications concerning the Parti Démocratique de Guinée and those of the Ministère de l'Education Nationale, des Finances, du Plan, du Travail, etc., are listed, all of more than 49 pages.

The journal plans to publish in its first issue each year a national bibliography covering publications of the preceding year.

1568 Mengrelis, Thanos. *Bibliographie générale de la région de N'zérékoré.* Conakry, Institut National de Recherches et de Documentation, 1964, 55 p.

1569 Organisation de Coopération et de Développement Economiques. Centre de Développement. *Bibliographie sur la Guinée. Bibliography on Guinea.* Paris [1965 ?] 46 l. (CD/D/Bibl./2)

Emphasis is mainly on economic, political and sociological matters. Listed by subject are books, monographs, government publications, chapters from composite works, and articles. A list of Guinea periodicals concludes the work.

Reference works

1570 Ameillon, B. *La Guinée : Bilan d'une indépendance.* Paris, F. Maspero, 1964. 205 p. (Cahiers libres, nos. 58–59)
In 1958 Guinea alone chose independence from France. Chapters on the aftermath consider Guinea itself, Guinea and France, the economy, relations with other countries, and socialism.

1571 American University, Washington, D.C. Special Operations Research Office. *Area handbook for Guinea.* Prepared by the Foreign Areas Studies Division. Washington, 1961. xii, 534 p. maps.
Prepared under contract with the Department of the Army. The carefully presented factual information is in four sections, on sociological, political, economic, and military background. Bibliographies of seven or eight pages follow each section. See also L. G. Cowan, ' Guinea ', in Carter's *African one-party states.* See also no. 531n.

1572 Guinea. *Journal Officiel de la République de Guinée.* 1958– . Conakry, Impr. Nationale ' Patrice Lumumba '. Semi-monthly.
Supersedes the *Journal Officiel de la Guinée Française*, which had been published since 1901. For other official publications before independence, see the Library of Congress, *Official publications of French West Africa,* no. 1494.

1573 *Guinée : Prélude à indépendance.* Paris, Présence Africaine, 1959. 175 p.
This report of the Conférence des Commandants de Cercle includes the opening address by Governor Ramadier, an address by President Sékou Touré, a report of the Minister of Finance and of the Commandant de Cercle de Labé, and a section ' Naissance de la République de Guinée '.
The conference here referred to, held in Conakry in 1957, preceded Touré's repression of the *chefferies* and led to his personal control of the country which brought about the vote of ' no ' in 1958.
A combined issue for December 1959 and January 1960 of the serial *Présence Africaine* was devoted to ' Guinée indépendante '.

1574 Holas, Bohumil. *Le culte de Zie : Eléments de la religion Kono (Haute Guinée française).* Dakar, IFAN, 1954. 275 p. illus. (Mémoires, no. 39)
' Ouvrages cités ': p. 231–242.
An important contribution to anthropological studies of Guinea.
Another volume relating to Guinean tribes is in the French series of the International African Institute, Monographies ethnologiques africaines: Monique de Lestrange, *Les Coniagui et les Bassari (Guinée française)* (1955, 86 p., illus.; maps; bibliography, p. [77]–82).

1575 Marty, Paul. *L'Islam en Guinée : Fouta-Diallon.* Paris, Leroux, 1921. 588 p. illus., maps, geneal. tables. (Collection de la *Revue du Monde Musulman*)
The author first provides a historical background and then discusses Islamic communities and groups, the Moorish influence, Islamic doctrine and religion, education, juridical institutions, social customs, rites and practices, and survivals from the past. There are 34 appendices, including maps. For note on Marty, see no. 1661.

1576 *Recherches Africaines : Etudes Guinéennes.* n.s. no. 1– . Conakry, Institut National de Recherches et de Documentation, République de Guinée. Quarterly.
This new serial, launched under the direction of M. Jean Suret-Canale, has

Part III: area guide (by colonial power, region and colony)

superseded the former *Etudes Guinéennes* of the Centre IFAN de la Guinée, the volumes of which were published irregularly from 1947 to 1955.

The Institut, one of the major research centres in French-speaking West Africa, also issues an irregular publication, *Mémoires*. The first number is an index to the archives of French Guinea for the period 1720 to 1935, compiled by the former archivist, Damien d'Almeida: *Premier répertoire des archives nationales de Guinée: Sér. A–N, 1720–1935* (1962, 224 p.). The archives are housed in the Institut, which has a library of over 8,000 catalogued items, several hundred rare books and pamphlets on the slave-trade, and a limited number of official documents of the Republic.

1577 Suret-Canale, Jean. *La République de Guinée*. Paris, Editions Sociales, 1970. 431 p., tables, illus., maps. Bibliography: p. 401–422.

The author, a well-known historian and geographer, examines the development of Guinea from a Marxist point of view, with special emphasis on economic and social history. He begins his study with a geographical survey, discusses the colonial experience, the achievement of independence and the subsequent development of Guinea to 1968. The value of this study is enhanced by numerous maps and sketches. The author, who assesses the colonial experience largely in negative terms, concludes by saying that the salvation of Guinea must ultimately be achieved by mobilizing its own human potential. For an earlier solid history, see André Arcin, *Histoire de la Guinée française: rivières du sud, Fouta-Dialo, région du sud du Soudan* (Paris, A. Challamel, 1911, 752 p.).

1578 Touré, Sékou. *L'action politique du parti démocratique de Guinée* [series]. Conakry, Impr. Nationale 'Patrice Lumumba', 1958– . illus. (v. 10, 1963)

1579 ——— *Expérience guinéenne et unité africaine*. Paris. Présence Africaine, 1959, 566 p. (Leaders politiques africains)

1580 ——— *Toward full re-Africanisation (policy and principles of the Guinea Democratic Party)*. Paris, Présence Africaine, 1959. 108 p.

The speeches, weekly press conferences, and other papers of President Touré in L'action politique du parti démocratique de Guinée are published in large volumes of offset print. The 1959 volume was brought out in these editions by Présence Africaine.

Ivory Coast

Note For specific references in earlier sections, see nos. 1465 and 1494. See also nos. 1483, 1484, 1492.

Bibliographies

1581 Organisation de Coopération et de Développement Economique. Centre de Développement. *Essai d'une bibliographie sur la Côte d'Ivoire*. By N. Novacco. Paris, 1964. 122 l.

The bibliography is divided into monographs and articles, and under these are two alphabetical listings, one by author, the other (for anonymous works) by title. There is no subject approach. Most of the 254 monographs and 407 articles deal with socioeconomic problems in the Ivory Coast. One of the four appendices lists French organizations that have done work in the Ivory Coast.

French Africa: French West Africa

1582 Schwartz, A. *Etudes des sciences humaines en Côte d'Ivoire : Essai de bibliographie.* Paris, ORSTOM, 1964. 47 l. (Sciences humaines)

A systematic listing of works (including articles) arranged in three chronological sections under each main subject heading and subdivision (i.e., publications issued before 1965, from 1945 to 1960, and from 1960 through early 1964). The seven main headings are general works, history, demography, economy, sociology, ethnology, and linguistics.

Reference works

1583 American University, Washington, D.C. Special Operations Research Office. *Area handbook for the Ivory Coast.* Prepared by the Foreign Areas Studies Division. Washington, U.S. Government Printing Office, Dec. 1962. xii, 485 p. maps, diagrs.

Another in the series of country handbooks prepared under contract with the Department of the Army. Comprehensive background information is given on social, economic and political institutions and on national security in four main sections, each of which is followed by an extensive bibliography (up to 12 pages). A glossary is included.

1584 Amin, Samir. *Le développement du capitalisme en Côte d'Ivoire.* Paris, Editions de Minuit, 1967. 330 p. maps, tables, diagrs. (Grand documents, no. 28) Bibliography: p. [309]–321.

Covers population and employment, growth of agricultural production, regional and social division of rural income, growth of industrial production and transportation, social division of urban income, volume, efficiency, and financing of investments (1950–65), public finance, and balance of payments. There is a good bibliography. Written from the Marxist standpoint.

1585 Amon d'Aby, F. J. *La Côte d'Ivoire dans la cité africaine.* Paris, Larose, 1951. 606 p. illus.

By the former government archivist of the Ivory Coast, a well-known African playwright. In this book he has given background history and analysis of political, economic, and cultural progress in the country under French administration, particularly of the changes following the Conference of Brazzaville in 1944 and the formation of the French Union. His viewpoint is one of enthusiasm for the fusion of French and African culture.

Two of the author's later studies are *Le problème des chefferies traditionnelles en Côte d'Ivoire* (Abidjan, 1957, 51 p.; Mémoires du CHEAM, no. 2778); and *Croyances religieuses et coutumes juridiques des Agni de la Côte d'Ivoire* (Paris, Larose, 1960, 184 p., plates, fold. map).

1586 Atger, Paul. *La France en Côte d'Ivoire de 1843 à 1893 : Cinquante ans d'hésitations politiques et commerciales.* Dakar, Faculté des Lettres et Sciences Humaines, Université de Dakar, 1962. 204 p. maps. (Publications de la Section d'Histoire, no. 2) Bibliography: p. 11–18.

In this study of the early French administration the lengthy bibliography lists archives, documents and printed sources for 19th-century history.

1587 Duprey, Pierre. *Histoire des Ivoiriens.* Abidjan, Imprimerie de la Côte d'Ivoire, 1961. 233 p., illus.

A short popular history. Traces the development of the Ivory Coast from ancient times to independence. The author argues that 'the fusion of the indigenous peoples, undertaken by France in order to turn Ivorian into French citizens, has not been in vain ' and that ' the cohesion of the Ivory Coast nation

317

is no less real than that of ancient African kingdoms or of the young nations of Central Europe and Latin America '.

1588 *Etudes éburnéennes.* no. 1– , 1950– . Abidjan (etc.), Institut Français d'Afrique Noire, Centre de Côte d'Ivoire. illus. Irregular.

This scholarly series, usually monographic, e.g., no. 8, consisting of Marguerite Dupire, *Planteurs autochtones et étrangers en basse-Côte d'Ivoire orientale*, and Edmond Bernus, *Kong et sa région* (Abidjan, 1960, 324 p.), was suspended at the time of independence. The Institut has been replaced by a new research organization, the Centre des Sciences Humaines, which has a collection of about 6,000 books, pamphlets, and periodicals on Africa. As of 1967, publication of the *Etudes* had not been resumed.

1589 Ivory Coast. *Journal Officiel de la République de Côte d'Ivoire.* no. 1– , Dec. 6, 1958– . Abidjan. Weekly.

The *Journal Officiel* superseded that published semi-monthly from 1895 to 1958 by the government of the former French colony.

The Imprimerie Nationale also published the annual *Budget* and the *Journal Officiel des Débats* of the Assemblée. An annual volume of *Lois* is issued in mimeographed form by the Assemblée's Services Législatifs. See also no. 1494.

1590 —— Direction de la Statistique et des Etudes Economiques et Démographiques. *Inventaire économique et social de la Côte d'Ivoire, 1947 à 1958.* Abidjan, Ministère des Finances, des Affaires Economiques et du Plan, Service de la Statistique, 1960. 283 p. maps (part col.), tables, diagrs.

An impressive publication of the former colonial government, in handsome makeup, with tables exhibiting all economic and social factors. The previous edition was issued by the Service de la Statistique Générale et de la Mécanographie under the title *Inventaire économique de la Côte d'Ivoire (1947 à 1956)*.

1591 Joseph, Gaston. *Côte d'Ivoire.* Paris, Fayard, 1944. 254 p. Bibliography: p. 207–213.

The Ivory Coast became a French colony by a decree of March 10, 1893. This survey, combining history, ethnology, administration, and economic and social aspects, was written as a 50-year balance sheet.

1592 Marty, Paul. *Etudes sur l'Islam en Côte d'Ivoire.* Paris, Leroux, 1922. 496 p. illus., plates, map. (Collection de la *Revue du Monde Musulman*)

A thorough study of Islam and its influence and survival in the Ivory Coast. Arrangement is by three regions – coastal, forest, and savanna. Seventeen appendices are included. For note on Marty, see no 1661.

1593 Wallerstein, Immanuel. *The road to independence : Ghana and the Ivory Coast.* Paris and La Haye, Mouton, 1964. xiii, 200 p. chart, tables. (Le monde d'outre-mer, passé et présent, 1st ser., Etudes, no. 20) Bibliography: p. [179]–200.

Study of social change under colonial rule in these two West African states, with the basic thesis that there were more similarities than differences in development of the countries under, respectively, British and French rule. Particular attention is given to the rule of voluntary associations and to the relation of élite groups to the rise of nationalism.

1594 Zeller, Claus. *Elfenbeinküste : Ein Entwicklungsland auf dem Weg zur Nation.* Freiburg im Breisgau, Verlag Rombach, 1969. 520 p. Bibliography: p. 442–456.

A study of what the author calls nation-building in the Ivory Coast. In the first two chapters the author traces the origins of French colonization, and the development of the Ivory Coast up to 1951. The second part of the book analyses social changes. The third part discusses the politics of the Ivory Coast, with special emphasis on the evolution of parties. The author stresses the creation of a political élite and of what he calls a ' counter-élite ' recruited from returning students. The appendices contain a chronology and statistical material.

1595 Zolberg, Aristide R. *One-party government in the Ivory Coast.* Princeton, N.J., Princeton University Press, 1964. xiv, 374 p. maps, tables, diagr. Bibliography: p. 343–360.

A thorough study of the government of the Ivory Coast under the Parti démocratique of President Houphouet-Boigny. Surveys the colonial period. The long bibliography includes books, pamphlets, and periodical articles, official documents, organizational reports and proceedings, and titles of unpublished material. See also Virginia Thompson, ' Ivory Coast ', in Carter's *African one-party states*, no. 531n.

Mauritania

Bibliographies

1596 Blaudin de Thé, Bernard, ed. *Essai de bibliographie du Sahara français et des régions avoisinantes.* 2d ed. Ed. with the assistance of the Organisation Commune des Régions Sahariennes. Paris, Arts et Métiers Graphiques, Librairie C. Klinksieck, 1960. 258 p.

A comprehensive catalogue of books, documents, pamphlets, monographs, and articles in French and other Western languages. Edited by an officer in the Service des Affaires Sahariennes, it combines a reprint of an earlier bibliography of the Territoires du Sud de l'Algérie, prepared by Lieutenant Moulias in 1923 and expanded by Lieutenant Thinières in 1930 (p. 1–61, 2,372 entries arranged chronologically under a variety of subjects) with his own compilation, parts of which had been published earlier. Commandant Blaudin de Thé's scope is wider than that of the first compilers, and he has brought together 9,301 references on the entire Saharan region, including Mauritania, upper Niger, and much of Mali and Chad. Entries are arranged alphabetically by author in sub-classifications under four main sections – travel and exploration before the 20th century, natural sciences, humanities, and ' varia ', the last including means of communication, economic exploitation, miscellany (travel narratives, general and regional studies, tourism, etc.), and unpublished documents. An author index is included, as well as an address list of French periodicals cited.

1597 Mauritanie. Ministère de l'Information et de la Culture. *Bibliographie Mauritanie.* Nouachott, 1971. 108 p.

Represents a revised and expanded version of Charles Toupet's work. While published *provisoire* it is still a useful bibliography. One section is devoted to the colonial period.

1598 Toupet, Charles. ' Orientation bibliographique sur la Mauritanie '. *Bulletin de l'Institut Français d'Afrique Noire, ser. B,* v. 31, no. 1–2, 1959: 201–239; July–Oct. 1962: 594–613.

An extensive bibliography, in subject classification, including maps, bibliography, general works, six rubrics of natural sciences, archaeology and history, Islam, linguistics, way of life, techniques and art, economics, regional and tribal studies, and general literature. A large proportion of the references is to articles in IFAN bulletins. The titles are almost without exception in French; a few have brief annotations. See also nos. 1484 and 1492.

Reference works

1599 Capot-Rey, Robert. *L'Afrique blanche française.* v. 2, *Le Sahara français.* Paris, Presses Universitaires de France, 1953. 564 p. illus., maps. (Pays d'outre-mer, 4th ser., Géographie de l'Union française, no. 1) Bibliography: p. 495–541.

Extensive and authoritative study of the Sahara, including Mauritania and regions of Mali, Niger and Chad. The first part is a thorough presentation of physical geography, climatology, and geology; the second part is on human geography; and the third part reviews the work of France as to capital equipment and production and prospects for future development. The long classified bibliography contains 818 numbered items in addition to maps, periodicals and collections. There is also an index of proper names.

A succinct survey of the Sahara's physical, human and economic geography appears as Part 5 (p. 419–510) of Jean Despois, *Géographie de l'Afrique du nord-ouest* (Paris, Payot, 1967, 570 p., maps). The book's select bibliography includes a section on the Sahara (p. 532–539) arranged by region.

1600 Cornet, Pierre. *Sahara, terre de demain.* Paris, Nouvelles Editions Latines, 1956. 270 p. illus., maps.

A councillor of the French Union here sets forth in explicit terms the plans for development of the Sahara, including the western Sahara and such projects as the irrigation works of the Office of the Niger and the proposed trans-Saharan railway. He ends with consideration of the projected French Saharan Region and its strategic connexion with the Fezzan. Two appendices cite pertinent parliamentary and other official texts from 1952 to October 1956, the last being the law proposed by M. Houphouët-Boigny, then Minister from the Ivory Coast, for the Organisation Commune des Régions Sahariennes, to include Mauritania, the French Sudan (now Mali), Niger, and Chad, together with Algeria.

1601 Désiré-Vuillemin, Geneviève. *Contribution à l'histoire de la Mauritanie de 1900 à 1934.* Dakar, Editions Clairafrique, 1962. 412 p. Bibliography: p. 353–404.

Only study of the important period of French dominance, written from archival sources. Excellent bibliography and guide to archives of West Africa and France with material on Mauritania.

1602 Etudes mauritaniennes. nos. 1–6. Saint-Louis, Institut Français d'Afrique Noire, Centre Sénégal-Mauritanie, 1948–55. Irregular.

At least two of the series are worth mention as reference sources: Mokhtar ould Hamidoun, *Précis sur la Mauritanie* (1952, 69 p.; no. 4), a geographical and ethnological introduction to the country; and Ahmad ibn al-Amin al-Shinqiti, *El Wasît : Littérature, histoire, géographie, moeurs et coutumes des habitants de la Mauritanie, par Ahmed Lamine Ech Chenguiti,* excerpts translated from the Arabic by Mourad Teffahi (1953, 150 p.; no. 5).

None of the series appears to have been issued since independence, and the library and archives of the IFAN Centre Mauritanie are still kept in Saint-Louis.

1603 Gerteiny, Alfred G. *Mauritania.* New York, Praeger, 1967. xi, 243 p. map. (Praeger Library of African Affairs) Bibliography: p. 225–234.

The first major publication in English on one of Africa's least-known countries. Professor Gerteiny, basing his work on extensive field and documentary research, ably handles a subject that has heretofore been almost exclusively the concern of French scholars. He first provides geographic and regional profiles and a historical background, examines the society, customs, beliefs, and language and literature of the Moors, and discusses the black minorities. A review of the era of French colonialism and the decolonization period follows, and the final portion of the volume is devoted to political, economic and administrative affairs.

1604 Gillier, L. *La pénétration en Mauritanie : Découverte, explorations, conquête, la police du désert et la pacification définitive.* Paris, Librairie Orientaliste Paul Geuthner, 1926. 359 p., maps. Bibliography: p. 354–56.
The author, a French army officer, traces the history of foreign settlement from the ancient Carthaginians to the French conquest of Senegal. He then deals with French penetration, properly speaking, from 1902, and continues the story to 1925. The second part of the book surveys the situation as it existed in 1925, with special emphasis on military problems.

1605 Gouraud, Général (Henri). *Mauritanie, Adrar : Souvenirs d'un Africain.* Paris, Plon, 1945. 349 p.
Useful reminiscences by a colonial official. See also his *Au Soudan : Souvenirs d'un Africain* (Paris, 1939).

1606 Husson, Philippe. *La question des frontières terrestres du Maroc.* Paris, 1960. 128 p.
Study by a French lawyer of the legal and political aspects of the boundaries of Morocco with the western Sahara, both the Spanish Sahara and Mauritania. The thorough examination of sources goes through 1958 only, before Mauritanian independence and well before the debated boundary question was brought before the United Nations in August–November 1960.

1607 Marty, Paul. *Etudes sur l'Islam et les tribus maures : Les Brakna.* Paris, Leroux, 1921. 399 p. illus., maps (part fold.), geneal. tables, facsims. (Collection de la *Revue du Monde Musulman*)

1608 —— *Etudes sur l'Islam maure : Cheikh Sidia, les Fadelia, les Ida ou Ali.* Paris, 1916. 252 p. plates, facsims. (Collection de la *Revue du Monde Musulman*)

1609 —— *L'Islam en Mauritanie et au Sénégal.* Paris, 1915–16. 483 p. 32 plates. (Collection de la *Revue du Monde Musulman*)
By a renowned authority on Islam and on Mauritania, the above three works form part of Marty's immense contribution to the study of Islam in West Africa. The first book is a specific study of the Brakna people of southwestern Mauritania. In the second specialized work Marty presents a detailed account of Shaikh Sidya and his 'way', of the Fadiliyya order and its followers, and of the Ida-ou-Ali people and the Tijaniyya sect. The third study, very likely a definitive one, covers not only the material on the second work but extends the subject to Senegal, with a discussion of the Tijaniyya sect among the Tukulors, Wolofs, and Mandingoes.

1610 Mauritania. *Journal Officiel de la République Islamique de Mauritanie.* 1959– . Saint-Louis. Semi-monthly.
Mauritania was the only AOF territory which had no official gazette. Legislation for the 1920–58 period appeared in the *Journal Officiel de l'Afrique Occidentale Française.*

Niger

Bibliographies

1611 Niger. [Outline of government reports issued since 1900, containing histories of tribes and cities, the census, and information on education, health, religion, etc.] Niamey [1967 ?] various pagings. See also nos. 1483, 1484, 1492.

1612 Urvoy, Yves F. 'Essai de bibliographie des populations du Soudan central (Niger français, nord de la Nigeria anglaise)', *Bulletin du Comité d'Etudes Historiques et Scientifiques de l'Afrique Occidentale Française*, v. 19, 1936: 243–333.
Complements Urvoy's historical study (see no. 1620, below).

Reference works

1613 Abadie, Maurice. *La colonie du Niger*. Paris, Société d'Editions Géographiques, Maritimes et Coloniales, 1927. 466 p., illus., maps, tables. Bibliography: p. 437–439.
The author, a French army officer, provides a survey concerning the country's geography; the various ethnic groups and their respective history; economic development, including flora, fauna, agriculture, industry and commerce; exploration, history of French occupation, administration, and military establishment. There are numerous appendices providing information on a great variety of topics, such as the budget of the colony, diseases, ceremonies, lists of chiefs, legislation, and so forth.

1614 Bonardi, Pierre. *La République du Niger: Naissance d'un état*. Paris, APD, 1960. 99 p. illus.
Informative survey of the new country, in feature-article style. The author, a journalist and travel writer, gives full accounts of government set-up, development plans, etc.

1615 Chapelle, Jean, *Nomades noirs du Sahara*, Paris, Plon, 1957. 449 p. illus., plates (1 col.), maps (1 fold. col.), tables. (Recherches en sciences humaines, no. 10) Bibliography: p. 411–417.
Excellent survey.

1616 *Etudes nigériennes*. no. 1– . Niamey, IFAN-CNRS (Centre Nigérien de Recherche Scientifique), 1953– . Irregular.
This series, begun in 1953 by the IFAN Centre du Niger with two numbers in 1953 and 1955, is being continued with valuable contributions since independence. The new centre is associated with the Musée de Niger. The *Etudes* are published in large processed brochures, illustrated lavishly with maps, charts, tables, and diagrams. Most are prepared at government request as working papers, some with assistance from ORSTOM or other French research organizations. Recent issues are mostly sociological studies. On the back page of each, the full list of titles is given.

1617 Marty, Paul. *L'Islam et les tribus dans la colonie du Niger (2e série)*. Paris, Paul Geuthner, 1931. 102 p. map, tables, geneal. table.
A concise survey in which Marty first examines the Kaoaur-Tibesti region (now parts of Niger and Chad) and four of its major personalities and then discusses doctrines and legal obligations, education, and the influence of Islam on social and juridical institutions.

1618 Niger. *Journal Officiel de la République du Niger.* 1959– . Niamey, Impr. Générale du Niger. Monthly.

Under the former colonial government, the *Journal Officiel du Territoire du Niger* (title varied), 1933–58, was printed for various periods by the government presses of other territories, i.e., in Ouagadougou, Porto Novo, Lomé, Koulouba, and Rufisque.

Niamey now has a national archives; and approximately 1,500 documents, some dating from the 1920s, are held in the library of the Bureau de la Documentation in the Présidence.

1619 Séré de Rivières, Edmond. *Histoire du Niger.* Paris, Berger-Levrault, 1965. 24 plates, 8 maps. (Mondes d'outre-mer, Série histoire) Bibliography: p. 295–297.

A survey of Niger's history from earliest times to the present by a former colonial officer who has served as a technical adviser to the Ministry of the Interior in Niamey. Part 1 describes the geographical and ethnical background and external relations (trade and exploration). Part 2, divided into ethno-geographic zones, extends the account from the early mediaeval kingdoms through the 19th century. Part 3 covers the French occupation and administration, the coming of independence, and contemporary social and economic conditions and prospects. There is an index of names.

The author contributed a brief survey of Niger as the second volume in the Pays africains series: *Le Niger* (Paris, Société d'Editions Géographiques, Maritimes et Coloniales, 1952, 94 p., plates, maps; bibliography, p. 92–94). See also no. 531, Thompson, ' Niger ', in Gwendolen M. Carter, ed., *National unity and regionalism in eight African states* (Ithaca, N.Y., Cornell University Press, 1966).

1620 Urvoy, Yves F. *Histoire des populations du Soudan central (colonie du Niger).* Paris, Larose, 1936. 350 p. plates, maps. (Publications Comité d'Etudes Historiques et Scientifiques de l'Afrique Occidentale Française, ser. A, no. 5)

A publication of the Comité which was the precursor of IFAN, this book by a French officer and ethnologist is a historical narrative of the tribes to the northeast of the Niger River. Captain Urvoy traces events from the 15th century to the 1930s.

Senegal

Bibliographies

1621 Boulègue, Marguerite. ' La presse au Sénégal avant 1939: Bibliographie '. *Bulletin de l'Institut Français d'Afrique Noire*, ser. B, v. 27, nos. 3–4, July–Aug. 1965: 715–754.

A comprehensive survey of 82 Senegalese periodicals, official publications, and bulletins of various societies issued before 1939. Mme Boulègue provides a seven-page introduction and then lists and describes the journals in order of appearance, including data such as title, subtitle, change of title, editor, administration, format, periodicity, and libraries where available. Included are a chronological and an alphabetical index. See also Arlette Fontaine, ' La presse au Sénégal, 1939–1960 ', Bibliographie (Dakar, Faculté des Lettres, 1967, 423 p.), a doctoral thesis.

Part III: area guide (by colonial power, region and colony)

1622 Dakar. Université. Ecole de bibliothécaires, archivistes et documentalistes. *Bibliographie nationale courante de l'année 1967 des pays d'afrique d'expression française d'après la production nationale imprimée du multigraphiée.* Dakar, 1969. 78 p.

Items (691) arranged by subject, then by country. Covers philosophy, religion, law, linguistics, science, applied science, fine arts, literature, history, geography and biography. Indexes for subject and author. See also nos. 1483 and 1484.

1623 Johnson, G. Wesley. 'Bibliographic essays: Senegal'. *Africana Newsletter*, v. 2, no. 1, 1964: 10–12.

Short but interesting bibliographical essay, with evaluative comment, on the main sources for bibliography, history, ethnography, politics, economics, education, literature, and periodical literature. Many of the references are general for French West Africa rather than relating specifically to Senegal. See also nos. 1480 to 1494.

1624 Sénégal. Archives Nationales Centre de Documentation. *Eléments de bibliographie sénégalaise, 1959–1963.* Comp. by Laurence Porges. Dakar, 1964. 141 p.

Bibliography of bibliographies and other reports and studies on Senegal undertaken since independence. Groupings are by major economic activities, the separate regions, and the scholarly research bodies involved. References are to works in the Archive Centre de Documentation at Dakar, including significant articles. The list may be supplemented by reference to the monthly bibliography of holdings issued by the Archives Nationales since 1962. See also no. 1492.

Reference works

1625 American University, Washington, D.C. Special Operations Research Office. *Area handbook for Senegal.* Washington, prepared by the Foreign Studies Division. Aug. 1963. xiv, 489 p. maps. Includes bibliographies.

Background study in the country series; research and writing completed on July 31, 1963. The four sections are on social, political, and economic background and national security. There are bibliographies at the end of the sections, and a glossary and an analytical index are included.

1626 Brigaud, Félix. *Histoire moderne et contemporaine du Sénégal.* Saint-Louis, CRDS-Sénégal, 1966. 149 p. maps (1 fold.), tables. (Etudes sénégalaises, no. 9, Connaissance du Sénégal, fasc. 11) Bibliography: p. [123]–146.

1627 ——— *Histoire traditionnelle du Sénégal.* Saint-Louis, CRDS-Sénégal, 1962. 335 p. maps (1 fold.), tables. (Etudes sénégalaises, no. 9, Connaissance du Sénégal, fasc. 9) Bibliography: p. 313–335.

Two excellent volumes on the history of Senegal, by the director of the Centre de Recherches et de Documentation du Sénégal (former Centre-IFAN). He brings together valuable material, much of it collected on various field trips around Senegal.

Brigaud has also contributed to other parts of the sub-series, Connaissance du Sénégal: fasc. 1 on geology (1960) and fasc. 2 on hydrology (1961), both by Brigaud; fasc. 3 on climate, soils, and vegetation (1965), by Brigaud and others; fasc. 5 on human geography (1963), by J. Lombard; and fasc. 6 on economy (1967), by Brigaud.

1628 Charpy, Jacques, ed. *La fondation de Dakar (1845–1857–1869)*. Paris, Larose, 1958. 596 p. plates (part col.), ports., fold. plans, facsims. (Collection des documents inédits pour servir à l'histoire de l'Afrique occidentale française, Recueil no. 1) Bibliographical footnotes.

This large volume of documents is a publication of the former Service des Archives du Haut-Commissariat en AOF, Dakar. The editor has provided a brief introduction and excellent indexes, a lengthy index to the founders of Dakar (with biographical data preceding page references) and both a chronological and a systematic index to the documents.

1629 Crowder, Michael. *Senegal: A study of French assimilation policy*. Rev. ed. London, Methuen, 1967. 151 p. map, tables. (Studies in African History, no. 1) Bibliography: p. 141–144.

This greatly revised edition of a work which first appeared in 1962 is a penetrating study of Senegal and its history, by a political historian with long experience in West Africa. His central theme in this concise account is that the French policy of assimilation and the resultant high culture reached only a small élite, who now in their doctrine of négritude have reacted, as has France, against this policy. See also E. Milcent, ' Senegal ', in Carter's *African one-party states*, no. 531n.

1630 Dakar. Chambre de Commerce, d'Agriculture et d'Industrie. *Bulletin Mensuel*. 1925– . Dakar.

The important Chambre de Commerce in French-speaking Africa's largest city also published a *Bulletin Quotidien*, a periodic report; *Economie du Sénégal* (2d ed., July 1965, 248 p.); and an annual *Condensé fiscal du Sénégal*.

1631 Deschamps, Hubert Jules. *Le Sénégal et la Gambie*. Paris, Presses Universitaires de France. 1964. 125 p. (' Que sais-je? ' no. 597)

A brief and somewhat summary account that concentrates on Senegal more than on Gambia.

1632 *Etudes sénégalaises*. no. 1– . Saint-Louis, Institut Français d'Afrique Noire, Centre Sénégal-Mauritanie, 1949– . Irregular.

This scholarly series has continued since independence. The first fascicle of *Connaissance du Sénégal*, part of the series, was issued in 1960. The Centre, since 1960 the Centre de Recherches et de Documentation du Senegal, has little connexion with the headquarters of IFAN, now an institute of the University of Dakar.

1633 Faidherbe, Louis Léon César. *Le Sénégal: La France dans l'Afrique occidentale*. Paris, Hachette, 1889. 501 p., illus., maps.

A history of French colonisation in Senegal by its leading proponent. The author gives a general account of chartered company activities in Senegal and of the slave-trade. The second part begins with the abolition of slavery in 1848 and continues the story of French colonization to the end of the 1880s, with special emphasis on military history. In his conclusion the author criticizes his compatriots for not having created any genuine settlement colonies, except in Canada. He calls upon France to create a new West African empire, whose future will hinge on the suppression of the Islamic slave-trade.

1634 Gamble, David P. *The Wolof of Senegambia, together with notes on the Lebu and the Serer*. London, International African Institute, 1957. 110 p. illus., maps. (Ethnographic Survey of Africa, Western Africa, pt. 14)

See general note on this series (no. 333).

1635 Gueye, Lamine. *Itinéraire africain*. Paris, Présence Africaine, 1966. 243 p.

Gueye was one of the founders of Jeunes Sénégalais, set up about 1912, probably the first modern political action group in French-speaking Africa. Gueye, later deputy and, by subsequent standards, a moderate, nevertheless claims to write this study ' *en témoin et en militant* '. The present work describes his early life, the development of Senegalese politics, the end of the Third Republic, the development toward the formation of the Union française, and finally toward independence. One of his earlier works was *Etapes et perspectives de l'Union française* (Paris, Editions de l'Union Française, [1955] 135 p.).

1636 Guyonnet, Marguerite. *La presse au Sénégal jusqu'à 1939.* Dakar, 1964. 340 l. Typescript. (Université de Dakar, Mémoire) Includes bibliography.

Historical survey of the Senegalese press to 1939 by M. Guyonnet née Boulègue.

A later period is covered in a doctoral thesis by Arlette Fontaine, *La presse au Sénégal, 1939–1960* (Dakar, Faculté des Lettres, 1967, 423 p.). A brief historical sketch, including a list of newspapers held by the Bibliothèque Nationale, is provided by Roger Pasquier in his article ' Les débuts de la presse au Sénégal ', *Cahiers d'Etudes Africaines*, no. 7, 1962, p. 477–490.

1637 Johnson, G. Wesley. *The emergence of black politics in Senegal: The struggle for power in the four communes, 1900–1920.* Stanford, Calif., Stanford University Press, 1971. 260 p. Bibliography: p. 244–255.

Good account of the work of the able black politician Blaise Diagne, elected to the French assembly in 1914, and of politics in the four communes.

1638 Klein, Martin A. *Islam and imperialism in Senegal: Sine-Saloum, 1847–1914.* Stanford, Calif., published for Hoover Institution by Stanford University Press, 1968. xvi, 285 p. maps, tables, diagrs. (Hoover Institution Publications) Bibliography: p. [265]–277.

An important ethno-historical monograph which, though concerned with a single region of Senegal, helps to elucidate much of contemporary African history. Professor Klein focuses on the two 400-year-old Serer states of Sine and Saloum (along with the adjacent Moslem Wolof state founded in 1861), offering an analysis of events in a region where three forces – the pagan African, the Moslem African, and the European Catholic – met. In the preparation of this account of the Serer's resistance to change and of their transition from traditional authority to the French colonial system and to reformist Islam, extensive use was made of archival documents and of oral tradition, as well as of a wide range of scholarly works. A glossary is included. See also Foltz, no. 1657; and Donal Cruise O'Brien, *The Mourides of Senegal: The political and economic organization of an Islamic brotherhood* (Oxford, 1970, 321 p.).

1639 Labouret, Henri. *Paysans d'Afrique occidentale.* 5th ed. Paris, Gallimard, 1941. 307 p. (Le paysan et la terre) Bibliography: p. 290–294.

Standard work by one of France's outstanding and scholarly colonial administrators on efforts to improve the economy of rural areas. Labouret wrote many other works, including *Colonisation, colonialisme, décolonisation* (Paris, Larose, 1952, 203 p.).

1640 Lavroff, Dimitri-Georges. *La République du Sénégal.* Paris, Librairie Générale de Droit et de Jurisprudence, 1966. 257 p., maps. Bibliography: p. 251–254.

A general survey, written by a law professor at the University of Bordeaux. The first part of the book deals with the history and development of Senegalese society; the second covers the political and administrative institutions of the Republic; the third concerns the political parties.

1641 Ly, Abdoulaye. *La compagnie du Sénégal.* Paris, Présence Africaine, 1958. 310 p. illus. (Enquêtes et études) Bibliography: p. 297–310.

By a Senegalese intellectual, nationalist, and political leader, whose historical writings give fervent expression to anticolonialism of a Marxist variety. In this study of French commerce with West Africa at the time of Colbert and his immediate successors, the author has made use of many little-known documents, some from departmental archives. In two previous studies he stressed French exploitation – political and economic in *Les masses africaines et l'actuelle condition humaine* (Paris, Présence Africaine, 1956, 254 p.; Enquêtes et études); and military in *Mercenaires noirs: Notes sur une forme de l'exploitation des Africains* (Paris, Présence Africaine, 1957, 67 p.; Collection ' Le colonialisme ').

1642 Marty, Paul. *Etudes sur l'Islam au Sénégal.* v. 1, *Les personnes*; v. 2, *Les doctrines et les institutions.* Paris, Leroux, 1917. 2 v. 412, 444 p. plates, maps, facsims. (Collection de la *Revue du Monde Musulman*)

A monumental work by a noted authority on Islam. In the first volume Marty examines the influence of the Moorish shaikhs and describes the Tijaniyya sect and its leaders among the Tukulors, Wolofs, and Mandingoes. The second volume is largely devoted to the Islamic doctrines and religious ethics, the mosques, the schools of the Marabouts, rites and practices, and Islamization as reflected in juridical institutions, in social customs, and in the economic domain. See also Paul Marty, *La politique indigène du Gouverneur Général Ponty* (Paris, 1915).

1643 Milcent, Ernest. *Au carrefour des options africaines: Le Sénégal.* Paris, Editions du Centurion, 1965. 223 p. plates, map. (Le poids du jour) Bibliography: p. 220–223.

By a journalist who spent eight years in Senegal, this is a sympathetic account of the country's colonial history, road to independence, and choice of government, and of the problems confronting the new nation.

1644 Monteil, Vincent. *Esquisses sénégalaises (Walo-Kayor-Dyolof-Mourides-un visionnaire).* Dakar, IFAN, 1966. 243 p. illus., maps (part fold.). (Initiations et études africaines, no. 21) Includes bibliographies.

A collection of five historical and socio-religious studies. In the first, a study of the Wolof kingdom of Walo (1186?–1855), Monteil introduces and comments upon a text by Amadou Wade. The remaining four essays deal, respectively, with the life of Lat-Dior, chief of the Cayor (1842–66), and the Islamization of the Wolofs; the province of Dyolof and its last king, Al-Bouri N'Diaye; religious and socio-economic aspects of the Muridiyya sect; and an analysis of the dreams, reveries, and visions of an anonymous Muslim visionary of Tukulor origin.

1645 Pélissier, Paul. *Les paysans du Sénégal: Les civilisations agraires du Cayor à la Casamance.* Saint-Yrieix (Haute Vienne), France, Impr. Fabrègue, 1966. 939 p. illus., plates, maps. Bibliography: p. 911–918.

A monumental and definitive volume on the environment and life and livelihood of the Senegalese peasant. Pélissier painstakingly and compassionately describes the ' dialogue ' between the peasant and his milieu, illustrating how through the ages the peasant has shown exceptional ingenuity, patience and flexibility in dealing with his environmental conditions. It is Pélissier's conclusion that Western-educated experts would do well to reconsider any plans to reform the remarkable cultural and technical pattern that has evolved. His observations derive both from his own intensive field work and from studies done by pedologists, agronomists, historians, sociologists, economists and other specialists. While the physical geography of each region forms the basis of the study, ample stress is put on such factors as historical evolution, religion, customs, and institutions involved in the settlement and development of the land. The volume has three main sections: peoples and regions of the ' peanut basin '; recent colonization and ancient enclaves in the Sudan zone; and landscapes and populations of the zone of the southern rivers. The numerous illustrations are excellent and there is a fine bibliography.

1646 Peterec, Richard J. *Dakar and West African economic development.* New York and London, Columbia University Press, 1967. 206 p. illus., maps, tables. Bibliography: p. [197]–202.

An analysis of the response of the ' Colonial port ' (not the city) of Dakar to recent political and economic changes in West Africa. Peterec, a professor of geography, first describes the physical and historic forces which conditioned the growth and development of the port, and then covers port facilities and traffic, the economic hinterland, and transportation links with the hinterland. In his concluding chapter he discusses the possible future role of this leading port in an independent West Africa. For views of a Senegalese intellectual regarding French exploitation, see Abdoulaye Ly, *Les masses africaines et l'actuelle condition humaine* (Paris, 1956, 254 p.); and *Mercenaires noirs: Notes sur une forme de l'exploitation des Africains* (Paris, 1957, 67 p.).

1647 Sénégal. *Journal Officiel de la République du Sénégal.* 1959– . Dakar, Impr. Nationale. Weekly.

The former *Journal Officiel du Sénégal* had been published in the French colonial capital of Saint-Louis, and under various titles had been issued since 1856, originally being published in Rufisque.

The Imprimerie Nationale in Dakar published the major official publications, including the *Débats assemblée nationale*, the *Recueil de législation et de jurisprudence,* and *Arrêts de la Cour suprême.* See also no. 1494.

1648 —— *Rapport général sur les prospectives de développement du Sénégal.* 3d ed. Dakar, 1963. 2 v.

Summary of a multi-volume economic study prepared for the government in 1959–60 by the French economist Father Louis J. Lebret and his staff.

The Service de la Statistique of Senegal publishes a *Bulletin Statistique et Economique Mensuel* and a monthly *Commerce Extérieur.* For publications of the former colony, see the Library of Congress, *Official publications of French West Africa* (no. 1494).

1649 Thomas, Louis V. *Les Diola: Essai d'analyse fonctionnelle sur une population de Basse-Casamance.* Dakar, IFAN, 1959. 2 v. plates, music. (Mémoires, no. 55) Bibliography: v. 2, p. 797–809.

This complete anthropological study is here cited because of its long bibliography, which includes recent work as well as earlier writings.

1650 Traoré, Bakary, Mamadou Lô, and Jean-Louis Alibert. *Forces politiques en Afrique noire.* Paris, Presses Universitaires de France, 1966. 312 p. (Travaux et recherches de la Faculté de Droit et des Sciences Economiques de Paris, Série ' Afrique ', no. 2)

Traoré traces the history of the political parties in Senegal since 1946 but also includes a brief introductory survey of the political stratification of traditional Senegal and the changes brought by colonial rule. Lô's study is devoted to the Union Progressiste Sénégalaise – its organization, doctrine of African socialism, position vis-à-vis opposition parties, and influence on administrative and economic structures. A documentary appendix lists the by-laws of the UPS.

Alibert's work covers the organizations in opposition to the established governments in independent black Africa – the traditional opposition groups as well as the modern ones (army, trade unions, students, etc.). Each of the first two studies includes a short bibliography.

A survey introducing the colony in the pre-independence post-war years was published in the Pays africains series: Edmond Séré de Rivières, *Le Sénégal: Dakar* (Paris, Editions Maritimes et Coloniales, 1953, 127 p., illus.; no. 4). A separate chapter is devoted to the French West African capital city, Dakar.

1651 Villard, André. *Histoire du Sénégal*. Dakar, Ars Africae, 1943. 264 p. illus., fold. maps. 'Note bibliographique': p. 227–249.
Standard history, dedicated to 'the young Frenchmen of A.O.F., European or African'. The work ends with an annotated bibliography. See also no. 1463.

Soudan (Mali)

Note Upon independence in November 1958, the former French Soudan became the République soudanaise. In 1959 it joined with Senegal to form the Federation of Mali, which was dissolved in August 1960. The country then took the name Republic of Mali.

Bibliographies

1652 Brasseur, Paule. *Bibliographie générale du Mali (ancien Soudan français et ancien Haut-Sénégal-Niger)*. Dakar, IFAN, 1964. 461 p. fold. map. (Catalogue et documents, no. 16)
Comprehensive model bibliography listing almost 5,000 titles, in subject classification, with index. See also nos. 1483, 1484, 1492.

1653 Cutter, Charles H. 'Mali: A bibliographical introduction', *African Studies Bulletin*, v. 9, no. 3, Dec. 1966: 74–87.
This bibliographic essay covers the best and most important works concerning Mali and at the same time stresses materials in English and those that have appeared since publication of Brasseur's monumental work.

Reference works

1654 Delafosse, Maurice. *Les frontières de la Côte d'Ivoire, de la Côte d'Or, et du Soudan*. Paris, Masson, 1908. 256 p.
One of many useful volumes by the great administrator-historian-ethnographer Delafosse.

A monument in French colonial studies of the early 20th century was *Haut-Sénégal-Niger (Soudan français): Séries d'études*, 1–2 sér., published under the direction of the Governor, M. F. J. Clozel (Paris, Larose, 1912, 5 v., illus., maps, plans; bibliographical footnotes). The first series was by Maurice Delafosse, *Le pays, les peuples, les langues, l'histoire* (3 v.), the second series, *Géographie économique*, by Jacques Méniaud (2 v.). See also Delafosse, *Les civilisations négro-africaines* (Paris, Stock, 1925, 143 p.).

1655 Dieterlen, Germaine. *Essai sur la religion bambara*. Paris, Presses Universitaires de France, 1951. 240 p. illus. (Bibliothèque de sociologie contemporaine)
Mme. Dieterlen, a former student of Professor Marcel Griaule, is one of the best-known French anthropologists. This work, based on extensive field research

Part III: area guide (by colonial power, region and colony)

in the region of Bamako, is a detailed ethnological treatise on religious myths, beliefs, and practices of a Sudanese tribe, the Bambara.

Other anthropological studies of the Bambara include the International African Institute volume in the Ethnographic Survey series, *Les Bambara*, by Viviana Paques (see no. 333); Dominique Zahan, *Société d'Initiation Bambara : Le N'domo, le Kore* (Paris, La Haye, Mouton, 1960, 439p., illus., plates, fold. maps, tables; Le monde d'outre-mer, passé et présent, 1st ser., Etudes, no. 8); and two books by Louis Tauxier, *Histoire des Bambara* (Paris, Paul Geuthner, 1942, 226 p., illus., map), and *La religion bambara* (Paris, Paul Geuthner, 1927). Another work by this last anthropologist is *Moeurs et histoire des Peuls* (Paris, Payot, 1937, 422 p., plates, map; Bibliothèque scientifique).

1656 *Etudes soudanaises.* no. 1– . Koulouba, Institut Français d'Afrique Noire, Centre du Soudan, 1953– . Irregular.

Only three monographs were issued in this series, the first two under the variant title *Etudes soudaniennes* (1953–54).

The IFAN Centre du Soudan has been replaced since independence by the Institut des Sciences Humaines in Koulouba, which is intended to serve as the legal depository for publications of the Malian government. The *Etudes* series had not been continued as of late 1967.

The Archives Nationales is also located in the Institut's headquarters. Most of its thousands of documents are as yet uncatalogued.

1657 Foltz, William J. *From French West Africa to the Mali Federation.* New Haven, Conn., London, Yale University Press, 1965. 235 p. Bibliography: p. 215–228.

Scholarly study of the short-lived Mali Federation of Senegal and the former Republic of the Soudan (later the Republic of Mali), by a first-hand observer of West African politics immediately after the break-up. Good historical survey of the two colonies before independence.

1658 Gallieni, Joseph S. *Gallieni pacificateur : Ecrits coloniaux de Gallieni.* Selection and notes by Hubert Deschamps and Paul Chauvet. Paris, Presses Universitaires de France, 1949. 382 p. (Les classiques de la colonisation, no. 13)

1659 ――― *Mission d'exploration du Haut-Niger : Voyage au Soudan français (Haut-Niger et pays de Ségou), 1879–1881.* Paris, Hachette, 1885. 632 p.

The above two works are classics of history of the Soudan from the French viewpoint. See also no. 1816 about Gallieni.

1660 Mali. *Journal Officiel de la République du Mali.* Sept. 1960– . Koulouba. Semi-monthly.

Supersedes the *Journal Officiel de la Fédération du Mali* (Apr. 1959–Aug. 1960, Dakar, weekly) and the *Journal Officiel de la République Soudanaise* (Nov. 1958–Sept. 1960), which had replaced the *Journal Officiel du Soudan Français* (1921–58, Koulouba, Impr. du Gouvernement) and the *Journal Officiel du Haut-Sénégal-Niger* (1906–21). See no. 1494.

1661 Marty, Paul. *Etudes sur l'Islam et les tribus du Soudan.* Paris, Leroux, 1920–21. 4 v. plates, ports., maps (part fold.), geneal. tables, facsims. (Collection de la *Revue du Monde Musulman*)

> v. 1, *Les Kounta de l'Est : Les Berabich, les Iguellad.* 1920. 358 p. (Bibliography: p. [352]–354.)

> v. 2, *La région de Tombouctou (Islam sonraï) : Dienné, le Macina et dépendances (Islam peul).* 1920. 334 p.

v. 3, *Les tribus du Sahel et du Hodh.* 1921. 475 p.

v. 4, *La région de Kayes : Le pays bambara, le Sahel de Nioro.* 1920. 295 p.

These four volumes constitute a portion of Marty's extensive and authoritative work on regional Islam – work which was officially encouraged by the French who then felt that Islam disrupted the religio-social order of Africans and was a threat to French hegemony. An account of the traditional religions vis-à-vis Islam and of France's efforts to avoid a clash between the two forces is given in Jules Brévié, *Islamisme contre 'naturisme' au Soudan français : L'essai de psychologie politique coloniale* (Paris, Leroux, 1923, xvi, 320 p.).

1662 Rouch, Jean. *Les Songhay.* Paris, Presses Universitaires de France, 1954. 100 p. fold. map. (Monographies ethnologiques africaines, no. 2) 'Essai de bibliographie analytique': p. 68–95.

See note on this series, published for the International African Institute (no. 333). Rouch's excellent annotated bibliography is accompanied by an author index.

Rouch, anthropologist and film director, is also the author of *La religion et la magie songhay* (Paris, Presses Universitaires de France, 1960, 325 p.), and of the second part (p. 121–259) of IFAN's Mémoire no. 29, *Un peuple de l'Ouest soudanien : Les Diawara,* by Gaston Boyer; *Contribution à l'histoire des Songhay,* by Jean Rouch (Dakar, IFAN, 1953, 259 p., illus., plates, maps; bibliography, p. [249]–252). Another interesting study of the Songhai is Jean Boulnois and Boubou Hama, *L'empire de Gao : Histoire, coutumes et magie des Sonraï* (Paris, A. Maisonneuve, 1954, 185 p., illus., fold. map).

1663 Snyder, Frank Gregory. *One-party government in Mali : Transition toward control.* New Haven, Conn., and London, Yale University Press, 1965. 178 p. (Yale College Series, no. 4) Bibliography: p. 161–170.

A detailed account of the history and structure of the Union Soudanaise, the only political party in Mali. The author based much of his material concerning this African political system on interviews in 1963 with government and political leaders and on party communiqués and documents. Part 1 traces the origins of the party (1936–47), covering the period of the Popular Front and of Vichy, World War II, and post-war political parties. Part 2, dealing with the period 1947–64, describes the founding of the *parti unique* and examines political ideology and perceptions. Part 3 consists of an analysis of the party's problems and prospects. Six useful appendices take up 42 pages.

1664 Spitz, Georges. *Sansanding: Les irrigations du Niger.* Paris, Société d'Editions Géographiques, Maritimes et Coloniales, 1949. 237 p. illus., fold. maps.

A comprehensive account of the irrigation works undertaken by the Office of the Niger, written by a former governor of Niger just after the completion in 1947 of the great dam near Sansanding in the Ségou region, now under the control of Mali.

1665 —— *Le Soudan français.* Paris, Editions Maritimes et Coloniales, 1955. 111 p. illus., maps. (Pays africains, no. 5)

An introductory survey that follows the pattern of the Pays africains series.

Togo

Note The former German colony of Togoland, which became a mandate under the League of Nations and a trust territory under the United Nations, was divided into two parts, the eastern section administered by France, the western by the United Kingdom. A plebiscite in British Togoland in 1956 decided for union with Ghana, which went into effect upon independence in 1960. As a result the present Togo is the French-speaking eastern state alone. In the older literature, especially in German works, the two parts are generally considered as a unit. In addition, in some cases studies relate to the two former German colonies of Togoland and Cameroons.

See also nos. 2103 to 2116 in German Africa section.

Bibliography

1666 France. Office de la Recherche Scientifique et Technique Outre-Mer (ORSTOM). Institut de Recherches du Togo. *Liste des travaux scientifiques, rapports et publications des chercheurs (concernant le Togo).* Paris, Sept. 15, 1962. 16 l. mimeo.

Some 150 reports and publications are listed in subject classes, including the physical sciences, sociology and ethnology. The Institut de Recherches du Togo in Lomé is an affiliate of ORSTOM and publishes monographic research studies in the fields of hydrology, geophysics, sociology, and nutrition. See also nos. 1483, 1484, 1492 and 1699.

1667 Guilleneuf, Raymond. *La presse au Togo, 1911–1966.* Dakar, Faculté des lettres et sciences humaines, 1967. 526 p.

A mimeographed thesis.

Reference works

1668 Chazelas, Victor. *Territoires africains sous mandat de la France: Cameroun et Togo.* Paris, Société d'Editions Géographiques, Maritimes et Coloniales, 1931. 240 p. plates.

Prepared by the Administrator-in-Chief of the Colonies for the International Colonial Exposition at Paris in 1931. The quarto volume presented a significant survey of physical and human geography, history and administration by France under the League of Nations mandate of the two colonies.

A later survey of the colonies, then U.N. trust territories under French administration, is Jean-C. Froelich, *Cameroun, Togo: Territories sous tutelle* (see no. 1744).

1669 Coleman, James S. *Togoland.* New York, Carnegie Endowment for International Peace, 1956. 91 p. (*International Conciliation*, no. 509, Sept. 1956)

In the autumn of 1956 the question of terminating the trusteeship of Togoland was to come up before the United Nations and preliminary choice was being offered to the people. This political review and analysis was written between the plebiscite in British Togoland in May 1956, which won the vote for union with the soon to be independent Gold Coast, and the referendum held in French Togoland in October 1956.

1670 Cornevin, Robert. *Histoire du Togo.* 3d ed. Paris, Berger-Levrault, 1969. 555 p. illus., maps, tables. (Mondes d'outre-mer, Série histoire) Bibliography: p. 475–528.

The author of *Histoire des peuples de l'Afrique noire* was commandant de cercle in Togo for eight years. His scholarship and intimate knowledge of the country are shown in this standard history, a third of which goes back to pre-

European times. He provides a major bibliography for the country. See also James Coleman, *Togoland* (New York, 1956, 91 p.), for a discussion on ending the trusteeship.

1671 Debrunner, Hans W. *A church between colonial powers : A study of the church in Togo.* Trans. by Dorothea M. Barton. London, Lutterworth Press, 1965. 368 p. maps. (World Studies of Churches in Mission) Bibliography: p. 345–353.

Outlines the growth of the Christian church under German and British rule. It seeks to elucidate the history and customs of the indigenous people, the impact of Christianity, and moral and religious conflicts the church faced in Togo.

1672 *Etudes togolaises.* v. 1, no. 1– . Lomé, Institut Togolais des Sciences Humaines, 1965– .

Initiated by the Institut Togolais des Sciences Humaines, which itself took the place of the IFAN Centre du Togo created in 1945. On IFAN see no. 1506.

1673 Faure, Jean. *Togo : champ de mission.* Paris, Société des missions évangéliques, 1943. 88 p.

Survey of French Protestant missionaries in Togo.

1674 France. *Rapport du Gouvernement Français à l'Assemblée Générale des Nations Unies sur l'administration du Togo placé sous la tutelle de France.* Paris, 1921–57. illus. Annual. (First produced for the League of Nations)

A lavish publication with many maps, charts, and tables of statistics. The last presented, for the year 1957, has 374 pages. Emphasis is on economic and social advances, with special attention to French aid.

1675 Froelich, Jean-Claude, Pierre Alexandre, and Robert Cornevin. *Les populations du nord-Togo.* With the collaboration of Pasteur J. Delord. Paris, published for the International African Institute by Presses Universitaires de France, 1963. 199 p. maps, tables. (Monographies ethnologiques africaines) Bibliography: p. [187]–193.

See general note on this series, no. 333.

A more specialized study is Froelich, *La tribu Konkomba du nord-Togo* (Dakar, IFAN, 1954, 255 p., illus., plates maps; Mémoires, no. 37).

1676 Great Britain. Colonial Office. *Report ... to the General Assembly of the United Nations on the administration of Togoland under United Kingdom trusteeship.* 1920/21–55. London. Annual.

Begun as a report to the League of Nations on the co-mandate. None was issued from 1939–46. Because of the referendum of May 1956 that announced British Togoland's union with Ghana, the report of 1955 was the last presented.

1677 Kuczynski, Robert R. *The Cameroons and Togoland : A demographic study.* London and New York, Oxford University Press, 1939. xviii, 579 p. ' Sources quoted ': p. 550–567.

Comprehensive technical work by a demographer connected with the British Foreign Office, undertaken under the auspices of the Royal Institute of International Affairs at the request of Lord Hailey, director of the African Research Survey. Kuczynski treated here with the utmost thoroughness all phases of population studies of the former German territories of Togoland and the Cameroons and their continuation under the French and British mandates of the League of Nations.

1678 Manoukian, Madeline. *The Ewe-speaking people of Togoland and the Gold Coast.* London, International African Institute, 1952. 63 p. map. (Ethnographic Survey of Africa, Western Africa, pt. 6)

See general note on this series (no. 333).

1679 Moberly, Frederick J. *Military operations in Togoland and the Cameroons, 1914–16.* London, H.M. Stationery Office, 1931. xxv, 469 p., maps, plates.

An official history compiled by a British brigadier-general under the direction of the Historical Section of the Committee of Imperial Defence, based on official documents.

1680 Pechoux, Laurent. *Le mandat français sur le Togo...* Paris, A. Pedrone, 1939. 405 p.

The most thorough study of French administration in Togo by a colonial official.

1681 Togo. *Journal Officiel de la République Togolaise.* 1956– . Lomé. Semi-monthly.

Superseded the *Journal Officiel de la République Autonome du Togo* which, under earlier titles, was published monthly from 1920 to 1926, then semi-monthly.

1682 United Nations. Trusteeship Council. Visiting Mission to the Trust Territories in West Africa, 1949, 1952. *Special report on the Ewe and Togoland unification problem.* New York, etc., 1950–52. 2 v. (T/463; T/1105)

1683 —— Visiting Mission to the Trust Territories in West Africa, 1949, 1952, 1955. *Report on Togoland under French administration.* New York, etc., 1950–55. 3 v. fold. maps. (T/464; T/1108; T/1211)

1684 —— Visiting Mission to the Trust Territories in West Africa, 1949, 1952, 1955. *Report on Togoland under United Kingdom administration.* New York, etc., 1950–55. 3 v. fold. maps. (T/465; T/1107; T/1210)

Title varies slightly; some issued from 1952 as Supplements to the Official Records of the Trusteeship Council. The Visiting Mission to Togoland, as to the Cameroons, made three inspection trips, 1949, 1952, 1955. Their examination also included the special consideration of the Ewe people of Togoland and the Gold Coast, who were pressing for unification. The last Visiting Mission recommended prompt self-determination. A plebiscite held in British Togoland on May 9, 1956, resulted in a decision for union with Ghana (March 1957). In a referendum of October 1956 (boycotted by the United Nations), French Togoland voted to end the trusteeship status and, under provisions of the *loi-cadre*, to become an autonomous state of the French Community. The independent republic of Togo came into being in April 1960.

For official documentation on Togo as a trust territory of the United Nations, see the *United Nations documents index*, 1950–58, and for brief résumés, the *Year book of the United Nations.* See also no. 1494.

Upper Volta (Haute-Volta)

Bibliography

1685 Izard, Françoise. *Bibliographie générale de la Haute-Volta, 1956–65.* Assisted by P. H. Bonnefond and M. d'Huart. Paris, Centre National de la Recherche Scientifique (CNRS); Ouagadougou, Centre Voltaïque de la Recherche Scientifique (CVRS), 1967. 300 p.

Lists 1,541 entries. A major source-book. See also nos. 1483, 1484, 1492.

Reference works

1686 Balima, Albert Salfo. *Genèse de la Haute-Volta.* Ouagadougou, Presses Africaines [1969]. 253 p., illus.
The author, an African scholar and diplomat, first of all outlines the condition of the territory in pre-colonial times, and then traces the story of the French colonial conquest and administration to the end of World War II. He subsequently outlines political development during the era of the Union Française (1945–1960) and the Communauté (1958–1960). Nearly one-half of the book consists of appended documents.

1687 Bassolet, François. *Evolution de la Haute-Volta.* Ouagadougou, 1968. 135 p.
Brief, popular history in outline form.

1688 Dim Delobsom, A. A. *L'empire du Mogho-Naba : Coutumes des Mossi de la Haute-Volta.* Paris, Domat-Montchrestien, 1932. 303 p. plates, map. (Institut de Droit Comparé, Etudes de sociologie et d'ethnologie juridiques, no. 2)
A classic study, based on many non-European sources – from archaeology, oral tradition, etc. A popular work by this West African scholar won a literary prize for French West Africa: *Les secrets des sorciers noirs* (Paris, Librairie Emile Nourry, 1934, 298 p., illus.; Collection science et magie, no. 5).

1689 Labouret, Henri. *Les tribus du rameau lobi.* Paris, Institut d'Ethnologie, 1931. 507 p. illus., plates, maps, plans. (Université de Paris, Travaux et mémoires de l'Institut d'Ethnologie, no. 15)

1690 ———— *Nouvelles notes sur les tribus du rameau lobi : Leurs migrations, leur évolution, leurs parlers et ceux de leurs voisins.* Dakar, IFAN, 1958. 295 p. maps. (Mémoires, no. 54)
The 1931 monograph is a detailed anthropological study of the Lobi peoples. Its paucity of linguistic material is well compensated for in the 1958 publication.

1691 Recherches voltaïques. no. 1– . Paris, Centre National de la Recherche Scientifique (CNRS); Ouagadougou, Centre Voltaïque de la Recherche Scientifique (CVRS), 1965– . Irregular.
A series devoted not only to research studies but also scheduled to include archival documents and heretofore unpublished old texts. Studies of the historical traditions of all the villages in the Mossi country, according to administrative units, are being published.
  The series supersedes *Etudes voltaïques* (1950–59; n.s. 1960–64), which was issued by the Centre IFAN-ORSTOM in Ouagadougou and presented monograph-length articles and bibliographies on various tribal groups, i.e., Bwa, Bisa, and Mossi.

1692 Skinner, Elliott P. *The Mossi of the Upper Volta: The political development of a Sudanese people.* Stanford, Calif., Stanford University Press, 1964. 236 p. illus., map. Bibliography: p. 225–227.
One of the few full-scale studies in English of Upper Volta, this scholarly work is a political and anthropological analysis of the only society of the western Sudan that has maintained almost to the present time the traditional structure of government of certain mediaeval kingdoms. A glossary is included.
  Among recent French studies of the Mossi are Gomboudougou V. Kabore, *Organisation politique traditionnelle et évolution politique des Mossi de Ouagadougou* (1966, 224 p., illus.), and Michel Izard, *Traditions historiques des*

villages du Yatenga, v. 1, *Cercle de Gourcy* (1965, 226 p., maps), which comprise, respectively, no. 5 and no. 1 of the series Recherches voltaïques; Yamba Tiendrebéogo, *Histoire et coutumes royales des Mossi de Ouagadougou*, ed by Robert Pageard (Ouagadougou, Larhallé Naba, 1964, 205 p., illus. [part fold.]); and Françoise Izard-Héritier and Michel Izard, *Les Mossi du Yatenga : Etude de la vie économique et sociale* (Bordeaux, 1959, 114 p.).

1693 Upper Volta. *Journal Officiel de Haute-Volta.* 1919–58. Weekly.
The initial *Journal Officiel de Haute-Volta* was issued in 1919–32 and 1953–58; from 1948 to 1953 official acts of the territory appeared in the *Journal Officiel de la Côte d'Ivoire*.

FRENCH EQUATORIAL AFRICA
(AFRIQUE EQUATORIALE FRANÇAISE)

Note The four states of former French Equatorial Africa (Central African Republic, Chad, the Congo-Brazzaville, and Gabon) in 1959 formed the Union Douanière Equatoriale (Equatorial Customs Union, franc zone). In 1961 Cameroun joined the UDE, which in December 1964 changed its name to Union Douanière et Economique de l'Afrique Centrale (UDEAC). It is especially because of the earlier commercial and administrative ties that Cameroun is here considered a part of Equatorial Africa rather than of West Africa. A good overview of Equatorial Africa is the essay by John A. Ballard in Carter, *National unity and regionalism* (no. 531). Especially useful are the publications of the Bureau pour le Développement de la Production Agricole Outre-Mer, INSEE, and ORSTOM. See nos. 1385, 1421, 1423.

Bibliographies

1694 Brasseur and Maurel. *Les sources bibliographiques de l'Afrique de l'ouest et de l'Afrique équatoriale...* See no. 1484 for annotation. See also no. 1363.

1695 Bruel, Georges. *Bibliographie de l'Afrique équatoriale française.* Paris, Larose, 1914. 326 p. (Gouvernement Général de l'AEF)
By the Chief Administrator for the Colonies, formerly the chief of the Geographic Service of the AEF, this is considered the authoritative bibliography of early material on French Central Africa. It contains over 7,000 references, 4,260 of which are for books, pamphlets, and signed periodical articles; the rest are content analyses of periodicals by year.

1696 French Equatorial Africa. Service de la Statistique Générale.
Bibliographie ethnographique de l'Afrique équatoriale française, 1914–1948.
By P. Sanner. Paris, Impr. Nationale, 1949. 107 p.
By the director of the Service, now director of documentation of the Banque Centrale des Etats de l'Afrique de l'Ouest, this is a list of 549 entries in the field of social or ' human ' sciences. Arrangement is in regional and subject classification with author index. It supplements the work of Bruel, above.

1697 Jacquot, André. *Catalogue des publications et rapports du service des sciences humaines (1949–67).* Brazzaville, Office de la Recherche Scientifique et Technique Outre-Mer (ORSTOM), 1968. 91 p.
Bibliography of a most valuable series of monographs and reports. See no. 1385.

1698 'Tableau de la littérature', by P. Bordarier, in Eugène Guernier, ed., *Afrique équatoriale française.* Paris, Encyclopédie Coloniale et Maritime, 1950.

1699   U.S. Library of Congress. General Reference and Bibliography Division. *Official publications of French Equatorial Africa, French Cameroons, and Togo, 1946–1958.* Comp. by Julian Witherell, African Section. Washington, 1964. xi, 78 p.

By examining available published sources, including French documentation, United Nations bibliographies, and listings in the *journaux officiels* and other publications of the governments concerned, the compiler has brought together over 400 titles of official publications of the AEF, its four former territories, and the two trust territories under French administration. Relatively few of the titles listed are held by American libraries.

Identification of official documents of these governments before World War II, other than those cited under special agencies as author, is almost impossible through the medium of published sources.

Reference works

1700   *Afrique centrale : Les républiques d'expression française.* Paris, Hachette, 1962. clxxxviii, 533 p. fold. map. (Les guides bleus) 'Indications bibliographiques ': p. clxx–clxxiv.

This handbook in Baedeker style – a guide edited by Gilbert Houlet – has 188 pages of introductory essays written by specialists on various subjects (geography, economics, prehistory, etc.). These are followed by a section on the several means of transportation and then the sections on the Congo, Gabon, the Central African Republic, Chad, and Cameroun. A large folded road map is inserted at the end.

1701   Aubréville, André. *Flore forestière soudano-guinéenne, A.O.F. – Cameroun – A.E.F.* Paris, Société d'Editions Géographiques, Maritimes et Coloniales, 1950. 523 p. illus., maps.

A botanical guide to the forests, which are a main source of wealth, particularly for the equatorial region. An earlier treatise on forests and forest industries by M. Aubréville, the inspector general of French colonial forests and waterways, is *Etude sur les forêts de l'Afrique équatoriale française et du Cameroun* (Paris, 1948, 131 p.; Ministère de la France d'Outre-Mer, Direction de l'Agriculture, de l'Elevage et des Forêts, Bulletin scientifique no. 2).

1702   Balandier, Georges. *Sociologie actuelle de l'Afrique noire : Dynamique des changements sociaux en Afrique centrale.* 2d ed. Paris, Presses Universitaires de France, 1963. xii, 532 p. illus., maps, tables. (Bibliothèque de sociologie contemporaine) Bibliography: p. 521–524.

An important study (1st ed., 1955, xii, 510 p.) based on extensive sociological research, which established its author as a foremost authority on the sociology of colonialism. See also his *Ambiguous Africa : Cultures in collision*, trans. from the French by Helen Weaver (New York, Pantheon Books, 1966, 276 p., illus., maps, plans). Trans. into English and publ. by A. Deutsch in 1970.

1703   Ballard, John. 'Equatorial Africa ', in Carter, *National unity and regionalism*, no. 531.

A good survey of the region and of the individual territories.

1704   Banque Centrale des Etats de l'Afrique Equatoriale et du Cameroun. *Etudes et statistiques.* 1956– . Paris.

1705   Banque Centrale des Etats de l'Afrique Equatoriale et du Cameroun. *Rapport d'activité.* Paris. Annual.

The above two publications are comparable, on a smaller scale, to those of the

Banque Centrale des Etats de l'Afrique de l'Ouest. The *Etudes et statistiques* does not, however, include documentation services.

1706   Bruel, Georges. *L'Afrique équatoriale française : Le pays, les habitants, la colonisation, les pouvoirs publics.* New ed. Paris, Larose, 1935. 558 p. illus., maps (6 fold. col.).

An exhaustive geographic survey of AEF by this geographer and bibliographer, epitomizing knowledge of the territory to the time of its first publication in 1918. The 1935 edition, which has slight changes to update it, mainly regarding colonial administration, was subsidized by the Gouvernement Général de l'AEF et du Cameroun. See also nos. 1418, 1463.

1707   Charbonneau, Jean and René. *Marchés et marchands de l'Afrique noire.* Paris, Editions du Vieux Colombier, 1961. 150 p.

A good survey on African and European traders and merchants and on European firms in A.E.F.

1708   Chemery, J. *Histoire de la mise en valeur minière des territoires d'Afrique centrale.* Paris, Bureau d'Etudes Géologiques et Minières Coloniales, 1960. 175 p. fold. map, tables. (Bureau d'Etudes Géologiques et Minières Coloniales, Publication no. 21)

Chemery's work covers an area of study for which information is difficult to get.

1709   Documents pour servir à l'histoire de l'Afrique équatoriale française [series]. Paris and La Haye, Mouton, 1966– .

Collection issued by the Ecole Pratique des Hautes Etudes, Sorbonne, 6e Section, Sciences économiques et sociales. The documents being published in the collection are drawn exclusively from public archives and will appear in three series: 1st ser., *La correspondance des commandants particuliers du Gabon de 1843 à 1886*; 2d ser., *Les documents sur Brazza et la fondation du Congo français*; 3d ser., *Les textes essentiels relatifs à la genèse de l'A.E.F.*

1710   Dreux-Brézé, Joachim de. *Le problème du regroupement en Afrique équatoriale (du régime colonial à l'Union Douanière et Economique de l'Afrique Centrale).* Paris, Librairie Générale de Droit et de Jurisprudence, 1968. 211 p. (Bibliothèque africaine et malgache, Droit et sociologie politique, v. 2) Bibliography: p. [205]–207.

Traces in detail the development of economic integration among the former AEF states and Cameroun. The volume is in three main parts: French colonization and the administrative and political construction of Equatorial Africa; internal autonomy and regroupment; and independence and regroupment.

1711   Eboué, A. Félix. *La nouvelle politique indigène pour l'Afrique équatoriale française.* Paris, Office Français d'Edition, 1945. 61 p. (La France des cinq parties du monde)

Short study by Governor Eboué, the black governor-general of AEF, which served as a guide to the important Brazzaville Conference of 1944. It was previously published under the title *Politique indigène de l'Afrique équatoriale française*. See also no. 1729, Brian Weinstein, *Eboué.*

1712   France. *Afrique équatoriale française.* n.p. Annual.

Not available for inspection, but was produced at least from 1922 to 1958.

1713   —— *Afrique équatoriale française.* Paris, 1950. 4 v.

Produced by the Ministère de la France d'Outre-Mer. Covers Gabon, le Moyen-Congo, l'Oubangui-Chari and Tchad.

1714   —— Ministère des Colonies. *Conférence africaine française de Brazzaville, 30 janvier–8 février 1944.* Paris, 1945.

An important meeting of all governors of French Africa and officials of the

Gaullist provisional régime. The Brazzaville conference prepared the way for political, social and economic reforms that shaped the history of French Africa until independence.

1715 French Equatorial Africa. *Journal Officiel de l'Afrique Equatoriale Française.* 1888–1904, 1904–58. Brazzaville, Impr. Officielle. Semi-monthly. From September 15, 1942, to August 1, 1942, the journal was titled *Journal Officiel de l'Afrique Française Libre et de l'Afrique Equatoriale Française.* This journal, now superseded by the *journaux officiels* of the separate states, is a primary source for historical research. Before 1910 it was called *Journal Officiel du Congo Français.*

1716 ——— Gouvernement-Général. *Histoire et organisation générale de l'enseignement en A.E.F.* Brazzaville, 1931.
Not available for examination.

1717 ——— ——— *Répertoire des textes en vigueur en Afrique équatoriale française.* Brazzaville, Gouvernement Général de l'A.E.F., 1954.

1718 ——— *Recueil de textes de l'Afrique équatoriale française, années 1935 à 1948.* Paris, Ch. Lavauzelle, 1949. 256 p.

1719 French Equatorial Africa. Haut Commissariat. *L'A.E.F. économique et sociale, 1947–1958.* Paris, Editions Alain, 1959. xxii, 112 p. illus. (part col.), maps, tables.
An official balance sheet stressing French contributions to the development of the territory on the eve of independence. See also no. 1708, *Histoire de la mise en valeur minière....*

1720 ——— Service de la Statistique Générale. *Annuaire statistique.* v. 1, *1936–1950.* Brazzaville, n.d. 289 p. maps, tables, diagrs.
Very comprehensive economic statistics, including population statistics, a map showing territorial organization, and another giving density of population (by district) in the Middle Congo and Gabon.

1721 Gamache, Pierre, ed. *Géographie et histoire de l'Afrique Equatoriale Française : Documentation.* Paris, F. Nathan, 1949. 304 p. illus., ports., maps.
Basic introduction to the area, including selections from various authors.

1722 Gide, André. *Travels in the Congo.* Trans. from the French by Dorothy Bussy. 2d ed. Berkeley, University of California Press, 1962 [c. 1957]. 375 p. illus.
The American edition above (reprint of the 1929 Knopf edition) comprises two books by this distinguished French literary figure and champion of social outcasts, *Voyage au Congo* and *Le retour du Tchad*, published in Paris in 1927 and 1928. The account of his long trip in the French tropical colony, with its challenging indictment of French exploitation and inefficient administrative control, exerted a strong influence on French opinion regarding colonial policy. In the June 10, 1950, issue of *France-Illustration* devoted to AEF, Gide, shortly before his death, expressed the belief that most of the abuses he had criticized in 1927 had been corrected and that present-day French policy, as related to both public administration and private business, was sincerely and intelligently directed to the welfare of the Africans.

1723 Guernier, Eugène, ed. *Afrique équatoriale française.* Paris, Encyclopédie Coloniale et Maritime, 1950.
See no. 1418.

Part III: area guide (by colonial power, region and colony)

1724 Institut d'Etudes Centrafricaines, Brazzaville. *Bulletin.* v. 1– . 1945– . Brazzaville. Irregular.

The Institut is the leading centre for scientific study of French-speaking Central Africa. The *Bulletin* is largely devoted to monograph-length studies in the natural sciences. The works of I.E.C. were listed in no. 19–20 of the *Bulletin*.

1725 ——— Mémoires. no. 1– . Brazzaville, 1948– .

The Mémoires series includes history, social sciences, and linguistics. An example of the sociological studies is that by Marcel Soret, *Démographie et problèmes urbains en A.E.F. : Poto-Poto, Bacongo, Dolisie* (Montpellier, Impr. Charité, 1954, 134 p., tables; Mémoires, no. 7). See also *Catalogue de la Bibliothèque de l'I.E.C. (matières, auteurs et périodiques)*, by Jeanine Lambert [bibliothécaire de l'IEC] (Montpellier, Impr. Charité, 1951, 152 p.; Mémoires, no. 4; bibliography, p. 71); and the *Supplément* to the *Catalogue* (no. 1– Jan. 1, 1951/Mar. 31, 1953–), Brazzaville.

1726 Maran, René. *Savorgnan de Brazza.* Paris, Editions du Dauphin, 1951. 246 p. illus.

Biography by a West Indian writer who won the Prix Goncourt in 1921 for his novel *Batouala*, an important anti-colonial book with echoes of black resistance and négritude. The book covers Brazza's life and explorations from his first expedition up the Ogooué River into Central Africa in 1875 to his death in 1905. This edition supersedes an earlier volume by Maran, *Brazza et la fondation de l'A.E.F.* (Paris, Gallimard, 1941). Henri Brunschwig is working on a major biography of Brazza based on newly uncovered material. See his *Brazza explorateur, L'Ogooué, 1875–1879* (Paris, Mouton, 1966, 215 p.).

1727 Thompson, Virginia, and Richard Adloff. *The emerging states of French Equatorial Africa.* Stanford, Calif., Stanford University Press, 1960. xii, 595 p. illus., ports., maps.

Notes (by chapters) p. 534–568; bibliography: p. 569–582.

The indispensable work in English, providing a broad background for study of the former French Equatorial Africa and its four states, now independent republics – the Central African Republic, Chad, Congo-Brazzaville, and Gabon. The authors glance hastily at history and largely bypass any anthropological considerations; but no phase of political, economic, and present-day social life has escaped their careful analysis exhaustively documented with chapter notes, bibliography, and index. At the time of the book's preparation, the four states were members of the French Community.

1728 Trézenem, Edouard. *L'Afrique équatoriale française.* 3d ed. Paris, Editions Maritimes et Coloniales, 1955. 208 p. illus. (Collection terres lointaines, no. 1) Includes a 3-page bibliography.

Third edition of a general survey of the AEF, previously published with Bertrand Lembezat's *Cameroun*. The 1955 version was revised to cover current conditions.

1729 Weinstein, Brian. *Eboué.* New York, Oxford University Press, 1971. viii, 350 p., illus. Bibliography: p. 321–337.

Eboué was governor of Chad in 1940, and subsequently governor-general of Afrique Equatoriale Française (AEF). An Afro-Guyanian by birth, he regarded himself as a black Frenchman, and played a major part in the history of AEF. Weinstein's bibliography, a major work, makes use of Eboué's papers and of information derived from his widow. See also René Maran, *Félix Eboué, grand commis et loyal serviteur, 1885–1944* (Paris, Editions Parisiennes, 1957. 128 p.); and Jean de la Roche, *Le Gouverneur-Général Félix Eboué, 1884–1944* (Paris,

Hachette, 1957, 189 p.). For Eboué's own views, see *La nouvelle politique indigène* ...; for some of his ethnographic work, see *Les peuples de l'Oubangui-Chari* ...

Cameroun

Note   See also German Africa section and no. 1484.

Bibliographies

1730   Institut de Recherches Scientifiques du Cameroun. *Liste bibliographique des travaux publiés par l'ancien Institut Français d'Afrique Noire, Centre Cameroun, et par l'I.R.CAM, 1935–1964.* Yaoundé [1965 ?] 19 p.

1731   ―――― *Quelques sources bibliographiques du Cameroun.* By Njikam Martin. Yaoundé [1967 ?] 11 l.
A list of important bibliographic material on Cameroun, of public and private Camerounian institutions offering research facilities, and of bibliographies in preparation.

1732   Mveng, E. ' Les sources de l'histoire du Cameroun: Contribution bibliographique des Missionnaires Pallotins '. *Abbia*, 1969, 127–137.

Reference works

1733   Billard, Pierre. *Le Cameroun Fédéral. Tome Second, Essai de géographie, humaine et économique.* Lyon, J. Tixier & Fils, 1968. 399 p. illus., tables. Bibliography: p. 367–371.
Covers the people, their religions, agriculture, cattle breeding and fishing, mineral resources, transportation system, industries, banking, communications system, radio broadcasting, political organization, education, health facilities, sports, tourist and judicial facilities.

1734   ―――― *Le Cameroun physique.* Lyon, Librairie Nambotin, 1964. 200 p. illus., plates, col. map.
Deals with physical geography.

1735   Cabot, Jean, and Roland Diziain. *Population du Moyen Logone (Tchad et Cameroun).* Paris, Office de la Recherche Scientifique et Technique Outre-Mer, 1955. 76 p. illus., plates, maps, diagrs. (L'homme d'outre-mer, no. 1)
Socio-demographic analysis in the ORSTOM series. See no. 1385.

1736   Cameroun. *Journal Officiel de la République Fédérale du Cameroun.* Yaoundé, Impr. Nationale. Every 2 weeks.
Supersedes the independent state's *Journal Officiel de la République du Cameroun*, which was a continuation of the *Journal Officiel du Cameroun Français* (Yaoundé, 1916– ; 45e année, 1960–).
   The monthly *Bulletin de la Statistique Générale*, begun in 1950 under the Service de la Statistique Générale of the French administration of Cameroun, was continued under the Republic through June 1962.

1737   *Le Cameroun : Aspect géographique, historique, touristique, économique et administratif du territoire.* Paris, Alépée, 1953. 225 p. illus., ports., maps (1 fold.). (Les documents de France)
Older but still useful survey.

341

Part III: area guide (by colonial power, region and colony)

1738 Costedoat, René. *L'effort français au Cameroun : Le mandat français et la réorganisation des territoires du Cameroun.* Paris, Imprimerie Jacques et Demontrond, 1930. 288 p.

Valuable for economic data before 1930. See also V. Chazelas, *Territoires africains sous mandat de la France : Cameroun et Togo* (Paris, Société d'Editions Géographiques, Maritimes et Coloniales, 1931. 240 p.). Another contemporary study is Pierre Chauleur, ed. *L'oeuvre de la France au Cameroun* (Yaoundé, Imprimerie du Gouvernement, 1936, 258 p., tables), which is particularly valuable for the wealth of its statistical material.

1739 Dugast, Idelette. *Inventaire ethnique du sud-Cameroun.* Douala, IFAN, 1949. xii, 159 p. maps. (Mémoires de l'IFAN, Centre du Cameroun, Série: Populations, no. 1) Includes bibliographies.

Ethnological analysis in systematic outline form, published as the first volume of a series of studies on population in the Camerouns. The writer identifies divisions and subdivisions of many tribes: pygmies, Duala, Bakundu, Bakoko and Basa, Bantu, Beti and Pahouins, Maka and Kozune, Soudano-Bantu, etc. Bibliographies and maps for each tribe are included at the end of sections, and there is a large map of the whole area.

1740 ———— *Monographie de la tribu des Ndiki (Banen du Cameroun).* v. 1 [subtitled *Vie matérielle*]; v. 2, *Vie sociale et familiale.* Paris, Institut d'Ethnologie, 1955–59. 2 v. xxiv, 824 p.; xx, 635 p. illus., maps (part fold.), geneal. tables, music. (Université de Paris, Travaux et mémoires de l'Institut d'Ethnologie, v. 58, 63) Bibliography: v. 1, p. xi–xxiv; v. 2, p. vii–xx.

In v. 1 an introduction surveys the physical and human geography as well as the characteristics of the Ndiki, a people of south-western Cameroun. The main part of the text covers first production and acquisitions and then consumption. Volume 2 discusses briefly the geographic setting, history, social structures, and habitat, and then offers a detailed socio-cultural study, along with two lengthy appendices, one on language and the other on divination. Each volume includes an excellent bibliography and an analytical index.

1741 Ethnographic Survey of Africa: Western Africa. London, International African Institute.

For the general note on this series, see no. 333. The following two volumes relate to populations of Cameroun:

> Part 9. *Peoples of the central Cameroons.* Tikar, by Merran McCulloch; Bamum and Bamileke, by Margaret Littlewood; Banen, Bafia, and Balom, by Idelette Dugast. 1954. 174 p. map (fold. col.), tables. (Includes bibliographies.)

> Part 11. *Coastal Bantu of the Cameroons (the Kpe-Mboko, Duala-Limba and Tanga-Yasa groups of the British and French trustee-ship territories of the Cameroons).* By Edwin Ardener. 1956. 116 p. maps (1 fold.), tables. (Bibliography: p. 109–111.)

There are also two volumes on Cameroun in the Monographies ethnologiques africaines series:

> *Le groupe dit Pahouin (Fang, Boulou, Beti).* By Pierre Alexandre and Jacques Binet. 1958. 152 p. fold. map, tables. (Bibliography: p. [137]–148.) English ed.: *The group called Pahouin. . . .* Trans. by Isabella Athey. New Haven, Conn., Human Relations Area Files, 1959. 185 p. illus., maps. (Bibliography: p. 173–181.)

French Africa: French Equatorial Africa

Les populations Païënnes de nord-Cameroun et de l'Adamaoua. By Bertrand Lembezat. 1961. 252 p. fold. map. (Bibliography: p. 243–247.)

1742 *Etudes Camerounaises.* 1948–58. Yaoundé. illus., maps. Quarterly.
Issued by the IFAN Centre du Cameroun, superseding an earlier *Bulletin* of the Société des Etudes Camerounaises; in turn superseded in 1960 by *Recherches et Etudes Camerounaises* (see below, no. 1755).

1743 France. *Rapport du Gouvernement Français à l'Assemblée Générale des Nations Unies sur l'administration du Cameroun placé sous la tutelle de la France.* 1920/21–57. Paris. illus., maps. Annual.
Former annual publication presented to the United Nations by France as an administering power, offering a survey of economic, political, social, and educational status and progress in the trust territory of the French Cameroons. The 'Annexe statistique', containing tables and graphic charts, and the second appendix, 'Répertoire des principaux textes de lois et règlements généraux', fill almost half the large, well-illustrated volumes. Begun in the 1920s under the League of Nations, the last submitted covers the year 1957.
Two background studies of the independent country were issued in the authoritative series of the French Direction de la Documentation, Notes et études documentaires: *La République du Cameroun* (Paris, 1961, 56 p.; no. 2746) and *Le Cameroun sous tutelle britannique à l'heure du plébiscite* (Paris, 1961, 13 p.; no. 2756).

1744 Froelich, Jean-C. *Cameroun, Togo : Territoires sous tutelle.* Paris, Berger-Levrault, 1956. 217 p. illus., maps. (L'Union française) Bibliography: p. 209–212.
Clear, well-balanced survey of the two trust territories under French administration. The coverage is of country, people, administration, economy, history, and culture.
Earlier semi-official surveys were *Le Cameroun: Aspect géographique, historique, touristique, économique et administratif du territoire* (Paris, Alépée, 1953, 225 p., illus., maps; Les documents de France) and Bertrand Lembezat, *Le Cameroun* (3d ed., Paris, Editions Maritimes et Coloniales, 1954, 208 p., illus.; Terres lointaines). See also no. 1418.
Victor Chazelas, administrator-in-chief of the colonies, prepared for the International Colonial Exposition at Paris in 1931 *Territoires africains sous mandat de la France : Cameroun et Togo* (Paris, Société d'Editions Géographiques, Maritimes et Coloniales, 1931, 240 p., plates).

1745 Gardinier, David E. *Cameroun : United Nations challenge to French policy.* London and New York, Oxford University Press, 1963. 142 p. Selective bibliography: p. 137–142.
Issued under the auspices of the Institute of Race Relations. This study of Cameroun under French administration during the trusteeship period, with slight background of earlier history, is concentrated on the period from 1946 to independence, January 1, 1960. The Southern Cameroons are considered only insofar as they influenced events in the French territory.

1746 Great Britain. Colonial Office. *The Cameroons under United Kingdom administration : Report ... to the General Assembly of the United Nations on the administration of the Cameroons under United Kingdom trusteeship.* 1920/21–61. London, H.M. Stationery Office. illus. Annual.
The strips of territory bordering on Nigeria known as Northern Cameroons and Southern Cameroons were placed under British administration after World

War I as a co-mandate of the League of Nations. Reports were issued annually to the League of Nations until World War II, after 1946 to the United Nations. The final report was that covering the year 1959 (London, 1961, 209 p., fold. maps).

1747 Hurault, Jean. *La structure sociale des Bamileke.* Paris, Mouton, 1962. 133 p. illus., maps (1 fold. col.), plans (part fold. col.), fold. geneal. tables, diagrs. (Le monde d'outre-mer passé et présent, 2e série: Documents, no. 1)
A detailed examination of the social structure of the Bamileke *chefferies* of Western Cameroun, covering habitat and agriculture, system of kinship, family customs and common law, the chiefdom, and districts. In appended sections the author describes the beliefs of the people and reflects on the future of Bamileke institutions.

For a comprehensive study of the traditional institutions of the Bamileke, see E. K. Kwayeb, *Les institutions de droit public du pays Bamileke* (Paris, Librairie Générale de Droit et Jurisprudence, 1960, 200 p., illus., maps).

1748 Kuczynski, Robert R. *The Cameroons and Togoland: A demographic study.*
See no. 1677.

1749 Labouret, Henri. *Le Cameroun.* Paris, Paul Hartmann, 1937, viii. 259 p., plates, maps. (Centre d'Etudes de Politique Etrangère, no. 6)
Labouret, a distinguished French Africanist, served for many years as Director of the International African Institute. The original purpose of the study was to compare the state of Cameroun under German rule in 1913 with the state of French Cameroun in 1937. The author found that the available data did not permit of such a comparison, but he provides instead a general survey that furnishes data on the period of German as well as French governance. The first part concerns the geography, the social conditions of the Africans, indigenous systems of justice, agriculture and medical services. The second part deals with the economy of the territory including such topics as labour, mining, communications, trade, finance, etc. The author considers that Cameroun's growing prosperity is the product of 'a prudent policy founded on experience and on trust'. Labouret was a prolific writer. Other semi-political studies from his pen include *À la recherche d'une politique indigène dans l'ouest africaine* (Paris, Editions du Comité de l'Afrique Française, 1931. 128 p.).

1750 Largeau, V. *Encyclopédie Pahouine.* Paris, Leroux, 1911. 700 p.
This remains a source of rare information on the Pahouin people, although it has been faulted – chiefly by Father H. Trilles, a noted authority on the Fang. The major work of Trilles is *Le totemisme chez les Fan* (Münster i.W., Aschendorff, 1912, xvi, 653 p., illus., music; Anthropos-Bibliothek, v. 1, fasc. 4).

Another comprehensive older work on the Pahouins is Günther Tessmann, *Die Pangwe: Völkerkundliche Monographie eines west-afrikanischen Negerstammes: Ergebnisse der Lübecker Pangwe-Expedition 1907–1909 und früherer Forschungen 1904–1907* (Berlin, Ernst Wasmuth A.-G., 1913, 2 v., illus., maps, music).

1751 Lebeuf, Jean-Paul. *L'habitation des Fali montagnards du Cameroun septentrional: Technologie, sociologie, mythologie, symbolisme.* Paris, Hachette, 1961. 607 p. illus. (part col.), maps, diagrs. (Bibliothèque des Guides bleus) Bibliography: p. 601–[604].
A detailed study of all aspects of the homes and home-life of the Fali people.

1752 Le Vine, Victor T. *The Cameroons, from mandate to independence.* Berkeley, University of California Press, 1964. xi, 329 p. maps, tables. Bibliography: p. 303–319.

A political history, which begins with a geographical and historical background and then goes on to analyse the rise of national politics in the inter-war period, the constitutional changes after the war, and political parties and politics through the consolidation of East Cameroun and the British Cameroons in 1960. The last two chapters look at problems in the two parts of the Federal Republic. There are useful appendices, references in notes, and a long bibliography. See also no. 1745.

1753 Mercier, A., and B. Paquier. *Développement industriel au Cameroun.* v. 1–2, *Rapport préliminaire, 1964–65.* Paris, Société d'Etudes pour le Développement Economique et Social [SEDES], 1965. 2 v. 159, 328 p. maps, tables, graphs.

This two-volume report on all aspects of industrial development updates a 1960 document drawn up by SEDES and includes detailed data on existing industries.

1754 Mveng, Engelbert. *Histoire du Cameroun.* Paris, Présence Africaine, 1963. 533 p. plates, maps, tables. Bibliography: p. [501]–526.

General history, synthesizing what was known on the Cameroun from pre-historic times through the reunification of the former British and French trust territories in 1961. The author is a Jesuit father deeply versed in the languages and folklore of the country. Unfortunately, he neglects British source material on the Northern Cameroons.

1755 *Recherches et Etudes Camerounaises.* no. 1– . 1960– . Yaoundé, Institut de Recherches Scientifiques du Cameroun. illus., plates, maps, diagrs. Semi-annual.

Journal of the Institut which succeeded the IFAN Centre du Cameroun (1935–60). On IFAN see no. 1506.

1756 Tardits, Claude. *Contribution à l'étude des populations Bamileke de l'ouest Cameroun.* Paris, Berger-Levrault, 1960. 140 p. illus., maps. (L'homme d'outre-mer, n.s. no. 4) Includes bibliography.

A work resulting from a survey of the *chefferies* in the prosperous agricultural regions of the Southern Cameroons, sponsored by the Office de la Recherche Scientifique et Technique Outre-Mer (ORSTOM).

1757 United Nations. Trusteeship Council. Visiting Mission to the Trust Territories in West Africa, 1949, 1952, 1955, 1958. *Report on the Cameroons under United Kingdom administration.* New York. 4 v. maps.

The Visiting Missions examined political, social, and economic conditions in the Cameroons on four visits, 1949, 1952, 1955, and 1958, reporting to the Trusteeship Council, which passed the reports on to the General Assembly. For discussion of reports and for the many other UN documents relating to the Cameroons, including innumerable petitions, see the annual *United Nations documents index* under 'Cameroons'.

Chad

Bibliographies

1758 Appert, Monique. *Essai de bibliographie concernant le Tchad jusqu'en 1913.* n.p., 1962. mimeo.

Has approximately 1,000 titles. No further information has been found.

Part III: area guide (by colonial power, region and colony)

1759 Lebeuf, J.-P. *Bibliographie du Tchad.* Fort-Lamy, Institut National Tchadien pour les Sciences Humaines, 1968. 243 p. (Etudes et documents tchadiens, ser. A, no. 4)

Lists in alphabetical order over 2,000 items (printed or cyclostyled), books, articles, pamphlets, etc. dealing with Chad. Also cites records and films. Contains a subject index.

1760 Moreau, Jacqueline. *Bibliographie du Tchad, Sciences Humaines.* 2d ed. Fort-Lamy, Institut National Tchadien pour les Sciences Humaines, 1970. 353 p.

Lists over 2,000 books, articles published up to 31 December 1969. Arranged alphabetically by author. Separate sections for maps, records, films. Subject index. See also no. 1484. The Moreau work is Lebeuf (no. 1759) with additions.

Reference works

1761 *Annuaire du Tchad, 1958.* Casablanca, Editions Fontana [1958 ?]. 161 p. illus. (part col.)

This presentation of Chad, ' constituting a practical guide to its economy, organization, and structure', was prepared by the Chambre de Commerce, d'Agriculture et d'Industrie du Tchad in Fort-Lamy. It is an updating of a similar work issued with the same title (the *Annuaire* is misleading) in 1950–51, to celebrate the 50th anniversary of the French installation in Chad. The book is handsomely made up and illustrated, with both pictures and advertising partly in colour. Coverage is general, including geography, history and archaeology, territorial organization, and economy, and there are chapters on the six largest cities.

The Chambre de Commerce also issues a weekly bulletin, *Informations Economiques.*

1762 Boisson, Jacques. *L'histoire du Tchad et de Fort-Archambault.* Paris, Editions du Scorpion, 1966. 249 p. maps.

A history of Chad, 1880–1966. The author traces the stages of French penetration, emphasizing the role of Fort-Archambault (created in 1899) in the region of the Sara people. There are 20 maps. See also chapter on Chad in no. 531.

1763 Chad. *Journal Officiel de la République de Tchad.* 1959– . Fort-Lamy, Impr. Officielle. Semi-monthly.

Formerly published as *Journal Officiel de l'Oubangui-Chari-Tchad,* 1907–1958.

Another publication of Chad, the *Bulletin Mensuel de Statistique,* begun in the 1950s by the Service de la Statistique of the colonial government, is continued under the Service de la Statistique Générale of the republic. It is issued in mimeographed form.

1764 Diguimbaye, Georges, and Robert Langue. *L'essor du Tchad.* Paris, Presses Universitaires de France, 1969. 400 p., maps, illus., tables. Bibliography: p. 373–384.

This study concentrates on the economic development of Chad during the post-colonial era. The authors do, however, supply a good deal of historical material. The first part of the book deals with the history and politics of Chad from 1944 to 1960. An additional chapter concerns the international dimensions. Economic and social growth are delineated sector by sector.

1765 Hugot, Pierre. *Le Tchad.* Paris, Nouvelles Editions Latines, 1965. 155 p. illus., map.

A concise political, social, and economic survey of Chad from its early history to the 1960s by a former commandant in Chad, especially good on the inter-war period.

1766 Institut National Tchadien pour les Sciences Humaines. [Publications]
The Institut was founded in January 1961 as the Centre Tchadien pour les Sciences Humaines, and the name was changed to the present form in 1963. The director is the archaeologist and anthropologist Jean-Paul Lebeuf. Lebeuf's work includes a socio-demographic study, *Fort-Lamy, Tchad, A.E.F. : Rapport d'une enquête préliminaire dans les milieux urbains de la fédération* (Paris, 1954, 64 p.).

1767 Lapie, Pierre O. *Mes tournées au Tchad.* London, J. M. Murray, 1943. 178 p., illus., tables.
Lapie, a former governor of Chad, describes the country during World War II, and provides a good deal of historical and ethnographic information cast in a popular form. His work was written at the suggestion of General de Gaulle, who asked him to ' write down what you have just told me '. Lapie also wrote a brief account of Chad's contribution to the Allied cause in World War II, *Le Tchad fait la guerre* (London, Distribution Hachette, 1943, 33 p., plates).

1768 Lebeuf, Annie M. D. *Les populations du Tchad (nord du 10e parallèle).* Paris, Presses Universitaires de France, 1959. 130 p. illus. (Monographies ethnologiques africaines) Bibliography: p. 119–124.
See note on the Monographies series, published for the International African Institute (nos. 333 and 1459). The present study covers the Saharan populations of northern Chad (Teda and Daza), those of the ancient kingdoms of Kanem, Kotoko, Boulala, Baguirmi, and Wadai (Ouadai), those termed Arabs, and regrouped peoples, whom the author classifies collectively as the Yedina, Kinga, and Dadjo.

1769 Lebeuf, Jean-Paul, and A. Masson Detourbet. *La civilisation du Tchad : Suivi d'une étude sur les bronzes Sao, par Raymond Lantier.* Paris, Payot, 1950. 198 p. illus.
M. Lebeuf and his wife, the former Mlle. Masson Detourbet, are among the foremost scholars concerned with archaeological, anthropological and sociological research on Chad. In 1962 he published a study of the remains of ancient civilizations, *Archéologie tchadienne : Les Sao du Cameroun et du Tchad* (Paris, Hermann, 1962, 146 p., plates). Another of his works is a socio-demographic study, *Fort-Lamy, Tchad, A.E.F. : Rapport d'une enquête préliminaire dans les milieux urbains de la fédération* (Paris, Editions de l'Union Française, 1954, 64 p., illus.).

1770 Le Cornec, Jacques. *Histoire politique du Tchad de 1900 à 1962.* Paris, Librairie Générale de Droit et de Jurisprudence (R. Pichon et R. Durand-Auzias), 1963. 374 p. illus., maps, tables. (Bibliothèque constitutionnelle et de science politique, v. 4) Bibliography: p. [321]–329.
A detailed work on the political and legislative history of Chad, by a former administrator in the French territory. Expanded from a doctoral thesis, the emphasis is on the role of the *chefferies* in the political evolution of the country from its conquest by the French until independence. See also the biography of Eboué, who served as governor of Chad (no. 1729).

1771 Le Rouvreur, Albert. *Sahéliens et Sahariens du Tchad.* Paris, Berger-Levrault, 1962. 467 p. illus., maps. (L'homme d'outre-mer, n.s. no. 5)
A broad study of the peoples of northern Chad and the neighbouring semi-arid regions of Niger, their country, history, ways of life, economic resources and needs, and development under French rule. The many tribes are grouped in two sets, the Sahelians (in semi-arid country) and the Saharans (in true desert) and

divided in each as sedentary, semi-sedentary, semi-nomad, and nomad. Among typical Sahelians are the Kanembou, Maba, and Kréda; among typical Saharans are the Kamadja, Téda-Tou, and Gaéda.

1772 Romeuf, Jean. *Vues sur l'économie de l'Oubangui (Essai sur une économie sous-développée).* Paris, 1958.
Settler account of economic development in Ubangi-Shari.

1773 Urvoy, Yves F. *Histoire de l'empire du Bornou.* Paris, Larose, 1949. 166 p. (Mémoires de l'IFAN, no. 7)
Authoritative study of the past civilizations of the western Sudanic region, including a 12-page index of peoples and tribes mentioned, many of whom are within the current boundaries of Chad. (The present province of Bornu is in Northern Nigeria; the culture area runs into Niger also.)

Gabon

Bibliographies

1774 Draguet, Zoë. *Le Gabon: Répertoire bibliographique des études de sciences humaines, 1967–1970.* Libreville, ORSTOM, 1970.

1775 Perrois, Françoise. *Le Gabon: Répertoire bibliographique des études de sciences humaines, 1960–1967.* Libreville, ORSTOM, 1969. 58 p.

1776 Perrot, Claude. *Le Gabon: Répertoire bibliographique relatif aux sciences humaines.* Paris, B.D.P.A., 1962. 40 p.

1777 Weinstein, Brian. 'Gabon: A bibliographic essay'. *Africana Newsletter,* v. 1, no. 4, Winter 1963: 4–9.
Description of basic books, articles, and periodicals. See also no. 1484.

Reference works

1778 Charbonnier, François, ed. *Gabon, terre d'avenir.* Paris, Encyclopédie d'Outremer, 1957. 151 p. illus.
An informative popular survey. Following each descriptive chapter (history, surface and vegetation, wild life, depopulation, etc.), there is a well-chosen excerpt from one of the important source works. See also no. 531.

1779 Deschamps, Hubert Jules. *Quinze ans de Gabon: Les débuts de l'établissement français, 1839–1853.* Paris, Société Française d'Histoire d'Outre-Mer, Librairie G. P. Maisonneuve and Larose, 1965. 98 p. (Bibliothèque d'histoire d'outre-mer) Extract from *Revue Française d'Histoire d'Outre-Mer,* 1963. fasc. 180–181: 283–345; 1965, fasc. 186: 92–126. Bibliographical footnotes.
Survey of the early period of French settlement in Gabon based only on French sources. Part 1 is a statement of sources; part 2 presents a yearly chronology of events from 1839 to 1853; and part 3 discusses the people, the French army and navy, public works, Protestant and Catholic missions, slavery, and the economy. See also Deschamps, *Traditions orales et archives du Gabon...* (Paris, Berger-Levrault, 1962, 172 p.).

1780 Lasserre, Guy. *Libreville, la ville et sa région (Gabon, A.E.F.): Etude de géographie humaine.* Paris, A. Colin, 1958. 346 p. illus., maps, tables, diagrs. (Cahiers de la Fondation Nationale des Sciences Politiques, no. 98) Bibliography: p. 327–343.
This valuable study is in three parts. The first, 'Présentation de Libreville', gives

a geographical description of the area, the European city and African villages, and a historical account of the city's growth. The second part centres on economic activities – communications and links with the surrounding regions and their rural societies, Libreville as the capital and port, and the exploitation of the forests and wood industries. Last are chapters on the European and African populations and the life of Libreville and culture contacts therein. See also Balandier, *Sociologie actuelle de l'Afrique noire*, which discusses the Fang people.

1781 Savorgnan de Brazza, Pierre, comte. *Brazza explorateur: L'Ogooué, 1875–1879*. [Edited] by Henri Brunschwig, with the collaboration of Jean Glénisson and others. Paris, La Haye, Mouton, 1966. 219 p. fold. map. (Documents pour servir à l'histoire de l'Afrique équatoriale française, 2d ser.: Brazza et la fondation du Congo français, no. 1) Bibliographical footnotes.

A valuable volume of previously unpublished archival material on the first of Brazza's three explorations of the Ogooué River. A brief biographical introduction, which emphasizes the French government's unwillingness to finance Brazza's expedition, is followed by two main parts. The first consists of Brazza's communications (1874–78) with officials of the French navy concerning the organization of the expedition. Part 2 is made up of his lengthy report (dated August 30, 1879) to the Ministère de la Marine after his return to France. This last document, well complemented with substantive and bibliographic footnotes, first describes the regions explored and then gives an account of the voyage during which the Ogooué basin and a part of the Congo basin were explored. Included is an index with descriptive notes preceding page numbers.

1782 Trilles, H. *Les pygmées de la forêt équatoriale*. Paris, Bloud & Gay, 1932. xiv, 530 p. (Anthropos, collection internationale de monographies ethnologiques, v. 3, fasc. 4) 'Index bibliographique': p. 517–521.

The text of a course given at the Institut Catholique de Paris by the missionary anthropologist, Father Trilles. This is one of the longest and most renowned studies of the Negrillos, among whom the author worked in Gabon. (They also live in the forests of Congo-Brazzaville.) The bibliographic index gives titles only, the full references being in the voluminous footnotes.

1783 Weinstein, Brian G. *Gabon: Nation-building on the Ogooué*. Cambridge, Mass., and London, MIT Press, 1966. xiv, 287 p. illus., map (on lining paper). Bibliography: p. 257–259.

An examination of the forces acting on Gabon and its people from without and from within, pushing the country both towards and away from national consolidation. Following a brief analysis of nation-building in general, Weinstein describes the motive force in Gabonese nation-building (an account of the French and the Fang people), and then considers national consolidation through shared experience (the development of a national culture, history, and belief system) and through decision-making. In concluding his sympathetic account, he admits that there is no way to predict the future, remarking that a former colonial governor estimated that it would take at least a thousand years to form a developed nation, whereas former President Mba stated that five years would be sufficient. There is an excellent, briefly annotated bibliography. See also André Raponda Walker, *Notes d'histoire du Gabon* (1959, 158 p.; Mémoires de l'Institut d'Etudes Centrafricaines), for a good historical survey of chiefs, kings, and tribes of Gabon as well as a chronological résumé to 1929. See also no. 1729, Brian Weinstein, *Eboué*. For a survey of the defects of the French educational system in Africa, see Marc Botti and Paul Venizet, *Enseignement au Gabon* (Paris, 1965).

Part III: area guide (by colonial power, region and colony)

Middle Congo (Congo-Brazzaville)

Bibliographies

1784 Bureau pour le Développement de la Production Agricole. *Répertoire bibliographique : République du Congo-Brazzaville*. Paris, BDPA, 1965. 112 p. processed.
Lists 867 works, including articles, arranged by subject (economics, history, geography, culture, ethno-sociology). There is an author index.

1785 Jacquot, André. *Catalogue des publications et rapports du service des sciences humaines (1948–70)*. Brazzaville, Office de la Recherche Scientifique et Technique Outre-Mer (ORSTOM), 1971. 80 p.
Lists published and unpublished books, articles, and reports, etc. by researchers and technicians associated with the Centre ORSTOM at Brazzaville. Arranged alphabetically by author, subject, and region.

Reference works

1786 Amin, Samir, and Catherine Coquery-Vidrovitch. *Histoire économique du Congo, 1880–1968 : Du Congo français à l'union douanière et économique de l'Afrique centrale*. Paris, Editions Anthropos, 1969. 204 p.
A specialized survey of economic developments in the Congo. Ms. Coquery-Vidrovitch covers the period from 1880 to 1914; Mr. Amin the Congo after 1960. See for Matswaism, Kimbanguism and other religious-political movements in the Congo, Martial Sinda, *Messianismes congolais* (Payot, Paris, 1972).

1787 Balandier, Georges. *Sociologie des Brazzavilles noires*. Paris, A. Colin, 1955. 274 p. illus. (Cahiers de la Fondation Nationale des Sciences Politiques, no. 67) Bibliography: p. 273–274.
Analysis of Central African urbanization in the two centres that have grown up around the small European capital city of the former AEF. See also Roland Devauges, *Le chômage à Brazzaville en 1957 : Etude sociologique* (Paris, 1958, 258 p.), which complements Balandier's work.

1788 Challaye, Félicien. *Le Congo français : La question internationale du Congo*. Paris, Felix Alcan, 1909. 311 p.
An important book by a man who went with Brazza to inspect Equatorial Africa in 1905.

1789 Coquery-Vidrovitch, Catherine, ed. *Brazza et la prise de possession du Congo : La mission de l'Ouest africain, 1883–1885*. Paris, Mouton and Company, 1969. 502 p.
Valuable collection of documents not only for French colonization of the Congo area but also for the history of the peoples in the region, especially the Bateke and the Bobangi.

1790 Londres, Albert. *Terre d'ébène : La traite des noirs*. Paris, Albin Michel, 1929. 268 p.
Describes the mistreatment of African labourers during the construction of the Congo-Océan railroad. See also Jules Lefébure, *Le régime des concessions au Congo* (Paris, 1904).

1791 Lucas, Gerard. *Formal education in the Congo-Brazzaville : A study of educational policy and practice.* Stanford, Calif., Comparative Education Center, School of Education, Stanford University, 1964. 287 p. illus. (Education as an Instrument of National Policy in Selected Newly Developing Areas, Phase 3)

A comprehensive description and thoughtful evaluation of the Congo's educational system. Policy and practice both during the French colonial period and in the post-independence years are examined in detail.

1792 Rouget, Fernand. *L'expansion coloniale au Congo français.* Paris, Larose, 1906. 942 p., maps, tables, illus. Bibliography: p. 901–928.

An elaborate study, compiled by a French archivist. The first part of the book deals with French expansion from 1842 to the end of the last century, including French penetration to the Upper Nile and Chad. The second part of the book covers geography and ethnography. The third part deals with French politics and administrative, military and political organization. The fourth part concerns economic development.

1793 Soret, Marcel. *Les Kongo nord-occidentaux.* Avec la collaboration d'André Jacquot pour les questions de linguistique. Paris, Presses Universitaires de France, 1959. 144 p. illus. (Monographies ethnologiques africaines) Bibliography: p. 117–139.

One of the French series of the International African Institute's Ethnographical Survey of Africa, this study is by a specialist on demography and ethnology of Equatorial Africa. The peoples surveyed in the monograph (following the pattern of the series, for which see no. 333) are on both banks of the Congo, chiefly in the former AEF. The sources in the long bibliography include Belgian studies, but those of the French regions predominate. M. Soret has also published several ethnic maps of AEF (Brazzaville, Secrétariat Général de l'AEF, 1957).

1794 Wagret, Jean-Michel. *Histoire et sociologie politiques de la République du Congo (Brazzaville).* Paris, Librairie Générale de Droit et de Jurisprudence (R. Pichon et R. Durand-Auzias), 1963. 250 p. (Bibliothèque constitutionnelle et de science politique, v. 3) Bibliography: p. 227–231.

An authoritative work by a political scientist, covering history and social development of the country from pre-colonial days to post-independence (September 1962 is the last date recorded, after the riots in Libreville that led to the ouster of Abbé Youlou as president). The volume is in two parts. The first, following a brief introductory statement on the geopolitical framework of the Congo, sketches briefly the political history; the second discusses ' political sociology '. The last three sections of the second part include: Congolese society, political parties, and parapolitical forces (including separatist churches, labour unions, youth movements, etc.). A 15-page who's who of political personnel ends the volume. A useful history of the work of Christianity in the area is by Efraim Andersson, *Churches at the grass roots : A study in Congo-Brazzaville*, translated by D. M. Barton (New York, 1968, 296 p.). See also no. 531.

Ubangi-Shari (Central African Republic)

Bibliography

1795 Jean, S. *République centrafricaine : Bibliographie relative aux sciences humaines.* Paris, B.D.P.A., 1961. 60 p. See also nos. 1363 and 1484.

Part III: area guide (by colonial power, region and colony)

Reference works

1796 Daigre, P. *Oubangui-Chari : Témoignage sur son évolution : 1900–1940.* Issoudin, Dillen et Cie, 1947. 163 p.
Interesting account by a Catholic missionary.

1797 Eboué, A. Félix. *Les peuples de l'Oubangui-Chari : Essai d'ethnographie, de linguistique et d'économie sociale.* Paris, Publications du Comité de l'Afrique Française, 1933. 104 p.
Governor Eboué served early in his career as an administrator in Ubangi-Shari.

1798 Kalck, Pierre. *Réalités oubanguiennes.* Paris, Berger-Levrault, 1959. 356 p. illus. (Mondes d'outre-mer, Série Nations) Bibliography: p. 329–343.
Well-balanced study of the country. Writing in 1958, the author uses the name of the former colony, Ubangi-Shari (in French, Oubangui-Chari). The first part deals with early history and anthropology. The second part treats the French colonial territory, including a table of population as of 1958, with concentration on the socioeconomic balance sheet. The last part, 'L'Oubangui décolonisé', is an analysis of economic and social problems facing the new government of the landlocked country. The book ends with a good classified bibliography. See also Kalck, *Central African Republic: A failure of decolonization* (New York, Praeger, 1971); and also two older books by René Maran, a colonial official: *Batouala* (1921) and *Le Livre de la brousse* (1934).

OTHER FRENCH COLONIES

Madagascar (Malagasy Republic)

Atlas

1799 Association des Géographes de Madagascar. *Atlas de Madagascar.* Tananarive, Bureau pour le Développement de la Production Agricole and Centre de l'Institut Géographique National à Madagascar, 1969. illus., maps (part col.).
A collection of 60 maps: one on location, 13 on human geography, 16 on physical geography, 5 on industry and resources, 9 on rural matters, 9 on transportation and communication, 5 on miscellaneous aspects, one on regional divisions, and one on zones of development.

Bibliographies

1800 Fleur, Guy. *Bibliographie de Madagascar.* Paris, Fondation Nationale des Sciences Politiques, 1962. 42 p.
Extract from *Revue Française de Science Politique*, v. 12, no. 4, Dec. 1962. Systematic bibliography of works on Madagascar published since 1940.

1801 Grandidier, Guillaume. *Bibliographie de Madagascar.* Paris, Comité de Madagascar, etc., 1906–57. 3 v.
The listing in v. 1 of this comprehensive bibliography by a French specialist on Madagascar covers the literature from the earliest Portuguese records in 1500 to 1904. It is in two parts, the first alphabetically arranged by author, the second including anonymous works and periodical articles. Volume 2, issued as a volume of the *Bibliographie générale des colonies françaises* by G. Grandidier and E. Joucla, was published in 1935 by the Société d'Editions Géographiques, Mari-

times et Coloniales, and covers writings from 1904 to 1933. A third volume, published in 1957 by the Institut de Recherche Scientifique de Madagascar and covering writings from 1934 to 1955, opens with a tribute to the author, who died in 1956. Volume 2 is arranged like v. 1, but in v. 3 anonyms and authors' names are combined in alphabetical arrangement. All have author and subject indexes, referring to the consecutively numbered references, which in the three volumes amount to 23,003 items.

1802 International African Institute. *South-east Central Africa and Madagascar : General, ethnography, sociology, linguistics.* Comp. by Ruth Jones, librarian, with the assistance of a panel of consultants. London, 1961. 53 l. (Africa Bibliography Series, Ethnography, Sociology, Linguistics, and Related Subjects) Madagascar: p. 38–46.

See note on series, no. 252.

1803 Jaeglé, Eugène. *Essai de bibliographie : Madagascar et dépendances, 1905–1927.* Tananarive, 1927. 213 p. illus.

Long list of titles, including many government publications, and content analysis of journals, extract from the *Bulletin Economique de Madagascar*. The author was chief of the Bureau de Documentation of Madagascar.

1804 Madagascar. Université. Bibliothèque. *Bibliographie annuelle de Madagascar.* 1964– . Prepared under the direction of Marie Simone de Nucé and Juliette Ratsimandrava. Tananarive, Bibliothèque Universitaire and Bibliothèque Nationale, 1966– .

1964 ed., 262 p. (2,788 entries); 1965 ed., 1968, 221 p. (2,067 entries).

An excellent bibliography listing books, monographs, government publications, journal and newspaper articles, and maps and atlases published during the relevant year both in Madagascar and abroad, as well as processed materials and theses. Many of the items cited deal with the colonial period.

1805 Molet, Louis. ' Bibliographie critique récente sur Madagascar '. *Canadian Journal of African Studies*, v. 1, no. 1, Mar. 1967: 51–63.

A systematic and evaluative listing of some 130 important publications (excluding articles) on Madagascar, all of them French titles except for eight in a section on English works. Selected on the basis of their accessibility, the references cover the period from the 1940s on. Included is an index of authors.

1806 Paris. Bibliothèque Nationale. *Périodiques malgaches de la Bibliothèque Nationale.* By Jean-Claude Poitelon, Germaine Razafintsalama, Rasoahanta Randrianarivelo. Paris, 1970. 199 p.

Alphabetical title list of periodicals from Madagascar held in the Bibliothèque Nationale. In all, 753 serials are listed, with, for most, title, address, periodicity, beginning date, and holdings in the library. The catalogue is preceded by a six-page subject classification by title (Presse politique et information, Sciences, etc.).

1807 U.S. Library of Congress. General Reference and Bibliography Division. *Madagascar and adjacent islands : A guide to official publications.* Comp. by Julian W. Witherell, African Section. Washington, U.S. Government Printing Office, 1965. xiii, 58 p.

Contains 927 entries and numerous subentries covering publications of French administrations in Madagascar, the Comoro Islands, and Réunion, those of British administration in Mauritius and Seychelles, selected documents issued by France and Great Britain relating to their respective territories, and official publications by individuals and government-sponsored organizations. The terminal date for entries in the Madagascar section is October 1958 (the date of the establishment of the Malagasy Republic); for the other islands, entries have been continued to 1964. Official publications received by the Library of Congress are the basis of the bibliography, supplemented by information on the holdings of other American libraries reporting to the *National union catalog* and by titles recorded in bibliographies issued by the governments of Madagascar, Mauritius, France, and Great Britain. Under each dependency, entries are arranged alphabetically by author and title, except that census reports and material on development planning are grouped by subject. An author and subject index is provided.

Reference works

1808 Académie Malgache, Tananarive. Mémoires. fasc. 1– . Tananarive, G. Pitot de la Beaujardière, 1926– . plates, maps, diagrs. Irregular.

The monographic volumes of the Mémoires series of the Académie deal with history, sociology, anthropology, archaeology, natural sciences, and other disciplines relating to Madagascar. The inside cover pages of each number carry the full list of titles in the series. A typical contribution is fasc. 40, by Louis Michel, *Moeurs et coutumes des Bara* (1957, 192 p.). The Académie also has a *Bulletin* (1902– , annual [irregular]), in which proceedings and the papers of the members appear, and in 1939 the *Collection de documents concernant Madagascar et les pays voisins* was begun.

1809 Bardonnet, Daniel. *La succession d'états à Madagascar : (Succession au droit conventionnel et aux droits patrimoniaux)*. Paris, R. Pichon and R. Durand-Auzias, 1970. 867 p. Bibliography: p. 681–741.

A detailed legal treatise concerning the public law of Madagascar from the colonial era to independence. The appendices contain lists of treaties, conventions, etc. bearing on Madagascar from 1817 to 1968.

1810 Boiteau, Pierre. *Contribution à l'histoire de la nation malgache*. Paris, Editions sociales, 1958. 431 p.

A Marxist-Leninist analysis of French activity in Madagascar. Much detail on land alienation, French investments and commercial activity, forced labour and the development of a class structure.

1811 *Bulletin de Madagascar*. no. 1– . Jan. 1950– . Tananarive, Impr. Nationale. illus., maps. Monthly.

Originally published twice a month by the Service Général de l'Information of the Haut Commissariat de la République Française à Madagascar et Dépendances, now issued by the Direction de l'Information. The journal has grown from 48 pages to around a hundred per issue. Malagasy life, from agriculture to linguistics to scientific research, is given attention in scholarly articles, with occasional emphasis on agricultural and economic subjects. Bibliographical material is often included.

1812 Chevalier, Louis. *Madagascar : Populations et ressources*. Paris, Presses Universitaires de France, 1952. 212 p. maps, tables. (Institut National d'Etudes Démographiques, Travaux et documents, cahier no. 15) Bibliography: p. 208–212.

Much-quoted study by a population expert who went to Madagascar with a mission sent to consider the island as a possible place for settlement of European refugees. Use was made of local records of administrative districts and other unpublished sources in a careful and comprehensive assessment of demographic factors, resources, and agricultural techniques and limitations.

1813 Decary, Raymond. *Moeurs et coutumes des Malgaches.* Paris, Payot, 1951. 280 p. illus. (Collection de documents et de témoignages pour servir à l'histoire de notre temps)

M. Decary, former chief colonial administrator in Madagascar, explains Malagasy ways and manners, illustrating them with his own drawings – family and social life, material culture, methods of work, industry and trade, games and amusements, customary law, sorcery and witch doctor medicine, religious ideas, and the prominent cult of the dead. The last chapter touches on social 'evolution' in the half-century of European influence.

Among M. Decary's many other writings are the following:

> *L'Androy (extrême sud de Madagascar): Essai de monographie régionale.* Paris, Société d'Editions Géographiques, Maritimes et Coloniales, 1930–33. 2 v.

A comprehensive study of the physical and human geography, history, and civilization of the extreme south of the island, inhabited by the most primitive of the cattle-raising tribes, the last to come under French control.

> *La faune malgache: Son role dans les croyances et les usages indigènes.* Paris, Payot, 1950. 236 p. illus. (Bibliothèque scientifique) (Bibliography: p. 231–234)

An interesting combination of natural history and folklore.

> *L'habitat à Madagascar.* Pau, Impr. Marrimpouey Jeune, 1958. 80 p. illus.

A study of Malagasy house-structure.

> *L'Ile Nosy Bé de Madagascar: Histoire d'une colonisation.* Paris, Editions Maritimes et d'Outre-Mer, 1960. 225 p.

A chapter in the early history of French occupation, written largely from study of unpublished documents in the archives of Madagascar and Paris.

1814 Deschamps, Hubert J. *Histoire de Madagascar.* Paris, Berger-Levrault, 1960. 348 p. illus. (Mondes d'outre-mer) Bibliography: p. 317–325.

Up-to-date and authoritative history from the obscure origins of the island to the immediate present of the Malagasy Republic. Two important older collections of essays and articles are *Notes, reconnaissances et explorations* (v. I–VI, 1896–1900), and *The Antananarivo Annual and Madagascar Magazine*, ed. by Rev. J. Sibre and Rev. R. Baron (1875–1900). See also no. 1418.

1815 Etudes malgaches. v. 1– . Tananarive, Faculté des Lettres et des Sciences Humaines, Université de Madagascar, 1960– . Irregular.

A solid series published by Editions Cujas, Paris, and including the subseries *Madagascar: Revue de géographie*, which is produced by the Faculté's Laboratoire de Géographie. By 1966, 16 volumes had appeared, most of them devoted to historical, juridical, or geographical studies.

1816 Gallieni, Joseph S. *Gallieni pacificateur: Ecrits coloniaux de Gallieni.* Choix de textes et notes, par Hubert Deschamps et Paul Chauvet. Paris, Presses Universitaires de France, 1949, 382 p. maps.

Reports, papers and speeches of the great general whose career in subduing, reconciling, and administering France's colonial empire included Senegal and Sudan (1876–88), Tonkin (1892–96), and, most notably, Madagascar (1896–1905). The material on Madagascar takes up more than half the text (p. 169–373).

Part III: area guide (by colonial power, region and colony)

A good account of Gallieni's work in Madagascar is that of General Jean Charbonneau, *Gallieni à Madagascar* (Paris, Nouvelles Editions Latines, 1950, 189 p.; Bibliothèque de l'Union française), based on documents and unpublished material gathered by Gallieni's daughter-in-law.

1817 Grandidier, Alfred [and others]. *Histoire physique, naturelle et politique de Madagascar.* Paris, Impr. Nationale, 1875–1955. 5 v.

The great name connected with the study of Madagascar is that of Grandidier. Alfred Grandidier, geographer and traveller, pioneered in explorations and mapping in the centre and south of the Grand Island in 1865–70, read its ancient history, and studied its people. The monumental series of the *Histoire physique*, carried on for many years after his death in 1921 with the co-operation of leading natural scientists, was edited with the aid of his son, Guillaume. The first volume, *Histoire de la géographie* (1875–92, 1 v. of text, 2 v. of maps), was by Alfred; v. 4, *Ethnographie*, was by Alfred and Guillaume (2 v. in 1908, v. 3 in 1917, v. 4, by Guillaume, in 1928). Volume 5, *Histoire politique et coloniale*, was by Guillaume.

1818 Grandidier, Guillaume. *Le Myre de Vilers, Duchesne, Gallieni : Quarante années de l'histoire de Madagascar, 1880–1920.* Paris, Société d'Editions Géographiques, Maritimes et Coloniales, 1923. 252 p.

Authoritative account of the French conquest, pacification, and organization of Madagascar.

1819 Institut de Recherches Scientifiques de la République Malgache, Tananarive. Mémoires: Sér. C, Sciences humaines. v. 1– . [Paris] 1952– . illus., maps, diagrs.

This series of Mémoires of the prominent Institut (variant name, Institut de Recherche Scientifique de Madagascar) – other series are concerned with natural sciences – began with a careful statistical study of the capital city, *Tananarive : Etude d'économie urbaine,* by H. Fournier (1952, illus.; v. 1, fasc. 1, p. 29–157).

1820 Kent, Raymond K. *From Madagascar to the Malagasy Republic.* New York, Praeger, 1962. 182 p. illus. (Books That Matter) Bibliography: p. 160–180.

Condensed general study, by an American scholar. It covers geography and demography and also includes the history of the colonial period.

1821 Madagascar. *Journal Officiel de Madagascar.* 1883–1958. Frequency varies. Title has varied; in 1959 became *Journal Officiel* of the Malagasy Republic.

1822 —— Haut Commissariat de la République Française à Madagascar et Dépendances. *Annuaire statistique de Madagascar.* v. 1, *1938–1951.* Tananarive, 1953. 186 p.

A long-term statistical report. For other statistical material, see the Library of Congress list of official publications, no. 1807.

1823 *Madagascar à travers ses provinces : Aspect géographique, historique, touristique, économique et administratif du territoire.* Paris, Alépée, 1954. 402 p. illus., ports., maps. (Les documents de France)

Systematic survey from official sources of geography, history, economy, and administration of the five provinces, Tananarive, Fianarantsoa, Tamatave, Majunga, and Tuléar.

1824 Malagasy Republic. Commissariat Général du Plan. *Economie malgache: Evolution, 1950–1960.* Tananarive, Impr. Nationale, 1962. 277 p. illus., maps.

A White Book on the economic development of the Malagasy Republic between 1950 and 1960. It covers all aspects of the economy: commercial, agricultural, industrial, mines, energy, transportation, investments, etc. There are numerous maps and charts.

For other official publications, see the Library of Congress list, no. 1807.

1825 Mannoni, Dominique O. *Prospero and Caliban: The psychology of colonization.* Trans. by Pamela Powesland. New York, Praeger, 1956. 218 p. (Books That Matter) 2d ed. (a reprint, with added Author's Note). 1964. 218 p. Bibliography: p. 210–214.

A much-quoted psychoanalytical study which appeared in French in 1950 under the title *Psychologie de la colonisation.* The concept is general for colonial societies. Using the Prospero-Caliban and Crusoe-Man Friday relationships as symbols and Madagascar as case history, the author argues that the primitive emerging from the security of the old static, ancestor-worshipping society attaches himself as a dependant to the European; the European, like Prospero, finds his own ' inferiority complex ' reassured by the colonial situation. He tries to explain the revolution of 1947–48 as ultimately due to the threat of abandonment which the Malagasy felt in the post-war gestures towards fuller self-government.

1826 Massiot, Michel. *L'administration publique à Madagascar: Evolution de l'organisation administrative territoriale de Madagascar de 1896 à la proclamation de la République Malgache.* Paris, Librairie Générale de Droit et de Jurisprudence, 1971. 472 p. (Bibliothèque Africaine et Malgache: Droit, Sociologie, Politique et Économie, v. 15)

Detailed survey of administrative history.

1827 Minelle, Jean. *L'agriculture à Madagascar: Géographie, climatologie, géologie, conditions d'exploitation des sols, botanique malgache, productions agricoles, colonisation et paysannat autochtone, possibilités agricoles, conjoncture et économie agricoles, statistiques agricoles.* Paris, Librairie M. Rivière, 1959. 379 p. illus., tables. Bibliography: p. 371–375.

Basic study by a specialist in tropical agriculture who worked in Madagascar for 25 years as an agronomist and had first-hand knowledge of all regions.

1828 Oliver, Samuel Pasfield. *Madagascar: An historical and descriptive account of the island and its former dependencies.* London, Macmillan, 1886. 2 v. 569, 562 p. illus. Bibliography: v. 2, p. 233–259.

This large comprehensive work, written just after the Franco-Malagasy war of 1885 by which the French took over the island, covers history, topography, natural history, economy, administration, and most other aspects of Madagascar. The long bibliography cites works in French and English from the earliest travels to contemporary documents.

1829 Pascal, Roger. *La République malgache: Pacifique indépendance.* Paris, Berger-Levrault, 1965. 202 p. plates, ports. (Mondes d'outre-mer, Série: histoire) Bibliography: p. 190–196.

In his book on the Malagasy Republic's road to independence, the author divided his discussion into three parts – causes, means, and effects. The political situation in 1895, nationalism, and anti-colonialism; the Brazzaville conference (1944), *loi-cadre*, and French heritage; the internal situation (political, legal, economic, cultural) and external relations – all are given consideration in the three parts. Problems, needs, and prospects are outlined in a conclusion. Appended material includes the preamble to the Malagasy constitution and the final resolution of the congress of Tamatave (1958).

1830 Le peuple malgache: Monographies ethnologiques. Directed by Hubert Deschamps. Paris, Presses Universitaires de France, 1959– .

A series complementary to the Monographies ethnologiques africaines of the International African Institute. Number 1 is *Les Malgaches du sud-est: Antemoro, Antesaka, Antambahoaka, peuples de Farafangana (Antefasi, Zafisoro, Sahavoai, Sahafatra)*, by Hubert Deschamps and Suzanne Vianès (xii, 118 p., 2 plates, maps). It is written more in essay style than the Ethnographic Survey volumes but covers the same ground. Sketch maps show the distribution and migrations of peoples in south-eastern Madagascar.

1831 Rabemananjara, Jacques. *Nationalisme et problèmes malgaches*. Paris, Présence Africaine, 1959. 219 p.

By a French-educated poet and writer, one of the leaders of the nationalist revolt, formerly Minister of State for the National Economy and since 1965 Minister of Agriculture, Land, and Food. In this volume he discusses his country and its aims, political, cultural, and religious.

1832 Rajemisa-Raolison, Régis. *Dictionnaire historique et géographique de Madagascar*. Fianarantsoa, Librairie Ambozontany, 1966. 383 p. illus., maps.

By a distinguished author and official of Madagascar. A most useful reference with numerous pictures, charts, maps, and illustrations. Contains valuable biographic sketches.

1833 Ralaimihoatra, Edouard. *Histoire de Madagascar*. v. 1, *Des origines à la fin du XIXème siècle*; v. 2, *Le XXe siècle*. Tananarive, Société Malgache d'Edition, 1965–66. 2 v. 227, 108 p. illus., ports., maps, geneal. tables, facsims.

An outline of Madagascar's history.

1834 *Revue de Madagascar*. 1933– . Tananarive, Impr. Nationale (originally Impr. Officielle). illus. (part. col.), plates. Quarterly.

Lavishly illustrated official review of general coverage, issued by the Service Général de l'Information.

1835 Robequain, Charles. *Madagascar et les bases dispersées de l'Union française: Comores, Réunion, Antilles et Guyane, Terres océaniennes, Côte des Somalis, Saint-Pierre et Miquelon, Iles australes, Terre Adélie*. Paris, Presses Universitaires de France, 1958. 586 p. illus., maps. (Pays d'outre-mer, Colonies, empires, pays autonomes, 4th ser.: Géographie de l'Union française, no. 3.) Bibliography: p. 541–572.

Comprehensive work in an authoritative series of physical and economic geographies.

1836 Thompson, Virginia, and Richard Adloff. *The Malagasy Republic: Madagascar today*. Stanford, Calif., Stanford University Press, 1965. xvi, 504 p. illus., ports., map. Bibliography: p. 485–494.

First comprehensive survey in English of developments in Madagascar since 1945. Part 1 covers Malagasy history and politics, colonial rule, the revolt of 1947, decolonization, and the post-independence period. Parts 2 and 3 treat typically internal developments in the fields of religion, education, economics, etc. A useful glossary, a list of abbreviations, and an index are included.

French Somaliland (French Territory of the Afars and the Issas) and Indian Ocean Islands

Note The islands in the Indian Ocean and the territory in the Horn of Africa, the only parts of the continent still under French administration, are frequently treated in conjunction with Madagascar, and not many books of reference character have been written on them individually. They are grouped here to avoid repetition of titles. Réunion, the former Ile Bourbon, has since 1946 been an overseas department of France, with three deputies elected to the French National Assembly and two senators to the Senate. The Comoro Islands, formerly administered from Madagascar, and the barren desert of French Somaliland (now called Territoire français des Afars et des Issas) behind the important port and railroad centre of Djibouti are overseas territories of France.

Bibliography

1837 France. Agence économique des colonies. Bibliothèque. *Côte française des Somalis.* n.p., n.d.
Handwritten bibliographic listing by Roger Janvier and Christian Dupont (colonial officials) of books, articles and government documents dealing with French Somaliland. Part 1 is alphabetically arranged; part 2 is organized by topic or subject. See also Library of Congress, *Madagascar and adjacent islands . . .*, no. 1807. Barbara Dubins published some bibliographical articles on the Comoros in *African Studies Bulletin*, Sept. 1969, ' The Comoro Islands: A bibliographical essay ', p. 131–137.

Reference works

1838 Aubert de la Rüe, Edgar. *La Somalie française.* Paris, Gallimard, 1939. 162 p. illus. (Géographie humaine, v. 14) ' Bibliographie sommaire ': p. 155–157.
The author, a literary man and expert photographer as well as a geographer, was interested in meteorology, natural history, and other physical sciences connected with country studies as well as with description. This is one of the few books of general coverage dealing exclusively with French Somaliland.

1839 Deschamps, Hubert J., Raymond Decary, and André Ménard. *Côte des Somalis, Réunion, Inde.* Paris, Berger-Levrault, 1948. 209 p. plates, maps. (L'Union française) Brief bibliographies at the end of each section.
This general study of outlying French possessions is considered among the most authoritative of recent works. Professor Deschamps was for some years Governor of French Somaliland and is thoroughly intimate with the country. M. Decary, the authority on Madagascar, is also an expert on Réunion.

1840 *La France de l'Océan indien : Madagascar, les Comores, la Réunion, la Côte française des Somalis, l'Inde française.* [By Raymond Decary and others] Paris, Société d'Editions Géographiques, Maritimes et Coloniales, 1952. 314 p. illus., maps. (Terres lointaines, no. 8) Includes bibliographies.
Volume in a popular series of descriptions of French overseas possessions, the first 225 pages, by Raymond Decary, are on Madagascar and its island dependencies to the south, where the Indian Ocean merges into the Antarctic – Saint-

Paul and Amsterdam, Kerguelen, Crozet, and, on the Antarctic continent, Terre Adélie. The Comoro Islands are described by the *administrateur supérieur*, Pierre Coudert (p. 227–242). The following chapter, by Hildebert Isnard, is on Réunion (p. 243–276), and the next to the last chapter (p. 277–297) on French Somaliland, by a colonial official, Robert Lemoyne.

1841 Thompson, Virginia, and Richard Adloff. *Djibouti and the Horn of Africa.* Stanford, Calif., Stanford University Press, 1968. xiii, 246 p. map. Bibliography: p. 235–241.

The standard work in English. Covers the history of the territory, the way of life followed by the country's nomads and sedentary people, the organization of government, politics and external relations, as well as social development, and the traditional and the modern economy.

BELGIAN AFRICA

Note The Congo Free State (*Etat Indépendant du Congo*) was primarily the product of the private colonization promoted by King Leopold II of Belgium. The king created a political façade, first of all the Association Internationale Africaine (1876–1878), then the Comité d'Etudes du Haut-Congo (1878–1882), finally the Association Internationale du Congo (1882–1885). In 1885 the Belgian legislature authorized the king to become head of a new political entity, the Congo Free State, which in practice was treated as the sovereign's personal patrimony. To all intents and purposes, the king acted as his own Secretary of State. He was assisted by the Conseil Supérieur de l'Etat Indépendant du Congo (set up in 1889), which carried out certain advisory and judicial functions. The central administration was organized in three departments, each under its own administrateur général. In 1894, the administration was further centralized with the appointment of a separate Secrétaire d'Etat, assisted by three Secrétaires Généraux and a Trésorier Général. (The archives of the Congo Free State and other related materials have been described in E. van Grieken and Madeleine van Grieken-Taverniers in *Les archives inventoriées au Ministère des Colonies*, (Brussels, Académie Royale des Sciences Coloniales, 1958).) Administration in the Congo was formally supervised by a Gouverneur Général. The main agent of de facto sovereignty was the Force Publique. Economic exploitation was organized through the *régime domanial* whereby the state became proprietor of the vacant lands. The domain lands were handed over to Leopold's agents, or they were leased to powerful concessionary companies. Bodies such as the Comité Spécial du Katanga, the Union Minière du Haut-Katanga and the Société Anversoise de Commerce au Congo continued to play an important role throughout the history of Belgian colonization. (For a general account see Georges Brausch, *Belgian administration in the Congo*, London, Oxford University sity Press, 1961). The administration was assisted by the Conseil Supérieur, which functioned from 1889 to 1925.

One of the main agents of sovereignty was in fact the Force Publique, a black mercenary force many of whose early volunteers came from West Africa (for early history of the Force Publique see Académie Royale des Sciences d'Outre-Mer, *La Force Publique de sa Naissance à 1914* ... Brussels, Académie Royale des Sciences d'Outre-Mer, 1952).

In 1908 Belgium took over the Congo Free State, which became a colony

360

subject to parliamentary legislation. Belgium created its own Ministère des Colonies, which was organized into several Directions Générales. The Ministère des Colonies also contained a special bureau founded in 1907 known as Office Colonial, which until 1947 collected statistical and other information of value to industry and commerce, organized exhibitions, and issued a separate *Bulletin*. The Ministère des Colonies was repeatedly reorganized. (For a history, see Julien Vanhove, *Histoire du Ministère des Colonies*, Brussels, Académie Royale des Sciences d'Outre-Mer, 1968, 168 p.) By 1960 the ministry contained the Administration Centrale, which controlled six Directions Générales, each concerned with a group of related subjects. The Services Extérieurs looked after the Musée Royale du Congo Belge, the Laboratoire de Recherches Chimiques and the Ecole d'Administration du Congo Belge et du Ruanda-Urundi. In 1960, as the Congo became independent, the ministry was transformed into the Ministère des Affaires Africaines, concerned above all with technical assistance. Foreign affairs and matters concerning intergovernmental contacts became the exclusive preserve of the Ministère des Affaires Étrangères. In 1961 the bulk of the ministry's work passed to the Ministère du Commerce Extérieur et de l'Assistance Technique.

The official publications of these bodies are too numerous to be summarized. The Ministry of Colonies, for instance, published the *Annuaire du Ministère des Colonies*, later the *Annuaire du Ministère du Congo Belge et du Ruanda-Urundi*, and series such as *La Situation Economique du Congo Belge et du Ruanda-Urundi* (1952–1959). There were also the *Rapports Annuels sur l'Administration du Congo Belge*, printed at Brussels. The Belgian parliamentary debates were published as *Annales Parlementaires*, both for the Chambre des Représentants and the Sénat.

The Belgians also set up a considerable number of research institutions, all of which put out a great variety of publications. Among these institutions were the Musée Royal du Congo Belge (known originally as the Musée Colonial, founded in 1904, renamed Musée Royal de l'Afrique Centrale in 1960), the Laboratoire de Recherches Chimiques created in 1928, and the Institut Royal Colonial Belge at Tervuren, started in 1928, known from 1954 as the Académie Royale des Sciences Coloniales, and from 1959 as the Académie Royale des Sciences d'Outre-Mer. The Musée Royal put out many different publications, such as the *Annales d'Ethnographie* (1899–). The Institut Royal published an extensive series of *Mémoires*, that is monographs concerned with history, ethnology, administration, bibliographic information, and other subjects. Other learned institutions included the Institut International des Sciences Politiques et Sociales, the Institut International des Civilisations Différentes (INCIDI, successor in 1948 of the Institut Colonial International, set up in 1894), the Institut de Médecine Tropicale Prince Léopold (founded in 1910 under the name of Ecole de Médecine Tropicale), and others.

Students of Belgian colonialism should consult also material derived from bodies located in the Congo itself, such as the Institut National pour l'Etude Agronomique du Congo (INEAC, set up in 1933), the Institut pour la Recherche Scientifique en Afrique Centrale (IRSAC dating from 1947), l'Institut Géographique du Congo Belge (IGCB), the Institut Royal des Relations Internationales (started 1947), and many others.

The Centre de Documentation Economique et Sociale Africaine (CEDESA, set up in 1957 at Brussels) co-ordinated the economic and social history of Africa, especially of the Congo. Material of private provenance is to be found among the publications of such societies as the Société Royale Belge de Géographie (founded 1876), which publishes the *Revue Belge de Géographie*, and in the archives and publications of missionary bodies and commercial companies. Important also are the records of the Société Antiesclavagiste de Belgique. (See Part I for details on libraries and archives.)

Until independence came suddenly to the former Belgian Congo in June 1960, practically all writing relating to the colony, as well as to the Belgian-administered trust territory of Ruanda-Urundi, had been published in Belgium. It was exhaustively catalogued, as appears from the following subsection of bibliographies. Since 1960 the increased international concern over the country's unsettled government has been reflected in a wide range of literature concerning the country.

On attaining independence, the former Belgian Congo was named the Democratic Republic of the Congo. In 1971 the country became officially known as the Democratic Republic of Zaïre (Zaïre being the historic name of the Congo river). In post-independence literature Zaïre was also referred to often as Congo-Kinshasa to distinguish it from Congo-Brazzaville, that is to say, the People's Republic of the Congo, formerly a French territory.

Belgian Congo (Zaïre)

Atlases

1842 Académie Royale des Sciences d'Outre-Mer. *Atlas général du Congo et du Ruanda-Urundi.* Bruxelles, 1948–63. 34 pts. maps (col. fold.).
Monumental work covering all aspects of the former Belgian territories; issued in parts, each consisting of explanatory text of 7 to 30 folio pages (two editions, in French and Flemish) and one or more large-scale folded maps. The introductory part, ' Avant-propos ' (2d ed., 1954, 28 p., map), includes an index of place-names, in which names of towns are followed by statistics of population as of 1953–54. The other parts, accompanying maps covering all aspects of country and life, are by subject specialists.

1843 Comité Spécial du Katanga. *Atlas du Katanga.* Bruxelles, 1929– . Five parts of the atlas were published in 1952. Scale is 1 : 200,000.

1844 Rouck, René de. *Atlas géographique et historique du Congo belge et des territoires sous mandat du Ruanda-Urundi.* 4th ed. Bruxelles, 1954. 11 p. maps (13 col.). 36 cm.
Forty-five maps and plans on 12 plates, with an alphabetic index of 5,972 names. The maps include physical geography, political and administrative divisions, history, economy, and plans of the seven chief cities.

Bibliographies

1845 Académie Royale des Sciences d'Outre-Mer. *Catalogue.* Bruxelles, Librairie Africaine Hubaut, 1970. 37 p.
The Institut Royal Colonial Belge was established in 1929. In 1954 its name was changed by royal decree to Académie Royale des Sciences Coloniales, and in December 1959 to the present form. (By royal decree it was attached on October 1, 1962, to the Ministère de l'Education Nationale et de la Culture; another decree in 1964 put in under royal patronage.) Its many publications, new series of which are dated from 1954, are listed in this periodically revised catalogue, which includes items out of print as well as those in stock.

Belgian Africa

1846 Belgium. Ministère des Affaires Africaines [until 1960 Ministère du Congo Belge et du Ruanda-Urundi]. *Liste des publications. Lijst der uitgaven.* Bruxelles. (Latest received, June 1959, 135 p.)

This periodically revised list covered official publications on the former Belgian colonies, including the many distinguished contributions in the fields of natural and human sciences that appear in the journals and monographic series of the government-sponsored organizations concerned with the Congo and Ruanda-Urundi. They are listed by agency or institution: the Direction de l'Agriculture of the Ministry with explanation of its serials, the outstanding *Bulletin Agricole du Congo Belge et du Ruanda-Urundi* and the related *Bulletin d'Information de l'INEAC,* followed by almost 30 pages of separate monograph titles; publications of other branches of the Ministry, including *Bulletin Officiel* and *Bulletin Administratif,* annual reports on administration, mapping services, etc.; publications of the Institut National pour l'Etude Agronomique du Congo Belge (INEAC), of the Institut des Parcs Nationaux du Congo Belge; the more general works issued by the Office de l'Information et des Relations Publiques pour le Congo Belge et le Ruanda-Urundi (INFORCONGO); the vast list of scientific publications of the Musée Royal du Congo Belge (now Musée Royal de l'Afrique Centrale); and the above-mentioned list of the Académie Royale des Sciences d'Outre-Mer.

1847 Berlage, Jean. *Répertoire de la presse du Congo belge (1884–1958) et du Ruanda-Urundi (1920–1958).* Bruxelles, Commission Belge de Bibliographie, 1959. 193 p. (Bibliographia belgica, no. 43)

Compilation of all periodicals issued in the Belgian African territories, including many with terminal dates, numerous ephemeral publications of mission presses in vernacular languages, etc. There are 662 titles.

In 1960 the Commissariat Générale à l'Information of the then Belgian Congo issued a *Répertoire de la presse au Congo et au Ruanda-Urundi, mis à jour en avril 1960* (Léopoldville, 1960, 38 l.). In addition, the Ministère de l'Education Nationale, Section Bibliothèque, of the Congolese Republic has issued a *Répertoire des périodiques congolais.* See also J. M. Van Bol, *La presse quotidienne au Congo belge* (Bruxelles, 1959, 112 p.).

1848 *Bibliographie ethnographique de l'Afrique sud-saharienne* [formerly... *du Congo belge et des régions avoisinantes*]. 1932– . Tervuren, Musée Royal de l'Afrique Centrale. Annual.

For annotation, see Part III, under Anthropology, no. 301.

Although the 'ethnographic' is signalized in the title of this voluminous annual listing, the subject matter covers a number of disciplines as well as a range of territory including much of black Africa. The selection of references is international in scope, though Belgian literature is of course very well represented.

1849 Boogaerts, Marcel, Martin Bruch, and Alois Seiler. *Bibliographien zur Erziehung, Politik und Geschichte im Kongo Kinshasa.* Freiburg im Breisgau, Bertelsmann Universitätsverlag, 1969. 169 p. (Materialien des Arnold – Bergstraesser – Instituts für kulturwissenschaftliche Forschung, v. 26)

Part of a larger research project designed to elucidate education and politics in Africa. The first section, compiled by Marcel Boogaerts, covers every aspect of education, including the history of education, educational methods, administration, statistics, training at different scholastic levels in elementary and high schools, higher education, missions, the role of women in education, foreign aid, and so forth. The second part, put together by Martin Bruch, lists printed material concerning politics in the Congo from 1960 to 1968. The third section, compiled by Alois Seiler, covers the history of the Congo from ancient times to independence, An additional section deals with linguistics and ethnography. There is also an index of names.

1850 Bustin, Edouard. *A study guide for Congo-Kinshasa.* Boston, African Studies Center, Boston University, 1970. 167 p.

An outstanding bibliographic guide divided into the following sections: General, Physical environment, Traditional societies, History, Colonial rule, Politics, Social change, The economy, Bibliographies. Each section has two parts – an evaluative essay and a bibliography. The Colonial rule section is divided into the Congo Free State and the Belgian Congo (1908–1960). For a useful listing of sources on education, see M. Boogaerts, 'Education in the Congo: A provisional systematical bibliography', *Cahiers Economiques et Sociaux*, v. 5, no. 2, June 1967, p. 237–265.

1851 Heyse, Théodore. *Bibliographie du Congo belge et du Ruanda-Urundi, 19—.* Bruxelles, G. van Campenhout, 1946–53. (Cahiers belges et congolais, nos. 4–7, 9–12, 16–22)

Pamphlets of about 40 to 70 pages listing by subject field writings on the Congo from 1939 to the date of publication. An article by Professor Heyse in *Zaïre* of June 1948, 'Le travail bibliographique colonial belge de 1876 jusqu'en 1933' (reprint, Bruxelles, Editions Universitaires, 1948, 20 p.), explains sources for earlier writings.

A separate list, published in the series Bibliographia belgica (no. 64, 1961), was *Bibliographie de H. M. Stanley, 1841–1904.*

1852 ——— *Bibliographie juridique du Congo belge et du Ruanda-Urundi, période 1939–51.* Bruxelles, 1953. 26 pts. in 1 v.

1853 ——— *Contribution au progrès des sciences morales, politiques et économiques relatives aux territoires d'outre-mer.* Relevés bibliographiques I–III. Bruxelles, Commission Belge de Bibliographie, 1957–61. 3 v. 104, 206, 190 p. (Bibliographica belgica, nos. 32, 57, 59)

Systematic bibliographies largely concerned with specific studies on the Congo and Ruanda-Urundi. The first volume contains 1,064 entries, the second 783, and the third 811, and each volume includes an author index.

1854 ——— *Documentation générale sur le Congo et le Ruanda-Urundi, 1950–1953.* Bruxelles, Commission Belge de Bibliographie, 1954. 31 p. (Bibliographia belgica, no. 4)

1855 ——— *Documentation . . . 1953–1955.* Bruxelles, G. van Campenhout, 1956. 56 p. (Cahiers belges et congolais, no. 26)

1856 ——— *Documentation . . . 1955–1958.* With the cooperation of Jean Berlage. Bruxelles, Commission Belge de Bibliographie, 1958. 84 p. (Bibliographia belgica, no. 39)

1857 ——— *Documentation . . . 1958–1960.* With the cooperation of Jean Berlage. Bruxelles, G. van Campenhout, 1960. 96 p. (Cahiers belges et congolais, no. 34)

The above four works are general listings supplementing the earlier special bibliographies.

1858 ——— *Index bibliographique colonial : Congo belge et Ruanda-Urundi; 1ère série 1937–38, 2e série 1938–39.* Bruxelles, G. van Campenhout, 1939, 1940.

Professor Heyse died on January 10, 1963. In the ARSOM *Bulletin des Séances*, no. 1, 1964, p. 137–155, there is a bibliography of his writings, prepared by

M. E. van Grieken. Many of the titles are concerned with bibliographical studies of the Congo.

1859 Huisman, M., and P. Jacquet. *Bibliographie de l'histoire coloniale, 1900–1930 : Belgique.* Paris, Société de l'Histoire des Colonies, 1932.

1860 Lemarchand, René. 'Selective bibliographical survey for the study of politics in the former Belgian Congo'. *American Political Science Review*, v. 54, Sept. 1960: 715–728.

Bibliographical essay by a political scientist. The references are to important works dealing with political developments in the Congo and with their geographical and historical background. Sources include the main official publications in addition to numerous articles in leading periodicals and in the *Encyclopédie du Congo belge*.

1861 Monheim, Christian. *Congo-bibliographie.* Antwerpen, Veritas, 1942. 211 p. Supplement, 1944. 40 p.

A systematic bibliography on the Belgian Congo based on the catalogue of the Bibliothèque de l'Université Coloniale de Belgique. Following introductory geographic references, the 1942 volume of some 4,000 entries is divided into four main subject classifications – politics and administration, economy, history, and literature and the arts.

1862 Simar, T. 'Bibliographie congolaise de 1895 à 1910'. *Revue Congolaise*, v. 1, 1910. Reprint: Brussels, Vroment, 1912. 61 p.

1863 Tervuren. Belgium. Musée Royal de l'Afrique Centrale. *Bibliographie géologique du Congo, du Rwanda et du Burundi.* v. 1– , Tervuren, 1952– .

Published in co-operation with the Commission de Géologie. Volumes are as follows: v. 1, 1818–1924 (1955); v. 2, 1925–34 (1953); v. 3, 1935–44 (1952); v. 4, 1945–54 (1955); v. 5, 1955–56 (1957); v. 6, 1957–58 (1959); v. 7, 1959–60 (1961); v. 8, 1961–62 (1963). Publication through v. 6 was under an early name of the Museum, Musée Royal du Congo Belge, and the bibliography title itself has varied somewhat. See also its *Catalogue*.

1864 Vandewoude, Emile J. L. M. *Documents pour servir à la connaissance des populations du Congo belge : Aperçu historique (1886–1933) de l'étude des populations autochtones, par les fonctionnaires et agents du service territorial, suivi de l'inventaire des études historiques, ethnographiques et linguistiques conservées aux Archives du Congo Belge.* Léopoldville, Section Documentation des Archives du Congo Belge, 1958. 246 l. (Archives du Congo belge, no. 2)

This large processed volume lists 563 papers preserved in the archives. Many are notes of two or three pages, others reports of considerable size. There are indexes of personal names, places, and ethnic and linguistic terms and appendices explaining official instructions for collecting and preserving the material.

1865 Walraet, Marcel. *Bibliographie du Katanga.* Fasc. I, *1824–1899.* Bruxelles, Institut Royal Colonial Belge, 1954. 136 p. map. (Section des sciences morales et politiques, Mémoires in-8°, v. 32, fasc. 3, Série historique)

1866 —— *Bibliographie du Katanga.* Fasc. II, *1900–1924.* Bruxelles, Académie Royale des Sciences Coloniales, 1956. 234 p. map. (Classe des sciences morales et politiques, Mémoires in-8°, n.s. v. 14, fasc. 1, Histoire)

1867 —— *Bibliographie du Katanga.* Fasc. III, *1925–1949.* Bruxelles, Académie Royale des Sciences d'Outre-Mer, 1960. 280 p. map. (Classe des sciences morales et politiques, Mémoires in-8°, n.s. v. 23, fasc. 4)

A comprehensive systematic listing, with alphabetical arrangement by author or title under each section. Entries in the first fascicle total 1,246, in the second, 2,168, and in the third 2,934. There is an author index for each fascicle, the one in Fasc. III being cumulative for all three; Fasc. II also contains a chronological index.

1868 Wattel, Pierre. *Bibliographie des mémoires de l'Institut des Territoires d'Outre-Mer.* Bruxelles, Commission Belge de Bibliographie, 1955. xi, 95 p. (Bibliographia belgica, no. 11) (903 entries)

Includes a geographical index and an author index. A list of very important works.

1869 Wauters, Alphonse-Jules. *Bibliographie du Congo, 1880–95 : Catalogue méthodique de 3,800 ouvrages, brochures, notices et cartes relatifs à la géographie et à la colonisation du Congo.* With the collaboration of M. Ad. Buyl. Bruxelles, Administration du Mouvement Géographique, 1895. xlix, 356 p.

A bibliography of the early writings on the Congo, beginning with ' Résumé chronologique des principaux faits de l'histoire du Congo '. Following the essay and the list of dates are references in subject classification.

Serials

1870 Académie Royale des Sciences d'Outre-Mer. Bruxelles.
The ARSOM series consists of the following:

> *Bulletin des Séances. Mededelingen der Zittingen.* v. 1– , 1930–54; n.s. v. 1– , 1955– .
>
> Annual volumes, published in varying numbers of fascicles that range from under 500 to over 1,700 pages per volume. Ten-year indexes have been issued, 1930–39, 1940–49, 1950–59. The volumes contain valuable articles and reports. The first number, ' Annuaire ', of each year includes a list of periodicals received by the Academy.
>
> Mémoires [monographs]:
>
> Classe des sciences morales et politiques. Mémoires. Verhandelingen.
> In-4°. v. 1– , 1933– . illus., maps.
> In-8°. v. 1– , 1933– . illus., maps.
>
> Classe des sciences naturelles et médicales. Mémoires. Verhandelingen.
> In-4°. v. 1– , 1931– . illus., maps.
> In-8°. n.s. v. 1– , 1932– . illus., maps.
>
> Classe des sciences techniques. Mémoires. Verhandelingen.
> In-4°. v. 1– , 1930– . illus., maps.
> In-8°. n.s. v. 1– , 1935– . illus., maps.

The Académie also issues a set of Publications hors-série. The list of all titles in the *Catalogue* fills over 26 pages. These publications are also included in the official Belgian government list, below.

1871 *Aequetoria: Mission Catholique.* 1937– . Coquilhatville, Congo. Quarterly. Publ. by the Mission Catholique de Coquilhatville.

1872 *Africa – Tervuren.* 1955– . Tervuren, Amis du Musée Royal de l'Afrique Centrale. Quarterly. Supersedes *Congo-Tervuren.*

Belgian Africa

1873 *Belgique d'Outre-Mer.* 1957– . Bruxelles. Monthly.
Leading review, published from 1945 to 1956 as *Revue Coloniale Belge*, the numbering of which it continues (1945–60).

1874 Belgium. Ministère des Colonies. Office Colonial. *Bulletin de l'Office Colonial.* Bruxelles. Monthly. (1910–40) For *Bulletin Officiel* and *Moniteur Congolais*, see no. 1941.

1875 ——— Ministère du Congo belge et du Ruanda-Urundi. *Rapport sur l'Administration Belge du Ruanda-Urundi.* 1921– . Bruxelles. Annual. (1921–60)

1876 *Bulletin Agricole du Congo.* 1910–61. Bruxelles. Quarterly, 1910–52; bi-monthly, 1953–61.
Issued by the Direction de l'Agriculture des Forêts et de l'Élevage of the Belgian Ministère des Affaires Africaines. Very important journal on all aspects of agriculture and rural life. Articles on other parts of Africa appear occasionally.

1877 *Bulletin des Tribunaux Coutumiers.* 1953–63. Elisabethville, Société d'Etudes Juridiques du Katanga.
Superseded by *Revue Juridique du Congo.*

1878 *Cahiers Economiques et Sociaux. Economic and Social Papers.* v. 1, no. 1– , Oct. 1962– . Léopoldville [Kinshasa], Institut de Recherches Economiques et Sociales (IRES), Université Lovanium. Quarterly.
The IRES (established in 1955) attempts to continue the work of research organizations that functioned in the Congo before independence, and includes among its publications several series devoted to works on African (especially Congolese) economic, social, and political affairs. The aim of its journal is not only to study isolated features of the economic and social changes taking place in Africa but also to establish and interpret the emerging patterns and structures of the economic and social order in Africa generally. Articles are either in French or in English and are followed by a summary in the other language.

1879 *Congo Mission News.* 1913– . Léopoldville. Quarterly.
Journal of the Congo Protestant Council.

1880 *Etudes Congolaises.* no. 1– , Mar. 1961– . Léopoldville, Institut National d'Etudes Politiques (Institut Politique Congolais); Bruxelles, Centre de Recherche et d'Information Socio-Politiques. Every 2 months.
Journal of political and social comments, published jointly by CRISP in Brussels and INEP in Léopoldville. Its regular sections are ' Dossier ' (a survey of the top question of the day), ' Chronique ', ' Les livres ', ' Textes et documents ', and ' Revue de presse '. Since 1970 called *Cahiers Congolais.*

1881 *Etudes d'Histoire Africaine.* 1970– . Annual. Kinshasa, ed. by the Université Lovanium de Kinshasa.

1882 *Folia Scientifica Africae Centralis.* v. 1, no. 1– , Mar. 1955– . Bukavu [etc.], IRSAC. Quarterly.
Bulletin of information on current activities of the Institut pour la Recherche Scientifique en Afrique Centrale, with sections on biological, human, and physical sciences, giving brief accounts of work done and titles of new publications. The bulletin did not cease with independence; combined nos. 2–3–4 (Dec. 31, 1960) of v. 6 were printed in Europe.

1883 Institut National pour l'Etude Agronomique du Congo. *Bulletin d'Information.* 1952–61. Bruxelles.

1884 ——— *Publication . . . Hors série.* Bruxelles.

367

Part III: area guide (*by colonial power, region and colony*)

1885 ———— *Publications . . . Série scientifique.* 1935– . Bruxelles.

1886 ———— *Publications. Série technique.* 1935– . Bruxelles.

1887 ———— *Spermatophytes.* 1948– . Bruxelles.

1888 ———— Bureau Climatologique. *Communication.* 1950– . Bruxelles.

1889 *Kongo-Overzee; Tijdschrift Voor en Over Belgisch-Kongo en Andere Overzeese Gewesten.* 1934– . Antwerpen. Bi-monthly (except Aug. and Sept.).

1890 Notre Colonie (Société Coopérative). *Revue Coloniale. Organ de l'Office Belge de Colonisation au Congo.* 1924–1957. Bruxelles. Irregular.

1891 *Problèmes d'Afrique Centrale.* 1947–59. Bruxelles. Quarterly. Title varies: 1947–50, *Bulletin*.
Bulletin of the Association des Anciens Etudiants de l'I.N.U.T.O.M.

1892 *Problèmes Sociaux Congolais.* 1946– . Lubumbashi, Centre d'Etude des Problèmes Sociaux Indigènes. Quarterly.
Has valuable articles on all aspects of the social life of the area. The Centre also publishes *Collection de Mémoires* irregularly.

1893 *Revue Belge de Géographie.* 1877– . Bruxelles, Société Royale Belge de Géographie. Bi-monthly until 1913, then quarterly.
Compte-rendu des actes de la société included in each volume. See also no. 1900.

1894 *La Revue Coloniale Belge.* 1945–1960. Bruxelles. Semi-monthly.
The leading popular journal on the Belgian Congo. Changed its title to *Belgique d'Outre-Mer* in 1957.

1895 *Revue Congolaise Illustrée.* 1929–66. Bruxelles, Association des vétérans de l'Etat indépendant du Congo. Monthly.
Title changed to *Revue Belgo-Congolaise Illustrée* with v. 33, no. 6, June 1962. Publication discontinued November 29, 1966.

1896 *Revue Judiciaire Congolaise.* Périodique trimestriel. 1962– . Léopoldville.

1897 *Revue Juridique du Congo.* 1933– . Elisabethville, Société d'Etudes Juridiques du Katanga. Monthly, 1933–63; bi-monthly, 1964.
Formerly called *Bulletin des Tribunaux Coutumiers* and *Bulletin des Juridictions Indigènes et du Droit Coutumier Congolais.*

1898 Société Belge d'Etudes Coloniales, Brussels. *Bulletin de la Société Belge d'Etudes Coloniales*, 1894–1919. Bruxelles. Bi-monthly, 1895–99; monthly, 1900–1919.
Continued as *Congo : Revue Générale de la Colonie Belge*, 1920–1940, then as *Zaïre*.

1899 Société d'Etudes et d'Expansion. *Bulletin.* 1907– . Liège. Frequency varies.
Many important Belgian officials published in this journal.

1900 Société Royale Belge de Géographie, Brussels. *Bulletin.* 1876– . Bruxelles.

1901 Tervuren, Belgium. Musée Royal de l'Afrique Centrale. Annales. Série in-8°. Sciences historiques. Annalen. Reeks in-8°. Historische Wetenschappen. no. 1– , Tervuren, 1964– .
Supersedes in part its Annales, Série in-8°, Sciences historiques et économiques. Among the other important series (Annales) produced by the Musée are the following: Botaniques (1898–1934); Sciences économiques (1947–); Sciences géologiques (1948–); Sciences zoologiques (earlier series started in 1898) (1948–); Archives d'ethnographie (1960–); Documentation économique (1962–).

Belgian Africa

See also no. 1903, *Catalogue* (Tervuren, 1966, 56 p.), and *Afrika-Tervuren* (1961– , quarterly; formerly *Congo-Tervuren*, 1955–61).

1902 —————— Annales. Série in-8°. Sciences humaines. Annalen. Reeks in-8°. Wetenschappen van de mens. no. 33– , Tervuren, 1960– .

Nos. 1–32, 1951–60, published in four subseries: Anthropologie, Ethnographique, Linguistique, Préhistoire. An outstanding series. Almost 60 volumes had appeared by 1968.

1903 ——— *Catalogue.* Tervuren, 1966. 56 p.

1904 —————— Monographies ethnographiques. Ethnographische Monographien. no. 1– , Tervuren, 1954– .

1905 *Voix du Congolais.* 1945– . Léopoldville, Kalina. Bi-monthly; monthly.

1906 *Zaïre : Revue Congolaise*; *Congoleesch Tijdschrift.* 1947–60. Bruxelles, Editions Universitaires. illus. Monthly (except Aug. and Sept.)

Important journal which superseded *Congo : Revue Générale de la Colonie Belge*, published from 1920 to the outbreak of World War II. Its bibliographical section was issued by the Ministère du Congo Belge as a separate entity. The periodical was really terminated with the independence of the Congo in 1960, although one issue appeared in 1962.

Reference works

1907 Académie Royale des Sciences d'Outre-Mer.

The Académie Royale was started in 1928 as the Institut Royal Colonial Belge, renamed in 1954 Académie Royale des Sciences Coloniales, finally becoming known in 1959 under its present title. The Académie published a bulletin and a large number of monographs on historical, anthropological, legal, bibliographical and related subjects. A selection of their monographs follows:

> Ceulemans, R. P. F. *La question arabe et le Congo (1883–1892).* 1959. 396 p. (Mémoire no. 22 : 1) Bibliography : p. 368–380.

An important study, based on extensive archival research. The author, a former missionary, seeks to do justice to the political and economic, as well as the humanitarian, issues involved in the relations between the Congo Free State and the so-called Arabs in the Congo.

> *La Force Publique de sa naissance à 1914 : Participation des militaires à l'histoire des premières années du Congo.* 1952. 585 p. (L'Institut Royal Colonial Belge, no. 27) Bibliography : p. 533–539.

A military history compiled by the Deuxième Section de l'Etat-Major de la Force Publique, based on archival as well as secondary material. The work is specifically designed to do justice to those who fought 'under grim conditions, without hope of reward for the purpose of pacifying barbarous tribes and opening the way to civilisation'. There is also detailed material concerning organization, recruitment and training; there are numerous statistical tables and an index.

> Grévisse, F. *Le centre extra-coutumier d'Elisabethville : Quelques aspects de la politique indigène du Haut-Katanga industriel.* 1951. 448 p. (Mémoire no. 21)

The author, a Belgian administrator, surveys the administrative organization, the economic life, the living conditions, the courts, the social life and other questions concerning the African townsmen in Elisabethville. The author looks forward to a new Belgo-African community in Katanga. A very different inquiry is Jean Sohier, *Essai sur la criminalité dans la province de Léopoldville : Meurtres et infractions apparentées* (1959, 311 p., Mémoire no. 21:2). The author, a Belgian judge, investigates felonies, especially homicides tried at courts in the province of Léopoldville.

Roeykens, P. A. *Les débuts de l'oeuvre africaine de Léopold II (1875–1879).* 447 p. (Mémoire no. 1:1)

In 1952 the Institut Royal Colonial Belge set up a historical commission to study the origins of Belgian colonialism. Roeykens, a Capuchin missionary, set out to publish the main archival documents available at the time in Belgium. He also determined to throw light on ' the internal or obscure work of the King and of his collaborators, without whom our colonial empire could never have been created '. In the back of all his publications the author listed the unpublished sources he had used. These derived mainly from the Archives du Ministère des Affaires Etrangères, the Archives du Ministère des Colonies, the Archives Générales du Royaume, and the Archives de l'Institut Royal Colonial Belge. Each of his publications also contained a detailed bibliography and maps.

Subsequent volumes included the following: *Le dessein africain de Léopold II : Nouvelles recherches sur la genèse et sa nature (1875–1876)* (1956, 264 p., Mémoire no. 10:1); *Léopold II et la Conférence Géographique de Bruxelles (1876)* (1956, 298 p., Mémoire no. 10:2); *La période initiale de l'oeuvre africaine de Léopold II : Nouvelles recherches et documents inédits (1875–1883)* (1957, Mémoire 10:3); *Léopold et l'Afrique 1855–1880 : Essai de synthèse et de mise en point* (1958, 411 p., Mémoire no. 14:2).

1908 Académie Royale des Sciences d'Outre-Mer (ARSOM). *Biographie coloniale belge.* Bruxelles, Librairie Falk Fils, 1948–58. 5 v. ports.

Published by ARSOM under its earlier name, Institut Royal Colonial Belge. The work is not confined to Belgians connected with the Congo (e.g., Leopold II), but includes entries for Livingstone, Stanley, and others – more than 2,000 biographies in all. All entries are signed, dated, and documented (normally with a bibliography, sometimes with references as well). Each volume has a separate alphabetic sequence of biographies of deceased persons. Volumes 4 and 5 both carry cumulative biography and author indexes to previous volumes as well as corrigenda and addenda. Volume 6 title changed to *Biographie belge d'outre-mer.*

1909 Académie Royale des Sciences d'Outre-Mer (ARSOM). *Livre blanc : Apport scientifique de la Belgique au développement de l'Afrique centrale.* [Title also in Flemish] Bruxelles, 1962–63. 3 v. map (fold. col.), tables.

v. 1, *Classe des sciences morales et politiques.* 503, xx p.

v. 2, *Classe des sciences naturelles et médicales.* 436, xvi p.

v. 3, *Classe des sciences techniques.* 183, xxxii p.

A collective work reviewing the Belgian contribution to the Congo and Rwanda and Burundi, undertaken by ARSOM after the former colonies became independent countries. The many articles in French and Flemish are by leading specialists in studies of the Congo. Each volume is separately indexed, and there is a final alphabetical index covering the whole work. The first volume contains an introduction by L. Guébels, president of ARSOM, and surveys of scientific research problems by L. van den Berghe, of colonial congresses by P. Coppens, of bibliography and documentation by Théodore Heyse, and of archives by Mme M. van Grieken-Taverniers.

1910 American University, Washington, D.C. Special Operations Research Office. *Area handbook for the Republic of the Congo (Léopoldville).* Prepared by Foreign Areas Studies Division. Washington, 1962. xii, 657 p. maps, tables. Includes bibliographies.

Country study prepared to provide basic factual background for American officers in the Congo, with comprehensive information presented objectively in short paragraphs. Sections are on sociological background, political background (through 1961), economic background, and national security. Each section is followed by a long bibliography.

1911 Andersson, Efraim. *Messianic popular movements in the Lower Congo.* Uppsala, Almqvist & Wiksells Boktr. (New York), 1958. xiii, 287 p. illus., plates (part col.) (Studia ethnographica Upsaliensia, no. 14) Bibliography: p. xi–xiii.

By a missionary who spent many years in Central Africa, this is the most comprehensive account in English of Simon Kimbangu and his cult, with data on other ' prophet movements ' in French Equatorial Africa. Most valuable study of impact of colonial rule and Christianity.

1912 *Annuaire des missions catholiques au Congo belge et au Ruanda-Urundi.* 3d ed. Ed. by the Rev. J. van Wing, S.J., and V. Goemé, S.J. Bruxelles, Edition Universelle, 1949. 671 p. maps.

Includes history, current organization, locations, number of converts, directory of priests, etc. The second edition was issued in 1935.

1913 Anstey, Roger. *King Leopold's legacy : The Congo under Belgian rule, 1908–1960.* Issued under the auspices of the Institute of Race Relations, London. London and New York, Oxford University Press, 1966. xiv, 293 p. illus., ports., plates, map. Bibliography: p. 265–272.

A sequel to Ruth Slade's *King Leopold's Congo* (see no. 1985), this is a well documented account of the origins, nature, and impact of Belgian rule in the Congo. Two opening chapters describe what Leopold's legacy comprised. The early period of Belgian rule is then covered, followed by a discussion of the inter-war years, with focus on African administration and the pressures of customary society, and on economic development and town growth. Following a chapter on prophet movements, the latter half of the book deals with the period 1940–60. An appendix consists of parts of Reverend J. van Wing's ' Evolution of Ba-Kongo custom ', first published in 1927.

1914 Artigue, Pierre. *Qui sont les leaders congolais?* 2d ed. Bruxelles, Editions Europe-Afrique, 1961. 375 p. (Collection ' Carrefours africains ')

Biographical sketches of Congolese personalities. A preliminary edition came out in 1960 (139 p.; ' Carrefours Africains ', no. 3). The greatly enlarged revision contains more than 800 biographies. They vary in length from 20 to several hundred words, including for many individuals a carefully dated account of education and pre-independence activities.

1915 Belgium. Parlement. Chambres des Représentants. *Compte-rendu analytique.*

1916 ———— ———— Sénat. *Compte-rendu analytique.*

Covers debates in both chambers. See also *Documents Parlementaires,* which contain reports of parliamentary committees on various topics on government in the Congo. Each year the minister of the colony presented to the chambers a *Rapport sur l'administration de la colonie.* These reports are basic to the history of Belgian rule in the Congo. They cover political, social and economic developments, and are useful also for records of major legislative proceedings, meetings of the advisory body of the governor general, lists of labour organizations, census figures and so forth. A major source for the economic and social conditions of the Congo are the *comptes-rendus analytiques des séances des conseils coloniaux*, and reports of the Conseil de Gouvernement made up of high officials and various representative interests in the Congo. Each year the governor-general gave a speech in the Conseil de Gouvernement – *Discours d'ouverture du Gouverneur Général* – which is valuable for information on the political objectives and policies of the administration.

1917 ———— Institut National de Statistique. *Annuaire statistique de la Belgique et du Congo Belge.* 1870–1960. Brussels.
See also *Bulletin mensuel des statistiques générales du Congo et du Ruanda-Urundi,* which provides an impressive amount of information on human and economic developments in the colony.

1918 ———— Ministère des Affaires Africaines. Direction de l'Agriculture, des Forêts et de l'Elevage. *Volume jubilaire du Bulletin Agricole du Congo Belge et du Ruanda-Urundi, 1910–1960.* Bruxelles, 1960. 226 p. illus. (part col.), maps, tables, diagrs.
Published by the Ministère under its earlier name, Ministère du Congo Belge et du Ruanda-Urundi; text in French only.
Fiftieth anniversary volume of the official journal, which has been the main source of current information on Congolese agriculture. The work, setting forth the history and accomplishments of Belgian agricultural endeavour in the Congo, appeared almost simultaneously with the independence proclamation.

1919 ———— ———— Direction des Etudes Economiques. *La situation économique du Congo belge et du Ruanda-Urundi.* 1950–59. Bruxelles, 1951–60. tables, charts. Annual. 1959 ed., 272 p. 84 tables.
Yearly survey of the economy, relating to the Congo only from 1950 to 1954, then including Ruanda-Urundi. All features of economic life are thoroughly covered in tabulated data from official and private sources.

1920 ———— Ministère des Colonies. *Annuaire officiel.* Brussels, 1959. 35th ed.

1921 ———— *La situation économique du Congo belge et du Ruanda-Urundi, 1950–59.* Brussels. 1960.

1922 ———— ———— *Recueil à l'usage des fonctionnaires et agents du service territorial au Congo belge.* Brussels. Many editions.

1923 ———— Ministère du Congo Belge et du Ruanda-Urundi. *Statistiques des mouvements de capitaux au Congo belge et au Ruanda-Urundi de 1887 à 1956.* Brussels, 1958. 308 p.
Excellent source for data on the colonial period.

1924 ———— Office de l'Information et des Relations Publiques pour le Congo Belge et le Ruanda-Urundi (INFORCONGO). *Belgian Congo.* [v. 1 trans. from the French by F. H. and C. Heldt, v. 2 by Claire van Gelder] Brussels, 1959–60. 2 v. 547, 187 p. illus., maps, tables. Bibliography: v. 2, p. 181–187.
Translation of the original French edition in 1958. Volume 1 is a digest of information on country and people, history, political institutions, economic and social life, etc. Volume 2 contains statistics; this part was designed to be revised periodically.

1925 ———— ———— *Congo belge et Ruanda-Urundi : Guide du voyageur.* 4th ed. Bruxelles, 1958. 798 p. illus., maps.
Formal guide-book, with itineraries and detailed regional descriptions preceded

Belgian Africa

by general articles. The first edition in 1949 and subsequent editions until 1956 were issued by the Belgian Office du Tourisme du Congo Belge et du Ruanda-Urundi. Two editions in English, titled *Traveller's guide for the Belgian Congo and Ruanda-Urundi*, were issued in 1951 and 1956.

1926 Bevel, Maurice Louis. *Le dictionnaire colonial (encyclopédie): Explication de plus de 8.000 noms et expressions se rapportant aux diverses activités coloniales, depuis l'époque héroïque jusqu'aux temps présents.* 3d ed. Bruxelles, Guyot, 1955. 202, 26 p. illus., port., maps (1 col. fold.)
Refers particularly to the Belgian Congo, giving, in alphabetical order, names of persons, places, and organizations and words and phrases connected with colonial activities. There is a supplement.

1927 Bézy, F. *Problèmes structurels de l'économie congolaise.* Louvain, Institut de Recherches Economiques et Sociales, 1957. 285 p.
An analysis of wage-rates and business practices. For mining and related activities, see A. Marthoz, *L'industrie minière et métallurgique au Congo belge* (Brussels, ARSC, 1955, 67 p.), and F. Bézy, *Changements de structure et conjoncture de l'industrie minière au Congo, 1938–1960* (Léopoldville, IRES, 1961, 30 p.). See also *L'Union Minière du Haut-Katanga, 1906–1956* (Brussels, Cuypers, 1956, 281 p.), and *Cominière, 1910–1960* (Brussels, Imprimerie Malvaux, 1962, 175 p.).

1928 Bilsen, A. A. J. van. *L'indépendance du Congo.* Tournai, Casterman, 1962. 236 p.
By a Belgian specialist on the Congo, professor at the Institut Universitaire des Territoires d'Outre-Mer, who in 1960 acted as adviser to Kasavubu at the Brussels Round Table Conference and afterward in Leopoldville. His ' Thirty-year plan for the political emancipation of Belgian Africa ', published in 1955, *Un plan de trente ans pour l'émancipation politique de l'Afrique belge* (Antwerp), was at the time considered an impossibility at long range. The 1962 volume is a compilation of articles and documents issued during the last period of hurried preparation for independence, including writings to the spring of 1961, after Lumumba's downfall and death. It supplements an earlier work, *Vers l'indépendance du Congo belge et du Ruanda-Urundi : Réflexions sur les devoirs et l'avenir de la Belgique en Afrique centrale* (Kraainem, 1958, 295 p.).

1929 Bouvier, Paule. *L'accession du Congo belge à l'indépendance : Essai d'analyse sociologique.* Bruxelles, Editions de l'Institut de Sociologie, Université Libre de Bruxelles, 1965. 392 p. tables. (Collection du Centre National d'Etudes des Problèmes Sociaux de l'Industrialisation en Afrique Noire) Bibliography: p. 365–378.
A sociological approach to decolonization in the Congo. Professor Bouvier's study is in five main parts: the social, economic, and political framework for emancipation; social factors involved in the behaviour of various Belgian and Congolese groups; characteristics of the Congolese political movements; metropolitan reactions and Congolese counterreactions (including a long section on the sociological components of the Brussels Round Table Conference); and events in the Congo from 1959 through 1962.

1930 Braekman, E. M. *Histoire du Protestantisme au Congo.* Bruxelles, Editions de la Librarie des Eclaireurs Unionistes, 1961. 391 p. plates, maps, tables. (Collection ' Histoire du Protestantisme en Belgique et au Congo belge ', v. 5) Bibliographical footnotes.
An outline history in which the author discusses the precursors of evangelization from the 16th to the late 19th century, traces the development of Protestantism through 1959, and describes Belgian missionary activities. Included are statistical

373

data, a chronological list of missionary societies and their stations, and both an onomastic and a geographical index.

1931 Brausch, Georges. *Belgian administration in the Congo.* London, Oxford University Press, 1961. 92 p.

An account of Belgian administration and decolonization by a former Belgian official, who outlines the shifts of Belgian policy preceding decolonization, shows how these were connected with changes in metropolitan politics, and demonstrates how the morale of the Belgian civil service was gradually eroded and finally broke.

1932 Bulck, G. van. *Les recherches linguistiques au Congo Belge : Résultats acquis, nouvelles enquêtes à entreprendre.* Bruxelles, G. van Campenhout, 1948. 767 p. fold. map. (Institut Royal Colonial Belge, Section des Sciences Morales et Politiques, Mémoires in-8°, v. 16)

Synthesis of results of linguistic studies for the Congo by a foremost authority on the subject. In 1949 Father van Bulck's *Manuel de linguistique bantoue* was published as fasc. 3 of v. 17 of this series. Many other papers on linguistics by him and by his colleagues, G. Hulstaert and L. de Boeck, are to be found in the indexes of the *Mémoires* of the Institut, now the Académie Royale des Sciences d'Outre-Mer.

1933 Bureau de l'Enseignement Catholique. *Où en est l'enseignement au Congo?* Léopoldville, 1960. 31 p.

Useful for an appraisal of the education system of the Congo at the time of independence.

1934 Centre d'Information et de Documentation du Congo Belge et du Ruanda-Urundi. *Liste des sociétés et institutions coloniales ayant un siège en Belgique et au Congo belge ou au Ruanda-Urundi.* Bruxelles, 1954. 74 p.

The many publications of INFORCONGO (previously called Centre d'Information et de Documentation – CID) were for general orientation purposes and included general reports, commercial statistics, maps, customs requirements, directories, etc. This directory shows the wealth of institutions concerned with the Congo during the Belgian régime.

1935 Centre de Recherche et d'Information Socio-Politiques. *Congo 19—.* Bruxelles, 1960– (Les dossiers du CRISP)

Eight annual volumes have been issued in this Dossiers series: *Congo 1959 : Documents belges et africains* (1960, 319 p.); ' Bibliographie politique sur le Congo en 1959 ', p. 303–309). (A second revised edition, edited by J. Gérard-Libois, was issued in 1961.)

CRISP, founded in 1958 by a group of Belgian scholars, journalists, and economists (and now including correspondents from other European countries, the United States, and the Congo), has undertaken this valuable sequence of annual documentary histories of Congolese politics. In addition to the Dossiers, CRISP publishes a number of special studies, a mimeographed bulletin, *Courrier Africain*, the bi-monthly journal *Etudes Congolaises* and the mimeographed monthly *Chronique des Evènements Relatifs au Congo*. In the series Les études du CRISP (see no. 1955), *Sécession au Katanga*, by J. Gérard-Libois (1963, 363 p.; English ed., *Katanga secession*, trans. by Rebecca Young, Madison, University of Wisconsin Press, 1966, 377 p.), was issued jointly with INEP. Also in this series, in collaboration with INEP and the Institut de Recherches Economiques et Sociales (IRES), Université Lovanium, Léopoldville, is *Rébellions au Congo*, v. 1, by Benoît Verhaegen (1966, 568 p., map; includes bibliographies), a major study based on documents and interviews.

Among other volumes in the Dossiers series are two on political parties in the Congo: *A.B.A.K.O., 1950–1960 : Documents*, edited by Benoît Verhaegen (1962, 367 p., illus., map), and *Parti solidaire africain (P.S.A.) : Documents, 1959–1960*, edited by Herbert Weiss and Benoît Verhaegen (1963, 315 p., map, tables). *Les partis politiques congolais*, by J. C. Willame (1964, 156 l., map), has appeared as the first volume of Dossiers documentaires in the series Travaux africains.

1936 Chronique de Politique Etrangère (periodical). *La crise congolaise, 1 janvier 1959–15 août 1960*. Bruxelles, Institut Royal des Relations Internationales, 1960. (*Its* v. 13, no. 4–6, July–Nov. 1960: 411–1012)

1937 —— *L'évolution de la crise congolaise de septembre 1960 à avril 1961*. (*Its* v. 14, nos. 5–6, Sept.–Nov. 1961: 565–1182)

1938 —— *L'O.N.U. au Congo, avril 1961 à octobre 1962*. (*Its* v. 15, nos. 4–6, July–Nov. 1962: 339–1108)

1939 —— *Conclusion de l'opération de l'O.N.U. au Congo, 1962–1963*. (*Its* v. 17, no. 1, Jan. 1964, 126 p.)

Solid documentation on political developments in the Congo before and since independence, in three sets of combined issues plus a single issue of this leading Belgian journal of international affairs.

1940 Clerfayt, A. *Le développement énergétique du Congo belge et du Ruanda-Urundi*. Brussels, Académie Royale des Sciences d'Outre-Mer, 1960. 437 p.

An analysis of the power infrastructure of the Congo.

1941 Congo, Belgian. *Bulletin Officiel. Amtelijk blad*. 1908– . Bruxelles. Monthly.

Supersedes *Bulletin Officiel* of the Congo Free State (1885–1908). Some numbers are accompanied by supplements. Superseded in 1960 by *Moniteur Congolais*. See also *Bulletin administratif* published at Léopoldville (1912–1959) for the Belgian Congo and earlier for the Congo Free State (1885–1910).

1942 Congrès Colonial National. Brussels.

The Congrès Colonial National was a voluntary organization composed of Belgian politicians, former civil servants, missionaries, industrialists, and others interested in promoting Belgian colonial enterprise. In 1921 the Congress founded a Comité permanent, which issued a *Bulletin* and also specialized reports on a great variety of subjects concerned with colonial questions. The Assemblée Générale of the Congress held periodic sessions at which colonial affairs were discussed. See also its *Rapports et comptes rendus* (1921–?).

1943 Congrès Scientifique du Cinquantenaire, Elisabethville, 1950. *Comptes-rendus*. Bruxelles, Comité Spécial du Katanga, 1951. 7 v.

These volumes, published in commemoration of the 50th anniversary of the Comité Spécial du Katanga, contain authoritative survey articles on all phases of scientific, geographical, economic, and social life of the territory. Contributors include all specialists on the Katanga.

The numerous scientific publications of the Comité are issued in several monographic series: Sér. A, Geography, geology, and mines; Sér. B, Natural history, etc. Titles will be found in the annual *Rapport de l'exercice* (1920– ; v. 1 covers 1910–19).

1944 Cornet, René J. *Terre katangaise : Cinquantième anniversaire du Comité Spécial du Katanga, 1900–1950*. Bruxelles, 1950. 317 p. illus., maps.

Published in a de luxe edition for the 50th anniversary of the Comité Spécial du Katanga and written by the son of the geologist whose pioneer work led to the discovery of Katanga's great mineral wealth. Cornet *père*'s standard history, *Katanga*, was issued in a third edition by Cuypers, Brussels, in 1946. The present book, lavishly illustrated with photographs and drawings, is a journalistic account, its author having been at the time editor of the leading popular journal devoted to the Belgian Congo, the *Revue Coloniale Belge*.

1945 Cornevin, Robert. *Histoire du Congo, Léopoldville-Kinshasa: Des origines préhistoriques à la République démocratique du Congo.* 2d ed., rev. and enl. Paris, Berger-Levrault, 1966. 348 p. 19 maps, 54 photos. (Mondes d'outre-mer, Série: Histoire) Bibliography: p. 316–329.

A most useful full-scale history of the Congo. The colonial period is well covered. Particularly valuable for students.

1946 Daye, Pierre. *L'empire colonial belge.* Bruxelles, Editions du 'Soir, 1923. 669 p.

Standard work on the economical, industrial and agricultural development of the Belgian Congo. Also useful for survey of medical care in the colony.

1947 De Craemer, Willy, and Renée C. Fox. *The emerging physician: A sociological approach to the development of a Congolese medical profession.* Stanford, Calif., Hoover Institution, 1968. 99 p. Bibliography: p. 97–99.

An original and valuable approach via the study of a career pattern as a key to understanding social change during the colonial period.

1948 Denis, Jacques. *Le phénomène urbain en Afrique centrale.* Bruxelles, Académie Royale des Sciences Coloniales, 1958. 407 p. (Classe des sciences morales et politiques, Mémoires in-8°, n.s. v. 19, fasc. 1) Bibliography: p. 371–394.

Study by a Jesuit priest and geographer of the new cities and the urban life and problems that have accompanied the rapid industrialization in the post-war era. The concern is chiefly with Congolese centres, though Father Denis includes some cities of neighbouring territories. He has used material from over 400 sources listed in his bibliography.

A more specialized study is the author's *Les Yaka du Kwango: Contribution à une étude ethno-démographique.* (Tervuren, Musée Royal de l'Afrique Centrale, 1964, xi, 107 p., maps, tables; Annales, Sér. in-8°, Sciences humaines, no. 53), an account of the diffusion of the Bayaka people over the *territoires* of Popokabaka, Kasongo-Lunda, and Kenge.

1949 Dumont, Georges-H. *La table ronde belgo-congolaise (janvier-février 1960).* Paris, Editions Universitaires, 1961. 308 p. map, tables, fold. chart. (Encyclopédie universitaire) At head of title: *Le Congo, du régime colonial à l'indépendance, 1955–1960.*

Description of the origins, composition, and proceedings of the Brussels Round Table. It was at this conference, attended by a Congolese delegation of almost 100 persons, representing some 15 different political groups, that the target date for Congo independence was eventually fixed for June 30, 1960. The resolutions of the conference are given in the body of the text and numerous documents appear in appendices. Both an analytical index and an index of personal names are included.

1950 *Elisabethville, 1911–1961.* Brussels, Cuypers, 1961. 265 p.

Historical survey of one of two largest cities in the Congo. See also L. Whyms, *Léopoldville, son histoire 1881–1956* (Brussels, Office de Publicité, 1956, 196 p.); and Valdo Pons, *Stanleyville: An African urban community under Belgian administration* (London, Oxford University Press, 1969, 376 p.).

Belgian Africa

1951 *Encyclopédie du Congo belge.* Bruxelles, Bieleveld, 1950(?)–52. 3 v. 722, 668, 862 p. illus., col. plates, maps (part col.), diagrs.

Synthesis of the then available knowledge about the Congo, prepared through the collaboration of about 50 specialists. Statistics are of 1948. Volume 1 covers history, ethnology, geology, climate and soils, botany, colonial agricultural industries; v. 2, forestry, fauna, animal husbandry, mines and mining; v. 3, colonial hygiene, diseases of animals, plants, applied entomology, economic life, political institutions, and education. At the end of v. 3 is an alphabetical index plus an index of 60-odd maps.

1952 Ethnographic Survey of Africa: Central Africa, Belgian Congo [series]. London, International African Institute (IAI).

For the general note on this series, see no. 333.

The studies relating to Congolese peoples were also published in the Annales du Musée Royal du Congo Belge, Tervuren, Sér. in-8°, Sciences de l'homme, Monographies ethnographiques. Some that have appeared are the following:

> *Les tribus Ba-Kuba et les peuplades apparentées.* By Jan Vansina. 1954. xiii, 64 p. fold. map. (Monographies ethnographiques, v. 1) (Bibliography: p. 57–61)
>
> *Les Bira et les peuplades limitrophes.* By H. van Geluwe. 1957. xiii, 165 p. fold. map. (Monographies ethnographiques, v. 2) (Bibliography: p. 155–161)
>
> *Mamvu-Mangutu et Balese-Mvuba.* By H. van Geluwe. 1957. xv, 195 p. fold. map. (Monographies ethnographiques, v. 3) (Bibliography: p. 175–182)
>
> *Les peuplades de l'entre Congo-Ubangi (Ngbandi, Ngbaka, Mbandja, Ngombe et Gens d'Eau).* By H. Burssens. 1958. 219 p. fold. map. (Monographies ethnographiques, v. 4) (Bibliography: p. 175–198)
>
> *Les Bali et les peuplades apparentées (Ndaka, Mbo, Beke, Lika, Budu, Nyari).* By H. van Geluwe. 1960. 130 p. fold. map. (Monographies ethnographiques, v. 5) (Bibliography: p. 115–122)

See also *The Lele of the Kasai,* by Mary Douglas (1963, xiv, 286 p., fold. map; IAI series; bibliography, p. 280–282).

An earlier study was issued in 1935 by the Musée Royal du Congo Belge (Publications du Bureau de Documentation Ethnographique, Sér. 2, Monographies idéologiques, v. 1): *Les peuplades du Congo Belge : Nom et situation géographique,* by Joseph Maes and Olga Boone.

1953 Franck, Louis. *Le Congo belge.* Bruxelles, La Renaissance du Livre, 1928. 2 v. 379, 489 p.

Monumental work. Profusely illustrated with large folding maps. Covers every aspect of Belgian colonization in the Congo.

1954 Ganshof van der Meersch, W. J. *Fin de la souveraineté belge au Congo : Documents et réflexions.* Bruxelles, Institut Royal des Relations Internationales; La Haye, M. Nijhoff, 1963. 684 p. plates, maps, charts. ' Bibliographie ': p. 671–676; ' Notice bibliographique de l'auteur ': p. 678–679.

The author, a lawyer and professor, was named Ministre des Affaires Générales en Afrique (Resident Minister in the Congo) without portfolio in May 1960 and resigned his post in July 1960. The tumultuous events in which he was involved during this two-month period are documented and his thoughts on them recorded in this useful volume of source material which was largely inspired by his official report, *Congo mai-juin 1960 : Rapport du Ministre*

Chargé des Affaires Générales en Afrique (Bruxelles, 1960, 482 p., maps, fold. charts, tables). A chronology from January 4, 1959, to April 6, 1962, is provided, with page references given for events covered in the volume. Included are 10 appendices and an index.

1955 Gérard-Libois, Jules. *Katanga secession.* Trans. by Rebecca Young. Madison, University of Wisconsin Press, 1966. 377 p.

The best of the Katanga secession studies of the period. The author, director of the Center for Socio-Political Research and Information (CRISP) at Brussels, has drawn on a wealth of unpublished material supplemented by personal information. He sketches in the background of pre-independence Katanga politics, analyzes the upheavals in the Katanga, the part played by the United Nations, and ends with an interesting chapter entitled ' Concluding observations ', cast in the form of questions and answers.

1956 Gevaerts, Franz. *Vade-Mecum à l'usage des fonctionnaires et agents territoriaux du Congo belge.* Costermansville, Belgian Congo, 1953. 585 p.

Important source for an assessment of Belgian colonization in the Congo. Contains the legislation on most subjects needed by the colonial officials in the different provinces of the Congo.

1957 Goffart, Ferdinand. *Le Congo : Géographie physique, politique et économique. Deuxième édition revue et mise à jour par George Morissens.* Bruxelles, 1908. 502 p. maps.

Excellent standard work. One of the most detailed sources for Congolese ethnology, ethnography, political structure, and economy of the period.

1958 Halewyck de Heusch, Michel. *La charte coloniale.* Bruxelles, 1919. 4 v.

A monumental survey of all aspects of the relationship between Belgium and the Congo. See also Jean-Pierre Paulus, *Droit public du Congo belge* (Bruxelles, Institut de Sociologie Solvay, 1959).

1959 —— *Organisation politique et administrative de la colonie.* Bruxelles, Bibliothèque Coloniale Internationale, 1936.

A full treatment of the administration of the colony. See also for the ' extra-customary ' centres Guy Baumer, *Centres indigènes extra-coutumiers* (Paris, 1939), which provides a valuable analysis of the relation between the European administrators and the chiefs and the indigenous population.

1960 Hertefelt, Marcel d', A. Trouwborst, and J. Scherer. *Les anciens royaumes de la zone interlacustre méridionale (Rwanda, Burundi, Buha).* London, International African Institute, 1962. 252 p. maps. (Ethnographic Survey of Africa, East Central Africa, pt. 14) Bibliographies: Rwanda, p. 99–111; Burundi, p. 165–169; Buha (of Tanganyika), p. 221–223.

1961 Hostelet, Georges. *L'oeuvre civilisatrice de la Belgique au Congo, de 1885 à 1945.* v. 1, *L'oeuvre économique et sociale.* Bruxelles, Institut Royal Colonial Belge, 1954. 512 p. maps (1 fold. in pocket), tables. (Section des sciences morales et politiques, Mémoires in-8°, v. 33, fasc. unique)

1962 —— *L'oeuvre civilisatrice de la Belgique au Congo, de 1885 à 1953.* v. 2, *Les avantages dont les blancs et les noirs ont bénéficié et bénéficieront de l'oeuvre civilisatrice de la Belgique au Congo.* Bruxelles, Académie Royale des Sciences Coloniales, 1954. 411 p. tables. (Section des sciences morales et politiques, Mémoires in-8°, v. 37, fasc. 2) ' Ouvrages consultés (Tomes 1 et 2) ': v. 2, p. 400–403.

In the above two volumes, the author, former director of the Institut de Sociologie Solvay, presents a review and appreciation of Belgian colonization in the

Congo from the economic and social standpoint. The introduction to the first volume includes a summary of Congolese conditions of life before the arrival of the Belgians. The text then outlines the political, administrative, economic, and social situation before and during World War II. In the second volume Hostelet first describes what he considers the many advantages gained by both the black man and the white man up to the eve of World War II, and then comments on the potential benefits to be derived from the 10-year plan decreed in 1949. Despite his optimistic interpretation, the author considers that there might be serious racial and political conflict.

1963 Jadot, J. M. *Les écrivains africains du Congo belge et du Ruanda-Urundi : Une histoire – un bilan – des problèmes.* Bruxelles, Académie Royale des Sciences Coloniales, 1959. 167 p. (Classe des sciences morales et politiques, Mémoires in-8°, n.s. v. 17, fasc. 2) Bibliography: p. 152–156.
A literary history covering the period 1885 to the late 1950s. Jadot traces the evolution of an oral literature into a written literature, reviews the various literary genres and themes, and analyses the problems facing new African writers. A good survey of colonial literature.

1964 Joye, Pierre, and Rosine Lewin. *Les trusts au Congo.* Brussels, Société Populaire d'Editions, 1961. 318 p.
Marxist interpretation of economic control during the colonial period.

1965 Lacroix, Jean-Louis. *Industrialisation au Congo : La transformation des structures économiques.* Paris and La Haye, Mouton, 1967. 358 p. map, tables, graphs. (Institut de Recherches Economiques et Sociales, Université Lovanium de Kinshasa, Recherches africaines, no. 1) Bibliographical footnotes.
A technical analysis in which Dr. Lacroix details and appraises three major developments that have occurred in the process of the Congo's industrialization: (1) the transformation of methods of production; (2) the establishment of rapport between various sectors of the national economy; and (3) the development of international economic relations. The principal sectors of Congolese industry are reviewed in a 50-page appendix.

1966 Lagergren, David. *Mission and state in the Congo : A study of the relations between Protestant missions and the Congo Independent State authorities with special reference to the Equator District, 1885–1903.* Uppsala, C. W. K. Gleerup Lund, 1970, 365 p. Bibliography: p. 350–359.
This is one of many missionary studies produced at Uppsala in the series entitled *Studia Missionalia Upsaliensia.*

1967 Lemarchand, René. *Political awakening in the Belgian Congo.* Berkeley, University of California Press; London, Cambridge University Press, 1964. xi, 357 p. plates, ports., maps. Bibliographical footnotes.
Survey of the factors in the Belgian-controlled territory that made for ' fragmentation ', tribal and linguistic divisions, different patterns of administration, centralization which undermined chiefly authority, etc. A detailed account that gives damning evidence of what the author considers to be Belgian mistakes.

1968 Lumumba, Patrice. *Congo, my country.* Trans. by Graham Heath. London, Pall Mall Press with Barrie and Rockliff, 1962. xxxii, 195 p. ports., facsim.
Congo, my country was written by Lumumba during 1956–57 and first published posthumously in 1961 in Belgium under the title *Le Congo, terre d'avenir – est-il menacé ?* A notable historical document, it not only provides a record of Lumumba's ideas (many of which he later discarded) and of his political develop-

Part III: area guide (by colonial power, region and colony)

ment, but also offers valuable insight into the attitudes of the Congolese *évolués* towards Belgian rule and the attitudes of the Congolese leaders on the eve of independence. The volume is enhanced by Colin Legum's foreword, 'The life and death of Patrice Lumumba '.

1969 —— *La pensée politique de Patrice Lumumba.* Texts and documents collected and presented by Jean Van Lierde. Paris, Présence Africaine, 1963. xlvi, 406 p. port.

1970 Masoin, Fritz. *Histoire de l'Etat Indépendant du Congo.* Namur, Impr. Picard-Balon, 1912–13. 2 v.
A monumental history of the Congo Free State. See also A. J. Wauters, *Histoire politique du Congo Belge* (Bruxelles, 1955) and Henry Morton Stanley, *The Congo and the founding of its Free State* (London, 1885, 2 v.).

1971 Merriam, Alan P. *Congo : Background of conflict.* Evanston, Ill., Northwestern University Press, 1961. 368 p. illus. (Northwestern University African Studies, no. 6) Includes bibliography.
Detailed study of the development of the national movement in the Congo, the parties and their leaders, and the Belgian background for relinquishing authority.

1972 Michiels, Albert, and N. Laude. *Congo belge et Ruanda-Urundi : Géographie et notice historique.* 18th ed., rev. and enl., of *Notre colonie.* Bruxelles, Edition Universelle, 1957. 370 p. illus., maps.
A comprehensive survey, originally published in the early 1920s and revised to include later statistics. Its arrangement follows the usual order: physical geography, anthropology, economics, and politics and administration. Ruanda-Urundi is treated in a separate section following the same order, and the very brief outline of chief historical events takes up the last 30 pages. There are chapter bibliographies, with references mostly in French.

1973 Monheim, Christian. *Le Congo et les livres: Anthologie coloniale.* Bruxelles, A. Dewit, 1928. 368 p.
Historical, political and social accounts.

1974 Morel, Edmund Dene. *History of the Congo reform movement.* Completed by Wm. Roger Louis and Jean Stengers. Oxford, Clarendon Press, 1968. 289 p. illus. Bibliography: p. 274–277.
Valuable survey of the reform movement that forced the Belgian government to take over the Congo Free State from Leopold II. See also his very important exposé that started the criticism of Leopold's rule: *Red rubber : The story of the rubber slave trade flourishing in the Congo* . . . (New York, 1969 reprint, 213 p.).

1975 Mosmans, Guy. *L'église à l'heure de l'Afrique.* Paris, Casterman, 1961. 225 p.
Intelligent review of Belgian policies and errors in the period before independence by a Catholic priest.

1976 Moulaert, G. *Problèmes coloniaux d'hier et d'aujourd'hui : Pages oubliées. 38 années d'activité coloniale.* Bruxelles, Edition universelle. 1939. 649 p.
Survey of 28 years of administrative, financial, social and economic developments in the Belgian Congo.

1977 Nicolai, H., and J. Jacques. *La transformation des paysages congolais par le chemin de fer : L'exemple du BCK.* Brussels, Académie Royale des Sciences d'Outre-Mer, 1954. 208 p.
A good study of social and economic change along the line of rail. See also for studies of rural development: *Promotion de la société rurale du Congo Belge et*

du Ruanda-Urundi : Rapport général des journées d'études coloniales tenues à l'INUTOM à Anvers, les 23, 24 et 25 Avril 1957 (Brussels, Ministère du Congo Belge et du Ruanda-Urundi, 1958, 282 p.); and *Vers la promotion de l'économie indigène* (Brussels, Institut de Sociologie, U.L.B., 1956, 600 p.).

1978 Petillon, L. A. M. *Témoignage et réflexions.* Brussels, La Renaissance du Livre, 1967. 443 p.

Belgian administrator in the Congo and Ruanda-Urundi from 1939 to 1958 here gives his account of Belgian rule. He succeeded Ryckmans as governor-general and earlier had been *chef de cabinet* to Ryckmans. The Ten-year Plans for the Congo and Ruanda were largely drafted by Petillon.

1979 Piron, P., J. Devas, et al., eds. *Codes et lois du Congo Belge.* Brussels, Larcier, 1959–1960. 3 v.

Basic collection (in its third edition). See also Jean-Pierre Paulus, *Droit public du Congo Belge* (Brussels, Institut de Sociologie, 1959, 519 p.).

1980 Robert, Maurice. *Le Congo physique.* 3d ed., rev. and completed. Liège, H. Vaillant-Carmanne, 1946. 449 p. illus., maps. Supplements: 1948, 83 p.; 1954, 15 p. Bibliography: p. 417–427.

By a professor of geology at the Université Libre of Brussels, author of many studies of Central Africa, this work was first published in 1919. It was brought up to date with a synthesis of existing information in two later editions and two supplements. Its coverage includes geology, mineralogy, climatology, hydrology, soils, and biogeography.

1981 ———— *Géologie et géographie du Katanga, y compris l'étude des ressources et de la mise en valeur.* Publ. under the auspices of the Union Minière du Haut-Katanga. Bruxelles, 1956. xvi, 620 p. illus., fold. maps. Bibliography: p. 589–601.

Folio volume prepared in honor of the 50th anniversary of the founding of the Union Minière. The author, an authority on development of Central Africa, describes it as a synthesis of available knowledge about this territory, which was perhaps the largest single contributor to Belgian prosperity. (He was himself responsible for about 30 of the studies recorded in the bibliography.) Part 1 is on the physical and biological geography of the area; Part 2 tells briefly the history of European penetration; and Part 3 (p 359–588) covers in detail the development of the Katanga's resources (mineral, vegetable, and animal) and 'sources of energy', including hydroelectric power and communications.

An anniversary volume, *Union Minière du Haut Katanga, 1906–1956 : Evolution des techniques et des activités sociales,* appeared in 1957.

1982 Ryckmans, Pierre. *Dominer pour servir.* New and rev. ed. Brussels, Edition Universelle, 1948. 189 p.

1983 ———— *La politique coloniale.* Louvain, Editions Rex. 1934. 117 p.

Ryckmans was a governor-general of the Belgian Congo. The above two works represent a defence of the Belgian colonial case, comparable in many respects, and similar in inspiration to Lord Lugard's famous *The dual mandate in British tropical Africa* (Edinburgh, W. Blackwood, 1922). See also his *Politique indigène* (Bruxelles, 1949).

1984 Slade, Ruth N. *English-speaking missions in the Congo Independent State (1878–1908).* Bruxelles, Académie Royale des Sciences Coloniales, 1959. 432 p. maps. (Classe des sciences morales et politiques, Mémoires in-8°, n.s. v. 16, fasc. 2) Bibliography: p. 409–414.

By an English scholar who has done extensive research in archival material, particularly that relating to the missionary activities, which are studied in detail in this work.

Part III: area guide (by colonial power, region and colony)

1985 —— *King Leopold's Congo : Aspects of the development of race relations in the Congo Independent State.* London and New York, Oxford University Press, 1962. xi, 230 p. illus., ports., maps. Bibliography: p. 215–219.

In this book, issued under the auspices of the Institute of Race Relations, Dr. Slade examines the first European contacts with the Congo, the acquisition and rule of the Congo by Leopold II, and the founding of the Congo Free State. Her account is carried through the annexation by Belgium in 1908 and up to World War I.

1986 Sohier, Jean. *Répertoire général de la jurisprudence et de la doctrine coutumières du Congo et du Ruanda-Urundi jusqu'au 31 décembre 1953.* Bruxelles, Maison F. Larcier, 1957. 975 p.

Standard compilation of the customary law of the Belgian colonies. A condensed version by Antoine Sohier was also issued by the same publisher: *Traité élémentaire de droit coutumier du Congo belge* (2d ed., rev. and enl., 1954, 206 p.).

1987 Sourdillat, Jacques. *Les chefferies au Congo belge.* Paris, Domat-Montchrestien, 1950. 440 p.

A valuable survey of native administration after the reforms of the 1930s. For the later period, see Victor Vermeulen, *Déficiences et dangers de notre politique indigène* (Brussels, 1953, 108 p.).

1988 Stengers, Jean. *Belgique et Congo : L'élaboration de la Charte Coloniale.* Bruxelles, Renaissance du Livre, 1963. 251 p. (' Notre passé ') Bibliography: p. 237–240.

The book outlines the steps and the work of the commission leading to the promulgation of the Charte Coloniale in 1908, when the territory became a formal colony of Belgium. Excerpts from the text of the charter are on p. 229–236. See also his excellent work, *Combien le Congo a-t-il coûté à la Belgique?* (Brussels, ARSOM, 1957).

1989 Turnbull, Colin M. *The forest people.* New York, Simon & Schuster, 1961. 288 p. illus.

In this book, authored by an anthropologist writing from personal experience, scholarly ethnological data on the pygmies of the Congo forest are set in a narrative so readable that it made the best-seller lists. See also his *The lonely African* (1962).

The standard works on the pygmies of Africa are those of Father Paul Schebesta, originally written in German and issued in English translation by Hutchinson, London: *Among Congo pygmies* (1932, 287 p.), *My pygmy and Negro hosts* (1936, 287 p.), and *Revisiting my pygmy hosts* (1936, 288 p.). They were given definitive publication in more scholarly form in the ARSOM Mémoires series (Coll. in-4°, v. 1, 2, 4, 5): *Die Bambuti-Pygmäen von Ituri : Ergebnisse zweier Forschungsreisen zu den zentral-afrikanischen Pygmäen* (Bruxelles, Hayez, 1938–50, 2 v. in 4, illus.).

1990 *Union Minière du Haut Katanga, 1906–1956 : Evolution des techniques et des activités sociales.* Bruxelles, L. Cuypers, 1957. 355 p. plates, col. maps, tables, col. diagrs.

Anniversary volume containing papers by members of the Union, some of which were presented at scientific congresses. The *Rapports du Conseil d'Administration* of the Union Minière were issued annually in Brussels, providing important information on the economy of the Katanga and the country as a whole.

1991 Van der Kerken, G. *La politique coloniale belge.* Antwerp, Editions 'Zaïre', 1943. 238 p.
A good analysis of Belgian policies in the Congo. See also his earlier work, *Les sociétés bantoues du Congo belge et les problèmes de la politique indigène* (Brussels, Bruylant, 1920. 462 p.).

1992 Vandewoude, Emiel J. L. M. *Documents pour servir à la connaissance des populations du Congo belge : Aperçu historique (1886–1933) de l'étude des populations autochtones, par les fonctionnaires et agents du service territorial, suivi de l'inventaire des études historiques, ethnographiques et linguistiques conservées aux Archives du Congo Belge.* Léopoldville, Section Documentation des Archives du Congo Belge, 1958. 246 l. (Archives du Congo belge, no. 2)
Beginning with an essay on the studies carried out by the agents of the administration in the Congo during the years from the creation of the Free State to 1933, this large processed volume lists 563 papers preserved in the archives.

1993 Vanhove, Julien. *Histoire du Ministère des Colonies.* Bruxelles, Académie Royale des Sciences d'Outre-Mer, 1968. 168 p. (Classe des sciences morales et politiques, n.s. v. 35, fasc. 3)
Most useful administrative history of the colonial ministry from its founding in 1908. The annexures list principal office holders and chart administrative structures.

1994 Vansina, Jan. *Introduction à l'ethnographie du Congo.* Kinshasa, Université Lovanium; Kisangani, Université Libre du Congo; Lubumbashi, Université Officiel du Congo; Bruxelles, CRISP, 1966. 228 p. maps. (Editions universitaires du Congo, no. 1) Includes bibliographies.
A concise study of the peoples of the Congo, describing their history, languages, economies, social and political structure, religion, and art. The four main sections of the volume are arranged by region – the northern savannas, the forest area, and so forth.

1995 Vermeulen, V. *Déficiences et dangers de notre politique indigène.* Bruxelles, Impr. Michel Ange, 1953. 108 p.
A critical review of Belgian policies towards the indigenous people of the Congo.

1996 Wauters, A. J. *Histoire du Congo belge.* Brussels, P. Van Fleteren, 1911. 435 p.
Good older account of Leopold and the Congo Free State.

1997 Willequet, Jacques. *Le Congo belge et la Weltpolitik, 1894–1914.* Bruxelles, Presses Universitaires de Bruxelles, 1962. 499 p. plates, maps. (Travaux de la Faculté de Philosophie et Lettres, no. 22) Bibliography: p. 451–466.
Detailed study of German, Belgian, and British policies towards the Congo and Portuguese Africa. Its thesis is that the Belgian Congo was never the primary concern of German foreign policy. This is an indispensable work for the study of the period.

1998 Wing, Joseph van. *Etudes bakongo : Sociologie, religion et magie.* 2d ed. Bruges, Desclée, De Brouwer, 1959. 512 p. illus. (Musée Lessianum, Section missiologique, no. 39) Bibliography: p. 15–17.
A celebrated study, published first in 1930–37, by a Jesuit priest who had been a missionary in Kisantu. The revision includes a number of additions. Other studies by Father van Wing have been published in the Mémoires series of ARSOM.

Part III: area guide (by colonial power, region and colony)

1999 Young, Crawford. *Politics in the Congo: Decolonization and independence.* Princeton, N.J., Princeton University Press, 1965. xii, 659 p. maps, tables. Bibliography: p. 609–644.

A lucid and readable analysis of the nature of an African political system. Professor Young first describes the colonial power structure and then successively discusses the Belgian vision of decolonization and the disintegration of the power structure, the Congolese response to colonialism, and the trends and forces emerging in the years of independence and strife, 1960–63. An interim assessment of the events of 1964 is offered in an epilogue.

Rwanda and Burundi

Note On July 1, 1962, the U.N. trust territory known as Ruanda-Urundi and administered by Belgium was divided into two parts, one becoming the Republic of Rwanda and the other the Kingdom of Burundi. Since much of the material below deals with them before independence, it is presented under a single heading.

For further specific references, see also the Congo section, above, wherein are listed so many materials that apply also to Ruanda-Urundi that their repetition here is considered unnecessary.

Bibliographies

2000 Boston University. African Studies Program. *Rwanda and Burundi: Selected bibliography.* Boston, 1964. 5 l. Processed.

2001 Clément, Joseph R. A. M. *Essai de bibliographie du Ruanda-Urundi.* [Usumbara, Service des Affaires Indigènes] 1959. 201, xxii p.

Published under the auspices of IRSAC (Institut pour la Recherche Scientifique en Afrique Centrale), this classed listing of books and periodicals covers ethnology, history, government, geography, agriculture, etc. An author index is included.

2002 Walraet, Marcel. *Les sciences au Rwanda: Bibliographie (1894–1965).* Bruxelles, Bibliothèque Royale de Belgique, 1966. 211 p. (Académie Royale des Sciences d'Outre-Mer, Classe des sciences morales et politiques, Mémoires in-8°, n.s. v. 34, fasc. 5)

This volume, the first extensive bibliography on Rwanda, was compiled by the head of the Centre de Documentation Africaine of the Bibliothèque Royale de Belgique. The 1,934 books and articles listed appear under five main sections: general bibliographies and documentation (including geography and scientific research); the humanities; physical sciences; life sciences (e.g., conservation, botany, zoology, medicine); and agronomic sciences. Arrangement is alphabetical by author. There is an index of authors, tribal names, and place-names, as well as a brief chronological index. See also Simon Nahayo, ' Contribution à la bibliographie des ouvrages relatifs au Burundi (Afrique Centrale) ', *Genève Afrique*, v. 10, no. 1, 1971, and v. 10, no. 2, 1971, a bibliography divided by topics.

Belgian Africa

Reference works

2003 Belgium. Ministère du Congo Belge et du Ruanda-Urundi. *Rapport sur l'administration belge du Ruanda-Urundi.* 1921– . Bruxelles. Annual. (1921–60)
Annual survey of Belgian mandate control.

2004 ——— Office de l'Information et des Relations Publiques pour le Congo Belge et le Ruanda-Urundi. *Le Ruanda-Urundi.* Bruxelles, 1959. 377 p. maps (18 col., 6 in pocket), tables, diagrs.
A general survey prepared by specialists, a number of them connected with IRSAC. The five parts treat geography, history, governmental organization, economic life, and social life. A translation into English by Goldie Blankoff-Scarr was issued in several parts by this office in 1960, all with the main title *Ruanda-Urundi : Economy* (2 v.), *Social achievements* (79 p.) and *Geography and history* (79 p.).

2005 Bourgeois, R. *Banyarwanda et Barundi.* Bruxelles, Académie Royale des Sciences Coloniales, 1954– . illus., maps. (Classe des sciences morales et politiques, Mémoires in-8°) Includes bibliographies.
The Banyarwanda dwell in Rwanda, the Barundi in Burundi. Four volumes have been published of this exhaustive anthropological study in the Mémoires series. Volume 1, *Ethnographie* (790 p.; n.s. v. 15), appearing in 1957, was not the first issued. The other volumes are v. 2, *La coutume* (1954, 472 p.; v. 35); v. 3, *Religion et magie* (1956, 376 p.; n.s. v. 4); v. 4, *L'évolution du contrat de bail à cheptel au Ruanda-Urundi* (1958, 60 p.; n.s. v. 9, fasc. 4).

2006 Centre de Recherche et d'Information Socio-Politiques. *Rwanda politique, 1958–1960.* Documents presented by F. Nkundabagenzi. Bruxelles, 1961. 423 p. map. (Les dossiers du CRISP) Bibliography: p. 407–412.
The first complete assemblage of facts and documents (many unpublished) relating to the political changes as the Tutsi-dominated feudal society broke down under the voting weight of the Hutu majority.

2007 *Décolonisation et indépendance du Rwanda et du Burundi.* Bruxelles, Institut Royal des Relations Internationales, 1963. 309 p. (*Chronique de Politique Etrangère*, v. 16, nos. 4–6, July–Nov. 1963: 439–748)
Survey with complete documentation from official sources.

2008 Lemarchand, René. *Rwanda and Burundi.* London, Pall Mall Press, 1970. xiv, 562 p.
According to the author, this is 'a trial essay in the sociology of revolutionary change in contemporary Africa'. The study specially investigates the colonial background and the sudden change in Belgian policy in 1959, the civil strife between Hutu and Tutsi, as well as the extent to which the new states do, or do not, differ from the older Tutsi monarchies.

2009 Leurquin, Philippe. *Le niveau de vie des populations rurales du Ruanda-Urundi.* Louvain, Institut de Recherches Economiques et Sociales, 1960. 420 p. illus., maps, tables, diagrs. (Publications de l'Université Lovanium de Léopoldville, no. 6) Bibliography: p. 353–376.
Excellent study by an outstanding Belgian economist.

2010 Louis, Wm. Roger. *Ruanda-Urundi, 1884–1919.* Oxford, Clarendon Press, 1963. xvii, 290 p. maps. Bibliographical note: p. 261–272; notes: p. 272–278.
A diplomatic and administrative history of the two countries, which the author

calls by the joint name under which they were administered until independence in 1962. During most of the period covered in this study, the kingdoms formed part of German East Africa.

2011   Maquet, Jacques J. *The premise of inequality in Ruanda : A study of political relations in a Central African kingdom.* London, published for the International African Institute by Oxford University Press, 1961. 199 p. illus., ports., maps. Bibliography: p. 186–194.

Professor Maquet, social anthropologist, was director of IRSAC in Elisabethville. This book, a synthesis of research carried out over some years, was published in part at Tervuren (Musée du Congo Belge) in 1954 as *Le système des relations sociales dans le Ruanda ancien.* It is regarded as an authoritative analysis of the respective roles of the ruling Tutsi and the subject Hutu in the former society of Ruanda-Urundi.

See also his *Elections en société féodale : Une étude sur l'introduction du vote populaire au Ruanda-Urundi* (1959, 231 p., maps, tables, illus., graphs; Mémoire no. 21:2).

In 1956 the Belgians organized the first elections in Ruanda-Urundi in which the entire male adult population was invited to take part. The author furnishes a detailed analysis of the election, of the candidates' places in society, and of the elections' impact on the country's ethnic problems. The writer believes that the elections helped to spread Western political concepts and that political life would continue to centre on the problem of ethnic ' castes '.

2012   Syracuse University. Maxwell Graduate School of Citizenship and Public Affairs. Program of Eastern African Studies. *The political development of Rwanda and Burundi.* By John B. Webster. Syracuse, N.Y., 1966. 121 p. (Occasional Paper, no. 16) Bibliography: p. 101–121.

An ethno-political history based primarily on resources available at Syracuse University. The author traces the development of the two countries from precolonial Tutsi rule to the mid-1960s.

GERMAN AFRICA

Note   This section lists items concerned with the relatively brief period of German colonial rule in Africa. Many of the titles could have been listed under the mandate country or power, but it was felt useful to present a coherent overview of German Africa as a unit. The same reasoning prompted us to do the chapter on Italian Africa. For more material on individual countries, see country sections and no. 476, Schiller, for legal material.

When Bismarck founded the German overseas empire, he intended to place the main responsibility for colonial governance on chartered companies that were to perform the bulk of the administrative work. Bismarck's design, however, did not work. The Deutsch-Ostafrikanische Gesellschaft had to relinquish its responsibility in 1890. (For the history of the Gesellschaft, see Bruno Kurtze, *Die Deutsch-Ostafrikanische Gesellschaft : Ein Beitrag zum Problem der Schutzbriefgesellschaften und zur Geschichte Deutsch-Ostafrikas*, Jena, G. Fischer, 1913.) The Deutsche Kolonialgesellschaft für Südwest Afrika refused altogether to shoulder the administrative responsibilities that Bismarck had wished to confer on the company. (See Ludwig Sander, *Geschichte der deutschen Kolonialgesellschaft für Südwest Afrika, von ihrer Gründung bis zum Jahre 1910 . . .* , Berlin, D. Reimer, 1912, 2 v.)

Between 1884 and 1890, a small group of officials within the Foreign Office supervised administration in the colonies. In 1890, a new section, the Kolonialabteilung, was set up within the Foreign Ministry. This section published the *Amtsblatt für die Schutzgebiete des Deutschen Reichs*, later known as *Deutsches Kolonialblatt*. In 1894, the Director of the Kolonialabteilung was empowered to represent his department in the legislature, and the colonial section began to take an ever-increasing part in supervising colonial budgets, organizing tours of inspection, drafting colonial legislation, and so forth. In 1907, after a period of colonial crises, the Kolonialabteilung was replaced by the Kolonialamt, a separate ministry. The Kolonialamt continued to operate for some years even after Germany had lost her colonies in the Great War. In 1919 it became known as the Reichskolonialministerium. In 1920 its functions were taken over by the Kolonialzentralverwaltung, which operated within the Ministerium für Wiederaufbau (Ministry for Reconstruction). Its work was finally completed in 1921, and the *Kolonialblatt* ceased publication.

The Kolonialamt published annual reports (known as *Jahresberichte*) and memorials (*Denkschriften*), which appeared as supplements to the *Kolonialblatt*. The Kolonialamt and its predecessor also put out a regular series, the *Mitteilungen aus den deutschen Schutzgebieten . . .* (1888–1919) which, from 1909 onward, were supplemented by special *Ergänzungshefte*. In addition the Kolonialamt produced a massive series of *Veröffentlichungen*, detailed monographs on a broad range of economic and scientific questions. These and similar publications (such as the *Medizinal-Berichte über die deutschen Schutzgebiete*) bore witness to the primacy which the Germans briefly attained in a vast range of colonial research.

In 1890, the Germans also set up an important advisory council of colonial experts that was known as the Kolonialrat. The Kolonialrat continued to operate until 1908, when the Kolonialamt decided to get rid of a body which had been so closely allied with the former colonial administration. The Kolonialrat dealt with a broad range of administrative, political, economic, and scientific matters; it also provided a forum for various colonial lobbies. The Kolonialrat issued reports on its work, which were published in the *Kolonialblatt*.

The Reichstag also played a major part in the machinery of German colonial supervision. In practice it initiated a good deal of legislation. It was a forum for discussion and it had to provide revenue. The high cost of colonialism and the need for grants-in-aid provided the Reichstag with added political leverage. In all probability, no colonial power during this period experienced as much parliamentary opposition to colonialism as Germany in the Reichstag. The Reichstag debates (*Verhandlungen des Reichstags*) thus provide detailed information concerning a broad range of colonial questions. So do the *Anlagebände* (appendices), which contain such items as committee reports, texts of treaties, consular reports and bills. Until 1900, these volumes also included the colonial budget; thereafter this information was published in separate volumes known as the *Haushalts-Etats für die Schutzgebiete*. All laws were brought together in a semi-official publication known as the *Deutsche Kolonialgesetzgebung . . .* (put out in 13 volumes, 1893–1910).

Students of German colonial history must also consult material produced by a considerable number of semi-official or private agencies. These include bodies as varied as the Deutsche Afrikanische Gesellschaft (the German branch of the International African Association), the Deutsche Gesellschaft zur Erforschung Aequatorialafrikas, the Deutsche Kolonial Eisenbahnbau- und Betriebsgesellschaft, the Komitee zur Einführung von Erzeugnissen aus den deutschen Kolonien, and a score of others. German humanitarian opinion found expression in the *Koloniale Rundschau*, which began publication in 1909. This journal was the organ of the Gesellschaft für Eingeborenenschutz; scholars such as Dietrich Westermann and Ernst Vohsen were associated with its publication.

The most important of all colonial societies was the Deutsche Kolonialverein (founded in 1882). In 1887 this body merged with Karl Peters's Gesellschaft für Deutsche Kolonisation; it finally became known as the Deutsche Kolonialgesellschaft. The Deutsche Kolonialgesellschaft was responsible for numerous publications. In 1899 it began to publish the *Beiträge zur Kolonialpolitik und Kolonialwirtschaft*, renamed after 1904 the *Zeitschrift für Kolonialpolitik, Kolonialrecht und Kolonialwirtschaft*. The Kolonialgesellschaft also put out a more general magazine, frankly propagandist in nature, known as the *Kolonialzeitung*, which carried information on all aspects of colonial policy. The Kolonialgesellschaft had a special economics committee, known as the Kolonialwirtschaftliche Komitee. This body was responsible for putting out a considerable number of publications which included *Der Tropenpflanzer* (an agricultural journal) and specialist monographs on subjects as varied as colonial trade or the production of hides. The committee created a Botanische Zentralstelle as a headquarters for plant research. In addition it set up a considerable number of subcommittees to study the production of particular commodities.

Space limits prevent us from surveying the various learned institutions which also concerned themselves with colonial research. The most important one was Kolonialinstitut at Hamburg, whose 43-volume series of *Abhandlungen* forms a major source of information on subjects such as demography, legislation, linguistics, hydrology, economics and geography. Another important source is the collection of proceedings of the various colonial congresses (*Verhandlungen des deutschen Kolonialkongresses*, Berlin, 1902, 1905, 1910 and 1924), which were sponsored by the Kolonialgesellschaft.

A complete survey concerning the newspapers and periodicals of interest to German colonization would require an article of its own. The principal journals issued in Germany itself have been listed in the text. Scholars should of course consult the main daily newspapers in Germany. In addition, there were local German organs in the colonies. These include the *Deutsch Südwestafrikanische Zeitung* (1901–14), known from 1898 to 1900 as *Windhuker Anzeiger*; the *Swakopmunder Zeitung* (1911–12), subsequently merged with the *Südwestafrikanische Zeitung*. These journals elucidate settler opinion in South-West Africa. The *Deutsch-Ostafrikanische Zeitung* (1899–1914), published at Dar es Salaam, the *Deutsch-Ostafrikanische Rundschau* (Dar es Salaam, 1908–14) and the *Usumbara Post* (Tanga, 1904–14) performed a similar function for East Africa. Local government gazettes include the *Amtlicher Anzeiger für Deutsch-Ostafrika* (Dar es Salaam, 1900–1916), the *Amtsblatt für das Schutzgebiet Kamerun* (1908–14), *Amtlicher Anzeiger für das südwestafrikanische Schutzgebiet* (Windhuk, 1910–1914), and *Amtsblatt für das Schutzgebiet Togo* (Lome, 1906–14). (See Part I for a description of German archival holdings.) Readers should also consult the entries for Rwanda and Burundi.

Bibliographies

2013 African Law Association in America, Inc. *Newsletter number 5*. April 15, 1967. n.p.
Contains a detailed bibliography concerning German colonial law and indexes to compilations and series. The bibliography is divided into general works and works concerning particular colonies. See also no. 476.

2014 Bridgman, Jon, and David E. Clarke. *German Africa : A select annotated bibliography.* Stanford, Calif., Hoover Institution, Stanford University, 1965. (Hoover Institution Bibliographical Series, no. 19)
A detailed bibliography going up to 1964. The work contains a general note on German official and semi-official publications, as well as annotated lists of general works, followed by annotated lists on each of the German African colonies. The authors provide nearly 1,000 titles. They also give a description of material dealing with German Africa contained in the British Confidential Prints prepared by the Colonial Office and the Foreign Office between the years 1888 and 1906, as well as an alphabetical list of serials and newspapers respectively.

2015 Brose, Max. *Repertorium der deutsch-kolonialen Literatur, 1884–1890.* Berlin, Winckelmann, 1891. 113 p.

2016 Carlson, Andrew R. *German foreign policy, 1890–1914, and colonial policy : A handbook and an annotated bibliography.* Metuchen, N.J., Scarecrow Press, 1970. vii, 333 p. maps, tables.
This annotated bibliography covers a variety of subjects, including German domestic and foreign policy, the franchise, leading personalities, naval and military questions, etc. There are short introductory essays and a table of ' events in German foreign and colonial policy 1884–1914 '. The colonial section, covering pages 285 to 333, is subdivided into a general section and portions concerning particular colonies. An indispensable guide to modern German history.

2017 Deutsche Kolonialgesellschaft. *Die deutsche Kolonialliteratur im Jahre : 1902–1908.* Berlin, Wilhelm Süsserott, 1904–9.
These bibliographies were published annually as special numbers of the *Beiträge zur Kolonialpolitik und Kolonialwirtschaft.* They were edited by Maximilian Brose, librarian of the German Kolonialgesellschaft, and later on by Hubert Henoch. The works cited include articles in learned journals, legal publications, etc., as well as books. The entries are grouped by territory and, within each territory, by topic.

2018 Deutsche Kolonialgesellschaft. *Die deutsche Kolonialliteratur von 1884– 95.* Berlin, Deutsche Kolonialgesellschaft, 1897. 158 p.

2019 Köhler, Jochen, ed. *Deutsche Dissertationen über Afrika : Ein Verzeichnis für die Jahre 1919–1959.* Bonn, K. Schroeder, 1962. unpaged.
Published under the auspices of the Deutsche Afrika Gesellschaft, Bonn. Lists 795 items.

2020 Pogge von Strandmann, Hartmut, and Alison Smith. ' The German empire in Africa and British perspectives : A historiographical essay ', in Prosser Gifford and Wm. Roger Louis, eds., with the assistance of Alison Smith, *Britain and Germany in Africa : Imperial rivalry and colonial rule,* p. 709–795. New Haven, Conn., Yale University Press, 1967.
A detailed and up-to-date essay which gives a general review of the printed literature concerning Anglo-American rivalry in the colonies, Germany's bid for the colonies, local aspects of German-British rivalry, the Heligoland-Zanzibar treaty, Anglo-German relations respecting the Transvaal, the Portuguese colonies and the Congo, as well as German and British war aims during and after the First World War. The author then discusses the literature concerning German, as well as British, administration; the study of the colonial period in general and of the German colonial period in particular. He also provides a great deal of information concerning German archival sources, printed material of official

provenance and so on. The essay also describes the structure of the German Colonial Office, lists the principal officials concerned with colonial affairs, and finally gives a list of titles extending over more than 20 pages. The author has brought the subject up to date in a more recent article entitled 'The German role in Africa and German imperialism', *African Affairs*, v. 6, no. 277, Oct. 1970, p. 381–389, which has an appended bibliography. See also Schramm, *Deutschland und Übersee* . . . , no. 2066; pages 476–600 contain a detailed bibliography illustrating various German connexions with Africa. See also no. 476 for legal bibliography.

2021 Reichskolonialbund. *Kolonien im deutschen Schrifttum : Eine Übersicht über deutsches koloniales Schrifttum unter Berücksichtigung nur volksdeutscher Autoren.* Berlin, Verlag die Brücke zur Heimat, 1936. 62 p.

A colonial bibliography deliberately selected for the purpose of acquainting German youth with colonial literature in accord with Nazi racialism. Lists novels and travelogues as well as imperialist works in the more restricted sense of the word. A similar production, *Deutsche Kolonien : Ein Bücherverzeichnis* (Leipzig, Institut für Leser und Schrifttumskunde, 1939, 80 p.), is an annotated and highly selective bibliography, designed to spread colonial propaganda. Relatively the most objective of these studies is *Koloniales Schrifttum in Deutschland*, published by the Kolonialpolitisches Amt (Munich, 1941, 109 p.). This covers the colonial enterprise of all European powers, with special reference to German colonialism. The bibliographical information covers books and monographs including studies concerning the indigenous population of the various territories, medicine, agriculture, history, politics, etc., giving special emphasis to pro-Nazi books.

2022 Streit, R. *Die katholische deutsche Missionsliteratur. Zweite Teil : Bibliographie, 1800–1924.* Aachen, Xaverius, 1925. 278 p.

The standard work on the subject.

Reference works

2023 *Allgemeine Missionszeitschrift.* 1874–1939. Berlin. Monthly.

A major missionary source. Ceased publication with v. 50 in 1923. It was then superseded by the *Neue Allgemeine Missionszeitschrift*.

2024 Bremen Mission. *Monatsblaetter.* Bremen. 1847–1941.

The Norddeutsche Missionsgesellschaft in Bremen was founded in 1836, one of the earliest Protestant missions in Germany. There were various other missionary journals dating from about the same period, for instance the *Allgemeine Missions-Zeitung*, published in Hamburg from about 1844.

2025 Brunschwig, Henri. *L'expansion allemande outre-mer du XV siècle à nos jours.* Paris, Presses Universitaires de France, 1957. 208 p. Bibliography: p. 189–193.

A general work which places special emphasis on the economic origins of German colonization. Earlier works of a general nature include Mary E. Townsend, *The rise and fall of Germany's colonial empire, 1884–1918* (New York, Macmillan, 1930, 424 p.). This is one of the first substantial studies to be written in English. It is not, however, based on archival research, and is now somewhat dated. Another earlier work is Paul Darmstädter, *Geschichte der Aufteilung und Kolonisation Afrikas seit dem Zeitalter der Entdeckungen* (Berlin, G. J. Göschen, 1913–20, 2 v.). It covers the colonization of Africa from the discoveries to 1919, and contains a great many references to German colonization.

2026 Calvert, Albert Frederick. *The German African empire*. London, T. W. Laurie, 1916. 335 p.

An economic, ethnic, and geographic survey of the German colonies seen in a militantly anti-German light. It forms part of an extensive wartime and post-war literature which includes studies such as Percy Evans Lewin, *The Germans in Africa : Their aims on the dark continent and how they acquired their colonies* (London, Cassell, 1915, 317 p.). Calvert also wrote *The Cameroons* (London, T. W. Laurie, 1917, 82 p.); *Togoland* (T. W. Laurie, 1918, 86 p.); *South-west Africa . . .* (T. W. Laurie, 1916, 105 p.); and other pamphlets.

2027 Class, Paul. *Die Rechtsverhältnisse der freien farbigen Arbeiter in den deutschen Schutzgebieten Afrikas und der Südsee*. Ulm, K. Höhn, 1913. 101 p.

An investigation into the German labour law in the colonies which also gives an account of reforms introduced by the German colonial administration in the treatment of indigenous workmen. Class's work was a doctoral dissertation submitted by a German jurist at Heidelberg. A comparative study is J. K. Julius Friedrich, *Kolonialpolitik als Wissenschaft* (Berlin, Walther Rothschild, 1909, 40 p.), submitted by a jurist as a doctoral thesis at Giessen. Friedrich argues that the study of indigenous law and its application in colonial governance must be regarded as a new field of jurisprudence.

2028 *Denkschriften zum Kolonial-Etat*. Berlin, Reichsdruckerei, 1885–1918 [?]. Annual, later biennial.

These memoranda were published by the *Kolonialabteilung* of the Auswärtiges Amt and its successors in order to assist members of the Reichstag in framing the colonial budgets. The series also includes special reports. The annual reports formed the continuation of the original *Weissbücher* mentioned below. The annual reports appeared as supplements to the *Deutsches Kolonialblatt*.

2029 Dernburg, Bernhard. *Zielpunkte des deutschen Kolonialwesens : Zwei Vorträge*. Berlin, E. S. Mittler, 1907. 88 p.

Dernburg, one of the most influential of German colonial secretaries, stood for a policy of economic rationalization, a more humane treatment of Africans and administrative reform. There is as yet no biography of Dernburg, but additional material concerning his views can be obtained in publications such as his *Koloniale Finanzprobleme* (Berlin, E. S. Mittler, 1907, 24 p.), *Koloniale Lehr-jahre* (Stuttgart, Union, 1907, 16 p.), and *Südwestafrikanische Eindrücke, industrielle Fortschritte in den Kolonien : Zwei Vorträge* (Berlin, E. S. Mittler, 1909, 87 p.). Various aspects of Dernburg's policy are critically discussed by Paul Rohrbach, a prolific nationalist and a militant protagonist of *Weltpolitik*, in *Dernburg und die Südwestafrikaner. Diamantenfrage, Selbstverwaltung, Landeshilfe* (Berlin, Deutscher Kolonialverlag, 1911, viii, 323 p.). Dernburg's thinking had much in common with that of Walther Rathenau, whose colonial views concerning East Africa, developed in collaboration with Dernburg, were expressed in *Reflexionen* (Leipzig, S. Hirzel, 1912, 270 p.).

2030 *Deutsches Kolonialblatt : Amtsblatt des Reichskolonialamtes*. Berlin, E. S. Mittler, 1890–1921.

This was the official German government gazette for the colonial empire as a whole. It was issued originally under the auspices of the Auswärtiges Amt (the German Foreign Ministry). In 1907 an independent Reichskolonialamt came into existence, which continued to publish the journal. In 1919 the ministry became known as Reichskolonialministerium, but this ceased to exist in 1920. Subsequently the journal was published by the Kolonialzentralverwaltung im

Reichsministerium für Wiederaufbau (the colonial section within the German Ministry of Reconstruction), and ceased publication in 1921.

The name of the journal changed several times. From 1890 to 1904 it was known as the *Amtsblatt für die Schutzgebiete des Deutschen Reiches*. In 1905 it became the *Amtsblatt für die Schutzgebiete in Afrika und in der Südsee*.

The *Kolonialblatt* published not only official legislation, but also a great deal of additional information derived from scholars, travellers, missionaries, planters, and so forth, especially in its earlier numbers. From 1898 it also issued supplementary volumes giving official reports for annual submission to the Reichstag. These contained an account of the development of each colony, together with numerous statistics. These reports were later issued independently by the Reichskolonialamt.

2031 *Die deutsche Kolonialgesetzgebung. Sammlung der auf die deutschen Schutzgebiete bezüglichen Gesetze, Verordnungen, Erlasse und internationalen Vereinbarungen, mit Anmerkungen und Sachregister.* . . . Berlin, E. S. Mittler, 1893–1910. 13 v.

A collection of the legislation and international treaties concerning the German colonies. The editors include authorities such as A. Zimmermann, E. Schmidt-Dargitz, O. M. Köbner, J. Gerstmeyer, and T. Riebow. The volumes are annotated, and there is a subject index. Volume 1 goes up to 1892; v. 2 to 13 go up to 1910. Lists of laws subsequent to 1909 were published in the *Zeitschrift für Kolonialpolitik* and elsewhere.

2032 *Deutsche Kolonialzeitung.* 1884–1942. Berlin. Irregular.

Published from 1884 by the Deutscher Kolonialverein (German Colonial League), which was founded in 1882 at Frankfurt; it later became known as the Deutsche Kolonialgesellschaft, with its headquarters at Berlin. The Kolonialgesellschaft aimed at promoting German colonization and a militant *Weltpolitik*. It published various other journals, including the *Koloniales Jahrbuch* (1889–99), the *Beiträge zur Kolonialpolitik und Kolonialwirtschaft*, which became known in 1904 as *Zeitschrift für Kolonialpolitik, Kolonialrecht und Kolonialwirtschaft*, and in 1913 as *Koloniale Monatsblätter*. The Colonial Economic Committee of the Society, known as Kolonial-Wirtschaftliches Komitee, founded in 1896, supported the propagandistic work of its parent society by numerous scientific studies. It formed separate commissions to deal respectively with cotton, technology in the colonies, rubber, oil, and sheep rearing. It also issued *Der Tropenpflanzer, Zeitschrift für Tropische Landwirtschaft*, an agricultural journal, and other works.

2033 Dove, Karl, *et al.*, eds. *Das überseeische Deutschland in Wort und Bild.* . . . Stuttgart, Union deutsche Verlagsgesellschaft, 1911. 2 v. illus. (incl. ports.), plates, maps (part col., fold.).

The first volume relates to Kamerun, South-West Africa, and Germany's Pacific possessions. The second volume deals with Togo, German East Africa, and Samoa. The books were compiled by persons considered experts at the time, many of them naval or military officers.

2034 Fabri, Friedrich. *Bedarf Deutschland der Kolonien? Eine politisch-ökonomische Betrachtung.* 3d ed. Gotha, Friedrich Andreas Perthes, 1884. 112 p.

A famous tract, written by a former mission inspector, and originally published in 1879. Fabri's work, widely credited with awakening German interest in the colonies, argued that Germany must find both colonies of settlement and colonies of trade. Trade colonies should be administered by Germany in the interest of the indigenous races, in the same spirit of ' genuine humanity ' shown by the British in India. In a subsequent book, entitled *Fünf Jahre deutscher Kolonialpolitik : Rück- und Ausblicke* (Gotha, F. A. Perthes, 1889, 153 p.), the author argued that rule by chartered companies had proved ineffective, and that Germany should set up a colonial ministry.

2035 Fischer, Ferdinand. *Die Industrie Deutschlands und seiner Kolonien.* Leipzig, Akademische Verlagsgesellschaft, 1908. 125 p. tables.

A statistical study of Germany's metropolitan and colonial economy with data concerning German capital investments in the colonies.

2036 Geographische Gesellschaft in Hamburg. *Mitteilungen.* 1874– . Hamburg. Frequency varies.

2037 *Geographische Zeitschrift.* 1895– . Wiesbaden, Franz Steiner. Quarterly. Publication suspended 1945–62 inclusive.

2038 Gifford, Prosser, and Wm. Roger Louis, eds., with the assistance of Alison Smith. *Britain and Germany in Africa.* New Haven, Conn., Yale University Press, 1967. 825 p. maps.

A detailed comparative study with contributions by many experts. The first part of the book is entitled ' Imperial Rivalry ' and looks upon British and German colonial expansion, Anglo-German rivalry in Morocco, the Transvaal, the Portuguese colonies and elsewhere primarily from the metropolitan point of view. It also has several essays which discuss the role of colonial issues in world diplomacy. Part II centres on colonial rule as exercised by the men on the spot. Some of the contributors attempt to deal with the subject from an Afrocentric point of view; others are more interested in what were primarily administrative questions. The book has a detailed bibliographical section to which reference has already been made. It is the most detailed and up-to-date study on the subject that exists at present.

2039 Hallgarten, Georg Wolfgang Felix. *Imperialismus vor 1914 : Die soziologischen Grundlagen der Aussenpolitik europäischer Grossmächte vor dem ersten Weltkrieg.* Rev. and extended ed. München, C. H. Beck, 1963, 2 v.

A massive study, based on copious bibliographical material, to interpret European, especially German imperialism, in sociological terms. Hallgarten's approach owes much to a brilliant book by a young, but prematurely deceased, German historian, Eckhart Kehr, *Schlachtflottenbau und Parteipolitik 1894– 1901 : Versuch eines Querschnitts durch die innenpolitischen, sozialen und ideologischen Voraussetzungen des deutschen Imperialismus* (Berlin, E. Ebering, 1930), in which the author tried to analyse German navalism in societal terms. Early socialist works included ' Parvus ' [Alexander Helphand], *Marineforderungen, Kolonialpolitik und Arbeiterinteressen* (Dresden, Verlag der Sächsischen Arbeiterzeitung, 1898, 35 p.), and *Die Kolonialpolitik und der Zusammenbruch* (Leipziger Buchdruck, 1907, 135 p.).

2040 Hassert, Kurt. *Deutschlands Kolonien : Erwerbungs und Entwicklungsgeschichte, Landes- und Volkskunde und wirtschaftliche Bedeutung unserer Schutzgebiete.* Leipzig, Seele und Co., 1910. xii, 657 p. illus., maps, photos.

A survey of the German colonies, written by an economic geographer of strongly imperialist leanings. The chapters on the various territories each contain a historical section, an ethnographic section, and a section concerned with economic geography. Hassert was also the author of *Beiträge zur Landeskunde der Grashochländer Nordwest-Kameruns* (Berlin, E. S. Mittler, 1917, 147 p.).

Part III: area guide (by colonial power, region and colony)

2041 Henderson, William Otto. *Studies in German colonial history.* London, Frank Cass, 1962, ix. 150 p., tables, maps. Bibliography: p. 123–128.
A collection of essays written by an economic historian. They deal mainly with economic questions, including chartered companies, British and German trade in the colonies, Germany's war economy in East Africa, German colonization and the colonial problems of the 1930s, and so forth. There are detailed statistical tables.

2042 Hildebrand, Klaus. *Vom Reich zum Weltreich: Hitler, NSDAP und koloniale Frage: 1919–45.* Munich, Wilhelm Fink Verlag, 1968. 955 p. (Veröffentlichungen des Historischen Instituts der Universität Mannheim, v. 1)
Discusses the continuity of German colonial policy during the Weimar Republic and the Nazi era. The author deals with the domestic and foreign policy connected with the colonial issue, as well as with Germany's colonial ambitions. The writer considers Nazism as the last stage of German imperialism. A major work.

2043 Ibbeken, Rudolf. *Das aussenpolitische Problem Staat und Wirtschaft in der deutschen Reichspolitik 1880–1914.* Schleswig, Johs. Ibbeken, 1928. 285 p. Bibliography: p. 281–285.
A study written in the tradition of the German historian Hermann Oncken. The author seeks to link German foreign policy, colonial policy, public opinion, and the requirements of German capitalism.

2044 Jacob, Ernst Gerhard, ed. *Deutsche Kolonialpolitik in Dokumenten: Gedanken und Gestalten aus den letzten fünfzig Jahren.* Leipzig, Dieterich'sche Verlagsbuchhandlung, 1938. 608 p. illus., maps, tables.
A collection of documents and essays, written partly to inform, and partly to promote colonial revisionism. The contributors include militant nationalists like Hans Grimm and Paul von Lettow-Vorbeck, as well as some persons of a more moderate outlook like Bernhard Dernburg. The book includes a chronology, a list of sources and a bibliography. Its principal value lies in the factual material presented, including statistics and treaties. The introduction was written by Heinrich Schnee, a former colonial governor and then Führer des Reichskolonialbundes, a pro-Nazi organization. Schnee also produced, among other works, a *Kolonialpolitisches Quellenheft: Die deutsche Kolonialfrage 1918–1935* (Bamberg, C. C. Buchner, 1935, 198 p.). This provided source material to substantiate German colonial claims.

2045 *Jahrbuch über die deutschen Kolonien, 1908–1914.* Essen, G. D. Baedeker, Verlagshandlung, 1908–1914. 7 v.
Valuable articles by specialists treating administration, military and medical developments in the German colonies. Many essays on Africa. Another reference work is R. Fitzner, *Deutsches Kolonialhandbuch* (Berlin, H. Paetel, 1901 ed., 412 p.). It was reissued repeatedly, and the publishers also put out occasional supplements known as *Ergänzungsbände.*

2046 Kolonialgeographisches Institut. *Forschungen zur Kolonialfrage.* Würzburg, K. Triltsch, 1939–42. 2 v.
The Kolonialgeographische Institut was part of the University of Leipzig. The present series, edited by K. H. Dietzel, mingled Nazi propaganda with scholarship of a more objective kind. The publications of the Institut included monographs on subjects as varied as transport in Africa, Germany's colonial demands, British and French attitudes concerning German colonial policy, colonies and industry, the German colonies and the press.

2047 Kolonialinstitut. *Abhandlungen.* Hamburg, L. Friederichsen, 1910–21. 43 v.

The *Abhandlungen*, monographs of the highest scientific value, concern mainly Africa, though not entirely so. They deal with subjects as varied as African linguistics, ethnography, hydrology, economics, education, folklore, agriculture, colonial legislation, and so forth. The publications are remarkable for their objectivity and completeness. The Kolonialinstitut issued two separate series: Series A covered law and political science, Series B with ethnography and languages.

2048 —— *Bericht über das Studienjahr.* 1908–21. Hamburg. Annual.

The Kolonialinstitut carried on investigations into various German colonial problems and issued regular reports concerning its work.

2049 *Koloniale Rundschau. Monatsschrift für die Interessen unserer Schutzgebiete und ihrer Bewohnen.* 1909–1943. Berlin. Monthly.

Organ of the Gesellschaft für Eingeborenenschutz. The journal spoke for humanitarian opinion in Wilhelminian Germany and forms an important source with many scholarly contributions from experts such as Dietrich Westermann.

2050 Kolonial-Wirtschaftliches Komitee. *Kolonialhandels – Adressbuch.* 1936. Berlin, W. Süsserott, 1898–1912, 1936.

Published as annual supplementary volumes for the *Deutsches Kolonialblatt*. The 1936 issue, edited by A. Marcus, has a special title *Mandatsgebiete in Afrika*.

For the years 1898 to 1909, these volumes provided the official report submitted by the Kolonialamt to the Reichstag each year. These reports contained accounts of the development of each colony, as well as numerous statistics. Before 1898 they were included in the *Anlagebände* of the Reichstag debates. Later on, the official reports were included in *Die deutschen Schutzgebiete in Afrika*... published by the Reichskolonialamt.

The Kolonial-Wirtschaftliches Komitee also published *Unsere Kolonialwirtschaft in ihrer Bedeutung für Industrie, Handel und Landwirtschaft* ... (Berlin, E. S. Mittler, 1909–10, 2 v.), based on material derived from the German Statistical Office.

2051 Kuczynski, Jürgen. *Studien zur Geschichte des deutschen Imperialismus.* (East) Berlin, Dietz Verlag, 1948–50. 2 v. Bibliography: v. 1, p. 323–373, contains a detailed bibliography by H. Alberts concerning German trusts and cartels. There is, however, no special section concerning colonialism.

A Marxist-Leninist study, published during the Stalinist era in Eastern Germany with the expressed object of unmasking the alleged machinations of German monopoly capitalism and of its subsequent American allies. The first volume covers the 19th-century trend towards the creation of economic 'monopolies' in Germany, and the development of employers' organizations. The second volume deals with the Alldeutsche-Verband (Pan German League), the Deutsche Kolonialgesellschaft, the Deutsche Flottenverein (Naval League), and other militantly nationalist bodies, as well as with the links between these organizations and German capitalism.

2052 Lepsius, Johannes, Albrecht Mendelssohn-Bartholdy, and Friedrich Thimme, eds. *Die grosse Politik der europäischen Kabinette, 1871–1914: Sammlung der diplomatischen Akten des Auswärtigen Amtes, im Auftrag des Auswärtigen Amtes.* Berlin, 1922–27. 40 v. in 54.

This collection was published by the German government after the First World War to elucidate German foreign policy before 1914. It covers German policy from the preliminary treaty with France in 1871 to the outbreak of the First World War. Colonial issues are mentioned, though the work is concerned above all with Germany's international relations. The editors, conscious of the contemporary 'War Guilt' issue, concentrated above all on events during the early 20th century, and paid less attention to the Bismarckian period. The documents are arranged by topics instead of in strict chronological order.

2053 *Marine Rundschau : Monatsschrift für Seewesen.* Berlin, later Frankfurt, 1890– .

The official organ of the German Navy, issued by the Reichsmarineamt, later by the Marineleitung im Reichswehrministerium and its successors. It now continues as a non-official publication under the title of *Marine Rundschau : Zeitschrift für Seewesen*, put out by the Arbeitskreis für Wehrforschung, published by E. S. Mittler, Frankfurt. The journal was primarily concerned with matters of naval interest, but there are references to colonial affairs during the imperial period.

2054 Meyer, Hans Heinrich Joseph, ed. *Das deutsche Kolonialreich : Eine Länderkunde der deutschen Schutzgebiete.* Leipzig, Bibliographisches Institut, 1909–10. 2 v. illus., maps, diagrs.

An encyclopaedic work which summarizes the geographical, ethnographic, geological, and related information available at the time concerning the German colonies. There is also some reference to economic and administrative matters. Meyer, himself an expert on railways and economic development in the colonies, called on leading experts to assist him in his work. The first volume, dealing with East Africa and Kamerun, was compiled by Meyer and Siegfried Passarge. The second volume, which treats Togo, South-West Africa, and Germany's Pacific possessions, was put together by Passarge, Leonhard Schultze, Wilhelm Sievers, and Georg Wegener. The editor wrote many other works including a study of railway policy entitled *Die Eisenbahnen im tropischen Afrika : eine kolonialwirtschaftliche Studie* (Leipzig, Duncker und Humblot, 1902, 186 p.).

2055 Müller, Fritz Ferdinand, ed. *Kolonien unter der Peitsche : Eine Dokumentation.* Berlin, Rütten and Loening, 1962. 173 p.

A collection of 87 documents drawn from the archives of the former Reichskolonialamt. They were selected in such a way as to give substance to the author's Marxist-Leninist approach to German colonial history. No reference is made to the more positive aspects of German colonization.

2056 Reichskolonialamt. *Die deutschen Schutzgebiete in Afrika und der Südsee.* 1909–13. Berlin. Annual.

These were official publications giving a general review of German colonial development. Earlier titles were *1906/7, Jahresbericht über die Entwicklung der deutschen Schutzgebiete* and *1908/9, Denkschrift über die Entwicklung der Schutzgebiete in Afrika und der Südsee.* These appeared as supplements to the *Deutsche Kolonialblatt.*

Before the Kolonialamt was set up as an independent agency in 1907, colonial affairs were handled under the auspices of the Auswärtiges Amt, which issued the *Jahresberichte* ... from 1903 to 1907. These *Jahresberichte* also contain valuable *Anlagen* or supplements. The German colonial authorities issued the *Deutsches Kolonialblatt*, which incorporated a good deal of information derived from missionaries, travellers, and soldiers. The *Kolonialblatt* contained annual supplements, starting with *1891–92, Entwicklung unserer Kolonien.*

German Africa

2057 —— *Mitteilungen aus den deutschen Schutzgebieten mit Benutzung amtlicher Quellen.* 1888–1919. Berlin. illus., plates, maps (part fold.). Annual. These were issued by official German agencies, mainly the Reichskolonialamt, as long as this office remained in existence. The compilers included Freiherr von Danckelmann and H. Marquandsen. The *Mitteilungen* were supplemented by *Ergänzungshefte* (1–25), dating from 1908 to 1921. The series provides extensive information concerning expeditions in the German colonies, and geographical, geological, and agronomic data.

2058 —— *Veröffentlichungen.* Jena, G. Fischer, 1911–17. 9 v. illus., maps (part fold.).
The Reichskolonialamt published a series of detailed monographs, all of considerable scientific value, concerning cotton cultivation, forestry, veterinary science, irrigation, domestic slavery, concessions, grants to companies, and similar questions. They were compiled by the leading experts of the day. The medical side of German colonialism is elucidated by *Medizinal-Berichte über die deutschen Schutzgebiete*, published annually by the Reichskolonialamt from 1903 onward.

2059 Reichskolonialbund. Gruppe deutscher kolonialwirtschaftlicher Unternehmungen. *Mitteilungen.* Berlin, W. de Gruyter, 1939–43. 11 v.
The Reichskolonialbund was a Nazi organization charged with producing revisionist propaganda. In addition to issuing tracts, such as *Deutschlands Recht auf Raum und Robstoffe* (Berlin, Fichteverlag, 1938, 73 p.), it also published more objective investigations into economic problems. The *Mitteilungen* deal with subjects as varied as the economics of banana culture, the study of soils in the colonies, the cotton-growing potential of the Niger Delta, the mineral industry in South-West Africa, pastoral farming in East and South-West Africa, tin mining in Africa, botanical investigations in Cameroun, etc.

2060 Reichstag. *Stenographische Berichte über die Verhandlungen des deutschen Reichstages.* Berlin, 1871–1938.
The Reichstag formed the lower house in the legislature of the German Reich. Its debates (*Verhandlungen*), the material placed before the House (Anlagebände) and official papers (*Drucksachen*) are an essential source, as the powers of the Reichstag in colonial matters were relatively great. This material and the *Beilagen* to the *Deutsches Kolonialblatt* include not only all the debates on colonial questions but also numerous documents, committee reports, correspondence, and the official reports on the colonies given by the Colonial Office.

The material dealing with the colonies as a whole has never been reprinted. There is, however, one valuable publication entitled *Die letzten Kolonialdebatten im aufgelösten Reichstag, November und Dezember, 1906* (Berlin, E. S. Mittler, 1907, 295 p.). These debates, in which the Catholic Centre Party and the Social Democrats opposed the government's policy in South-West Africa, provide a great deal of material containing real and alleged abuses committed under the German colonial régime. (They also contributed both to German colonial reforms and also to the 'Hottentot elections' of 1907, in which a conservative-liberal coalition defeated the Centre and the Socialists.)

2061 Schack, Friedrich. *Das deutsche Kolonialrecht in seiner Entwicklung bis zum Weltkrieg. Die allgemeinen Lehren: Eine berichtende Darstellung der Theorie und Praxis nebst kritischer Bemerkungen.* Hamburg, L. Friederichsen, 1923. 434 p. (Abhandlungen aus dem Gebiet der Auslandkunde, no. 12) Bibliography: p. 395–431.
An exhaustive study of German colonial law. Contains a very extensive bibliography on German colonial law.

397

Part III: area guide (by colonial power, region and colony)

2062 Schlunk, Martin. *Die Schulen für Eingeborenen in den deutschen Schutzgebieten am 1. Juni 1911...* Hamburg, L. Friedrichsen, 1914. xiv, 365 p. tables. (Abhandlungen des Hamburgischen Kolonial Instituts, v. 18)
The state of African education in the German colonies as of 1911.

2063 Schmokel, Wolfe W. *Dream of empire: German colonialism, 1919–1945.* New Haven, Yale University Press, 1964. 204 p. illus. Bibliography: p. 185–196.
Reviews German colonial revisionist claims until the end of the Second World War. The author concludes that colonialism was primarily the casualty of the Second World War, and might have lasted longer had the British and French decided on a policy of more extensive appeasement. The Marxist-Leninist interpretation is provided by Horst Kühne, *Faschistische Kolonialideologie und zweiter Weltkrieg* (Berlin, Dietz, 1962, 226 p.).

2064 Schnee, Heinrich. *German colonization, past and future: The truth about the German colonies by Dr. Heinrich Schnee...with an introduction by William Harbutt Dawson.* London, Allen & Unwin, 1926.
An influential book putting the German case for German colonialism. Written by a former German colonial governor. Schnee also wrote *Erinnerungen als letzter Gouverneur in Deutsch-Ostafrika* (Heidelberg, Quelle und Meyer, 1964, 186 p.). This autobiography provides a good account concerning the making of a senior colonial civil servant. The author also writes about his stint in the Zentralverwaltung in Berlin, and his experiences at the Seminar für Orientalische Sprachen. See also no. 2100 for other works by Schnee.

2065 ———, ed. *Deutsches Kolonial-Lexikon.* Leipzig, Quelle und Meyer, 1920. 3 v. xxx, 776, 698, and 778 p. illus., photos., maps, tables.
Schnee was a senior German official who served successively as Deputy Governor of Samoa, as Ministerialdirektor in the Kolonialamt, and finally as Governor of German East Africa. He took a major role as propagandist for the 'colonial idea', and was a leading defender of Germany's colonial record. One of his many books was characteristically entitled *Die koloniale Schuldlüge* (München, Buchverlag der Süddeutschen Monatschefte, 1924). The *Kolonial-Lexikon* is the most important reference work of its kind for the German colonies. Schnee drew on the services of more than 80 experts. His work sheds light on every aspect of German colonial enterprise.

2066 Schramm, Percy. *Deutschland und Übersee: Der deutsche Handel mit den anderen Kontinenten, insbesondere Afrika, von Karl V. bis zu Bismarck. Ein Beitrag zur Geschichte der Rivalität im Wirtschaftsleben.* Braunschweig, Westermann, 1950. 639 p. fold. maps. Bibliography: p. 476–600.
A history of German overseas trade with special reference to Africa, from the 16th to the late 19th century.

2067 Schultz-Ewerth, Erich, and Leonhard Adam, eds. *Das Eingeborenenrecht: Das Sitten und Gewohnheitsrecht der Eingeborenen der ehemaligen deutschen Kolonien in Afrika und der Südsee.* Stuttgart, Schrecker und Schröder, 1929–30. 2 v.
A classical study concerning indigenous customary law based on questionnaires and inquiries issued before the Great War. The project was started by Felix Meyer and continued after his death in 1925 by other editors. The first volume, edited by Bernhard Ankermann, deals with East Africa. The second volume, edited by Adolf Schlettwein, Julius Lips, Berengar Zastrow, and others, covers South-West Africa, Togo, Kamerun, and the South Sea Islands. It is partly a work of jurisprudence and partly a work of ethnology. The coverage is uneven;

for instance, few replies were received from Kamerun. It is nevertheless the most complete survey of its kind for the German colonies.

2068 Seitz, Theodor. *Vom Aufstieg und Niederbruch deutscher Kolonialmacht.* Karlsruhe im Breisgau, C. F. Müller, 1927–1929. 3 v., illus., maps.

The author became governor of Kamerun in 1907, and governor of South-West Africa in 1910. In 1915 he was forced to surrender South-West African troops. In 1920 Seitz was made president of the Deutsche Kolonialgesellschaft, and soon made his name as a leading spokesman for German colonial revisionism. The first two volumes deal with Kamerun, the third mainly with South-West Africa. For other examples of German gubernatorial reminiscences see, for instance, no. 2109, Jesko von Puttkamer, *Gouverneursjahre in Kamerun*; no. 2127, Theodor Leutwein, *Elf Jahre Gouverneur in Deutsch Südwestafrika*; and Eduard von Liebert, *Aus einem bewegten Leben : Erinnerungen* (Munich, 1925).

2069 Spellmeyer, Hans. *Deutsche Kolonialpolitik im Reichstag.* Stuttgart, Kohlhammer, 1931. 140 p.

A study of the links between German colonial and domestic politics between the years 1884 and 1914. The author gives special emphasis to the role played by the Social Democrats.

2070 Taylor, A. J. P. *Germany's first bid for colonies, 1884–1885 : A move in Bismarck's European policy.* Hamden, Conn., Archon Books, 1967. 103 p.

An early work by a British historian, who argues that Bismarckian colonialism derived primarily from diplomatic motives involving Europe. According to Taylor, the German empire was the by-product of an abortive Anglo-French entente directed against Great Britain. Sybil Eyre Crowe, *The Berlin West Africa Conference, 1884–1885* (London, Longmans, Green, 1942, 249 p.), provides a detailed diplomatic study based on British Foreign Office documents. She shows, however, that the Franco-German co-operation achieved before the Berlin Conference disintegrated when the conference started, and that the outcome of the conference was more in the nature of an Anglo-German understanding.

There are many other works, however, which place the main emphasis for Bismarck's policy on domestic issues. See, for instance, William Osgood Aydelotte, *Bismarck and British colonial policy : The problem of South West Africa, 1883–1885* (Philadelphia, University of Pennsylvania Press, 1937, 179 p.), and, in a different context, no. 2074, Hans-Ulrich Wehler, *Bismarck und der Imperialismus.*

The Marxist-Leninist interpretations current in East Germany likewise place the main emphasis on internal German developments and the structure of German capitalism. East German historiographers are particularly concerned with the question whether German colonization was dominated by premonopolistic capitalism of the mercantile variety or by imperialist capitalism of the monopolistic kind. For contributions to this question, see, for instance, no. 2051, Jürgen Kuczynski, *Studien zur Geschichte des deutschen Imperialismus.* Another Marxist work is Manfred Nussbaum, *Vom ' Kolonialenthusiasmus' zur Kolonialpolitik der Monopole : Zur deutschen Kolonialpolitik unter Bismarck, Caprivi, Hohenlohe* (Berlin, Akademieverlag, 1962). The author argues that Bismarckian expansion overseas represented a pre-imperialist colonial policy, the original acquisition of the colonies having preceded the consolidation of monopoly capitalism. A recent Soviet-Russian work, translated into German, is Arkadie Samsonovich Jerussalimski, *Bismarck : Diplomatie und Militarismus* (Berlin, Dietz, 1970).

Part III: area guide (by colonial power, region and colony)

2071 Tesch, Johannes. *Die Laufbahn der deutschen Kolonialbeamten.* Berlin, Otto Salle, 1902. 231 p.

A complete résumé of the German colonial machinery as it existed at the turn of the century, the conditions under which the officials served, their salaries, as well as the relevant legislation on the subject. An earlier account is by Max Beneke, 'Die Ausbildung des Kolonialbeamten', published in *Mitteilungen der Gesellschaft für vergleichende Rechts- und Staatswissenschaften* (Berlin, 1894). This study was commissioned by the Kolonialgesellschaft in an effort to provide more carefully selected and better officials for the colonies after numerous abuses in Kamerun and elsewhere. A more general work is Otto Köbner, *Einführung in die Kolonialpolitik* (Jena, G. Fischer, 1908, 227 p.), which provides a survey of administrative systems. The subject was further elucidated by E. Backhaus, *Das Verordnungsrecht in den deutschen Kolonien* (Berlin, W. Süsseroth, 1909, 45 p.), originally a doctoral dissertation. A critical study by a German official during the period was Karl Theodor Helfferich, *Zur Reform der kolonialen Verwaltungsorganisation* (Berlin, E. S. Mittler, 1905, 47 p.). A doctoral dissertation by Eugen Kade, *Die Anfänge der deutschen Kolonial-Zentralverwaltung* (Würzburg-Aumühle, Triltsch, 1939, 186 p.), gives an account concerning the development of Germany's administrative machine and early colonial policy, such as there was.

2072 *Das überseeische Deutschland: Die deutschen Kolonien in Wort und Bild.* Stuttgart, Union Deutsche Verlagsgesellschaft, 1911. 2 v. illus., photos., maps, tables.

An encyclopaedic compilation prepared by leading experts of the time. The first volume contains an account of Kamerun and South-West Africa. The second volume deals with Togo and German East Africa respectively. Each chapter is subdivided by topics such as administration, labour, ethnography, economy, defence, and so forth. There is a good deal of statistical material. Bibliographical notes are appended to various chapters.

2073 Warneck, Gustav. *Missionstunden.* Gütersloh, C. Bertelsmann, 1890. 2 v. Bibliographical notes: v. 2, p. 345–352.

Warneck's first volume discusses missionary enterprise and the Bible. The second volume deals with Protestant missionary enterprise in Africa and the South Seas. Warneck was a prolific writer who played an important part as a theoretician of Protestant mission work, as well as a militant polemicist against Catholic claims during the *Kulturkampf.* Warneck was also the author of a study, *Welche Pflichten legen uns unsere Kolonien auf? Ein Appell an das christlich deutsche Gewissen* (Heilbronn, Henniger, 1885, 123 p.; *Zeitfragen des christlichen Volkslebens*, nos. 75–76), in which he argues that the Germans must protect, educate, and Christianize the indigenous people. Another interesting work written rather later is Johann Karl Vietor, *Geschichtliche und kulturelle Entwicklung unserer Schutzgebiete* (Berlin, D. Reimer, 1913, 144 p.). The author was particularly interested in social conditions, race relations and African policy. He considered that the missions should play a major role in Germany's colonial development. See also Religion and Mission section in Part II.

2074 Wehler, Hans-Ulrich. *Bismarck und der Imperialismus.* Cologne, Kiepenheuer und Wietsch, 1969. 582 p. Bibliography: p. 520–566.

Standard study on the origins of German colonialism. The author links Germany's 'social imperialism' to German domestic policies in the widest sense, especially Bismarck's desire to create a nationalist consensus. In addition to the bibliography the study contains an appended bibliographical essay (p. 507–516) and a note concerning archival material in Germany (p. 517–520).

2075 *Weissbücher über Kolonialangelegenheiten.* Berlin, Reichdruckerei, 1883–85. 13 v.
These were published by the Kolonial-Abteilung des Auswärtigen Amts, and dealt with a great variety of African matters of interest to German parliamentarians. The series was continued later as *Denkschriften zum Kolonial-Etat*, mentioned previously.

2076 Wertheimer, Mildred S. *The Pan-German League, 1890–1914.* New York, Columbia University Press, 1924. 256 p. Bibliography: p. 219–228.
The author examines the origins and politics of the Pan-German League, as well as the social background of its members and officials. She stresses the fact that workers and peasants played but a small role in the League. Businessmen were considerably more important. The largest membership group, however, derived from the academic and liberal professions. For an interesting comparison with the ' colonial party ' in France, see Henri Brunschwig, *Mythes et réalités de l'impérialisme colonial français 1871–1914* (Paris, Librairie Armand Colin, 1960).

2077 Zache, Hans, ed. *Das deutsche Kolonialbuch.* Berlin, Wilhelm Andermann Verlag [1926]. 512 p. illus., maps, tables.
An apologia for Germany's colonial record, with many distinguished contributors from Germany's former colonial establishment. The work contains interesting factual and statistical material, as well as polemical articles, essays, and poems written in a nationalist vein. The first part deals with general topics such as administration and defence; the remaining portions cover, respectively, West Africa, East Africa, and the Far East. Pages 508–512 contain a list of collaborators with valuable biographical data.

2078 *Zeitschrift für Eingeborenen-Sprachen.* 1910–20. Berlin. Irregular.
A valuable linguistic journal. In 1920 it was superseded by the *Zeitschrift für Kolonialsprachen*, and in 1952 by *Afrika und Übersee : Sprachen, Kulturen.*

2079 *Zeitschrift für Ethnologie.* 1869–1944. Berlin. 1950– . Braunschweig. Annual ? (irregular).
Published until 1944 as the organ of the Berliner Gesellschaft für Anthropologie, Ethnologie und Urgeschichte. In 1944 it was suspended with v. 7. In 1950 it was revived with v. 75, as the organ of the Deutsche Gesellschaft für Völkerkunde. A major ethnographic source for Africa and other regions. Another important source is *Zeitschrift für Morphologie und Anthropologie* (1899– , Stuttgart).

2080 *Zeitschrift für Kolonialpolitik, Kolonialrecht und Kolonialwirtschaft. Herausgegeben von der Deutschen Kolonialgesellschaft.* Berlin, W. Süsserott, 1899–1914. 16 v.
Each volume contains much information concerning the most varied aspects of German colonization, including a good deal of legal material. Volumes 15 and 16 were bound separately under the title *Zeitschrift für Kolonialrecht*, with separate pagination. A major source.

2081 *Zeitschrift für Missionswissenschaft und Religionswissenschaft.* 1911– . Münster. Quarterly.
Issued by the Allgemeine Evangelisch-Protestantische Missionsverein, a valuable source.

2082 Zimmermann, Alfred. *Geschichte der deutschen Kolonialpolitik.* Berlin, E. S. Mittler, 1914. 336 p.
The work formed the last in a five-volume series *Geschichte der europäischen Kolonien* (1895–1914), dealing with the history and policy of the various colonial powers. The author, who had previously served on the staff of the German legation in London and in the Colonial Section of the German Foreign Ministry, was

likewise an expert on the history of Prussian and of German commercial policy. His work thus stresses economic as well as political aspects of contemporary colonialism. Earlier works by the author include *Kolonialgeschichtliche Studien* (Oldenburg, Schulzesche Hof-Buchhandlung, A. Schwartz, 1895, viii, 417 p.), and *Kolonialpolitik* (Leipzig, C. L. Hirschfeld, 1905, xxii, 421 p.).

East Africa

Note The best bibliographical publications remain Schiller, no. 476; Bridgman, no. 2014; Gifford and Louis, no. 2020; and Carlson, no. 2016. A few important titles are listed below for each colonial territory. See also Rwanda and Burundi.

2083 Austen, Ralph Albert. *Northwest Tanzania under German and British rule : Colonial policy and tribal politics, 1889–1939.* New Haven, Conn., Yale University Press, 1968. 307 p. map.
Case study of German and subsequent British colonial policy and indigenous responses in one area of a German colony. Based on detailed archival research. Important alike for the knowledge of the German background and its comparative data on British colonial rule.

2084 Bald, Detlef. *Deutsch-Ostafrika 1900–1914 : Eine Studie über die Verwaltung, Interessengruppen und wirtschaftliche Erschliessung.* Munich, Weltforum Verlag, 1970. 238 p. (Ifo-Institut für Wirtschaftsforschung, Afrika-Studien, no. 54) Bibliography: p. 216–229.
A monograph, based on archival sources on Germany and Tanzania, which tries to elucidate the complex relations between the administration and the German settlers. The author considers the settlers' organizations to have been doctrinaire, reactionary, militantly nationalist, and protectionist in their economic policy. The author diverges, however, from the Afrocentric interpretation of German policy put forward by John Iliffe, and argues that German policy was affected only to a very limited extent by the Maji Maji rising.

The book contains an excellent little historiographical essay in the form of a *Literaturbesprechung*, which outlines the principal problems that historians of German colonialism have hitherto discussed. The bibliography contains a detailed description of the archival material available, as well as detailed information concerning published reminiscences, official publications, bibliographies and secondary works.

2085 Blöcker, Hans. *Deutsch-Ostafrika einst und jetzt : Eine wirtschaftliche Monographie.* Berlin, Sacher und Kuschel, 1928. 91 p.
Compares the German administration with the first five years of British mandatory governance.

2086 Büttner, Kurt. *Die Anfänge der deutschen Kolonialpolitik in Ostafrika : Eine kritische Untersuchung an Hand unveröffentlicher Quellen.* Berlin, Akademie-Verlag. 1959. vii, 166 p. ('Studien zur Kolonialgeschichte und Geschichte der kolonialen Befreiungsbewegung', v. 1) Bibliography: p. 151–156.
Written from the Marxist-Leninist point of view, part of a wider project designed to reassess Western colonial history in a strictly negative light. The study is based on Kolonialamt material.

The early literature on the origins of German East Africa is extensive. It includes works written by colonial pioneers themselves, such as no. 2098, Karl Peters, *Die Gründung von Deutsch-Ostafrika*; Graf Joachim von Pfeil, *Zur*

Erwerbung von Deutsch-Ostafrika : Ein Beitrag zur Kolonialgeschichte (Berlin, K. Curtius, 1907, 232 p.); Rochus Schmidt, *Geschichte des Araberaufstandes in Ost-Afrika : Seine Erstehung, seine Niederwerfung und seine Folgen* (Frankfurt an der Oder, Trowitzsch, 1892, 360 p.); and others. All of them are pro-colonial in their approach.

Bruno Kurtze, *Die Deutsch-Ostafrikanische Gesellschaft : Ein Beitrag zum Problem der Schutzbriefgesellschaften und zur Geschichte Deutsch-Ostafrikas* (Jena, G. Fischer, 1913, 198 p.), is an enlarged version of the author's doctoral dissertation submitted at Jena. An earlier work on the subject is J. Wagner, *Deutsch-Ostafrika : Geschichte der Gesellschaft für deutsche Kolonisation, der deutsch-ostafrikanischen Gesellschaft und der deutsch-ostafrikanischen Plantagengesellschaft* (Berlin Mitscher und Rostell, 1886, 124 p.). The most detailed of these early accounts is Paul Reichard, *Deutsch-Ostafrika* (Leipzig, O. Spamer, 1891, 524 p.).

2087 Fonck, Heinrich. *Deutsch-Ostafrika : Eine Schilderung deutscher Tropen nach zehn Wanderjahren.* Berlin, Vossische Buchhandlung, 1910.
Five short monographs bound in a single volume; they cover subjects as varied as defence, geography, agriculture, ethnography, etc.

2088 Götzen, Gustav A. von. *Deutsch-Ostafrika im Aufstand 1905–1906.* Berlin, D. Reimer, 1909. xxiii, 274 p. illus., maps.
An account of the Maji Maji rising, written from the point of view of a German governor. Götzen gives an account of his policy in the interior, but basically blames the rebellion on what he believed to be African superstition.

2089 Gouvernmentsrat des Deutsch-Ostafrikanischen Schutzgebietes. *Verhandlungen...* Dar es Salaam, 1912–.
In 1904 the Germans set up a Gouvernementsrat containing both official and unofficial members. The Gouvernementsrat was in effect an advisory rather than a legislative council, but the settler element became increasingly powerful, especially when, in 1913, all Europeans, irrespective of their nationality, became eligible for the franchise. From 1912 onwards, the proceedings of the council were published. They are particularly valuable for a study of settler politics.

2090 Great Britain. Naval Staff. Naval Intelligence Division. *A handbook of German East Africa. Comp. by the Geographical Section of the Naval Intelligence Division, Naval Staff, Admiralty.* London, H.M. Stationery Office [printed by Frederick Hall], 1923. 440 p. illus., plans, diagrs.
An account with special emphasis on geographical and related features.

2091 Gwassa, G. C. K., and John Iliffe, eds. *Records of the Maji Maji rising.* Nairobi, East African Publishing House, 1967–. Bibliography: Pt. 1, p. 31–32.
Covers the major African rising against the Germans, 1905–1907.

2092 Iliffe, John. *Tanganyika under German rule, 1905–1912.* London, Cambridge University Press, 1969. 236 p. map. Bibliography: p. 211–223.
A detailed study based on extensive archival sources. Elucidates the causes and effects of the Maji Maji rising, the impact of German settlement, attempts at administrative and social reform, and the various contradictions that beset German policy. There is an excellent, detailed bibliography that contains a short description of relevant material in the Tanzania National Archives at Dar es Salaam; the University College, Dar es Salaam; the Tanzania Area Offices; Makerere University College, Kampala; as well as in the Deutsche Zentralarchiv, Potsdam, and in the archives of the United Society for the Propagation of the Gospel, London.

Part III: area guide (by colonial power, region and colony)

2093 Kaiserlich-Biologisch-Landwirtschaftliches Institut Amani. *Jahresberichte...* 1903–14.

The Research Institute at Amani, founded in 1902, was probably the foremost institution of its kind existing at the time in sub-Saharan Africa. Its object was to study the flora and fauna of German East Africa and to conduct practical experiments in agriculture. The Institute also helped to put out *Der Pflanzer : Ratgeber für tropische Landwirtschaft...*, an agricultural journal (1905–14). The journal provided additional information to the material contained in *Der Tropenpflanzer: Zeitschrift für tropische Landwirtschaft*, published by the Kolonialwirtschaftliches Komitee. A general account of the state of European plantations in 1904 is given in Kaiserliches Gouvernement von Deutsch-Ostafrica. *Nachweisungen über die in Deutsch-Ostafrika vorhandenen Privat-Pflanzungen und deren ungefährer Stand am 1. April 1904* (Dar es Salaam, 1906). F. Stuhlmann, head of the Institute, also wrote numerous articles under his own name in scientific journals concerning various plantation products.

2094 *Die Landesgesetzgebung des Deutsch-Ostafrikanischen Schutzgebietes...* Dar es Salaam, 1911. 2 v.

A compilation of the legislation concerning the colony. Volume 1 covers ordinances and regulations. Volume 2 publishes the circulars and orders issued to the various departments and subordinate offices.

2095 Methner, Wilhelm. *Unter drei Gouverneuren : 16 Jahre Dienst in den deutschen Tropen.* Breslau, Korn, 1938. 452 p.

The author was chief secretary in the German East African administration, and his account gives an interesting picture of the administrations of Governors Götzen, Rechenberg and Schnee, respectively.

2096 Meyer, Hans, ed. *Das deutsche Kolonialreich : Eine Länderkunde der deutschen Schutzgebiete.* v. 1, *Ostafrika und Kamerun.* Leipzig, Bibliographisches Institut, 1909. 909 p. illus., map, diagrs.

A detailed account, with special reference to geographic, ecological and geological features. The portion dealing with German East Africa was compiled by the editor.

2097 Müller, Fritz Ferdinand. *Deutschland-Zanzibar-Ostafrika : Geschichte einer deutschen Kolonialeroberung 1884–1890.* (East) Berlin, Rütten und Loening, 1959. 581 p. illus., maps. Bibliography: p. 555–567.

A massive study written from the Marxist-Leninist standpoint. The author also wrote a brief, polemical work, *Bwana : Deine Zeit ist um. Der Freiheit Flamme brennt im Herzen Afrikas* (Berlin, Kongress Verlag, 1960, 166 p.).

2098 Peters, Karl. *Die Gründung von Deutsch-Ostafrika : Kolonialpolitische Erinnerungen und Betrachtungen.* Berlin, C. A. Schwetschke und Sohn, 1906. viii, 276 p.

Peters, a pioneer of German colonization and one of its most controversial figures, compiled this work in an autobiographical style. His book concerns the German colonization in East Africa until 1890. Peters was a prolific writer. Other works include, for instance, *Lebenserinnerungen* (Grossenwörden, Rüh'sche Verlagsbuchhandlung, 1918, 147 p.), a work of self-exculpatory reminiscences. His collected works appeared as *Gesammelte Schriften...* (Berlin, C. H. Beck, 1943–44, 3 v.).

2099 Redeker, Dietrich. *Journalismus in Deutsch-Ostafrika 1899–1916. Beitrag zur Geschichte der Presse...* Frankfurt, Diesterweg, 1937. 135 p.

A history of the press in East Africa, written from the pro-settler point of view.

2100 Schnee, Heinrich. *Als letzter Gouverneur in Deutsch-Ostafrika.* Heidelberg, Quelle und Meyer, 1964. 186 p.

Schnee was the last governor of German East Africa. His reminiscences form a valuable source for the history of German East Africa, and also for the career of a senior colonial civil servant, with details concerning his stint in the Zentralverwaltung in Berlin, in the Seminar für Orientalische Sprachen, etc. See also no. 2064, Schnee, *German colonization, past and future.* . .

Schnee's experiences in World War I were described in *Deutsch-Ostafrika im Weltkrieg: Wie wir lebten und kämpften* (Leipzig, Quelle und Meyer, 1919, 439 p.). His account of German campaigning in East Africa forms part of an extensive wartime literature. This includes Paul Emil von Lettow-Vorbeck, *East African campaigns* (New York, R. Speller, 1957, 303 p.), which is a translation of the author's *Meine Erinnerungen aus Ostafrika*; and also Ludwig Boell, *Die Operationen in Ostafrika: Weltkrieg 1914–1918* (Hamburg, W. Dachert, 1951, 444 p.).

Another example of German official reminiscences is Eduard von Liebert, *Aus einem bewegten Leben: Erinnerungen* (Munich, J. F. Lehmann, 1925, 226 p.). Liebert, a Prussian general, a militant opponent of the Social Democratic Party, and founder of the Reichsverband gegen die Sozialdemokratie, was governor of East Africa from 1897 to 1901, and a hard liner in German colonial policy.

2101 Tetzlaff, Rainer. *Koloniale Entwicklung und Ausbeutung: Wirtschafts- und Sozialgeschichte Deutsch-Ostafrikas 1885–1914.* Berlin, Duncker und Humblot, 1970. 295 p. (Schriften zur Wirtschafts- und Sozialgeschichte, v. 17).

An economic history, written from a Marxist standpoint. The author seeks to show that Germany's early attempts to modernize the colony had small success, but had the effect of destroying the pre-colonial systems of trade and production. The second part of the book deals with the period 1902 to 1914, when the Germans were more successful in exacting profits from their colony. The final section considers the social problems resulting from the creation of a colonial economy based on wage labour. The writer's general approach stresses the settlers' self-interest which, he believes, stood in the way of long-term African development.

2102 Wright, Marcia. *German missions in Tanganyika, 1891–1941: Lutherans and Moravians in the southern highlands.* Oxford, Clarendon Press, 1971. 249 p., maps. (Oxford Studies in African Affairs) Bibliography: p. 227–240.

A Eurocentric work based on detailed research into German government archives and missionary records. Traces the story from the beginnings of missionary enterprise to what the author calls ' the crisis years 1933–1939 '.

Kamerun and Togo

2103 Dominik, Hans. *Kamerun, Sechs Kriegs- und Friedensjahre in den deutschen Tropen.* Berlin, E. S. Mittler, 1901. viii, 315 p. illus., maps.

Dominik's book was one of many reminiscences written by German colonial pioneers. Another work that falls into a comparable category is Eugen Zintgraff, *Nordkamerun* (Berlin, 1895).

2104 Full, August. *Fünfzig Jahre Togo.* Berlin, D. Reimer, 1935. 280 p. illus., plates, maps, diagrs.

A history of Togo written from the German colonial point of view by a former official of the Togolese administration. The author deals with both historical and administrative aspects of German colonization. See also Meyer, no. 2054.

Part III: area guide (by colonial power, region and colony)

2105 Gärtner, Karl. '*Togo*', *finanztechnische Studie über die Entwicklung des Schutzgebietes unter deutscher Verwaltung.* Darmstadt, Oppeln, Erdmann, Raabe, 1924. 57 p.

A study of the financial administration of Togo. An appendix outlines the author's experiences as a British prisoner of war.

2106 Hausen, Karin. *Deutsche Kolonialherrschaft in Afrika: Wirtschaftsinteressen und Kolonialverwaltung in Kamerun vor 1914.* Zürich, Atlantis, 1970. 340 p. (Beiträge zur Kolonial und Überseegeschichte, no. 6)

A study of German economic policy in Kamerun, based on original sources in both East and West Germany. The author argues that in Kamerun, as in other African colonies at a comparable rate of economic development, there was a conflict between the short-term goal of maximizing initial profits by brute exploitation, and the long-term interest of the administration in scientific colonization for the wider benefit of the metropole. According to the author, the administration became an increasingly autonomous factor during the last decade of German rule as against the planters and merchants.

2107 Metzger, O. F. *Unsere alte Kolonie Togo.* Neudamm, Verlag J. Neumann, 1941. 295 p. illus., maps.

Written by a former German colonial official, who had been governor of Togo during World War I, this book came out when German hopes of recovering former colonies were high. It is a compendium of information, emphasizing potential wealth in forest products, palm-oil and agriculture.

2108 Meyer, Hans, ed. *Das deutsche Kolonialreich: Eine Länderkunde der deutschen Schutzgebiete.* v. 1, *Ostafrika und Kamerun.* Leipzig, Bibliographisches Institut, 1909. 909 p., illus., maps, diagrs.

See no. 2096.

2109 Puttkamer, Jesko von. *Gouverneursjahre in Kamerun.* Berlin, G. Stilke, 1912. 331 p. illus., maps.

Puttkamer governed Kamerun during its formative years from 1895 to 1906. For additional literature written from the 'gubernatorial' standpoint, see v. 2 of Theodor Seitz, *Vom Aufstieg und Niederbruch deutscher Kolonialmacht* (Karlsruhe, C. F. Müller, 1927–29).

2110 Rudin, Harry Rudolph. *Germans in the Cameroons, 1884–1914: A case study in German imperialism.* London, J. Cape, 1938. 465 p. fold. map. Bibliography: p. 427–437.

The classical work on German Kamerun written by an American historian. This book is based on extensive source material in Germany and the Cameroons and is provided with a detailed bibliography.

2111 Ruppel, Julius. *Die Landesgesetzgebung für das Schutzgebiet Kamerun* ... Berlin, E. S. Mittler, 1912. xxxii, 1,263 p.

A complete collection of the treaties, laws, ordinances and circulars in force at the time. See also the *Amtsblatt für das Schutzgebiet Kamerun.*

2112 Schlunk, Martin. *Die Norddeutsche Mission in Togo.* Bremen, Verlag der Norddeutschen Missionsgesellschaft, 1910–12. 2 v. Bibliography: v. 2, p. 169–170.

A standard work concerning Protestant mission work among the Ewe. The first volume deals with the author's own journey, the second with general problems.

2113 Seidel, August. *Deutsch-Kamerun : Wie es ist und was es verspricht; historisch, geographisch, politisch, wirtschaftlich dargestellt.* Berlin, H. J. Meidinger, 1906. xv, 367 p. illus., maps.

A historical, political and economic account by an expert who had also written extensively on African languages and African economic problems.

2114 Stoecker, Helmuth, ed. *Kamerun unter deutscher Kolonialherrschaft.* Berlin, Rütten und Loening, 1960. 2 v. illus., maps, tables, geogr. index.

A co-operative project which seeks to interpret the history of Kamerun from the Marxist-Leninist point of view. The collaborators include Hans-Peter Jaeck, Adolf Rüger, Hella Winkler, Rudi Kaeselitz, Hartmut and Ellen Mehls. Despite its marked political bias, the work provides an extensive amount of information on subjects as varied as the German annexation, the development of the local black proletariat, indigenous resistance against the Germans, the German concession companies, and so forth. The work is based on detailed archival research. For a French view see no. 1749.

2115 Trierenberg, Georg. *Togo : Die Aufrichtung der deutschen Schutzherrschaft und die Erschliessung des Landes.* Berlin, E. S. Mittler, 1914. vii, 216 p. maps. Bibliography: p. vii.

A short study of German colonization in Togo.

2116 Westermann, Diedrich. *Die Glidyi-Ewe in Togo : Züge aus ihrem Gesellschaftsleben.* Berlin, Walter de Gruyter, 1935. xv, 332 p. (Mitteilungen des Seminars für orientalische Sprachen an der Universität Berlin, Beiband zum Jahrgang 38)

Professor Westermann's long and distinguished career as an Africanist began with a dictionary of Ewe published in 1905, while he was a missionary among the Ewe in Togoland. The anthropological treatise on a particular tribe of the Ewe group was one among many of his works on the Ewe. Westermann was also author of a pioneer history of pre-colonial states in sub-Saharan Africa, *Staatenbildungen südlich der Sahara* (Cologne, 1952).

South-West Africa

Bibliographies

2117 Bielschowski, Ludwig. *List of books in German on South Africa and South West Africa published up to 1914, in the South African Public Library, Cape Town.* Cape Town, School of Librarianship, 1949, vi, 84 p.

This study is part of the Cape Town School of Librarianship Bibliographical Series.

2118 Spohr, Otto H., comp. *German Africana : German publications on South and South West Africa, compiled and indexed by Otto H. Spohr, assisted by Manfred R. Poller.* Pretoria, State Library, 1968. 332 p. (Pretoria, State Library, Bibliographies, no. 14)

This bibliography, the most complete of its kind, covers 3,423 entries arranged in alphabetical order by author. There is also an index for personal names (including joint authors, illustrators and editors), a subject index for South-West Africa and one for South Africa. Readers are also provided with an indication of the South African library in which any particular book is to be found. The subjects covered include every conceivable topic – ethnography, history, geography, mining, agriculture, linguistic studies, and so forth. The entries are confined to published material; archival sources are not included.

Part III: area guide (by colonial power, region and colony)

Reference works

2119 Bley, Helmut. *Kolonialherrschaft und Sozialstruktur in Deutsch-Süd-westafrika 1894–1914.* Hamburg. Leibniz-Verlag, 1968. 390 p. (Hamburger Beiträge zur Zeitgeschichte, v. 5)
Based on extensive archival and published material. Bley's study is influenced by the socio-psychological theories elaborated by Fanon and Mannoni. The author argues that German colonial governance possessed some of the features that distinguish modern totalitarianism and that German colonialism in turn helped to poison the political climate at home. Little reference is made, however, to the more positive aspects of German colonization. The book has a detailed bibliography and an index of persons. See also no. 664, *Cambridge history of the British Empire*, v. 8, chap. XXVI, on German South-West Africa. Bley's work has since been translated into English by Hugh Ridley under the title *South-West Africa under German Rule 1894–1914* (Evanston, Northwestern University Press, 1971, 303 p.). It has been reviewed by L. H. Gann in an article entitled 'South West Africa and German Colonialism', *International Journal of African Historical Studies*, no. 1, 1973.

2120 Drechsler, Horst. *Südwestafrika unter deutscher Kolonialherrschaft : Der Kampf der Herero und Nama gegen den deutschen Imperialismus (1884–1915).* Berlin, Akademie-Verlag, 1966. 372 p. maps. Bibliography: p. 291–321.
Drechsler's book, which is based on extensive archival research, interprets the history of South-West Africa from the Marxist-Leninist point of view. He considers that the intrusion of Germany aborted the natural development of indigenous states, that German colonization was linked to the inner contradictions of German capitalism, and that the history of South-West Africa would be interpreted, above all, in terms of a liberation struggle waged by the indigenous tribes against foreign imperialism. The book has a detailed bibliography and notes on archival sources.

2121 Dove, Karl. *Deutsch Südwest-Afrika.* Berlin, W. Süsseroth, 1903. 208 p., illus., maps.
The writer, a German geographer, exhausted all the sources available at the time. His work deals successively with the history, geography, minerals, climate, flora, fauna, African population, and white population of the territory. Other works by the same author include *Südwest-Afrika : Kriegs- und Friedensbilder aus der ersten deutschen Kolonie* (Berlin, Allgemeiner Verein für deutsche Literatur, 1896, 348 p.); this is an interesting travelogue.

2122 Esterhuyse, J. H. *South West Africa, 1880–1894 : The establishment of German authority in South West Africa.* Cape Town, Struik, 1968. 282 p. Bibliography: p. 240–251.
A history of the founding of the colony, based on extensive use of archives in South and South-West Africa.

2123 François, Curt von. *Deutsch-Südwest-Afrika : Geschichte der Kolonisation bis zum Ausbruch des Krieges mit Witbooi, April 1893.* Berlin, D. Reimer, 1899. xi, 223 p. illus.
The author, a former explorer, was appointed to the command of the German forces in South-West Africa in 1889. He was subsequently promoted to be administrator of the territory, but was replaced by Theodor Leutwein, who in 1894 finally suppressed the Witbooi rising.

2124 Grosser Generalstab. Kriegsgeschichtliche Abteilung. *Die Kämpfe der deutschen Truppen in Südwestafrika.* Berlin, E. S. Mittler, 1906–7. 2 v. illus., maps, tables.

The official account of the German General Staff of the German campaigns in South-West Africa. The first volume deals with operations against the Herero; the second covers the campaigns against the Hottentots. The German account stresses the high quality of Germany's opponents in the field. The authors considered, for instance, that ' the Herero were equal in skill and marksmanship to the Boers, but exceeded them in military efficiency and resolute action ' (v. 2, p. 19). The work is of considerable interest, both for the study of war and for the study of Germany's strategy of annihilation (*Vernichtungsstrategie*) against the Herero.

2125 Hintrager, Oskar. *Südwestafrika in der deutschen Zeit.* Munich, Kommissionsverlag R. Oldenbourg, 1955. 261 p. illus., map.

A senior German colonial official in retirement, Hintrager writes from the German colonial point of view, stressing the positive aspects of German colonial rule and providing a good deal of statistical material to substantiate his interpretation. The book contains a chronology, an index of places, and an index of names.

2126 *Landratprotokolle.* Windhuk. 1910–14.

A Gouvernementsbeirat, that is to say, an advisory council with settler representation, was first created in 1904. It was subsequently raised to the dignity of a Landrat, and its proceedings were published.

2127 Leutwein, Theodor. *Elf Jahre Gouverneur in Deutsch Südwestafrika.* Berlin, E. S. Mittler, 1908. 589 p. illus., maps, photos.

The author, a former governor of the territory, relates successively the history of German colonization, of the various indigenous risings, and of military, economic, and administrative development. He assumes that colonization must in the last instance be considered as a ' business venture ', that a policy of brutal repression is ultimately unprofitable, and that colonial government must rely on indigenous chiefs. (Leutwein's attitude towards the Herero insurgents starkly contrasted with the strategy of annihilation adopted by the German General Staff and General L. von Trotha, as depicted in *Die Kämpfe der deutschen Truppen in Südwestafrika* (Berlin, E. S. Mittler, 1906–7, 2 v.). Leutwein's book contains appendices with government circulars and ordinances. There is a biography of the author written by his son Paul Leutwein, *Afrikanerschicksal, Gouverneur Leutwein und seine Zeit* . . . (Stuttgart, Union Deutsche Volksgemeinschaft [1929 ?], 184 p.).

2128 Loth, Heinrich. *Die christliche Mission in Südwestafrika : Zur destruktiven Rolle der Rheinischen Missionsgesellschaft beim Prozess der Staatsbildung in Südwestafrika, 1842–1893.* Berlin, Akademischer Verlag, 1963. 180 p.

An attack against the role of the Rheinische Mission, written from the Marxist-Leninist standpoint. The author has also written more specialized articles on African independent churches, and on the relations between missions and government. For a more traditional interpretation, see H. Driessler, *Die Rheinische Mission in Südwestafrika* (Gütersloh, Buchhandlung der Rheinischen Missionsgesellschaft, 1932, 323 p.); and Walther Spiecker, *Die Rheinische Missionsgesellschaft in ihren volks- und kolonialwirtschaftlichen Funktionen* (Gütersloh, C. Bertelsmann, 1922, 84 p.).

Part III: area guide (by colonial power, region and colony)

2129 Oelhafen, H. von. *Die Besiedlung Deutsch Südwestafrikas bis zum Weltkrieg*. Berlin, D. Reimer, 1926. 132 p.

A brief account of the German migration to South-West Africa with sections on railways, water, land, etc., as well as documents. Other books of interest include Paul Barth, *Südwestafrika : Wirtschaftlicher Ratgeber und allgemeine Anleitung, besonders für Auswanderungslustige* (Windhoek, J. Meinert, 1926, 304 p.), a handbook for settlers. Hermann Hesse, *Die Landfrage und die Frage der Rechtsgültigkeit der Konzessionen in Südwestafrika* (Jena, H. Costenoble, 1906, 2 v.), deals with the land law as it affected the settlers; the second volume contains documents. There are numerous reminiscences by German colonists, for instance Helene von Falkenhausen, *Ansiedlerschicksale : Elf Jahre in Deutsch Südwestafrika, 1893–1904* (Berlin, D. Reimer, 1906, 260 p.). South-West German colonization also produced a good deal of semi-fictional and fictional writing, for instance Hans Grimm, *Das deutsche Südwester-Buch* (Munich, A. Langen, 1929, 429 p.), a series of sketches concerning life in South-West Africa; and *Volk ohne Raum* (Munich, A. Langen, 1932, 1,352 p.), a once-famous novel whose title became an expansionist slogan.

2130 Reichskolonialamt. *Die Behandlung der einheimischen Bevölkerung in den kolonialen Besitzungen Deutschlands und Englands : Eine Erwiderung auf das englische Blaubuch vom August 1918 : Report on the natives of South-West Africa and their treatment by the Germans*. Berlin, Kommissionsverlag H. R. Engelmann, 1919.

An official German defence of Germany's colonial record against what the Germans called *die Kolonialschuldlüge*, the lie of colonial guilt. The official British case was embodied in Great Britain, Parliament, Accounts and Papers, *Union of South-Africa – report on the natives of South-west Africa and their treatment by Germany*, prepared by the Administrator's Office, Windhoek, South-West Africa (Jan. 1918; Cmd. 9146).

2131 Sander, Ludwig. *Geschichte der deutschen Kolonial-Gesellschaft für Südwestafrika von ihrer Gründung bis zum Jahre 1910*. Berlin, Reimer, 1910. 2 v.

The first volume covers the history of the enterprise. The second volume is a collection of documents. The author also edited *Die deutschen Kolonien in Wort und Bild* . . . (Leipzig, H. Hillger, 1906, xxiv, 737 p.).

2132 Schwabe, Kurd. *Im deutschen Diamantenland : Deutsch-Südwestafrika von der Errichtung der deutschen Herrschaft bis zur Gegenwart (1884–1910)*. Berlin, E. S. Mittler, 1910. xii, 443 p. illus., maps.

A history of German colonization from the standpoint of a German settler. The author also wrote *Der Krieg in Deutsch-Südwestafrika 1904–1906* (Berlin, C. A. Weller, 1907, 440 p.), and *Mit Schwert und Pflug in Deutsch-Südwestafrika* . . . (Berlin, E. S. Mittler, 1899, x, 448 p.).

2133 Vedder, Heinrich. *South-West Africa in early times : Being the story of South-West Africa up to the date of Maharero's death in 1890*. Ed. and trans. by Cyril G. Hall. London, Oxford University Press. 1938, 525 p.

A standard work on the early history and ethnology of South West Africa. The author concentrates on the history of the various African communities; his treatment of the early European activities is somewhat superficial and disjointed. His work as a whole, however, ranks as a missionary classic. See also Wellington in the South African section, no. 1317.

2134 Walter, Heinrich. *Die Farmwirtschaft in Deutsch-Südwest-Afrika : Ihre biologische Grundlagen.* Berlin, P. Parey, 1940. 5 v., plates, diagrams.
An exhaustive treatise on the agricultural economics of South-West Africa. The first volume deals with climatic conditions, the second with pastoral farming, the third with arable farming and market gardening, the fourth with the food value of South-West African grasses and bushes, the fifth with the flora of South-West African grazing lands. An early study, and an excellent source regarding the beginnings of German settlement and the nature of German policy, is Paul Rohrbach, *Deutsche Kolonialwirtschaft.* Vol. 1. *Südwest-Afrika* (Berlin, Buchverlag der 'Hilfe', 1907, 510 p., illus., maps). Rohrbach, a firm believer in a policy designed to turn tribesmen into proletarians, represented the settlers' standpoint as against the big concessionary companies.

ITALIAN AFRICA

Note Italian travellers and missionaries were among the earliest explorers of Africa. Their doings are recorded in an extensive body of secondary literature, as well as in numerous archives. Part of this material is described in Richard Grey and David Chambers, *Materials for West African history in Italian archives* (see no. 28). Modern Italian colonialism, however, dates only from the unification of Italy. In 1882 the Italians acquired Assab on the Red Sea. In the same year, a special section was created within the Italian Foreign Ministry, the Ministero degli Affari Esteri, to take charge of colonial matters. This section, which became increasingly important, was reorganized in 1908 as the Direzione Centrale degli Affari Coloniali. The archives of the Ministry of Foreign Affairs (which at the time of writing were open to researchers up to 1896) remain of major importance for the study of Italian colonialism. The ministry also published an extensive series of Green Books, including the *Documenti Diplomatici concernenti Assab* (1870–1882); *Documenti Diplomatici. Massaoua (1888)*; *Documenti Diplomatici. Etiopia (1889–1890)*; *Amministrazione Civile della Colonia Eritrea (1895)*; *Avvenimenti d'Africa (1895–1896)*, and others. (J. L. Miège, *L'impérialisme colonial italien de 1870 à nos jours*, Paris, Société d'Enseignement Supérieur, 1968, 412 p., provides a brief outline for those students unable to read Italian. The book also has an extensive bibliography.)
In 1912, following upon the conquest of Libya, colonial affairs were entrusted to a separate ministry, the Ministero delle Colonie. This body was assisted by the Consiglio Superiore Coloniale (originally set up in 1903 within the Foreign Ministry). In 1937 the Ministry as a whole was reorganized under fascist auspices as the Ministero dell'Africa Italiana, with separate *Direzioni*, respectively, for political affairs, civil affairs, economic and financial matters, colonization and labour, personnel and general affairs, police, defence, research and justice. (From 1913, the Ministero delle Colonie published its own *Bolletino* with slightly varying titles, and from 1927 the *Rivista delle Colonie*. The Ministero dell'Africa Italiana continued to put out an extensive amount of material, including *Annali* 1938–1943.)
In 1935 Italian troops invaded Ethiopia, and a year later the newly conquered kingdom was amalgamated with Italy's existing colonies in a single territorial bloc known as Africa Orientale Italiana, subject to a viceroy, who in turn was assisted by provincial governors. In 1940 Italian troops also occupied British

Somaliland; but the following year British troops, assisted by Ethiopian levies, occupied Italian East Africa, and the Italian colonial empire collapsed. After the war, African affairs once more reverted to the Ministero degli Affari Esteri. In 1952 this body instituted a separate commission for the study of Italy's colonial past, known as the Comitato per la Documentazione dell'Opera dell'Italia in Africa. From 1958 onward, the Comitato put out a major publication, *L'Italia in Africa*, with specialized series designed to illustrate Italy's colonial enterprise in its various aspects, historical, military, administrative, scientific, and so forth. At the time of writing, the original archives derived from the Ministry of Colonies that were used for these series remained officially closed to private researchers.

Students of Italian colonialism, however, can use numerous private reminiscences, often of a propagandistic character, as well as a vast amount of semi-official material. This includes publications put out by the Istituto Coloniale Italiano (founded in 1906, and known from 1929 as the Istituto Coloniale Fascista). The institute aimed at co-ordinating the work of other scientific and patriotic societies interested in promoting Italian colonialism. These included bodies such as the Società Dante Alighieri, Lega Navale, Società Geograficà, Società Africana di Napoli, Società d'Esplorazioni di Milano, and others, all of which also issued publications in their own right. (For an account of the work done by the Istituto see Cesare Cesari, *L'Istituto Coloniale Fascista : A Trenta Anni dalla sua Costituzione*, Rome, Fratelli Palombi, 1936.) In addition, an extensive body of missionary literature in the Italian language, as well as a considerable number of learned journals and other works of erudition, is available for students. The colonies of former north-east Italian Africa were Eritrea, Ethiopia, and Italian Somaliland. After World War II the Italian government lost power over Eritrea and Ethiopia : Eritrea was reunited to Ethiopia by the United Nations. Italy was allowed to administer Somaliland until July 1, 1960, when British and Italian Somaliland were joined to form the independent nation of Somalia. See also Ethiopia, nos. 2444–2468.

Atlas

2135 Agostini, Giovanni de. *Italy and her empire : Perforated pocket atlas, with 16 colored maps and explanatory text.* Trans. by E. Cope. Genoa, E. E. Ortelli, 1937. 34 p. col. illus., col. maps.

Bibliographies

2136 ' Bibliografia dell'Africa orientale italiana 1936–1939 in ... Anno III, numero 2, 1940 ', in *Annali dell'Africa italiana*, p. 1269–1313. Verona, A. Mondadori.

2137 *Bibliografia dell'Istituto Fascista dell'Africa Italiana; elenco completo di tutte le opere pubblicate dall'I.F.A.I. dalla sua fondazione (1906) al Gennaio 1939 (XVII) e degli articoli apparsi nelle Riviste edite dall'Istituto (Rivista Coloniale – l'Oltremare – Africa Italiana).* Roma, 1939. 89 p.
Catalogue of publications of the Institute (formerly Istituto Coloniale Italiano, then Istituto Coloniale Fascista) from its founding in 1906 to January 1939. Part one is a listing of periodicals, conference proceedings, and monographs. Part two lists articles appearing in periodicals of the Institute, arranged by geographical area and topic. Geographic areas covered include Eritrea, Somalia, Ethiopia, and the Belgian Congo.

Italian Africa

2138 *Bibliografia dell'Italia d'oltremare.* Spoleto, Istituto Nazionale per le Relazioni Culturali con l'Estero, 1940.
Not available for examination.

2139 Hess, Robert L. *Italian colonialism in Somalia.* Chicago, University of Chicago Press, 1966. 234 p., maps, tables. Bibliography: p. 213–226.
The author's ' Annotated Bibliography ' gives a general account of existing bibliographical aids, unpublished sources, official sources, books concerning travel and exploration, memoirs of officials and secondary works. Many entries are annotated.

2140 *Guide bibliografiche dell'Istituto Coloniale Fascista.* Rome, Istituto Coloniale Fascista, 1928.
Excellent bibliography on Italian Africa.

2141 Istituto Nazionale per le Relazioni Culturali con l'Estero. Centro Studi di Diritto e Politica Coloniale Fascista. *Bibliografia dell'Italia d'oltremare.* Anno 1939–40. Roma, 1940–42.

2142 Italy. Ministero degli Affari Esteri. *Raccolta di pubblicazioni coloniali italiane : Primo indice bibliografico.* Rome, Tipografia della Camera dei Deputati, 1911.
The Ministry published also a bibliography of maps, *Raccolta cartografica*, at the same time.

2143 U.S. Library of Congress. General Reference and Bibliographical Division. *North and northeast Africa: A selected, annotated list of writings, 1951–1957*, comp. by Helen F. Conover. Washington, D.C., 1957. 182 p.
Contains separate sections, respectively, on ' Ethiopia and Eritrea ', ' The Somalilands ', as well as ' Libya '.

2144 Varley, Douglas H. *A bibliography of Italian colonisation in Africa, with a section on Abyssinia.* London, Royal Empire Society and the Royal Institute of International Affairs, 1936. 92 p.
Prepared in connexion with the international interest occasioned by the Italo-Abyssinian war in 1936, which added Ethiopia to the former Italian possessions in Africa – Libya, Eritrea, and Somaliland. There was subsequently set up the central administration of Italian East Africa, combining Ethiopia, Eritrea, and Somalia. This list, pages 72–92 of which relate to Ethiopia, cites books and periodical material, particularly those relating to modern political developments. Reprinted in 1970 by Dawsons of Pall Mall, London. See also Schiller, no. 476, for legal material.

2145 Zanutto, S. *Pubblicazioni edite dall'amministrazione coloniale e sotti i suoi auspici, 1882–1937.* Rome, Società Anonima Italiana, 1938.

Reference works

2146 *Africa.* 1882–1940. Irregular.
The official bulletin of the Società Africana d'Italia. Had an annual index. Also called *L'Africa Italiana*.

2147 Agostino Orsini, Paolo d'. *La colonizzazione africana nel sistema fascista, i problemi della colonizzazione nell'Africa italiana.* Milano, Fratelli Bocca, 1941. 164 p. Bibliography: p. 157–161.
An overview of Italian colonization from the Fascist point of view.

Part III: area guide (by colonial power, region and colony)

2148 *Annuario delle colonie italiane* (*e dei paesi vicini*). Rome, Cooperativa Tipografica ' Castaldi ' [etc.], 1926–39. 13 v. plates, maps, facsims.
This annual publication was issued by the Istituto Coloniale Italiano (later known as Istituto Coloniale Fascista) in Rome. The title varies: 1926–27, *Annuario delle colonie italiane* ...; 1937, *Annuario dell'impero italiano*; 1938–39, *Annuario dell'Africa italiana*. The yearbook is valuable for a study of Fascist policies and preconceptions, as well as statistical material.

2149 Becker, George H. *The disposition of the Italian colonies, 1941–1951.* Annemasse, Imprimerie Granchamp, 1952. 270 p. Bibliography: p. 265–270. See no. 2195 for annotation.

2150 Bertola, A. *Il regime dei culti nell'Africa italiana.* Bologna, Cappelli, 1939.

2151 Cattaneo, Vincenzo. *La giustizia italiana in Africa : Somalia, Harar, Galla e Sidama, Eritrea, Amara, Scioa.* Rome, A. Signorelli, 1942. 395 p.
Provides much information concerning Italian courts and administrative practices in Italian East Africa, though by the time the book came out, the empire had already collapsed.

2152 Centro di Studi Coloniali. *Atti del primo congresso di studi coloniali.* Florence, 1931. 6 v.
Proceedings and collected papers delivered at the Congress on all aspects of Italian colonialism. Particularly valuable because the papers are authentic scholarly contributions, generally free of Fascist propaganda and hyperbole. See also proceedings of other colonial congresses held in Naples (1934), Naples-Rome (1937) and Florence (1946). (See also no. 2221.)

2153 Ciasca, Raffaele. *Storia coloniale dell'Italia contemporanea : Da Assab all'Impero.* Milano, U. Hoepli. 1938, 570 p., maps.
A standard scholarly politico-diplomatic survey, with strongly nationalist and pro-fascist sympathies, which ends with Mussolini's conquest of Ethiopia.

2154 Cucinotta, Ernesto. *Diritto coloniale italiano.* 2d rev. ed. Rome, Società Editrice del Foro Italiano, 1933.
A detailed account of colonial law during the Fascist period.

2155 Dainelli, Giotto. *Gli esploratori italiani in Africa.* Torino, Unione Tipografico-Editrice Torinese, 1960. 2 v., maps, illus.
The standard work on the subject. The first part concerns Italian exploration from the Roman era to the eighteenth century; the second part deals with the early years of modern exploration. The main part of the study outlines the classical era of Italian exploration, especially in East Africa. The last part of the work is entitled ' the epigoni ', and makes mention of Italian expeditions up to the 1950s. There is an index of names. See also the journal *L'Esplorazione commerciali e l'esploratore*, 1886–1928. Milan. Monthly. A bulletin of the Società Italiana di Esplorazioni Geografiche e Commerciali (after 1928 was incorporated into *L'Oltremare*).

2156 *Enciclopedia italiana di scienze, lettere ed arti.* Pubblicata sotto l'Alto Patronato di S. M. il Re d'Italia. Milan, Istituto Giovanni Treccani, 1927–37. 36 v.
The first volume of appendices came out in 1938. Two more volumes, covering all letters from A to Z, appeared in 1949. These cover the years 1938 to 1948 under the auspices of the Istituto della Enciclopedia Italiana.

2157 Folchi, Alberto Enrico. *L'ordinamento amministrativo dell'Africa italiana.* Milan, G. Martucci, 1936. 111 p. (Opere politiche, Giurdiche, economiche, no. 3)

Italian Africa

2158 Fossa, Davide. *Lavoro italiano nell'Impero.* Milan, Mondadori, 1938. 571 p., illus., tables. Includes bibliography.
Written by a former Inspector of Production and Labour in Italian East Africa. In addition to Fascist propaganda, the work contains a great deal of factual information, including statistical tables. The author surveys labour legislation, Italian economic policy and Italian enterprises. He describes the various official organizations including the Legioni Lavoratori, and the work done by the Genio Militare. He provides data concerning road construction, urbanization, agriculture and settlement, etc. The appendices contain labour legislation.

2159 Gaibi, Agostino. *Manuale di storia politico-militare delle colonie italiane.* Roma, Provveditoria Generale dello Stato, Libreria, 1928. 579 p. illus., plans, fold. tables.
Published under the auspices of the Ministry of War to give a general account of the political and military problems of the empire. The author was official historian of the General Staff.

2160 *Guida dell'Africa orientale italiana.* Milano, 1938. maps.
An excellent work – much more than a mere guide. Coverage includes Ethiopia, Eritrea and former Italian Somaliland.

2161 *La formazione dell'impero coloniale italiano.* Milan, Fratelli Treves, 1938. 3 v., maps, illus.
A product of the Fascist era, designed to provide Italian families with a complete account of the labours performed ' by our miraculous people guided by the infallible genius of the Duce '. Despite its propagandistic flavour, this work contains a great deal of factual material, especially regarding Italian military history. The editors provide contemporary source material drawn from military communiqués, reports and memoirs. The first volume deals with Italian colonialism up to the end of World War I. The second volume covers the conquest of Ethiopia, while the third volume continues the military history, and also provides a general account of the Italian colonial empire.

Another work of this period is Giovanni Vitali, *Le guerre italiane in Africa: La conquista dell'Eritrea e della Somalia : La conquista della Libia; la conquista dell'Ethiopia* (Milano, Sonzogno, 1936, 472 p., illus., ports., fold. col. map). It is written, according to the editor, ' with the love of the scholar and the passion of an Italian '. A military history in the narrow sense of the word.

2162 *L'Italia Coloniale. Organo delle nostre colonie di Diretto Dominio e della Gente Italiana negli Altri Paesi.* 1924– . Monthly.
Published in Milan, later in Rome. Presents the Fascist point of view, both on colonies under direct Italian rule, and on Italians in other countries. Copiously illustrated. Contains biographical, statistical, and other types of information, as well as Fascist propaganda. Popular in style.

2163 Italy. Commissione per la Pubblicazione dei Documenti Diplomatici. *I documenti diplomatici italiani.* Rome, Libreria dello Stato, 1952– .
The Italians only began to publish their diplomatic documents well after the Germans and British had done so. They hope to produce a complete collection dating from the foundation of the kingdom of Italy to 1943. This collection will naturally include a great deal of information concerning colonial diplomacy and other related matters. But so far only a limited number of volumes have appeared. These cover only selected periods, and there are as yet many gaps. The arrangement is purely chronological.

The collection as a whole is divided into several series, each covering a specific period. Each series in turn is subdivided into several volumes.

Part III: area guide (by colonial power, region and colony)

The first series covers the period January 8, 1861, to September 20, 1870; the fifth, August 2, 1914, to October 16, 1914; the sixth, November 4, 1918, to January 17, 1919; the seventh, October 31, 1922, to September 23, 1928; the eighth, May 23, 1939, to September 3, 1939; the ninth, September 4, 1939, to June 10, 1940. The documents are useful for an understanding of Italian imperialism, though they do not throw much light on the colonies as such.

2164 Italy. Istituto Coloniale Italiano.

The Institute was founded in 1906 in Rome. It was renamed Istituto Coloniale Fascista during the Fascist era, and occupied a semi-official position. The Institute aimed at promoting Italian colonialism, and published a variety of journals and also documentary collections, including the following:

> *Annuario delle Colonie Italiane e dei Paesi Vicini* (1926–1936), 11 v.
> *Rivista Coloniale* (1906–1927).
> *L'Oltremare* (1927–1934, a continuation of the *Rivista Coloniale*).
> *Annuario dell'Italia all'Estero e delle sue Colonie* (1911), 1 v.
> *Atti del Congresso Coloniale Italiano in Asmara* (1905), 2 v.
> *Atti del primo Congresso degli Italiani all'Estero* (1908), 2 v.
> *Atti del secondo Congresso degli Italiani all'Estero* (1911), 4 v.
> *Atti del Convegno Nazionale Coloniale pel dopo guerra delle Colonie* (1919), 1 v.
> *Indici della Rivista Coloniale* (1906–1920).
> *Elenco degli articoli pubblicati dalla Rivista Coloniale e dalla Rivista L'Oltremare* (1922–1932).
> *Le Colonie*, publ. by the Agenzia Quotidiana d'Informazioni Coloniali, 1928–1936).

See Cesare Cesari, *L'Istituto coloniale fascista a trenta anni della sua Costituzione* (Rome, Fratelli Palombi, 1936), for an account of the work of the institute.

2165 Italy. Ministero degli Affari Esteri. Rome.

In 1882 a special section within the Italian Ministry of Foreign Affairs took charge of colonial affairs. In 1908 this was reorganized as the Direzione Centrale degli Affari Coloniale. This continued to control colonial questions until 1912, when the colonies were entrusted to a separate Ministero delle Colonie.

The Italian Ministry of Foreign Affairs published an extensive series of documents, including the following:

> Agnesa, G., and V. Deciani, eds., *Trattati, Convenzioni, Accordi, Protocolli ed altri Documenti Relativi all'Africa, 1825–1906*, Rome, 1906–1909, 4 v.
> *Amministrazione Civile della Colonia Eritrea*, 15-7-1895.
> *Corrispondenza tra il Governo Centrale e il Governo dell'Eritrea*, 20-3-1896.
> *Avvenimenti d'Africa* (1895/3–1896), 27-4-1896.
> id. (March–April 1896), 27-4-1896.
> *Condizioni e Amministrazione del Benadir, 21-5-1903, etc....*
> *Documenti Diplomatici Concernenti Assab (1870–1882)*, 12-6-1882.
> *Documenti Diplomatici. Massaoua.* 1° ser. 24-4-1888.
>   2° ser. 8-11-1888.
> *Documenti Diplomatici. Etiopia.* 1° ser. 17-12-1889.
>   2° ser. 5-5-1890.
> *Protocolli 24-3 a 15-4-1891 relativi alla Delimitazione della Zone di Influenza tra Italia e Inghilterra nella Regione a Sud e a Nord dell'Ethiopia e dell'Eritrea, 16-4-1891.*

Italian Africa

The Italians also published a more extensive series of diplomatic documents known as *I Documenti Diplomatici Italiani*. The following series are of interest concerning the Italian colonial empire. Series 3: 1896–1907; 4: 1908–1915; 5: 1915–1921; 6: 1921–1922; 7: 1922–1925; 8: 1936–1938; 9: 1939–1943. In addition, researchers should consult the *Bollettino Consolare*.

2166 Italy. Ministero degli Affari Esteri. *L'Africa italiana al parlamento nazionale.* 1882–1905.
This is useful as a summary and as a reference on debates on Africa in the Italian parliament. Use indexes by subject and name of speaker.

2167 Italy. Ministero degli Affari Esteri. Comitato per la Documentazione delle attivita italiane in Africa. *L'Italia in Africa.* Rome, Istituto Poligrafico dello Stato, 1955– .
This series, issued under the auspices of the Italian Ministry of Foreign Affairs, is highly uneven in quality, but nonetheless remains a standard reference work. The best of the volumes that have appeared are serious, interpretive works by professional historians who have made critical use of unpublished materials. The less satisfactory volumes, often written by former civil servants of the Ministry, use published sources uncritically, and the volumes sometimes amount to little more than compilations of official regulations and decrees.

> *L'Italia in Africa.* Rome, Istituto Poligrafico dello Stato, 1955. 2 v.
> Covers early exploration, the acquisition of Assab, economic penetration of East Africa in the second part of the 19th century, and so forth. Original documents are appended.

> *L'Italia in Africa. Serie civile.* Rome, Istituto Poligrafico dello Stato, 1965– .
> Two volumes have appeared up to now; they deal with sanitary and veterinary administration. Include bibliographies.

> *L'Italia in Africa. Serie giuridico-amministrativa.* Rome, Istituto Poligrafico dello Stato, 1963– .
> The first volume covers certain aspects of judicial and civil administration in the Italian colonies (later trusteeship territories) between 1869 and 1955. There is information regarding the central organs of government, the civil service and other aspects.

> *L'Italia in Africa. Serie scientifico-culturale.* Rome, Istituto Poligrafico dello Stato, 1963– .
> The first volume concerns the contribution made by Italy to our knowledge of Africa. An additional volume published in 1964 deals with the development of colonial cartography.

> *L'Italia in Africa. Serie storica.* Rome, Istituto Poligrafico dello Stato, 1958– .
> The series comprises an extensive number of documents, excerpts from parliamentary debates, private letters, and so forth. There is also a great deal of bibliographical information, as well as editorial annotation.

> *L'Italia in Africa. Serie storico-militare.* Rome, Istituto Poligrafico dello Stato, 1960–64. 5 v.
> Covers the history of the army in the colonies from 1885 to 1943; naval operations connected with the colonies between 1868 and 1943; operations of the air force, 1888–1932, in Libya and Eritrea; and the army's part in civil administration.

Part III: area guide (by colonial power, region and colony)

2168 Italy. Ministero dell'Africa Italiana. *Gli annali dell'Africa italiana.* Rome, Casa Editrĭce A. Mondadori, 1938–43. 20 v.

This series deals with subjects as varied as administration, agriculture, colonial history, settlement in Italian Africa, and so forth. There are also articles of a more general propagandistic kind extolling the supposed virtues of Fascist policy. The series is, nevertheless, a valuable historical source. Includes maps, plates, portfolios, charts, diagrams and bibliographies.

2169 Italy. Ministero delle Colonie, Rome.

In 1912 the Italians formed a separate Colonial Ministry. In 1936 the Ministry was renamed Ministero dell'Africa Italiana. (In 1957 the archives of the Ministry were transferred to the Ministero degli Affari Esteri.)

Bollettino Officiale (1913–).

Printed the major administrative measures and legislative measures and legislative enactment concerning the Ministry. See S. Zanutto, *Pubblicazioni edite dall'Amminstrazione Coloniale o sotto i suoi Auspici* (1882–1937). v. 1, 1938; v. 2, 1940.

This work provides a full list of the publications of the Ministry.

2170 Italy. Ministero delle Colonie. *Bollettino di informazioni.* Rome, 1913–22.

Title changes and series added: *Bollettino di informazioni economiche*, 1923–27; *Rassegna economica delle colonie*, 1928–37; *Rassegna economica dell'Africa italiana*, 1937–41?

One of the most valuable series for information on Italian colonialism.

2171 Italy. Senato. *Memorandum sulla situazione economica e finanzaria dei territori italiani in Africa.* Rome, 1946. 53 p.

Indispensable for the official estimates of Italian investments in East Africa and Libya.

2172 Micus, Ingeborg. *Die Presse des italienischen Kolonialreiches.* Würzburg, K. Triltsch, 1941. 64 p. plates, facsims.

A general account of the colonial press, supplied with bibliographical footnotes.

2173 Miège, J. L. *L'impérialisme colonial italien de 1870 à nos jours.* Paris, Société d'Edition d'Enseignement Supérieur, 1968. 419 p., maps. Bibliography: p. 285–308.

The most up-to-date work on the history of Italian colonialism, written from a Eurocentric standpoint. The study is based on a series of lectures delivered at the Faculté des Lettres at Aix between 1965 and 1968; it covers modern Italian colonialism from the legacy of the *Risorgimento* to the collapse of the Italian empire during the Second World War. There is a detailed note on published archival sources (p. 281–283); there are appended documents, and a list of the principal office-holders concerned with colonial affairs in Italy. An indispensable introduction to the subject. The reference material must be used with caution because of the enormous number of misprints.

2174 Mondaini, Gennaro. *La legislazione coloniale italiana nel suo sviluppo storico e nel suo stato attuale (1881–1940).* Milano, Istituto per gli Studi di Politica Internazionale, 1941. (Manuali di Politica Internazionale, no. 30)

Reviews the colonial legislation within their historical context. This is a revised edition of the author's *Manuale di storia e legislazione coloniale del regno d'Italia (1924–1927).* Includes a bibliography.

2175 Parlamenghi-Crispi, Tommaso. *L'Italia coloniale e Francesco Crispi . . .* Milano, Fratelli Treves, 1928. 247 p.

Includes documents from the Crispi archives.

Italian Africa

2176 Parpagliolo, A. *Raccolta dei principali ordinamenti legislativi delle colonie italiane.* Rome, Ministero delle Colonie, 1930–32. 2 v.

2177 Piccioli, Angelo. *La Nuova Italia d'Oltremare e l'opera del fascismo nelle colonie italiane. . . .* 2d ed. Verona, Mondadori, 1934. 2 v.
This work was commissioned by the colonial ministry and is the official history of the colonial accomplishments of Fascism in the first decade of Mussolini's rule.

2178 Preti, Luigi. *Impero fascista : Africani ed ebrei.* Milano, 1968.
A popular but suggestive account of the origins of fascist imperial ideology and the relationship between Mussolini's racism in Africa and the evolution of Italian domestic anti-semitism.

2179 *Rivista Coloniale. Organo dell'Istituto Coloniale Italiano.* 1906–27. Rome. Monthly.
The 1920 volume contains an index for the years 1906–20. The early issues especially contain interesting articles by colonial pioneers.

The Italians subsequently published: *Rivista delle Colonie : Rassegna dei Possedimenti Italiani e Stranieri d'Oltremare* (1927–43, Rome, monthly). This journal was published for the first eight years by the Ministero delle Colonie under the title *Oltremare,* then under the title *Rivista delle Colonie Italiane.*

2180 *Rivista di agricoltura subtropicale e tropicale.* 1907. Firenze. Monthly.
Up to 1944 the title was *L'Agricoltura coloniale.* Issued by Istituto Agricolo Coloniale Italiano. This journal, while devoted primarily to technical aspects of tropical agriculture, also contains valuable articles on Italian land colonization policies and occasional commentary on general colonial policy.

2181 *Rivista Geografica Italiana.* 1893– . Firenze, Società di Studi Geografici e Coloniali. Frequency varies.

2182 Società Geografica Italiana. *Memorie della Reale Società Geografica Italiana.* v. 1– . 1878– . Roma, Reale Società Geografica Italiana.
Useful accounts by travellers, geographers and colonial officials, and missionaries. See Enrico De Agostini, *La Reale Società Geografica Italiana e la sua opera dalla fondazione ad oggi (1887–1936)* (Rome, Reale Società Geografica Italiana, 1937), an official history of the Italian Geographical Society. The Society also publishes *Bollettino* (1868–).

2183 Traversi, Carlo. *Storia della cartografia coloniale italiana.* Roma, Istituto Poligrafico dello Stato, 1964. 294 p. plates. maps (part fold., part col.), facsims. (Comitato per la Documentazione dell'Opera dell'Italia in Africa, l'Italia in Africa, Serie scientifico-culturale) Bibliography: p. 247–257.
Standard history of the subject. The author first covers Eritrea, then Somaliland and Libya. He gives an account of the various scientific expeditions in the Italian colonies, and of the role played by cartography in the course of military operations. He provides details concerning the work of Italian topographers and of the part taken by various ministries and specialized institutions.

2184 *Vademecum africana.* Roma, Istituto fascista dell'Africa italiana. 1943. 2 v.
Covers the Italians in Africa 1939–1945.

2185 Villari, Luigi. *The expansion of Italy.* London, Faber & Faber, 1930. 290 p.
Covers Italian expansion from the Middle Ages to the Fascist period. The book seeks to convince the reader that Italian expansion harms no one and develops everyone.

Part III: area guide (by colonial power, region and colony)

2186 Zoli, Corrado. *Espansione coloniale italiana (1922–37).* Rome, L'Arma, 1949.
A succinct historical account with special attention to military affairs. Written from a pro-colonial point of view.

2187 ──── *Relazione generale dell'Alto Commissario per l'Oltre Giuba a S.E. il Principe Pietro Lanza di Scalea, Ministro delle Colonie (Riservato).* Rome, Arti Grafiche, 1926.

Ethiopia and Eritrea

Note See also separate entries for Ethiopia and Somalia.

Bibliographies

2188 Dainelli, Giotto, Marinelli Olinto, and Attilio Mori. ' Bibliografia geografica della colonia Eritrea, 1891–1906 '. *Rivista Geografica Italiana*, v. 14, 1907. 72 p.

2189 Haskell, Daniel Carl, comp. *Ethiopia and the Italo-Ethiopian conflict, 1936 : A selected list of references.* New York, New York Public Library, 1936. 13 p.

2190 Italy. Ministero degli Affari Esteri. Istituto Agronomico per l'Africa Italiana. *Contribution to an Italian bibliography on Ethiopia, 1935–1950 (agriculture and arguments relative to).* Trans. from Italian by P. Gemma. Florence, n.d. 154 l.
Translation of a work published in Florence by the Istituto Agronomico in 1953 (84 p.; 1,500 entries).

Reference works

2191 Baer, George W. *The coming of the Italo-Ethiopian war.* Cambridge, Mass., Harvard University Press, 1967. 404 p. map. Bibliography: p. 379–400.
A standard work. Outstanding not merely for its treatment of the subject but also for the wealth of its bibliographical information.

2192 Baratieri, Oreste. *Mémoires d'Afrique (1892–1896).* Paris, C. Delagrove, 1899. 542 p. port., maps.
Reminiscences of the Italian general who commanded the Italian forces during the disastrous Aduwa campaign, and who was subsequently tried and censured by a military tribunal. The work throws light on Eritrea as well as on Ethiopia and on general Italian policy.

2193 Bardi, Pietro Maria. *Pionieri e soldati d'A.O. dall'acquisto di Assab all'Impero romano di Etiopia : Antologia di scritti, documenti e illustrazioni.* Milan, U. Hoepli, 1936. 580 p. illus., ports., facsims.
Bardi's work is a propagandistic venture that seeks to glorify Mussolini and his ' most humane enterprise in undertaking the immense labour of founding the Empire '. Despite the author's bias, he provides a good deal of biographical material as well as documents, newspaper articles, etc., dating from the birth of Italian colonialism in the middle of the last century to 1936.

2194 Battaglia, Roberto. *La prima guerra d'Africa.* Turin, Einaudi, 1958. 819 p., maps, illus.
An important study, with a strong Marxist bias, of the Italian attempt to conquer

Ethiopia during the Crispi era. The author discusses the origins of Italian coloniza-tion, its domestic causes, the political motivation and effects of Crispi's regime; he ends with the Adua campaign and its aftermath. The ' official ' story is told in T. Parlamenghi-Crispi, ed., *Francesco Crispi : La prima guerra d'Africa : Documenti e memorie dell'Archivio Crispi* (Milan, Fratelli Treves, 1914, 419 p.).

2195 Becker, George H. *The disposition of the Italian colonies, 1941–1951.* Annemasse, Imprimerie Granchamp, 1952. 270 p. Bibliography : p. 265–270.
Prepared as a thesis at the Institut Universitaire des Hautes Etudes Internationales in Geneva, this work reviews the post-war settlements for the former Italian colonies, Eritrea, Somaliland, and Libya. A short background section on pre-war and wartime administration is followed by a discussion of the economic, strategic and prestige value of the colonies and the efforts of the Council of Foreign Ministers, the Paris Peace Conference, and finally the General Assembly to settle the problems.

2196 Berkeley, George Fitz Hardinge. *The campaign of Adowa and the rise of Menelik.* New ed. London, Constable and Co., 1935. 403 p. maps.
Originally published in 1902. The author, a British expert on Italy, used largely Italian sources. The 1935 edition, which was no longer favourable to the Italians, contains a brief sketch of Abyssinian history up to the Italian campaign of 1895–96. This is subsequently studied in considerable detail.

2197 Conti Rossini, Carlo. *Etiopia e genti di Etiopia.* Firenze, R. Bemporad, 1937. 402 p. plates, maps.
Conti Rossini, considered the leading Italian exponent of Ethiopian studies, com-bined two careers as a scholar and civil servant. His government posts included a position as director of civil affairs in Eritrea, 1899–1903. His publications on lan-guages and literature of Northeast Africa led to his membership in the Accademia dei Lincei.
  Among the writer's numerous works, another important volume is his compre-hensive account of customary laws of the peoples of Eritrea, *Principi di diritto consuetudinario della colonia Eritrea* (Rome, Tipografia dell'Unione Editrice, 1916, 802 p.).

2198 —— *Italia ed Etiopia. Dal trattato d'Ucciali alla battaglia di Adua.* Rome, Pubblicazioni dell'Istituto per l'Oriente, 1935. 494 p. maps.
A history of Italo-Ethiopian relations compiled by one of the most distinguished Italian authorities on Ethiopia, who had previously written many works on the early history, languages and the ethnography of Abyssinia.

2199 Del Boca, Angelo. *The Ethiopian war, 1935–1941.* Chicago, University of Chicago Press, 1969. 289 p.
Primarily a military account of the Ethiopian war by an Italian journalist who interviewed many of the surviving Ethiopian leaders and shows a strong sym-pathy for their side of the story. The book deals generously with Italy's use of poison gas and the realities behind Ethiopian slavery and war ' atrocities ', thus debunking the Fascist propaganda stories that Del Boca had experienced as a youth. Equally important is the author's skilful presentation of the Italian popular view of Ethiopia as a kind of ' wild west ' land of opportunity.

2200 Great Britain. Foreign Office. Historical Section. *Eritrea.* London, H.M. Stationery Office, 1920. 32 p. (Handbooks . . ., no. 126)

2201 Howard, William Edward Harding. *Public administration in Ethiopia : A study in retrospect and prospect.* Groningen, J. B. Wolfers, 1956. 204 p. map.
A detailed study for the Italian period and after.

Part III: area guide (by colonial power, region and colony)

2202 Longrigg, Stephen Hemsley. *A short history of Eritrea*. Oxford, Clarendon Press, 1945. 188 p. illus., maps.
The author was a brigadier-general in the British army. After the British conquest of Eritrea, he became chief administrator of the occupied area.

2203 Martini, Fernando. *Nell'Africa italiana : Impressioni e ricordi*. Milano, Fratelli Treves, 1891. 291 p. fold, imps.
Impressions by a fine prose stylist and minor literary figure who became an ardent convert to the colonial cause. Martini, who eventually served a brief term as Minister of Colonies, described a long and constructive term as governor of Eritrea in his indispensable *Il diario eritreo* (Florence, Vallecchi, 1947, 4 v.).

2204 Mori, Angiolo. *Manuale di legislazion e della colonia Eritrea: Indici generali, 1869–1912*. Roma, 1915. 846 p.

2205 Quaranta di San Severino, Ferdinando, Barone. *Ethiopia : An empire in the making*. With a foreword by the Rt. Hon. Lord Hailey. . . . London, P. S. King and Son, 1939. 120 p. illus., plates, fold. maps.
Review of the economic and social development during the first three years of Italian civil administration, written by an official in the Ministry of Italian East Africa. A more technical analysis of Italy's administrative organization in conquered Ethiopia appears in an article by an American political scientist, Arthur H. Steiner, 'The government of Italian East Africa', *American Political Science Review*, v. 30, Oct. 1936, p. 884–902.

2206 Rainero, R. *I primi tentativi di colonizzazione agricola e di popolamento dell'Eritrea, 1890–95*. Milan, Marzorati, 1960. 255 p., 2 maps.
This study, originally a thesis, details the earliest attempts to settle landless peasants in the Eritrean highlands – a forerunner to Mussolini's later experiments in Ethiopia. The appendix contains many of the unpublished documents on which the work is based.

2207 *Rassegna di Studi Etiopici*. 1941– . Rome, Istituto Studi Orientali, Centro di Studi Etiopici e Cristiano-Orientali.
Major journal for Ethiopian studies.

2208 Rodd, Francis James Rennell. Baron Rennell. *British military administration of occupied territories in Africa during the years 1941–1947*. London, H.M. Stationery Office, 1948. 637 p. maps.
The official British account. The author was a recognized authority on the Sahara, the Tuareg people and other aspects of Africa.

2209 Trevaskis, Gerald Kennedy Nicholas. *Eritrea : A colony in transition, 1941–1952*. London, Oxford University Press, 1960. 137 p. maps.
Written by a former official in the British occupation service. Describes briefly the period of transition from Italian Fascist to British military rule, and finally to semi-independence within a greater Ethiopian Federation.

Somalia

Bibliographies

2210 Camera di Commercio Industria ed Agricoltura della Somalia. Sezione Fiere e Mostre. Mogadiscio. *Bibliografia Somala*. Mogadiscio, Scuola Tipografica Missione Cattolica, 1958. 135 p. illus.
This bibliography, prepared under the auspices of the Mogadishu Chamber of Commerce, 'aims at being a complete bibliography of Somalia'. The work was

compiled by Professor Apollonio, head of the Dipartimento Studi of the Somalia government, and by Dr. Pirone, administrative director of the Istituto Superiore di Diritto ed Economia della Somalia, with the assistance of various outside scholars and institutions. The bibliography lists more than 2,000 items and is divided into two main sections. The first covers books and monographs. The second lists articles and similar material. The sections are subdivided by topics, including agriculture and related subjects; anthropology and other social studies; bibliography; hunting, fishing, and zoology; accounts of journeys; economics and statistics; geology and related subjects; military affairs; education and linguistics; legislation and law; literature; medicine and nutrition; history, politics and religion; works of general interest; veterinary sciences; maps. The work is supplied with a general index, and forms the most extensive bibliography of the country available.

2211 Caroselli, Francisco Saverio. *Catalogo del Museo nella Garesa a Mogadiscio.* Mogadishu, Stampa della Colonia, 1934. 727 p.

A descriptive list of Arabic descriptions in Somalia, and of documents pertaining to the Filonardi Company. The author wrote on numerous aspects of Italian colonial history, and his works include *Ferro a fuoco nella Somalia* (Rome, Arti Grafiche, 1931), in which he relates the career of Muhammad Abdullah Hassan, a famous dervish revolutionary, known to the British as the ' Mad Mullah '.

2212 Italy. Ministero degli Affari Esteri. Istituto Agronomico per l'Africa Italiana. *Contributo ad una bibliografia italiana su Eritrea e Somalia con particolare referimento all'agricoltura ed argomenti affini.* Firenze, 1953. 239 p. (4,000 entries)

2213 Papieri, Mario. *Contributo alla bibliografia e cartografia della Somalia italiana.* Roma, Istituto Coloniale Fascista, 1932. 90 p.

2214 U.S. Library of Congress. General Reference and Bibliographical Division. *Official publications of Somaliland, 1914–1959: A guide.* Compiled by Helen Conover. Washington, D.C., 1960. 41 p.

Covers works on British and French, as well as on Italian, Somaliland. Most of the literature cited is, however, in Italian. See also Hess, no. 2225.

Reference works

2215 Angeloni, Renato. *Principi di diritto amministrativo somalo.* Milan, A. Giuffrè Editore, 1965. 390 p. (Istituto universitario della Somalia, Facoltà di diritto ed economia, Collana scientifica, no. 10)

Technical study on administration, administrative law, and judicial matters of the Somali state.

2216 Bono, E. *La residenza di Bur Hacaba.* Mogadishu, Stamperia della Colonia, 1930.

The author of this work was the resident of Bur Hacaba, and describes actual local administrative practices there.

2217 ――― *Vade mecum del R. residente in Somalia.* Mogadishu, Stamperia della Colonia, 1930.

Intended as a manual of regulations for local administrators in Somalia.

2218 Castagno, Alphonso A. *Somalia.* New York, Carnegie Endowment for International Peace, 1959. 61 p. tables. (*International Conciliation*, no. 522, p. 339–400)

Concentrated review of the stages of political, educational, and economic development of the trust territory of Somalia during the decade after the United Nations decision in 1949 to give the country its independence in 1960. Emphasis is on relations of the Amministrazione Fiduciaria Italiana della Somalia (AFIS) with the United Nations. A chapter on 'International problems' considers the boundary dispute with Ethiopia and the 'Greater Somalia' issue. Documents are cited in footnotes.

2219 Cerulli, Enrico. *Somalia: Scritti vari editi ed inediti.* Roma, published for the Amministrazione Fiduciaria Italiana della Somalia by Istituto Poligrafico dello Stato, 1957–59. 2 v. Bibliographical footnotes.

By an Italian colonial administrator and scholar noted for his studies of northeastern African peoples and letters. These two volumes bring together writings on many aspects of Somalia. In the first volume are essays on history and legend, Islam, religious literature and astronomy, and the Arab text and translation in Italian of a Somali chronicle, 'The book of Zengi'. The second volume is on customary law, ethnography, linguistics, and the tribal way of life.

2220 Constanzo, Giuseppe A. *Problemi constituzionali della Somalia nella preparazione all'indipendenza (1957–1960).* Milano, A. Giuffrè Editore, 1962. 146 p.

Concerns work on constitutional problems in anticipation of Somalia's independence. Among the many aspects covered are the agreement on fiduciary administration, the establishment and work of the political and technical committees, the legislative assembly, the constituent assembly, the plan for gradual transformation of powers, and the question of Somalia before the United Nations. The work concludes with the proclamation of independence.

2221 Convegno di Studi Coloniali. 2d Florence, 1947. *Amministrazione fiduciaria all'Italia in Africa, atti del secondo convegno di studi coloniali, Firenze, 12–15 maggio.* 1947. 415 p.

Papers and discussions cover many aspects of Italian administration.

2222 Corni, Guido, ed. *Somalia italiana.* Milano, Editoriale Arte e Storia, 1937. 2 v. illus (part col.), maps.

A large general survey of Italian Somaliland under the Fascist government, lavishly produced in two volumes of articles by Italian specialists. The first volume has a general sketch and papers on history, geology, flora and fauna, peoples, primitive agriculture, stock raising and diseases, and fishing. The second volume is on the Fascist administration and its measures of physical and economic development.

The editor was a former governor of Italian Somaliland who also wrote *Problemi coloniali* (Milan, 1933).

2223 Gaibi, Agostino. *Manuale di storia politico-militare delle colonie italiane.* Rome, 1928.

2224 Great Britain. Foreign Office. Historical Section. *Italian Somaliland.* London, H.M. Stationery Office, 1920. (Handbooks..., no. 128)

A useful summary. There is a list of authorities on p. 26–27.

2225 Hess, Robert L. *Italian colonialism in Somalia.* Chicago, University of Chicago Press, 1966. 234 p. maps, tables. Bibliography: p. 213–226.

A brief but extremely well-documented account with an excellent bibliographical essay. Hess provides details, for instance, regarding official Italian reports. See also his more recent work, *Ethiopia: The modernization of autocracy* (Ithaca, Cornell University Press, 1970, 272 p., maps).

2226 Istituto Agricolo Coloniale. *Per le nostre colonie.* Firenze, Vallecchi, 1927. A high-level collection of essays by Cantalupo, Maugini, De Cillis, Cavazza, etc. on problems of colonization and settlement as well as on colonial political policy.

2227 Istituto Coloniale Italiano. *Atti del 2° Congresso degli Italiani all'Estero (11–20 giugno 1911).* 4 v.

2228 Italy. Ministero degli Affari Esteri. *Rapport du gouvernement italien à l'Assemblée Générale des Nations Unies sur l'administration de tutelle de la Somalie.* 1950– . Rome. illus., maps. Annual.

These reports are almost encyclopaedic in their coverage, providing details on every aspect of life. For instance, the 1953 report begins with a general description, followed by an account of the legal system, a survey of international and regional relations, law and order, political progress, economic advance, social progress, education, etc. The statistical appendices are of great value.

2229 Pankhurst, Estelle Sylvia. *Ex-Italian Somaliland.* London, Watts and Co., 1951. 460 p. illus., ports., maps.

A partisan publication written by a veteran British suffragette leader who later became a militant advocate of Ethiopian claims. She wrote also on many other aspects of history and politics in the Horn of Africa. Her works include a massive book, *Ethiopia : A cultural history*, with a foreword by Canon John A. Douglas (Essex, Lalibela House, 1955), which touches also on adjacent areas.

2230 Rossetti, Carlo. *Manuale di legislazione della Somalia italiana.* Rome, Ministero delle Colonie, 1912–14. 3 v.

A general compendium of Italian legislation in Somaliland. The author was a noted legal scholar.

2231 Technical Assistance Mission to the Trust Territory of Somaliland under Italian Administration. *The trust territory of Somaliland under Italian administration.* Report prepared jointly for the government of Italy by an expert appointed by the United Nations Technical Assistance Administration and by experts appointed respectively by the Food and Agriculture Organization of the United Nations, the United Nations Educational, Scientific, and Cultural Organization, and the World Health Organization. New York, 1952. 343 p. illus., maps, tables. (United Nations [Document] ST/TAA/K Somaliland/1) Includes bibliographies.

Processed publication of the United Nations. Six experts had spent three months making an extended survey of the economic needs of the territory, touring the country widely, talking with local officials and representatives on all levels, visiting all institutions. They reported in great detail, offering advice on many points. Their impressions were not optimistic regarding the possibility of a viable economy.

2232 U.S. Operations Mission to Italy. [Reports] Rome, 1950– .

This mission, later under the International Cooperation Administration, began operations in 1950 as the ECA Special Mission to Italy. In that year the United States suggested to the Italian Foreign Office that Somaliland be included in the Dependent Overseas Territory Program, and visits of inspection to Somaliland by American technicians were undertaken at once. Their reports were brought out as mimeographed pamphlets, in limited editions. Among them are the following:

> U.S. Economic Cooperation Administration. Special Mission to Italy. *Somalia agricultural projects.* By W. E. Corfitzen and Grover Kinsey. Rome, Sept. 1950. 36 l.

Part III: area guide (by colonial power, region and colony)

U.S. Economic Cooperation Administration. Special Mission to Italy. *A reconnaissance ground-water survey of Somalia, East Africa.* By Thomas P. Ahrens. Rome, 1951. 270 p. illus.

U.S. Operations Mission to Italy. [International Cooperation Administration] *Road study in Somalia, East Africa.* By H. A. Van Dyke. Rome, Dec. 31, 1953. 105 l.

U.S. Operations Mission to Italy. [International Cooperation Administration] *Port survey in Somalia, East Africa.* By Frederick G. Reinicke. Rome, Jan. 10, 1954. 40 l.

U.S. Operations Mission to Italy. [International Cooperation Administration] *The mineral deposits of Somalia.* By Ralph J. Holmes. Rome, Mar. 1954. 56 l. illus.

U.S. Operations Mission to Italy. [International Cooperation Administration] *Plans and schedules for Somalia economic development.* By W. E. Corfitzen. Rome, June 28, 1954. 34 p.

U.S. Operations Mission to Italy. [International Cooperation Administration] *Proposed program for agricultural technical assistance for Somalia.* By W. W. Worzella and A. L. Musson. Rome, Aug. 9, 1954. 17 l.

U.S. Operations Mission to Italy. [International Cooperation Administration] *A fisheries reconnaissance, Somalia, East Africa.* By Ralph L. Johnson. Rome, June, 18, 1956. 29 l.

U.S. Operations Mission to Italy. [International Cooperation Administration] *Livestock survey, Somalia, East Africa.* By C. L. McColloch. Rome, Feb. 1, 1957. 15 l.

U.S. Operations Mission to Italy. [International Cooperation Administration] *Forestry and range management survey, Somalia, East Africa.* By Marvin Klemme. Rome, Feb. 28, 1957. 23 l. map.

2233 U.S. Operations Mission to the Somali Republic. *Inter-river economic exploration: The Somali Republic.* Washington, 1961. xxxi, 347 p. illus., maps, tables, diagrs.

The Mission has continued under the new name after the independence date of Somalia, through 1961 under the International Cooperation Administration, from 1962 under AID (Agency for International Development). This long report contains economic data and estimates for development by irrigation and other measures of the land between the Giuba and Uebi Scebeli rivers (these names have varied spellings) in southern Somalia. There are somewhat optimistic forecasts of what might be accomplished in a 20-year program with large investment.

PORTUGUESE AFRICA

Note During their long history of colonial conquest, the Portuguese again and again attempted to govern their African territories as an integral part of the Portuguese state. The most thoroughgoing attempt at administrative assimilation derived from the Liberal Revolution, which in 1821 placed all colonial affairs without exception in the charge of metropolitan ministries, with the Ministério da Justicia taking over judicial questions, civil administration falling under the

426

Ministério do Reino, and military affairs being controlled by the Ministério da Guerra. Administrative assimilation failed to work, and when the absolutist régime was restored, the Portuguese went back to an older pattern whereby the colonies were run through the Secretário do Estado da Marinha e Conquistas. The Ministry of Marine was repeatedly reorganized, but colonial affairs were controlled essentially by two Direcções Gerais, the Direcção Geral da Marinha and the Direcção Geral do Ultramar. By 1910 this administrative machinery also included the Inspecção Geral da Fazenda do Ultramar, the Sétima Repartição da Direcção da Contabilidade Pública, and the Direcção dos Caminhos de Ferro Ultramarinos (the last two offices dealing respectively with public audits and railroads).

The new Portuguese Republic tried to introduce reforms into the Portuguese empire, and also reorganized the ministerial system. In 1910 the Ministério da Marinha e Ultramar was renamed Ministério da Marinha e Colonias, the change of title expressing an attempted new orientation in colonial policy. Until 1972, when Angola and Mozambique became formally known as ' states ', the colonies were styled Províncias Ultramarinas, whose administrative organization was similar in form with that of the metropolitan provinces. In 1911, the Overseas Ministry became the Ministério das Colónias (renamed after World War II Ministério do Ultramar). The Ministry produced numerous published reports, such as the *Relatórios apresentado ao Congresso da República* (Lisbon, Imprensa Nacional, 1912–), which provided a considerable amount of information of a statistical, administrative and economic nature.

The Ministry was repeatedly reorganized during the Salazar régime. A major step was taken in 1929 when the departmental services were grouped into two major divisions, sections directly subordinate to the Ministry, such as accountancy, cartography and military affairs, and bureaus subject to the Secretária Geral das Colónias, including civil administration, public works, and so forth. (For a detailed account see Júlio Monteiro and Paulo Roque da Silveira, *Lições da Cadeira de Administração Colonial* . . . , Lisbon, Escola Superior Colonial, 1931, 287 p.). The Ministério do Ultramar continued to publish a considerable amount of material, particularly books of a legal and administrative kind, as *Legislação Mandada Aplicar ao Ultramar Portuguesa, 1926 a 1963* (Lisbon, Agência-Geral do Ultramar, 1965–).

The Ministry was assisted in its work by a variety of subsidiary organizations. These included the Conselho Superior das Colónias and more specialized bodies such as the Junta Central de Trabalho e Emigração, the Conselho Superior de Obras Públicas e Minas, the Conselho Superior Judicário das Colónias, and the Comisão de Cartografia.

Another major agency was the Agência-Geral do Ultramar, set up in 1924 and reorganized in 1932. The Agência-Geral put out its own *Boletim Geral do Ultramar*; it published over 1,500 monographs, such as Vicente Ferreira, *Estudos Ultramarinos* (Lisbon, Divisão de Publicações e Biblioteca, Agência-Geral do Ultramar, 1953–55, 4 v.), as well as works bearing on legislation and administration in the colonies. (See its *Catálogo*, no. 2247.)

In 1936 the Portuguese set up the Junta das Missões Geográficas e de Investigações Coloniais, renamed in 1951 the Junta das Missões Geográficas e de Investigações do Ultramar. The Junta aimed at co-ordinating existing research and at expanding their scope. The Junta undertook a considerable amount of geographical work with publications such as the great *Atlas de Portugal Ultramarino e das Grandes Viagens Portugueses de Descobrimento e Expansão* (1938). It promoted all manner of scientific studies in agronomy, botany, including the

Part III: area guide (by colonial power, region and colony)

Contribuições para o Conhecimento da Flora da Moçambique (1950–); zoological studies, historical, ethnological and anthropological investigations, for instance, the *Estudos sobre a Etnologia do Ultramar Português* (1960–). The Junta administered numerous research institutions and centres, including, among others, the Centro de Estudos Históricos Ultramarinos set up 1955, and the Centro de Estudos Políticos e Sociais, founded 1956. (For an administrative history, see *Presidência do Conselho, 25 Anos de Administração Pública : Ministerio do Ultramar*, Lisbon, Imprensa Nacional, 1955, 358 p.)

Other learned institutions of an official character included the Arquivo Histórico Ultramarino, founded in 1931, the Museu Etnográfico do Ultramar at Lisbon, and similar bodies. Formal training on the graduate and postgraduate level was provided by the Instituto Superior de Estudos Ultramarinos (previously the Escola Superior Colonial) which offered courses in judicial and administrative studies, finance and economics, history, and also in engineering, tropical hygiene, and tropical agriculture. The teaching of African languages was concentrated in the Instituto de Linguas Africanas e Orietais. The Instituto put out a variety of publications including its *Anuário* (1954–).

Students of Portuguese colonialism should consult also material derived from institutions based in the colonies themselves, such as the Museu de Angola, founded in 1938, the Missão Geográfica de Angola, established 1941, the Instituto de Investigação Científica de Angola, established 1955, and the Arquivo Histórico de Moçambique. There is also a wealth of material that originated with semi-private bodies like the Sociedade de Geográfia de Lisboa, incorporated in 1876, and Portuguese missionary societies, concessionary companies, and other organizations.

The great majority of works on the Portuguese in Africa are in Portuguese and are not widely available to students. There is no Portuguese equivalent to Hewitt's guide to British sources, although a listing of official colonial reports, legislation, and journals concerned with the overseas territories and published by the Library of Congress (see no. 2260) is very useful.

Atlases

2234 Portugal. Centro de Estudos Históricos Ultramarinos. *Atlas missionário português [de] Junta de Investigações do Ultramar e Centro de Estudos Históricos Ultramarinos.* 2d ed. Lisbon, 1964. 184 p. plates, maps.
Valuable maps and charts of Catholic and Protestant missions in the Portuguese empire. Gives locations of stations and descriptions of dioceses.

2235 Portugal. Ministério das Colónias. *Atlas de Portugal ultramarino e das grandes viagens Portuguesas de descobrimento e expansão.* Lisbon, Junta das Missões Geográficas e de Investigações Coloniais, 1948. 110 plates, maps.
A completely revised edition of the *Atlas Colonial* published by the former Commissão de Cartografia do Ministério das Colónias in 1914. The atlas provides information on ethnography, linguistics, geology, economic activity, imports and exports, physical geography, communications, as well as on colonial history, with information concerning the routes taken by the principal Portuguese explorers.

Portuguese Africa

Bibliographies

Note See also Schiller, no. 476.

2236 Carvalho Dias, Fernando de. 'Notícias dos documentos da Secção dos Reservados, Fundo Geral, da Biblioteca Nacional de Lisboa respeitantes as províncias ultramarinas de Angola, Cabo Verde, Guiné, Macau, Moçambique, S. Tomé e Príncipe e Timor'. *Garcia de Orta*, v. 5, nos. 2–3, 1957.

2237 —— 'Ultramar português e a expansão na Africa e no Oriente: Breve notícia dos documentos manuscritos de Fundo Geral da Biblioteca Nacional de Lisboa; extracto do fíchero geral'. *Garcia de Orta*, v. 3, nos. 3–4, 1955; v. 4, nos. 1–4, 1956.

2238 Centro de Estudos Políticos e Sociais da Junta de Investigações do Ultramar. Biblioteca. *Catálogo*. Lisbon, 1968. 276 p.
A simple alphabetical listing of items held in the library.

2239 Chilcote, Ronald H. *Emerging nationalism in Portuguese Africa: A bibliography of documentary ephemera through 1965.* Stanford, Calif., Hoover Institution, Stanford University, 1969. 114 p. (Hoover Institution Bibliographical Series: XXXIX)
This bibliography presents a wide range of viewpoints, including the official Portuguese position, the various African nationalist movements, and Portuguese in opposition. The bibliography covers Portuguese Africa in general, the various territories, and United Nations documents on Portuguese Africa, as well as other sources. The publication distinguishes between ephemera and other material. This major bibliographical work has now been complemented by the author's *Emerging nationalism in Portuguese Africa: Documents* (Hoover Institution Press, 1972, 646 p.).

2240 'Documenting Portuguese Africa'. *Africana Newsletter*, v. 1, no. 3, Summer 1963: 16–36.
This survey of sources, archives, and movements concerned with the Portuguese in Africa is in four main parts: serial publications of Portugal and Portuguese Africa; archives, libraries, and institutes, with country subdivision; bibliography of general works published since 1945; and political groups in Portuguese Africa, with country subdivision.

2241 Gonçalves, José Júlio. *Bibliografia antropológica do ultramar Português.* Lisbon, Agência-Geral, 1960. 95 p.

2242 —— 'Bibliografia antropológica do Ultramar português'. *Boletim Geral do Ultramar*, no. 37, Mar.–Apr. 1961: 483–499; Oct.–Dec. 1961: 431–471.
A set of references printed in the form of cards that might be clipped for use in a file, though the entries appear on both sides of the pages.

2243 Gonçalves, Francisco, and Jaime Caseiro. *Bibliografia geológica do Ultramar português.* Lisboa, Junta de Investigações do Ultramar, 1959. lxxiii, 272 p.

2244 Moser, Gerald M. *A tentative Portuguese-African bibliography: Portuguese literature in Africa and African literature in the Portuguese language.* University Park, Pennsylvania State University Libraries, 1970. 148 p. (Pennsylvania, State University, Libraries. Bibliographical series no. 3)
Covers sub-Saharan Africa literature from earliest times through 1969: books, pamphlets, parts of larger works, manuscripts, some periodical articles. The

Part III: area guide (by colonial power, region and colony)

author-index contains very useful biographical information on each author cited. Material is arranged under three headings: folk literature, art literature, history and criticism of literature.

Subject headings are subdivided by geographical area, i.e., Angola, Cape Verde Islands, Mozambique, Portuguese Guinea, São Tomé and Príncipe.

2245 Pélissier, René. 'Eléments de bibliographie: L'Afrique portugaise dans les publications de la Junta de Investigações do Ultramar (Lisbonne) '. *Genève Afrique*, v. 4, no. 2, 1965: 249–270.

By a specialist on Spanish and Portuguese Africa. He presents a classified list, extensively annotated, of the important monographs published by the Portuguese office for overseas research.

2246 ———— 'Etat de la littérature militaire relative à l'Afrique australe portugaise.' *Revue Française d'Etudes Politiques Africaines*. no. 74, Feb. 1972, pp. 58–89.

A survey of writing on the Portuguese-African nationalist struggle in Angola, Mozambique and Guinea with critical evaluations.

2247 Portugal. Agência-Geral do Ultramar. *Catálogo das edições*. Lisbon, 1966. 49 p. *Suplemento*, 1969. 49 p.

Lists all their published books and articles.

2248 Portugal. Agência-Geral do Ultramar. *Elementos para uma bibliografia da literatura e cultura portuguesa ultramarina contemporânea*. Lisbon, Agência-Geral, 1968. 180 p.

2249 Portugal. Centro de Estudos de Antropobiologia. *Bibliografia do Centro de Estudos de Etnología do Ultramar*. By M. Emília de Castro e Almeida, M. Cecília de Castro and José D. Lampreia. Lisbon. 1964. 163 p.

2250 Portugal. Instituto Nacional de Estatística. *Bibliografia sobre economia portuguesa*, 1948/49– . Lisboa, 1958– . Annual.

Covers fully Portuguese overseas provinces. Cites books, articles, newspaper articles, government documents. A most important source.

2251 Portugal. Junta de Investigações do Ultramar. *Catálogo didascálico das publicações editadas e subsidiadas pela Junta*. . . . Lisboa, 1959, 45 p.

Supplement to Dec. 1960. 17 p. (Separate from *Garcia de| Orta*, v. 8, 1960) This comprehensive catalogue of the many works published or sponsored by the Junta is supplemented from time to time in *Garcia de Orta*.

2252 Portugal. Junta de Investigações do Ultramar. Centro de Documentação Científica Ultramarina. *Bibliografia científica da Junta de Investigações do Ultramar*. v. 1– . 1958– . Lisboa, 1960– . Annual.

As complete as possible a list of studies and papers, along with analytics of contents of the journal *Garcia de Orta*. The first compilation, covering the period 1936–58, contained 1,697 references, based on the card file of the Centro, printed on one side only (371 l.) and suitable for clipping for a card file. The volumes for publications of 1959 added 382 card references. Entries are classed by the Universal Decimal Classification, mainly in the social sciences, pure and applied sciences, and geography. There is an author index.

2253 Portugal. Junta de Investigações do Ultramar. Centro de Documentação Científica Ultramarina. *Boletim Analítico*. no. 1– . 1959– . Lisboa. Bi-monthly.

2254 Portugal. Junta de Investigações do Ultramar. Centro de Documentação Científica Ultramarina. *Boletim Bibliográfico*. no. 1– . 1958– . Lisboa. mimeo. Bi-monthly.

Portuguese Africa

2255 Portugal. Junta de Investigações do Ultramar. Centro de Documentação Científica Ultramarina. *Catálogo das publicações periódicos e seriados existentes na biblioteca de Junta.* Lisboa, 1958. 158 p.

2256 Portugal. Junta de Investigações do Ultramar. Centro de Documentação Científica Ultramarina. *Documentação especial elaborada pelo Centro de Docum. Cient. Ultram. (Nos. D1 a D199, 1957 a 1966).* Lisboa, Dec. 31, 1966. 13 l.

2257 Portugal. Junta de Investigações do Ultramar. Centro de Documentação Científica Ultramarina. *Instituições portuguesas de interesse ultramarino.* Lisboa, 1964. 138 p. Processed.

2258 Portugal. Junta de Investigações do Ultramar. Centro de Documentação Científica Ultramarina. *Periódicos portugueses de interesse ultramarino actualmente em publicação.* 2d ed. Lisboa, 1967. 59 p. Processed.
The last two entries are comprehensive listings of Portuguese institutions and periodicals concerned with overseas development. Both are classified according to the Dewey decimal system. The list of periodicals includes official and unofficial serials published in Portugal and overseas. Many items from this list are included in the Library of Congress list *Serials for African studies.* Three indexes are included in both these Junta publications.

2259 Portugal. Ministério do Ultramar. Junta de Investigações do Ultramar. Missão de Estudo do Rendimento nacional do Ultramar. *Bibliografia sobre economia do Ultramar Português.* Lisbon, 1963–64. 2 v.
Covers the period 1958–1963 and lists articles, series, books and theses on all aspects of economics. Volume 1 is an author listing; v. 2 is a listing by title and subject and by each overseas province.
An important earlier work is *Elementos de geografia militar das colónias portuguesas administração colonial e organização dos exércitos nas colonias organização militar colonial portuguesa.* Lisbon, Agência-Geral, 1945. 2 v.

2260 U.S. Library of Congress. General Reference and Bibliography Division. Reference Department. *Portuguese Africa : A guide to official publications.* Comp. by Mary Jane Gibson, African Section. Washington, 1967. 217 p.
An extensive listing of documents of Portuguese Africa from 1950 to 1964 published in Africa. Unfortunately it leaves out much of the massive publication program of the Lisbon Imprensa Nacional. In addition to government documents, the guide includes municipal and provincial documents as well as publications either attributed to or subsidized by government agencies. Arrangement is in six parts: Angola, Cape Verde Islands, Mozambique, Portuguese Guinea, São Tomé e Príncipe, and Portugal. At the end of each part is an ' Other authors' section which cites works written by individuals and issued by a government agency or government-affiliated organization.

Serials

2261 Centro de Estudos Históricos Ultramarinos, Portugal. *Studia : Revista Semestral.* 1958– . Lisboa. Semi-annual.
A big volume, usually on historical studies. Most of the essays are furnished with footnote references or bibliographies. An occasional article is in English. The Centre also issues *Documentação ultramarina portuguesa* (1960– , annual).

Part III: area guide (by colonial power, region and colony)

2262 Estudos Ultramarinos. no. 1– , 1948– . Lisboa, Instituto Superior de Estudos Ultramarinos. Quarterly.
Review originally titled Estudos Coloniais. Carries valuable contributions on political, economic, and social aspects of overseas Portugal.

2263 Garcia de Orta: Revista da Junta de Investigações do Ultramar. v. 1– , 1953– . Lisboa. illus. Quarterly.
The journal of this scholarly official body, carrying monograph-length articles on natural and human sciences. The last pages often give the impressive list of publications of the Junta, including contents of earlier volumes of Garcia de Orta.
In some issues in the 1950s the journal included lists of 'Publicações de interesse ultramarino entradas na Biblioteca Nacional de Lisboa por obrigação de depósito legal' as occasional special bibliographies.

2264 Lisbon. Instituto Superior de Estudos Ultramarinos. Anuario. 1919– . Lisbon.

2265 O Mundo Português. 1934– . Lisbon. Monthly.
Edited by the Agência-Geral das Colónias and the Secretariado da Propaganda Nacional. Important for official views and policies and programs for the overseas territories.

2266 Portugal. Agência-Geral do Ultramar. Boletim Geral do Ultramar. no. 1– , July 1925– . Lisboa. illus., maps (fold. col.). Monthly.
This official journal is of first importance for the study of administrative matters relating to the overseas territories. It also contains specialist articles of general coverage, a regular review of missionary activity, a section of news and notes, a review of the press, and other features, including summary sections in English and French. Many issues contain bibliographies which in some cases are complete listings of publications of the Agency and records of books received, in other cases specialized bibliographical entries, 'Fichas bibliográficas', printed in a form to be cut for files (see, for instance, the work by José Júlio Gonçalves cited above, no. 2242).
The Agência, which was formerly known as the Agência-Geral das Colónias, operates under the Ministério do Ultramar, formerly the Ministério das Colónias, at Lisbon. It has sponsored numerous publications of an historical, legal, and ethnographic nature. It has also published a good many studies defending Portugal's colonial record.

2267 Portugal. Ministério do Ultramar. Arquivo das Colónias. illus. Monthly, July 1917–June 1919; quarterly, April/June 1922– . (Publication suspended July 1919–March 1922, July 1922–1928)
The earlier numbers were issued by the Ministry under its original name Ministério das Colónias. See also Portugal, Junta das Missões Geográficas . . . , no. 2316.

2268 Portugal colonial. Revista mensal de propaganda e expansão do Império Português. 1931. Lisbon. Monthly.

2269 Portugal em Africa. 1894–1910. 2d ser., 1946– . Lisbon. Monthly, formerly bi-monthly.
The former title of the journal was Portugal em Africa: Revista Illustrada e Científica. Published under Catholic auspices. Contains a wealth of information concerning the colonies, with special reference to missionary work.

2270 Revista do Gabinete de Estudos Ultramarinos. Lisbon, 1951–1960.
A journal published three times a year by the Centro Universitário de Lisboa da Mocidade Portuguesa, contains articles, notes, bibliographical information,

and also news concerning the activities of the Instituto Superior de Estudos Ultramarinos. Succeeded by *Ultramar*. 1960– . Quarterly.

2271 *Revista militar*. 1849– . Lisbon. Monthly.
An illustrated magazine basic to the military and administrative history of the Portuguese empire. Especially valuable are accounts by participants in wars of pacification and conquest in Africa. See also the journal *Defesa nacional*.

2272 *Revista Portugueza Colonial e Marítima, 1897–1910*. Lisbon.

2273 Sociedade de Geografia de Lisboa. *Boletim*. 1876– . Lisbon. Monthly.
Very important journal especially for the period of the partition. The Sociedade was an active propagandist for colonial expansion. The *Boletim* had learned articles on travel, geography, ethnography, military conquest, etc.

Reference works

2274 Abshire, David M., and Michael A. Samuels, eds. *Portuguese Africa : A handbook*. London, Pall Mall Press, 1969. xiii, 480 p. maps, charts, tables.
The first part covers the physical, human, and economic setting, the age of discoveries, the era of colonization, the scramble for Africa and the *Estado Novo*, as well as the Portuguese racial legacy and the African peoples. The second part concerns government and society, including labour policies, education, health, welfare, and various aspects of multi-racialism. The third part deals with the economy, including the infrastructure, primary production, and the consequences that might ensue from a Portuguese withdrawal from Africa. And the last part concerns political and international issues, including the role of the nationalist parties, international pressures, and the strategic role of the Portuguese colonies. Contributors include the editors, as well as Norman A. Bailey, Frank Brandenburg, George Martelli, Andrew W. Green. The book is written from a generally pro-Portuguese point of view. It is the most comprehensive of its kind in English.

2275 Almada, José de. *Tratados aplicáveis ao ultramar. Coligidos e anotados*.
Lisbon, Agência-Geral, 1942–1943. 8 v. and 2 v. of maps.
Basic collection of treaties dealing with the overseas territories.

2276 Almada Negreiros, António de. *Colonies portugaises : Les organismes politiques indigènes*. Paris, A. Challamel, 1910. 320 p.
Traces the evolution of Portuguese colonial rule.

2277 *Anuário católico do Ultramar português (1960)*. Lisboa, Centro de Estudos Políticos e Sociais, Junta de Investigações do Ultramar, 1962. 433 p. (Estudos de ciências políticas e sociais, no. 57)
The Catholic yearbook of overseas Portugal, giving names and statistical data of missions and parishes in Africa, Asia, and Oceania.

2278 *Anuário estatístico do Ultramar. Annuaire statistique d'outre-mer*. Prepared by the Portuguese Instituto Nacional de Estatística. [1945?–] Lisboa, Tipografia Portuguesa.
Annual volume covering in detailed tables all aspects of population and economic life in the Portuguese overseas territories. There is a full index with subject breakdown under each country.
The *Anuário do Ultramar português* (with which this is not to be confused), issued by the Anuário Comercial de Portugal in Lisbon, is a business directory, with data on regions and administration (29th ed., 1963/64, 1,056 p.).

Part III: area guide (by colonial power, region and colony)

2279 Anuário do Instituto Superior de Estudos Ultramarinos. Lisbon, 1954–.
The Anuário reviewed the work of the Instituto, printed notes concerning lectures and conferences given under its auspices, published legislation concerning the colonies and provided information concerning the personnel employed in colonial administration.

2280 Axelson, Eric Victor. Portugal and the scramble for Africa, 1875–1891. Johannesburg, Witwatersrand University Press, 1967. 318 p. plates, maps. (Publications of the Ernest Oppenheimer Institute of Portuguese Studies of the University of Witwatersrand)
Readable scholarly account of Portugal's efforts to hold on to its possessions in Africa and to expand its empire.

2281 Azevedo Guimarães, Rui de. Lei orgânica do Ultramar. Lourenço Marques, Imprensa Nacional, 1953. 314 p.
An annotated edition of the Portuguese Organic Law concerning the colonies by a professional jurist. The work is indexed. The Portuguese introduced numerous changes in their basic legislation. Earlier publications include, for instance, Ministério das Colónias, Carta orgânica do império colonial portugues . . . 1933 (Lourenço Marques, Imprensa Nacional, 1933, 246 p.); and Les lois organiques de l'empire colonial portugais (Brussels, Bibliothèque Coloniale Internationale, 1932, 229 p., in French and Portuguese).
A more recent publication in French is André Durieux, La loi organique de l'outre-mer portugais modifiée par la loi du 24 juin 1963 (Brussels, Académie Royale des Sciences d'Outre-Mer, 1966, 48 p.).

2282 Brásio, Antônio D., ed. Monumenta missionaria africana: Africa ocidental [series]. 2d ser., v. 1– . Lisboa, Divisão de Publicações e Biblioteca, Agência-Geral do Ultramar, 1958– . illus.
A collection of source accounts for Portuguese missions, in Latin and Portuguese. The first series was published in nine volumes, 1952–56.

2283 Caetano, Marcelo. Colonizing traditions, principles and methods of the Portuguese. [Translation from the Portuguese; translation also in French] Lisboa, Agência-Geral do Ultramar, 1951. 54 p.
Official statement of Portuguese colonial policy. The writer, a distinguished professor of law, and later Rector, at the University of Lisbon, was at one time Minister of Colonies and is now Prime Minister.
A later study by Professor Caetano was on the question of African labour in Mozambique and Angola, Os nativos na economia africana (Coimbra, Coimbra Editora, 1954, 144 p.); also, O conselho ultramarino: Esbôço da sua historia (Lisbon, Agência-Geral, 1967, 176 p.).

2284 Casimiro, Augusto. Angola e o futuro: Alguns problemas fundamentais. Lisbon, Depositária Livrolândia, 1958. 346 p.
A classic study critical of the labour policy of the Portuguese government. Casimiro was a Portuguese democrat and former governor of Portuguese Congo.

2285 Chilcote, Ronald H. Emerging nationalism in Portuguese Africa: Documents. Stanford, Hoover Institution Press, 1972. 646 p.
A major documentary collection describing the origin, organization, leadership and ideology of nationalist groups in Portuguese Africa. Translations are provided for 179 documents (the 2499 documents of the total collection are deposited in the Hoover Institution). The introduction with numerous tables and charts places the African movements in time and topography for each part of the Portuguese Empire. Charts show the origin and growth of each party. The

appendix gives capsule histories on opposition, pre-nationalist and nationalist organizations with interests in Portuguese Africa.

2286 Chilcote, Ronald H. *Portuguese Africa.* Englewood Cliffs, N.J., Prentice-Hall, 1967. 149 p. maps. (A Spectrum Book: The Modern Nations in Historical Perspective) Bibliography: p. 129–141.

A short and readable introduction sympathetic to African nationalist aspirations. There is an excellent bibliographical essay. The author's attitude regarding the Portuguese is reminiscent in some ways of British missionaries, humanitarians, and chauvinists during the Victorian era.

2287 Congresso Internacional de História dos Descobrimentos. *Actas.* Lisbon, Comissão Executiva dos Comemoracões do V centenário da Morte do Infante D. Henrique, 1961. 6 v.

Publications of the proceedings of this learned Congress on the history of discoveries and the problems of overseas expansion. The Congress had two sections: History of Discoveries and the Expansions Overseas.

The former has four subsections on maps and cartography, nautical science, voyages of discovery, and the causes and consequences of discoveries.

The section on the overseas expansion has three subsections covering expansion to the end of the 16th century, the 17th and 18th centuries and the 19th and 20th centuries. Volume 6 deals with the modern period and has some valuable essays on Africa, mostly Portuguese Africa.

2288 Congresso Militar Colonial. 1st, Oporto, 1934. *Primeiro congresso militar colonial, julho 1934 : Relato dos trabalhos realizados.* Pôrto, Impr. Moderna, 1934. 466 p., illus.

Provides a history of military activity in the colonies.

2289 Cordeiro, Luciano. *Questões histórico-coloniais.* Lisboa, 1958. 3 v.

Important work on all aspects of Portuguese colonialism. Based on archival research.

2290 Duffy, James. *Portuguese Africa.* Cambridge, Mass., Harvard University Press, 1959. 389 p. illus., maps.

The classic, well-written survey. The 1968 reprint has a preface which discusses events of 1959 to 1967. The author, a critic of Portugal's record in Africa, also published various other studies, including *Portugal in Africa* (Baltimore, Md., Penguin Books, 1963, 240 p.); and *A question of slavery* (Oxford, Clarendon Press, 1967, 240 p.).

2291 Ennes, António. *O ' Ultimatum ' visto por António Ennes, com um estudo biográfico por F. A. Oliveira Martins.* Lisbon, A. M. Pereira, 1946. 410 p. port.

Articles published in *O Dia* between 1888 and 1890 concerning a vital period in Anglo-Portuguese relations regarding Africa.

2292 Exposição Colonial Portuguesa. 1st, Oporto, 1934. *Angola,* Pôrto, 1934. 1093 p.

A major handbook on all aspects of Angolan life.

2293 Ferreira, Vicente. *Estudos ultramarinos.* Lisboa, Agência-Geral do Ultramar, 1953–55. 4 v.

v. 1. *Os sistemas monetários e o crédito.* 1953. 334 p.

v. 2–3. *Angola e os seus problemas.*

v. 4. *Colonização e diversos.*

Part III: area guide (by colonial power, region and colony)

2294 Figueirido, Antonio de. *Portugal and its empire: The truth.* London, V. Gollancz, 1961. 159 p.
A harsh inside view by a well-educated Portuguese who knew Mozambique society thoroughly. He now lives in exile in London.

2295 Galvão, Henrique. *Por Angola: Quatro anos de actividade parlamentária, 1945–1949.* Lisbon, Depositária: Livraria Popular, 1949. 367 p.

2296 —— and Carlos Selvagem. *Império ultramarino português (monografia do império).* Lisboa, Empresa Nacional de Publicidade, 1950–53. 4 v. illus., maps, tables. Includes brief bibliographies.
Survey of the Portuguese overseas territories, with emphasis on political and economic geography. The two writers are both literary men who have written extensively in the fields of drama, history, and colonial literature. Senhor Galvão was at the time of writing Inspector Superior of Colonial Administration. (He later became a prominent opponent of the Salazar government.) A report he made in 1947 on conditions in Angola, which was a violent denunciation of the government, was suppressed.

2297 Gonçalves, José Júlio. *Criação e reorganização do Instituto Superior de Estudos Ultramarinos.* Lisbon, Agência-Geral, 1962. 2 v.
Covers all aspects of the history, organization, courses and staff of the institute.

2298 Hammond, Richard James. *Portugal and Africa, 1815–1910: A study in uneconomic imperialism.* Stanford, Calif., Stanford University Press, 1966. 384 p. illus., maps. Bibliographical references in 'Notes': p. 343–375.
An outstanding account by a British economic historian from an avowedly Eurocentric point of view, based on a thorough study of archival sources and published secondary material. Emphasis is on Mozambique and the period 1870 to 1910. Stresses non-economic factors in Portuguese colonialism.

2299 Leal, Francisco Pinto da Cunha. *O colonialismo dos anticolonialistas.* Lisbon, Petrony, 1961. 165 p.

2300 —— *Novas coisas da Companhia de diamantes de Angola* (Diamang). Lisbon, 1959. 189 p.
Leal was one of the leading critics of Portugal and of its rule in Africa. He was an able writer-politician and a member of the anti-Salazar opposition. See his valuable autobiography *As minhas memórias* (Lisbon, 1966–1968, 3 v.).

2301 Martins, Joaquim Pedro de Oliveira. *História de Portugal.* 7th ed., Lisbon, Parceria A. M. Pereira, 1908. 2 v.
Oliveira Martins was one of the most distinguished Portuguese historians. He also wrote *As raças humanas e a civilisação primitiva* (Lisbon, 1883, 2 v.), and many other works that are of great value for the general background and ideology of colonial expansion. See also his *Portugal contemporaneo.*

2302 Mendes Corrêa, Antônio Augusto. *Ultramar português.* v. 1, *Sintese da Africa.* Lisboa, Divisão de Publicações e Biblioteca, Agência-Geral das Colónias, 1949. 437 p. maps.
The first volume of a projected general survey of all Portuguese territory (for v. 2, see no. 2414). Among the subjects covered are physiography, climate, ethnography, and economy. The book contains good maps and bibliographies and summaries of each chapter in French and English.

2303 Monteiro, Júlio, and Paulo Roque da Silveira. *Lições da Cadeira de Administração Colonial* . . . Lisbon, Familição, 1931. 287 p.
A survey of Portuguese administrative history (seen from the metropolitan standpoint), colonial legislation, and colonial administration, with comparative

notes on the colonial institutions of other colonial powers. This work is based on lectures given at the Escola Superior Colonial by Gonçalo de Santa-Rita. Portuguese colonial literature is replete with legal and administrative treatises. These include works such as Ministério das Colónias. Secretária Geral. *Administração Civil e Financeira das Províncias Ultramarinas* (Loanda, Imprensa Nacional, 1914), a collection of laws; and J. J. da Silva, *Repertório Alphabético e Chronológico ou Indice Remissivo da Legislação Ultramarina* (Lisbon, F. F. Pinheiro, 1904).

Another study was Miguel Lourenço Aleixo Carmo da Sá, *Recurso para o Supremo Tribunal Administrativo Conselho Colonial, Conselho Superior das Colónias* (Macau, Imprensa Nacional, 1929). This work examined the workings of the Conselho Superior das Colónias whose decisions were listed alphabetically, by subject.

2304 Moreira, Adriano. *Portugal's stand in Africa.* New York, University Publishers, 1962. 265 p

Explanation of Portugal's overseas policy, prepared in an English-language edition to counter what the author considered American misunderstanding of trends that led to unrest and nationalist revolt in Portugal's African territories. The author, ex-Overseas Minister of Portugal, is also a professor at the Instituto Superior de Estudos Ultramarinos in Lisbon. His book is largely made up of addresses delivered in various Portuguese institutions from 1958 to 1961 and includes texts of the major colonial decrees of 1961 that were intended to ameliorate conditions. Portugal's multiracial concepts are emphasized.

Another expression of the Portuguese position is by the ex-Foreign Minister Dr. Franco Nogueira, *The United Nations and Portugal : A study in anticolonialism* (London, Sidgwick & Jackson, 1963, 188 p.).

2305 Portugal. Laws, statutes, etc. *Legislação novíssima do ultramar, 1864– .* Lisbon. Annual. Title changes.

2306 —————— *Collecção de legislação relativa as colónias portuguesas em Africa.* Lisbon. Annual.

2307 —————— *Legislação mandada aplicar ao ultramar português, 1926–1963.* Lisboa, Agência-Geral do Ultramar, 1965– .

2308 —————— *Nova legislação ultramarina.* Lisboa, Agência-Geral do Ultramar, 1953– .

Various annual compilations of legislation applying to the overseas provinces were published by the Portuguese. Occasionally a compendium was also issued.

2309 Portugal. Agência-Geral do Ultramar. *Administração da justicia aos indígenas.* By Adriano Moreira. Lisbon, Divisão de Publicações e Biblioteca, Agência-Geral do Ultramar, 1955. 275 p. Bibliography: p. 273–275.

This study deals with both customary and statutory law respecting Africans in the Portuguese colonies.

2310 Portugal. Agência-Geral do Ultramar. *Bases orgânicas da administração, civil e financeira das colónias, codificadas por J. M. L. Prazeres da Costa.* Lisbon, Agência-Geral das Colónias, 1926. 48 p.

2311 Portugal. Agência-Geral do Ultramar. *Colonização, projectos de decretos.* Ed. by José Francisco Vieira Machado. Lisbon, Agência-Geral das Colónias, 1940. 376 p.

Part III: area guide (by colonial power, region and colony)

2312 Portugal. Agência-Geral do Ultramar. *Estudos ultramarinos.* By Vicente Ferreira. Com prefácio do Prof. Doutor Marcello Caetano. Lisbon, Divisão de Publicações e Biblioteca, Agência-Geral do Ultramar, 1953–55. 4 v.
The first volume deals mainly with financial questions, the second and third with Angola, the fourth with miscellaneous problems.

2313 Portugal. Agência-Geral do Ultramar. Divisão de Publicações e Biblioteca. *Colecção pelo império.* No. 1–131. Lisbon, 1935–61.
Biographies, usually brief (under 75 pages) of Portuguese colonial administrators, governors, military, and missionary leaders, etc.

2314 Portugal. Conselho Superior de Disciplina do Ultramar. *Colecção de acórdãos doutrinários do Conselho Superior de Disciplina do Ultramar.* Lisbon, Agência-Geral. v. 1, 1934–35, v. 2, 1936–37, v. 3, 1949–50, v. 4, 1951–53.

2315 Portugal. Conselho Ultramarinos. *Acórdãos doutrinários do Conselho Ultramarino.* Lisbon, Agência-Geral. 1959– .

2316 Portugal. Junta das Missões Geográficas e de Investigações do Ultramar. This body was earlier known as the Junta das Missões Geográficas e de Investigações Coloniais, and also as the Junta de Investigações do Ultramar. It was first established in 1936 at Lisbon and operates under the Ministério do Ultramar, formerly the Ministério das Colónias. It administers numerous research institutes and centres. These include the following, whose respective founding dates are given in parentheses: Instituto de Investigação Científica de Angola (1955), Luanda; Instituto de Investigação Científica de Moçambique (1955), Lourenço Marques; Centro de Biologia Piscatória (1959), Lisbon; Centro de Botânica (1948), Lisbon; Centro de Documentação Científica Ultramarina (1957), Lisbon; Centro de Estudos de Etnologia do Ultramar (1954), Lisbon; Centro de Estudos Históricos Ultramarinos (1955), Lisbon; Centro de Estudos de Pedologia Tropical (1960), Tapada d'Ajuda; Centro de Estudos Políticos e Sociais (1956), Lisbon; Centro de Geografia do Ultramar (1946, 1955), Lisbon; Centro de Investigação das Ferrugens do Cafeeiro (1955), Oeiras; and the Centro de Zoologia (1948), Lisbon. Smaller research centres, missions, and laboratories have also been established by the Junta.
The Junta is also responsible for an extensive publications program covering natural sciences, social sciences, history, and so forth.
The Junta likewise issued several series of *Memórias.* Initially these were published in separate runs, known respectively as *Série de agronomia tropical, Série antropológica . . . , Série geológica,* and so forth. In 1958 the earlier *Memórias* were united into a single set known as *Memórias, 2 Ser.*
In addition the Junta was responsible for putting out: *Anais* (1946–), *Estudos, ensaios e documentos* (1950–), *Estudos de ciências políticas e sociais* (1956–).
Some important studies published in these series are the following:

> Nunes Barata, *Localização da sede dos organismos de coordenação económica no Ultramar* (E.C.P.S., No. 54, 1961, 155 p.).

> *Estudo sobre o absentismo e a instabilidade da mão-de-obra africana* (E.C.P.S., No. 20, 35, 44).

> Oliveira, Jorge E. da Costa, *Aplicação de capitais nas provincias ultramarinas* (E.C.P.S., No. 50, 1961, 374 p.).

2317   Portugal. Junta das Missões Geográficas e de Investigacões do Ultramar. *Glossário toponímico da antiga historiografia portuguesa ultramarina.* Por Visconde de Lagoa. Lisbon, 1953. 3 v. *Corrigenda e adenda.* 1954.

Lists and identifies: The kings, princes and persons of the historic Portuguese overseas connections, the countries, provinces, districts, cities, towns, ports, houses, villages, rivers, lakes, bays, estuaries, etc., as cited in books and manuscripts and gives the current or correct name if they differ.

2318   Portugal. Junta de Investigações do Ultramar. *Ensaio de Iconografia das Cidades Portuguesas do Ultramar.* Lisbon, c. 1952, plates, illus., maps, 4 v.

This major work, compiled by Luís Silveira, covers the history of cities in the Portuguese empire from ancient times to the present. The second volume covers East and West Africa. In addition to explanatory notes, the author provides a wealth of illustrations, city plans, plans of fortifications, sketches, etc.

2319   Portugal. Junta de Investigações do Ultramar. *Estudos sôbre a etnologia do Ultramar português.* Lisboa, 1960–63. 3 v. plates, maps. (Estudos, ensaios e documentos, nos. 81, 84, 102.) Includes bibliographies.

A collection of scholarly papers on many aspects of ethnology and history in Portuguese Africa, by leading scholars.

2320   Portugal. Junta de Investigações do Ultramar. *Junta de Investigações do Ultramar : Seus organismos, pessoal científico, técnico e auxiliar.* 8th ed. Lisboa, Centro de Documentação Científica Ultramarina, 1968. 153 p.

Directory of the Junta, including the Executive Commission and Secretariat, research groups, personnel of research institutes, scientific missions, etc., with indexes of institutions, of personal names, and of scientific organizations and subject indexes. The headings in Portuguese are repeated in French and English translation. Research groups include those in fields of engineering, geography and cartography, etc. Study groups include centres for phytosanitary research, Biological Center for Fisheries, Botanical Center, Overseas Scientific Documentation Center, Research Center for Anthropobiology, Cultural Anthropology Center, Cabo Verde Research Center, Community Development Research Center, Overseas History Research Center, Missionary Research Center, and Political and Social Research Center.

2321   Portugal. Ministério das Colónias. *Relatório apresentado ao Congresso de República....*

From 1912 onward the Ministério das Colónias presented lengthy reports to the Portuguese Parliament, in compliance with article 87 of the Constitution. These reports contained statistical tables, information concerning military matters, economic development, railways, administrative questions, and so forth. They were commonly indexed.

Before the creation of the Ministério das Colónias in 1911, the Ministério e Secretário d'Estado dos Negocios da Marinha e Ultramar issued various reports, such as the voluminous and comprehensive *Relatório de propostas de lei e documentos relativos aos possessões ultramarinas . . .* 1899, which was presented to the Cámara dos Deputados.

More recent reports include publications such as *Presidência do Conselho : 25 Anos de Administração Pública : Ministério do Ultramar* (Lisbon, Imprensa Nacional, 1955), which gives a general narrative and statistical account, arranged according to the different territories. See also Jesus Nunes dos Santos, *A centralização na estatística colonial* (Lisbon, 1942, 236 p.).

Part III: area guide (by colonial power, region and colony)

2322 Portugal. Ministério do Ultramar. *Anuário colonial de 1916– .* Lisbon, Imprensa Nacional, 1917– .

Published irregularly. Organized into three parts. Part 1 deals with the organization in the metropole that handles colonial affairs and provides a list of persons in the ministry and a chronology of former ministers. Part 2 describes the administrative organization and services of the colonies, as well as listing commercial companies and banks. Part 3 treats in detail, with many statistical tables on each colony, imports, exports and population. There are useful bibliographies in each issue. It lasted into the 1930s. For another valuable earlier publication of the Ministry of Colonies, see *Collecção dos boletins militares do Ultramar, 1878–1917.*

2323 Portugal. Ministério do Ultramar. *Legislação mandada aplicar ao Ultramar português, 1926 a 1963.* v. 1, A–C. Lisbon, Agência-Geral do Ultramar, 1965. 585 p.

2324 Rego, António da Silva. *Curso da missionologia.* Preface by Adriano Moreira. Lisbon, Agência-Geral do Ultramar, 1956. 700 p. Bibliography: p. xxvii–xlv.

The standard work by a distinguished colonial historian who is himself a clergyman and sympathizes with the Portuguese colonial record. See also his *Lições de missionologia* (1961, 564 p.).

2325 Rego, António da Silva. *O ultramar português no Seculo XIX, 1834–1910* . . . Lisbon, Agência-Geral do Ultramar, 1966. 446 p.

A chronological history covering the Portuguese colonial empire from 1834 to 1910. The study is written from the Portuguese metropolitan point of view, and pays special attention to the evolution of Portuguese colonial policy, Portuguese foreign relations, and Portuguese colonial problems, including the question of slavery. There are three chapters specifically concerned with the development of Mozambique, and three with Angola.

2326 Ribeiro, [Coronel] Gaspar do Couto. *História Colonial.* Grandes Atelieres Gráficos, Lisbon, 1937–38. 2 v.

A useful general and popular survey of Portuguese colonial history by a professor at the Escola Superior Colonial. Volume 2 treats of the modern period.

2327 Silva, J. J. da. *Repertório alphabético e chronológico ou índice remissivo da legislação ultramarina desde a epoca das descobertas até 1902 inclusivo.* Lisbon, Typografia de J. F. Pinero, 1904. 457 p.

An alphabetical reference work to Portuguese colonial legislation up to 1902, with headings such as 'public credit', 'exports', 'museums'. References to legislative enactments are provided under each entry.

Portuguese colonial literature contains a good many of these compilations. Another work of this type is António M. de Castilho Barreto, *Indice remissivo da legislação ultramarina desde 1446 até 1878* (Cidade da Praia, Cabo Verde, Imprensa Nacional, 1882, 117 p.). The author explains in the preface that Portuguese legislation is so extensive, and that the sources are so scattered, that a systematic perusal of the laws requires such a guide. See also Ernesto Luiz Dias Lobo, *Indice alfabético e chronológico de todos os diplomas de caracter permanente . . . de 1902 a 1928* (S. Tomé, Imprensa Nacional, 1929, 200 p.), which provides this type of information for one particular region, the Colónia de S. Tomé e Príncipe.

The work of Francisco Augusto Martins de Carvalho, *Diccionário bibliográphico militar portuguez* (Lisbon, Imprensa Nacional, 1891, 331 p.), is similar in nature, though it specializes in military affairs. The *Diccionário* provides not only information on individual officers and their respective careers, but also entries on subjects such as official journals and military literature.

2328 Sociedade de Geografia de Lisboa. *75 anos de actividades ao serviço da ciência e da nação : 1875–1950.* Lisbon, 1950, illus. 171 p.

The Sociedade, incorporated in 1876, played an important part in the history of Portuguese expansion during the era of the 'New Imperialism' (see its *Boletim*, no. 2273). This report illustrates its past activities, provides details with regard to its various publications, conferences held, and so forth. Especially valuable are the various catalogues and indexes prepared for Exposicões Coloniais or of its journal and library holdings.

2329 United Nations. General Assembly. Special Committee on Territories under Portuguese Administration. *Report,* 15 August 1962. New York, 1962. 144 p. annexes. (A/5160)

The Committee, consisting of representatives from Bulgaria, Ceylon, Colombia, Cyprus, Guatemala, Guinea and Nigeria, had received 'no cooperation' from the Portuguese government, which had supplied no reports as directed for the Administering Power in the Charter. After obtaining information from sources outside the territories, they concluded that the situation 'warrants the serious concern of the international community in every respect' and called for United Nations action against Portugal. See also more recent reports: A/AC.109/ L.451/Add.1.2: 1968 and A/AC.109/L.538: 1969.

For many other papers of the United Nations relating to the overseas possessions of Portugal, see the United Nations documents index, i.e., United Nations. General Assembly. Special Committee on the Situation with Regard to the Implementation of the Declaration on the Granting of Independence to Colonial Countries and Peoples. Sub-committee I. *Supplementary report : The activities of foreign economic and other interests which are impeding the implementation of the declaration on the granting of independence in the territories under Portuguese Administration.* New York, 1966. 278 p. (A/AC.109/L.334/Add.1).

2330 Wilensky, Alfredo Héctor. *Tendencias de la legislación ultramarina portuguesa en Africa : Contribución para su estudio en los países de habla hispana.* Braga [Portugal], Editora Pax, 1968. 269 p. Bibliography: p. 261–269.

A doctoral dissertation which traces Portuguese legislation from 1911 to the period 1961 to 1962. The author devotes special attention to African policy. He distinguishes three distinct periods, the legislation of 1911 involving compulsory labour, the legislation of 1928 limiting compulsory labour solely to works of a public nature, and the reforms of the early 1960s, which insisted on free labour. The writer links Portuguese legislation to external influences, such as challenges to the integrity of the empire as a whole. The appendix contains a detailed analysis of constitutional legislation during the early 1960s.

Angola

Bibliographies

Note Several slight reading lists on Angola were put out in the early 1960s, consisting mainly of periodical articles on the revolt and later outdated by events, e.g. (1787) United Nations, Secretariat, *Angola : A bibliography, 1963* (New York, 1963, 11 p.; Document ST/LIB/10). For bibliographical references other than those cited below, see the general bibliographies on Portuguese

Part III: area guide (by colonial power, region and colony)

Africa cited above. The Boston University Press issued *Western African history* (1969), which has a chapter by Douglas L. Wheeler, 'Towards a history of Angola: Problems and sources'. See also no. 2260.

2331 Angola. Comissão para a Exposição Histórica da Ocupação, 1st, Lisbon, 1937. *Catálogo do documentário coligido pela Comissão de Luanda para a Exposição Histórica da Ocupação a realizar em Lisboa, em 1937.* Remetido pelo govêrno geral de Angola. Luanda, Imprensa Nacional, 1937. 107 p. plates, ports., maps, facsims.

2332 Borchardt, Paul. *Bibliographie de l'Angola (bibliotheca angolensis), 1500–1910.* Bruxelles, Institut de Sociologie, 1912. 61 p. (Monographies bibliographiques, no. 2)
Cites some 1,000 references concerned primarily with geography and economics.

2333 Cosme, Leonel. *Primeira exposição de bibliografia angolana.* Catálogo. Sá da Bandeira, Câmara Municipal, 1962. 125 p.
Cites over 700 items, distributed among six sections: history and sociology, ethnography, literature and fiction, travels and narratives, various studies and anthropology.

2334 Greenwood, Margaret Joan. *Angola : A bibliography.* Cape Town, School of Librarianship, Cape Town University, 1967. 52 p. (*Its* Bibliographical Series)

2335 Werner, Manfred W. *Angola: A selected bibliography, 1960–1965.* Washington, D.C., Library of Congress, 1965.
A useful list of articles in English. See also no. 2260. For current nationalist war in Angola, see no. 2246.

Serials

2336 Angola. Instituto de Angola. *Boletim Informativo.* Luanda. Monthly.

2337 Angola. Instituto de Investigação Científica. *Memorias e Trabalhos.* 1960– . Luanda, Imprensa Nacional de Angola. Irregular.

2338 Angola. Instituto de Investigação Científica. *Relatórios e Comunicações.* 1962– . Luanda.

2339 Angola. Museu de Angola. *Arquivos de Angola,* 1933– , and *Boletim Cultural.* Luanda. Irregular.

2340 *Boletim Cultural da Câmara Municipal de Luanda.* 1934– . Luanda. Issued about 5–6 times a year.

2341 *Trabalho.* 1963– . Luanda. Issued by the Instituto do Trabalho, Providência e acção social. Quarterly.

Reference works

2342 Albuquerque Felner, Alfredo de. *Angola : Apontamentos sôbre a colonisação dos planaltos e litoral do sul de Angola : Extraidos de documentos históricos.* Lisboa, Divisão de Publicações e Biblioteca, Agência-Geral dos Colónias, 1940. 3 v. illus.
Documentary history of European settlement in the highlands and littoral of the south of Angola, in continuation of the author's earlier-published work (see next entry). Volume 1 deals with colonization and the indigenous people; v. 2 has documents for the period 1801–55; and v. 3 covers the period 1856–93.

Portuguese Africa

2343 Almeida, João de. *Sul de Angola, relatório de um governador de distrito* (1908–1910). Lisbon, Agência-Geral, 1936. 643 p.

Portuguese governors often published *Relatórios*, which were reports of their administration for a period of one or two years. Included were usually speeches made before various colonial councils.

2344 Amaral, Ilídio do. *Aspecto do povoamento branco de Angola*. Lisbon, Agência-Geral, 1960. 83 p.

Short but valuable survey of poor whites in Angola from the *degredados* through the colonization of the Huíla Plateau with Madeirians in 1845, to trek Boers in 1880 to modern times.

2345 American University, Washington, D.C. Foreign Areas Study Division. *Area handbook for Angola*. Co-authored by Allison Butler Herrick [and others]. Washington, D.C., 1967. 426 p. map, tables. ([U.S. Department of the Army] Pamphlet no. 550-59) Bibliography: p. 391–424.

The most up-to-date compendium in English, with separate sections on social, political, economic, and military problems respectively. The bibliography is similarly subdivided by topics. See also no. 2274.

2346 Andrade, Mario de, and Marc Ollivier. *La guerre en Angola : Etude socio-économique*. Paris, François Maspero, 1971. 161 p.

Andrade is a leader of a Marxist-oriented African nationalist movement (Movimento Popular de Libertação de Angola, MPLA). This book in addition to discussing the war analyses the economic and social causes and effects of the war from a Marxist point of view. The authors argue that Western capitalism is saving Portuguese imperialism.

2347 Angola. *Boletim Oficial*. 1845– . Luanda. Weekly.

At first the *Boletim* contained articles of general interest, reports submitted by officials, details concerning exploration, wars, ethnohistory, missionary work and economic activities in addition to legislation. Gradually it became more specialized in content and confined itself to laws, ordinances and decrees. There are indexes for each year: *Indice alfabético e cronológico dos Boletins oficiais*.

2348 Angola. Instituto de Investigação Científica de Angola, and Centro de Estudos Históricos Ultramarinos. *Angolana (Documentação sôbre Angola)*. 1970– . 3 v.

In 1968 the Instituto and the Centro began work on a major series designed to illustrate the history of Angola from the end of the eighteenth century onward. The first volume covered the years 1783 to 1883; the second dealt with the period 1883 to 1887, with special emphasis on the conference of Berlin, 1884–1885. The documents were provided with annotations compiled by Mário António Fernandes de Oliveira and Carlos Alberto Mendes do Couto. The material is fully indexed.

2349 Araújo, A. Correia de. *Aspectos do desenvolvimento económico e social de Angola*. Lisbon, Agência-Geral, 1964. 217 p.

The author claims that Portugal can only develop and survive if it channels emigration to the overseas provinces to exploit the land and resources there. See also the excellent survey by Amadeu de Castilho Soares, *Política de bem-estar rural em Angola* (Lisbon, Agência-Geral, 1961, 278 p.).

2350 Boavida, Américo. *Angola : Cinco séculos de exploração portuguesa*. Río de Janeiro, Civilização Brasileira, 1967. 138 p.

A Marxist-Leninist, Fanonesque attack, this work is fully documented from Portuguese sources and is a kind of historical document in itself. No other

Part III: area guide (by colonial power, region and colony)

systematic work of this size written by an Angolan nationalist has yet appeared. For a pro-Portuguese account, see F. Clement C. Egerton, *Angola in perspective* (London, Routledge and Kegan Paul, 1957, 272 p.).

2351 Childs, Gladwyn M. *Umbundu kinship and character.* London, published for the International African Institute by Oxford University Press, 1949. 245 p. illus., map.
A description of social structure and individual development of the Ovimbundu, especially in relationship to the impact of Christianity.

2352 Companhia de Diamantes de Angola [Diamang]. *Angola Diamond Company : A short report.* Lisbon, The Company, 1963. 168 p. illus., map.
English-language public-relations report on the company which plays a preponderant part in the economy of Angola. The company also issues its annual *Rapports* (French and Portuguese editions) and sponsors a series prepared by the Museu do Dundo, Luanda, Angola: Publicações culturais (1946–).

2353 Davezies, Robert. *Les Angolais.* Paris, Les Editions du Minuit, 1965. 259 p.

2354 ——— *La guerre d'Angola.* Bordeaux, G. Ducros, 1968. 189 p.
Tape-recorded accounts of African guerrilla fighters provide the data for these books.

2355 Estermann, Carlos. *Etnografia do sudoeste de Angola.* 2d ed., corr. Lisboa, 1960– . illus., map (fold. col.). (Junta de Investigações do Ultramar, Memórias, Série antropológica e etnológica, nos. 4–5)
These comprehensive scholarly volumes are the first two of a trilogy concerned with peoples of southeastern Angola. Volume 1 takes in the Bushmen and kindred tribes and the ethnic group of the Ambo (Ovambo). In v. 2 Father Estermann studies the Nhaneca-Humbe group, covering all phases of history, tribal and family life, mores, art, and religious beliefs and practices. The third volume will deal with the northern Herero. At the end of each volume is a short list of sources used. A 15-page list of the writings of this anthropologist, *Bibliografia do etnólogo padre Carlos Estermann, S. Sp.*, compiled by Afonso Costa, was published by the Instituto de Angola in Luanda in 1961.

2356 Felgas, Helio. *Guerra em Angola.* Lisbon, Livraria Clássica Editora, 1968.
Basic book for war in Angola during 1961.

2357 Institute of Race Relations, London. *Angola : A symposium, views of a revolt.* London, Oxford University Press, 1962. 160 p.
Excellent survey of people, movements and events of 1961.

2358 Lima, Raul de, ed. *Manual das administrações dos concelhos e circunscrições da Colónia de Angola.* Lisbon, 1941. 2 v.
Basic manual for administrative officials.

2359 Lopo, Júlio Castro de. *Jornalismo de Angola : Subsídios para a sua história.* Luanda, Centro de Informação e Turismo de Angola, 1964. 127 p. illus., ports., facsims.
Valuable survey of the press in Angola in the 19th and 20th centuries. There are useful lists of journals published. Also included is a section on African journalists.

2360 McCulloch, Merran. *The Ovimbundu of Angola.* London, International African Institute, 1952. 50 p. (Ethnographic Survey of Africa, West Central Africa, pt. 2) Bibliography. p. 48–50.

2361 ———— *The southern Lunda and related peoples* (*Northern Rhodesia, Belgian Congo, Angola*). London, International African Institute, 1951. 110 p. (Ethnographic Survey of Africa, West Central Africa, pt. 1) Bibliography: p. 101–109.
Two monographs in this authoritative series (see no. 333), synthesizing existing studies. The southern Lunda and related peoples occupy most of the eastern half of Angola, spreading over its borders into northwestern Rhodesia (Zambia) and the Katanga province of the Congo (Zaïre). Their total population in the early 1950s was estimated at around 63,000, of whom 10,000 lived in Angola, 10,000 in the Congo, and the rest in two districts of what was then Northern Rhodesia. The Ovimbundu are an important autochthonous race of Angola, their homeland being the Benguela Highland in the west-central part of the country, though they are found as far as the coast. It is estimated that more than a third of Angola's total population of about four million are Ovimbundu.
A more recent specialized study is by Adrian C. Edwards, *The Ovimbundu under two sovereignties: A study of social control and social change among a people of Angola* (London, published for the International African Institute by Oxford University Press, 1962, 169 p.).

2362 Marcum, John. *The Angolan revolution.* v. 1, *Anatomy of a revolution, 1950–1962.* Cambridge, Massachusetts Institute of Technology, 1969.
A major study of African resistance to Portuguese rule.

2363 Nevinson, Henry Woodd. *A modern slavery.* See no. 2413n.

2364 Okuma, Thomas Masaji. *Africa in ferment: The background and prospects of African nationalism.* Boston, Beacon Press, 1962. 137 p. illus. Bibliography: p. 127–131.
In 1961–62 there was an outpouring of books, mainly from the African nationalist viewpoint, regarding the Angola revolt. This work, by a writer who had been for some years a missionary in Angola, is among the best-balanced reviews of the background of Portuguese policy and events of early 1961.
A useful pamphlet was *Angola: A symposium* (London, published for the Institute of Race Relations by Oxford University Press, 1962, 160 p.); in a collection of views there were included the official Portuguese statement, the impressions of Protestant missionaries, reports from the Catholic press, etc. Another work is by two Swedish authors, Anders Ehnmark and Per Wästberg, *Angola and Mozambique: The case against Portugal*, translated by Paul Britten-Austin (New York, Roy, 1963, 176 p.).

2365 Paiva, Arturo de. *Arturo de Paiva.* Lisbon, Divisão de Publicações e Biblioteca, Agência-Geral das Colónias, 1938. 2 v. plates, maps, plans, tables.
Contains a bibliographical sketch as well as much material concerning Paiva's military campaigns in Angola during the 1880s and 1890s and matters of wider interest.

2366 Pélissier, René. 'Campagnes militaires au Sud-Angola (1885–1915)'. *Cahiers d'Etudes Africaines.* Paris, v. 9, no. 1, 1969. pp. 4–73.
A careful, thoroughly documented account of the Portuguese efforts to pacify southern Angola. See also his bibliographical survey of the modern struggle, no. 2246.

2367 Portugal. Agência-Geral das Colónias. Belo de Almeida, ed., *Eduardo da Costa: colectânea das suas principais obras militares e coloniais.* Lisbon, Agência-Geral das Colónias. Divisão de Publicações e Biblioteca, 1938–1939. 4 v., illus., tables.
Eduardo da Costa, a distinguished Portuguese soldier, became governor general

of Angola in 1906. The study, compiled by a Portuguese army officer, traces his career. A great variety of official memoranda, reports, and other works compiled by da Costa are reprinted in extenso. An important source-book for Portuguese military and administrative history, written for the purpose of reconstructing the career of ' one of those great fighters who have rendered such valiant service to the Fatherland both in the military and the governmental sphere '.

2368 Portugal. Agência-Geral do Ultramar. *Luanda, sua organização e occupação.* Ed. by Alberto de Almeida Teixeira. Lisbon, Divisão de Publicações e Biblioteca, Agência-Geral das Colónias, 1948. 258 p. illus., ports., map.

Useful historical monograph.

2369 Portugal. Agência-Geral do Ultramar. *As operações militares no sul de Angola em 1914–1915.* Lisbon, Divisão de Publicações e Biblioteca, Agência-Geral das Colónias, 1937. 198 p.

A useful historical monograph on military operations in southern Angola.

2370 Samuels, Michael A. *Education in Angola, 1870–1914: A history of culture transfer and administration.* New York, Teacher's College Press, 1970. 185 p.

A history of education and culture and race relations in Angola up to 1914. The author concludes the Portuguese did little to educate the African.

2371 Santos, Eduardo dos. *Ideologias políticas africanas.* Lisbon, Centro de Estudos Político-Sociais, 1968, 238 p.

———— *A questão da Lunda, 1885–1894.* Lisboa, Agência-Geral do Ultramar, 1966. 413 p.

Important works by a leading Portuguese scholar. See also his *Maza : Elementos do etno-história para a interpretação do terrorismo do noroeste de Angola* (Lisbon, 1965).

2372 Santos, Martin dos. *História do ensino em Angola.* Luanda, Edição dos Serviços de Educação, 1970. 361 p.

A preliminary survey of the history of education in Angola written in a popular style without footnotes or bibliography. A useful overview from the official point of view which deals historically with teaching by the missionaries and government education on the primary, secondary and university levels. Appendices include historical documents and a chronology. See also the author's *A história de Angola através dos seus personagens principais* and his forthcoming *Assistência sanitária em Angola.*

2373 Wheeler, Douglas L., and René Pélissier. *Angola.* New York, Praeger, 1971. ix, 296 p. illus., maps.

The most up-to-date survey of Angola. The first half of the book deals with the pre-1961 period concentrating on the origins of political consciousness, 1800–1960. The second half gives a detailed account of the Angolan independence movements. The survey is critical but objective about Portuguese rule. An extensive set of notes and bibliography add to the value of this work of synthesis, which also has sections of original research.

Mozambique

Atlas

2374 Moçambique. Direcção dos Serviços de Agrimensura. *Atlas de Moçambique.* Lourenço Marques, Empresa Moderna, 1960. 43 p. maps (chiefly col., part fold.). 38 cm. ('Exemplar no. 4697')
Scale of maps: 1:1,000,000 or 1:6,000,000.

Bibliographies

2375 Costa, Mário Augusto da. *Bibliografia geral de Moçambique (contribução para um estudo completo).* v. 1. Lisboa, Divisão de Publicações e Biblioteca, Agência-Geral das Colónias, 1946– . 359 p.
A long bibliography classed under 35 headings in alphabetical order (administration, agriculture, veterinary sciences, voyages and travels, etc.), some with from two to twenty subdivisions. A detailed table of contents is complemented by indexes of personal and organizational names (onomástico) and of subjects. References are to monographic publications and separates from reviews or collected volumes.

2376 Eça, Filipe Gastão de Moura Coutinho de Almeida de. *Achegas para a bibliografia de Moçambique : Novos subsídios para um estudo completo.* Lisboa, Agência-Geral das Colónias, 1949. 134 p.
List of 428 numbered entries for books and separately issued papers, including many works of the 19th century. Arrangement is alphabetical, and indexes of names and subjects are included.
See also bibliographies in the serial *Moçambique : Documentário Trimestral,* no. 2395.

2377 —— *Subsídios para uma bibliografia missionária moçambicana (católica).* Lisboa, Depositários: Livraria Petrony, 1969. 157 p.

2378 International African Institute. *South-east Central Africa and Madagascar : General, ethnography, sociology, linguistics.* Comp. by Ruth Jones, librarian, with the assistance of a panel of consultants. London, 1961. 53 l. (Africa Bibliography Series, Ethnography, Sociology, Linguistics, and Related Subjects) Moçambique: p. 28–37.
See note on series, no. 252.

2379 Rita-Ferreira, António. *Bibliografia etnológica de Moçambique (das origens a 1954).* Lisboa, Junta de Investigações do Ultramar, 1962. 254 p.
Bibliography of 968 numbered entries for books and articles in all languages on the ethnology of the races of Mozambique and of south-eastern Africa in general. Introductory chapters are on South and East Africa (p. 1–61), Republic of South Africa (p. 62–64), Rhodesia and Nyasaland (p. 65–79), and Tanganyika (p. 80–91). Then division is by tribal groups living within Mozambique and also in the rest of the area (p. 92–230). Ethnology is broadly interpreted, including references on music, medicine, and travel, as well as folklore, customs, magic, religion, and language. Some entries are briefly annotated. There are indexes of authors and of periodicals cited.

2380 Souto, C. E. M., ed. *Indice alfabético da principal legislação publicada no 'Boletim Oficial' de Moçambique desde 1912–1945.* Lourenço Marques, Imprensa Nacional, 1955–57. 3 v.

Part III: *area guide* (*by colonial power, region and colony*)

2381 *Sinopse das matérias oficiais publicadas no 'Boletim Oficial' da Província de Moçambique.* By José Knópfli Júnior. 1923– . Lourenço Marques. Annual.

Valuable summary of official legislation and proclamations published in the official journal or gazette. See also nos. 2246, 2260 and 2385n.

Reference works

2382 American University, Washington, D.C. Foreign Areas Study Division. *Area handbook for Mozambique.* Washington, D.C., 1969. 351 p. maps, tables. Includes bibliography.

The most up-to-date compendium in English, with separate sections on social, political, economic, and military problems, respectively. The bibliography is similarly subdivided by topics. See also no. 2274.

2383 *Anuário Católico de Moçambique.* Lourenço Marques, 1961– . 468 p. In 1957 the Archdiocese of Lourenço Marques began to publish the *Anuário da Arquidiocese.* In 1961 this publication was reorganized and its scope was extended. The publication aimed at providing 'a better knowledge concerning the life of the Church in Moçambique, and the work of civilisation carried on by Catholic missionaries who so often have been unjustly criticised'. The *Anuário* gives details concerning evangelical work, education, ecclesiastical organization, and so forth.

2384 *Anuário da Província de Moçambique.* 43d ed. Lourenço Marques, A. W. Bayly & Co., 1962. cvi, 1522 p. maps, plans. Annual.

Comprehensive business register of the city of Lourenço Marques and other districts of Mozambique, including an encyclopaedic survey of the colony as well as directory by towns and districts. It begins with indexes of subjects, addresses of government offices, business and industries, local names, and economic activities (the last-named in English translation also). The main text includes folded maps, town plans, etc. (interspersed with advertisements). The separately numbered pages at the end are an index of advertisers. There is also an English edition, begun in 1899 as *Delagoa directory* and since 1943 titled *Lourenço Marques directory.*

2385 *Boletim Oficial da Colónia de Moçambique.* 1854– . Moçambique, later Lourenço Marques. Irregular, later weekly.

The *Boletim* first began publication in Mozambique on May 13, 1854. From January 5, 1855, it appeared as a regular weekly. At first it contained articles of general interest, reports submitted by senior officials, details concerning agricultural production, missionary work, statistical information, and so forth, in addition to legislation. Gradually it became more specialized in content and confined itself to laws.

The earlier numbers were indexed in great detail in Alberto Cota Mesquita, *Índice alfabético e cronológico da principal legislação publicada nos 'Boletins Oficiais' da Colónia de Moçambique, desde 1854 a 1920* . . . (Lourenço Marques, Imprensa Nacional, 1941, 63 p.). The first part contains a subject index arranged alphabetically. The second consists of a chronological index, listing all legislation concerning the colony between 1761 and 1920.

See also *Legislação da metrópole em vigor na província de Moçambique, publicada no 'Boletim Oficial' 1900 a 1964,* comp. by J. da Silva Rodrigues Carrazola (Lourenço Marques, Imprensa Nacional de Moçambique, 1965, 414 p.).

Portuguese Africa

2386 Companhia de Moçambique. *Território de Manica e Sofala . . . Monografías apresentadas na Exposição Colonial International de Paris.* Lisbon, Sociedade Nacional de Tipografia, 1931. 1 v.

In French. The Companhia de Moçambique was incorporated in 1888, and received an extensive territorial concession, with far-reaching administrative powers in Mozambique. The company issued all manner of reports (see especially its annual reports). The present series comprises ten monographs, which deal respectively with its history, the soil and climate within its concession, administration and finance, the indigenous peoples, education, medical services, ports and transportation, agriculture and pastoral farming, surveys, commerce and industry. See also its *Boletim do governo do Território da Companhia de Moçambique.* Beira. 1892–1942. Other companies were Companhia do Nyassa, ruled from 1891 to 1929, and Companhia da Zambezia (1890–1916?).

2387 Costa, Mário Augusto da. *Voluntários de Lourenço Marques.* Lourenço Marques, Imprensa Nacional, 1928. 90 p. illus.

Provides a military history of Mozambique.

2388 Dias, Raul Neves. *A imprensa periódica em Moçambique 1854–1954 : Subsídos para a sua história.* Lourenço Marques, Impr. Nacional de Moçambique, 1956. 110 p.

A useful survey of the daily press.

2389 Ferreira, A. Rita-. *O movimento migratório de trabalhadores entre Moçambique e a África do Sul.* Lisbon, Agência-Geral, 1963. 193 p.

An historical and sociological survey of migrant labour from Mozambique to South Africa from 1872 on. Labour migration through official channels (the Witwatersrand Native Labour Bureau) and by clandestine means is analysed in social, economic, and psychological terms.

2390 Freitas, Antônio Joaquim de. *A geologia e o desenvolvimento económico e social de Moçambique.* Lourenço Marques, Imprensa Nacional de Moçambique, 1959. 396 p. illus., fold. maps, tables. Includes bibliographies.

Extended economic and technical survey of geology and mining developments in Mozambique. The author was formerly Chief of the Services of Industry and Geology of the province.

2391 Liesegang, Gerhard Julius. *Beiträge zur Geschichte der Gaza Nguni im südlichen Moçambique 1820–1895.* Cologne University, 1967. 292 p. illus., map, tables. (Doctoral dissertation) Bibliography : p. 254–287.

A pioneer study based on unpublished archival sources. It traces the growth and destruction of the Gaza kingdom in Mozambique. The bibliography contains a detailed description of the archival sources which the author consulted in the Arquivo Histórico Ultramarino at Lisbon, the Biblioteca da Sociedade de Geografia at Lisbon, the Royal Geographical Society and the Public Record Office in London.

2392 Martins, E. A. Azambuja. *O Soldado Africano de Moçambique.* Lisbon, Agência-Geral, 1936. 127 p.

Not available for examination.

2393 Mondlane, Eduardo. *The struggle for Mozambique.* Baltimore, Md., Penguin Books, 1969. 221 p., illus., maps.

Mondlane (assassinated in 1969) was founder and head of the Frente de Libertação de Moçambique (FRELIMO). He was a nationalist leader, but FRELIMO became a Marxist-oriented pro-Soviet organization. Compare Nuno Rocha, *Guerra em Moçambique* (Lisbon, 1970).

Part III: area guide (by colonial power, region and colony)

2394 Mouzinho de Albuquerque, Joaquim. *Moçambique : 1896–1898*. Lisbon, Manuel Gomes: Livreiro de Suas Majestades e Altezas. 1899, xvl, 365 p., maps.

Mouzinho de Albuquerque made his name in a series of campaigns conducted in Mozambique during the 1890s. In 1896 he was made governor-general of Mozambique. In addition to being an outstanding soldier, Mouzinho de Albuquerque was a gifted writer. His book *Moçambique* contains a general account of the area, a history of its colonization and an account of its administration and natural resources, as well as appended documents. Other published works from his pen include *Campanha contra os Namarrais : Relatórios enviados ao Ministro e Secretário dos Negócios da Marinha e Ultramar pelo Commissário Régio da Província de Moçambique* (Lisbon, Imprensa Nacional, 1897, 176 p.). See also *Livro de Centenário de Mouzinho de Albuquerque 1855–1955* (Lisbon, Commissão Nacional para as Commemorações ..., 1955, 317 p.), a patriotic eulogy; but the work contains a fully annotated bibliography (p. 285–294). See, for a compendium, Mouzinho de Albuquerque, *Escritos sobre Moçambique* (Lisbon, Biblioteca Colonial Portuguesa, 1934–35, 2 v., plates, ports., plans).

2395 Mozambique. *Moçambique : Documentário Trimestral*. 1935– . Lourenço Marques. illus., plates (part col.), maps, music. Quarterly.

This official quarterly, which carries excellent articles on many aspects of history, economy, and culture, is a valuable source for information on Mozambique. The issues include regular bibliographies of works published in Mozambique and received on legal deposit by the Arquivo Histórico.

2396 Pinto, Frederico da Silva. *Roteiro histórico-biográfico da cidade de Lourenço Marques*. Lourenço Marques, Moçambique Editora, 1965. 206 p.

A biographical survey of important men in the history of Lourenço Marques.

2397 Oliveira Boleo, José de. *Moçambique*. Lisboa, Divisão de Publicações e Biblioteca, Agência-Geral do Ultramar, 1951. 562 p. plates, maps. (Monografias dos territórios do Ultramar) Bibliography: p. 539–558.

Like others of the series, this study surveys factors of physical geography, geology, climate, flora and fauna, anthropogeography, history, politics and social welfare under the Portuguese, and economic development. Chapters are followed by résumés in French and English. In conclusion there is a long bibliography, classified by subject field and including writings in various languages.

2398 Portugal. Agência-Geral do Ultramar. *História das guerras no Zambeze, Chicoa e Messangano, 1807–1888*. By Filipe Gastão de Moura Coutinho de Almeida de Eça. Lisbon, Divisão de Publicações e Biblioteca, Agência-Geral das Colónias, 1953–54. 2 v. illus., ports., map, plan, facsims. Bibliography: v. 1, p. 471–475; v. 2, p. 683–684.

2399 Portugal. Agência-Geral do Ultramar. *Moçambique: Relatório apresentado ao govêrno*. 3d ed. By António Ennes. Lisbon, Divisão de Publicações e Biblioteca, Agência-Geral das Colónias, 1946. 625 p.

This report was first published in 1893. Its author, a Royal Commissioner in the colony at the time, played an important part in the affairs of the colony.

2400 Portugal. Agência-Geral do Ultramar. *O trabalho indígena: Estudo de direito colonial*. By Joaquim Moreira da Silva Cunha. Lisbon, Divisão de Publicações e Biblioteca. Agência-Geral das Colónias, 1949. 295 p. Bibliography: p. 279–289.

Standard study of Portuguese labour legislation in the colonies before the period of post-war reform.

Portuguese Africa

2401 Portugal. Laws, statutes, etc. *Principal legislação aplicável aos indígenas da Província de Moçambique.* Lourenço Marques, Imprensa Nacional de Moçambique, 1960. 385 p.
Survey of laws governing the African population of Mozambique.

2402 Santos, Joaquim Rodrigues dos. *Contribuição para o estudo da antropologia de Moçambique : Algumas tribos do distrito de Tete.* Pôrto, Tipografia Mendoça, 1944. 412 p. illus., fold. maps, tables. (República Portuguêsa, Ministério das Colónias, Junta das Missões Geográficas e de Investigações do Ultramar, Memórias, Série Antropológica, no. 2) Bibliographical notes: p. 361–387; bibliography: p. 389–397.
This scholar, a professor at the University of Pôrto, was a noted anthropologist and author of many works relating to East Africa. In the 1930s he conducted Portuguese expeditions studying and photographing tribes of Mozambique, an account of which was published by the Agência-Geral das Colónias in 1940, *Missão antropológica de Moçambique... 2a. Campanha, agosto de 1937 a Janeiro de 1938* (por J. R. dos Santos Júnior, Lisboa, 1940, 91 p., 95 plates on 48 l.). The present book is an extensive study of the physical anthropology of tribes of Zambesia, particularly of the district of Tete. It ends with anthropometric tables and almost 40 pages of bibliographical notes, in which the author's own contributions are entered under the name Santos Júnior (J. R. dos).

2403 Santos, Rui Martins dos. *Uma contribuição para a analise da economia de Moçambique.* Lisboa, Companhia de Cimentos de Moçambique, 1959. 373 p. tables, diagrs.
Full-scale statistical study of all phases of economic life in Mozambique.

2404 Serra, Aniano Mendes. *Sinopse dos diplomas oficiais de carácter permanente publicados no 'Boletim Oficial' da colónia de Moçambique.* Lourenço Marques. Annual.

2405 Spence, C. F. *Moçambique (East African province of Portugal).* Cape Town, Timmins, 1963. 147 p. illus.
An overall picture of Mozambique by a travel writer and interpreter of southern Africa. Spence had published in 1951 an economic survey of Mozambique, which this supersedes and covers more broadly. His chapters cover historical background, geographical information, game, the tsetse fly and its influence on the economy, population, government and citizenship (the rate of *assimilação* had been slow), education, health, and many aspects of the economy.

2406 Teixeira Botelho, José Justino. *História militar e política dos portugueses em Moçambique de 1833 aos nossos dias.* 2d ed. Lisbon, Centro Tipográfico Colonial, 1936. 742 p. illus.
This work is a continuation of the author's standard work *História militar e política dos portugueses em Moçambique da descoberta a 1833* (Lisbon, Centro Tipográfico Colonial, 1934, 637 p., illus.). Both are rigidly Eurocentric in conception. For a political biography of an African leader, see Wheeler, 'Gungunhana', in no. 1021, *Leadership in Eastern Africa.*

Portuguese Guinea, Cape Verde Islands, São Tomé and Príncipe

Bibliographies

2407 Lampreia, José D. *Catálogo inventário da Secção de Etnografia do Museu da Guiné Portuguesa.* Lisboa, Junta de Investigações do Ultramar, 1962. 91 p. illus.

2408 Tenreiro, Francisco. 'Bibliografia geográfica da Guiné'. *Garcia de Orta,* v. 2, no. 1, 1954. See also nos. 2246 and 2260.

Reference works

2409 Amaral, Ilídio do. *Santiago de Cabo Verde. A terra e os homens.* Lisbon, Agência-Geral, 1944. 444 p.

A detailed study, richly illustrated, of the assimilated people of Cape Verde, their history, geography and economics.

2410 Barreto, João. *História da Guiné 1414–1918.* Lisbon, The Author, 1938. 452 p., tables, illus.

The standard history of the territory, written entirely from a Eurocentric standpoint. The author traces the development of the colony from the age of discoveries to the Portuguese Republic. There are special chapters concerning the administration of justice, religious missions, and finance. For a contemporary travelogue in English, written in a somewhat nostalgic manner, see Archibald Lyall, *Black and white make brown : An account of a journey to the Cape Verde Islands and Portuguese Guinea* (London, William Heinemann, 1938, 303 p.). A popular Portuguese account of more recent vintage is António Alberto de Andrade, *História breve da Guiné Portuguesa* (Lisbon, Agência-Geral, 1968, 50 p.).

2411 *Boletim Cultural da Guiné Portuguesa.* v. 1– , 1946– . Bissau, Centro de Estudos da Guiné Portuguesa. illus. Quarterly.

A distinguished review, organ of the prominent centre for study and research on Portuguese Guinea, edited at its headquarters in the Museu Guiné Portuguesa in Bissau. The numbers carry substantial articles on ' what is considered of interest ... of an historical, ethnographic, scientific, literary, or artistic character '. There are also regular sections of chronicle of the province, economic statistics, news and notes, and list of publications received at the museum. On the back cover, titles are given of the Centro's monographic publications (Memórias).

2412 Chaliand, Gérard. *Armed struggle in Africa : With the guerrillas in 'Portuguese' Guinea.* New York, Monthly Review Press, 1969. 142 p., tables. Bibliography: p. 141–142.

A translation of *La lutte armée en Afrique.* Written from the pro-guerrilla standpoint, with the professed objective ' to outline the inner sociology of an African *maquis* '. The first two portions of the book discuss the struggle in Guinea; the third portion deals with wider problems of guerrilla warfare in Africa. The author emphasizes the need for adequate political, psychological and organizational preparations before guerrillas can successfully take up arms. Appendices include Portuguese psychological warfare circulars, and data concerning foreign firms in Guinea. Amilcar Cabral, founder and secretary-general of the pro-Soviet and Marxist-oriented Partido Africano da Indepêndencia da Guiné e Cabo Verde (PAIGC), published his version in *Selected texts by Amilcar Cabral : Revolution in Guinea. An African people's struggle* (London, ' Stage 1 ', 1969, 142 p.). A more popular account also written from the pro-Marxist point of view, is Basil Davidson, *The liberation of Guiné : Aspects of an African revolution* (Harmondsworth, Middlesex, Eng., Penguin Books, 1969, 169 p.).

For the Portuguese side, see, for instance, Amândio César, *Guiné 1965 : contra-ataque* (Braga, Editoria Pax, 1965, 229 p.). António de Spínola, commander in chief of the Portuguese armed forces in Guinea, issued a collection of speeches, interviews and communiqués entitled *Por uma Guiné melhor* (Lisbon, Agência-Geral do Ultramar, 1970, 385 p.). For a brief introduction in Portuguese see António Alberto de Andrade, *História breve da Guiné portuguesa* (Lisbon, 1968, 50 p.). Andrade published in English a defence of Portugal's position entitled *Many races but a sole nation : Outline of the theory of Portuguese humanism* (Lisbon, Agência-Geral do Ultramar, 1969, 101 p.).

2413 Instituto Superior de Ciências Sociais e Política Ultramarina. *Cabo Verde, Guiné, São Tomé e Príncipe : Curso de extensão universitária; ano lectivo de 1965–1966.* Lisbon, Universidade Técnica, 1966, 1,036 p., tables, maps.

A standard work, the third in a series of lecture courses, each designed to acquaint students with one particular region. There are articles by twenty-three experts, dealing with different aspects of the various territories, including their history, geography, labour, settlement, natural resources, and so forth. There is also a chapter on ' subversive movements '. Some of the chapters are provided with detailed bibliographies.

A much earlier account is Manuel Ferreira Ribeiro, *A província de S. Tomé e Príncipe e suas dependencias...* (Lisbon, Imprensa Nacional, 1877, 705 p.). The author, a medical doctor, tried to cover every aspect, including geography, agriculture, navigation, trade, but devoting special attention to health conditions.

For a bitterly critical account of Portuguese administration and African labour conditions, see Henry Woodd Nevinson, *A modern slavery* (London, Harper, 1906, 215 p.), a work famous in the history of British humanitarianism. Nevinson provided a description of a journey through Angola, São Tomé and Príncipe between 1904 and 1905, and of real and alleged evils in these colonies.

2414 Mendes Corrêa, Antônio A. *Ultramar português.* v. 2, *Ilhas de Cabo Verde.* Lisboa, Divisão de Publicações e Biblioteca, Agência-Geral do Ultramar, 1954. 262 p. illus., maps.

Detailed coverage of the physical and human geography of the Cape Verde Islands. The first eight chapters are on natural science, the remaining seven on ethnology, demography, social conditions, languages, culture and education, politics and government, and economy. Each chapter is followed by résumés in French and English. An earlier work by Professor Mendes Corrêa (anthropology, University of Pôrto) is concerned with ethnology of the tribes of Portuguese Guinea : *Uma jornada científica na Guiné portuguesa* (Lisboa, Divisão de Publicações e Biblioteca, Agência-Geral das Colónias, 1947. 193 p.).

2415 Mota, Avelino T. da, and Mario G. V. Neves, eds. *A habitação indígena na Guiné portuguesa.* Bissau, 1948. 538 p.

Useful publication of the Centro de Estudos da Guiné portuguesa.

2416 Portugal. Agência-Geral do Ultramar. *Estatuto político-administrativo da província S. Tomé e Príncipe.* Lisbon, Agência-Geral do Ultramar, 1965. 40 p.

2417 Portugal. Agência-Geral do Ultramar. *S. Tomé e Príncipe, pequena monografia.* Lisbon, Agência-Geral do Ultramar, 1964. 108 p. plates, ports., maps.

The above two entries, though official surveys, are useful.

2418 Portugal. Junta de Investigações do Ultramar. Centro de Estudos Políticos e Sociais. *Colóquios cabo-verdianos.* Lisboa, 1959. 182 p. (Estudos de ciências políticas e sociais, no. 22)

Proceedings of a conference on Cape Verde studies held by the Centro. The papers cover a broad perspective. Eight are reproduced here, beginning with a discussion of literary trends in Cape Verde and including talks on Creole society, on bilingualism, on education and culture, and on economic problems.

2419 Portuguese Guinea. *Boletim Oficial da Guiné.* 1880– . Imprensa Nacional, Bissau (Bolama until 1942).

Carries Portuguese legislation applicable to the overseas territories, local legislation, notices, etc.

2420 Portuguese Guinea. Conselho do Governo. *Acta.* 1919– . Bissau.

2421 —— Conselho Legislativo. *Actos do sessões.* 1925.

2422 São Tomé e Príncipe. *Boletim oficial.* 1857– . Imprensa Nacional, São Tomé. Frequency varies.

Carries Portuguese legislation applicable to the overseas territories, local legislation, notices, etc.

2423 São Tomé e Príncipe. Curadoria Geral dos Servicais e Colónos. *O trabalho indígena nos ilhas de S. Tomé e Príncipe : Relatório apresentado as Govêrno da colónia.* S. Tomé, Imprensa Nacional, 1919. 460 p.

Report by the office of the governor of the island on the condition of the indigenous workers.

2424 Silva, Hélder Lains e. *São Tomé e Príncipe e a cultura do café.* With the collaboration, on soil studies, of José Carvalho Cardosa. Lisboa, Junta de Investigações do Ultramar, 1958. 499 p. plates, fold. map (in pocket), tables. (Memórias, 2d ser., no. 1) Bibliography: p. 391–403.

Scholarly ecological study beginning with a general account of the province in geographical, geological, climatological, and economic aspects and then analysing in detail its agriculture generally and the coffee culture specifically. A summary in English is given on pages 353–387.

2425 Teixeira da Mota, Avelinó. *Guiné portuguesa.* Lisboa, Divisão de Publicações e Biblioteca, Agência-Geral do Ultramar, 1954. 2 v. (Monografias dos territorios do ultramar) Bibliography (by subject classes): v. 2, p. 251–286.

An impressive survey giving wide coverage to physical features – geology, hydrography, climate, flora and fauna, etc. – and to ethnological aspects in Portuguese Guinea and the islands of São Tomé and Príncipe, as well as to economic and social development under the Portuguese administration. All chapters are followed by summaries in French and English; some are also followed by bibliographies.

2426 Tenreiro, Francisco. *A ilha de São Tomé.* Lisboa, Junta de Investigações do Ultramar, 1961. 279 p. 73 plates, maps, diagrs. (Memórias, 2d ser., no. 24) Bibliography: p. 243–278.

A comprehensive geographical survey, with chapters on climate and soils, colonization and agriculture, peoples, socioeconomics, and economic position, with particular reference to the export crops of coffee and cocoa. There is a long classified bibliography, largely of articles in Portuguese journals but including a handful of writings in English.

SPANISH GUINEA (EQUATORIAL GUINEA)

Note The only Spanish possession in sub-Saharan Africa had been this region of two territories under one governorship, the mainland Río Muni and the large island of Fernando Po (Fernando Póo in Spanish) some 20 miles from the coast. The administration of Fernando Po included four smaller islands, Annobón, Corisco, and Great and Little Elobey. The seat of government was at Santa Isabel on Fernando Po. Since October 12, 1968, Spanish Guinea has been the independent republic of Equatorial Guinea.

Atlas

2427 Spain. Dirección General de Marruecos y Colonías. *Atlas histórico y geográfico de Africa española.* Madrid, 1955. 197 p. maps (part col.).
This folio atlas is in two parts, historical (p. 13–67) and geographical. In the first section, 31 coloured maps showing stages of the history of Spain in Africa are interspersed with explanatory text. In the geographical atlas, the maps, physical, geological, political-administrative, on double-page spreads with explanatory text, cover practically all details of geographical information about Spanish African possessions. There is a comprehensive index of place-names.

Bibliographies

2428 Berman, Sanford. *Spanish Guinea: An annotated bibliography.* Washington, D.C., Catholic University of America, 1961. 597 l. typescript.
A unique contribution to African studies, invaluable for research on Spanish Guinea. Microfilm copies of this master's thesis in library science may be obtained from the Catholic University of America. After an introductory essay on the literature relating to the region, the bibliography proper, occupying over 330 pages, is arranged under alphabetical subject headings, with a preliminary section of general works. Mr. Berman has analysed practically all entries in evaluative annotations, often of several hundred words. He has provided an extended glossary (p. 434–490), a chronology (p. 491–527), a directory of publishers, periodicals, and institutions, and finally a full index of authors and subject matter.

2429 Guinea, Spanish. Laws, statutes, etc. *Indice legislativo de Guinea.* [Prepared by Francisco Martos Avila] Madrid, Instituto de Estudios Políticos, 1944. xxii, 249 p.
An index to legislation published in the *Boletín Oficial* from 1907 to 1944. Entries total roughly 3,500. See also Schiller, no. 476, for listing of legal material.

Reference works

2430 *Africa* [*Revista de Acción Española*]. v. 1– , Jan. 1942– . Madrid, Instituto de Estudios Africanos [IDEA]. illus., maps. Monthly.
IDEA, an institute of the official Spanish Consejo Superior de Investigaciones Científicas, in 1950 took over publication of this review from a non-governmental organization, the Instituto de Estudios Políticos. In 1960 the subtitle was dropped to fit with wider Spanish interest in other parts of Africa. The

455

Part III: area guide (by colonial power, region and colony)

journal is the most ready source of information about Spanish possessions in Africa. Besides articles and news notes, *Africa* carries a regular section on a press review, a list of new publications including contents of periodicals, and a section of laws and decrees.

2431 Alvarez García, Heriberto R. *Historia de la acción cultural en la Guinea española, con notas sobre la enseñanza en el Africa negra.* Madrid, Instituto de Estudios Africanos. 1948. 557 p. illus., maps, diagrs. Bibliography: p. 543–545.

Study of Spanish educational work in West Africa by the chief inspector of education of these tropical colonies. The account is largely historical.

2432 *Fernando Póo.* 1961– . Santa Isabel. (Fernando Póo, Spanish Guinea, Diputación Provincial)

The contents of this periodical have been analysed in the ' Reseña de revistas ' in the IDEA monthly *Africa.* Also noted in *Africa* are occasional articles from the information bulletin *La Guinea Española* (1903– , Santa Isabel, Misioneros Hijos del Immaculado Corazón de María, semi-weekly), which has a new title, *La Guinea Ecuatorial.*

2433 France. Direction de la Documentation. *Les territoires espagnols d'Afrique.* By René Pélissier. Paris, La Documentation Française, 1963. 40 p. (Notes et études documentaires, no. 2951, Jan. 3, 1963)

Spanish ed., *Los territorios españoles de Africa.* Madrid, 1964.

In the official French series of background documentation, this brochure gives a concise survey of the three territories held by Spain: Ifni (p. 7–12); Spanish Sahara (p. 13–19); Spanish Guinea (p. 20–37). A short reading list is given. Aspects of Guinea considered are general conditions with outline of geography, history, and people; evolution of political and administrative institutions; economic and financial development; and cultural and social evolution.

2434 Guinea, Spanish. Laws, statutes, etc. *Leyes coloniales.* Ed. by Agustín Miranda Junco. Madrid, Imprensa Succesores de Rivadeneyra, 1945. 1,462 p.

Compilation in chronological order of all legislation of the Territorios Españoles del Golfo de Guinea from the acquisition by Spain in 1778 through the year 1944. The new constitution and some of the material from the Constitutional Conference appear in *Textos fundamentales de Guinea Ecuatorial* (Madrid, Servicio Informativo Español, 1968, 150 p., illus.; 'Documentos históricos', no. 5).

2435 Martínez García, Tomás. *Fernando Póo : Geografía, historia, paisaje, la Guinea española.* Santa Isabel, Ediciones Instituto ' Claret ' de Africanistas, 1968. 119 p. illus., map, plan. Includes bibliography.

A basic survey.

2436 Pélissier, René. ' Spanish Guinea: An introduction '. *Race* (London), v. 6, Oct. 1964: 117–128.

This article in the journal of the Institute of Race Relations describes the political and economic situation in Guinea in mid-1964. An earlier account, ' La Guinée espagnole ', by Pélissier, appeared in the *Revue Française de Science Politique*, v. 13, Sept. 1963, p. 624–644. He also contributed an article on ' Spain's discreet decolonization ' to *Foreign Affairs*, v. 43, Apr. 1965, p. 519–527. See also his *Etudes hispano-guinéennes* (Paris. n.p., 1969, unpaged [61 p.]).

2437 Prothero, G. W., general ed. *Spanish Guinea*. Prepared under the direction of the Historical Section of the Foreign Office. London, H.M. Stationery Office, 1920. 60 p. (Handbooks, no. 125)
Useful older work.

2438 Spain. Consejo Superior de Investigaciones Científicas. Instituto de Estudios Africanos. *Archivos*. no. 1– , June 1947– . Madrid. illus., maps. Quarterly.
Archivos was the scholarly review of IDEA (ceased publication in 1966), carrying articles by experts in varied subject fields. In most numbers there is printed the list of 300-odd monographs published by the Institute since its establishment in the early 1940s, together with titles of articles in previous issues of *Archivos*. Among the earlier titles there appear many items on Spanish Guinea in varied fields of human and physical sciences. Replacing *Archivos* is a series of pamphlets, *Colección monográfica africana*.

2439 —— Instituto de Estudios Africanos. *Catálogo de publicaciones*. Madrid, 1965. 51 p.
The *Catálogo de publicaciones*, which is revised periodically, is available from the Institute.

2440 —— Instituto de Estudios Africanos. *Resúmenes estadísticos del gobierno general de la Región Ecuatorial, provincias de Fernando Póo y Río Muni, 1959–60*. Madrid, 1962. 479 p. maps, diagrs. (Publicaciones)
A joint publication of IDEA and the Dirección General de Plazas y Provincias Africanas. This is a separate publication from the overall *Resúmen estadístico del Africa española*, which has appeared periodically since 1954 (1963–64 ed., 1965, 528 p., map); until 1958 section was entitled *Resúmenes . . . de los territorios del Golfo de Guinea*. The overall volume includes official data on Spanish Guinea and on most subjects, for example, industry, labour, social welfare, justice, etc.

2441 Unzueta y Yuste, Abelardo de. *Geografía histórica de la Isla Fernando Póo*. Madrid, Instituto de Estudios Africanos, 1947. 494 p. illus., maps. Bibliography: p. 435–462.

2442 —— *Guinea continental española*. Madrid, Instituto de Estudios Políticos, 1944. 394 p. illus., maps. Bibliography: p. 381–378.

2443 —— *Islas de Golfo de Guinea* (*Elobeyes, Corisco, Annobón, Príncipe y Santo Tomé*). Madrid, Instituto de Estudios Políticos, 1945. 386 p. illus., maps. Bibliography: p. 373–378.
The above three entries are standard encyclopaedic surveys of the Spanish possessions in West Africa by an authority on colonial trade, professor of economic geography at the Institute of Political Studies. The coverage includes historical, physical, and human geography as well as ethnology, social welfare, political administration, and economy.

ETHIOPIA

Note A separate section on Ethiopia is included in this bibliography because Ethiopia was both a colonized and a colonial nation. Menelik participated in the process of territorial expansion along with the European colonial powers, and then Italy conquered Ethiopia. See also items on Ethiopia listed under Italian Africa, nos. 2135–2233.

Bibliographies

2444 African Bibliographic Center, Washington, D.C. *A current bibliography on Ethiopian affairs.* Comp. by Daniel G. Matthews. Washington, Mar. 1965. 46 p. (Special Bibliographic Series, v. 3, no. 3)
Supersedes two earlier bibliographies, *Ethiopia, 1950–1962* (1962, 7 l.) and *Ethiopian survey*, compiled by Annette Delaney (Jan. 1964, 12 l.). Although emphasis is on English-language publications, included also are those in Russian (titles transliterated and translated), French, German, Italian, and other languages. Entries are arranged by subject, and there is an author index.

2445 Baylor, Jim, comp. *Ethiopia: A list of works in English.* Berkeley, Calif. (privately circulated), Mar. 1966. 60, 6 l. mimeo. 2d ed. 1967. 60, 10 l.
Works listed are grouped by subject. Periodical articles are not included unless printed separately. There are selected governmental publications. In the first edition the addenda consist of two pages of 'Additions, changes, and deletions' and a four-page index; in the second edition, additional entries only.

2446 Fumagalli, Giuseppe. *Bibliografia etiopica: Catalogo descrittivo e ragionato degli scritti pubblicati dalla invenzione della stampa fino a tutto il 1891, intorno alla Etiopia e regioni limitrofe.* Milano, U. Hoepli, 1893. xi, 288 p.
Usually cited as the most comprehensive and renowned bibliography of Ethiopica and Amharica from the earliest records to the end of the 19th century.
   This work was supplemented by Silvo Zanutto in his *Bibliografia etiopica, in continuazione alla 'Bibliografia etiopica' die G. Fumagalli* (Roma, published for the Ministry of Colonies by the Sindicato Italiano Arti Grafiche, 1929, 2 v.). The first volume, *1. Contributo* (54 p.), which was reprinted in a 1936 edition, is a bibliography of bibliographies, a general survey organized according to broad subject fields, including catalogues and reading lists in published studies. The second, *Contributo* (1932, 178 p.), lists 'Manoscritti etiopici' – presumably those discovered since 1891.
   In the chief 19th-century English work on Ethiopia, published following the punitive expedition against the Emperor Theodore in 1867, *Abyssinia and its people: or, Life in the land of Prester John*, ed. by John Camden Hotten (London, 1868, 384 p.), the last 15 pages were given to a 'Bibliography of all the known works relating to Abyssinia', comprising, according to the editor, 'a tolerably perfect list of the books and tracts which have been published upon that country'. For a major bibliography by Harold Marcus, see Addenda.

2447 Laborde, Marquis Léon E. S. J. de. *Voyages en Abyssinie: Analyse critique des voyages qui on été faits dans ce pays et des ouvrages qu'on a publié sur son histoire, sa religion et ses moeurs.* [n.p.] 1938. 87 p. (150 entries)

2448 Simon, J. 'Bibliographie éthiopienne, 1946–1951'. *Orientalia*, v. 21, 1952: 47–66, 209–230.
This list of 411 references is a continuation of Carlo Conti Rossini's 'Pubblicazioni etiopica dal 1936 al 1945', *Rassegna di Studi Etiopici*, 1944, p. 1–132.

2449   Somer, John. *A study guide for Ethiopia and the Horn of Africa.* Boston, Boston University, 1969. 94 p.
Prepared for the Agency for International Development. Each section contains a general note drawing attention to the most important work on a particular topic, followed by a bibliography. The main headings are physical environment, early external influences, traditional societies, colonial rule and nationalism, politics, social change, and the economic system. There is also a general bibliography.

2450   Wright, Stephen G., comp. *Ethiopian incunabula [a bibliography of pre-1936 printed material produced in Ethiopia].* Compiled from the collections in the National Library of Ethiopia and the Haile Selassie I University. Addis Ababa, Commercial Printing Press, 1967. 107 p.
'Incunabula' is defined in this case as all books printed in Ethiopia before the Italian occupation of 1936–41. Newspapers and other serials are excluded and only books found in the National Library and the University Library are covered by the 223 items. Section 1 consists of a subject index. In the body of the bibliography, Section 2, entries are arranged by town of printing, then by printing press. Detailed bibliographical data are given for the entries, virtually all of which are in Amharic (others are in Italian). Section 3 is a rough chronological listing of the books. A second, more comprehensive edition is planned.

Serials

2451   *Ethiopia Observer : Journal of Independent Opinion, Economics, History and the Arts.* v. 1, no. 1– . Dec. 1956– . Ed. by Richard and Rita Pankhurst. Addis Ababa. illus. Quarterly.
Articles on a wide range of topics concerned with Ethiopia are sometimes of monograph length. A chronology, 'Ethiopian record', occupies the last pages.
Among the most important organs for study of Ethiopian culture and Ethiopica is the journal founded by the late Italian Ethiopicist, Carlo Rossini, *Rassegna di Studi Etiopica* (1941– , Istituto Studi Orientali, Centro di Studi Etiopici e Cristiano-Orientali, Università di Roma).

2452   *Ethiopian Economic Review.* no. 1– . Dec. 1959– . Issued by the Imperial Ethiopian Government Ministry of Commerce and Industry. Addis Ababa. tables. Irregular.
Official journal reviewing the economic life of Ethiopia. A large, well-printed magazine, its text is equally divided between articles on general and specific aspects of economic life and statistical tables of external trade, industry, finances, etc. In no. 5, Feb. 1962, an inserted green-paper section lists businesses in the empire of Ethiopia. The periodical follows and supersedes *Economic handbook*, also published by the Ministry of Commerce and Industry (Dec. 1958, 93, 119 p.), which in turn superseded an illustrated volume, *Economic progress of Ethiopia* (Addis Ababa, 1955, 171 p.).

2453   *Ethiopian Geographical Journal.* v. 1, no. 1– . June 1963– . Addis Ababa. Semi-annual.
Scholarly journal published by the Mapping and Geography Institute of Ethiopia. The text is in Amharic and English.

2454   *Journal of Ethiopian Law.* v. 1– . 1964– . Addis Ababa, Faculty of Law, Haile Selassie I University, in co-operation with the Ministry of Justice. Semi-annual.
Each issue of the journal includes a table of cases reported, case reports, current

Part III: area guide (by colonial power, region and colony)

issues, articles commenting on various aspects of Ethiopian law, and a book review section that first appeared in 1966. The last issue each year has an annual index to cases reported and an index of laws cited.

2455 *Journal of Ethiopian Studies.* no. 1– . 1963– . Addis Ababa, Institute of Ethiopian Studies, Haile Selassie I University. Semi-annual.

The Institute, established in January 1963 and directed by Dr. Richard Pankhurst, serves as the University's principal institution for research in all fields relating to Ethiopia.

Reference works

2456 American University, Washington, D.C. Foreign Areas Study Division. *Area handbook for Ethiopia.* By George A. Lipsky and others. 2d ed. Washington, June 1964. xi, 621 p. maps, charts, graphs, tables. Includes bibliographies.

One of a series of country surveys, this handbook was originally published in October 1960, and the 1964 edition appears to be an unaltered reprint. It presents basic background information in four sections: social (including physical setting and historical data), economic, political, and military. Each section is followed by a bibliography, the longest running eight pages. (A 1971 revised edition was issued.)

2457 Food and Agriculture Organization of the United Nations. *Agriculture in Ethiopia.* Comp. by H. P. Huffnagel, consultant to FAO. Rome, 1961. xv, 484 p. illus., maps (part fold.), tables. Bibliography: p. 481–484.

Exhaustive survey of Ethiopian agriculture, covering physical characteristics, economic conditions, agricultural practices, production of specific crops, animal husbandry, marketing and processing, forestry, fisheries, agricultural administration, research and education, and agricultural credit.

2458 Greenfield, Richard. *Ethiopia: A new political history.* New York, Praeger, 1965. 515 p. illus., maps, tables. (Praeger Library of African Affairs) Bibliographical footnotes.

An interpretative, readable account by a former dean and assistant to the president of Haile Selassie I University. Ethiopia's complicated history is carefully traced from earliest times to the 1960s (Ethiopian roots, Ethiopia emergent, war with Italy, etc.). Appendices include the Ethiopian calendar, Ethiopian titles and modes of address, and statistical tables. An index is included.

2459 Huntingford, George W. B. *The Galla of Ethiopia: The kingdoms of Kafa and Janjero.* London, International African Institute, 1955. 156 p. (Ethnographic Survey of Africa, North-eastern Africa, pt. 2) Bibliography: p. 145–147.

See general note on this series, no. 333.

The Galla, a pastoral people whose original home was possibly in what used to be British Somaliland, invaded and have spread widely over southern and eastern Ethiopia during the past 400 years, and now form one of the more important stocks of that country. For this handbook the main sources were the important older works of French, German, and Italian authorities. The author readily admitted that because of the difficult nature of the Galla country and the lack of recent studies, it was impossible to say whether the mores he described were still prevalent. For more recent works see Herbert S. Lewis, *A Galla monarchy: Jemma Abba Jifar, Ethiopia, 1830–1932* (Madison, University of Wisconsin Press, 1965, 148 p., illus., maps; bibliography, p. 135–142); and

Ethiopia

Eike Haberland, *Galla Süd-Aethiopiens* (Stuttgart, W. Kohlhammer, 1959, xix, 815 p., illus., plates, maps; Frobenius Institut, Frankfurt am Main, *Völker Süd-Aetiopiens*, v. 2), which includes an English summary.

2460 International Conference of Ethiopian Studies, 2d, Manchester University, 1963. *Ethiopian studies: Papers read at the Second International Conference of Ethiopian Studies, Manchester University, July 1963.* Prepared under the patronage of His Imperial Majesty the Emperor of Ethiopia. Manchester, Eng., Manchester University Press, 1964. xv, 264 p. (*Journal of Semitic Studies*, v. 9, no. 1)

There are 31 articles in English, French, German, and Italian, more than half of them concerned with archaeology and linguistics. The Proceedings of the Third International Conference, Addis Ababa, 1966, were at the press in 1969.

2461 Levine, Donald Nathan. *Wax and gold: Tradition and innovation in Ethiopian culture.* Chicago, University of Chicago Press, 1965. xvi, 315 p. plates, map, tables. Bibliographical footnotes.

A thorough, well-written account of Amharic culture rather than of Ethiopian society. A brief historical summary from 1270 is followed by a detailed discussion of Amharic life and of the many and great contradictions between tradition and modernity in present-day Ethiopia. A four-page glossary and an index are included.

2462 Lipsky, George A., in collaboration with Wendall Blanchard, Abraham M. Hirsch, and Bela C. Maday. *Ethiopia: Its people, its society, its culture.* New Haven, Conn., HRAF Press, 1962. 376 p. maps, tables, diagrs. (Survey of World Cultures, no. 9) Bibliography: p. 343–357.

Intended to meet the need for a 'comprehensive reliable volume' synthesizing the most authoritative materials on Ethiopia in all aspects of behavioural sciences. The presentation is encyclopaedic, with chapters divided into sections with subheadings, the writing in easy narrative style. The book concludes with tabulated statistical data, a selected bibliography, and a full index.

2463 Marein, Nathan. *The Ethiopian empire: Federation and laws.* Rotterdam, Royal Netherlands Printing and Lithographing Co., 1955. 456 p. port.

A compendium for Ethiopian lawyers and judges and for foreigners concerned with laws relating to Ethiopian commerce and finance, by the Advocate General and General Adviser to the Imperial Ethiopian Government. This 1955 volume superseded two earlier guides, *Handbook to the laws of Ethiopia* (Addis Ababa, 1949, 207 p.) and *The judicial system and the laws of Ethiopia* (Rotterdam, Royal Netherlands Printing and Lithographing Co., 1951, 288 p.).

2464 Pankhurst, Estelle Sylvia. *Ethiopia: A cultural history.* Essex, Eng., Lalibela House, 1955. xxxviii, 747 p. illus. (part col.), ports.

Monumental tome presenting a 'comprehensive' survey of Ethiopian history and culture. Based on careful study and including much good archaeological and artistic material, as exemplified in the plates, it is a basic account in English, with an enormous amount of detail. Much of this is in the form of long quotations from Ethiopian records, papers, and documents testifying to the glories of the past and the virtuous accomplishments of the present. Richard Pankhurst is preparing a volume on the economic history from 1800 to 1935. See also Richard Pankhurst, *An introduction to the history of the Ethiopian army* (Addis Ababa, 1967).

2465 Perham, Margery. *The government of Ethiopia.* London, Faber and Faber, 1948. xxiii, 481 p. Reprinted 1969. Bibliography: p. 457–464.

Standard work on Ethiopian government and political history up to the post-war Restoration. In the introduction of her skilful, far-ranging study the author comments that the book was designed to offset the distortions of propaganda regarding Ethiopia, which since the Italian aggression had become the subject for an emotional approach unsupported by 'serious information'.

2466 Trimingham, John S. *Islam in Ethiopia.* London and New York, Oxford University Press, 1952. xv, 299 p. maps. Reissue, New York, Barnes & Noble, 1965. xv, 299 p.

A major contribution to Islamic studies, surveying Islam, its history and extent in the entire region of the Horn of Africa, including Eritrea and the Somalilands as well as the highland kingdom, which is designated as Abyssinia. Canon Trimingham begins with an account of the region, its peoples, and distribution of religions, then considers in historic terms the centuries-old conflict of Islam with the Christian religion that had been brought to Abyssinia in the days of the Early Church. His third part is a detailed analysis of the tribal distribution of Islam in Ethiopia – Beni Amir, Danakil, Galla, Somali, and many minor groups, including Negroid tribes. Last, the special characteristics of Islam in Ethiopia are examined, as well as the interplay of influence with paganism and Westernism.

A booklet by this author, *The Christian Church and missions in Ethiopia (including Eritrea and the Somalilands)* (London and New York, World Dominion Press, 1950, 73 p., fold. maps; Survey Series), contains a short statement of the general religious background and of the National Church of Ethiopia, which since 1951 has been distinct from the Coptic Church in Egypt and has an Ethiopian Coptic archbishop. There follows a systematic examination of missions and their work in the Horn of Africa before, during, and since the Italian occupation, their connexion with the Ethiopian National Church, and their proselytizing efforts among pagans and Muslims.

The standard work on the Ethiopian Coptic Church is by Harry M. Hyatt, *The Church of Abyssinia* (London, Luzac, 1928, 302 p.).

2467 Trudeau, E. *Higher education in Ethiopia.* Montreal, 1964. 195 l. graphs, tables. Processed. Bibliography: p. 186–195.

This doctoral project first surveys the overall development of education in Ethiopia and the foundations and progress of higher education (1951–61). The author then describes Haile Selassie I University and concludes with a discussion of problems and prospects in planning the future development of higher education.

2468 Ullendorff, Edward. *The Ethiopians: An introduction to country and people.* London and New York, Oxford University Press, 1960. 232 p. illus. Rev. ed. 1964. Bibliography: p. 207–213.

By an Ethiopicist who has spent over 20 years in the study of Ethiopian languages and civilizations. His survey begins with a review of explorations and studies, followed by a background of country and people and then by an outline of history. The focus is on cultural factors, explained in chapters on religion, languages, literature, art and music, daily life and customs; only the last chapter, 'Ethiopia today', touches on modern politico-economic matters. The work is dedicated to Haile Selassie, by whose 'high example . . . no one living in Ethiopia can fail to be inspired'.

A book on the Emperor, by Leonard O. Mosley, a British writer of popular histories and biographies, is *Haile Selassie: The conquering lion* (Englewood Cliffs., N.J., Prentice-Hall, 1965, 288 p., illus.).

ADDENDA

PART I: GUIDE TO REFERENCE MATERIALS

LIBRARIES AND ARCHIVES

WESTERN EUROPE

Belgium

2469 Geeraerts, Pierre. *La Bibliothèque Africaine : Quatre-vingt-cinq ans d'activité bibliographique africaine.* Bruxelles, Bibliothèque Africaine, 1972. 90 p.
A useful history of the library founded by Léopold II and a listing (44 pages) of rare works housed in the library. La Bibliothèque Africaine houses over 300,000 volumes, 800 periodical titles, a large collection of maps and microfilms dealing with Central Africa from the 16th century to the present. Various bibliographies, findings, and accounts of the library are listed also in this pamphlet. The library and archives are under the Ministère des Affaires Etrangères.

France

2470 Tantet, V. *Catalogue méthodique de la Bibliothèque du Ministère des Colonies.* Melun, 1905. 652 p.
Not available for examination.

Great Britain

2471 Matthews, Noel, and M. Doreen Wainwright, comps. *A guide to manuscripts and documents in the British Isles relating to Africa.* Edited by J. D. Pearson. London, Oxford University Press, 1971. 321 p.
' Africa ' refers to Africa south of the Sahara. The guide lists papers, official and unofficial, of ' explorers, traders, missionaries, politicians, administrators, soldiers, sailors, doctors, nurses, natural historians ' . . . Papers listed are not necessarily open to scholars. Arrangement is by city. For each depository the guide gives address, brief history and/or description and period of access if known. This volume is the United Kingdom contribution to the series ' Guide to the Sources of the History of Africa ', published under the auspices of UNESCO by the International Council on Archives. The last section of the guide lists ' Papers in Private Ownership '. There is an index.

Addenda

AFRICA

West Africa

Nigeria

2472 Northern Nigeria, Archives. *Finding aids at the National Archives, Kaduna, Northern Nigeria.* Kaduna, 1971. 13 p.
A listing of major record groups for which simple lists have been prepared: Secretariat Northern Provinces Papers; Northern Nigerian Government Papers, Provincial Offices Papers, Special Lists, Inventories and Handlists and Arabic manuscripts.

Sierra Leone

2473 Howard, Allen, 'Survey of provincial and district archives, Northern Province, Sierra Leone.' *Sierra Leone Studies*, July 1966: 124–45.

French West Africa

2474 *Inventaire méthodique des cartes et croquis, imprimés et manuscrits relatifs à l'Afrique occidentale existant au Gouvernement Général de l'A.O.F. à Dakar; établi sur l'ordre de M. le Gouverneur Général de l'A.O.F. par le Commandant Ed. de Martonne.* Laval, Goupil, 1926. 139 p.

Senegal

2475 Senegal. Archives Nationales. *Répertoire des archives sous série 2G: Rapports périodiques, 1895–1940.* Dakar, Archives Nationales, 1967. 2 v.
A guide to the files and reports (monthly, quarterly and annual) of the governors and chiefs of divisions of the colonies of French West Africa. Arranged chronologically. Compiled by Abdoulaye Gamby N'Diaye.

PART II: SUBJECT GUIDE FOR AFRICA IN GENERAL

ECONOMICS

2476 Baltzer, Franz. *Die Kolonialbahnen mit besonderer Berücksichtigung Afrikas.* Berlin and Leipzig, 1916. 462 p.
Covers railway construction and development in Africa and economic connections with the colonies, especially North Africa, Ethiopia, German East Africa, Mozambique, South Africa, Angola, Cameroun and West Africa. Standard work on the subject with tables, statistics, maps, illustrations.

Addenda

SOCIOLOGY

2477 Ajaegbu, Hyacinth I., comp. *African urbanization: A bibliography.* London, International African Institute, 1972. 78 p.
Nearly 3,000 references covering books, articles, research papers and government publications arranged by region and country. There is an index to individual towns and an author index. Replaces the 1965 work *African urbanization : A reading list of selected books, articles and reports* (London, International African Institute, 1965, Africa Bibliography, Series B).

PART III: AREA GUIDE

BRITISH AFRICA

Reference work

2478 Masefield, G. B. *A history of the Colonial Agricultural Service.* Oxford, Clarendon Press, 1972, 176 p.
The Colonial Agricultural Service was founded in 1935 and lasted for 31 years. During the term of its existence nearly 1,000 graduate agricultural scientists served in the African territories under British colonial sway. This is the history of its achievements.

WEST AFRICA

Nigeria

Bibliography

2479 Ombu, Jigekuma A., comp. *Niger Delta studies, 1627–1967 : A bibliography.* Ibadan, Nigeria, Ibadan University Press, 1970. 138 p. map. (Ibadan University Library. Bibliographical series 2)
Covers all types of literature on the Niger Delta. E. J. Alagoa has provided a note on archival material.

Reference works

2480 Afigbo, A. E. *The warrant chiefs : Indirect rule in southeastern Nigeria 1891–1929.* New York, Humanities Press, 1972. 338 p. Bibliography: p. 319–27. (Ibadan History Series)
A major political history of the Ibo, Ibibio, Ijo and Ogoja peoples under colonial rule. Afigbo has written a first-rate piece of revisionist history: revisionist in supplying proof that indirect rule was introduced into Southern Nigeria as well as into Northern Nigeria, and revisionist in its devastating analysis of how flawed indirect rule was in south-eastern Nigeria. The British did not in fact rule through indigenous chiefs or political organizations. The warrant chiefs, created by the colonial administration, in some cases from slaves, cheated, abused and extorted forced labour and money from their charges. Only the Natives Court system eventually became a beneficial part of the warrant chief system.

465

Addenda

2481 Murray, David John, ed. *Studies in Nigerian administration.* London, Hutchinson Educational Ltd., 1970. lx, 324 p., tables.

Contributors include the editor, L. Adamolekun, R. O. Teriba, F. J. Fletcher, O. Nwanwene, R. K. Harrison, G. M. Walker and R. L. Harris. The work provides details on such subjects as organization of the service, its social background, ministerial control and taxation. It is intended to be of practical use to administrators, and was published under the auspices of the Institute of Administration at the University of Ife.

2482 Whitaker, Jr., C. S. *The politics of tradition: Continuity and change in Northern Nigeria 1946–1966.* Princeton, Princeton University Press, 1970. 563 p. Bibliography: 509–46.

Whitaker focuses on internal political experiences of Northern Nigeria between 1946 and 1966. He stresses continuity and change of the traditional political system of the North during the colonial period. The impact of colonial rule on the emirates is the central subject of the study. Part one treats of why and how officials fashioned a program of reform based on both traditional and modern conceptions of government. Part two deals with the political results of the policy; and Part three is concerned with the regional emirate politics and how they influenced one another. A long bibliography and a biographical directory of Northern Nigerian political leaders add to the value of this major study.

BRITISH CENTRAL AFRICA

Southern Rhodesia

2483 Murray, David John. *The governmental system in Southern Rhodesia.* Oxford, Clarendon Press, 1970. xxi, 393 p., map. Bibliography: p. 372–384.

The author seeks to interpret the governmental system as ' one significant part of the general political and administrative system of the society '. He considers that whereas the pre-UDI system had emphasized the pursuit of separate white occupational interests, the post-UDI system replaced the old ruling group for the purpose of safeguarding whites against Africans.

SOUTHERN AFRICA

Reference works

2484 Houghton, D. Hobart, and Jenifer Dagut. *Source material on the South African economy: 1860–1970.* Cape Town, Oxford University Press, 1972– . 3 v.

A basic collection of documentary extracts. There is a general introduction for each volume, with short explanatory preludes for each section. Though forced to be selective, the compilers have tried to make their material ' representative of all shades of opinion '. There is an index to sources cited, as well as a general index.

Volume 1 covers the period 1860 to 1899. The first portion of the book illustrates the state of the economy in the early 1860s; the second illustrates the mining revolution, in both its economic and social aspects. At the time of writing, only the first volume had appeared. Houghton, a leading South African free enterprise economist, is the author also of *The South African economy* (Cape Town, Oxford University Press, 1964).

Addenda

2485 Hyam, Ronald. *The failure of South African expansion 1908–1914.* New York, Africana Publishing Corporation, 1972. 219 p. illus., maps.

A thorough, scholarly study that outlines the reasons for South Africa's inability to absorb the British High Commission territories and expand its borders to the Zambezi. The author is concerned only with political expansion, and not with the development of South Africa's indirect influence through trade, diplomacy and investments. Hyam also wrote *Elgin and Churchill at the Colonial Office 1905–1908* (London, Macmillan, 1968).

2486 Laidler, Percy Ward, and Michael Gelfand. *South Africa; its medical history : A medical and social study.* Capetown, C. Struik, 1971. xii, 536 p. illus., ports.

Standard history with detailed references to wider problems concerning social conditions and public welfare. A medical success story. Michael Gelfand is the author also of medico-social histories of Malawi (no. 919), Rhodesia (no. 965) and Zambia (no. 941).

2487 MacCrone, I. D. *Race attitudes in South Africa : Historical, experimental and psychological studies.* Johannesburg, Witwatersrand University Press, 1957. Bibliography: p. 311–317.

Reprint of a classic first published in 1937. The author provides a detailed historical analysis, and presents experimental data compiled in the 1930s, based on social distance testing as between South Africans of differing ancestry.

2488 Marks, Shula. *Reluctant rebellion : The 1906–08 disturbances in Natal.* Oxford, Clarendon Press, 1970, xxv, 404 p., maps. (Oxford Studies in African Affairs.) Bibliography: p. 366–382.

A detailed analysis of the Zulu rebellion, based on extensive archival material in the Public Record Office, London, in the Natal Archives, in missionary and other private collections. The author tries to see the Zulu rising in its wider social and political setting. She concludes that the disturbances helped to orient politically conscious Africans toward ' a wider political organization which would embrace Africans all over Southern Africa '.

2489 Saron, Gustav, and Louis Hotz, eds. *The Jews in South Africa; a history.* Cape Town, Oxford University Press, 1955. xvii, 422 p., illus. Bibliographical note: p. 405–408.

Standard work on the subject. An older book, still valuable, is Louis Herrman, *The Jews in South Africa from the earliest times to 1895* (London, Victor Gollancz, 1930). Specialized studies include Israel Abrahams, *The birth of a community : A history of Western Province Jewry from earliest times to the end of the South African war, 1902* (Cape Town, Hebrew Congregation, 1955); and Frieda H. Sichel, *From refugee to citizen : A sociological study of the immigrants from Hitler Europe who settled in southern Africa* (Capetown, A. A. Balkema, 1966). A. A. Jonker, *Israël : Die Sondebok* (Capetown, Central News Agency, 1940) is a pro-Jewish work that pays special attention to the role of Jews among the Afrikaners.

2490 Wilson, Francis. *Labour in the South African gold mines, 1911–1969.* Cambridge University Press, 1972. xviii, 218 p., tables, illus. (African Studies Series, no. 6)

An investigation concerning the economics of migrant labour and of the colour bar in mining. The author argues that African cash earnings were no higher in 1969 than they had been in 1911, possibly even lower. Wilson's study was compiled in the liberal tradition of scholars such as Sheila T. van der Horst, author of *Native labour in South Africa* (London, Oxford University Press, 1942,

Addenda

340 p.), a classic, based on a London University dissertation; and *African workers in town : A study of labour in Cape Town* (Cape Town, Oxford University Press, 1964, 140 p.).

FRENCH AFRICA

Note French government bodies directly concerned with the administration of overseas possessions, c. 1848–1964: Under the Second Republic, colonial affairs were the responsibility of the Direction des Colonies of the Ministère de la Marine. In 1858, the government of the Second Empire placed the direction under the newly created Ministère de l'Algérie et des Colonies. It was reunited with the Ministère de la Marine in 1860, and in 1881 was made part of the Ministère du Commerce et des Colonies. In 1882, it was again attached to the Ministère de la Marine. Constituted an 'autonomous administration' in 1885, it was placed under the Ministère du Commerce et de l'Industrie in 1889. In 1892, it was attached to the Ministère de la Marine and was placed again under the Ministère du Commerce et de l'Industrie later that year. In 1894, the Administration des Colonies (the successor of the Direction des Colonies) was raised to ministerial level.

The Ministère des Colonies was responsible for colonial affairs from 1894 to 1946, when it was superseded by the Ministère de la France d'Outre-Mer. Beginning in 1959, this ministry was gradually dissolved, and many of its functions were assumed by agencies attached to the office of the Prime Minister. In 1960, affairs of the overseas departments and territories (e.g., Réunion and the Comoro Islands) were the responsibility of the Ministère d'État Chargé du Sahara, des Départements et Territoires d'Outre-Mer.

Reference works

2491 Cohen, William B. *Rulers of Empire : The French Colonial Service in Africa.* Stanford, Hoover Institution Press, 1971. xv, 279 p., maps, tables illus. Bibliography: p. 249–272.
The standard history of the subject and the only one of its kind. The author covers the background, training, career structure and organisation of the service, changing doctrines of government, the role of the Ecole Coloniale, and related subjects. The author has not only used archival material, but has also made wide use of interviews. Appendices provide a list of colonial ministers and under-secretaries, a sample questionnaire used by the writer, and detailed notes. There is a wealth of monographs on more detailed subjects. One of them is Gérard Peureux, *Le Haut Conseil de l'Union Française : Sa constitution et son oeuvre (1946–1958),* Paris, Librairie Générale de Droit et de Jurisprudence, 1960.

FRENCH WEST AFRICA

Reference works

2492 French West Africa. Grand Conseil. *Bulletin. Procès-verbaux.* no. 1– . 1948– . Dakar, Grand Impr. Africaine.
Established in 1947, the Grand Conseil had broader powers than its predecessor, the Conseil de Gouvernement. It decided the federal Budget and the bases of

assessment of all taxes, and it advised the High Commissioner (Governor General) on the allocation of funds for public works and agricultural development. Following the enactment of the Loi-Cadre in 1956, many of its powers were transferred to the territorial assemblies. It was composed of forty members (five elected by each territorial assembly), and it usually held two sessions a year. A commission permanente carried on its work between sessions. The Grand Conseil published various series, for example, *Allocution prononcée par ... à la séance d'ouverture de la ... session*. Rufisque. 1948–59.

2493 Lenfant, Eugene A. *Le Niger: Voie ouverte à notre empire africaine.* Paris, Hachette, 1903. 252 p.

An important source for the French occupation, the services of the Niger Company and British activities in the area. A wealth of details on trade and commerce. Lenfant was a leading French explorer and authority on Niger and Chad. See also his *La découverte des grandes sources du centre de l'Afrique* (Paris, 1909, 283 p.).

2494 O'Brien, Rita Cruise. *White society in black Africa: The French of Senegal.* London, Faber and Faber, 1972. 320 p. Maps, tables, illus. Bibliography: p. 304–313.

An historical, economic and sociological study of the French residents, based on both written sources and field work. The author pays special attention to race relations and to the expatriates' role in the economy.

2495 Tauxier, Louis. *Moeurs et histoire des Peuls.* Paris, Payot, 1937. 422 p.

———— *Le noir de Bondoukou, Koulangos, Dyoulos, Abrons...* Paris, E. Leroux, 1921. 770 p. (Etudes soudanaises)

———— *Le noir du Soudan. Pays mossi et Gourounsi. Documents et analyses.* Paris, Larose, 1912. 796 p.

———— *Le noir du Yatenga.* Paris, Larose, 1917. 790 p. (Etudes soudanaises)

———— *La religion bambara.* Paris, Guenther, 1927. 472 p. (Etudes soudanaises)

Important anthropological works by a scholar-administrator of A.O.F.

Mauritania

2496 Van Maele, Bernard. *Bibliographie Mauritanie. Avec la collaboration de Adam Heymowski. Edition provisoire.* Nouakchott, Ministère de l'Information et de la Culture, Ministère de la Planification et de la Recherche, 1971. 108 p. Mimeo.

Some 1,400 titles of books articles and government publications arranged under the following headings: social sciences, Islam, archaeology and pre-colonial history (contact with Europeans) and geography.

Niger

2497 Centre Nigérien de Recherches en Sciences Humaines, IFAN-C.N.R.S.H. *Bibliographie sommaire de la République du Niger.* Niamey, 1970. 50 p.

Lists books and periodical articles. Arranged alphabetically by author. Cites works from the 19th century to 1970.

Addenda

BELGIAN AFRICA

Belgian Congo (Zaïre)

Reference works

2498 Belgium Corps Législatif. *Table alphabétique décennale des pièces imprimées par ordre de la Chambre de Représentants et du Sénat, 1901–1902 à 1910–1911 ... suivie de la table analytique des documents relatifs à l'origin et à l'annexation de l'Etat Indépendant du Congo.* Bruxelles, Hayez, 1912. 488 p.

2499 Na Wundu, Lutumba-Lu–Vilu. *Histoire du Zaïre: L'administration centrale du Ministère Belge des Colonies 1908–1940. Structure et fonctionnement.* Kinshasa, Editions Okapi, 1972. Bibliography: p. 7–20.
A detailed administrative history covering, in fact, the period from 1885 to 1940. The author first describes the administrative structure of the Etat Indépendant du Congo and then the organization of the Belgian colonial system. In each case he provides data concerning general organizations, the various departments, personnel (including details concerning their background and salaries) and financial administration, as well as relations between the government and other bodies. The bibliographical information is supplemented by more than a thousand footnotes.

2500 Peemans, Jean-Philippe. *Diffusion du progrès économique et convergence des prix : Le cas Congo-Belgique, 1900–1960.* Louvain, Editions Nouwelaerts, 1969. 520 p.
A major attempt to analyse changes in both the European and African economic sectors of the Belgian Congo from 1900 to 1960.

2501 Schwetz, Jacques. *L'évolution de la médecine au Congo Belge.* Bruxelles, Office de Publicité, 1946. 129 p. (Université Libre de Bruxelles. Institut de Sociologie Solvay. Actualités sociales. Nouv. sér.)
The author, a physician, traces the development of the Congolese medical service, and also the various campaigns against individual diseases, such as sleeping-sickness and malaria. The writer has contributed also an essay, ' Le peuplement blanc du Congo : le point de vue médical ', in *Deux études sur le Congo Belge* (Université Libre de Bruxelles. Institut de Sociologie Solvay, 1945).

GERMAN AFRICA

Bibliography

2502 Dresler, Adolf. ' Die deutsche koloniale Presse in Afrika ', in Paul Rohrbach, ed., *Afrika : Beiträge zu einer praktischen Kolonialkunde.* Berlin, Werner and Co., 1943, pp. 294–301.
A complete review concerning the German journals published in the African colonies, grouped by territory.

Addenda

Togo

2503 Schlunk, Martin. *Die Norddeutsche Mission in Togo.* Bremen, Verlag der Norddeutschen Missions-Gesellschaft, 1910–12. 2 v., illus., maps, ports. Bibliography: v. 2, p. 169–170.
The Norddeutsche Missions-Gesellschaft, a Lutheran group founded in Hamburg in 1836, concentrated its activities on the Ewe people. Schlunk's study, a basic work, describes in the first volume a journey through the Ewe country, and in the second volume deals with wider missionary problems. Schlunk was the author also of *Das Schulwesen in den deutschen Schutzgebieten* (Hamburg, Friedrichsen, 1914), as well as of no. 2062, both of which deal with African education.

ITALIAN AFRICA

Reference works

2504 Italy. Corte di Assise, Rome. *Processo Graziani.* Rome, Ruffolo, [1948–1950]. 3 v., illus., tables.
Marshal Rodolfo Graziani, who had campaigned widely in the Italian colonies, became viceroy of Italian East Africa, and later commander-in-chief of the Italian forces in North Africa during World War II. Although subsequently tried by an Italian court for collaborating with the Germans, he was released in 1950. The trial, first conducted before the Corte di Assise, was later transferred to the Tribunale Militare Territoriale at Rome. The first volume contains Graziani's own defence, with references to his colonial record. The second and third volumes comprise testimony given at the court and other documents.

2505 Italy. Ministerio degli Affari Esteri. Direzione Centrale degli Affari Coloniali. *Raccolta di pubblicazioni coloniali italiane : Primo indice bibliografico.* Rome, Tip. della Camera dei Deputati, 1911. ix, 357 p.
Lists a total of 1,501 items in Italian that have a bearing on Italian colonization. The first section lists publications concerning East Africa in general, Ethiopia and Eritrea arranged alphabetically by author. The second part deals with Italian Somaliland and its neighbours. The third section, which is arranged according to topic, includes biography and bibliography, exploration, linguistics and letters, history, natural sciences, periodical publications and miscellanea.

2506 Rochat, Giorgio. *Militari e politici nella preparazione della campagna d'Etiopia : Studio e documenti 1932–1936.* Milano, Franco Angeli, 1971. 514 p., maps, documents: p. 276–509.
The best existing book on Italian military preparations for the Ethiopian campaign, copiously annotated, with extensive documentation, based on archival sources, especially the Badoglio papers in the Archivio Centrale dello Stato. The author seeks to place Italian military preparations in the wider context of Italian society under the Fascist regime. Rochat is author also of a standard work on the earlier history of the Italian army entitled *L'esercito italiano da Vittorio Veneto a Mussolini (1919–1925)* (Bari, Laterza, 1967. 609 p.).

Addenda

PORTUGUESE AFRICA

Bibliography

2507 Nunes, José Lucio, and José Júlio Gonçalves. *Bibliografia historico-militar do ultramar português.* Lisbon, 1956. 398 p.
A simple listing of 1,802 books, articles and pamphlets that treat of military history in the Portuguese empire. The majority of items deal with Africa. Contains an index organized by colonies.

Reference works

2508 Andrade Corvo, João de. *Estudos sobre as províncias ultramarinas.* Lisbon, Academia Real das Sciencias, 1883–87. 4 v., tables.
Portuguese colonization is first discussed by region, including Cabo Verde, S. Tomé, Angola, and Mozambique. The second part of the study deals with the indigenous peoples, with special regard to economic and administrative questions. Contains valuable statistics. A more succinct work, dating from the same period, is Manuel Chagas Pinheiro, *As colónias portuguezas no século XIX (1811–1890)* (Lisbon, A. M. Pereira, 1890).

2509 Nunes Barata, José Fernando. *Estudos sobre a economia do ultramar.* Lisbon, Centro de Estudos Políticos e Sociais, 1963. 232 p., tables.
A series of articles dealing with demographic development, the economy of Guinea, general problems of economic growth, Catholic doctrine and imperial economic development. Especially valuable for the statistical tables. An older work, valuable for trade statistics, is *A evolução comercial da metrópole e das colónias* (Lisbon, Agência-Geral das Colónias, 1928). A highly critical study, which questions the efficacy of Portuguese economic development and suggests that the Portuguese colonies might be turned into League of Nations Mandates, is Elemér Böhm, *La mise en valeur des colonies portugaises* (Paris, Presses Universitaires de France, c. 1935. 231 p.).

Angola

Reference works

2510 Macedo, José de. *Autonomia de Angola: Estudos de administração colonial.* Lisbon, Typographia Leiria, 1910. 278 p. tables.
An administrative as well as an economic study furnished with bibliographical footnotes. The author wrote a more general work also: *As nossas riquezas coloniaes; memória* (Lisbon, Impr. Nacional, 1901), published under the auspices of the Congresso Colonial Nacional.

2511 Mendes, Afonso. *A Huíla e Moçâmedes: Considerações sobre o trabalho indígena.* Lisbon, Centro de Estudos Políticos e Sociais, 1958, 208 p. Bibliography: p. 207–208.
A defence of Portuguese labour policies. The author investigates what he regards as the problem of native labour shortage, and then considers health problems, the workmen's own attitudes, problems of labour productivity, industrial accidents

Addenda

and so forth. He strongly opposes the influence of 'foreign' trade unions and of the United Nations.

Mozambique

Reference works

2512 Ennes, António. *A Guerra d'Africa em 1895 : Memórias.* Lisbon, Typographia do 'Dia ', 1898. 573 p., maps.
A detailed study of Luso-African struggles in the Lourenço Marques region and of the campaign against Gungunhana, written by the Portuguese victor. Appended documents provide details concerning Portuguese military and administrative dispositions. Another work dealing with the pacification era from the gubernatorial standpoint is Albino Fernandes de Sá, *João de Almeida : Governador da Huíla* (Sá da Bandeira, 1963).

2513 Isaacman, Allen F. *Mozambique, the Africanization of a European institution : The Zambesi prazos, 1750–1902.* Madison, University of Wisconsin Press, 1972. xviii, 260 p. Bibliography: p. 238–252.
A thoroughly documented work; outlines how prazo owners came increasingly to resemble indigenous chiefs. Giuseppe Papagno, *Colonialismo e feudalismo : La questione del prazos da coroa nel Mozambique alla fine del secolo XIX* (Turin, 1972), another detailed study with an excellent bibliography, covers the same subject from a different perspective.

2514 Maugham, R. C. F. *Portuguese East Africa : The history, scenery and great game of Manica and Sofala.* New York, E. P. Dutton and Co., 1906. 340 p., maps, illus.
Written by a member of the British consular service, for the benefit of 'the traveller, the sportsman, and for him whose delight lies in ... scenes of natural, unembellished beauty ', but furnished also with more general information. The author wrote several other works, including *Zambezia : A general description of the valley of the Zambezi river from its delta to the river Aroangwa* (London, Murray, 1910). A contemporary Portuguese study, written by a provincial governor, is Ernesto Jardim de Vilhena, *Companhia do Nyassa : Relatórios e memórias* (Lisbon, Typographia da ' A Editora ', 1905), which provides a detailed account of various African peoples, agriculture, industry, commerce and Islamic influence. Economic aspects are emphasized in R. N. Lyne, *Mozambique : Its agricultural development* (London, T. F. Unwin, 1913).

2515 Warhurst, Philip R. *Anglo-Portuguese relations in south-central Africa 1890–1900.* Published for the Royal Commonwealth Society. London, Longmans Green, 1962. xii, 165 p., maps. Bibliography: p. 157–165.
An Oxford B. Litt. thesis, based on extensive archival research, this study outlines a crucial period in Anglo-Portuguese relations. The author indicates why Rhodesia failed to secure a coveted outlet to the sea, and how the Anglo-Portuguese entente was restored after a prolonged crisis. For an older Portuguese work illustrating the background to the crisis, see Manuel Chagas Pinheiro, *As negociaçoes com a Inglaterra* (Lisbon, 1890).

Addenda

ETHIOPIA

Bibliography

2516 Marcus, Harold G. *The modern history of Ethiopia and the Horn of Africa: A select and annotated bibliography.* Stanford University, Hoover Institution Press, 1972, 641 p. (Hoover Institution Bibliographical Series, no. 56)

A monumental study, containing 2,042 annotated entries drawn from a great variety of books and journals in English, French, Italian, German, Russian, Italian and other languages. The work is fully indexed, and supplied with explanatory appendices listing geographical journals and some of the more important books cited in book reviews and similar entries. In his introduction the author stresses the value of lesser known publications, such as minor geographical journals, for the student of African history.

INDEX

Note This is an index to authors, titles, institutions, organizations, colonies, government agencies and major geographical areas; it is not a subject index. The numbers refer to entries not to pages. An n after a number refers to the annotation or note of that entry. When a page reference is given the letter p will appear before the number.

Index

Index

477

Index

479

Index

482

Index

Behn, Hans Ulric, 708
Beiträge zur Geschichte der Gaza Nguni im südlichen Moçambique 1820–1895, 2391
Beiträge zur Kolonialpolitik und Kolonialwirtschaft (Berlin), 2032n; Note, p. 388
Beiträge zur Landeskunde der Grashochländer Nord-west-Kameruns, 2040n
Belgian administration in the Congo, 1931; Note, p. 360
BELGIAN AFRICA
archival and library sources on, p. 42–44
general, p. 360–362
research on, p. 25–27
Belgian Congo (Zaïre), p. 362–384; archival and library sources on, p. 71
Rwanda and Burundi, p. 384–386
' Belgian centers of documentation and research on Africa ', 8
BELGIAN CONGO, *see* Congo, Belgian
Belgian Congo, 1924
Belgique d'Outre-Mer (Brussels), 1873, 1894n
Belgique et Congo: L'élaboration de la charte Coloniale, 1988
Belgium, p. 25–27, p. 42–44
Archives Générales du Royaume, 34; Note, p. 42
Conseil de Gouvernement, 1916n
Corps Législatif, 2498
Institut National de Statistique, 1917
Ministère des Affaires Africaines, 1846; Note, p. 42, p. 361; Bibliothèque, 35; Direction de l'Agriculture, des Forêts et de l'Elevage, 1876n, 1918; Direction des Etudes Economiques, 1919
Ministère des Affaires Etrangères, Note, p. 361; Dépôt Centrale des Archives, Note, p. 42
Ministères des Colonies, 1920–1922; Note, p. 42, p. 361; Office Colonial, 1874; Note, p. 361
Ministère du Commerce Extérieur et de l'Assistance Technique, Note, p. 361

Ministére du Congo Belge et du Ruanda-Urundi, 36, 1846, 1875, 1918n, 1923, 2003
Office de l'Information et des Relations Publiques pour le Congo Belge et le Ruanda-Urundi (INFOR-CONGO), 1924, 1925, 1934n, 2004
Parlement: Chambre des Représentants, 1915; Note, p. 361; Sénat, 1916; Note, p. 361
Belgium. Université Coloniale, p. 26
Bell, Sir Hesketh, 1478n
Bell, J. Bowyer, 423
Bell, R. D., 921
Belton, E. J., 166
Bemba and related peoples of Northern Rhodesia, 937n
Benedict, Burton, 1159, 1173
Beneke, Max, 2071n
Benians, E. A., 664
Benin kingdom and the Edo-speaking peoples of south-western Nigeria, The, 825n
Bennett, George, 435n, 1062
Bennett, Norman R., 3n, 421, 453n, 1021
Bennion, Francis A. R., 771
Benoist, J. de, 711n
Bentley, H. Margo, 584
Berg, Elliot J., 727n
Bericht über das Studienjahr [Kolonialinstitut, Hamburg], 2048
Berkeley, George Fitz-Hardinge, 2196
Berlage, Jean, 1847, 1856, 1857
Berlin Universität
Institut für Bibliothekswissenschaft, 66n
Seminar für orientalische Sprachen, p. 12, p. 22–23
Berlin West Africa Conference, 1884–1885, The, 2070n
Berliner Gesellschaft für Anthropolgie, Ethnologie und Urgeschichte, 2079n
Berman, Sanford, 2428
Bernard, Augustin, 411n
Bernus, Edmond, 1588n
Bertin, A., 1434n
Bertola, A., 2150
Bertrand, Albert J., 1399n
Besiedlung Deutsch Südwestafrikas bis zum Weltkrieg, Die, 2129
Besterman, Theodore, 230, 232n
Bevel, Maurice Louis, 1926
Bey, Anisse Salah, 466

Beyond the reefs, 1174n
Bézy, F., 1927
Bianqués, Jean, 1446n
Bibliografia antropológica do Ultramar português, 2241
' Bibliografia antropológica do Ultramar português ', 2242
Bibliografia científica da Junta de Investigações do Ultramar, 2252
Bibliografia colonial: Contribución a un índice de publicaciones africanas, 257
' Bibliografia dell'Africa orientale italiana 1936–1939 ...', 2136
Bibliografia dell'Istituto Fascista dell'Africa Italiana ..., 2137
Bibliografia dell'Italia d'oltremare, 2138, 2141
Bibliografia di studi africani della missione dell'Africa centrale, 1198
Bibliografia do Centro de Estudos de Etnologia do Ultramar, 2249
Bibliografia do etnologo padre Carlos Estermann, S. Sp., 2355n
Bibliografia etiopica ..., 2446
Bibliografia etiopica, in continuazione alla ' Bibliografia etiopica ' di G. Fumagalli, 2446n
Bibliografia etnológica de Moçambique (das origens a 1954), 2379
' Bibliografia geográfica da Guiné ', 2408
' Bibliografia geografica della colonia Eritrea, 1891–1906 ', 2188
Bibliografia geológica do Ultramar português, 2243
Bibliografia geral de Moçambique ..., 2375
Bibliografia historico-militar do Ultramar português, 2507
Bibliografia Missionaria (Rome), 551
Bibliografia sôbre economia do Ultramar português, 2259
Bibliografia sôbre economia portuguesa ..., 2250
Bibliografia Somala, 2210
Bibliografie van Afrikaanse Boeke, 1240
Bibliografie van die Bantoetale in die Unie van Suid-Afrika, 1239
Bibliografiia Afriki, 280
Bibliographic aid to the study of the geography of Africa, A, ..., 400

483

' Bibliographic essays: Senegal ', 1623

Bibliographical Bulletin (Paris), 380n

' Bibliographical control of African manuscripts and archives collections ', p. 15 (n 7)

Bibliographical introduction to legal history and ethnology, 471

Bibliographical Series [Cape Town, University, School of Librarianship], 876

Bibliographical sources for Nigerian studies, 801

' Bibliographie africaine et malgache: Ecrivains noirs d'expression française ', 1365

Bibliographie annuelle de l'histoire de France, p. 24

Bibliographie annuelle de Madagascar, 1804

Bibliographie: Auteurs africains et malgaches de langue française, 1352

Bibliographie cartographique internationale, 310

' Bibliographie congolaise de 1895 à 1910 ', 1862

Bibliographie critique de l'Afrique occidentale française, 1493

Bibliographie critique des sources imprimées d'histoire de la Guinée publiées avant 1914, 1566

' Bibliographie critique récente sur Madagascar ', 1805

Bibliographie de H. M. Stanley, 1841–1904, 1851n

Bibliographie de la condition de l'Africaine en Afrique en Afrique noire, 589n

Bibliographie de la France (Paris), 296; Note, p. 94–95, p. 282

Bibliographie de l'Afrique équatoriale française, 1695

Bibliographie de l'Afrique occidentale française, 1486

Bibliographie de l'Angola (bibliotheca angolensis), 1500–1910, 2332

Bibliographie de l'histoire coloniale, 1900–1930: Belgique, 1859

Bibliographie de Madagascar [Fleur, G.], 1800

Bibliographie de Madagascar [Grandidier, G.], 1801

Bibliographie de Maurice, 1502–1954, 1157, 1158n

Bibliographie démographique, 1945–1962 . . . , 1358

Bibliographie démographique, 1945–1964 . . . , 345, 1359

Bibliographie des études démographiques relatives au pays en voie de développement . . . , 346

Bibliographie des mémoires de l'Institut des Territoires d'Outre-Mer, 1868

Bibliographie des ouvrages relatifs à la Sénégambie et au Soudan occidental, 1485

Bibliographie des ouvrages relatifs à l'Afrique et à l'Arabie . . . , 258

' Bibliographie des recherches psychologiques conduites en Afrique ', 498n

Bibliographie d'histoire coloniale (1900–1930), 419, 1364

Bibliographie d'ouvrages ayant trait à l'Afrique en général dans ses rapports avec l'exploration et la civilisation de ces contrées, 418

Bibliographie du Congo, 1880–95 . . . , 1869

Bibliographie du Congo belge et du Ruanda-Urundi, 19—, 1851

Bibliographie du Katanga [1824–1949], 1865–1867

Bibliographie du mouvement syndical ouest-africain d'expression française, 1482

Bibliographie du Tchad, 1759

Bibliographie du Tchad, sciences humaines, 1760

' Bibliographie éthiopienne, 1946–1951 ', 2448

Bibliographie ethnographique de l'Afrique équatoriale française, 1914–1948, 1696

Bibliographie ethnographique de l'Afrique sud-saharienne, 327, 1848

Bibliographie ethnographique du Congo belge et des régions avoisinantes, 327n, 1848

Bibliographie française sur l'Afrique au sud du Sahara [196–], 240n, 241

Bibliographie générale de la Haute-Volta, 1956–65, 1685

Bibliographie générale de la région de N'Zérékoré, 1568

Bibliographie générale des colonies françaises, 1810n

Bibliographie générale du Mali . . . , 1652

Bibliographie géologique du Congo, du Rwanda et du Burundi, 1863

Bibliographie internationale d'anthropologie sociale et culturelle, 329

Bibliographie juridique du Congo belge et du Ruanda-Urundi, période 1939–51, 1852

Bibliographie linguistique de l'année, Note, p. 103

Bibliographie Mauritanie, 1597, 2496

Bibliographie nationale courante de l'année 1967 des pays d'Afrique d'expression française . . . , 1622

Bibliographie Sélective des Publications Officielles Françaises (Paris), 296n, 1357, 1422n

Bibliographie sélective d'ouvrages de langue française sur les problèmes gouvernementaux et administratifs (notamment en Afrique), 623

Bibliographie sommaire de la République du Niger, 2497

Bibliographie sur la Guinée, 1569

Bibliographie sur les classes sociales en Afrique, 590

' Bibliographie sur l'histoire de l'Afrique et la colonisation européenne de sources principalement soviétiques ', 415

Bibliographien zur Erziehung, Politik und Geschichte im Kongo Kinshasa, 1849

Bibliographies of West Africa, The, 702, 757n

' Bibliography ' [on Cecil Rhodes], 875

Bibliography for the study of African history in the nineteenth and twentieth centuries, A, 420

Bibliography of Africa, The, . . . , 110

Bibliography of African anthropology, 1937–1949, 334n

Bibliography of African bibliographies, 232

Bibliography of African bibliographies covering territories south of the Sahara, A, 233, Note, p. 80

Index

Bibliography of African education in the Federation of Rhodesia and Nyasaland, 1890–1958, A, 876n

Bibliography of African education south of the Sahara, A, 386

Bibliography of African geography, 1940–1964, 403

Bibliography of African government, 1950–1966, A, 522

Bibliography of African law [African Law Association of America], 469

Bibliography of African law . . . [Allott, A. N.], 988

Bibliography of African statistical publications, 1950–1965, 363

Bibliography of agriculture, land use and surrounding conditions in Ghana and adjacent territories, 1930–1959, 799n

Bibliography of articles . . . on colonies and other dependent territories, appearing in American geographical and kindred journals, A, 284

Bibliography of Basutoland, 1321

Bibliography of Bechuanaland, 1324

Bibliography of British Somaliland, A, 1184

Bibliography of East African literature on bilharziasis . . . , 497

Bibliography of economics in East Africa . . . , 992

' Bibliography of Ghana, A : 1958–1964 ', 760n

Bibliography of Ghana, 1957–1959, 762

Bibliography of Ghana, 1930–1961, A, 760

Bibliography of historical writings published in Great Britain and the Empire, 1940–1945, 610

Bibliography of Italian colonisation in Africa, with a section on Abyssinia, A, 2144

Bibliography of Kenya, A, 1006n, 1057

Bibliography of labor migration in Africa south of the Sahara, A, 461

Bibliography of land tenure [Uganda], 1126

Bibliography of Malawi, A, 915, 1057n

Bibliography of Mauritius, 1502–1954 . . . , 226

' . . . Bibliography of modern African religious movements ', 571n

Bibliography of neo-African literature from Africa, America, and the Caribbean, A, 485

Bibliography of Nigerian history, A, 804

Bibliography of non-periodical literature on Sierra Leone, 1925–66, A, 865

' Bibliography of periodical literature ' [on Arab world], 1180n

Bibliography of psychological research and writings on Africa, A, 498

Bibliography of published sources relating to African land tenure, 612

Bibliography of Sierra Leone, 1925–1967, A, 864

Bibliography of Sierra Leone, preceded by an essay on the origin, character and peoples of the colony and protectorate, A, 861

Bibliography of South African government publications, 1910–1968, 1243

' Bibliography of Sudan law, 1 ', 1199

' Bibliography of Tanganyika, 1959–64, A ', 1085n

Bibliography of the Anglo-Egyptian Sudan, from the earliest times to 1937, A, 1191

Bibliography of the Bantu languages in the Republic of South Africa, 1239

Bibliography of the distribution of disease in East Africa . . . , 499

Bibliography of the Federation of the Rhodesias and Nyasaland, up to June 30th, 1949, A, 876n

Bibliography of the Gold Coast, A, 757, 760n

' Bibliography of the Masai ', 998

Bibliography of the National Archives Library, Ibadan, A, . . . , 140

Bibliography of the Negro in Africa and America, 267

Bibliography of the Society for African Church History, 1, 560

Bibliography of the status of South-West Africa up to June 30th, 1951, 1306n

Bibliography of the Sudan, 1938–1958, A, 1197

Bibliography on anthropology and sociology in Tanzania and East Africa, A, 1006

Bibliography on anthropology and sociology in Uganda, A, 1124

Bibliography on Bechuanaland, A, 1325

Bibliography on development planning in Nigeria, 1955–1968, A, 803n

Bibliography on Guinea, 1569

Bibliography on politics and government in Uganda, A, 1125

' Bibliography on special problems in education in tropical Africa, A ', 392, 393n

Bibliography on spirit possession and spirit mediumship, 561

Bibliography Series [Padmore Research Library on African Affairs], 761

Biblioteca di Studi Coloniali, p. 29

' Biblioteche e archivi d'Angola ', 194n, 197

Bibliotheca missionum, 558

Bibliothèque Africaine, La: Quatre-vingt-cinq ans d'activité bibliographique africaine, 2469

Bibliothèque du Ministère des Affaires Africaines, La, . . . , 41

Bibliothèques publiques au Congo, Les, 165

Bielschowski, Ludwig, 2117

Billard, Pierre, 1733, 1734

Bilsen, A. A. J. van, 1928

Binet, Jacques, 1741n

Biobaku, Saburi O., 823n

Biographical dictionary of the Anglo-Egyptian Sudan, A, 1211n

Biographical dictionary of the Sudan, A, 1211

Biographie belge d'outre-mer, 1908n

Biographie coloniale belge, 1908

Biography catalogue of the library of the Royal Commonwealth Society, 285

Bira et les peuplades limitrophes, Les, 1952n

Birds of eastern and north eastern Africa, 517

Birds of tropical west Africa, 511n

485

Index

Bulletin [African Studies Association of the United Kingdom, Birmingham], 5, 13n; Note, p. 40

Bulletin [Comité Central Française pour l'Outre-Mer, Paris], 1380n

Bulletin [Comité d'Etudes Historiques et Scientifiques de l'Afrique Occidentale Française, Gorée], p. 24

Bulletin [Congrès Colonial National, Brussels], 1942n

Bulletin [France, Agence Générale des Colonies, Paris], 1384, 1431n

Bulletin [IFAN, Dakar], 1502; p. 25

Bulletin [Imperial Institute, London], 644

Bulletin [Institut d'Etudes Centrafricaines, Brazzaville], 1724

Bulletin [Inter-African Conference on Statistics, London], 376n

Bulletin [Inter-African Labour Institute, London], 463, 464n; p. 32

Bulletin [Mauritius, Archives Dept., Port Louis], 227n

Bulletin [Mauritius Institute, Port Louis], 1166

Bulletin [Société de Géographie, Paris], 1375, 1398

Bulletin [Société des Etudes Camerounaises, Yaoundé], 1742n

Bulletin [Société d'Etudes et d'Expansion, Liège], 1899

Bulletin [Société Royale Belge de Géographie, Brussels], 1900

Bulletin [Society for African Church History, Nsukka], 577

Bulletin [University of Zambia, Institute for Social Research, Lusaka], 905n

Bulletin Administratif (Léopoldville), 1941n

Bulletin Agricole du Congo (Brussels), 1876

Bulletin Analytique Africaniste (London), 236n, 325

Bulletin Bibliographique (Paris), 1360

Bulletin Bibliographique des Archives du Sénégal (Dakar), 154

Bulletin de la Société Belge d'Etudes Coloniales (Brussels), 1898

Bulletin de la Statistique Générale (Yaoundé), 1736n

Bulletin de l'Office Colonial (Brussels), 1874

Bulletin de Madagascar (Tananarive), 1811

Bulletin des Juridictions Indigènes et du Droit Coutumier Congolais (Elisabethville), 1897n

Bulletin des Séances (Brussels), 32n, 415n, 1858n, 1870n; p. 26

Bulletin des Tribunaux Coutumiers (Elisabethville), 1877, 1897n

Bulletin d'Information [INEAC, Brussels], 1883

Bulletin d'Information [Société de Africanistes, Paris], 20, 301n

Bulletin d'Information sur les Recherches dans les Sciences Humaines Concernant l'Afrique (Brussels), 6, 589n

Bulletin Information et Liaison (Paris), 301n

Bulletin Mensuel (Dakar), 1630

Bulletin Mensuel de Statistique (Fort-Lamy), 1763n

Bulletin Mensuel de Statistique d'Outre-Mer (Paris), 1425

Bulletin Mensuel des Statistiques Générales du Congo et du Ruanda-Urundi (Brussels), 1917n

Bulletin of Hygiene (London), 501: p. 18

Bulletin of Information on Current Research on Human Sciences Concerning Africa (Brussels), 6

Bulletin of News [Historical Society of Nigeria, Ibadan], 126n

Bulletin of the Africa Institute of South Africa (Pretoria), 1248

Bulletin of the School of Oriental and African Studies (London): 631; p. 12

Bulletin of the Scottish Institute of Missionary Studies (Edinburgh), 571n

Bulletin Officiel [Belgian Congo; Brussels], 1941

Bulletin Officiel [Congo Free State; Brussels], 1941n

Bulletin Officiel [France, Ministère de la France d'Outre-Mer, Paris], 1431

Bulletin: Procès-Verbaux [French West Africa, Grand Conseil, Dakar], 2492

Bulletin Quotidien (Dakar), 1630n

Bulletin Scientifique (Nogent-sur-Marne-Seine), 1385n

Bulletin Statistique et Economique Mensuel (Dakar), 1648n

Bulletin, Série A: Sciences Naturelles [IFAN, Dakar], 1505, 1506n; p. 25; Note, p. 142

Bulletin, Série B: Sciences Humaines [IFAN, Dakar], 1506; p. 25

Bulpin, Thomas V., 1174

Bundesarchiv und seine Bestände, Das, . . . , 62

Burden of empire: An appraisal of Western colonialism in Africa south of the Sahara, 434

Bureau de l'Enseignement Catholique, 1933

Bureau of Ghana Languages, Note, p. 103

Bureau of Hygiene and Tropical Diseases, London, p. 18

Bureau pour le Développement de la Production Agricole, 1421, 1784; Note, p. 336

Burke, E. E., 188, 875; p. 16

Burns, Sir Alan Cuthbert, 820

Burridge, William, 564

Burrows, H. R., 1276n

Burssens, H., 1952n

BURUNDI, p. 384–386

Bustin, Edouard, 523, 1850

Butler, Jeffrey, 425

Butt, Audrey J., 1030n, 1205n

Butterfield, Harry F., 989, 1086n

Butterworth's African Law Series, 481

Büttner, Kurt, 2086

Butts, Patricia, 287

Bwana: Deine Zeit ist um . . . , 2097

CADULAC, see Kinshasa, Congo. Université Lovanium. Centres Agronomiques . . .

CARDAN, see Centre d'Analyse et de Recherche Documentaires pour l'Afrique Noire

CAS, see Cambridge University. African Studies Centre

CCTA, see Commission for Technical Cooperation in Africa [South of the Sahara]

Index

Index

491

Index

493

Index

494

Index

Index

498

Index

Emerging nationalism in Portuguese Africa: Documents, 2239n

Emerging physician, The: A sociological approach to the development of a Congolese medical profession, 1947

Emirates of Northern Nigeria, The: A preliminary survey of their historical traditions, 831

Empire (London), 640

Empire colonial belge, L', 1946

Empire de Gao, L': Histoire, coutumes et magie des Sonraï, 1662n

Empire du Mogho-Naba: Coûtumes des Mossi de la Haute-Volta, L', 1688

Enciclopedia italiana di scienze, lettere ed arti, 2156

Encyclopédie coloniale et maritime, 1418

Encyclopédie de l'Afrique française, 1418n

Encyclopédie de l'Empire français, 1418n

Encyclopédie de l'Union française, 1418n

Encyclopédie du Congo belge, 1951; p. 26 (n 18)

Encyclopédie Pahouine, 1750

Encyclopédie permanente de l'administration française, 1420n

Enfant africain, L', . . . , 594

Engelborghs-Bertels, Marie, 526

England, Europe and the upper Nile, 1217

English, Patrick T., 180

English-speaking missions in the Congo Independent State (1878–1908), 1984

Ennes, António, 87n, 2291, 2399, 2512

Enquêtes bibliographiques [series], 589n

Ensaio de iconografia das cidades portuguesas do ultramar, 2317

Enseignement au Gabon, 1783n

Enseignement supérieur et la recherche scientifique en Afrique intertropicale, L', 388

Entwicklung unserer Kolonien, 2056n

Environment and land use in Africa, 381

Enwere, J. C., 147n

Epidemic disease in Ghana, 1901–1960, 796

Epstein, Arnold L., 938, 939

Epstein, Fritz T., 61n

EQUATORIAL AFRICA, see French Equatorial Africa; Congo, Belgian Equatorial Africa', 1703

EQUATORIAL GUINEA, see Spanish Guinea

Erinnerungen als letzter Gouverneur in Deutsch-Ostafrika, 2064n, 2100

ERITREA, p. 420–422

Eritrea, 2200

Ernest Oppenheimer and the economic development of southern Africa, 1262n, 1275n

Erreurs et brutalités coloniales, 1401

Errington, Kathleen, 1068

Escola Colonial, p. 27. See also Escola Superior Colonial

Escola Médico-Cirurgia, p. 27

Escola Polytéchnica, p. 27

Escola Superior Colonial, p. 27; Note, p. 428

Escritos sôbre Moçambique, 2394n

Esercito italiano da Vittorio Veneto a Mussolini (1919–1925), L', 2506n

España: Guía de fuentes para la historia de Africa subsahariana, 29n; Note, p. 57

Espansione coloniale italiana (1922–37), 2186

Esploratore, Giornale de Geografia Commerciale (Milan), p. 29

Esploratori italiani in Africa, Gli, 2155

Esplorazioni Viaggi, e Geografia Commerciale (Milan), 2155n

Esquisses sénégalaises (Walo-Kayor-Dyolof-Mourides-un visionnaire), 1644

Essai de bibliographie concernant le Tchad jusqu'en 1913, 1758

' Essai de bibliographie des populations du Soudan central . . . ', 1612

Essai de bibliographie du Ruanda-Urundi, 2001

Essai de bibliographie du Sahara français et des régions avoisinantes, 1481, 1596

Essai de bibliographie: Madagascar et dépendances, 1905–1927, 1803

Essai d'une bibliographie sur la Côte d'Ivoire, 1581

Essai sur la criminalité dans la province de Léopold-ville . . . , 1907n

Essai sur la religion bambara, 1655

Essai sur le Dahomey, 1550

Essay on the economics of detribalization in Northern Rhodesia, An, 951n; p. 20

Essays in imperial government, 695

Essor du Tchad, L', 1764

Estatuto político-administrativo da província S. Tomé e Príncipe, 2416

Esterhuyse, J. H., 2122; Note, p. 48

Estermann, Carlos, 2355

Estudo sôbre o absentismo e instabilidade de mão-de-obra africana, 2316n

Estudos Coloniais (Lisbon), 2262

Estudos de ciências políticas e sociais [series; Junta das Missões Geográficas e de Investigações do Ultramar], 2316n; p. 28

Estudos, ensaios e documentos [series; Portugal, Junta das Missões Geográficas e de Investigações do Ultramar], 2316n; p. 28

Estudos sôbre as províncias ultramarinas, 2508

Estudos sôbre etnologia do Ultramar português, 2318; Note, p. 428

Estudos ultramarinos, 2293, 2312; Note, p. 427

Estudos Ultramarinos (Lisbon), 2262; p. 27

Etapes et perspectives de l'Union française, 1635n

Etat actuel et perspectives de la recherche scientifique française en Afrique et à Madagascar . . . , 1419

' Etat de la littérature militaire relative à l'Afrique australe portugaise ', 2246

ETHIOPIA, p. 420–422, p. 457–462

archival and library sources on, p. 73

Ethiopia: A cultural history, 2229n, 2464

Ethiopia: A list of works in English, 2445

Ethiopia: A new political history, 2458

501

Index

Index

French Africa: A decade of
progress, 1948–1958 ...,
1429n
French aid, 1429n
' French colonial rule in
Africa: A bibliographical
essay ', 1363
French colonies in Africa: A
list of references, 1371
FRENCH EQUATORIAL
AFRICA
archival and library sources
on, p. 70–71
general, p. 336–341
Cameroun, p. 341–345;
archives on, p. 71
Chad, p. 345–348
Gabon, p. 348–349
Middle Congo (Congo-
Brazzaville), p. 350–351
Ubangi-Shari (Central
African Republic), p. 351–
352
See also French Africa
French Equatorial Africa,
1715, 1718
Gouvernement-Général,
1716, 1717
Haut Commissariat, 1719
Service de la Statistique
Générale, 1696, 1720
' French provincial centers of
documentation and
research on Africa ', 9
FRENCH SOMALILAND
(French Territory of the
Afars and the Issas), p.
359–360
French-speaking West Africa:
A guide to official publi-
cations, 1494
French-speaking West Africa –
from colonial status to
independence, 1547n
FRENCH SUDAN, see
Soudan
FRENCH TERRITORY OF
THE AFARS AND THE
ISSAS, see French
Somaliland
FRENCH WEST AFRICA
archival and library sources
on, p. 62–63
general, p. 300–311
Dahomey, p. 311–314
Guinea, p. 314–316;
archives on, p. 64–65
Ivory Coast, p. 316–319
Mauritania, p. 319–321;
library sources on, p. 65
Niger, p. 322–323
Senegal, p. 323–329;
archival and library
sources on, p. 69–70

Soudan (Western Sudan;
Mali), p. 329–331;
archival and library
sources on, p. 63–64, p. 65
Togo, p. 331–334
Upper Volta, p. 334–336
See also French Africa
French West Africa, 1500,
1526
Grand Conseil, 2492
Service des Archives, 120,
121
See also Comité d'Etudes
Historiques et Scienti-
fiques de l'Afrique
Occidentale Française
French West Africa ...
[Great Britain, Naval
Intelligence Division], 1534
French West Africa [Thomp-
son, V. M., and Adloff,
R.], 1547
Frenkel, M. Y., 455n
Frewer, Louis B., 78n, 610
Friedland, William H., 460
Friedrich, J. K. Julius, 2027n
Fripp, Constance E., 901n
Froelich, Jean Claude, 323,
324, 567, 1668n, 1675,
1744
From French West Africa to
the Mali Federation, 1657
From Madagascar to the
Malagasy Republic, 1820
From protest to challenge:
A documentary history of
African politics in South
Africa, 1882–1964 ...,
1273
From refugee to citizen: A
sociological study of the
immigrants from Hitler
Europe who settled in
southern Africa, 2489n
From tribal rule to modern
government, 905n
Fromont-Guieysse, G., 1418
Frontières de la Côte d'Ivoire,
de la Côte d'Or, et du
Soudan, Les, 1654
Full, August, 2104
Fumagalli, Giuseppe, 2446
Fünf Jahre deutscher Kolon-
ialpolitik: Rück- und
Ausblicke, 2034n
Fünfzig Jahre Togo, 2104
Fung, Karen, 815n
Furon, Raymond, 514
' Further additions to Materials
for West African history
in the archives of
Belgium and Holland ',
37n
' Future of African law, The ',
483n

Future of customary law in
Africa, The, 478
Fyfe, Christopher, 869
Fynn, J. T., 714n

GABON, p. 348–349
' Gabon: A bibliographic
essay ', 1777
Gabon: Nation-building on
the Ogooué, 1783
Gabon, Le: Répertoire biblio-
graphique des études de
sciences humaines, 1960–
1967, 1775
Gabon, Le: Répertoire biblio-
graphique des études de
sciences humaines, 1967–
1970, 1774
Gabon, Le: Répertoire biblio-
graphique relatif aux
sciences humaines, 1776
Gabon, terre d'avenir, 1778
Gaffarel, Paul, 1437–1440
Gaibi, Agostino, 2159, 2223
Gailey, Harry A., 127n, 157,
413n, 745
Gaitskell, Arthur, 1208
Gale, William Daniel, 963
Galla monarchy, A: Jemma
Abba Jifar, Ethiopia,
1830–1932, 2459n
Galla of Ethiopia, The: The
kingdoms of Kafa and
Janjero, 2459
Galla Süd-Aethiopiens, 2459n
Gallagher, John, 452
Gallieni, Joseph Simon, 1528,
1529, 1658, 1659, 1816
Gallieni à Madagascar, 1816n
Gallieni pacificateur: Ecrits
coloniaux de Gallieni,
1529, 1658, 1816
Gallois, L., 411n
Galvão, Henrique, 2295, 2296
Gamache, Pierre, 1721
GAMBIA, p. 187–188
archives on, p. 64
Gambia, 128
Gambia colony and protec-
torate, The: An official
handbook, 747n
Gambian-Fula verb list, 746n
Gamble, David P., 741, 746,
1634
Game animals of Africa, The,
512n
Game animals of southern
Africa, The, 512n
Game fishes of Africa, The,
512
Gandolfi, Alain, 1441
Ganiage, Jean, 433
Gann, Lewis H., 186, 423n,
434, 435, 888, 889, 933n,
940, 950n, 964, 2119n;
p. 13 (n 6)

505

Index

Index

507

Index

Index

511

Index

Hopkins, J., 498n
Hopkins, Terence K., 1121
Hopkinson, Emilius, 749
HORN OF AFRICA, archival and library sources on, p. 73–74. *See also* Ethiopia; French Somaliland; Somalia; Sudan (Anglo-Egyptian)
Horne, A. J., 619
Horrell, Muriel, 601n, 1289n
Horton, James Africanus B., 720; p. 12
Hoskyns, Catherine, 547
Hostelet, Georges, 1961, 1962
Hotten, John Camden, 2446n
Hotz, Louis, 2489
Houghton, D. Hobart, 1262n, 1287n, 1289n, 1303n, 2484
Houis, Maurice, 1418n
Houlet, Gilbert, 1700n
Hovet, Thomas, 361n
Howard, Allen, 2473
Howard, Cecil, 721
Howard, William Edward Harding, 2201
Howard University. Library. The Moorland Foundation, 272
Howell, P. P., 1221n
Hoyle, B. S., 1036
Huart, M. d,' 1685
Hudson, W., 326
Huffnagel, H. P., 2457
Huggins of Rhodesia: The man and his country, 889
Hughes, A. J. B., 967
Hughes, Judith M., 1455n
Hugot, Pierre, 1765
Huíla e Moçâmedes, A: Considerações sôbre o trabalho indígena, 2511
Huisman, M., 1859
Hulstaert, G., 1932n
Human factors of productivity in Africa, The, . . . , 464n
Human Problems in [British] Central Africa, see *Rhodes-Livingstone Journal*
Human Relations Area Files (HRAF), 337n
Humboldt, Alexander von, p. 5
Hunt, John A., 1184n, 1185
Hunter, A. P., 573n
Hunter, Guy, 595
Huntingford, George W. B., 1030n, 1205n, 2459
Hunwick, J. O., 124
Hurault, Jean, 1747
Hurwitz, Nathaniel, 1276n
Husson, Philippe, 1606
Hutchinson, John, 515
Hutton, J., 38n

Huxley, Elspeth, 1067
Hyam, Ronald, 2485
Hyatt, Harry M., 2466n

IAI, *see* International African Institute
ICA, *see* International Council on Archives
IDEA, *see* Spain. Conejo Superior de Investigaciones Científicas. Instituto de Estudios Africanos
IEC, *see* Institut d'Etudes Centrafricaines
IFAN, *see* Institut Français [Fondamental] d'Afrique Noire
IGCB, *see* Institut Géographique du Congo Belge
INCIDI, *see* Institut International des Civilisations Différentes
INEP, *see* Institut National d'Etudes Politiques
INEAC, *see* Institut National pour l'Etude Agronomique du Congo
INFORCONGO, *see* Belgium. Office de l'Information et des Relations Publiques pour le Congo Belge et le Ruanda-Urundi
INSEE, *see* France. Institut National de la Statistique et des Etudes Economiques
IRAD, *see* Institut de Recherches Appliquées du Dahomey
IRES, *see* Kinshasa, Congo. Université Lovanium. Institut de Recherches Economiques et Sociales
IRSAC, *see* Institut pour la Recherche Scientifique en Afrique Centrale
I speak of freedom: A statement of African ideology, 790, 791n
Ibadan. University Institute of African Studies. Centre of Arabic Documentation, 114
Library, 802
Ibbeken, Rudolf, 2043
Ibo and Ibibio-speaking peoples of south-eastern Nigeria, The, 825n
Ibrahim, Asma, 1192
Ibrahim-Hilmy, Prince, 1193
Ideologias políticas africanas, 2371
Ike, Adebimpe O., 803
Ikime, Obaro, 714n, 832

Ila-Tonga peoples of north-western Rhodesia, The, 937n
Ile Nosy Bé de Madagascar, L': Histoire d'une colonisation, 1813n
Ilha de Sao Tomé, A, 2426
Iliffe, John, 2084, 2091, 2092
Illustrated social history of South Africa, An, 1271
Ilyasu, M. S. D., 147n
Im deutschen Diamantenland: Deutsch-Südwestafrika von der Errichtung der deutschen Herrschaft bis zur Gegenwart (1884–1910), 2132
Immelman, R. F. M., 207
Imperial Institute, 644
Imperial Institute Journal (London), 644
Imperialism and nationalism in the Sudan: A study of constitutional and political development, 1889–1956, 1200
Imperialism and the scramble for Africa, 431n
Imperialism reader, The, 697
Impérialisme colonial italien de 1870 à nos jours, L', 2173; Note, p. 411
Imperialismus vor 1914 . . . , 2039
Império ultramarino português . . ., 2296
Impeno fascista: Africani ed ebrei, 2178
Imprensa periódica em Moçambique 1854–1954, A, . . . , 2388
Invo Zabantsundu (Johannesburg), 1251
Indépendance du Congo, L', 1928
Index bibliographique colonial: Congo belge et Ruanda-Urundi . . . , 1858
Index Cards: Selected Current Bibliography (Paris), 380n
Index-digest of the reported cases determined by the Court of Appeal for Eastern Africa . . . 1900 to 1938, 1010
Index digest of the reported cases determined by the Court of Appeal for Eastern Africa . . . 1900–1952, 989
Index Islamicus, 1906–1955 . . . [and supplements], 259, 552

512

Index

Index

Index

Index

518

Index

Index

D.G.—18

Index

Lugard, Frederick J. D.
Lugard, baron, 689, 836n, 838, 1040, 1983n; p. 4, p. 20 (n 15)
Lugard, 692, 1040n
Luke, Harry C., 861, 864n, 865n
Lumumba, Patrice, 1968, 1969
Luo of Kenya, The: An annotated bibliography, 1055
Lury, D. A., 1041
Luthuli, Albert J., 1275n
Lutte armée en Afrique, La, 2412n
Luwel, Marcel, 47, 48
Ly, Abdoulaye, 1522n, 1641, 1646n
Lyall, Archibald, 2410n
Lydekker, Richard, 512n
Lynch, Hollis R., 725n
Lyne, R. N., 2514n
Lynes, Tony, 1171
Lystad, Robert, 776n

Ma, John T., 556
Maberly, Charles T. Astley, *see* Astley Maberley, Charles T.
Mabogunje, Akin L., 837, 839
Macaulay, Thomas B., 68n
McAuslan, J. P. W. B., 1065
McCall, Daniel F., 31
McColloch, C. L., 2232n
MacCrone, I. D., 2487
McCulloch, Merran, 597n, 873, 1741n, 2360, 2361
Macdonald, John F., 969
Macedo, José de, 2510
McEwan, P. J. M., 446
MacGibbon, Iain, 1309
McGowan, Patrick J., 529
MacGregor, J. C., 1349n
Mackay, Ian K., 840
McKay, Vernon, 254n
McKee, Malcolm, 250n
MacKenzie, John, p. 8
Mackenzie, William J. M., 543
Mackey, Alexander M., 68n
Mackinnon (Sir William) Papers, 38n
Mackintosh, Catherine Winkworth, 584n
Mackworth-Praed, Cyril W., 517
MacMichael, Sir Harold A., 1216
Macmillan, Gary D., 101
Macmillan, William M., 544, 1294n; p. 12
McNair, James I., 896
McPhee, Allan, 730
Macphee, Marshall Archibald, 1062n
Macpherson, Margaret, 1042

MADAGASCAR (Malagasy Republic), p. 352–358, p. 359
archival and library sources on, p. 78–79
Madagascar, 1821
Haut Commissariat de la République Française à Madagascar et Dépendances, 1822
Madagascar. Université. Bibliothèque, 1804
Madagascar, 1463n
' Madagascar ', 1364n
Madagascar à travers ses provinces . . ., 1823
Madagascar: An historical and descriptive account of the island and its former dependencies, 1828
Madagascar and adjacent islands: A guide to official publications, 1172, 1807
Madagascar et les bases dispersées de l'Union française . . ., 1835
Madagascar: Populations et ressources, 1812
Madagascar: Revue de géographie (Tananarive), 1815n
Maday, Bela C., 2462
Madden, F., 695
Maes, Joseph, 1952n
' Mahdist archives and related documents ', 185
Mahdist state in the Sudan, 1881–1898, The, . . ., 1214
Main-d'oeuvre dans les colonies françaises de l'Afrique occidentale et du Congo, La, 1520
Mair, Lucy Philip, 341n, 435n, 447, 604n
Makerere Institute of Social Research, 1002, 1027n.
See also East African Institute of Social Research
Makerere University. Library, 1001
Making of a nation, The: A history of the Union of South Africa 1910–1961, 1303n
Making of modern Uganda, The, 1136
Making of Northern Nigeria, The, 852
Making of Rhodesia, The, 893
Makings, S. M., 371n
MALAGASY REPUBLIC, *see* Madagascar
Malagasy Republic. Commissariat Général du Plan, 1824

Malagasy Republic, The: Madagascar today, 1836
Malan, S. I., 306
Malaria in Africa, 503
Malaria in Tanzania, 503n
MALAWI, *see* Nyasaland
Malawi
Dept. of Antiquities, 923
National Archives, 186n
Malawi: A political and economic history, 928
Malcolm, Dougal, 882n
Malgaches du sud-est, Les, . . ., 1830n
MALI, *see* Soudan
Mali, 1660
Archives Nationales, 1656n
' Mali: A bibliographical introduction ', 1653
Malinowski, Bronislaw, 336
Malinowski's sociological theories, 336n
Malvezzi de Medidi, A., 540n
Mamvu-Mangutu et Balese-Mvuba, 1952n
Manchester Guardian, Note, p. 172
Manchka, P., 532n
Mandat français sur le Togo, Le, . . ., 1680
Mandated territory of South West Africa in relation to the United Nations, The, 1308
Mandatsgebiete in Afrika, 2050n
Mangat, J. S., 1043
Mangin, Charles Marie Emmanuel, 1455
Mannoni, Dominique O., 1825
Manoukian, Madeline, 776n, 1678
Manual das administrações dos concelhos e circunscrições da Colónia de Angola, 2358
Manuale di legislazione della colonia Eritrea: Indici generali, 1869–1912, 2204
Manuale di legislazione della Somalia italiana, 2230
Manuale di storia e legislazione coloniale del regno d'Italia (1924–1927), 2174n
Manuale di storia politico-militare delle colonie italiane, 2159, 2223
Manuel d'agriculture tropicale (Afrique tropicale et équatoriale), 373
Manuel de législation coloniale, 1400
Manuel de linguistique bantoue, 1932n

Index

Index

Meebelo, Henry S., 948
Meek, Charles K., 475, 620;
    p. 19 (and n 13)
Mehls, Ellen, 2114n
Mehls, Hartmut, 2114n
Meillassoux, Claude, 730n
*Meine Erinnerungen aus
    Ostafrika*, 2100n
Méjan, François, 1457, 1476n
Melland, F. H., 318n
Mémoires [series; ARSOM],
    32n, 1870n, 1998n
  Classe des sciences morales
    et politiques, 1870n; p. 26
  Classe des sciences naturelles
    et médicales, 1870n; p. 26
  Classe des sciences tech-
    niques, 1870n; p. 26
Mémoires [series; Académie
    Malgache], 1808
Mémoires [series; IEC], 1725
Mémoires [series; IFAN],
    1503, 1576n; p. 25
Mémoires [series; IRAD],
    1555n
Mémoires [series; Institut de
    Recherches Scientifiques
    de la République
    Malgache], 1819
Mémoires [series; Institut
    Royal Colonial Belge],
    1907, 1932n; Note, p. 361
*Mémoires d'Afrique (1892–
    1896)*, 2192
*Memorandum of Books
    Printed in Mauritius and
    Registered in the Archives
    Office*, 1155
*Memorandum on the native
    tribes and tribal areas of
    Northern Rhodesia*, 936n
*Memorandum sulla situazione
    economica e finanzaria dei
    territori italiani in Africa*,
    2171
Memórias [series; Centro de
    Estudos da Guiné Portu-
    guesa], 2411n
Memórias [series; Portugal,
    Junta das Missões Geo-
    gráficas e de Investigações
    do Ultramar], 2316n
Memórias e Trabalhos
    (Luanda), 2337
Memorie [Società Geografica
    Italiana, Rome], p. 29
*Memorie della Reale Società
    Geografica Italiana*
    (Rome), 2182
*Men of the times: Old
    colonists of the Cape
    Colony and Orange River
    Colony*, 1275

*Men of the times: Pioneers
    of the Transvaal and
    glimpses of South Africa*,
    1275n
Ménard, André, 1839
*Mende of Sierra Leone, The:
    A West African people in
    transition*, 872n
Mendelssohn, Sidney, 1235
Mendelssohn-Bartholdy,
    Albrecht, 2052; Note,
    p. 48
Mendes, Afonso, 2511
Mendes Corrêa, Antônio
    Augusto, 2302, 2414
Mendes do Couto, Carlos
    Alberto, 2348n
Mendonça, L., 1128
Mengrelis, Thanos, 1568
Méniaud, Jacques, 1539, 1654n
Méniaud, Jean, 1478n
*Mercenaires noirs: Notes sur
    une forme d'exploitation
    des Africains*, 1522n,
    1641n, 1646n
Merchant adventure, 834n
Mercier, A., 1753
Mercier, René, 1458
Mercier, Robert, 495n
Mercier, Roger, 1365
Merle, Marcel, 1419n
Merriam, Alan P., 1971
Mes tournées au Tchad, 1767
*Messianic popular movements
    in the Lower Congo*, 1911
Messianismes congolais, 1786n
Metcalfe, G. E., 787; p. 17
Methner, Wilhelm, 2095
*Méthodes et les doctrines
    coloniales de la France,
    du XVIe siècle à nos jours,
    Les*, 1412
Metzger, O. F., 2107
Meyer, Felix, 2067n
Meyer, Hans H., 410, 2054,
    2096, 2108
Meynaud, Jean, 466
Mezger, Dorothea, 1003
Michel, Louis, 1808n
Michiels, Albert, 1972
Microfilm Abstracts, Note,
    p. 94
Micus, Ingeborg, 2172
MIDDLE CONGO (Congo-
    Brazzaville; Republic of
    Congo), p. 350–351
Middle East Journal (Wash-
    ington, D.C.), 246, 1180
Middleton, Coral, 1323
Middleton, John, 435n, 536n,
    1030n, 1115
Miège, J. L., 2173; Note,
    p. 411
Migliorini, Elio, 411

*Migrant cocoa-farmers of
    southern Ghana, The*, 782
*Migrant labour and tribal
    life: A study of conditions
    in the Bechuanaland Pro-
    tectorate*, 1339n
*Migrant labour in Africa
    south of the Sahara . . .*,
    464
Migrants and malaria, 503n,
    508
'Migration in West Africa:
    The political perspective',
    727n
Milcent, Ernest, 1402n, 1629n,
    1643
Miliavskaiia, S. I., 280n
*Militari e politici nella pre-
    parazione della campagna
    d'Etiopia . . .*, 2506
Militaria (Pretoria), 1252
'Military history of British
    Central Africa . . .', 924n
*Military operations in Togo-
    land and the Cameroons,
    1914–16*, 1679
Miller, Ronald, 896
Milligan, S., 944
Minelle, Jean, 1827
Miner, Horace M., 602, 727n
*Mineral deposits of Somalia,
    The*, 2232n
*Mineral resources of Africa,
    The*, 513
Minhas memórias, As, 2300n
*Mining in Northern
    Rhodesia . . .*, 934
Minutes [League of Nations,
    Permanent Mandates
    Commission], 541
*Minutes of the proceedings
    and ordinances (1st–7th
    Council, May 15, 1889–
    October 11, 1923)*
    [Southern Rhodesia], 984
*Mise en valeur des colonies
    françaises, La*, 1475
*Mise en valeur des colonies
    portugaises, La*, 2509n
*Missão antropológica de
    Moçambique . . .*, 2402n
*Mission and state in the
    Congo . . .*, 1966
*Mission d'études forestières
    envoyée dans les colonies
    françaises . . .*, 1434
*Mission d'exploration du
    Haut-Niger . . . 1879–1881*,
    1528, 1529n, 1658
*Missionary biography: An
    initial bibliography*, 557
*Missionary factor in East
    Africa, The*, 1035n
*Missionary impact on modern
    Nigeria, 1842–1914, The*,
    . . ., 813

524

Index

Moyse-Bartlett, Hubert, 924
MOZAMBIQUE, p. 447-451
    archival and library sources,
    on, p. 76
Mozambique, 2395
    Direcção dos Serviços de
    Agrimensura, 2374
    Direcção dos Serviços de
    Instrução. Arquivo
    Histórico, Note, p. 76,
    p. 428
    Instituto de Investigaçao
    Científica, 2316n
*Mozambique: Its agricultural
    development*, 2514n
*Mozambique, the Africaniza-
    tion of a European institu-
    tion: The Zambesi prazos,
    1750-1902*, 2513
Muffett, D. J. M., 714n
*Muhammadan emirates of
    Nigeria, The*, 831n
Mulford, David C., 949
Muller, C. F. J., 1236
Müller, Fritz Ferdinand,
    2055, 2097
Müller, Karl, 587n
Multitribal society, The, 905n
Mundo Português, O (Lisbon),
    2265
Mungeam, G. H., 1077
Murdock, George Peter, 324n,
    337
Murphree, Marshall W., 970
Murray, Andrew C., 585n
Murray, David John, 2481,
    2483
Murray, S. S., 925
Musée Colonial, *see* Tervuren,
    Belgium. Musée Colonial
Musée de l'Homme, *see* Paris.
    Musée de l'Homme
Musée Royal de l'Afrique
    Centrale, *see* Tervuren,
    Belgium. Musée Royal de
    l'Afrique Centrale
Musée Royal du Congo Belge,
    see Tervuren, Belgium.
    Musée Royal du Congo
    Belge
Museo Canario, *see* Canary
    Islands
Museu Agricola do Ultramar,
    see Lisbon: Jardim e
    Museu Agricola . . .
Museu de Angola, *see* Angola
Museu della Garese, *see* Moga-
    discio
Museu do Dundo, *see* Luanda
Museu Etnográfico do Ultra-
    mar, *see* Lisbon: Museu
    Etnográfico . . .
Museu Militar, *see* Lisbon:
    Museu Militar

*Museums in Africa: A direc-
    tory*, 11
Musiker, Reuben, 206, 1237,
    1238
*Muslims and chiefs in West
    Africa* . . . , 738a(n)
Musson, A. L., 2232n
*Musulmans d'Afrique noire,
    Les*, 567
Mveng, Engelbert, 1732, 1754
My pygmy and Negro hosts,
    1989n
Mylius, Norbert, 261
*Myth of ' Mau Mau ', The:
    Nationalism in Kenya*,
    1063n
*Myth of the guerrilla, The:
    Revolutionary theory and
    malpractice*, 423
*Mythes et réalités de l'impérial-
    isme colonial français
    1871-1914*, 2076n

NADA (Salisbury), 971
*Nachlässe in den Bibliotheken
    der Bundesrepublik
    Deutschland, Die,* . . . ,
    66n
*Nachlässe in den deutschen
    Archiven, Die,* . . . , 66
Nachtigal, Gustav, p. 5
*Nachweisungen über die in
    Deutsch-Ostafrika vor-
    handenen Privat-Pflan-
    zungen und deren
    ungefährer Stand am 1.
    April 1904*, 2093n
Nahayo, Simon, 2002n
*Naissance d'un état noir:
    L'évolution politique et
    constitutionnelle du
    Dahomey* . . . , 1556
el-Nasri, Abdel Rahman, 1192,
    1197
Natal. University, Pietermaritz-
    burg. Dept. of Economics,
    1276n
Natal Regional Survey [series],
    1276
Nathan, M., 1275n
*Nation et voie africaine du
    socialisme*, 548n
' National Archives of
    Rhodesia and Nyasaland,
    The ', 186
National atlas of Kenya, 1053
*National bibliography of
    Botswana, The*, 1319
National Library Occasional
    Publications Series
    [Nigeria], 804n
' National Library of Ethiopia,
    The ', 183
National union catalog, Note,
    p. 93

*National union catalog of
    manuscript collections,
    1959-61, The* [plus supple-
    ments and indexes], 102
*National unity and regionalism
    in eight African states*
    . . . , 531
Nationalism in colonial Africa,
    538, 539n
*Nationalisme et problèmes
    malgaches*, 1831
*Native administration in the
    British African territories*
    . . . , 319, 1335
Native African medicine . . . ,
    506
Native labour in South Africa,
    2490n
*Native life in South Africa,
    before and since the Euro-
    pean war and the Boer
    rebellion*, 1279
Native policies in Africa, 447
*Native policy in Southern
    Africa: An outline*, 447n
Native problem in Africa, The,
    317
Native reserves of Natal, The,
    1276n
*Native states of the Gold
    Coast, The: History and
    Constitution* . . . , p. 19
    (n 14)
*Native tribes of South West
    Africa, The*, 1277
*Nativos na economia africana,
    Os*, 2283n
*Natural resources and develop-
    ment potential in the
    southern provinces of the
    Sudan: A preliminary
    report, 1954*, 1221
*Nature du mouvement syndical
    ouest-africain d'expression
    française, La*, 1514
*Nature of African customary
    law, The*, 670
Na Wundu, Lutumba-Lu-Vilu,
    2499
N'Diaye, Abdoulaye Gamby,
    2475n
*Negociaçoes com a Inglaterra,
    As*, 2515n
Neill, Stephen Charles, 448
*Nell'Africa italiana: Impres-
    sioni e recordi*, 2203
*Neoafrikanische Literatur,
    Die: Gesamtbibliographie
    von den Anfängen bis zur
    Gegenwart*, 485n
*Neo-colonialism: The last
    stage of imperialism*, 791
Neres, Philip, 1547n
Nersesov, G. A., 455n

526

Index

Index

531

Index

Index

Index

Index

535

Index

Relatório apresentado ao Congresso da Repúblico . . . , 2321; Note, p. 427

Relatório de propostas de lei e documentos relativos aos possessões ultramarinas . . . , 2321n

Relatórios e Comunicações (Luanda), 2338

Relazione generale dell'Alto Commissario per l'Oltre Giuba a S.E. il Principe Pietro Lanza di Scalea, Ministro delle Colonie (Riservato), 2187

Religion and art in Ashanti, 794, 795n; p. 19 (n 13)

Religion bambara, La, 1655n, 2495

Religion en Afrique (Leiden), 571

Religion et la magie songhay, La, 1662n

Reluctant rebellion: The 1906–08 disturbances in Natal, 2488

Rennell, Baron, see Rodd, Francis James Rennell

Renner, Peter Awoonor, 778

Répertoire bibliographique de la littérature militaire et coloniale française depuis cent ans, 1355

Répertoire bibliographique: République du Congo-Brazzaville, 1784

Répertoire de la presse au Congo et au Ruanda-Urundi, mis à jour en avril 1960, 1847n

Répertoire de la presse du Congo belge (1884–1958) et du Ruanda-Urundi (1920–1958), 1847

Répertoire des archives [Senegal], 156; p. 16

Répertoire des archives [series; French West Africa, Service des Archives], 120

Répertoire des archives, bibliothèques et écoles de bibliothéconomie d'Afrique, 107

Répertoire des archives sous série 2G: Rapports périodiques, 1895–1940, 2475

Répertoire des périodiques congolais, 1847n

Répertoire des principales institutions s'intéressant à l'Afrique noire, 14

Répertoire des textes en vigueur en Afrique équatoriale française, 1717

Répertoire général de la jurisprudence et de la doctrine coutumières du Congo et du Ruanda-Urundi jusqu'au 31 décembre 1953, 1986

Repertório alphabético e chronológico ou índice remissivo do legislação ultramarina desde a época das descobertas até 1902 inclusivo, 2303n, 2327

Repertorium der deutsch-kolonialen Literatur, 1884–1890, 2015

Report [Ghana, National Archives], 130

Report [Great Britain, East Africa Royal Commission], 1032

Report [Great Britain, Rhodesia-Nyasaland Royal Commission], 944n

Report [Inter-African Conference on Housing and Urbanization, 2d session, Nairobi, 1959], 596

Report [Kenya, African Affairs Department], 1072

Report [Mauritius, Archives Department], 227, 1156, 1158n

Report [Mauritius Sugar Industry Research Institute], 1167

Report [Nigeria, National Archives], 147

Report [South Africa, Commission of Enquiry into South West African Affairs, 1962–63], 1311

Report [South Africa, South West Africa Commission], 1311n

Report [United Nations, General Assembly, Committe on South West Africa], 1315

Report [United Nations, General Assembly, Special Committee on Territories under Portuguese Administration], 2329

Report [Zanzibar, Archives and Museum Department], 179

Report by the chief archivist [Southern Rhodesia, Central African Archives], 189

Report made for the year . . . with a view to exhibit the past and present state of H.M.'s colonial possessions, 672n

Report of the commission appointed to enquire into the financial and economic position of Northern Rhodesia, 677n, 921n, 944; p. 10

Report of the commission appointed to enquire into the financial position and further development of Nyasaland, 677n, 921

Report of the commission to investigate . . . the strike amongst African employees of the Rhodesian railways . . . , p. 10

' Report of the International Committee of Experts on Native Labor ', p. 31

Report of the Northern Nigeria Lands Committee . . . , p. 10

Report of the Secretary for Native Affairs and Chief Native Commissioner [Southern Rhodesia], 980

Report on African materials and activities in some European institutions, A, 31

Report on African participation in the commerce of Sierra Leone . . . , 867

Report on an economic survey of Nyasaland, 1958–1959, 929

Report on native affairs [Kenya], 1072n

Report on Seychelles, 1175

Report on the Cameroons under United Kingdom administration, 1757

Report on the Company's proceedings and the condition of the territories within the sphere of its operations [British South Africa Company], 882n

Report on the East Africa High Commission, 1046

Report on the preservation and administration of historical records and the establishment of a Public Record Office in Nigeria, 139

Report on the press in West Africa, 711

Report on the public records of the Gambia, April 1966, 128

Report . . . to the General Assembly of the United Nations on the administration of Togoland under United Kingdom trusteeship, 1676

536

Index

Index

Index

Index

Index

Index

Welman, C. W., p. 19 (n 14)
Welsh, David, 1303n
Welsh, Doris V., 103
Werner, Manfred W., 2335
Wertheimer, Mildred S., 2076
WEST AFRICA, archival and
  library sources on, p. 61–
  62. *See also* British Africa:
  West Africa; French West
  Africa
West Africa, 731
*West Africa: A Weekly News-
  paper* (London), 456, 707,
  815n
*West Africa: General, ethno-
  graphy, sociology, linguis-
  tics*, 252n, 701
*West Africa: The former
  French states*, 718n, 1536
*West Africa under colonial
  rule*, 713
West African botany, 516
West African Cacao Research
  Institute, 782n
*West African chiefs: Their
  changing status* . . , 714n
*West African countries and
  peoples: British and
  native* . . . , 720; p. 12
West African explorers, 721
' West African history in
  German archives ', 65
West African Institute of
  Social and Economic
  Research, 813n; p. 21
*West African intellectual com-
  munity, The*, . . . , 722
*West African kingdoms in the
  nineteenth century*, 717
West African Language Com-
  mittee, Note, p. 103
West African Libraries
  (Ibadan), 117n
West African Library Associa-
  tion, 117n; Note, p. 40
West African Pilot (Lagos),
  815
West African psychology . . . ,
  734, 735n
West African religion . . . ,735
West African resistance . . . ,
  714
West African Review (London),
  662
*West African Shipping Trade,
  1909–1959, The*, 731n
West African trade . . . , 365
West African urbanization . . . ,
  728
Westermann, Diedrich, 739,
  2049n, 2116; p. 8; Note,
  p. 388
Western African history, Note,
  p. 442

Western Lacustrine Bantu, The,
  . . . , 1030n
WESTERN SUDAN, *see*
  Soudan
Wheeler, Douglas L., 883n,
  2373, 2406n; Note, p. 442
*Whispers from a continent:
  The literature of con-
  temporary black Africa*,
  486n
Whitaker, C. S., Jr., 531n, 2482
White and coloured, 593n
*White man's country: Lord
  Delamere and the making
  of Kenya*, 1067
White settlers in the tropics,
  451
*White settlers in tropical
  Africa*, 434n
*White society in black Africa:
  The French of Senegal*,
  2494
Whiteley, Wilfred H., 937n,
  1011
Whittington, G. W., 382
*Who's who in Midwestern
  Nigeria Legislature*, 858n
Who's who in Nigeria . . . , 858
*Who's who, Northern Region
  of Nigeria Legislature*,
  858n
*Who's who of Southern
  Africa* . . . , 1302
*Who's who of the federal
  House of Representatives
  [Nigeria]*, 858n
*Who's who, Western Nigeria
  Legislature*, 858n
Whyms, L., 1950n
Widstrand, Carl G., 550
Wieschhoff, Heinrich A., 261n,
  266
Wight, Martin, 798
Wiid, J. A., 1297
Wilensky, Alfredo Héctor,
  2330
Wilks, Ivor, 129
Willame, J. C., 1935n
Willan, Sir Harold, 1337
Willequet, Jacques, 1997
Williams, Basil, 897n
Williams, Geoffrey J., 864
Wills, A. J., 912
Wills, J. Brian, 799
Willson, F. M. G., 956, 976n;
  p. 21 (n 16)
Willson, Jean, 956, 976n
Wilson, C. J., 1052
Wilson, Charles, 834n
Wilson, F. B., 1027n
Wilson, Francis, 1303n, 2490
Wilson, Gail, 73
Wilson, Godfrey, 951n; p. 20
Wilson, John, 740

Wilson, Monica Hunter, 448n,
  1303
Winchell, Constance M., 254n,
  318n, 529n, 615n; Note,
  p. 80
Windhuker Anzeiger (Wind-
  hoek), Note, p. 388
Wing, Joseph van, 1912, 1913n,
  1998
Winkler, Hella, 2114n
Winks, Robin W., 626, 1236n
*Wirtschaftswissenschaftliche
  Veröffentlichungen über
  Ostafrika in englischer
  Sprache: Eine Biblio-
  graphie* . . . , 1003
Wissenschaft in Afrika, 25
Witchcraft, 339n
*Witchcraft and sorcery in
  Rhodesia*, 961
*Witchcraft, oracles and magic
  among the Azande*, 1207
Witherell, Julian W., 764,
  1494, 1699, 1807
Wolfson, Freda, 132
*Wolof of Senegambia, together
  with notes on the Lebu
  and the Serer, The*, 746,
  1634
Women of tropical Africa, 340
*Women's role in the develop-
  ment of tropical and sub-
  tropical countries*, 601
Woodhouse, C. M., 897, 1275n
Woodruff, Harry W., 881n
Woods, C. A., 1276n
Woody plants of Ghana, 784
Work, Monroe N., 267; Note,
  p. 85
*Work of an African chief in
  Kenya, The*, . . . , 1073
*Work of the missionaries of
  die Nederduits Gere-
  formeerde Kerk van Suid-
  Afrika up to year 1910:
  An annotated bibliography*
  . . . , 1246
*World bibliography of bibliog-
  raphies and of biblio-
  graphical catalogues,
  calendars, abstracts,
  digests, indexes, and the
  like, A*, 230
Worthington, Edgar B., 520,
  521, 1152; p. 11 (n 4);
  Note, p. 142
Worthington, Stella, 1152
Worzella, W. W., 2232n
Wraith, R. E., 800
Wright, Harrison M., 626n
Wright, Marcia, 178, 2102
Wright, Stephen, 184

551

Index